J Tyler Friedman and Sebastian Luft
The Philosophy of Ernst Cassirer

New Studies in the History and Historiography of Philosophy

Edited by
Gerald Hartung and Sebastian Luft

Volume 2

The Philosophy of Ernst Cassirer

A Novel Assessment

Edited by
J Tyler Friedman and Sebastian Luft

DE GRUYTER

ISBN 978-3-11-055477-9
e-ISBN (PDF) 978-3-11-042181-1
e-ISBN (EPUB) 978-3-11-042183-5
ISSN 2364-3161

Library of Congress Cataloging-in-Publication Data
A CIP catalog record for this book has been applied for at the Library of Congress.

Bibliographic information published by the Deutsche Nationalbibliothek
The Deutsche Nationalbibliothek lists this publication in the Deutsche Nationalbibliografie; detailed bibliographic data are available on the internet at http://dnb.dnb.de.

© 2017 Walter de Gruyter GmbH, Berlin/Boston
This volume is text- and page-identical with the hardback published in 2015.
Printing and binding: CPI books GmbH, Leck

♾ Printed on acid-free paper
Printed in Germany

www.degruyter.com

Table of Contents

Editors' Introduction —— 1

Part I: Cassirer and the Philosophy of Science

Massimo Ferrari (Torino)
Ernst Cassirer and the History of Science —— 11

Thomas Mormann (San Sebastián)
From Mathematics to Quantum Mechanics – On the Conceptual Unity of Cassirer's Philosophy of Science (1907–1937) —— 31

Thomas Ryckman (Palo Alto)
A Retrospective View of *Determinism and Indeterminism in Modern Physics* —— 65

Alan W. Richardson (Vancouver)
Holism and the Constitution of "Experience in its Entirety" Cassirer contra Quine on the Lessons of Duhem —— 103

Jeremy Heis (Irvine)
Arithmetic and Number in the Philosophy of Symbolic Forms —— 123

Scott Edgar (Halifax)
Intersubjectivity and Physical Laws in Post-Kantian Theory of Knowledge Natorp and Cassirer —— 141

Norbert Andersch (London)
Symbolic Form and Mental Illness: Ernst Cassirer's Contribution to a New Concept of Psychopathology —— 163

Part II: Epistemology and the History of Philosophy

Samantha Matherne (Santa Cruz)
Marburg Neo-Kantianism as Philosophy of Culture —— 201

Steve G. Lofts (London/ON)
Cassirer and Heidegger: The Cultural-Event The *Auseinandersetzung* of Thinking and Being —— 233

Pierre Keller (Riverside)
Cassirer's Retrieval of Kant's Copernican Revolution in Semiotics —— 259

Simon Truwant (Leuven)
The Concept of 'Function' in Cassirer's Historical, Systematic, and Ethical Writings —— 289

Guido Kreis (Bonn)
The Varieties of Perception Non-Conceptual Content in Kant, Cassirer, and McDowell —— 313

Part III: The Philosophy of Culture Today

Anne Pollok (Columbia/S.C.)
The First and Second Person Perspective in History: Or, Why History is 'Culture Fiction' —— 341

J Tyler Friedman (Milwaukee)
Cassirer's Critique of Culture and the Several Tasks of the Critic —— 361

Sebastian Luft (Milwaukee)
The A Priori of Culture: Philosophy of Culture Between Rationalism and Relativism. The Example of Lévi-Strauss' *Structural Anthropology* —— 381

Curtis L. Carter (Milwaukee)
After Cassirer: Art and Aesthetic Symbols in Langer and Goodman —— 401

Jennifer Marra (Milwaukee)
Humor as a Symbolic Form: Cassirer and the Culture of Comedy —— 419

Fabien Capeillères (Paris/Princeton)
Cassirer on the "Objectity" of Evil The Symbolic Constitution of *Der Mythus des 20 Jahrhunderts* —— 435

Subject index —— 469

Index of names —— 473

Editors' Introduction

The present volume collects the majority of the papers that were based on talks delivered at the conference in Milwaukee, June 18–21, 2014, that had the same title as this volume.¹ This was the first large-scale conference on the philosophy of Ernst Cassirer in North America. This in itself is a remarkable fact. For, not too long ago, people would have scoffed at such an attempt at reviving Cassirer, his thought, his legacy, and his potential relevance for contemporary philosophy.² Looking at newer interest in Cassirer, both in North America and elsewhere in the world, it is safe to say that this is no longer the case. Indeed, it is now generally recognized that Cassirer is one of the most important philosophers of the 20th century and has been unrightfully forgotten, only to be revitalized in the last decades. The conference in 2014 had the intention of reassessing his legacy and his importance for contemporary thought. In an age in which "culture" is the most sought-for word in internet searches,³ displaying both an irritated puzzlement and a curious ambivalence towards the very word that defined Cassirer's philosophy, an express *philosophy of culture* certainly has the potential to play a vital role in today's world, both within the academy as well as—as Cassirer would have insisted—in the broader world of culture.

As mentioned, this novel interest in Cassirer is not entirely new. Such a revival as we are experiencing it today would, no doubt, have been impossible without the efforts on the part of selfless scholars who have been editing Ernst Cassirer's papers (in ECW and ECN). Regarding this work, one should recognize the work of the late John Michael Krois (1943–2010). It is no exaggeration to say that the Cassirer who resurfaces in these impressive editions is new similar to the way in which Husserl became an entirely new philosopher after the publication of his literary estate. Regarding Cassirer, what is new is not so much the

---

1 With one exception: Thomas Mormann could not attend the conference but kindly submitted a paper to be included in this volume.
2 Indeed, Hans Sluga's review of the 2010 book by Peter Gordon, *Continental Divide* (reviewed in NDPR in 2011.02.31), while laudatory of Gordon's achievement, concludes: "Attempts to revive his fortunes are, I am afraid, doomed to failure." The history of Cassirer's reception, both in the present volume and other recent publications, has, hopefully, made amply clear that this judgment was premature.
3 Cf. Joshua Rothman's article "The Meaning of 'Culture'" (http://www.newyorker.com/books/joshua-rothman/meaning-culture), in which he points to Merriam-Webster's selection of "culture" as word of the year 2014, which, in turn, was motivated by the largest "hit" on internet searches. Rothman's article makes a nice case for both the ambivalence of the term "culture" and the necessity for a sustained reflection on it.

general philosophical standpoint, but our ability to witness the impressive breadth and depth of his scholarship in many areas of intellectual inquiries, within philosophy and in other scholarly disciplines, both "hard" and "soft" sciences. Finally, the monumental edition of Cassirer's correspondence makes manifest a scholar who was in close contact with the intellectual luminaries of his day, causing one to wonder, once again, how such a towering figure could be so forgotten in the decades after World War II.

The editors would be remiss were we not to emphasize that many of the authors present in this volume were instrumental for this Cassirer-renaissance, and indeed it could not have happened without their work, and some of the younger authors represented here will no doubt continue in this effort in their own forthcoming work. Thus, this is a happy moment for Cassirer, his philosophy and its ethos. The editors are pleased that this joint effort has come together for an international conference to celebrate the philosophy of Ernst Cassirer, and that the fruit of these labors are now available in printed form.

A few initial words to motivate a turn to the philosopher Cassirer.

It was said at the outset that it is "generally recognized" that Cassirer is one of the most important philosophers of the 20th century. Let us start here with a few reflections on what it can mean to be "important" as a philosopher, what the very notion of an *important philosopher* implies. What is the measure of importance, when it comes to philosophy and philosophers as the human beings conceiving philosophy? *Can* such a measure at all exist, let alone be applied? One can perhaps approach the question differently by asking whether or not Cassirer can be considered a *classic*, for surely one will consider a classic philosopher important. If we follow Gadamer's definition of the classical – that it speaks to us now and always, vis-à-vis that which goes, as ephemeral, into the gargantuan trash bin of history – can we call Cassirer a classical philosopher in the way we consider Kant and Hegel to be? If he may not measure up to these towering figures, may he perhaps be considered, more modestly, a classic of the 20th century alongside other classics of this century, such as—in standard accounts—Husserl, Heidegger, or Wittgenstein?

Regarding one of these figures just mentioned, perhaps one may draw an analogy to someone whose fate has been similar. Edmund Husserl, like Cassirer, was a Jew who suffered from the ascendance of Nazism in 1933 and whose literary estate only became known after World War II. In his opening speech of the conference celebrating Husserl's 150th birthday in Leuven in 2009, the famous Husserl scholar Robert Sokolowski made the following observation:

"We all agree [we want to stress the 'we'] that Husserl's phenomenology is now safely ensconced in the cultural firmament, far from the turbulence of our sublunar world, where authors devour or clamber over one another in the struggle for survival."

Of course, Sokolowski was preaching to the choir. But can we ("we" here being the *pluralis maiestatis* for the group of scholars surrounding Cassirer) all agree on the same terms similar to the way in which the Husserl crowd agrees on Husserl? And even if we can get ourselves to agree to this assessment: Would Cassirer even *want* to be considered part of the "cultural firmament" and not rather of the "rich bathos" of culture? A problem with such an assessment is precisely that it is one striking feature of Cassirer's philosophizing that he rarely clambers over others in a struggle for survival. It is for this reason that he has been called "the Olympian," which can be considered, in truth, a backhanded critique on the part of those who might have wished that he had engaged in a more spirited exchange from time to time. This judgment makes it seem as if Cassirer never really was of this sublunar world and always had his head in the cultural firmament.

But is this really a fair assessment? Is it not rather the case that Cassirer seems so far removed from our current concerns that he, to his own disadvantage, *appears* to be a classic to us today, precisely because it is hard for us today to revitalize the world Cassirer lived in? But is this not just a repetition of the old critique that Cassirer was a citizen of the Wilhelminian Germany and then the Weimar Republic, defending it staunchly as it exuded its last breath? That his philosophy died the moment the Weimar Republic died? Seen in this light, Cassirer might well be a classic but in a dubious sense, namely in that sense in which Goethe is a classic too, such that one can peacefully let the dust continue to settle on the tomes in our grandparents' library. It is in this sense that the term "classical" is readily used to pronounce someone dead instead of "timely" or "vital." Moreover, the problem with this characterization of Cassirer as "Olympian" or "classical" obscures that he was very much engaged in the times he lived in, although these times are so far removed from ours. One has forgotten that Cassirer was anything but aloof but engaged with the best minds of his day.

But to be fair to Gadamer, this was clearly not what he meant when he defined the classical as something that continues to speak with equal strength and power to humans as long as they live. To Gadamer, "the classic" was a decidedly positive category, designating someone's continuous and normative relevance, and to belong to this small crowd is not only rare, but also something over which the author of classical works has no control. It is not something someone can *wish to be*, but a classic is something that takes on the shape of the classical over the course of time. Now, if we take *this* criterion of the classical as a yardstick for someone's importance, what can we say with respect to Cassirer's importance?

Defining the classical in the way Gadamer does presupposes a separation of the author's intention from the history of its effects, the *Wirkungsgeschichte*. So let us approach the question as to Cassirer's importance, by asking, what Cassirer would presumably say about his own effectiveness, were he to be able to witness it today. Apart from the apparent contributions he has made to the history of philosophy and the way of writing it, to the philosophy of science, to individual cultural studies, we may ask: Would he be dismayed by the little effect he has exerted on cultural life as a whole and the philosophy of this culture in particular? Would he really have such a high regard for his own work, such that he would even *want* to be in a position of having to answer this question? We think it is one sign of Cassirer's incredible modesty that he presumably would have been quite uncomfortable in being asked to assess his own importance. As much as one may personally find this trait in him *très sympathique*, it is also something that has worked against him, especially in comparison with his charismatic teacher Hermann Cohen, with the aggressive and ambitious Heidegger and perhaps other problematic human beings who come to mind. Indeed, it is the lacking cult of personhood surrounding Cassirer that may well be the most striking feature of the man and the philosopher. He would presumably have abhorred a cult around him, a cult that exists around Heidegger to this day. Indeed, the cult around the philosopher who asked his "ownmost" (*einzigste*) question of being, on the one hand, and the tireless worker in the vineyards of culture, on the other—the contrast could not be starker.

Polemics aside, a point is to be made that Cassirer, who saw himself as a philosopher of culture—as someone, that is, who witnesses cultural work and then assesses it philosophically, but in constant dialogue with scholars of culture—would not have considered Gadamer's criterion at all applicable to his own work, as much as he admired the literary and philosophical classics, such as Goethe and Kant and the other representatives of the European life of spirit, and he presumably would have rejected this label outright.

Instead, if we scan the scope and breadth of his work, in the philosophy of science, in theoretical philosophy, the study of myth, the philosophy of language, the historiography of philosophy—and lots of this work is dealt with in this volume—what we discover is not a novel philosophical system that "sublates," say, Kant or Hegel or Cohen or Natorp, into a new unified vision. We also do not find a new philosophical method and research program as in Husserl, such that Cassirer's contribution could be easily identifiable with a novel title. Instead, we find a philosophical meditation on these different expressions of the human spirit as the symbolic forms we create and live in and through which alone we can be what we are, in Cassirer's words, as *animalia symbolica*. At the same time, Cassirer remained a firm Kantian, which is to say, he wanted to involve himself in the sphere of culture without relinquishing the properly philosophical, that is, transcendental standpoint, and indeed to accomplish for culture writ large and for cultural studies, as he submits in his late work *Zur Logik der Kulturwissenschaften*, what Kant had accomplished for the natural sciences.

But despite this ambitious claim, what Cassirer wanted at the end of the day, was (we believe) not a *new* philosophy, a new system that would encompass philosophically the entire realm of the sciences and, even more so, all reality. Cassirer instead wanted a philosophy that should understand itself as what it is and can be, to the full extent of its capacities and in the full realization of its limits. That is, Cassirer wanted a philosophy that finally gives full expression to and rises to the level of what we as symbolic creatures are and what we ought to be. In this sense, philosophy should not be separate from, but *continuous with* the best work of culture that we as a species are capable of. This is the deep Enlightenment humanism of Cassirer's philosophy. It is not the naïve vision of a visionary sage calling from the desert to remind us of the good old days. Rather, it is the ethos of someone who has immersed himself in all aspects of culture to bring out the specifically human side in all these forms, the human which may not be reduced to the rational. So if there is something that can be called classical in Cassirer, it is his philosophical ethos, which we may call humanistic or enlightened, again, not in a naïve understanding of the term, but in the way in which another Neo-Kantian, Jürgen Habermas, speaks of "Modernity, an unfinished project."

This form of humanistic ethos has not only experienced enormous blowback from its post-modern critics; it has also let itself get on the defensive, instead of turning the tables on these critics. Its neglect to go on the offensive has worked very much to its disadvantage. Indeed, is it not rather the case that the critics of a humanistic modernity, in decrying the Enlightenment stance, stand on its very ground when making these allegations? Have they really understood what modernity means to its defendants? Are they not benefactors of one of modernism's most powerful virtues – tolerance – in critiquing what they themselves take for granted as enabling their critique? It may be hard to "sell" this ethos nowadays and that it may sound, to some, quaint and old-fashioned. But again one can turn the tables on this sentiment and ask why it should be old-fashioned. Is not the call to a "new humanism" that Heidegger issued after World War II, in which he called for such a new humanism based on a new understanding of the human being as being *gelassen zu den Dingen*, much more old-fashioned today, and much more helpless? This critique of modern technology may be essentially correct, but can it be a solution to the present crisis? Can a primitivistic celebration of idyllic pre-industrial nature be more persuasive than facing culture and its subcultural discontents head-on?

The editors believe that they speak for all authors represented in this volume that Cassirer's vision of humanity and humankind is much more attractive and much more timely today, in a time when we come to realize that global problems cannot be tackled alone, neither by individuals or individual groups or even nations, nor can we sit around and wait until a God saves us. But of course this is in good Marburg fashion an *Aufgabe,* it is our task to show that this is the case. To be at work at culture is more than ever a moral demand for us today, as we see the achievements of culture being destroyed and our sense of feeling at home in the world ever more alienated. To return to the question, "what is culture?," a philosophical reflection on this question is ever more timely today, in a time where fundamentalism in its various forms is on the rise and where even—the head of the hydra we had all hoped to be chopped off for good—Anti-Semitism has become fashionable once again in certain parts of the world.

***

The volume is divided into *three* sections. The *first* section is devoted to the philosophy of science, a theme that occupied Cassirer from his first published work – *Leibniz' System in seinen wissenschaftlichen Grundlagen (Leibniz' System in its Scientific Foundations,* of 1902) – to his last, *Galileo's Platonism,* of 1946. In *Ernst Cassirer and the History of Science,* Massimo Ferrari considers the development of scientific thought as a theme for Cassirer's philosophy as well as Cassirer's relationship to other contemporary historians of science. Thomas Mormann's piece, *From Mathematics to Quantum Mechanics – On the Conceptual Unity of Cassirer's Philosophy of Science (1907–1937),* examines Cassirer's philosophical treatment of the two scientific revolutions in 20th century physics – Einstein's theory of relativity and the development of quantum physics. Alan W. Richardson's *Holism and the Constitution of "Experience in its Entirety": Cassirer contra Quine on the Lessons of Duhem* considers the adaptability of the Neo-Kantian framework to scientific progress, especially the status of the a priori in the wake of paradigm shifts. Jeremy Heis' contribution is an in-depth study of the philosophy of arithmetic contained in Cassirer's *Philosophy of Symbolic Forms*, whose neglect has led scholars to overlook the new ideas absent from Cassirer's earlier work on mathematics. Scott Edgar considers the basis of the intersubjectivity of physical laws and the way that the accounts offered by Cassirer and his Neo-Kantian contemporary Paul Natorp overcome the epistemic idiosyncrasy that hinders the intersubjective reach of a representation. In *Symbolic Form and Mental Illness: Ernst Cassirer's Contribution to a New Concept of Psychopathology*, Norbert Andersch places Cassirer's overlooked account of the constitution of consciousness and psychopathology in conversation with other 20th century accounts and its implications for classificatory systems such as the DSM and ICD.

The authors in the *second* section treat two more themes that were central to Cassirer's philosophizing: epistemology and the history of philosophy. Samantha Matherne considers Cassirer's Neo-Kantian pedigree and the precedence set by his Marburg colleagues in recognizing the necessity of a philosophy of culture and delimiting its task. Stephen Lofts takes a fresh look at the fabled Cassirer-Heidegger relationship, and by eschewing the traditional paradigm of the Davos dispute, suggests directions for further research. Pierre Keller undertakes a detailed study of Kant's theory of signs and considers its significance for Cassirer's celebrated work on the symbolic forms. Simon Truwant highlights the pervasiveness of the concept of 'function' throughout Cassirer's work and argues that it plays the central, unifying role usually accorded to 'the symbol.' Placing Cassirer in conversation with Kant and McDowell, Guido Kreis argues that his *Philosophy of Symbolic Forms* provides untapped resources for weighing in on the long-standing debate over the conceptuality or non-conceptual nature of perception.

The *third* section, concerning "The Philosophy of Culture Today," authors consider prospects and possibilities for Cassirer's thought as well as some of the posthumous influence it has exercised. After presenting Cassirer's account of historical reconstruction, Anne Pollok considers the intersubjective dimension of history. J Tyler Friedman focuses on the different meanings of critique and the corresponding tasks for the philosopher and the critic that derive from Cassirer's project of critiquing culture. Sebastian Luft examines the possibility of merging a transcendental philosophy of culture with empirical cultural studies, using the example of Claude Lévi-Strauss' structural anthropology. Curtis Carter examines Cassirer's few, yet substantial writings on art and traces their influence on philosophers of art working in his wake. Jennifer Marra applies the concept of symbolic forms to intractable problems in the philosophy of humor, namely finding a unified ground for defining humor as such. Fabien Capeillères takes an in-depth look at the symbolic form of myth and its reemergence in the political actuality and theoretical underpinnings of National Socialism.

J Tyler Friedman & Sebastian Luft, Milwaukee, January 2015

Part I: **Cassirer and the Philosophy of Science**

Massimo Ferrari (Torino)
Ernst Cassirer and the History of Science*

1 Philosophy of Science and the History of Science

The importance attributed to Cassirer as a philosopher of cultural, symbolic forms has often led the scholarship to underestimate the role played by science in the framing of his thought. Until recently, therefore, the historical development of scientific knowledge as a pivotal point in his thought has largely been neglected. More specifically, many critical studies devoted to Cassirer seem to overlook the fact that not only was he capable of offering illuminating interpretations of Goethe's, Schiller's or Humboldt's works, but he could also provide profound accounts of the origins of modern science from Galileo to Newton, as well as Einstein's or Heisenberg's physical theories. In his late article "Mathematical Mystique and Mathematical Science of Nature" (1940), Cassirer stressed that not only is the history of science a crucial issue for both the philosopher and the historian of philosophy, but that the question of the *origins* of the exact sciences represents a philosophical focus which cannot be ignored.[1] Moreover, this question, which Cassirer considered to be fundamental, is already present at the very beginnings of his intellectual development. His first, great book on Leibniz, published in 1902, is devoted to an inquiry into the 'scientific foundations' of Leibniz's system and breaks with the traditional image of Leibniz as the author of a metaphysical novel about the Monadology.[2] Thus, this investigation of Leibniz as a seminal mathematician and physician of his time constitutes Cassirer's first attempt at grasping the scientific roots of modern science and philosophy. The next step in his project devoted to the 'prehistory of pure reason' is even more impressive—the masterful book *The Problem of Knowledge in the Philosophy and Science of the Modern Time*, which appeared in 1906–1907. These two volumes serve as a testament to Cassirer's very fruitful insights into the historical and systematic development of epistemology in its connection with, and in its reliance on, the modern mathematical science of nature.[3]

---

* I would like to warmly thank Shimon Shemtov for having helped me with the English corrections of this paper.
1 Cassirer (2006a), 284.
2 Cassirer (1998).
3 Cassirer (1995).

This central feature of Cassirer's work is closely related to his commitment to Marburg Neo-Kantianism which is, in turn, either scarcely considered by scholarship or solely remembered more as a biographical, rather than properly philosophical, background of Cassirer's thought. In reality, however, the legacy of Hermann Cohen's and Paul Natorp's Neo-Kantianism represents the basic framework of Cassirer's intellectual enterprise—not only biographically, but also with respect to the entire development of his thinking, including his later 'philosophy of culture'.[4] While there are certainly many important differences that gradually emerge on the road from early Neo-Kantianism to the final outcome of his 'philosophy of symbolic forms,' Cassirer always remains faithful to at least the essential methodological premise of the Neo-Kantianism which Cohen and Natorp formulated. According to Cohen, whose 1871 book *Kant's Theory of Experience* is doubtless the 'Bible' of the Marburg School, transcendental philosophy rests on the *'Faktum'* of the mathematical science of nature. This 'fact', as Cohen suggests, is both historically determined and steadily changing, and demands an analysis which uncovers the conditions of its possibility, thereby discovering the synthetic principles and epistemological foundations of mathematical science itself.[5] This is the reason why Cohen maintains that the commonly used term 'theory of knowledge' is misleading, whereas the proper description of Kant's reformulated project would be 'the critique of knowledge' (*Erkenntniskritik*).[6] Thus, transcendental philosophy deals neither with the constitution of the human subject, nor with his ability to know, but rather with the 'meta-level' of philosophical and epistemological reflection about the a priori conditions of scientific knowledge. In short, 'the critique of knowledge' aims to uncover the a priori presuppositions and foundations of scientific thought beginning with the given, historically determined 'fact' of natural science. This is precisely what Cohen, and the Marburg School in general, call the 'transcendental method'.[7] To some extent, this method can be considered an early attempt to perform the 'logical analysis of science' practiced later by Rudolf Carnap and Logical Empiricism, all of whom rejected an account of scientific knowledge still committed to psychologism.[8] But Marburg Neo-Kantianism was particularly devoted to an investigation of the history of mathematics, especially mathematical science, which aimed to show, for instance, how infinitesimal analysis, non-

---

4 On this topic I allow myself to refer to my book: Ferrari (1988).
5 We refer to Cohen (1987).
6 Cohen (1884), 4–6.
7 See Cohen (1987), 93–110. An illuminating overview is offered by Natorp (1912).
8 See my paper "Versteckte Verwandtschaften. Erkenntniskritik und Wissenschaftsanalyse— Cohen und der logische Empirismus" (forthcoming).

Euclidean geometries, modern logic, and profound transformations in physics at the turn of the 20th century had radically changed the *'Faktum'* to which transcendental philosophy refers. As is demonstrated by Natorp's studies on Copernicus, Descartes, Hobbes, and Leibniz, this was also connected with the ambitious project of revisiting the history of philosophy with regard to its relationship to the development of science or, in other words, to the changing 'fact' of science.[9]

Yet it was Cassirer who first understood the true significance of the historical and mutable dimensions of this 'developing fact' for a Kantian epistemological project, and in so doing, he bound, more deeply than his Marburg predecessors, the fate of critical philosophy to its relationship with the development of the exact sciences. Cassirer thus located the sole enduring task of a critical inquiry based on the transcendental method in the "continually renewed examination of the fundamental concepts of science, [...] which simultaneously involves a thorough subjective self-examination of the critique itself."[10] But if the 'fact' of science is "in its nature a historically developing fact",[11] then philosophical reflection about the forms of knowledge that underlie this 'fact' and make it possible must be characterized by a fundamental *dynamism*—a dynamism which is intrinsic to the formation of the transcendental method and also enables its extension to all areas of cultural objective forms. In his 1906 *Introduction* to the first volume of *The Problem of Knowledge*, Cassirer writes:

> The 'fact' of science is, and will of course remain, in its nature a historically developing 'fact'. If this insight does not yet appear explicitly in Kant, if his categories can still appear as *finished* 'core concepts of reason' in both number and content, the modern development of critical and idealistic logic [here he's referring to Cohen's *Logik der reinen Erkenntnis*] has made this point perfectly clear. By the *forms of judgment* are meant the unified and active *motivations* (*Motive*) of thought which course through the manifold particular formations and are continually put to use in the generation and formulation of new categories.[12]

Thus, Cassirer's impressive reconstruction of the problem of knowledge in modern times from the historical and systematic standpoint is the result of his Neo-Kantian apprenticeship and, at the same time, the highest proof of his very original approach to the epistemological reflection about the scientific *'Faktum'* with which the transcendental method deals. On the one hand, Cassirer's main idea is

---

9 We refer especially to Natorp (1985), 3–14; (1882b) 193–229; (1882a) 355–375. The importance of Natorp's early historical works is extensively illustrated by Sieg (1994).
10 Cassirer (2001), 37.
11 Cassirer (1995) vol. 1, 14.
12 Cassirer (1995) vol. 1, 14–15.

that science and philosophy must be mutually connected; modern philosophy and modern science constitute a unique whole and, more precisely, the understanding of the problem of knowledge must consider both philosophers such as Descartes or Leibniz as well as scientists such as Galileo, Kepler or Newton. According to Cassirer, the traditional history of philosophy has, for the most part, neglected the essential ways in which the rise of modern science contributed to the deep changes that have occurred in philosophical thought. In the early modern age, scientists and philosophers worked together on a new image of both nature and the universe, which also entailed a radical break from the previous conception of man. For Cassirer, the final outcome—and the final goal—of this history is Kant's critical philosophy. To some extent, Cassirer deals here with a kind of 'history of pure reason' in the Kantian sense, which is based on—as Cassirer emphasizes—the strict collaboration between the epistemological standpoint and historical enquiry.[13] On the other hand, Cassirer intended to continue the ambitious project which the young Natorp had sketched in his early book on Descartes' theory of knowledge, namely, to outline the prehistory (*Vorgeschichte*) of Kant's critical philosophy through a philosophical and historical examination of its sources in the philosophy and scientific thought of Descartes, Galileo, Kepler and Leibniz, the founders of the idealistic tradition in the sense of Marburg 'logical idealism', whose origins Cohen, and later Natorp himself, saw in Plato's theory of ideas.[14] Surely, nobody will deny that Cassirer goes far beyond the original conception of the history of philosophy and the history of science endorsed by Cohen and Natorp. Nevertheless, it would be quite impossible to outline Cassirer's own achievement in this field without taking into account his former apprenticeship in Marburg and the enduring influence of Neo-Kantianism on his work. Insofar as it is plausible to speak of a Neo-Kantian tradition in the history of science in the first decades of the 20th century, Cassirer is surely both its most representative interpreter and its first promoter. But it is not only for these reasons that Cassirer is still of greatest interest to the wide contemporary community of professional historians of science.

---

13 Cassirer (1995) vol. 1, VII.
14 See in particular Natorp (1921). The decisive role played by the epistemological interpretation of Plato's theory of ideas within the Marburg Neo-Kantianism is doubtless a crucial one in understanding its interpretation of modern mathematical science of nature. A good survey is available in the excellent book by Lembeck (1994). See also Servois (2004).

2 The Question of Continuity and Progress in Scientific Thought

Since its very beginnings, Cassirer's work on the history of science is not only deeply connected with the history of epistemology, but rests also on the firm belief that—as he already states in the introduction to *The Problem of Knowledge*—modern science is also a cultural form, a way in which the spirit of early modern culture shows one of its most typical characteristics. According to Cassirer, science is connected to the various "intellectual energies" which have contributed to the rise of the early modern age, from Humanism to the Scientific Revolution. In this sense, science represents the core—as Cassirer says—of the "theoretical self-awareness" of a new era in human culture.[15] This insight constitutes a kind of *leitmotiv* in Cassirer's work: even in the later period of his intellectual life he stresses the break represented most notably by Galileo, whose main achievement was the essential transformation of scientific thought thanks to a new concept of truth which resulted in an "ethics of science".[16]

In his wonderful book on Renaissance thought published 20 years after the *Erkenntnisproblem*, Cassirer offers a more detailed account of the intrinsic relationship between the rise of modern science and the heritage of Renaissance culture. *Individuum und Kosmos in der Philosophie der Renaissance* is a work composed in connection with the *milieu* of the Warburg Library and influenced by the image of the Renaissance which Aby Warburg himself had elaborated in his fascinating inquiries into the rebirth of Paganism and ancient astrological beliefs in the early 15th century.[17] Here Cassirer emphasizes the wide context of symbolic forms (religion, art, mythical thought) which constitute the cultural background that has enabled the rise of the modern scientific image of the universe, from Nicholas Cusano to Giordano Bruno. According to Cassirer, both a new sentiment of life as well as the increasing emancipation of natural science from the dark power of magic and astrology made it possible to conceive of nature in a new light, namely, as the object of mathematical measurement rather than something which could only be approached purely qualitatively. In a broader sense, the scientific worldview is therefore the result of a new image of man, now placed at the centre of the world as a Prometheus unbound.

---

15 Cassirer (1995) vol. I, p. XI.
16 Cassirer (2007a), 5–19.
17 Cassirer (2002).

On the other hand, one has to ask whether Cassirer's highly sophisticated reconstruction of the origins of modern science during the Renaissance can be interpreted in the sense of a revolutionary break or as a kind of linear progress towards the final goal of pure reason. To be sure, Cassirer was convinced that reason essentially means—quite similarly to Cohen's own insight—*continuity*, namely, that reason is the continuous process thanks to which the development of scientific thought does not involve a relativism which is opposed to the universality of the "logical functions of knowledge".[18] Nevertheless, Cassirer is fully aware that scientific progress is not simply cumulative. In the first pages of *The Problem of Knowledge*, Cassirer suggests very clearly that in the "critical periods" during which scientific knowledge changes its fundamental standpoints we are not witness to a mere "quantitative growth" but, on the contrary, to a "strong dialectical contradiction" between the different insights at issue. "A concept earlier considered as untenable," Cassirer adds, "can later become both a means and a necessary condition of knowledge". Put in other words, what has been a basic principle of empirical knowledge is not timelessly valid, on the contrary, it seems quite possible that its previous fundamental function in explaining phenomena will be overthrown by a new conceptual framework, which may even make the former one appear "absurd."[19]

It would not be an exaggeration to suggest that Cassirer's conception of the conflict between opposed principles of knowledge anticipates a sort of "transition from one paradigm to another" in Thomas Kuhn's sense. No wonder, therefore, that in his essay, which we have already quoted, "Mathematical Mystique and Mathematical Science of Nature", Cassirer speaks explicitly of *revolution* in science (and perhaps, in doing so, he is echoing Koyré's use of this term in the *Études galiléennes*, that appeared one year earlier). He writes:

> The history of human knowledge repeatedly shows us new, particular ages (the more important ones, to be sure), in the course of which knowledge doesn't simply increase its extent as much as change both its overall conceptual tools and its sense. Instead of a mere quantitative growth, there suddenly appears a qualitative "change" (*Umschlag*). Rather than dealing with an evolution, we are dealing with an unexpected *revolution*. The very ideal of exact knowledge of nature arises from just such a revolution.[20]

Nevertheless, it must be stressed that, for Cassirer, a conceptual "revolution" in no way signifies a sudden break from the previous scientific age. On the contrary,

---

18 Cassirer (1995) vol.1, 13.
19 Cassirer (1995) vol. 1, 4 (my emphasis).
20 Cassirer (2006a), 285.

Cassirer argues that it would be "misleading" to consider the rise of modern natural science as being totally independent from its roots in the Middle Ages. "We are never truly dealing with an interruption in the continuity", he states.[21] Both continuity and discontinuity are, therefore, the two faces of scientific progress, although Cassirer does underline that the "jump" accomplished by scientific thought in the modern age would not have been possible in *vacuo*. Yet Cassirer questions the usefulness of the concept of continuity as featured in Pierre Duhem's historical account of the development of science from the Middle Ages to Galileo. Whereas Duhem, in his outstanding works on the history of mechanics before Galileian science, surely has great merit in pointing out the undeniable importance of the theory of *impetus*, in Cassirer's judgement it is "audacious and doubtful" to place the prehistory Duhem is dealing with on the same level as the rise of the new science that represents, in Cassirer's mind, both an enormous change from mathematical and empirical standpoints as well as the birth of a very different image of the universe.[22]

Cassirer refuses, therefore, Duhem's thesis of radical continuity. This in no way implies that Cassirer underestimates Duhem's excellent contributions to contemporary history of science, not to mention Cassirer's commitment to Duhem concerning his epistemological holism as it is formulated by Duhem in his book about the structure of physical theory.[23] In *The Problem of Knowledge*, Cassirer refers with the greatest appreciation to Duhem's studies on Leonardo and Kepler,[24] but evidently disagrees with some of Duhem's epistemological assumptions, especially with regard to the motto "sozein ta phainomena" (*salvare apparentia*) which summarizes his view of scientific change. This seems to be of some importance, inasmuch as Duhem attempted through this principle to de-

---

21 Cassirer (2006a), 285.
22 Cassirer (2006a), 286. See also Cassirer (2006b) 185–193. We refer furthermore to Cassirer (2007b), 5–19.
23 To Cassirer, two main aspects of Duhem's epistemological approach seem to be particularly apt in outlining a critical framework according to 'logical idealism' (although Duhem had nothing to do with the Kantian tradition). First of all Duhem has the great merit to have understood the *holistic* character of scientific theories, so that their empirical confirmation can be gained only when the individual concepts are considered as members "of a theoretical complex" Cassirer (1953), 146–147. Secondly, Cassirer particularly admires Duhem's profound insight into the unavoidable intellectual function of forming scientific experience. "The intellectual work of understanding, which connects the bare fact systematically with the totality of phenomena—as Cassirer sums up Duhem's account—only begins when the fact is represented and replaced by a mathematical *symbol*" Cassirer (1953), 146–147 [my emphasis]. Regarding this latter aspect in particular, see Duhem (1974), 159.
24 See, for instance, Cassirer (1995) vol 1., 267.

prive the astronomical revolution from Copernicus to Kepler of either a break or interruption from the pre-Copernican conception of universe. According to Duhem, Andrea Osiander was right when he stressed, in his preface to the *Revolutionibus orbium coelestium*, that Copernicus's theory was merely a new way of arranging astronomical data in a more harmonious and clear system, without giving up the previous cosmology.[25] Cassirer opposes this claim by emphasizing the properly critical view according to which the new science involves something very different from a mere reorganization of mathematical data, and offers, by contrast, an essentially new account of phenomena thanks to a new concept of natural law. Why, otherwise, Cassirer wonders rhetorically, would Bruno and Galileo have devoted their lives to the simple cause of "salvare apparentia"?[26]

In this sense, Duhem represents a case study enabling us to understand what Cassirer means when he speaks both of revolution and epoch-making changes in the history of science. However, this cannot be reduced to a purely historical question. The very idea which Cassirer endorses in his epistemological and historical work is, in fact, tied to the change of paradigm that he highlights, in *Substance and Function*, as the crucial transition from "substance" to "function". "The conception of function," Cassirer argues, "constitutes the general schema and model according to which the modern concept of nature has been moulded in its progressive historical development".[27] At the same time, this is the main idea on which Cassirer bases his admirable reconstruction of the problem of knowledge since the Renaissance,[28] aimed at showing how the long road from the concept of substance to Kant's 'functional' theory of knowledge is a very complicated one. According to this view, Kant himself appears as the result of an historical process whose final outcome would not have been possible without Galileo and Kepler, Leibniz and Descartes, Euler and Newton, etc.

One of the most influential heroes of the philosophical history told by Cassirer is doubtless Galileo, the great father of modern science and the modern concept of scientific law. The main question here is how Galileo conceived of scientific experience in its relationship to mathematical procedures and, more generally, to reason as such. In short, Cassirer's explanation of this crucial issue is centered, broadly speaking, on the Kantian account of knowledge as the result of the spontaneous activity of reason, both in organizing empirical phenomena and in submitting them to purely functional mathematical laws. Given the fact that, according to Galileo, experience is grounded in mathematics, it is possible then

---

25 On this topic, see Carrier (2001), 129.
26 Cassirer (2010), 41.
27 Cassirer (1953), 21.
28 See Cassirer (1995), vol. 1, 303.

—Cassirer suggests—to consider the fundamental role played by mathematical laws within the tradition of Platonism, a Platonism interpreted, in turn, within the framework of 'logical idealism' which Cohen had formulated in the early days of the Marburg School. This kind of Platonism—as we shall see again further on—views mathematics as being applied to experience thereby providing a complete 'functionalization' to the conceptual equipment of scientific thought.[29] Thus, Galileo embodies, in Cassirer's eyes, the first scientist able to grasp the fundamental concept of function and, consequently, overcome the metaphysical concept of substance.

Something similar characterizes, in Cassirer's mind, the core of Kepler's astronomical work.[30] Both the concept of harmony and the aesthetic image of the universe can be assumed—Cassirer points out—to be the background of the veritable *epistemological* problem posed by Kepler. Kepler refers explicitly to Plato as well as the tradition of Renaissance Platonism insofar as his main scientific goal consists of finding a connection between the pure thought and the experience or, in other words, between an idealism quite similar to the Platonic one and the scientific experience.[31] Thus, the concept of *law* makes it possible to consider Kepler as a modern scientist, devoted to going beyond—as Cassirer says— the usual predominance of geometry in favor of a physics resting rather on principles. The latter, and not the geometrical forms, are the "constants" which constitute the modern concept of science, and provide its very peculiar theoretical feature with regard to the ancient metaphysics.[32]

Are we dealing here with a 'Cassirerian' Kepler? To be sure, or, at least to some extent, it seems undeniable that it is so. Nevertheless the core issue is that Cassirer, once again, attempts to show a very decisive development in the "fact of science". However, in this context Cassirer calls into question Cohen's typical interpretation of Kant's transcendental philosophy as depending on, and essentially referring to, Newton's *Principia*.[33] At issue here is primarily the crisis of the Newtonian theory of experience, which Cassirer sees in the unresolved tension between the absolute character of both space and time and the *regulae philosophandi*.[34] The scientific and philosophical answer that Cassirer believes to be capable of solving this fundamental question consists, essentially, of recognizing the objectivity of space and time according to the view expressed

---

29 Cassirer (1995) vol. 1, 324–325, 356–358.
30 Cassirer (1995) vol. 1, 268–270.
31 Cassirer (1995) vol. 1, 275, 281–283, 291–292.
32 Cassirer (1995) vol. 1, 287, 297, 306–313.
33 See Cohen (1987), 94, 518.
34 Cassirer (1995) vol. 2, 391.

by Leibniz in his famous polemic against Newton. What is even more interesting here is that Cassirer extends his inquiry to include a great overlooked figure like Leonard Euler, who was the protagonist of an enormously influential debate and who proposed a functional solution to the metaphysical and scientific problems of his time.[35] The result of Cassirer's exciting reconstruction of this debate is to demonstrate how Kant, in his critique of reason with its strict connection to contemporary science, elaborated on 'material' that had already existed previously (for instance, the proper nature of space and time, the antimonies of divisibility, or even the concept of a thing in itself).[36] In contrast, Kant's 'revolution in the way of thinking' consists of the profound transformations of both concept of being and the relationship between subject and object. According to Cassirer, both the historical and theoretical presuppositions representing the sources of Kant's new philosophy are, therefore, the necessary conditions for properly understanding what Kant has done.[37] Hence, Kant is for Cassirer not only the starting point of a new insight into philosophical reflection, but also the outcome of a previous revolution—the Scientific Revolution to which the history of science must go back if it is to truly understand the origins of thought.

3 Cassirer and the Contemporary History of Science

Since the publication of *The Problem of Knowledge*, Cassirer has assumed an eminent place within the history of science.[38] His subtle, well-documented analyses concerning the origins of both scientific thought and philosophical development in connection with mathematical sciences can still be considered a fundamental contribution to contemporary historical scholarship. At the beginning of the 20th century Cassirer offered, for the first time, an extensive account of—among others—Leonardo's, Galileo's, Kepler's, Newton's, Descartes', Leibniz's, Euler's, and Kant's scientific and philosophical insights, viewing the history of science as an essential aspect of the history of philosophy and, especially, the

---

35 Cassirer (1995) vol. 2, 388–389, 396, 401.
36 Cassirer (1995) vol. 2, 358, 410–411, 633.
37 Cassirer (1995) vol. 2, 437, 489.
38 Surprisingly enough, Cassirer is only incidentally quoted in the excellent book by H.F. Cohen (1994), see in particular p. 11.

history of epistemology.³⁹ Nonetheless, the Neo-Kantian philosophical background of Cassirer's work has led the scholarship to underestimate his quite original contribution and is responsible, to some extent, for the fact that even today Cassirer is still seen as more of a pure philosopher with a great interest in the history of philosophy, rather than as a true historian of science. No wonder, then, that in the introduction to his book *The Metaphysical Foundations of Modern Physical Science* (1924) Edwin Burtt wrote: "Professor Cassirer [...] has done work on modern epistemology which will long remain a monumental achievement in its field. But a much more radical historical analysis needs to be made".⁴⁰ One can share Burtt's desire for a "more radical historical analysis", but it would be difficult to maintain that Cassirer was unfamiliar with proper historical inquiries. Interestingly enough, Arthur O. Lovejoy, among others, was also acquainted with Cassirer, at least with Cassirer as a Leibniz scholar.⁴¹ More generally, the American community of historians of science during the 1940 s manifested a high regard for Cassirer's studies on Renaissance thought, Leibniz, Newton, Galileo, etc., which he published during the painful years of his exile in the United States.⁴² This is of some importance inasmuch as Cassirer not only contributed to the very influential *Journal for the History of Ideas*, but the volume presented to George Sarton includes one of his last essays, once again on *Galileo's Platonism*, which remains—as we shall see—the final outcome of his long research activity in this field.⁴³

In contrast, Cassirer was well known by the leading figures of philosophy and the history of science in France. Brunschvicg, Meyerson, and Koyré are particularly worthy of being considered here because of their acquaintance with

---

39 See, in particular, the section of the *Problem of Knowledge* devoted to the long scientific and philosophical road "from Newton to Kant" Cassirer (1995) vol. 2, 372–397. Cassirer deals here with, at that time, little known thinkers such as—among others—Henry More. Moreover, he even bases his inquiry on the handbooks on mechanics published in the age of Newton's triumph. Obviously, the history of science has since made enormous progress in this field of research, but Cassirer's outstanding work remains a pioneering example that even today demands closer consideration.
40 Burtt (1954), 28.
41 On Cassirer and Lovejoy see Meyer (2006), 234–235. In his *opus magnum*, Lovejoy never refers to Cassirer's Problem of Knowledge or any other works by him, though Lovejoy does quote the two volumes of Leibniz's writings edited by Cassirer and Arthur Buchenau between 1904 and 1906 (see Lovejoy (1936), 349 fn. 1). Moreover, Lovejoy had already published a review of this Leibniz edition in *The Philosophical Review*, 15, 1906, 437–438. Nevertheless, the question of whether Lovejoy was indeed influenced in some way by Cassirer's interpretation of Leibniz remains open.
42 See for instance Cassirer (1942), Cassirer (2007a), and Cassirer (2007c).
43 Cassirer (2007b).

Cassirer's works concerning the historical development of modern science. No wonder, for instance, that Brunschvicg, in his masterful history of mathematical philosophy (*Les étapes de la philosophie mathématique*), repeatedly refers to Cassirer's *Problem of Knowledge*,[44] while also endorsing his plea for an historical analysis of mathematical and scientific thought based only on what Brunschvicg calls "the historical method" (*la méthode historique*).[45] Quite similarly to Cassirer, at issue here, according to Brunschvicg, is a view of scientific knowledge as a kind of historical dynamics. It is no accident, therefore, that in 1936 Brunschvicg will contribute to the volume devoted to Cassirer on the occasion of his 60th birthday with a paper aimed at showing that at the turn of the 20th century the exact sciences (probability calculus, thermodynamics, theory of relativity) exhibited a new form—the "form of history". So history was no longer a mere appendix to knowledge, but an intrinsic, immanent feature of scientific thought. For Brunschvicg, this perspective, very close to Cassirer's own, was essentially tied to a philosophy of mind (*philosophie de l'esprit*), which opens the domain of reason to the dimension of historical development.[46]

In contrast, Meyerson does not agree with Cassirer's Neo-Kantian standpoint. In his review of *The Problem of Knowledge* published in 1911 in the *Revue de Métaphysique et de Morale*, Meyerson insists on the independence of "objective reality" from any epistemological framework; the permanent connection between epistemology and ontology is, according to him, the missing aspect of Cassirer's conception of science and, more generally, the essential assumption on which science is based.[47] Nevertheless, Meyerson praises the enormous achievement that Cassirer has offered to scholarship with his masterful work and its careful historical reconstruction of modern science. Moreover, Meyerson remarks in his review, that Cassirer's excellent book is the outcome of an "immense knowledge" (*immense savoir*), embracing not only the history of philosophy, but also the history of science in its many different aspects and topics. So, in Meyerson's opinion, Cassirer's work represents both a great novelty and a veritable model for scholarship devoted to analyzing scientific thought from an historical standpoint, a standpoint—we may add—which at the time was not as familiar to philosophers or historians of philosophy as it is today.

---

44 Brunschvicg (1912), especially p. 262. See also p. 205, where Brunschvicg quotes Cassirer's book on Leibniz and laments the fact that both Bertrand Russell and Louis Couturat didn't at all understand "l'exactitude fondamentale et la profondeur" of this illuminating work.
45 Brunschvicg (1912), 3.
46 Brunschvicg (1936), 27–34.
47 Meyerson (1911), 100–129. With regard to Meyerson's epistemology see Fruteau de Laclos (2009).

Thus, both Meyerson and Brunschvicg are the French philosophers who, at the beginning of 20th century, contributed to the acknowledgment of Cassirer as an eminent historian of science.[48] This is the reason why Alexandre Koyré—one of the most important historians of science in the first half of 20th century—also refers often to Cassirer, especially in his *Galileo Studies*, though he disagrees with him on the matter of Galileo's Platonism and, more specifically, with regard to the status of the law of inertia as Galileo and Descartes conceived of it.[49] Although Koyré recognizes Cassirer's great merit (along with Duhem, Brunschvicg, and Meyerson) for having pointed out in his writings both the extraordinary importance of the modern Scientific Revolution and its relevance for philosophy,[50] it is remarkable, nonetheless, to see the difference that emerges from a comparison between Koyré's and Cassirer's understanding of the history of science. On the one hand, Koyré tries, quite differently from Cassirer, to grasp the inner process of the growth of scientific thought "by comprehending its development—as he said in 1951—in the course of its own creative activity".[51] In other words, Koyré aims at showing the specific procedure by which a scientist, e. g. Galileo, Descartes or Newton, builds a scientific theory by weaving together, so to speak, the individual, abstract pieces upon which the said theory depends. On the other hand, Koyré is not committed to a Kantian way of thinking and it is not by accident that he was deeply influenced, above all, by Meyerson.[52] Scientific thought has to be illuminated, according to Koyré, by considering both its intrinsic conceptual equipment and reality as it is given, without referring to a kind of transcendental subject constituting reality itself. This in no way signifies that Koyré's account of the Scientific Revolution does not share a common research field with Cassirer or that his view is still indebted either to old positivism or to Ernst Mach's conception of the history of science. On the contrary, Koyré and Cassirer are both firmly convinced that mathematical Platonism, and not experimental outcomes as such, lie at the core of exact science since the days of the rise of modern scientific thought.[53] The question is rather how Platonism should be un-

---

48 An overview of this issue is provided by Seidengart (1995).
49 Koyré (1966), 8–9, 90–91.
50 Koyré (1966), 11.
51 Koyré (1986), 14.
52 Regarding Koyré and Meyerson, see Koyré (1931), 197–217. We refer also to Jorland (1981), 23–70.
53 Koyré, "Galilée et la révolution scientifique", in: Koyré (1986), 210: "C'est la pensée pure et sans mélange, et non l'expérience et la perception des sens, qui est à la base de la 'nouvelle science' de Galileo Galilée". See, furthermore, Koyre's seminal essay "Galileo and Plato" (which for the first time made available to the American scholarship the essential theses of his *Études Galiléennes*).

derstood and, to some extent, in what way mathematics plays a pivotal role in grounding physical science. According to Koyré, in fact, mathematics is first and foremost geometry and he consequently identifies the very origins of the modern scientific image of the world with both the "geometrisation" of space and the "destruction of the Cosmos" inherited by the Greeks.[54] For Cassirer, however, mathematics essentially means the quantification of natural phenomena (through infinitesimal calculus, for example). Thus, the main feature of mathematics is that of applied mathematics in a broader, transcendental Kantian sense, rather than only belonging to a realm of pure mathemata, as Koyré seems to believe, in agreement with his former teacher in Göttingen, Edmund Husserl.[55] Moreover, in the later years of his intellectual life, Koyré stressed—not accidentally—that his great admiration for Brunschvicg's book *Les étapes de la philosophie mathématique* didn't exclude a fundamental objection to a Kantian account of mathematics. For Koyré, numbers are not, as Brunschvicg or Cassirer himself believed, the result of a specific activity of mind, but something belonging to another realm or, in Husserlian terms, to the pure sphere of 'essences'. Only God has created the numbers, Koyré affirmed, although for the rest, mathematics depends on the "invention" of human mind.[56]

During the interwar period, the history of science was also dominated by fundamentally philosophical insights regarding, in particular, the relationship between mathematics and experience. Accordingly, the question about the specific role that Platonism or, to some extent, Neo-Platonism played in the origins of modern science, from Galileo's revolution onwards, was at issue again and again. As Cassirer wrote in his essay "Mathematical Mystique and Mathematical Science of Nature", where he refers, among others, to Koyré, Burtt, Edward Strong, and Dietrich Mahnke, a crucial aspect was simply to point out what Platonism means and why it could be considered the essential framework within which the Scientific Revolution is rooted. Interestingly enough, Cassirer distanced himself from both Burtt's and Strong's interpretations. On the one hand, Cassirer argues that Burtt overestimates the "Neo-Platonic speculations

---

54 Koyré repeatedly insisted on these twofold presuppositions of the Scientific Revolution, constituting, at once, a metaphysical as well as theoretical change in approaching nature: see Koyré (1965) 6, and Koyré (1943), 404. This main issue is also the foundation of Koyré's most famous book, *From the Closed World to the Infinite Universe*.
55 Koyré's early days in Göttingen and his relationship to Husserl are well documented by Zambelli (1998), 303–354.
56 See Koyré's speech on the occasion of the conference "Commémoration du cinquantenaire de la publications des *Étapes de la philosophie mathématique* de Lèon Brunschvicg", Koyré (1963), 11.

as well as the Pythagorean mystique of numbers" which he believes to be very influential on Galileo's mathematical physics. On the other hand, Cassirer maintains that Strong, for his part, has not really understood the extent to which the empirical side of Galileo's inquiries was quite insufficient for founding the new science. Cassirer, however, aims at clearly distinguishing the mere "symbolic" aspects constituting the wide cultural background of scientific thought from their properly rational components that lie at the core of both the mathematical and empirical investigations of nature. Accordingly, the main character of Galileo's theory of science consists in the "correlation" between experience and thought, which in no way signifies that mathematics can be reduced to a simple "technical application", as Strong suggests.[57]

Hence, it is not by accident that Cassirer—both as a great historian of scientific thought and as a Neo-Kantian philosopher—devotes his last intellectual energy to discussing once more the question of the significance of Galileo's Platonism. In his contribution to the volume presented to George Sarton, Cassirer takes into account Koyré's "excellent article" on Galileo and Plato, stressing his essential agreement with his French colleague. Koyré had criticized Burtt's interpretation by distinguishing between two kinds of Platonism: the first being a purely mathematical Platonism, while the second is strictly connected to the mystical-speculative tradition that flourished within the Florence Academy, to which Galileo was totally foreign.[58] According to Koyré, Galileo was, therefore, engaged in the founding of exact science through a straightforwardly oriented mathematical Platonism, a circumstance that Koyré summarized provocatively by stressing that "the new science is for him [Galileo] an experimental proof of Platonism".[59] In answering Koyré, Cassirer emphasizes a modified account of this story or, at the very least, a more sophisticated point of view. In his mind, Galileo's Platonism represents a *third* kind of Platonism, one that is neither a metaphysical or mystical, nor simply a mathematical Platonism. Beginning with a stimulating historical reconstruction, Cassirer tries to outline, quite differently from Koyré, the *physical* Platonism underlying Galileo's scientific revolution. What is at stake here is the use of the method of geometrical analysis as a basic conceptual

---

57 Cassirer (2006a), 290, 297. According to Eugenio Garin, Cassirer is wrong in proposing this distinction, since "mathematical Platonism and mystique of numbers" are quite similar: see Garin (2007), 312.
58 See Koyré (1986), 212, as well as Koyré (1943), 425 fn. 64. In this footnote Koyré refers to the distinction between two different traditions of Platonism which Brunschvicg had rightly proposed in Brunschvicg (1912), 67–70. See, by contrast, Burtt (1954), 68.
59 Koyré (1943), 428. Koyré's interpretation of Galileo is discussed with perspicacity by Galluzzi (1994), 241–261.

tool of natural science which enables Galileo to conceptualize empirical phenomena while avoiding any commitment to both the Aristotelian tradition and traditional Platonism. Cassirer writes:

> Galileo [...] acted and spoke as a faithful disciple of Plato's. He followed the same method that Plato used in his "Meno" [...] Galileo simply transferred the method of "problematical analysis" that had stood its ground in the history of geometrical and astronomical thought [...] He had to deviate both from the principles of Platonism and Aristotelianism. He accepted Plato's hypothetical method but he gave this method a new *ontological* status; a status which it had never possessed before.[60]

It has often been remarked that, in his later work, Cassirer is irremediably far from his former Neo-Kantianism. When reading this essay on Galileo, one is led to modify this received view. Here Cassirer seems to still be in agreement with the interpretation which Paul Natorp offered more than sixty years earlier in his seminal article *Galileo as Philosopher* (*Galilei als Philosoph*), which basically built on Hermann Cohen's very peculiar way of rethinking Plato through the lens of critical idealism.[61] Now, what Cassirer has never left out, although his extraordinary historical awareness might disguise it, is the focus on the crucial theoretical problem regarding the conditions of mathematical science, i.e., the very idea of mathematics as the structure of pure thought (as Cohen would have said) which constitutes the reign of physical laws. This is also the reason why Cassirer is still remembered as an eminent but, unfortunately, outdated historian of science. Thomas Kuhn once pointed out that Cassirer surely had a great influence on the subsequent history of science in spite of his "profound [...] limitations".[62] However, it should be remembered that Kuhn's teachers were Meyerson, Koyré, Anneliese Meyer, and Hélène Metzger, that is, historians not influenced—as Kuhn pointed out—by Kantianism or Neo-Kantianism (demonstrated, in particular, by the case of Meyerson).[63] But the story is more complicated than the usual reconstruction might suggest. Without doubt, during the golden age of its pioneering work, studies on the history of science were more philosophically oriented than they have become since the field's professionalization. Nevertheless, Kuhn himself—one of the field's most illustrious scholars—endorsed a kind of evolutionis-

---

60 Cassirer (2007b), 351. One must remember that Cassirer clearly disagrees with John Randall's opinion, according to which the Aristotelanism of Padua would have exercised a decisive influence on Galileo.
61 See Natorp (1882b), 193–229.
62 Kuhn (1977), 108, 149.
63 Kuhn (1970), VI. Regarding Kuhn and Meyerson, see Friedman (2003), 19–44, especially 31–34 as well as Gutting (2005), 71–83, especially 80.

tic Kantianism which, while surely not in agreement with Cassirer's views, still testifies to the fact that every account of the history of science requires, to some extent, a philosophy of science or, at least, philosophical assumptions regarding revolutions, paradigms, continuity as well discontinuity in the development of scientific thought. This is the fundamental insight that Cassirer articulated throughout his work and it is a compelling reason for rethinking not only his contribution to our contemporary debates, but also the essential character of his still-relevant philosophy.[64]

Bibliography

Brunschvicg (1912): Léon Brunschvicg, *Les étapes de la philosophie mathématique*, Paris: Alcan.
Brunschvicg (1936): Léon Brunschvicg, "History and Philosophy", in: R. Klibansky, H. J. Paton (eds.), *Philosophy and History. Essays Presented to Ernst Cassirer*, Oxford: Clarendon Press, 27–34.
Burtt (1954): Edwin Arthur Burtt, *The Metaphysical Foundations of Modern Physical Science*, New York, Anchor Books.
Carrier (2001): Martin Carrier, *Nikolaus Kopernikus*, München: Beck.
Cassirer (1942): Ernst Cassirer, "G. Pico della Mirandola. A Study in the History of Renaissance", *Journal of the History of Ideas* 3, 123–144, 319–346.
Cassirer (1953): Ernst Cassirer, *Substance and Function*, William C. Swabey and Marie C. Swabey (trans.), New York: Dover.
Cassirer (1995): Ernst Cassirer, *Das Erkenntnisproblem in der Philosophie und Wissenschaft der neueren Zeit*, 2 vols., reprint: Darmstadt: Wissenschaftliche Buchgesellschaft, 1995.
Cassirer (1998): Ernst Cassirer, *Leibniz's System in seinen wissenschaftlichen Grundlagen*, in: *Gesammelte Werke* (henceforth: ECW). Hamburger Ausgabe, B. Recki (Ed.) vol. 1, Hamburg: Meiner.
Cassirer (2001): Ernst Cassirer, "Kant und die moderne Mathematik (Mit Bezug auf Bertrand Russells und Louis Couturats Werke über die Prinzipien der Mathematik)", in: ECW, vol. 9, op. cit.
Cassirer (2002): Ernst Cassirer, *Individuum und Kosmos in der Philosophie der Renaissance*, in: ECW, vol. 14, op. cit.
Cassirer (2006b): Ernst Cassirer, "Wahrheitsbegriff und Wahrheitsproblem bei Galilei", in: ECW, vol. 22, op. cit.
Cassirer (2006a): Ernst Cassirer, "Mathematische Mystik und mathematische Naturwissenschaft", in: ECW, vol. 22, op. cit.
Cassirer (2007a): Ernst Cassirer, "Galileo Galilei: A New Science and a New Spirit", in: ECW, vol. 24, op. cit.
Cassirer (2007b): Ernst Cassirer, "Galileo's Platonism", in: ECW, vol. 24, op. cit.
Cassirer (2007c): Ernst Cassirer, "Leibniz and Newton", in: ECW, vol. 24, op. cit.

---

64 Friedman (2010), 177–191.

Cassirer (2010): Ernst Cassirer, *Vorlesungen und Vorträge zu philosophischen Problemen der Wissenschaften 1907–1945*, J. Fingerhut, G. Hartung and R. Kramme (eds.), Hamburg: Meiner.
Cohen (1984): Hermann Cohen, *Das Prinzip der Infinitesimal-Methode und seine Geschichte*, Hermann-Cohen-Archiv (ed.), vol. 5, Hildesheim- Zürich,-New York: Olms.
Cohen (1987): Hermann Cohen, *Kants Theorie der Erfahrung*, Hermann-Cohen-Archiv (ed.), vol. I/3, Hildesheim-Zürich-New York: Olms.
Cohen (1994): H. Floris Cohen, *The Scientific Revolution. A Historiographical Inquiry*, Chicago and London: Chicago University Press.
Duhem (1974): Pierre Duhem, *The Aim and Structure of Physical Theory*, Philip P. Wiener (trans.), New York: Atheneum.
Ferrari (1988): Massimo Ferrari, *Il giovane Cassirer e la scuola di Marburgo*, Milano: Franco Angeli.
Friedman (2003): Michael Friedman, "Kuhn and Logical Empiricism", in: Thomas Nickles (ed.), *Thomas Kuhn*, Cambridge: Cambridge University Press, 19–44.
Friedman (2010): Michael Friedman, "Ernst Cassirer and Thomas Kuhn: The Neo-Kantian Tradition in the History and Philosophy of Science", in: R. A. Makkreel, S. Luft (eds.), *Neo-Kantianism and Contemporary Philosophy*, Bloomington and Indianapolis: Indiana University Press, 177–191.
Fruteau de Laclos (2009): Frédéric Fruteau de Laclos, *L'épistémologie d'Émile Meyerson. Une anthropologie de la connaissance*, Paris: Vrin.
Galluzzi (1994): Paolo Galluzzi, "Gli studi galileiani", in: Carlo Vinti (ed.), *Alexandre Koyré. L'avventura intellettuale*, Napoli: Edizioni Scientifiche Italiane, 241–261.
Garin (2007): Eugenio Garin, *Rinascite e rivoluzioni. Movimenti culturali dal XIV al XVIII secolo*, Roma-Bari: Laterza.
Gutting (2005): Gary Gutting (ed.), *Continental Philosophy of Science*, Oxford: Blackwell, 2005.
Jorland (1981): Gérard Jorland, *La science dans la philosophie. Les recherches épistémologiques d'Alexandre Koyré*, Paris: Gallimard.
Koyré (1931): Alexandre Koyré, "Die Philosophie Emile Meyersons", *Deutsch-französische Rundschau*, 4, 197–217.
Koyré (1943): Alexandre Koyré, "Galileo and Plato", *Journal of the History of Ideas* (4), 400–428.
Koyré (1963): Alexandre Koyré, "Commémoration du cinquantenaire de la publications des *Étapes de la philosophie mathématique* de Lèon Brunschvicg", *Bulletin de la Société française de philosophie*, 57.
Koyré (1965): Alexandre Koyré, *Newtonian Studies*, Cambridge: Harvard University Press.
Koyré (1966): Alexandre Koyré, *Études galiléennes*, Paris: Hermann.
Koyré (1986): Alexandre Koyré, "Orientation et projects de recherches", in: *Études d'histoire de la pensée scientifique*, Paris: Gallimard.
Kuhn (1970): Thomas Kuhn, *The Structure of Scientific Revolutions*, Chicago: The University of Chicago Press.
Kuhn (1977): Thomas Kuhn, *The Essential Tension: Selected Studies in Scientific Tradition and Change*, Chicago: The University of Chicago Press.

Lembeck (1994): Karl-Heinz Lembeck, *Platon in Marburg. Platonrezeption und Philosophiegeschichtsphilosophie bei Cohen und Natorp*, Würzburg: Konigshausen & Neumann.

Lovejoy (1936): Arthur Oncken Lovejoy, *The Great Chain of Being. A Study of the History of an Idea*, Cambridge: Harvard University Press.

Meyer (2006): Thomas Meyer, *Ernst Cassirer*, Hamburg: Eller & Richter, Verlag.

Meyerson (1911): Emile Meyerson, "L'histoire du problème de la connaissance de M. Cassirer", *Revue de Métaphysique et de Morale* 19.

Natorp (1882a): Paul Natorp, "Die kosmologische Reform des Kopernikus in ihrer Bedeutung für die Philosophie", *Preussische Jahrbücher*, 41, 355–375.

Natorp (1882b): Paul Natorp, "Galilei als Philosoph. Eine Skizze", *Philosophische Monatshefte*, 18, 193–229.

Natorp (1912): Paul Natorp, "Kant und die Marburger Schule", *Kant Studien*, 17, 193–221.

Natorp (1921): Paul Natorp, *Platos Ideenlehre. Eine Einführung in den Idealismus*, Leipzig: Meiner.

Natorp (1985): Paul Natorp, "Leibniz und der Materialismus", H. Holzhey (ed.), *Studia Leibnitiana* 17, 3–14.

Seidengart (1995): Jean Seidengart, "Cassirer et la philosophie des sciences en France", *Rivista di storia della filosofia*, 50, 753–783.

Servois (2004): Julien Servois, *Paul Natorp et la théorie platonicienne des idées*, Lille: Presses Universitaires du Septentrion.

Sieg (1994): Ulrich Sieg, *Aufstieg und Niedergang des Marburger Neukantianismus. Die Geschichte einer philosophischen Schulgemeinschaft*, Würzburg: Königshausen & Neumann.

Zambelli (1998): Paolo Zambelli, "Alexandre Koyré. Alla scuola di Husserl a Gottinga", *Giornale critico della filosofia italiana*, 78.

Thomas Mormann (San Sebastián)
From Mathematics to Quantum Mechanics – On the Conceptual Unity of Cassirer's Philosophy of Science (1907–1937)

1 Introduction

The two fundamental scientific revolutions that shaped the modern physics of the 20th century took place in Cassirer's lifetime; first Einstein's theory of relativity, and secondly quantum physics. Cassirer reacted to both events with contributions that can claim, even today, the attention not only of philosophers of science but also of physicists who are interested in philosophical and historical reflections concerning their discipline. Cassirer's pertinent works in this respect are *Zur Einsteinschen Relativitätstheorie*[1] (henceforth ERT) and *Determinismus und Indeterminismus in der modernen Physik*[2] (henceforth DI). In these two works Cassirer attempts to come to terms philosophically with the just mentioned two characteristic revolutions of modern physics, relativity theory and quantum theory.

The following list shows a rough time-table of the most important "revolutionary" events in the evolution of physics in the first quarter of the 20th century and the publication dates of some of Cassirer's most important works in philosophy of science:

Physics	Cassirer's Philosophy of Science
1900 Planck's Law of Black Body Radiation	
1905 Special Theory of Relativity	
	1907 Kant und die moderne Mathematik
	1910 Substanzbegriff und Funktionsbegriff
1915 General Theory of Relativity	
	1921 Zur Einsteinschen Relativitätstheorie
1925 Heisenberg's Matrix Mechanics	
1926 Schrödinger's Wave Mechanics	
	1923–1929 Philosophie der symbolischen Formen I–III
	1937 Determinismus und Indeterminismus in der modernen Physik

---

1 Cassirer (1923a).
2 Cassirer (1956).

Although Cassirer played an active role in the attempts to contribute a philosophical understanding of the most recent developments in physics, perhaps somewhat surprisingly during his whole career as a philosopher of science he saw no reason to abandon the basic convictions of his philosophy of science that he had developed in *Substanzbegriff und Funktionsbegriff*[3] (henceforth SF) on the basis of <u>classical</u> 19th century physics. On the contrary, in DI he put forward the thesis:

> The fundamental viewpoint, in accordance with which I have dealt with these problems [the philosophical problems posed by quantum physics], does not differ essentially from that of my *Substance and Function*. This viewpoint is, I believe, still justifiable. Indeed, I think I can now justify it better and formulate it more precisely on the basis of the developments in modern physics than I formerly could.[4]

To put it bluntly, in DI Cassirer was engaged in interpreting quantum mechanics in the same neo-Kantian frame that he used more than fifteen years earlier in ERT to make philosophical sense of Einstein's relativity theory. Even more, in DI he put forward the thesis that quantum mechanics provided a further proof of the relational character of the concepts of modern physics. This entailed that the relational (or functional) *Ansatz* of his philosophy of science—first elaborated in SF—remained unaffected by the scientific revolutions of the 20th century. Taking into account the early programmatic paper *Kant und die moderne Mathematik*[5] (henceforth KMM) one may even go further and claim that from KMM (1907) onwards to SF (1910) and DI (1937) Cassirer's philosophy of science is characterized by a thoroughgoing conceptual continuity or even invariance. The aim of this paper is to make explicit this thesis by detailed textual comparisons. Moreover, I want to show that this invariance cannot be simply dismissed as a philosopher's excuse for not keeping up with the novel conceptual challenges of his time. More precisely I propose to read Cassirer's KMM, SF, ERT, and DI as integral parts of a comprehensive and coherent "idealist" philosophy of science of the early 20th century. In this interpretation, KMM plays the role of a programmatic overture where essential ideas and themes are already suggested in an early stage; SF may be seen as an execution of this program in the realm

---

3 Cassirer (1923b).
4 Cassirer (1956), xxiii.
5 Cassirer (1907).

of classical physics, while ERT and DI may be taken as resumptions of the classical themes in the fields of modern physics.⁶

As I want to argue in detail in the following, in particular the connections between KMM and SF on the one hand, and DI on the other, are surprisingly close. This shows that Cassirer's functional or relational account can be applied in a fruitful way to classical *and* modern physics. It is therefore a fundamental misunderstanding of Cassirer's philosophy of science to read it as an epigonal attempt to immunize an obsolete neo-Kantian account in such a way that is confirmed by just any new scientific achievement. Rather, the insight in the relational character of scientific concepts should be considered as a lasting contribution of Cassirer to philosophy of science. This does not mean, of course, that one has to subscribe to all details of his approach.

The outline of the paper is as follows. To set the stage, in section 2 we briefly recall the basic ideas of Cassirer's philosophy of science as expounded programmatically in his early paper KMM and presented in mature form in SF. For him, the relational character of physical concepts had become visible already in classical physics, the formation of radically relational concepts in quantum mechanics was only a confirmation and further clarification of this tendency.

In section 3, *How Not to Understand Idealization and the Ideal Character of Scientific Knowledge*, we deal with Cassirer's refutation of certain misconceptions that threatened a correct understanding of the roles of idealization and ideal concepts in science. In SF Cassirer critizised the account of the mathematician

---

6 For reasons of space I deal with ERT only briefly. The point I want to make is that Cassirer's relational philosophy of science covers classical and non-classical physics. To argue for this claim it may suffice to deal with DI and the issue of quantum mechanics.
In matters of philosophy of science (and philosophy of mathematics) Cassirer's *opus magnum Philo–sophy of Symbolic Forms* (henceforth PSF) follows SF rather closely. The essential ideas of SF are rehearsed in PSF III, sometimes in extensive quotations. Although ERT had already appeared in 1921, in PSF III Einstein's theories are mentioned only in passing. This is evidence that Cassirer saw no need to alter the fundamentals of his philosophy of science, as he had presented them in SF in the light of the theory of relativity. In other words, he interpreted the "new relativistic physics" as a confirmation of his functional account. There is, however, one point in PSF III which goes beyond SF. On the last pages of PSF III he deals with the concept of field that first emerged in the context of Maxwell's theory of electromagnetic fields. Cassirer conceives fields as a striking example for the growing tendency in modernity to replace "thing-concepts" with "relation-concepts": "The reality that we designate as a field is no longer a complex of physical things, but an expression for an aggregate of physical relations." Cassirer (1957), 465. Later, in DI he dealt with fields in more detail in the context of quantum theory.
When writing PSF Cassirer was already acquainted with the "old" quantum theory. He mentions briefly and in passing through the works of Bohr, Planck, and Sommerfeld (cf. Cassirer (1957), 445, 446, 475n). Heisenberg and Schrödinger are not mentioned at all.

Paul du Bois-Reymond who claimed to have shown in his *Allgemeine Functionentheorie* that the concepts of idealization and limit necessarily possessed certain aporetic features which directly threatened the very feasibility of Cassirer's "critical idealist" approach of SF that basically relied on "limiting concepts" (*Grenzbegriffe*).

Almost 30 years later, in DI, Cassirer took sides again against the account of idealization that the brothers du Bois-Reymond had propagated since the last decades of the 19th century. In DI Cassirer primarily attacked Emil du Bois-Reymond's account of causality that the latter had derived from the idealized model of science based on the thought-experiment of the almost omniscient Laplacian demon. Cassirer argued that du Bois-Reymond's arguments rested on a confused concept of causality that had been rendered obsolete by modern science.

In section 4 *The Principle of Causality and the Problem of Reality* we deal with Cassirer's conception of causality as presented in DI. According to general wisdom, the most important revolutionary feature of quantum theory was that it forced us to abandon the classical concept of causation. Cassirer disagreed. According to him, causality was a relation within the realm of conceptual objects and not between of objects in nature. In modern science causality has to be attributed to a model which the science constructs out of concepts. It does not directly refer to "reality". Hence quantum theory does not urge us so much to give up the concept of causality but to rethink the concepts of object and objectivity in a way that takes into account in a more thoroughgoing way the relational character of the concepts of exact empirical sciences. Section 5 deals with the complex reception that DI had in 20th century philosophy of science up to the present. On the basis of DI, in some philosophical quarters, Cassirer is considered as a forerunner of contemporary structural realism (in the philosophy of quantum mechanics and beyond). This topic is discussed in detail in section 6. It is argued that recruiting Cassirer posthumously for the camp of structural realism does not do full justice to his approach. Rather, he probably would have felt more at home with a kind of structural empiricism[7], or so I want to argue.

---

7 Cf. van Fraassen (2006b) and van Fraassen (2008).

2 Philosophy of Science as a Theory of Scientific Concepts

"The investigations contained in this volume were first prompted by studies in the philosophy of mathematics."[8] This is the very first sentence of SF. This assertion should be taken seriously. Cassirer's philosophy of science is inspired more profoundly by mathematics than any other philosophy of science of the 19th and 20th century.

The most characteristic feature of Cassirer's philosophy of science is how the relation between mathematics and physics is conceptualized, or, more generally, the relation of mathematics and the (mature) empirical sciences. As he pointed out in KMM, philosophy of science has to concentrate neither on mathematics, as a science of ideal objects, nor on physics, as a science of empirical objects, but rather:

> If one is allowed to express the relation between philosophy and science in a blunt and paradoxical way, one may say: The eye of philosophy must be directed neither on mathematics nor on physics; it is to be directed solely on the connection of the two realms.[9]

According to Cassirer, the basic task of philosophy of science is to look for the common root from which both physical and mathematical concepts spring. This common root is identified as the activity of constructing ideal concepts or limit concepts (*Grenzbegriffe*) that are necessary to order and unify the wealth of experiences. The main organon for this endeavor is the new relational logic inaugurated by Frege, Peano, Russell, and others. This logic had emerged from the evolution of mathematics itself. For Cassirer, being a member of the Marburg school of neo-Kantianism, this was no coincidence. Rather, it confirmed the basic neo-Kantian thesis that the history of science plays an eminent role for the philosophy of science. It led the critical idealism of the Marburg school to a genetic epistemology that regarded the process of the conceptual evolution of science as essential, not so much the certainty and truth of the temporary results of science.

Cassirer's philosophy of science treated mathematics and physics as a conceptual unity. More precisely, his approach was based on the general "idealist" thesis

---

8 Cassirer (1923b), iii.
9 Cassirer (1907), 44.

> that the same foundational syntheses on which logic and mathematics rest also govern the scientific construction of experiential knowledge, that only they enable us to speak of a strict, lawful ordering among appearances and therewith of their objective meaning, only then the true justification of the principles is attained.[10]

Thus, to put it bluntly, according to Cassirer, mathematical knowledge and physical knowledge are basically of the same kind. Both are characterized by the introduction of "ideal elements" which in both areas play essentially the same role. This thesis may be dubbed the "sameness thesis". It may be considered as an invariant feature of his philosophy of science from the beginning to the end. For the first time, Cassirer put forward the sameness thesis in KMM,[11] with only slight simplification one may read the whole of SF as an ample elaboration of this thesis. Eventually, in DI it is argued that one may even go further and claim that from the sameness thesis is confirmed and clarified in light of the new revolutionary achievements of quantum physics. For instance, when resuming the achievements of DI in the penultimate chapter of this work, Cassirer contended that quantum mechanics has brought to the fore once again the fundamental similarity between mathematical and physical concepts, in particular, the conceptual similarity between geometrical points and material points, namely, that both are implicitly constituted as aggregates of relations.[12] In other words, mathematics was not a "logical oddity" or a "logical exception" (*logisches Unikum*)[13] but an integral component of the philosophy of science as a whole. More specifically, the formation of mathematical concepts was to be considered as the prototype of the formation of scientific concepts in general.

> What "Critical Idealism" seeks and what it must demand is a logic of objective knowledge. Only when we have understood that the same foundational syntheses on which logic and mathematics rest also govern the scientific construction of experiential knowledge, that only they enable us to speak of a strict, lawful ordering among appearances and therewith of their objective meaning: only then the true justification of the principles is attained.[14]

---

10 Cassirer (1907), 44.
11 Cassirer (1907), 44.
12 Cf. Cassirer (1956), 195.
13 Cassirer (1923b), 230. The expression "logisches Unikum" is difficult to translate: Taking into account the Latin origin of "Unikum", it may be translated simply as "something unique". "Being unique" in the sense of "Unikum" carries with it, however, the connotation of "being odd" or "being an exception". Hence, in a more pronounced manner "logisches Unikum" may be rendered "logical oddity" or "logical exception".
14 Cassirer (1907), 44.

Although the principles of the processes of the formation in mathematics and physics are basically the same, they are not identical. Rather, the formation of mathematical concepts may be conceived of as a "finite" version of the more open formation of physical concepts: In contrast to the mathematical concept, however, in empirical science the characteristic difference emerges that the construction which within mathematics arrives at a fixed end, remains in principle incompletable within experience.

It is important to note that for Cassirer "ideal gases", "perfect fluids" and their (idealized) relatives are not just approximated by the more or less ideal gases and the more or less perfect fluids "to be found in nature". Rather, idealizing concepts such as ideal gases or perfect fluids play an epistemological role essentially different from their non-ideal counterparts. Ideal concepts provide conceptual perspectives that allow the formulation of general relational laws and thereby they help make sense of reality as a manifold of experiences. The indispensability of idealization for scientific knowledge entails that the factual and theoretical components of scientific knowledge cannot be neatly separated. In a scientific theory, "real" and "non-real" components are inextricably interwoven:

> The relation between the theoretical and factual elements at the basis of physics is a ... peculiar interweaving and mutual interpenetration of the theoretical and the factual, that prevails in the actual structure of science and calls for clearer expression logically of the relation between principle and fact.[15]

This entails that no single concept of physics is confronted with reality but a whole system of concepts:

> We do not have physical concepts and physical facts in pure separation, so that we could select a member of the first sphere and enquire whether it possessed a copy in the second; but we possess the "facts" only by virtue of the totality of concepts, just as, on the other hand, we conceive the concepts only with reference to the totality of possible experience.[16]

Surely, this holism is not breaking news for philosophy of science in the second decade of 21th century, but for a fair assessment of the novelty of this claim one should take into account that is was put forward in 1910.[17] Moreover, quite re-

---

15 Cassirer (1923b), 130.
16 Cassirer (1923b), 147.
17 In DI, Cassirer put great emphasis on the fact that his holism is, so to speak, an articulated holism that takes into account the different kinds of physical statements, statements of results of measurement, of laws, and of principles. This articulation is not to be thought, however, as a

cently, this holism plays an important role in the relations between Cassirer and contemporary "ontological structural realism" (OSR) (see section 6).

In line with the historicist orientation of Neo-Kantianism, conceptualizing the philosophy of science as a theory of the formation of scientific concepts entails that it has to study the evolution of scientific concepts in the course of their historical development. From the time of his earliest publications, Cassirer endorsed the thesis that for the development of modern mathematics the concept of function was of the outmost importance[18]. For him the concept of function encapsulated the essence of modern scientific thought. The conceptual evolution of modern science could be described as the emergence of the functional character of scientific concepts.

In light of the methods and the results of modern structural mathematics, it is not too difficult to accept the thesis of the relational character of mathematical concepts. According to common wisdom, all mathematical objects may be conceived as relational structures. Less plausible is the stronger thesis that this also holds for the concepts of empirical science. Cassirer is well aware of the fact that this step from mathematics to physics is the most difficult obstacle that his theory of the formation of scientific concepts has to overcome. In chapter 4, the largest chapter of SF, he tackled this challenge. After having argued in the preceding chapters for the relational character of mathematics, in this central chapter of SF Cassirer attempted to generalize his relational theory of concepts of mathematics to a comprehensive theory of the formation of concepts of physics and chemistry:

> The exact scientific concepts only continue an intellectual process already effective in pure mathematical knowledge. ... The theoretical concepts of natural science are in no sense merely purified and idealized word-meanings; ... They always contain reference to an exact serial principle, that enables us to connect the manifold of intuition in a definite way, and to run through it according to a prescribed law.[19]

It is one of the basic tenets of the Marburg Neo-Kantian philosophy of science that this "intellectual process" of scientific concept formation has no end. Scientific concepts in the understanding of the Marburg school were always preliminary concepts, to be replaced by better ones in the course of the evolution of science. Or, in the words of Paul Natorp, science was a fact in becoming (*Werde-*

---

hierarchical structure: "If we choose a spatial analogy for the structure of physics, we must not liken this structure to a pyramid ... but to the "well-rounded sphere" with which Parmenides compared his universe..." Cassirer (1956), 35.
18 Cf. Cassirer (1902), Cassirer (1907), Cassirer (1923b), Cassirer (1957).
19 Cassirer (1923b), 233.

faktum). Hence for Cassirer, the dynamical character of scientific concepts became most clearly visible in the formation of the concepts of empirical science.[20]

More precisely, Cassirer contends that the conceptual evolution of the empirical sciences had the tendency that the "thing-concepts", characteristic of the more primitive stages of a science, are transformed into relational or functional concepts.[21] Thus it is an important task of the philosophy of science to render the relationalization of this process explicit. As a paradigmatic example for this process he discusses in SF the conceptual evolution of chemistry:[22]

> [I]f the chemical concept of a certain body is given by its constitution-formula, in which it is grasped as a particular material in its characteristic structure, it is at the same time brought under the various chemical "types", and is thus set in a definite relation to the totality of remaining bodies.[23]

A paradigmatic example of a relational concept in physics was for Cassirer the concept of *energy*. The utility of the concept of energy is not to describe any new class of objects, alongside the already known physical objects such as light and heat, electricity and magnetism. Rather, the concept of energy signifies an objective lawful correlation, in which all these "objects" stand. The meaning of the concept of energy resides in the equations that it establishes among different kinds of events and processes. Energy in the sense of modern science is not an object in the traditional sense, but a unifying perspective that sheds light on a manifold of experiences. This is rendered most evident by the functional identity of potential and kinetic energy through which states are identified with temporal processes:

> The two [moments of kinetic and potential energy] are "the same" not because they share any objective property, but because they occur as members of the same causal equation, and thus can be substituted for each other from the standpoint of pure magnitude.[24]

Theoretical concepts such as *energy* cannot be understood as the conceptual counterpart of something empirical out there. Rather, it is to be understood as an order-generating principle. In this respect it resembles the notion of number by which we make the sensuous manifold unitary and uniform in conception.[25]

---

20 Cassirer (1923b), 113.
21 Cassirer (1923b), 225.
22 Cf. Cassirer (1923b), chapter IV.
23 Cassirer (1923b), 224.
24 Cassirer (1923b), 199.
25 Cassirer (1923b), 189.

In contrast to the concept of number, the concept of energy is a genuine concept of the empirical sciences. Hence, since "number" and "energy" both served as order-generating principles in essentially the same manner, this was considered as another argument in favor of the Marburg thesis that mathematics *and* mathematized empirical sciences followed the same rules of one and the same transcendental logic This endeavor is taken up again in a more radical vein on the basis of non-classical examples from quantum mechanics in DI.

The thesis that mathematical concepts and concepts of exact empirical sciences are intimately related lies at the heart of Cassirer theory of the formation of scientific concepts. It may explain the wide spectrum of his philosophy of science ranging from philosophy of mathematics to philosophy of quantum physics including philosophy of chemistry and touching even philosophy of biology. This variety of concepts did not simply amount to a juxtaposition of concepts of unrelated disciplines, rather, from Cassirer's point of view it exhibited a conceptual unity that is hardly visible from the perspective of philosophical mainstream.

According to Cassirer concepts should be characterized functionally, i.e., by what they achieved for the evolution of scientific knowledge. From this perspective, mathematical concepts as well as theoretical concepts of physics have similar roles:

> Concepts do not gain their truth by being copies of realities presented in themselves, but by expressing ideal orders by which the connection of experiences is established and guaranteed. The "realities," which physics affirms, have no meaning beyond that of being ordering concepts. They are not grounded by pointing out a particular sensuous being, that "corresponds" to them, but by being recognized as the instruments of strict connections and thus of thoroughgoing relative determinateness of the "given".[26]

As we shall see later (cf. section 6), this instrumentalist interpretation of the role of theoretical concepts brings Cassirer's account in the conceptual neighborhood of van Fraassen's project of a "structuralist empiricism",[27] or so I want to argue.

---

26 Cassirer (1923b), 319.
27 Cf. van Fraassen (2006b) and van Fraassen (2008).

3 How Not to Understand Idealization and the Ideal Character of Scientific Knowledge

Cassirer's emphasis on the importance of idealization for scientific knowledge evidences that for him idealization was not an issue that should be taken lightly by the philosophy of science. Indeed throughout his career as a philosopher of science he was committed to fighting against conceptions of idealization that, as he was convinced, would lead us astray in our effort to understand the complex "fact of science" and the various roles that idealizations play in it.

Throughout his life Cassirer was engaged in the task of elaborating a "realist" concept of idealization that did justice to the way of how idealization "really" worked in "real" science. A part of this endeavor was to criticize the flaws and shortcomings of the attempts of other philosophers to cope with this problem. A preferred target of Cassirer's criticisms were the proposals that the brothers Paul and Emil du Bois-Reymond had put forward in the last decades of the 19th century. Cassirer extensively dealt with the theses of the du Bois-Reymonds in SF, PSFIII, and DI. This may be taken as evidence that he considered their theses as important, although philosophically mistaken claims.

The common point of departure for Cassirer's SF and Paul du Bois-Reymond's *Die Allgemeine Funktionentheorie* (1882) was the fact that the theoretical laws of modern science do not directly refer to perceptual data. Rather, the scientific image of the world is grounded on a wealth of idealizations in which the indefinite empirical data are replaced by strict conceptual limits. The ways of Cassirer and du Bois-Reymond parted when it came to the problem of determining the "ontological status" of these idealizations or limit concepts.

According to du Bois-Reymond there existed two different ways to tackle the problems posed by such limiting concepts.[28] The first he called the way of idealism, the second the way of empirism. Du Bois-Reymond characterized the idealist approach by the assumption that conceptual limits, which are required by our cognizing activity, exist in the same way as the objects of our perceptions. On the other hand, du Bois-Reymond's "empirism" only recognized what can be perceived. This stance, however, is too austere to adequately describe the knowledge of modern science because it depends on the assumption that ideal objects such as the absolutely rigid body, the atom, or the force of a distance do exist in the same way as particular data exist. On the other hand, the idealist's candid claims of the existence of ideal objects seem to be extravagant and unjustifiable, be-

---

28 Cf. P. du Bois-Reymond (1882), 3, 78–176.

cause the existence of these ideal entities clearly transcends the accessible world of sensuous appearances. In sum, du Bois-Reymond's idealist as well as his empirist seem to be trapped in an aporetic dilemma.

Contemporary philosophers with empiricist inclinations use to express this dilemma by saying that the idealizing scientific concepts are "lying" or "falsifying" reality but nevertheless are needed for the scientific endeavor. Other scholars, with less empiricist qualms assert that the idealized theories of science do not apply to the actual world but to some mysterious 'ideal worlds'. An extreme example is provided by Leszek Nowak's "(supra-)realism". Nowak argues for a strong realism with respect to ideal objects:

> [A]ll our idealizational "constructs" are not constructs but true descriptions of some existing ideal worlds. ... As it were, we are unable to theoretically invent something which would not hold nowhere, in no world.[29]
>
> ...
>
> Our thinking consists only in finding some thing that holds somewhere, in some world. And the idealizational thinking straightforwardly falls under this rule.[30]

According to Nowak, we are able to perceive "somehow" facts of ideal worlds in the same way as we are able to perceive facts in the real world. Cassirer vigorously protested against du Bois-Reymond's allegedly unescapable dilemma. both interpretations of the role of idealizations. He neither accepted the stance of du Bois-Reymond's conceptually consumptive "empirism" that accepted idealizations only with bad conscience as (perhaps) necessary lies, nor was he prepared to buy into an overstated "idealism" that indulged in the existence of countless phantastic ideal worlds populated by more or less phantastic ideal objects. Rather, rightly understood,

> [The] ideal concepts of natural science affirm nothing regarding a new realm of separate absolute objects, but they only want to establish the inevitable, logical lines of direction, by which alone complete orientation is gained within the manifold of the phenomena. They only go beyond the given, in order to grasp more sharply the systematic structural relations of the given.[31]

Cassirer would have considered Nowak's account of idealization as a wildly overstated idealism put forward by an extravagant "idealist à la du Bois-Reymond" who has not understood the complex relation between the real and the ideal. For

---

29 Nowak (1995), 236.
30 Nowak (1995), 238.
31 Cassirer (1923b), 128.

Cassirer, the "worlds" where we find ideal gases, ideal planes, point masses and so on, are worlds only in a highly metaphorical sense. Moreover, these "ideal worlds" do not have much to do with the processes of idealization that the scientists carry out to come to terms with the real world. In these processes the indefinite data of sensations are supplanted by their strict conceptual limits. Nevertheless the assertion of the objective validity of these processes should not be confused with the assertion of the existence of a new class of objects, to say nothing about the existence of a new class of worlds.

According to Cassirer the fundamental flaw of du Bois-Reymond's idealist consists in reifying the ideal. The ideal concepts, which real science employs for the logical interpretation and mastery of the manifold of sensations, are transformed into mysterious realities behind, and independent, of the phenomena. This is paradigmatically exemplified by Nowak's "supra-realism". This species of an idealist, Cassirer remarks, "has permitted his conception (of the ideal) to be perverted by his opponent the 'empiricist'".

Cassirer offered the following proposal of a reconciliation between the two extreme stand–points: (i) The empiricist should admit the necessity of idealizing if he wants to come to terms with the real world. Without introducing certain appropirate idealizations science is simply not possible:

> This reduction of the manifold and ceaselessly changing material of perception to ultimate constant relations must be granted by even the most radical "empiricism." For the assumption of this fundamental relation is all that remains for empiricism of the concept of the "object," and thus of the conception of nature.[32]

The necessity of idealizing does not entail, however, the recognition of ideal objects as objects of "real" ideal worlds. This is to say, in order to achieve a peaceful coexistence with the empiricist the idealist has to recognize only the irreality of ideal concepts and being content with the objectivity of the activity of idealizing.

In virtually all his important contributions to the philosophy of science Cassirer argued that "critical idealism" escaped du Bois-Reymond's dilemma according to which one had to choose between an anorexic empiricism and an extravagant idealism. He contended that his "critical idealism" put forward an adequate understanding of what idealization really meant and what its real function was for modern science. In brief, the critical idealist approach showed—contra du Bois-Reymond—that it was possible to describe the idealizing practice of real science in a plausible and non-aporetic way.

---

[32] Cassirer (1923b), 260.

Ideal concepts such as point-masses, frictionless planes and so on are not the only ingredients of scientific knowledge for which idealization plays essential role. Idealization also plays a role in the philosophy of science proper, namely, in the highly idealized models of science that philosophers of science employ in their speculations about science. These models may be characterized as *global* idealizations. In contrast, ideal concepts such as point-masses, perfect fluids etc. are *local* idealizations—they affect only relatively small areas of scientific knowledge.

Pertinent examples of such "global idealizations" are the various accounts of an "ideal physics", models of ideal neuroscience and psychology that ignore the embarrassing but allegedly inessential shortcomings and deficiencies that at present still hamper these sciences. One may distinguish between negative and positive global idealizations. Negative idealizations are concerned with some allegedly "absolute" limitations of science according to which science will never be able to answer certain questions or solve certain problems. Which problems science allegedly will never solve varies, of course, widely with time and ideological background of those who put forward such a thesis.

Positive global idealizations claim that for understanding the essence of science it is expedient to ignore certain inessential limitations of present day science, for example our limited capacities of calculations, limited precision of measurements etc. which certainly affect the results of present day science but can be ignored *sub specie aeternitatis* for an ideal science.

Perhaps the most important and most influential example of such a global idealization that Cassirer's critical idealism was confronted with was the model of scientific knowledge encapsulated in the metaphor of the Laplace's demon and his immense physical knowledge concerning the whole past and future of the world. In the last decades of the 19th century the prominent physiologist and philosopher Emil du Bois-Reymond (and his brother Paul du Bois-Reymond) used this model of an ideal physics to argue for the existence of some unsurmountable limits ("Ignoramus et ignorabimus") for human scientific knowledge. The negative part of their argument is simple: Clearly, the demon's physical knowledge is at least as comprehensive and profound as that which mankind can ever hope to achieve. Thus, if there are problems that the demon is unable to solve then these are unsolvable for mankind a fortiori. The positive part of du Bois-Reymond's argument is less trivial but philosophically more interesting. Du Bois-Reymond takes it for granted that the demon's physical knowledge can be considered as a faithful, although idealized model of human physical knowledge.

Over the decades, du Bois-Reymond's thesis had an immense repercussion in the German academia and beyond.[33] In DI, Cassirer vigorously attacked du Bois-Reymond's Laplacian model of an ideal science arguing that it lead to a confused and obsolete conception of causality. In particular, he critizised du Bois-Reymond's "Ignorabimus"-thesis as an artifact of bad metaphysics and approvingly quoted Richard von Mises[34] according to whom du Bois-Reymond's "ignorabimus" "has no other significance for us than the sober kowledge that the mathematician has of the impossibility of squaring the circle and of other similar problems... ."[35] For Cassirer, the idea of an ideal science, suggested by Laplace's demon was an idealization that lead us astray. Rather, faithful to the Marburg maxim of learning from the history of science what science is, he proposed to look at the most promising scientific theory then available for clues about how an ideal science would look. For Cassirer, quantum mechanics was a compelling argument that we have to formulate the ideal of science in a different way:

> We must formulate the ideal and principle of scientific knowledge differently and from a new point of view if the principle is to be logically coherent and empirically useful, applicable to the procedure of "actual" physics and its formation of concepts.[36]
>
> ...
>
> The causal problem must be grasped as a problem of "discursive," not of "intuitive," understanding, of a finite, not of an infinite intellect. If this finite intellect is limited, this limtation implies by no means a merely negative, but rather a positive, characterization. ...

---

33 Still in 1930 David Hilbert felt called to contradict du Bois-Reymond at the meeting of the German Mathematical Society in Königsberg: "We must not believe those, who today, with philosophical bearing and deliberative tone, prophesy the fall of culture and accept the ***ignorabimus***. For us there is no ***ignorabimus***, and in my opinion none whatever in natural science. In opposition to the foolish ***ignorabimus*** our slogan shall be: *Wir müssen wissen – wir werden wissen!*" In different ways, logical empiricists such as Carnap and Frank argued against du Bois-Reymond's *ignorabimus* (cf. Carnap (1928), Frank (1949)).
34 Cf. Cassirer (1956), 9.
35 It may be interesting to note that the young Carnap had no qualms in applying Laplace's model of ideal scientific knowledge, see his *Die Aufgabe der Physik und das Prinzip der Einfachstheit* (1923). In contrast, Carnap's fellow empiricist Neurath vigorously rejected the Laplace's model of scientific knowledge ("The system is the great scientific lie"). Somewhat ironically then, Cassirer, aiming at a realist model of science "as it is practiced by scientists", sided with Neurath with respect to the issue of idealization. Carnap was never very much interested in the task of overcoming the possibly distorting features of the philosophically and logically overidealized models of science that philosophers are prone to deal with instead of "real" science. On the other hand, all logical empiricists agreed that du Bois-Reymond's *Ignorabimus*, i.e., his forever unsolvable "world riddles" were meta–physical pseudo-problems.
36 Cassirer (1956), 10.

It rather delimits the domain in which alone our thinking and knowing find fulfillment, in which alone they win concrete significance.[37]

In other words, acknowledging the necessity of idealizing does not amount to adopting a "God's eye" point of view. On the contrary, idealization in science is justified by an argument which draws its strength from another, quite different source, namely, the insight into the finiteness of the human mind and its conceptual achievements. In other words, the necessity of idealization in human "discursive" science is the key ingredient for doing justice to the essential aspect of its finiteness. Laplace's model of an ideal science freed of all limitations that beset real science, seriously misrepresents it. Idealization is a central issue for every kind of philosophy of science that aims to understand "real" science and is not content with a metaphysical surrogate inspired not by science but rather by some sort science fiction. As will be explained in detail, Laplace's model destroys an essential feature of any finite human science, namely, its nonintuitive discursive character of science.[38]

4 The Causality Principle and the Problem of Reality

The starting point for Cassirer's account of causality is the assumption that causality is to be found not in nature but is to be conceived as an ingredient of our theories about nature. Or, as Victor Lenzen put it:

> Causality is a relation within the realm of conceptual objects. The relation of cause and effect refers to conceptual events regardless of the relation of the latter to reality. ... In the sophisticated age of science causality must be attributed to a model which the scientist constructs out of concepts.[39]

---

[37] Cassirer (1956), 23.
[38] In their opposition to the Laplacian model of science again we find Cassirer and Neurath on the same side. They expressed their convictions, of course, in quite different ways. While for Neurath the Laplacian system was "the great scientific lie", Cassirer characterized Laplace's model taken as the limiting point to which real science would converge, as a deceiving *focus imaginarius* (cf. Cassirer (1956), 24).
[39] Cassirer (1956), xii.

Indeed, Cassirer explicitly contended that in light of modern science it is no longer possible to maintain that causal relations have empirical content.[40] Nevertheless, they are not superfluous. Rather, the principle of causality is a methodological principle. Evidently, this thesis is in need of further explication. Causality is concerned with all domains of physical knowledge and all aspects of scientific knowledge, but not in the same kind. In order to understand how it works it is necessary to investigate in some detail the structure of physical knowledge. For this purpose Cassirer distinguished between three types of physical statements:
- Statements of results of measurements
- Statements of laws
- Statements of principles

We may say that statements of results of measurements are individual, statements of law are general, and statements of principles are universal.[41] Cassirer insists that these three types of statements are statements of different types. There is no "continuous" path from one level to the other, rather, what is required, is a "jump".[42]

Statements of the results of measurements are the first step in the transition from the realm of "given" to the realm of scientific knowledge, or, in other words "from the world of sense to the world of physics"[43]. How this transition from "percepts" to "concepts" is to be thought has been explained in sufficient detail in SF (*The Concepts of Natural Science* (Chapter IV)) and therefore need not be repeated in DI. The essential point of this theory of the formation of physical concepts is that the concepts of science cannot be understood simply as "copies" or "abbreviations" of sensuous percepts but as constructions.[44] In the following problems of the formation of physical concepts are left aside. DI will be essentially dealing not with questions concerning physical concepts but with questions concerning physical statements.

With respect to statements of measurement results, the first thing one observes is that the experimental observation in physics and other sciences has resulted in an immense extensional enrichment of our knowledge. Thus, it seems

---

40 Cf. Cassirer (1956), 60.
41 Cassirer (1956), 54.
42 Cassirer (1956), 54.
43 Cassirer (1956), 31.
44 As more recent literature on the issue of the formation of physical concepts Cassirer recommends Carnap's *Physikalische Begriffsbildung* (Carnap (1926)) and Hermann Weyls *Philosophie der Mathematik und der Naturwissenschaft* (Weyl (1927)).

natural to understand the importance of all our physical measuring instruments as their improvement of the capacities of our natural sense organs. This aspect of physical measurement is particularly visible in the case of visual perception. In this realm, microscopes, telescopes and other apparatuses appear simply to be devices that help overcome the contingent restrictions of our sense organs. This is, however, only one aspect of the use of instruments. At least as important is another, complementary aspect of physical experimentation:

> For over against the broadening of our world picture, ... there comes about also a highly significant concentration. ... To the growing extensive range of knowledge there corresponds an ever stronger intensive penetration and mastery.[45]

Shaped by a basic conviction of Marburg Neo-Kantianism, Cassirer claims that these two tendencies—extension vs. concentration—are not in perfect equilibrium but the latter dominates the former. That is to say the history of physical knowledge is characterized by a tendency toward concentration and condensation as its organizing principle. This feature shows up in the formation of all physical concepts and judgments, be they statement of results of measurements, of laws, or of principles.[46]

In other words, there is a kind of dialectic between the extension and the condensation of scientific knowledge. This dialectic has a direction in so far as the tendency of concentration and unification is dominant. It takes place on all three levels of physical knowledge, beginning already on the level of measurement statement, and continuing in specific ways on the levels of statements of laws and of principles. The driving force in this dialectical evolution of scientific knowledge lies on the side of condensation, i.e., according to the Neo-Kantian perspective on the evolution of scientific knowledge the primary feature of this evolution is the ever-growing condensation und conceptual deepening of scientific knowledge.

Statements of laws lead to further condensation and extension of scientific knowledge. Already in SF Cassirer had discussed as pertinent examples mathematical, physical, and chemical formulas.[47] In DI he emphasizes that the transition from a particular case—expressed as a statement of the result of a measure-

---

[45] Cassirer (1956), 33.
[46] Cf. Cassirer (1956), 34.
[47] Cf. Cassirer (1923b), Chapter IV. In this respect, grist for Cassirer's mill would have been Wigner's well-known dictum of "the unreasonable effectiveness of mathematics in the natural sciences". Instead of Wigner's "unreasonable effectiveness" Cassirer spoke of "the indwelling "sagacity" (*Spürkraft*) of formulas, which he considered as "... one of the most remarkable and fascinating problems in the epistemology of science." Cassirer (1956), 39.

ment—to a statement of a law should not be conceived of as a merely extensional generalization but as a transition to another type of physical knowledge. Analogously, the transition from the level of statements of laws to the level of statements of principles is to be conceived of not as a "continuous" process of expansion, but as a discontinuous jump, i.e., as a *metábasis eis allo génos*.[48]

The distinction between "laws" and "principles" seems new. In SF Cassirer had not yet distinguished between laws and principles, rather, the two types of physical judgments laws were lumped together. In DI he clearly distinguished between the two levels, probably in the order to pave the way for the elucidation for the "principle of all principles", namely, the principle of causality. Laws have empirical content, principles tend to be empirically empty. They are not themselves laws, but rules for seeking and finding laws.[49] The higher one ascends in the hierarchy of scientific propositions, the harder it becomes to distinguish between these propositions and the summit of the hierarchy, the principle of causality.[50] Cassirer treats in detail the historical evolution of the principle of least action and the principle of the conservation of energy.[51]

In order to understand the principle of causality as the highest principle of all principles it is expedient to recall the general characterization of the role of principles that Cassirer gave above: "Principles are ... rules for seeking and finding laws." This general characterization leads to a principle of causality tailor-made for the needs of method-centered Marburg Neo-Kantianism:

> The principle of causality is not a new insight concerning content, but solely one concerning method.[52] It is a postulate of empirical thought that specifies that the evolution of scientific knowledge can and should go on without limitation. The prinicple assumes that phenomena of nature do not withstand in principle the possibility of being ordered by science. The causal principle is a principle *sui generis* insofar as it is a statement about measurements, laws, <u>and</u> principles. It says that all these can be so related and combined with one another that from this combination there results a system of physical knowledge and not a mere aggregate of isolated observations.[53]

---

48 Cf. Cassirer (1956), 42.
49 Cf. Cassirer (1956), 52.
50 Cassirer (1956), 55.
51 Cf. Cassirer (1956), 48 ff.
52 Similarly Thomas Nagel: According to him the principle of causality is a methodological rule of heuristic value which "bids us to analyze physical processes in such a way that their evolution can be shown to be independent of the particular times and places at which those processes occur." Nagel insists the principle of causality is a maxim for inquiry rather than a statement with definite empirical content (cf. Nagel (1961), 320) with reference to DI. In Frank (1932) one finds similar contentions.
53 Cassirer (1956), 60.

The transcendental character of principle of causality entails that philosophy of science can never treat this issue in isolation. Rather, what is understood by causality always depends on certain assumptions concerning the nature of the objects of science and the concept of physical "reality" that is presupposed. For the case of quantum mechanics this means that the allegedly grave crisis of the concept of causality by that theory suggests a new understanding of the concept of the physical object, and, more globally, of the concept of physical reality. Indeed, Cassirer put forward the following radical thesis:

> The essential problems posed by quantum mechanics for epistemology ... deal primarily not with the category of cause and effect but with the category of thing and attribute, of substance and accident. It appears that we must here carry through a more far-reaching transformation and relearn much more radically than we had to in the case of the causal concept.[54]

According to the classical criterion of the real, to which virtually all pre-quantum epistemologies subscribe, something is real only if it is temporally and spatially completely determined. According to the *Critique of Pure Reason:*

> Every thing ... is subject to the principle of complete determination, according to which if all the possible predicates of things be taken with their contradictory opposites, then one of each pair of contradictory opposites must belong to it.[55]

In the light of quantum mechanics, this principle of complete determination of every "real" thing had to be given up. Quantum theory requires a new concept of physical state that is incompatible with that of classical physics.[56] Insofar as "empiricist" and "rationalist" philosophers of science alike subscribed to a strict Kantian correspondence between complete determination and reality they clash with the new results of non-classical physics. In DI Cassirer mentions Natorp's *Die logischen Grundlagen der exakten Wissenschaften*[57] and Schlick's *Allgemeine Erkenntnislehre*[58] as two contemporary examples whose criteria of reality are seriously affected (or even rendered obsolete) by the new results of quantum mechanics.[59]

---

[54] Cassirer (1956), 188.
[55] Kant (1933) A572/B600.
[56] Cf. Cassirer (1956), 190.
[57] Natorp (1910).
[58] Schlick (1985).
[59] Cf. Cassirer (1956), 189f.

This is not the case for "critical idealism", Cassirer argues. The epistemological framework of "critical idealism" is sufficiently flexible to cope with the new challenge that quantum mechanics represents. According to Cassirer, quantum mechanics, or, more precisely, the uncertainty relations of quantum mechanics teaches us "the impossibility of drawing a sharp line between nature itself and our knowledge of nature. ... Nothing that is not ... for physical knowledge in any sense, is any longer in "itself" in nature."[60] Cassirer intends to render plausible this breakdown of the Aristotelian difference between "for us" and "in itself" by invoking the close affinity between physical and mathematical concepts put forward already in KMM and explicated later in SF and other works. According to him, one of most important advances of modern mathematics was the insight that mathematical objects such as points, lines, and curves

> no longer have a firmly determined existence or a definite significance ascribed to them independently of their mutual relations. All these structures do not exist in order subsequently, to enter into certain relationships; rather, it is these relations themselves which determine and completely exhaust the being expressed in mathematical concepts. Likewise concepts like atoms or electrons fully share the logical character of these geometrical concepts. They do not admit of an explicit definition but basically can only be defined implicitly. In this respect there is no difference between the material point and the ideal mathematical point. To such a point also no being in itself can be ascribed; it is constituted by a definite aggregate of relations, and consists in this aggregate.[61]

The contemporary structural realists French and Ladyman comment that this "structural dissolution of physical objects leads to a blurring of the line between the mathematical and the physical".[62] This may well be true, but it certainly does not adequately express the full content of Cassirer's original sameness thesis. On the other hand, it should be noted that Cassirer does not contend that physical and mathematical concepts are identical:

> The difference between mathematical and physical concepts consists solely in the way they are constituted: Mathematical concepts can be obtained by construction; we "create" these concepts by means of the conditions which we impose on them, by means of the systems of axioms which they have to satisfy. In physics the place of these logical axioms is taken by the hypothetical formulation of the basic concepts, and by hypothetical deductions.[63]

---

60 Cassirer (1956), 194.
61 Cassirer (1956), 195.
62 French and Ladyman (2003), 41.
63 Cassirer (1956), 195–196.

At the end of DI we eventually have come full circle back to the point from which we have started: Clearly, these considerations just rehearse for quantum mechanics the "sameness thesis" that Cassirer had put forward for classical physics already in KMM and SF, namely, that mathematical and empirical concepts are of the same kind. In other words, at the end of DI it becomes evident that Cassirer reads quantum theory as the strongest available confirmation of the fundamental thesis of his version of the Marburg Neo-Kantian philosophy of science according to which mathematical and empirical concepts spring from the same origin, namely, the conceptual activity of the mind.

From KMM through both SF and DI, Cassirer holds fast to the thesis of the conceptual sameness of mathematical and physical concepts. He even claimed that quantum mechanics further confirmed this contention. This basic methodological thesis of his "critical idealism" survived all the revolutions that took place in the course of the physics of 20th century.

By emphasizing the role of implicit definitions for physical concepts quantum mechanics confirms also for post-classical physics the close affinity between mathematical and empirical concepts. Thereby the basic thesis of Cassirer's philosophy of science, namely, that the formation of mathematical and physical concepts follows the same pattern, is validated also for post-classical physics.

5 On the Reception of Determinism and Indeterminism

When Cassirer published DI in 1937 the political and cultural circumstances were anything but favorable for the success of such a book. Cassirer had been exiled from Germany for four years and was living in Sweden. DI, although written in German, could not be published in any German-speaking country, but had to appear in a Swedish publishing house. Taking these negative factors into account, nevertheless, the book was rather successful in its original German version.

In contrast to Cassirer's treatise on Einstein's relativity theory (ERT) some fifteen years prior, DI did not meet strong opposition from the camp of the logical empiricists. On the contrary, in a review of DI, Philipp Frank, one of the hardliners of logical empiricism, somewhat grudgingly felt obliged to admit that he essentially agreed with Cassirer's account of quantum mechanics.[64] More precisely, he conceded that Cassirer's interpretation of quantum mechanics was fully in line with the logical empiricist interpretation of this theory that the members

---

64 Cf. Frank (1938).

of the Vienna Circle had "always" maintained. From Frank's perspective, DI was evidence that one of the leading representatives of "school philosophy" was on his way toward a truly scientific world view. Needless to say, this interpretation did not fully coincide with that of Cassirer who, to repeat it again, considered quantum mechanics as another confirmation for the feasibility of his idealist relational philosophy of science.

In 1956, ten years after Cassirer death, an English translation of DI was released. In the preface of the English edition, Henry Margenau, Cassirer's colleague at Yale and one of the leading quantum physicists of the time, praised his work in enthusiastic terms as follows:

> The book [DI] was ahead of its day; its thesis was revolutionary and radical, not, like so many philosophical commentaries, a wordy echo of the scientists' own pronouncements. For at a time when every physicist spoke of the uncertainty principle as a restrictive injunction on the process of measurement, ... Cassirer saw more deeply and perceived a basic change in the meaning of reality. ... he showed that the causal controversy which raged at the time was not itself of crucial importance but was an outgrowth of a more fundamental issue.[65]

Margenau, playing the role of Cassirer in his preface of DI, describes as the main merit of this book the fact that it reminded the physicists of the following urgent issues on their agenda:

> Your interpretation of uncertainty is a halfway concession. You cannot continue to use the classical models in your reasoning and make your peace with the new doctrine by admitting errors of observation forever beyond human control. You must grant that the very concepts of "physical system" and "physical state" have changed. By going to this deeper level of analysis, you can retain what most philosophers have regarded as causal description.[66]

Margenau even used the expression "prophetic" with respect to DI. Meanwhile, much time has passed and Cassirer's "prophetic" thesis that quantum particles should be considered, in some sense, not as individuals, has become the "received view".[67] Some physicists were convinced that this loss of individuality is something much more fundamental, and much more difficult to digest than the change from classical space and time to the relativistic space-time concept.[68]

---

65 Cassirer (1956), x.
66 Cassirer (1956), x.
67 French and Rickles (2003), 221.
68 French and Rickles (2003), 221.

> [Cassirer's] view has stood the test of two decades and enjoys greater popularity today than when it was propounded.[69]

Margenau's contention that Cassirer's interpretation of quantum mechanics was "ahead of its day" has been confirmed in an unexpected way much later. Cassirer is the only classical philosopher of science whom contemporary structuralist philosophers of quantum mechanics recognize as a precursor of the contemporary structuralist approach. This appropriation has, however, some paradoxical features. While Cassirer was at pains to present his philosophical interpretation of quantum mechanics as a confirmation and deepening of his Neo-Kantian *Ansatz*, the structuralists of the 21th century try hard to play down the genuinely Neo-Kantian ingredients in Cassirer's thought that lead him to a structural interpretation of the new physics.

Be this as it may, in the most recent version of the entry on quantum mechanics in the *Stanford Encyclopedia of Philosophy*,[70] which may be considered as an authoritative source for the general philosophical public, DI is mentioned as a classical work of philosophy of quantum mechanics. This may be taken as convincing evidence that Margenau was right with his assessment.

Nevertheless, the reception of DI in contemporary philosophy of science exhibits some almost paradoxical features. While quite a few philosophers of science with explicit anti-Kantian inclinations welcome Cassirer's explicitly Neo-Kantian contributions to the philosophy of quantum mechanics, in the camp of the avowed partisans of Neo-Neo-Kantian philosophy of science DI has been largely ignored. For instance, Michael Friedman, one of the leading exponents of this current, does not even mention DI once his *Dynamics of Reason*.[71] Despite his high esteem for Cassirer's philosophy he contends that up to now the philosophy of science has not provided a sufficiently philosophically profound interpretation of quantum mechanics—in contrast to the other non-classical theory, i.e., relativity theory. For quantum mechanics we allegedly lack the means "to rationally bridge the gap between prerevolutionary and post-revolutionary conceptual landscapes".[72] As it seems, Friedman opines that DI was of no help in overcoming this shortcoming.

This pessimistic view is in stark contrast with Cassirer's own assessment of the state of the art. The later Cassirer argued in DI that the gap bewween quantum and pre-quantum physics could be rationally bridged although many philoso-

---

69 Cassirer (1956), x, xi.
70 Cf. Ismael (2015).
71 Friedman (2001).
72 Friedman (2001), 120.

phers and scientists were inclined to deny this. It should be noted that Cassirer did not undertake lightly his strong "no-revolutionary thesis". He was well aware of the fact that his thesis that his Neo-Kantian relational account scientific knowledge was able to overcome the apparent gap between classical and non-classical physics did not find unanimous agreement. For instance, he was well aware of the fact that Planck, one of the founding fathers of the new theory, had characterized his *"Quantenhypothese"* as a "dangerous explosive" for classical physics, far more dangerous than Einstein's theories. In sum, the *Rezeptionsgeschichte* of DI is anything but simple and univocal and remains an interesting task for the history of the philosophy of science.

6 A Structural Realist *avant la lettre?*

DI is recognized as an important early work in the philosophy of quantum mechanics. In light of contemporary discussions, one may say with only a bit of exaggeration that Cassirer has had an impressive posthumous career as a structuralist philosopher of quantum physics. Quite a few contemporary philosophers of quantum theory have proposed considering Cassirer as an early representative of a structuralist philosophy of science.[73] These authors propose considering Cassirer's approach as closely related to the so-called "ontological structural realism" (OSR).

In contemporary philosophy of science, in particular in the philosophy of quantum mechanics, one finds a bewildering profusion of "structuralisms". One of the most prominent is "structural realisms" (SR).[74]

In this section I'd like to deal first with one member of SR, namely, the "ontological structural realism" (OSR) of French, Ladyman, and others. These authors have come to recognize Cassirer as a precursor of this subspecies of structural realism. In the second half of this section I'll tentatively argue that Cassirer's idealist structuralism may have affinities not so much with some version of SR, but rather with another species of structuralism, namely, the one which van Fraassen has characterized as "empiricist structuralism" (ES).[75]

---

[73] Cf. French and Ladyman (2003), Ladyman and Ross (2007), Cei and French (2009), French (2014).
[74] Frigg and Votsis list no less than six subspecies XSR of structural realism SR (Frigg and Votsis (2011), 238).
[75] Cf. van Fraassen (2006) and van Fraassen (2008).

Let us start with a rough and informal sketch of OSR.[76] In first approximation, OSR may be characterized by assertions such as "Only (relational) structures are real", or, a bit more cautiously, "There are relations in which the relation is primary, while the things are secondary",[77] or "There are only relations and no relata".[78]

For Ladyman and French "the claim that relata are constructed as abstractions from relations" does not imply that there are no relata; "rather the opposite"(!). This somewhat enigmatic contention is explained as follows:

> A core aspect of the claim that relations are logically prior to relata is that the relata of a given relation always turn out to be relational structures themselves on further analysis.[79]

In other words, OSR contends that, in one way or other, all the way down there are only relations. How can this bold thesis be reconciled with the fact that most people consider it as impossible to think of a relation without relata? Among the various proposals to overcome this difficulty one finds the following ingenious proposal of Ross and Ladyman:

> Speculating cautiously about psychology, it is possible that dividing a domain up into objects is the only way we can think about it. ... We may not be able to think about structure without hypostatizing individuals as the bearers of structure, but it does not follow that the latter are ontologically fundamental.[80]

Whether Ladyman and Ross's "cautious psychological speculation" is compelling, it is certainly not new. Almost one hundred years ago one finds it as an essential ingredient of an elaborated Neo-Kantian epistemology in SF that aims to elucidate the complex relation between objects and objectivity:

> ... we do not know "objects",—as if they were already independently determined and given *as objects*,—but we know *objectively*, by producing certain limitations and by fixating certain permanent elements and connections within the uniform flow of experience. The concept of object in this sense constitutes no ultimate limit of knowledge, but is rather its fundamental instrument, by which all that has become its permanent possession is expressed and established.[81]

---

[76] Cf. French (2014), Ladyman and Ross (2007), Frigg and Votsis (2011).
[77] Ladyman (2007), 152.
[78] French (2014).
[79] Ladyman and Ross (2007), 154–155.
[80] Ladyman and Ross (2007), 155.
[81] Cassirer (1923b), 303, and Cassirer (1956), 137.

Indeed, the distinction between "knowing objects" and "objective knowledge" was the cornerstone of Marburg Neo-Kantianism namely, the primacy of an objective scientific method over allegedly "real" objects that exist "out there". Cassirer considered this distinction as essential for the critical idealist approach *überhaupt*, as is evidenced by the extensive self-quotation concerning of the pertinent passage in DI taken from SF. Moreover, this link between DI and SF provides unmistakable evidence that DI is to be considered as a continuation of his earlier work.

Although the partisans of OSR are readily prepared to give a place of honor to Cassirer in the "prehistory of structuralism" they shy away from close conceptual contact with his Neo-Kantian philosophy of science. For instance, in the section *What we can take from Cassirer* in *The Structure of the World*,[82] Cassirer's legacy is summarized succinctly in the following general insights.[83]
- Relations are conceptually prior to objects.
- The locus of objectivity shifts from objects to laws and symmetries.

In "On the Transposition of the Substantial into the Functional: Bringing Cassirer's Philosophy of Quantum Mechanics into the 21st Century",[84] Cei and French contextualize these two contentions as consequences of the following three theses that encapsulate the allegedly neutral, non-Neo-Kantian essence of Cassirer's philosophy of science:[85]
- *Holism.* Cassirer distinguishes between three different types of statements of statements in physics: statement of the results of measurement, statement of laws, and statements of principles.[86]
- *Functional coordination.* All the statements of physics are determined through one another, the mutually condition and support one another, and their specific "truth" is due precisely to this mutual interconnection. This reciprocal interweaving and bonding constitutes one of the basic features of the system of physics. There is only a functional coordination in which all the elements ... uniformly participate.[87]
- *Centrality of the notion of Law.* The laws are the features that in the theoretical set-up bring about the coordinative component. They express the pattern that we then find instantiated in the various singular cases. In this sense the

---

82 French (2014).
83 French (2014), 99 ff.
84 Cei and French (2009), 114.
85 Cf. Cassirer (1956), 35.
86 Cassirer (1956), chapter 3.
87 Cf. Cassirer (1956), 35.

principles just replicate this coordinate "move" at the more general level of the laws themselves.[88]

Cei and French explicitly state that they do not want to suggest that "the debate on structuralism should move in a Neo-Kantian direction".[89] Rather, Cassirer's work is said to present elements of interest in a more general sense for the agenda of structuralism.[90] According to them, Cassirer's conclusions about quantum mechanics are not consequences of his Neo-Kantianism. All that is needed to conclude that quantum objects are not individuals are the just mentioned ingredients holism, functional coordination, and the centrality of the notion of law.[91]

This thesis is at variance with Cassirer's own interpretation of DI, according to which DI was a continuation and clarification of the account of scientific knowledge that he had formulated for classical physics some 25 years ago in SF.[92] In particular, the ingredients of holism, functional coordination, and the centrality of law already appear in SF. It seems, however, difficult to deny that SF is a genuine Neo-Kantian work.

Some further remarks on the relation of Cassirer's acount and the OSR-interpretation of it are in order. With respect to Cassirer's holism one may note that, in DI, he insisted on the importance of <u>three</u> types of statements of physical knowledge, namely, statements of the results of measurements, statements of laws, and statements of principles.[93]

Cassirer's expression of a "reciprocal interweaving and bonding" (DI) is taken up several times in French (2014) and Cei and French (2009) as evidence of the close affinity between Cassirer's and their account of structuralism. Neventheless a certain change of meaning seems to have taken place surreptiously. While Cassirer insisted on the holistic character of physical knowledge that comprised all three types of physical statements, Cei and French show a tendency toward a two-tiered approach that only recognizes laws and principles as generators of the entire system of physical knowledge:

---

[88] Cei and French (2009), 113.
[89] Cei and French (2009), 113.
[90] Rather vaguely, they adumbrate that Cassirer could teach contemporary philosophy of science that the concept of law of nature should play a major role in the debate on structuralism (cf. Cei and French (2009), 114, and French (2014)). Be this as it may, a realization of this project presupposes that Cassirer's Neo-Kantian concept of law could be reformulated in an appropriate Non-Neo-Kantian way.
[91] Cei and French (2009), 113–114.
[92] Cf. Cassirer (1956), xxiii.
[93] Cassirer (1956), 35.

The putative objects of the theory emerge from the interplay of the laws and the principles of the theory itself because they encapsulate the kind of constant patterns that ties together the empirical features that in different ways we consider to be properties of the object or consequences of the dynamics that the theory ascribes to its objects. In this sense, a working theory "generates" its own objects, and objectivity is grounded in the universality of laws and principles.[94]

Cei and French's claim that the objects of a theory emerge from the "interplay of the laws and the principles of the theory" is at variance with Cassirer's more thoroughgoing holism. Cassirer insists on the indispensible role of measurement statements.[95] If we characterize "laws" and "principles" as more idealized ingredients in a theory (in a sense that should be further specified, of course) one may say that the contemporary ontological structural realism subscribes to a more radical, eliminative structuralism that aims to eliminate objects completely.

Finally one should observe that Cassirer's structuralism is more comprehensive. While the contemporary structural realists rely on quantum physics as principal evidence for the structuralist character of scientific knowledge, Cassirer's structuralism considers quantum physics only as one among many arguments for a structuralist interpretation of physical knowledge. For Cassirer, quantum theory is only the most recent, although perhaps the most powerful argument for the structural character of scientific knowledge. Cassirer not only asserts that quantum objects are relationally defined non-individuals, but quite generally that classical and non-classical (quantum) physics are relational knowledge.

From the perspective of Cassirer's "critical idealism" the structural realism of OSR amounts to a version of idealism in du Bois-Reymond's sense, which Cassirer had critizised as overstated and distorted already in SF. Thus one may doubt, whether Cassirer's moderate idealist structuralism really is compatible with (OSR).

Fortunately, structural *realism* is not the only game in town. There are also other structuralisms available. In the rest of this section I'd like to deal tentatively with van Fraassen's Empiricist Structuralism (ES). For van Fraassen, the motivation for giving ES a try in *Scientific Representation*[96] is similar to that of Cassirer in SF and subsequent works, namely, to make sense of mathematization as one of the characteristic tendencies of modern science.

Van Fraassen opens the chapter on ES with the thesis that one of the major tasks of the philosophy of modern science is to make sense of "the mathemati-

---

94 French (2014), 99.
95 Cf. Cassirer (1956), 35.
96 van Fraassen (2008).

zation of the (scientific) world-picture that culminated in the twentieth century".[97] As he rightly points out, this transition incites the philosophy of science to develop views of science that help justify and explain the ever growing impact of mathematics on the sciences. Although the various structuralist attempts in the history of the philosophy of science cannot be said to have coped with this task in a fully satisfying way, van Fraassen is convinced that there is still hope to set up a version of structuralism that really works. Not surprisingly, he is convinced that only a structuralism in an empiricist setting will do.[98] ES is defined as follows. Essential to an *empiricist structuralism* is the following core construal of the slogan that *all we know is structure:*
- Science represents the empirical phenomena as embeddable in certain *abstract structures* (theoretical models).
- Those abstract structures are describable only up to structural isomorphism.[99]

Since *The Scientific Image*[100] the concept of "embedding empirical phenomena in abstract structures" has been one of the most interesting and difficult concepts of van Fraassen's constructive empiricism. What exactly does it mean that empirical structures can be embedded (or represented) as substructures of more complex structures that include theoretical ingredients? I think that the idea of such an "embedding" is sufficiently flexible to allow different interpretations. In the rest of this section I propose to interpret it in a way that is suggested by Cassirer's relational account of physical knowledge, namely, the embedding of empirical phenomena corresponds to the replacement of empirical concepts by idealized or limiting concepts. For instance, physical space is replaced by homogeneous and isotropic mathematical space, physical bodies are replaced by their mathematical models, etc. The crucial point here is that according to van Fraassen's "constructive empiricism" as well as to Cassirer's "critical idealism" there is no need to ascribe to the embedding structure a reality that renders them structural entities "out there". As Cassirer put it:

---

[97] van Fraassen (2008), 237.
[98] van Fraassen (2008), 238.
[99] The abstract character of these structures, i.e., the fact that they can be described only "up to structural isomorphism" evidences that it is not important what these structures "are", but what they are good for, i.e., what is their functional role. This is quite in line with Cassirer's conception of ideal concepts.
[100] van Fraassen (1980).

> Also the ideal concepts of natural science affirm nothing regarding a new realm of separate absolute objects, but they would only establish the inevitable, *logical lines of direction*, by which alone complete orientation is gained within the manifold of phenomena. They only go beyond the given, in order to grasp the more sharply the systematic structural relations of the given.[101]

The only "reality" that one can claim for them is their "objectivity" in the sense that they achieve their purpose, namely, to order the phenomena in an ever more comprehensive and perspicuous manner. But, as Cassirer pointed out already in SF "reality" and "objectivity" should not be confused (see section 3).

This kind of flexible empiricism concerning the role of the theoretical (idealizing) ingredients of a theory such as laws and principles, seems more in line with Cassirer's modest idealism than the rather robustly realist assumptions of OSR. Thus, tentatively, I'd like to conclude that ES may be more congenial to Cassirer's idealist structuralism than OSR.

To be sure, these two sketches of possible affinities between Neo-Kantian structuralism and and contemporary versions of structuralism such as ORS and ES in no way claim to have settled the issue of determining definitively Cassirer's place in the landscape of the many versions of structuralism presently available. Their only purpose was to show that this problem is still an unsolved and interesting problem in history of philosophy of science.

In sum, the project of the partisans of OSR to "bring Cassirer's philosophy of quantum mechanics into the twenty-first century" by eliminating its Neo-Kantian content of the twentieth century looks a bit quixotic, to say the least.

Bibliography

Bueno et al. (2002): Otávio Bueno, Steven French and James Ladyman, "On Representing the Relationship between the Mathematical and the Empirical", *Philosophy of Science 69*, 452–73.
Carnap (1923): Rudolf Carnap, "Über die Aufgabe der Physik und die Andwendung des Gundsatze der Einfachstheit", *Kant-Studien 28*, 90–107.
Carnap (1926): Rudolf Carnap, *Physikalische Begriffsbildung*, Karlsruhe: G. Braun.
Cartwright (1999): Nancy Cartwright, *The Dappled World. A Study of the Boundaries of Science*, Cambridge: Cambridge University Press.
Cassirer (1902): Ernst Cassirer, *Leibniz' System in seinen wissenschaftlichen Grundlagen*, Hamburg: Felix Meiner.

---

101 Cassirer (1923b), 128.

Cassirer (1907): Ernst Cassirer, "Kant und die moderne Mathematik (Mit Bezug auf Bertrand Russells und Louis Couturats Werke über die Prinzipien der Mathematik)", *Kant-Studien* 12, 1–49.
Cassirer (1923a): Ernst Cassirer, "Einstein's Theory of Relativity", in: *Substance and Function and Einstein's Theory of Relativity*, Chicago and LaSalle, Open Court.
Cassirer (1923b): Ernst Cassirer, "Substance and Function", in: *Substance and Function and Einstein's Theory of Relativity*, Chicago and LaSalle, Open Court.
Cassirer (1955a): Ernst Cassirer, *The Philosophy of Symbolic Forms, Volume One: Language*, Ralph Manheim (trans.), New Haven: Yale University Press.
Cassirer (1955b): Ernst Cassirer, *The Philosophy of Symbolic Forms, Volume Two: Mythical Thought*, Ralph Manheim (trans.), New Haven: Yale University Press.
Cassirer (1956): Ernst Cassirer, "Determinism and Indeterminism in Modern Physics. Historical and Systematic Studies", New Haven: Yale University Press.
Cassirer (1957): Ernst Cassirer, *The Philosophy of Symbolic Forms, Volume Three: The Phenomenology of Knowledge,* Ralph Manheim (trans.), New Haven: Yale University Press.
Cei and French (2009): Angelo Cei and Steven French, "On the Transposition of the Substantial into the Functional: Bringing Cassirer's Philosophy of Quantum Mechanics into the 21st Century", in M. Bitbol, P. Kerszberg, and J. Petitot (eds.), *Constituting Objectivity, Transcendental Perspectives on Modern Physics*, Dordrecht: Springer, 95–115.
du Bois-Reymond (1974): Emil du Bois-Reymond, *Über die Grenzen des Naturerkennens*, in Emil du Bois-Reymond, *Vorträge über Philosophie und Gesellschaft*, Hamburg: Meiner.
du Bois-Reymond (1882): Paul du Bois-Reymond, *Die Allgemeine Funktionentheorie, Erster Teil*, Tübingen: Verlag der H. Laupp'schen Buchhandlung.
du Bois-Reymond (1890): Paul du Bois-Reymond, *Über die Grundlagen der Erkenntnis in den exacten Wissenschaften*, Tübingen: Verlag der Laupp'schen Buchhandlung.
Frank (1932): Philipp Frank, *Das Kausalgesetz und seine Grenzen*, Vienna: Springer.
Frank (1949): Philipp Frank, "Determinism and Indeterminism in Modern Physics, (Review of Cassirer 1937)", in *Modern Science and its Philosophy*, Cambridge: Harvard University Press, 172–185.
French and Ladyman (2003): Steven French and James Ladyman, "Remodelling Structural Realism: Quantum Mechanics and the Metaphysics of Structure", *Synthese* 136, 31–56.
French (2014): Steven French, *The Structure of the World*, Oxford: Oxford University Press.
Friedman (2001): Michael Friedman, *The Dynamics of Reason*, Stanford: CSLI Publications.
Frigg and Votsis (2011): Roman Frigg and Ioannis Votsis, "Everything you always wanted to know about structural realism but were afraid to ask", *European Journal of Philosophy of Science* 1, 227–276.
Ihmig (1999): Karl-Norbert Ihmig, "Ernst Cassirer and the Structural Conception of Objects in Modern Science: The Importance of the 'Erlanger Program'", *Science in Context* 12, 513–29.
Ihmig (2001): Karl-Norbert Ihmig, *Grundzüge einer Philosophie der Wissenschaften bei Ernst Cassirer*, Darmstadt, Wissenschaftliche Buchgesellschaft.
Ismael (2015): Jenann Ismael, "Quantum Mechanics", in: *The Stanford Encyclopedia of Philosophy*, Edward N. Zalta (ed), URL=<http://plato.stanford.edu/entries/qm/>.
Kant (1933): Immanuel Kant, *Critique of Pure Reason*, London, Macmillan and Co.

Ladyman and Ross (2007): James Ladyman and Don Ross, *Every Thing Must Go. Metaphysics Naturalized*, Oxford: Oxford University Press.
Margenau (1935): Henry Margenau, "Methodology of Modern Physics, 2 parts", *Philosophy of Science* 2, 48–72 and 164–178.
Margenau (1950): Henry Margenau, *The Nature of Physical Reality: A Philosophy of Modern Physics*, New York: McGraw Hill.
Nagel (1961): Thomas Nagel, *The Structure of Science: Problems in the Logic of Scientific Explanation*, New York: Harcourt.
Natorp (1910): Paul Natorp, *Die logischen Grundlagen der exakten Wissenschaften*, Leipzig und Berlin: Teubner.
Norton (2007): John Norton, "Causation as Folk Science", in H. Price and R. Corry (eds.) *Causation, Physics and the Constitution of Reality*, Oxford: Oxford University Press, 11–44.
Nowak (1995): Leszek Nowak, "Antirealism, (Supra-) Realism and Idealization", *Poznarí Studies in the Philosophy of Sciences and the Humanities* 44, 225–242.
van Fraassen (2006a): Bas van Fraassen, "Representation: the Problem for Structuralism", *Philosophy of Science* 74, 536–547.
van Fraassen (2006b): Bas van Fraassen, "Structure: its substance and shadow", *British Journal for the Philosophy of Science* 57, 275–307.
van Fraassen (2008): Bas van Fraassen, *Scientific Representation*, Oxford: Oxford University Press.
Ryckman (1991): Thomas Ryckman, "*Conditio sine qua non? Zuordnung* in the early epistemologies of Cassirer and Schlick", *Synthese* 88, 57–95.
Ryckman (2005): Thomas Ryckman, *The Reign of Relativity. Philosophy in Physics 1915–1925*, Oxford: Oxford University Press.
Schlick (1921): Moritz Schlick, *Kritizistische oder empiristische Deutung der neuen Physik?*, Kant-Studien 26, 96–111.
Schlick (1985): Moritz Schlick, *General Theory of Knowledge*, Chicago: Open Court.
Schlick (1961): Moritz Schlick, "Causality in Contemporary Physics", *British Journal for the Philosophy of Science* 12, 177–193.
Stamatescu (1997): Ion-Olimpiu Stamatescu, "Cassirer und die Quantenmechanik", in E. Rudolph und I.O. Stamatescu (eds.) *Vor der Philosophie zur Wissenschaft. Cassirers Dialog mit der Naturwissenschaft*, Hamburg: Meiner, 17–35.
Stöltzner (2009): Michael Stöltzner, "The Logical Empiricists", in H. Beebee, C. Hitchcock, P. Menzies (eds.), *The Oxford Handbook of Causation*, Oxford: Oxford University Press, 108–127.
Torretti (1999): Roberto Torretti, *The Philosophy of Physics*, Cambridge: Cambridge University Press.
Weyl (1927): Hermann Weyl, *Philosophie der Mathematik und Naturwissenschaft*, München: Oldenbourg.

Thomas Ryckman (Palo Alto)
A Retrospective View of *Determinism and Indeterminism in Modern Physics*

> "It is everywhere the striving of ontology ... to transpose problems of meaning into problems of pure being"[1]

Section I

1 Background

Quantum mechanics originated in the summer of 1925 in a paper by the 24 year-old Werner Heisenberg seeking "to establish a quantum-theoretical mechanics entirely based on relations between observable quantities". Heisenberg's guiding idea was to let observable spectroscopic data of the hydrogen atom, the simplest atomic system, dictate the structure of the new theory. Algebraically manipulating "arrays" of intensities and frequencies of radiation corresponding to the transition of energy levels by the atom's sole electron, Heisenberg infamously did not realize he was multiplying matrices and so "matrix mechanics" is really due to the influential *"Drei Männer Arbeit"* of Born, Heisenberg and Jordan later that autumn. However, in matrix formulation, everything appeared discontinuous. In a quick follow-up paper the three authors had to admit that the abstract matrix representation of the relations between observable quantities was not at all amenable to a "geometrically visualizable (*anschauliche*) interpretation" of an atomic system and in fact the authors emphatically renounced any description of electron motions in terms of the concepts of space and time. At Cambridge, in November, Dirac independently derived the quantum commutation relations $pq - qp = (h/2\pi i)$ 1 while reformulating the theory of Heisenberg's initial paper as a generalization of the Poisson algebra (see §§) of canonically commuting variables of Hamiltonian classical mechanics. From January to June 1926, Schrödinger completed six papers developing a theory of the hydrogen atom as a "wave mechanics". Schrödinger's approach used a mathematical tool (a complex-valued wave equation, a continuous function) much more familiar to physicists. Following his (not entirely rigorous) demonstration in March that the new

---

[1] Cassirer (1957), 94.

wave mechanics and matrix mechanics are "completely equivalent from the mathematical point of view", wave mechanics rather quickly supplanted matrix mechanics whose methods, as well as those of Dirac's algebra, many physicists found obscure as well as difficult to apply to actual physical problems (in particular, to the helium atom, the next simplest atomic system). Heisenberg, however, did not concede the superiority of wave mechanics, responding to Schrödinger in a paper of 1927 in which a purely particle interpretation of matrix mechanics is used to formulate the uncertainty relations that bear his name. A controversy ensued over whether quantum mechanics was or could be a "visualizable" (*anschauliche*) theory (and if so, in what sense of "visualizable") and whether it concerned particles or waves. Bohr's complementarity, proclaimed at a conference at Lake Como in September, 1927, effected something of a reconciliation between the "particle" and "wave" approaches but at the cost of concurrent employment of both kinematical and dynamical concepts in the description of quantum systems. Both were necessary though employing one group of these concepts precluded simultaneous use of the other:

> The very nature of the quantum theory thus forces us to regard the space-time coordination and the claim of causality, the union of which characterizes the classical theories, as complementary but exclusive features of the description, symbolizing the idealization of observation and definition respectively.[2]

Complementarity proved a comforting panacea to Born, Heisenberg, Jordan and even to the hypercritical Pauli, but it failed to settle the lingering controversy concerning whether quantum mechanics was a fundamentally acausal and indeterministic theory, a principal topic of debate at the Fifth Solvay Conference in Brussels in October, 1927. Here Bohr and Born together with the younger Heisenberg and Dirac categorically supported the purely probabilistic and acausal interpretation they had developed, while an old guard consisting of H.A. Lorentz, Einstein, Schrödinger and Paul Langevin insisted on finding a causal version of wave mechanics. Indeed a causal theory was presented there, Louis De Broglie's "pilot wave theory", in which a free particle's motion is determined by the wave equation's complex phase, yet it failed to win support from any of the old guard. Under sharp criticism from Pauli, De Broglie quickly abandoned his approach; it was utterly forgotten until David Bohm (1952) revived it a quarter of a century later.

By the late 1920's nearly all founders of quantum mechanics had staked out a position in the debate concerning the problem of causality in quantum me-

---

[2] Bohr (1928), 89–90.

chanics. There was widespread consensus that, when the total energy of the quantum system S is known (and so long as no observations are made), the time dependent linear Schrödinger equation characterized continuous propagation of the probability density describing the relative likelihood of the different possible states S would be found to be in on measurement of a given quantum observable. Broadly speaking, this continuous evolution of probability ("unitary evolution") for observable events was viewed as having the essential features of a causal law; since the Schrödinger equation is a first-order differential equation in time (and again, as long as the system remains unobserved) the state (whatever it is, perhaps a superposition of eigenstates) of S at one time t_1 uniquely determined S's state at any later (or earlier) time t_2. In his seminal book, von Neumann termed "processes of type 2" such "automatic changes which occur with the passage of time".[3] However, and in sharp contrast, the Schrödinger equation was not supposed to hold at all for "reduction of the wave packet", i.e., for measurement of S. Measurement involves not observation of S alone but (following von Neumann, who based his discussion on Bohr's account of measurement) required the intervention of some instrument of measurement M; the result is an interaction between S and M. But here lay some grounds disagreement, including of terminology. May it be presumed that S was in some definite state or other prior to interaction with M? Not according to complementarity. And all von Neumann required is that "processes of type 1", describing S transitioning into a definite eigenstate of the operator corresponding to the chosen observable, were "discontinuous, non-causal and instantaneously acting"; this was also largely in line with Bohr's emphasis on "discontinuous transitions" in measurement. But others still viewed measurement as a causal interaction, though not describable by the Schrödinger equation. Dirac, to take a highly influential example, continued to use the concept of cause in describing the non-linear measurement interaction as "the disturbance involved in the act of measurement caus(ing) a jump in the state of the dynamical system".[4]

At this juncture the principal issues were two: 1) whether quantum mechanics as currently understood demonstrated the failure of the causal law as applied to the fundamental micro dynamics underlying the observable world described by classical physics; and 2) if it did, whether or not the theory might be supplemented to satisfy the causal law by the addition of 'hidden variables', essentially degrees of freedom that do not appear in the standard quantum formalism. To the first point, Heisenberg, Born, and Jordan all decisively answered 'yes'. So

---

[3] Neumann (1932), chapter V.
[4] Dirac (1958), 36.

also did Dirac and von Neumann, each of whom subsequently contributed to the modern Hilbert space formalism encompassing both matrix mechanics and Schrödinger's 1926 wave mechanics. After 1932, nearly all quantum physicists gave a negative answer to the second point following von Neumann's 'proof' in his book that there could be no empirically adequate 'hidden variable' causal completion of quantum mechanics. This dogma continued until John S. Bell (1964) who showed that von Neumann's proof depended on an unnecessary and in fact unreasonable assumption.

In any case, by the late 1920s the attention of most leading quantum theorists had turned from philosophical issues like causality, where clear progress no longer seemed likely, to generalizations and extensions of quantum theory, first to relativistic particles, then to fields, and to the newly discovered complexities of the atomic nucleus. Nonetheless, echoes from the unresolved earlier discussions resonated into the early 1930s, and several (e.g., von Laue, Schrödinger[5]) continued to write essentially philosophical papers related to the causal controversy. Around 1930 Einstein, having rejected his own unpublished 1927 attempt to give a causal interpretation of Schrödinger's wave equation, remained virtually alone in his opposition to quantum theory; a succession of arguments that the existing theory was incomplete culminated in the 1935 EPR paper coauthored with Boris Podolsky and Nathan Rosen. Following Bell's work in the 1960s, this would become one of the most cited papers of twentieth century physics, but with the exception of Bohr (who was critical) and Schrödinger (who was intrigued), it elicited little interest at the time. In large measure the target of Cassirer's monograph is the quantum physicists' talk of "crisis of the concept of causality"; no mention is made of Einstein's dissent. As we will see below, Einstein rehearsed the EPR incompleteness argument in a letter to Cassirer of 16 March 1937.

According to Toni Cassirer's memoir,[6] Cassirer began work on *Determinismus und Indeterminismus in der modernen Physik* (*D&I*)[7] whilst still in Hamburg; after the Cassirers left Germany on 12 March 1933 most of the monograph was written in exile at Oxford in 1934 and 1935. We learn from Cassirer's Foreword that the manuscript was completed in April 1936 at Göteborg, where Cassirer had taken

---

5 Cassirer ((1956), 180–1) refers to von Laue (1933, 1934) and (1956, p. 166) to Schrödinger (1934). There is an unfortunate typo (*Anwendbarkeit* should be *Unanwendbarkeit*) in the title of this 1934 paper of Schrödinger in the text of *D&I* (Cassirer (1957) 318), carried over into the English translation.
6 Cassirer (1981), 189.
7 Unless otherwise noted, all references to *D&I* are to the 1956 English translation by O. T. Benfey.

up a position with the University the previous August. It appeared in the original German in November 1936 in the *Göteborgs Högskolas Årsskrift*, a journal understandably little known outside of Sweden; a *separatum* by *Elanders Boktryckeri Aktiebolag* was published in Göteborg early in 1937.

2 Précis

D&I is principally concerned to establish two related theses, the first more general, the other, quite specific. The broader thesis forms a backdrop, claiming a methodological and architectonic continuity between classical and quantum physics. The second and narrower thesis identified the principal epistemological innovation of quantum mechanics not as the failure of the causal concept but as the transformation of the concept of physical state. Both theses are developed in tandem with a knowledgeable presentation of the historical routes to, and development of, quantum theory from Planck's radiation law and discovery of the quantum of action (1900), continuing through the Bohr atom's explanation of the Balmer series of the spectrum of hydrogen in 1913 (the first real success of what would become known as the "old quantum theory"), and culminating in the contributions of Born, Heisenberg, Jordan, Schrödinger and Dirac in 1925–7.

Four of the five parts of *D&I* (up to chapter 12) have the broader aim of demonstrating methodological and architectonic continuity between classical and quantum physics. Of course the then, and still prevailing, opinion most familiar today from the writings of Thomas Kuhn, is of a complete epistemological "rupture" or "paradigm shift". Cassirer's argument can be summarized in a superficially simple way.[8] The "crisis of causality" occasioned by quantum mechanics is better termed a "crisis of visualization" (*Krise der Anschauung*) for it does not pertain to the concept of cause itself. Rather the so-called "crisis" stems from the fact that the causal concept cannot be combined with space-time description. Here lay an apparent incompatibility (at which Cassirer barely hints) with the *Critique of Pure Reason* or at least with the chapter on "the schematism of the concepts of the pure understanding" (A137–47/B176–87) in the Analytic of Principles. There the schema of cause-and-effect of a thing in general is the *a priori* time determination according to the rule that wherever something is posited, something else always follows. However, unlike Bohr who proclaimed the fissure between causal and space-time descriptions to be the distinguishing feature of quantum mechanics, Cassirer traced it back to the foundations of the differential

---

[8] Cassirer (1956), 163–165.

calculus beginning with Leibniz and culminating in Weierstrass's demonstration that continuity (space-time description) and differentiability (the basis of causal description via differential equations) need not coincide. The further development of physical theory by quantum mechanics only exacerbated this fissure, showing that former assumptions of "uniformity" and "equiformity" in nature must be abandoned. But it is important to Cassirer's argument to establish that these trends were already underway within classical physics.

As Cassirer obliquely alerted the reader in his "Foreward", guiding *D&I* is the Marburg neo-Kantian postulate of the fact of physical science (*Faktum der Wissenschaft*) with the implication that epistemology must always be prepared to revise its presuppositions to be in step with the advance of science. The result is a selective epistemological reading of Kant informed by critical analysis of conceptual transformations within modern physics, i.e., relativity and quantum theory. In place of focusing on the *a priori* Kantian category of causality and an alleged necessity to structure experience in terms of the relation of cause and effect, Cassirer proceeded from the standpoint of "a scientific clarification of causality", pointing to "universal laws" that are "the real components of the assumed causal connection" between events. Unlike the concept of cause, all too easily and dogmatically taken to be applicable to 'things', the mathematized laws of physics possess their "own symbolic language, which is far removed from the language of 'things'".[9] Distancing critical philosophy from the metaphysical trappings inherent in the very concept of cause, Cassirer, drew from the Transcendental Dialectic and the role of reason in the construction of science in employing a purely methodological notion of causal *principle*. And he showed that within classical physics Helmholtz, in particular, clearly underscored that the operative significance of the causal concept is found within the regulative principle of a "general conformity to law". To motivate this otherwise surprising claim, Cassirer argued that the causal concept of classical physics is in any case not at all adequately captured by a Laplacian ideal of causal determination that, everyone agreed, utterly fails in quantum physics. Rather, and contrary to the usual assumptions, the Laplacian ideal within classical physics itself is largely a metaphysical fiction, not an empirically attestable notion. To the extent that it finds limited application there, it is seen to pertain to systems that can be treated as highly idealized point masses or perfectly rigid bodies; however, it is neither required nor implementable in systems that cannot, i.e., in most classical physical theories. Hence the causal concept applicable in both classical and quantum physics is

---

9 Ibid., 22.

better expressed by the demand for order according to law, in accordance with the regulative principle of unity of knowledge of nature.

3 Laplace or Helmholtz?

A "Historical Introduction" dialectically sets the stage for all that follows. Paraphrasing the following famous passage from Laplace's *Essai philosophique sur les probabilités*,

> An intelligence which, for one given instant, would know all the forces by which nature is animated and the respective situation of the entities which compose it, if also it were sufficiently vast to submit all these data (?) to mathematical analysis, would encompass in the same formula the motions of the largest bodies in the universe as well as those of the lightest atom; for it, nothing would be uncertain and the future, as the past, would be present to its eyes.[10]

Cassirer immediately observed that the "true grounds"[11] of the Laplacian intelligence lay not in the classical particle mechanics of which Laplace was a master, but in metaphysics, in particular in the "Leibnizian conception of destiny as a thoroughgoing, at once mathematical and metaphysical, determination of world events"; to Cassirer, of course, this manner of determination is an "inadmissible hypostasis of an ideal of pure reason".[12] This is a metaphysics rooted in the principle of sufficient reason and indeed, the "true grounds" of Laplace's formula are readily apparent to the reader of Laplace's essay who considers the paragraph immediately preceding the famous one quoted above:

> Current events are connected with preceding ones by a tie based upon the evident principle that a thing cannot come into existence without a cause that produces it. This axiom, known by the name of *the principle of sufficient reason,* extends even to the most indifferent acts. The most free will cannot give rise to these indifferent acts without a determinative motive. ... We ought then to regard the present state of the universe as the effect of its anterior state and as the cause of the one that is to follow. An intelligence which *etc.* ...

But from the standpoint of the practice of classical physics, not only is the "Laplacian formula" a metaphysical concept of causal determination, it is also largely an "empty concept", a *"focus imaginarius"* with no bearing on epistemological

---

10 Laplace (1814), 2–3.
11 Cassirer (1956), 11.
12 Ibid., 24.

questions concerning determinism in actual systems. Although Cassirer does not explicitly tell us this, implementing the Laplacian ideal presupposes that there exist ordinary differential equations of motion for each system of particles of the form

$$F(r) = \frac{d^2r}{dt^2}$$

that have a unique solution for given initial conditions of position and velocity, $r(t_0) = r_0$ and $\frac{dr}{dt}(r_0) = v_0$. Apparently Laplace himself knew, already in the 1770s, there are many examples of physical systems for which no such equations of motion can be obtained,[13] and indeed, satisfaction of the above requirement presupposes in turn existence and uniqueness theorems for solutions of ordinary differential equations that were developed only later on in the 19th century, long after Laplace's death.[14] In view of these facts, the 20th century pioneer of continuum mechanics and historian of physics Clifford Truesdell[15] went so far as to register a suspicion that in the 1814 passage "Laplace was teasing" simply for the purpose of contrasting the kind of knowledge of which humans are capable (i.e., merely probable knowledge) with the unattainable limit idea of a complete knowledge of nature. In any event, Cassirer did call attention to the extremely limited applicability in physics of the Laplacian ideal, referring[16] to the earlier discussion of the same issue in Philipp Frank's (1932) book on the law of causality. There Frank underscored the point that Laplace's ideal may have validity in restricted domains such as celestial mechanics (where planetary motions can be treated by an ideal system of point masses), but not in many others, like the mechanics of continua, hydrodynamics, or the theory of elasticity. To Cassirer, due to the "Laplacian Spirit (*Geist*)" lurking in the background,

> the causal concept of classical physics was by no means that simple and completely harmonious structure so frequently represented, but … it embraced a good many problems and a wealth of dialectical tensions.[17]

---

13 van Strein (2014).
14 These theorems generally require, after Rudolf Lipschitz (1876), a "Lipschitz continuity condition": *If $F(r) = \frac{d^2r}{dt^2}$ is a bounded continuous function in a domain D, then it has a unique solution iff there is a finite K > 0 such that $\forall r_1, r_2 : |F(r_1) - F(r_2)| \leq K|r_1 - r_2|$.* See e.g., Birkhoff and Rota (1962), 19.
15 Truescell (1984), 89.
16 Cassirer (1956), 65.
17 Ibid., 168.

On the other hand, invoking the Laplacian ideal of causal determination served still another purpose to Cassirer who further argued that the widespread idea of it as *the* exemplification of causal determinism in both philosophy and the physical science is of rather later vintage, stemming from Emil du Bois-Reymond's famous 1872 lecture "On the Boundaries of Knowledge of Nature". Cassirer recalled to the reader the intellectual climate of du Bois-Reymond's speech, *viz.*, a period of intense controversy over materialism and whether philosophy (or the *Geisteswissenschaften* more generally) could offer an alternative but equally genuine mode of cognition to that provided by the sciences of nature. Du Bois-Reymond's position was starkly unambiguous: legitimate scientific knowledge was attainable only through employ of the methods of mathematical physics. His speech was a neural physiologist's *cri de coeur*, a passionate rejection of any and all vitalist accounts of consciousness on the grounds that the sole epistemologically acceptable account of consciousness must be a causal explanation proceeding from the mathematized theories of electricity and chemistry. In a dialectical twist, du Bois-Reymond then summoned the specter of the Laplacian spirit to affirm that even the epitome of these methods, the fearsome intelligence itself, could be no wiser than we are concerning such intractable problems as the explanation of consciousness and freedom of the will. And since in the hands of its undisputed master, the one method appropriate to knowledge of nature could not yield the only possible explanation, du Bois-Reymond concluded, notoriously, that we shall never know (*"ignorabimus"*) the answer to the most tantalizing of questions, an answer that remains "transcendent" to the legimate methods of inquiry. As Cassirer duly noted, du Bois-Reymond's *"ignorabimus"* largely served to promote an irrational skepticism regarding the aims and extent of scientific knowledge of nature.

Cassirer's discussion of Du Bois-Reymond has occasioned one of the few recent references to *D&I* in the philosophy of science literature. In several recent writings on the rise of statistical thinking in the 19th century, Ian Hacking (e.g., 1990) has cited "Cassirer's thesis", that Cassirer in effect claimed that the du Bois-Reymond lecture established "when determinism began"[18] and that "efficient cause determinism—the doctrine of necessity—became a serious universal proposition only in 1872".[19] Hacking's treatment is both an overstatement and a misreading of Cassirer. It is clearly an overstatement since, although Cassirer pointed to Du Bois-Reymond's "strong influence both on metaphysics and on the theory of scientific principles" in the period in question, he clearly

---

[18] Hacking (1990), 150.
[19] Ibid., 154.

pointed out[20] that the Laplacean formula merely affirmed a "logic of facts of objective reason" that is Spinozist in origin, an admittedly metaphysical conception but then to Cassirer, so was the Laplacian spirit. Cassirer was also careful to observe that in hypothetically referring to the limit idea of the Laplacian intelligence, Du Bois-Reymond had invoked a contradictory idol for mathematical physics. For this being is an intelligence that, unlike humans, has no need of discursive calculation, but whose intuitive understanding of the Newtonian laws of motion enables it to grasp past, present initial conditions, and future at one fell swoop. Of course, this is just the other side of the coin of Truesdell's assessment (above) in judging that Laplace, by conjuring his spirit, was almost certainly "teasing". But Hacking's reference to "Cassirer's thesis" also misreads or elides a crucial aspect of Cassirer's discussion linking the Laplacian spirit with the philosophy of symbolic forms. Citing his monograph on language and myth, Cassirer viewed the dualistic coupling together of powerful image (the Laplacian spirit) with symbol (the language of differential equations) as a paradigmatic instance of investing the symbolic with magical properties, such that "the symbolic turns into the magical". As "not even the most abstract symbol is free from this compulsion to be visualized, and consequently free of the urge towards 'reification'",[21] the Laplacian spirit engendered the mythic illusion of magical knowledge and control of reality. The implication, surely, is not that "efficient cause determinism—the doctrine of necessity" was for Cassirer a "serious universal proposition only in 1872", but rather, as a substantialized and hypostatized one encapsulated by the Laplacian spirit, it should never have been entertained as a "universal proposition" in the first place.

As noted above, it was not in Laplace but in Herman von Helmholtz that Cassirer found "a truly representative statement of what classical physics understood by the concept of cause and of the sense in which it used this concept" (*D&I*, p.63). Among his many talents, Helmholtz was also a physiologist and electrochemist as well as a colleague and intimate friend of Emil Du Bois-Reymond. In this capacity Helmholtz was an antivitalist; his seminal 1847 essay *"Über die Erhaltung der Kraft"* established a key bulwark against vitalism, the rejoinder that vitalist accounts of consciousness violated the principle of conservation of energy ("force") deemed universally valid in the rest of science. Only a few years after Du Bois-Reymond's speech and in much the same intellectual climate of materialist controversy, when writing of the "causal law" in his 1878 rector's address *"Die Tatsachen in der Wahrnehmung"* Helmholtz made no appeal to

---

20 Cassirer (1956), 5.
21 Ibid., 8.

the Laplacian spirit but considered it to be merely a regulative principle of our thought. Cassirer took care to closely paraphrase the following passage from Helmholtz's 1878 address:

> Every inductive inference is based upon the trust that a lawful relation observed up to now will be confirmed in all cases not yet observed. This is a trust in the lawfulness of all phenomena (*Geschehens*). But trust in lawfulness is the condition of comprehension. Lawfulness is therefore at the same time trust in the comprehensibility of natural phenomena. However if we suppose that the comprehension can be carried to completion, that we can make out an ultimate invariant (*letztes Unveränderliches*) as *cause* of observed changes, then we call this regulative principle of our thought, that drives us to this supposition, the *causal law*. We can say that it expresses a trust in the *complete comprehensibility* of the world.
>
> ... The causal law is actually an *a priori* given, a transcendental law. A proof of it from experience is not possible, for the first steps of experience are not possible, as we have seen, without application of inductive inferences, i.e., without the law of causality ... Here the only valid advice is: have trust and act (*Vertraue und handle*)![22]

In referring to the law of causality as a "transcendental law" Helmholtz intended that the comprehensibility of nature must be presupposed by all scientific inquiry, in the very search for particular scientific laws. Without this presupposition, one would have no reason to think that the presumed aim of science, the characterization of wider and wider classes of phenomena in terms of ever more general lawful statements, was at all reasonable or could ever be carried out. This presupposition is supplemental to the synthesis of the manifold of sensible representation through the categories, including that of causality, since this synthesis precedes "all empirical cognition" (A130). It does not follow from this synthesis that nature is a *system* comprehensible to human cognition through empirical laws. In short, the conditions of the possibility of experience, the schematized pure categories of the understanding characterized in the Transcendental Analytic, are "very far from being conditions of the possibility of science".[23] Science, while requiring the understanding, is above all a construction of reason.

The Helmholtzian line of argument, endorsed by Cassirer, lies within the frame of the doctrine of the function of regulative principles in the Transcendental Dialectic. Particularly in the section on the Antinomies of Pure Reason, Kant held that only in virtue of the "law of nature" that everything that happens has a cause (the rule employed in the schematism of the Analytic of Principles, see

---

[22] Helmholz (1878), 133–134; my translation. The passage is repeated, nearly *verbatim*, in Helmholtz (1896), 593–594.
[23] Neiman (1994), 52.

above) that the order we call *nature* is constituted from appearances through the empirical determination of events (A542/B570). Yet in *application* to the scientific study of nature, this law must be constrained on pain of falling into antinomies. Such constraints are precisely the function of regulative principles, in this case halting the regress from the search for particular empirical laws (causal conditions) of phenomena to the unconditioned totality of causal laws (as a thing-in-itself). The latter can never be given, but only 'set as a task' (*nicht gegeben, sondern aufgegeben*) (A508/B536). Regulative principles therefore can have only a "doctrinal" (A516/B544), i.e., *methodological,* use, not a *constitutive* one. They are hypothetical rules projecting the systematic unity of the understanding's cognitions, but not in any sense guaranteeing or claiming universal validity for it (A647/B675). It is precisely in this regulative sense of the Transcendental Dialectic, clearly articulated by Helmholtz, that Cassirer reformulates the law (or better, principle) of causality to show a similarity, indeed isomorphism, between the architectonic of statements of classical and of quantum physics.

4 Architectonic Isomorphism of Statements of Classical and of Quantum Physics

With the methodological reformulation in place, Cassirer identified a regulative "general principle of causality", the proposition expressing the demand for order according to law, and so a proposition concerning cognitions rather than things and events, as the innermost core of a structure of physical statements characterizing respectively classical and quantum physics. In each case the structure is "not a pyramid" but consists of onion-like concentric layers of distinct types of physical statement emanating outward from the "general principle of causality". The broad function of this principle is to enable the search for more and more general laws governing the phenomena by regulating two-way dynamical transitions or "jumps" ("μεταβασις εις αλλο γενος") between all other layers, whereby statements in one layer are informed, revised by, or derived from, those in another. Naturally, the particular statements of classical and quantum physics in their respective layers differ in detail. Outermost in both are statement of measurement and observation; in quantum mechanics these are statistical statements of possible measurement outcomes. Working inward, the next layer in classical physics is comprised by particular force laws (Newton, Maxwell-Lorentz), the statistical laws of gas theory (e.g., the Maxwell-Boltzmann distribution law) and the second law of thermodynamics, while in quantum mechanics the layer contains both particular statistical laws (Planck's radiation law for blackbodies, the laws of radioactive decay for different elements) and the dynamical law (Schrödinger wave equation) for quantum systems. The latter is the "causal law of quantum mechanics", i.e., the continuous dynamic unitary (probability preserving) evolution of the undisturbed quantum state formulated by the time-dependent Schrödinger equation. This dynamical law satisfies the postulate of "comprehensibility of nature" contained within the general causal principle.[24]

Within the layer of particular laws lies a further layer of meta-laws or principles; these are "means of orientation ... for surveying and gaining perspective".[25] Initially these have only hypothetical validity, either in enabling derivation of particular force laws (in classical physics: Hamilton's principle, principle of conservation of energy, prohibition of perpetual motion machines) or by informing their interpretation (in quantum mechanics: the Heisenberg uncertainty relations, the Born rule, unitarity, the Pauli "*Verbot*" (exclusion principle), and "the Archimedean point", the Einstein-De Broglie relation $E = h\nu$ of proportionality between energy and frequency). But as these principles inherit the ever-increasing confirmation of the particular laws they inform or govern, they become more and more entrenched rendering them presuppositions of further inquiry. One is understandably struck by an almost complete similarity to the Quinean's "web of belief": each layer (except the innermost) is revisable from either direction. However, at the center of the whole, the "general principle of causality", understood methodologically as above, remains invariant, not because it is grounded in our mental organization, but as a "postulate of empirical thought".

> What it demands and what it axiomatically presupposes, is only this: that the completion can and must be sought, that the phenomena of nature are not such as to elude or to withstand in principle the possibility of being ordered by the process [structure of statements, TR] we have described.[26]

Each layer, as well as the transitions between layers, presupposes a methodological understanding of the causal principle. And so at the center of both onion-like structures lies the regulative directive to seek lawfulness (*Gesetzlichkeit*) in the connection of experiences. In this way, the structure of law statements of classical physics can easily accommodate both the dynamical laws of mechanics and electrodynamics and the statistical laws of gas theory according to Maxwell and Boltzmann, whereas that of quantum mechanics permits irreducibly statistical laws such as the Born probabilities for measurement outcomes. According

---

[24] Cassirer (1956), 188.
[25] Ibid., 53.
[26] Ibid., 60.

to the purely methodological significance of the causal law, claims concerning the "crisis of the causal concept" could be shown to be metaphysical statements hardly consistent with the guiding positivist or at least overtly non-metaphysical philosophy of nearly all quantum physicists.

5 "The essential problems posed for epistemology by quantum mechanics"[27]

To Cassirer, the principal epistemological departure from classical physics required by the quantum theory is a far more radical change than that resulting from the "critical" reformulation of the causal concept discussed above. From his perspective, the so-called "crisis of the causal concept" has far more to do with a new concept of physical object resulting from a fundamental transformation in the very concept of physical state itself. Cassirer's remarkable conclusion is that the quantum mechanical concept of 'physical state' has continued and at the same time radically deepened the already underway transformation of substance-concepts into functional concepts within classical physics he had highlighted as long ago as 1910. This process necessarily reached a halting point in the classical concept of physical state that remained a paradigmatic substance-concept pertaining to thing and attribute, substance and accident.

Cassirer pointed to the thing-attribute logic, criticized already in *Substance and Function*, underlying the notion of physical state in classical physics. He recognized[28] that notion as deriving from the "axiom" of classical logic that "the state of a thing in a given moment is completely determined in every way and with respect to all possible predicates", reminding the reader that Kant's "ideal of pure reason" (A574/B602) rests upon the metaphysical principal of thoroughgoing determination", (A571/B579) essentially identifying the two concepts of 'reality' and 'complete determination'. Elaborating Cassirer's exposition a bit, we recall that the 'object' of classical physics is a bearer of determinate properties, and in classical physics it is taken for granted that properties refer to a definite class of physical quantities, with values lying in specified ranges. The epistemological question of how knowledge of properties of an object is obtained is answered by measurement, a particular type of interaction designed to display the value of a specific physical quantity that, as a property of the object, is intrinsically attached to the object (at a given time) independently of the measure-

---

27 Ibid., 188.
28 Ibid., 188–189.

ment. (We recall that 'perfect' measurements in classical physics are an allowable ideal.)[29] Some properties of an object are not inherent but 'change in time' in a *deterministic* manner, i.e., knowledge of the laws and a *sufficiently complete* set of properties of an object at one time t_1 suffices to predict with certainty the values of the properties at any later (or earlier) time t_2. Given the deterministic laws, failure to predict the behavior of the object with certainty at t_2 is accorded as due to an incomplete knowledge of the object's properties at t_1. In broader compass, the concepts of *physical quantity* and *property* are encompassed in the notion of the space S of *states* of a system of one or more objects, with the understanding that, at a given time, a unique state $s \, \varepsilon \, S$ can be assigned to the system. A state assignment must satisfy the condition that the specification of a state s at any time suffices to determine the values of *all* physical quantities belonging to the system, and that the state at any time t_2 is determined uniquely by the state at any earlier time t_1.

On account of the quantum principle of superposition, and due to the limitations on simultaneous assignment of precise values of conjugate observables formulated by the Heisenberg uncertainty relations, the notion of a physical state in quantum mechanics has radically changed. In short, a quantum object does not possess the form of spatiotemporal connection taken over from macroscopic objects that characterizes the classical notion of physical state, of occupying a definite point of space at a definite moment of time. According to the principle of superposition, a quantum object is in general not in a determinate state at a given time, unless it has been put into a definite state by a preparation process (e.g., passing through a Stern-Gerlach device) or a measurement has been made. The superposition principle also entails that the part-whole relations of quantum systems are completely different from those of classical systems; e.g., knowledge of the separate states of the component quantum systems Ψ_1 and Ψ_2 at time t_1 does not determine the state of the joint system Ψ_{12} that, in general, is a superposition at t_2. The notion of physical state is further constrained by the Heisenberg uncertainty relations setting bounds on what can be simultaneously known about an object's canonically conjugate quantities with obvious implications for what can be predicted about the object's state at a later time. Since within quantum mechanics only statistical predications are possible, the very notion of an "individual" object has been transformed and the different families of quantum

---

[29] The separation of *observer* and *system* has no fundamental significance in classical physics; both are considered parts of a single, objectively existing world, potentially describable by the same laws.

objects (fermions, bosons) require different and non-classical methods of quantum statistics, of determining "what is to be counted as 'one'".[30]

All of this demonstrated to Cassirer that quantum mechanics has taken a decisive further step in the functionalization of the concept of a physical state. On account of the Heisenberg uncertainty relations as well as the principle of superposition, the notion of *absolute determination* has to be abandoned; what replaces it is still determination by law, a relative determination that must satisfy these quantum conditions. Cassirer called attention to Dirac's (1930) presentation of quantum mechanics, in particular, for Dirac's emphasis on the novel transformation of the notion of physical state. Quoting from section 4 of Dirac's *Principles of Quantum Mechanics* (1930),

> We must now imagine the states of any system to be related in such a way that whenever the system is definitely in one state, we can equally well consider it as being partly in each of two or more other states. The original state must be regarded as the result of a kind of *superposition* of the two or more new states, in a way that cannot be conceived on classical ideas. Any state may be considered as the result of a superposition of two or more other states, and indeed in an infinite number of ways.[31]

Cassirer applauded Dirac for placing principle of superposition at the center of his treatment. The new notion of state shows that quantum physics has adopted a principle of relative determination yet it is the "highest degree of relative determination of which physical knowledge is capable":

> if, in the determination of a physical system we admit only such elements of determination as satisfy the conditions expressed in the uncertainty relations, if we are satisfied with maximum observations … we can bring these into a sharply defined relationship with each other. We can then establish the principle that when a maximum observation of a physical system is made, its subsequent state is completely determined by the result of this observation.[32]

The relative determination characterizing the quantum state results from the Heisenberg uncertainty relations' placement of epistemic "conditions of accessibility" on any attribution of physical properties to an object. Abiding the transcendental formula, 'the conditions of the possibility of experience are the conditions of the possibility of the object of knowledge', in quantum mechanics the conditions of the possibility of knowledge are "conditions of accessibility" necessarily

---

30 Ibid., 187.
31 The passage is retained with inessential changes in the last (4th) edition of Dirac's text (1958), 12.
32 Cassirer (1956), 191–192.

bounding the concept of the 'object of experience'. By formulating "conditions of accessibility" restricting physical knowledge to attestable phenomena rather than metaphysically latent properties, the Heisenberg uncertainty relations acquire a 'critical' significance in place of the skeptical message they appear to have according to the classical concept of physical state.

6 Replies to Individual Quantum Physicists

We are now in a position to understand the direct responses to particular quantum physicists that pepper Cassirer's text. Only a few need be cited to see how resetting the epistemological situation in quantum mechanics in the context of a further development from substance to function concepts within physical theory enabled a consistent reply to their claims of a quantum "crisis of causality".

The earliest such claim Cassirer addressed had been made by Max Born in the 1926 paper on collision processes that first formulated the probabilistic interpretation of the Schrödinger wave function (and for which Born received the Nobel prize in 1954). Affirming that the "the motion of particles follows probability laws but the probability itself propagates according to the laws of causality" (i.e., the unitary evolution of the Schrödinger equation), Born then noted that from the fact that no determinate answer could be antecedently given to the question concerning the state of a particle after the collision process, he himself was "inclined to give up determinism in the world of atoms".[33] To this, Cassirer simply replied[34] that in a later 1927 paper, Born declared that the statistical statements of quantum mechanics are thoroughly "strict" statements in that "they are strictly determined by the formalism of the quantum theory", i.e., by the Born rule.[35]

Cassirer was rather less charitable to Dirac's reported statement, at Solvay in 1927, to the effect that a quantum measurement (finding the wave function in a definite eigenstate of an observable) shows "at certain moments nature makes a choice".[36] To Cassirer, this was an "inadmissible anthropomorphism".[37] But it is

---

33 Born (1926), 54.
34 Cassirer (1956), 116.
35 See part II below for discussion of the Born rule.
36 Cassirer ((1956), 119) cited a French report of Dirac's remark by Paul Langevin. According to the recently published proceedings of the conference (Bacciagaluppi and Valentini, 2009) what Dirac actually said was "The value of the suffix n that labels the particular Ψ_n chosen may be the result of an experiment, and the result of an experiment must always be such a number. It is a

to Heisenberg's remarks on causality that Cassirer repeatedly returned. In Heisenberg's 1927 paper first stating the uncertainty relations, Heisenberg expressly denied what he termed "the precise formulation" of the "law of causality", that "when we know the present precisely, we can predict the future".[38] Presciently, Cassirer observed what has since become obvious in the classical theory of deterministic chaos, that causality is not identical with exact predictability. And Cassirer did not fail to point out that the "precise form" of the law of causality cited by Heisenberg has the logical form of a material conditional, which remains true even if its antecedent is false. But Cassirer's considered response to Heisenberg's denial of causality invoked the broader thesis:

> If we express the demand of causality merely by the general requirement of conformity to law, then Heisenberg's uncertainty relations no longer constitute an exception".[39]

Cassirer also responded, or rather, made a series of responses to Bohr. In his "Preface" to the 1956 English translation of *D&I*, Yale physicist Henry Margenau (see further below) suggested that in many respects "the causal doctrine" of *D&I* appeared compatible with Bohr's complementarity and indeed noted several passages where Cassirer wrote approvingly of complementarity.[40] As seen above Cassirer indeed highlighted the mutual exclusivity between causal and space-time descriptions of the course of events that is the core of complementarity although, unlike Bohr, Cassirer traced the roots of this fissure to lie already in the foundations of the differential calculus. But Margenau also noted that Cassirer's text contained as well "a measure of apprehension" regarding complementarity, and indeed that is the case. The broad theme of *D&I* seeking to establish methodological and architectonic continuity between classical and quantum physics is utterly at odds with complementarity's emphasis on "non-negligible" disturbances induced by measurement of atomic phenomena, or as Bohr said in his Como lecture, that "every observation introduces a new uncontrollable element." The disturbance interpretation of the Heisenberg uncertainty relations,

---

number describing an irrevocable choice of nature, which must affect the whole future of events."

37 Cassirer (1956), 119.
38 Heisenberg (1927), 197.
39 Cassirer (1956), 123.
40 In particular, Cassirer (1956), 115: "In consonance with the nature of quantum theory we must be satisfied with conceiving the space-time representation and the demand of causality as complementary but mutually exclusive features of the description of experience, symbolizing the idealization of the possibilities of observation and of definition respectively." There follows a footnote to Bohr.

seemingly presumed by Bohr, was no doubt viewed by Cassirer as metaphysical, pertaining to 'things' rather than to conditions of accessibility governing knowledge of quantum objects. Similarly, Cassirer did not restrict the concept of observation to the use of classical concepts as did complementarity; rather with the evidence cited of the continuing functionalization of concepts within physical theory, Cassirer drew the implication that "there seems to be no return to the lost paradise of classical concepts" and the need of physics "to undertake the construction of a new methodological path".[41] Attempts to position *D&I* as congenial to Bohr's complementarity are accordingly misguided.

Finally, it remains to briefly characterize the response to Ernst Schrödinger, who, of all the founders of quantum mechanics, did not receive a single critical comment though his name appears in Cassirer's text more than those of Heisenberg, Bohr, or Born. From Cassirer's letter of 11 September 1936 to the Warburg Institute's Fritz Saxl, we learn that Schrödinger, also present in Oxford from October 1933 until the summer of 1936, had read a preliminary version of the manuscript. In the letter, Cassirer inquired whether Saxl knew Schrödinger's present address as Cassirer wished to send the now-completed manuscript to be read "once again" before publication.[42] Cassirer apparently knew that Schrödinger had been recently appointed *Ordinarius* in physics at the Karl Franzen University of Graz but in the letter to Saxl we learn that Cassirer's attempt to reach him there had been returned with the stamp "Unknown at the University". Apparently Schrödinger was still in transit; his post was not to begin until 1 October 1936.[43] Cassirer's inquiry to Schrödinger in Graz was consequently a few weeks too early and this second reading of the manuscript apparently did not occur. But it is of considerable interest that while both were in Oxford, there is evidence that Schrödinger may have had input into Cassirer's monograph, in particular given the rather extensive treatment[44] accorded to Franz Exner, Schrödinger's Vienna teacher and in many ways, intellectual mentor. Exner is not a figure discussed, to my knowledge, in any earlier Cassirer texts relevant to the philosophy of the natural sciences. But, as Cassirer took pains to point out, Exner's 1919 lectures on the physical foundations of natural science sought to re-formulate the concept of law of nature so that exception-less, universal dynamical laws were considered merely as laws of averages lacking validity 'in the small', i.e., in regions of space and time smaller than experimental error. Exner's attempt to abolish the dualism between dynamic and statistical laws by reducing the former to

---

41 Ibid., 194.
42 Cassirer (2009), 152.
43 Moore (1989), 322.
44 Cassirer (1956), 79–87.

the latter had been taken up by Schrödinger in his 1922 Inaugural Lecture at the University of Zürich.[45] Schrödinger's lecture, "What is a Law of Nature?" was not published until after Schrödinger acquired a world reputation; it first appeared in *Die Naturwissenschaften* in 1929. Cassirer duly cited this lecture in a footnote[46] accompanying his discussion of Exner.

7 Initial Reception

Due to the Cassirers' exile and the troubled times, but surely also to an obscure locus of publication, *D&I* was scantily reviewed on its appearance. Nonetheless, three reviews arguably set the tone for the book's neglect in the two decades before it appeared in English translation in 1956. Two were by notable philosophers, Ernst Nagel, then a rising star in the nascent sub-discipline of philosophy of science, and Philipp Frank, physicist, prominent logical empiricist and a founding member of the so-called "First Vienna Circle". From different vantage points, each attempts to position *D&I* as bordering on, or adjacent to, the main current trends in philosophy of science, viz., logical empiricism and (for Nagel), "naturalistic pragmatism". Writing in *Philosophy of Science*, the leading journal in the field upon the demise of *Erkenntnis* occasioned by the emigration of logical empiricists Rudolf Carnap and Hans Reichenbach, Nagel dismissively commented upon Cassirer's "Kantian piety" in a patently tepid review.

> ... nothing essentially new emerges ...[and] one can legitimately ask for a somewhat more precise and detailed handling of some of the issues involved. ...on many important points, it is only his Kantian terminology and Kantian piety which distinguishes Cassirer from many naturalistic pragmatists and logical empiricists ...[47]

Philipp Frank's review is more detailed. It is also more collegial, befitting his personal association with Cassirer. Yet it stands as an exemplar of Frank's pet theme of the "disintegration" of traditional or "school" philosophy and the subsumption of anything remaining of value into logical empiricism. Already in his book of 1932 on the law of causality (see the discussion below) Frank had singled out Cassirer's 1921 monograph on relativity as a leading example of the "process of self-destruction" ("*inneren Zersetzungsprozeß*") of "school philosophy" that

---

45 See Moore,(1989), 152–156.
46 Cassirer (1956), 79.
47 Nagel (1938), 230.

Frank considered a progressive intellectual trend.[48] Now with respect to Cassirer's book of 1936, Frank set his task as that of judging "Cassirer's exposition from the standpoint of logical empiricism, according to which only those statements may occur in science that can be justified through logical derivation or empirical tests".[49] In virtue of his finding that "almost all" of Cassirer's statements are "scientific statements as understood by logical empiricism", Frank's verdict is commensurate:

> Cassirer's book is to be welcomed from the standpoint of logical empiricism as a highly successful attempt to continue the adjustment of traditional idealist philosophy to the progress of science, which in my opinion can end only with the complete disintegration of the traditional philosophy.[50]

This is, of course, a rather backhanded compliment and we have seen above that, anticipating Quine, Cassirer's analysis of the structure and content of physical cognition rejects the logical empiricist dogma of a clean partition of scientific statements into the disjoint classes of analytic and synthetic-empirical.

In many ways the most substantive but also perhaps most curious review appeared in *Physikalische Zeitschrift,* a leading physics journal. Written by Carl Friedrich von Weizsäcker, well-known in post-war Germany as a physicist of Kantian proclivities, von Weizsäcker chastens Cassirer for seemingly contradictory reasons. On the one hand, Cassirer had not given sufficient recognition to the fact that, due to the change in meaning of the term 'physical state' in quantum mechanics, most quantum physicists regard the causal law as not "false" (as von Weizsäcker insinuated Cassirer alleged) but simply "inapplicable" in certain cases.[51] This charge appears to presuppose that Cassirer is concerned to demonstrate the falsity, rather than the inappropriateness, of the metaphysical Laplacian concept of causality in most of physical science, including in the new quantum mechanics. On the other hand, von Weizsäcker, an adherent of Bohr's complementarity, according to which measurement outcomes must be described in the language of classical physics, complains that complementarity presupposes the "narrow" (i.e, Laplacian) concept of cause that Cassirer considered metaphysical. Further puzzling is von Weizsäcker's parting comment that Cassirer's "critical" reformulation of the causal law as 'conformity to law' is not in accord

---

48 Frank (1932), 283.
49 Frank (1938), 173.
50 Ibid., 184–185.
51 Weizsäcker (1937), 860.

with a more orthodox reading of Kantian texts, and so with the views of physicists who attempt to adhere to this more orthodox reading:

> It seems to me that here the physicists require fewer "concessions" ("*Entgegenkommen*") from the *a priori* thinking philosophers than Cassirer is prepared to admit.[52]

Although Einstein, in Princeton, read and highly praised *D&I*, as did Max von Laue in Berlin, neither reviewed it.[53] Nor, despite Cassirer's efforts, did Schrödinger.[54] Indeed after the initial reviews, the book was largely ignored until the English translation appeared in 1956. There appears to have been but one significant exception, Max Born's Waynflete Lectures at Magdalen College, Oxford in 1948. Already on its appearance, Born had read *D&I* with "the greatest interest and most eager attentiveness" (*größten Interesse und gespannter Aufmerksamkeit*), as he wrote to Cassirer on 19 March 1937.[55] Reporting that he was "by and large and on the whole" (*Im Großen und Ganzen*) in agreement with Cassirer, Born's only complaint echoed von Weisäcker's earlier criticism that it was difficult to accept Cassirer's interpretation of Kant's "clear statements". As seen above, Cassirer, following Helmholtz, filtered Kant's remarks on the "law of causality" through the meditational lens of the Transcendental Dialectic, setting an example continued later by Kantian scholars such as Gerd Buchdahl and Susan Neiman. Born's Waynflete lectures were published in 1949 as *Natural Philosophy of Cause and Chance*, where, in a brief appendix, Born commented on the implications of quantum theory on the problem of freedom of will. Here Born is content to simply refer to Cassirer although tacitly suggesting Cassirer's treatment of the problem is somehow on a par with that of Bohr's complementarity:

> A book I have recently read with some care is Cassirer's *Determinismus* … (1937) which gives an excellent account of the situation, not only in physics itself but also with regard to possible applications of the new physical ideas to other fields. … My short survey of these difficult problems [ethical consequences of physical indeterminism] cannot be compared with Cassirer's deep and thorough study. Yet it is a satisfaction to me that he also sees the philosophical importance of quantum theory not so much in the question of indeterminism but in the possibility of several complementary perspectives or aspects in the description of the same phenomena as soon as different standpoints of meaning are taken. There is no unique image of our whole world of experience.[56]

---

52 Ibid.
53 See Cassirer's correspondence with von Laue, in Cassirer (2009), documents 131 and 133–4.
54 See Cassirer's letter to Fritz Saxl, cited above.
55 Cassirer (2009), 160.
56 Born (1949), 207–208.

The war years, followed by cultural hysteria engendered by the new atomic age and ensuing McCarthyism in the postwar period, were hardly a congenial climate for discussions of epistemological and foundational issues in quantum mechanics. David Bohm in 1952 initiated a sea change in this period of intellectual complacency with his two papers on a proposed deterministic interpretation of quantum mechanics in terms of 'hidden variables', the beginnings of what is now known and developed as "Bohmian mechanics". Arguably Bohm's initiative re-invigorated earlier efforts of Henry Margenau, physicist, friend and colleague of Cassirer at Yale, to oversee an English translation of *D&I*. In his Preface to the 1956 English edition, Margenau noted that just several months prior to Cassirer's death in April, 1945, he had been asked by Cassirer to prepare a bibliography and to collaborate in writing a new chapter on "developments concerning the causality problem after 1936", both to appear in an English translation of the original. As we learn from O.T. Benfey's "Translator's Note", dated September 1956, a first draft of a translation by two others had been undertaken but not completed. Apparently after some lapse of time, Margenau then passed on this draft to Benfey, a respected physical chemist, to complete it. Taking as evidence his brief discussion of Bohm's theory in his Preface, Margenau may be understood to imply that Bohm's initiative had given renewed relevance to Cassirer's 1936 work, in particular regarding Bohm's reference to his theory as "the causal interpretation" of quantum mechanics. Margenau notes that, in light of Cassirer's discussion, Bohm's claim is "a misnomer", failing to distinguish between Bohm's own view, pertaining to a causal interpretation of the state variables (e.g., position) of a quantum system, and the usual view of quantum dynamics, that the Schrödinger equation for a quantum state Ψ gives a linear, continuous, and deterministic unitary evolution of Ψ into a new state Ψ', uniquely determined by Ψ and the Hamiltonian operator $\hat{H}$ on Ψ.[57] As discussed above, dynamical Schrödinger evolution accords well with Cassirer's interpretation of the law of causality as 'conformity to law'. To be sure, by the mid-1950s, Margenau also had a stake in the interpretation game of quantum theory, for he (wrongly) believed that Cassirer's account favorable to his "latency" interpretation of quantum mechanics in terms of "unfolding state" causation.[58] This is essentially a dispositional interpretation of the quantum state, holding that a quantum system in a state Ψ that is not an eigenstate of the corresponding Hermitian (self-adjoint) operator

---

57 Such "automatic changes which occur with the passage of time" are called (following von Neumann (1932/1955, 351)) processes of type 2. Famously, von Neumann distinguished these from those of type 1, "arbitrary changes by measurements". A unitary operator leaves invariant the Born probabilities for the state, see part 2 below.
58 E.g., Margenau (1954).

(hence not in a definite state of an observable) has nonetheless the 'disposition' or 'capacity' to be found in a particular eigenstate of that operator on measurement, a capacity or propensity given by the Born probabilities for the various eigenstates. But it was a misreading of Cassirer to find grounds for this dispositional interpretation in *D&I* which, in point of fact, offers no "interpretation" at all, at least in in the usual sense of what an interpretation of quantum mechanics is, that is, a possible world in which that interpretation is true. As we have seen, Cassirer regarded as "metaphysical" any attempt to reverse the methodological or "critical" finding that in modern physics the concept of 'object' has been subordinated to that of 'law'.[59] This, of course, is just what an interpretation of quantum mechanics purports to do.

Section II

In this section, we shall attempt without inordinate mathematical detail to show why the existence of uncountably many unitarily inequivalent representations of the canonical commutation relations (CCRs) in quantum field theory (QFT) poses a fatal challenge to ontic structural realism (OSR). OSR is a relatively recent view in metaphysics and philosophy of physics; it has been motivated by the non-classical conditions of individuality and identity of quantum particles. But it finds a more congenial home in QFT where

> The metaphysical packages of individuality and non-individuality would then be viewed in a similar way to that of particle and field in QFT, namely as two different (metaphysical) representations of the same structure.[60]

OSR is a realism about all and only structure; its slogan holds "all that there is, is structure". This is of relevance to *D&I* precisely because this and other texts of Cassirer are frequently cited as lending support to the OSR claim concerning the sole reality of structure. Steven French, for example, has recently claimed that Cassirer's

> analysis of quantum theory in *Determinism and Indeterminism* has not received the attention it deserves. ... As far as Cassirer is concerned, it is the notion of a substantival object that must be given up in the face of [the devastating impact of quantum physics], rather than the principle of causality, and a broadly structuralist—if Kantian—understanding of objectivity adopted.

---

59 Cassirer (1956), 131.
60 French and Ladyman (2003), 37.

while further praise for *D&I* is found a few pages later,

> Cassirer makes a fundamental demand that is analogous to the tailoring of our metaphysics to epistemology that underlies OSR, namely that we take the 'conditions of accessibility' as 'conditions of the objects of experience'. ... Bringing this demand forward, it rules out any epistemically inaccessible objects hiding behind the structures which we can know.[61]

The qualification "if Kantian" is of course important. But we shall try to show that if that qualification is removed, nothing of Cassirer's position remains and that the OSR attempt to "tailor our metaphysics to epistemology" is incompatible *tout court* with the entire complexion of Cassirer's text, as characterized in part 1.

However, to do this responsibly will require a bit of background. We begin with the fact that the ordinary quantum mechanics of non-relativistic particles can be derived as a generalization of classical Hamiltonian mechanics by quantizing the commutation relations among canonical dynamical variables; this essentially corresponds to Dirac's original presentation of quantum mechanics in 1925/26. We then see that in ordinary quantum mechanics, there is in fact a strong structuralist criterion of theories: according to the Stone-von Neumann theorem, physically equivalent quantum theories have unitarily equivalent Hilbert space representations of the CCRs. However, it turns out that this purely structuralist characterization of theories fails for quantum theories with infinitely many degrees of freedom, e.g., in quantum field theories. Since a particular concatenation of QFTs underlies the Standard Model (SM) of fundamental interactions, for the structural realist, the QFTs of the SM must be exemplars of theories toward which realist claims about structure are justified. We briefly point out some of the difficulties here and show that the extant structural characterization of QFTs compatible with the existence of unitarily inequivalent representations is in terms of an abstract algebra of observables. However, this structure has an operationalist and instrumentalist complexion incompatible with OSR's realism about world structure. We conclude with the observation that this structuralist but hardly realist outcome is nicely accommodated within Cassirer's "demand that we use ... the conditions of accessibility as conditions of the objects of experience".[62]

---

[61] French (2014), 126, 138–139.
[62] Cassirer (1956), 178–179.

1 From Lagrange to Hamilton.

Recall that a classical system can be described in terms of generalized coordinates, $\{q_k\} = q_1, ..., q_k$, defining the position or configuration of the system as a function of time. Such coordinates are selected to match the conditions of the problem to be solved (there is, in general, no rule for doing this) but the number of independent generalized coordinates must match the system's total number of degrees of freedom in order to uniquely define the position of a system. Corresponding to the $\{q_k\}$ are generalized velocities $\{\dot{q}_k\}$. Simultaneous specification of $\{q_k\}$ and $\{\dot{q}_k\}$ determines (in the sense of Laplace) the mechanical state of the system at a particular time, while the system's subsequent motion is obtained by the solutions $q_k(t)$ of the appropriate equations of motion. These solutions may be found through Hamilton's variational principle, which asserts that the actual motion of a particle (or system of particles) from its initial configuration at time t_1 to its configuration at time t_2 is given by vanishing of the infinitesimal variations of the integral

$$\delta S = \delta \int_{t_1}^{t_2} L(q_k, \dot{q}_k) dt = 0 \quad (\star)$$

where $q_k = q_k(t)$ and L, a function of q_k and $\dot{q}_k$, is the *Lagrangian* for the system is equal to $T-V$ (kinetic energy–potential energy). $S = \int_{t_1}^{t_2} L dt$ is called the *action integral* and so here is the statement of the *Principle of Least Action*, according to which among the infinitely many *possible* trajectories through configuration space connecting the end points $q(t_1)$ and $q(t_2)$, the *actual* (physical) path is the one yielding a stationary value for the action integral. One can find all actual $q(t)$ satisfying the boundary conditions that the trajectories pass through the end points by solving the Euler-Lagrange equations, derivable by a variational technique from $(\star)$.

Hamilton showed that by defining generalized (or canonical) momenta and forces by, respectively,

$$p_k = \frac{\partial L}{\partial \dot{q}_k} \text{ and } F_k = \frac{\partial L}{\partial q_k},$$

Lagrange's equations can then be considered a generalized version of Newton's second law where generalized force equals the rate of change of canonical momentum. Hamilton then demonstrated that Lagrange's equations could then be simplified by replacing them (a set of n second-order ordinary differential equations) with a set of $2n$ first-order differential equations, now called Hamilton's canonical equations of motion. Defining a new function $H(q_k, p_k)$ with the same physical and geometrical content as $L(q_k, \dot{q}_k)$, Hamilton's equations

$$\dot{q}_k = \frac{\partial H}{\partial p} \text{ and } \dot{p}_k = \frac{\partial H}{\partial q_k}.$$

can be derived using the same variational technique as before. For a conservative system (...), the Hamiltonian equals the total energy of the system ($H = T + V$).

2 Poisson Brackets

Hamilton's canonical variables are q (position) and p (momentum); other dynamical variables such as kinetic energy are (once the system is specified) functions of these, hence the name 'canonical'. The kinematic laws and symmetries of a classical Hamiltonian system are reflected in stable relationships of the dynamical variables to one another. In particular these relationships are encoded in an algebraic structure arising from the Poisson bracket $\{f, g\}$ formed by two dynamical quantities f, g defined on the state space coordinated by the canonical magnitudes (q_k, p_k). The Poisson bracket is defined

$$\{f, g\} := \sum_{k=1}^{n} \left\{ \frac{\partial f}{\partial q_k} \frac{\partial g}{\partial p_k} - \frac{\partial f}{\partial q_k} \frac{\partial g}{\partial q_k} \right\}$$

with f and g being functions (linear combinations, products, limits of sequences of linear combinations or products) of one set of canonical coordinates q_k and p_k for the purpose of differentiation, itself independent of which set of canonical coordinates are used. Any two dynamical variables (or functions of them) u_i and v_i are said to be *canonically conjugate* if

$$\{u_i, u_k\} = \{v_i, v_k\} = 0 \text{ and } \{u_i, v_k\} = \delta_{ik}$$

where δ_{ik} is the so-called *Kronecker* delta function defined by

$$\delta_{ik} = 1 \text{ if } i = k; = 0 \text{ if } i \neq k$$

The quantities q_j and p_j are canonically conjugate variables since $\{q_j, p_k\} = \delta_{ik}$ and $\{q_j, q_k\} = \{p_j, p_k\} = 0$.

3 Quantum Theory

Dirac's method of quantizing a classical theory tells us to find a suitable quantum analog to the Poisson bracket relations for classical dynamical variables. In quantum mechanics, however, physical magnitudes that can be measured are called *observables* and are represented by linear operators in Hilbert space, so the commutation relations are stated in terms of operators, not dynamical variables. Dirac's recipe then states that the Poisson bracket of two dynamical quantities of classical mechanics are linked by a kind of principle of correspondence to the commutator bracket of the operators associated to these quantities by quantum mechanics. Schematically

$$\{,\} \rightarrow [,]$$

where '[,]' is defined $[A, B] = AB-BA$ for arbitrary operators, A, B.
or

(Poisson bracket) = $ih/2\pi$ (commutator bracket)

Quantizing a classical theory then converts the canonical Poisson brackets of the classical theory to canonical commutation relations between linear operators of the quantized theory. Where p, q, are now operators for momentum $\hat{p}$ and position $\hat{x}$ (in quantum mechanics, operators wear 'hats'), the canonical commutation relations (CCRs) are

$[\hat{p}, \hat{p}] = [\hat{x}, \hat{x}] = 0$ and $[\hat{p}, \hat{x}] = i\hbar \mathbf{1}$ where $\mathbf{1}$ is the unit matrix.

The latter identity is more familiar when occurring in the statement of the Heisenberg uncertainty relations (HUR), according to which simultaneous exact values of certain canonical observables cannot be known (or do not exist, depending on interpretation) to greater precision than $ih/2\pi$. In the most simple case, the HUR state that the uncertainties (Δ) in the simultaneous measurement of the position x of a particle along the x axis and its corresponding momentum in this direction, p_x, cannot be less than $ih/2\pi$, i.e., $\Delta x \Delta p_x \geq h/2\pi$.

Once the CCRs are set up through Dirac's correspondence, to complete the quantization requires finding a Hilbert space H on which operators satisfying the CCRs act, i.e., to find a representation of the CCRs. This representation generates an algebra isomorphic to the algebra of bounded operators B (H). As noted above, operators in quantum mechanics represent observables so B (H) may be referred to as an algebra of observables. Such operators must be linear, self-adjoint (Hermitian), and unitary. Finally, it remains to show that the states on B (H) allow for all physically possible assignments of expectation values to the dynamical magnitudes.

4 The Significance of Unitarity

Recall that a matrix or operator U is *unitary* if it is equal to the inverse of its own adjoint, $UU^\dagger = U^\dagger U = 1$. Unitary operators leave invariant the inner product between the vectors on which they act. Then to say that a process, operator or transformation in quantum mechanics is *unitary* means that it respects the transition probabilities between states given by the rule posited by Born in 1926, and in particular that the total sum of probabilities of outcomes of measurements of certain physical processes is unity. In updated terminology, the Born rule states that if a system is in a state represented by a normalized Hilbert space vector ψ and a measurement (of an observable represented by the corresponding operator) is performed putting the system into any one of the set of possible values (eigenstates) represented by one of the eigenvectors $\{\varphi_i\}$ of that operator, then the probability of finding the system in a particular eigenstate φ_i is given by

$$Prob\ (\psi \to \varphi_i) = |(\varphi_i, \psi)|^2$$

where $|(\varphi_i, \psi)|^2$ is the modulus squared of the inner product (yielding c, a generally complex scalar) of the two vectors. The Born probabilities $|c|^2$ for any operator are real-valued and sum to 1.

There are two important aspects of unitarity. First, the time evolution of states of an isolated (undisturbed) system is unitary. Time evolution for an undisturbed system is given by the time-dependent Schrödinger equation,

$$i\hbar \frac{\partial \psi(x,t)}{\partial t} = \hat{H}(\psi(x,t)),$$

where $\hat{H}$ is the Hamiltonian operator for the system, obtained from the classical energy expression

$$H = \frac{p^2}{2m} + V(x)$$

by replacing the momentum p and position x by their corresponding operators. $\hat{H}$ is unitary and so the Schrödinger evolution of the state vector Ψ from t to t' can be represented by the unitary operator/matrix U,

$$\psi(x,t) = U(t,t')\psi(x,t')$$

where

$$U\psi(x,t') = e^{\frac{-2\pi i}{\hbar}} U\psi(x,t)$$

showing that U is a complex function of the Hamiltonian operator $\hat{H}$. The Schrödinger equation is linear and deterministic is the precise sense that the time evolution of a state is completely fixed once the state is known at any one time (Schrödinger evolution is Process 2, in von Neumann's classification). The alleged failure of determinism occurs elsewhere, in interventions (measurements) (Process 1) performed on the system. The Schrödinger equation, like other fundamental dynamical laws of physics, is time-reversal invariant; however, time-reversal corresponds to the *anti-unitary* transformation between states (see below).

Secondly, any symmetry of a quantum system, essentially any change in viewpoint regarding the system (e.g., by translating the laboratory in space or time, rotating it) should leave invariant the transition probabilities $|(\varphi_i, \psi)|^2$. Unitary operators are then Hilbert space generalizations of rotation vectors in ordinary 3-space. They are of particular importance in quantum mechanics on account of a peculiar kind of underdetermination of description of physical states in Hilbert space, a vector space over the field C of complex numbers. In consequence, a physical state in quantum mechanics is determined only up to an arbitrary factor of phase. Though this fact can usually be conveniently ignored, it means that quantum states are not represented by a unique normalized vector in Hilbert space, but by a ray, that is, a whole class of normalized vectors that differ from one another by phase factors. Symmetry transformations (displacements in space or time) accordingly map rays into rays preserving transition probabilities: if Ψ and Φ are state vectors belonging to the rays representing two different physical states, and a symmetry transformation takes these two rays into two other rays containing the state vectors Ψ' and Φ', then

$$|(\Psi', \Phi')|^2 = |(\Psi, \Phi)|^2.$$

This is a condition only on rays; if it is satisfied by a given set of state vectors, it is also satisfied by any other set differing from the first only by arbitrary phase. According to a theorem of Wigner (1939) the condition will be satisfied for all Ψ and Φ just in case phases are related either by unitary transformations $\Psi \to U\Psi$ and $\Phi \to U\Phi$ or if U is an anti-linear and anti-unitary operator $U(c_1\Psi + c_2\Phi) = c_1^* \Psi + c_2^* \Phi$, where * indicates complex conjugation. A unitary transformation corresponds to a rotation of axes in Hilbert space leaving the state vector ψ unchanged but with different components. An antiunitary transformation represents the symmetry of a *reversal* in the flow of time, as seen in the absence of a minus sign in the exponential:

$$U\psi(x, t') = e^{\frac{2\pi i}{\hbar}} U\psi(x, t).$$

5 The Stone–von Neumann Theorem

In view of the fundamental role of the criterion of unitarity in quantum mechanics, it is not entirely surprising that it enables a unique structural characterization of a quantum theory. In the ordinary quantum mechanics of particles, where there are finitely many degrees of freedom, the *Stone–von Neumann theorem* (1931) (and the Jordan-Wigner theorem for antiunitary transformations) tells us that a quantum system with finitely many degrees of freedom has only one (irreducible) Hilbert space representation of the canonical (anti-) commutation relations (CCRs, CARs respectively) governing its operators, a representation that is unique up to unitary equivalence. Formally, unitary equivalence states that there is a one-one linear norm-preserving map from Hilbert space to Hilbert space U: $\mathcal{H} \to \mathcal{H}'$ such that all operators $\hat{O}'_i$ of $\mathcal{H}'$ are unitary transforms of operators $\hat{O}_i$ of $\mathcal{H}$:

$$\forall_i, U^{-1}\hat{O}'_i U = \hat{O}_i.$$

The philosophical significance of unitary equivalent representations of the CCRs follows from the reasonable assumption that two structurally identical quantum theories are physically equivalent. The *Stone–von Neumann theorem* then tells us that given any state $\psi \in \mathcal{H}$, there is a physically equivalent state $U\psi \in \mathcal{H}'$ and that Dirac's recipe for quantizing a classical particle theory leads to a unique result. This is precisely how Von Neumann employed the theorem to order to show the physical equivalence of matrix mechanics and wave mechanics.

The purely structural characterization of quantum mechanics is grist for the mill of OSR and, even independently of OSR, has been described as "a triumph of the structuralist point of view":

> ... the Stone-von Neumann theorem tells us that wave mechanics and matrix mechanics are just different representations of the same algebraic structure .... [It is] a triumph of the structuralist point of view.[63]

6 Quantum Field Theory

Quantum field theory is the structuralist exemplar for OSR. After all, the three quantum field fields comprising the Standard Model (SM) of elementary interactions is a reasonable target of realist desire since every high-energy experiment performed to date has confirmed the SM, most recently the finding announced

---

[63] Howard (2011), 231.

on July 4, 2013, of a particle that the majority of theorists are willing to call the long-sought "Higgs boson", the last remaining unobserved particle predicted by the Standard Model. The OSR supposition, of course, is that *there is something that is the structure* of QFT.

> the (quantum) field is nothing but structure. We can't describe its nature without recourse to the mathematical structure of field theory.[64]

However, we shall see that this transparently structural realist state of affairs does not really obtain in QFT and more generally, in quantum theories with infinitely many degrees of freedom. Von Neumann noted the problem already in 1938 but it took a much longer time for its significance to be recognized. A brief argument, due to Haag (1996, pp. 54–5), shows how unitarily inequivalent representations can arise; a more detailed treatment would require technical background that is inappropriate here.[65]

The standard quantization procedure of a classical field theory leads to field quantities that satisfy the CCRs at a fixed time. The simplest example of such a theory is a single scalar field in Minkowski space-time and a Lagrangian density, where g is a parameter ≥ 0:

$$\mathcal{L} = \frac{1}{2}\partial_\mu \varphi(x) - \frac{1}{4}g\varphi(x)^4.$$

The wave equation of such a field is

$$\Box \phi(x) + g\phi(x)^3 = 0.$$

where $\Box$ is the familiar differential operator (D'Alembertian) of electromagnetic wave equations and special relativity,

$$\Box = \partial^\mu \partial_\mu = \frac{1}{c^2}\frac{\partial^2}{\partial t^2} - \frac{\partial^2}{\partial^2 x} - \frac{\partial^2}{\partial^2 y} - \frac{\partial^2}{\partial^2 z}.$$

For $g = 0$, there is a free field, but for $g \neq 0$ the wave equation is a non-linear equation with interacting particles. The dynamical variables are the field amplitudes at each point x, $\phi(t, \vec{x})$, and their conjugate relativistic momenta $\pi(t, \vec{x}) = \partial \varphi(t, \vec{x})/\partial t$. With an appropriate Hamiltonian, the equal time commutation relations, stated in terms of the Poisson brackets, are $\{\phi(t, \vec{x}), \phi(t, \vec{y})\} = 0 = \{\pi(t, \vec{x}), \pi(t, \vec{y})\}$ and $\{\phi(t, \vec{x}), \phi(t, \vec{y})\} = \delta(\vec{x} - \vec{y})$. Quantization now requires a representation of these commutation relations in a Hilbert space $\mathcal{H}$. This must be an irreducible represen-

---

[64] Ladyman and Ross (2007), 140.
[65] See in particular, Ruetsche (2011).

tation since the field at an arbitrary time is determined by the canonical quantities due to the field equations and consequently all observables can be described in terms of $\phi(t,\vec{x})$ and $\pi(t,\vec{x})$. However, the representations must be inequivalent for different values of g. For each g there is one physically distinguished state, the physical vacuum. Its state vector Ψ_g must depend on g because the vacuum state is the lowest eigenstate of the Hamiltonian and the Hamiltonian depends on g. But any operators $U(a)$ representing a translation a in 3-space do not depend on g since for any g they yield the same transformation of the canonical quantities,

$$U(a)\psi(x)U^{-1}(a) = \psi(x + a), \; U(a)\pi(x)U^{-1}(a) = \pi(x + a).$$

The result is that if $\Psi_g \neq \Psi_{g'}$, the representations must be inequivalent. And so it is that

> the most important difference between quantum mechanics and quantum field theory ... is that for infinitely many degrees of freedom [as in QFT] there exist non-denumerably many unitarily inequivalent representations.[66]

The existence of unitarily inequivalent representations in quantum field theory has also been emphasized by Arthur Wightman. Wightman, who more than perhaps any other mathematician, has sought to place quantum field theory on a mathematically rigorous axiomatic basis, speaks of a *"maze"* of them:

> In general, two different Hamiltonians, even though they differ [only] in the value of a parameter such as [g], will require two inequivalent irreducible representations of the [Weyl] commutation relations. ... a mathematically more precise version ... [is] that the canonical commutation relations possess a *maze* of irreducible representations ... the space of unitary equivalence classes of irreducible representations of the commutation relations does not possess a separable Borel structure.[67]

And this fact leads to further problems of interpretation in relativistic QFT. For the simple case of a non-interacting free field, described in "Fock space", there is no unique Fock-space representation of the CCRs for existence of local number operators. Nor is there a total particle number operator. This is patently manifest in the so-called "Unruh" effect, the fact that in curved space-times, the particle number (Fock representation) attributed to the system will vary from observer reference frame to observer reference frame. Distinct freely-falling and accelerating observers will come up with different particle number attributions.

---

66 Rohrlich (1999), 362.
67 Wightman (1976), 198.

Unitarily inequivalent representations of the CCRs mean that there is no real notion of 'particle' or 'vacuum state' in QFT.

> One of the key insights ["into the nature of quantum theory itself"] is that—apart from stationary space-times or space-times with other special properties—there is no unique, natural notion of a 'vacuum state' or of 'particles'.[68]

OSR of course recognizes the problem.[69] The problem then becomes a question of privilege: which of the uncountably many unitarily inequivalent representations of the CCRs is one to be a realist about? There are ways to single out particular representations, but all known ways to do this are ad-hoc.[70] The problem seems even worse for the physically relevant case of interacting fields. There a famous theorem, due to Haag (1955), states that there is no unitary temporal evolution from a free field to an interacting field; moreover unitarily inequivalent representations of the CCRs are required to describe interacting fields.

In general, therefore, one cannot use the structuralist criterion of unitary equivalence of ordinary quantum mechanics to structurally characterize QFTs. Yet ontological structuralism (OSR) requires a univocal structuralist characterization of quantum field theories since there *must* be a univocal structure about which one can be a realist. At this juncture, the problem becomes intractable for the realist who now faces two unpalatable options. First there is the core assumption that *there is* such a structure of quantum field theories, a highly important constituent of the structure of the world. But if such a structure exists, it remains as yet unknown to several generations of mathematicians who have spent careers attempting to find out if there is a mathematically consistent union of relativity and quantum theory.[71] Undoubtedly, quantum theories are highly confirmed, yielding for example some of the most precise predictions in all of science. But these quantum theories (call them, physicists' quantum field theories), despite their remarkable accuracy, are known to be not mathematically well-defined; a case in point is the Feynman integral of the physicist's Lagrangian field

---

[68] Hollands and Wald (2010), 85–86.
[69] E.g., French (2010).
[70] For example, one can use the Poincaré invariance of Minkowski space-time to choose a unique vacuum state representation of a free field, but vacuum states are degenerate, as seen in the preceding quotation from Hollands and Wald (2010).
[71] See Fields medalist Richard Borcherds' talk "What is a Quantum Field Theory?" on the video *2007 UCLA Fields Medalists Symposium*, available on *iTunes U*, as well as the papers of Wightman's' student, Harvard mathematician Arthur Jaffe, e.g., Jaffe (2008).

theory: it has no known measure.[72] As mathematicians from Wightman, to Arthur Jaffe to Richard Borcherds have emphasized, there is no known non-trivial physically relevant four-dimensional interacting quantum field theory (in particular, the three theories of the SM, QED, QCD, electro-weak) that satisfies any proposed definition or axiomatization of quantum field theory, as mathematical rigor requires.

Secondly, quantum field theories can be given a univocal structural characterization if 1) the requirement of unitary equivalence is given up, and 2) attention is restricted to the bounded observables of the theory. Beginning in the 1950s, Segal and others have shown that the self-adjoint elements of a C^* algebra are a natural model for the bounded *observables* of a quantum field.

> An important conclusion ... is that a physical system is completely specified operationally by giving the abstract algebra formed by the bounded observables of the system, i.e., the rules for forming linear combinations of and squaring observables. In particular, operationally isomorphic algebras of observables that are represented by concrete C^* algebras on Hilbert spaces, do not at all need to be unitarily equivalent.[73]

In this setting the canonical variables are first and foremost the elements of an abstract algebra of observables, and it is only with respect to a particular state of this algebra that they become operators in Hilbert space. Isomorphic C^*-algebras then correspond to observationally equivalent systems but there is no requirement that the isomorphic algebras of observables that are represented by concrete C^*-algebras on Hilbert space must be unitarily equivalent. The requirement of unitary equivalence is, in Segal's terms, "irrelevant and impractical". In fact, a transformation of the observables determined by a unitary operator in a concrete representation is an automorphism of the algebra but the latter notion is a proper generalization of the conventional dynamics of unitary equivalence. It bears emphasis that a C^*-algebra structure is a fundamentally a structure of *observables* and as such, stands in accord with Cassirer's dictum that "conditions of accessibility" yield the conditions of possibility of the object of experience. It is *not* the structure of a quantum reality underlying measurement and observation. And it is instructive to point out that the algebraic approach to quantum field theory is rife with operationalist and instrumentalist maneuvers that should be anathema to any self-respecting realism, leave alone a realism about structure.

---

[72] For a discussion of these difficulties and a physicist's pragmatic solution, see Zee (2003), chapter IV.7.
[73] Segal (1959), 343.

I conclude that Cassirer's structuralism culminating in D&I in the subordination of the concept of object to that of law and conformity of law, in the further functionalization of the concept of physical state within ordinary quantum mechanics is, and should be properly understood, solely as an epistemology not a metaphysics, structuralist or otherwise. Historically informed, Cassirer's epistemology of physics is subject to the continued developments in physical theory. It helps to chart a course for contemporary philosophy of physics that proceeds towards analysis of conceptual change, through critical scrutiny of methodological assumptions, and by excavation of implicit presuppositions rather than towards a metaphysics that, in trespassing conditions of epistemic accessibility, must always be judged dogmatic.

Bibliography

Bacciagaluppi and Valentini (2009): Guido Bacciagaluppi and Anthony Valentini, *Quantum Theory at the Crossroads: Reconsidering the 1927 Solvay Conference*, Cambridge: Cambridge University Press.
Bell (1964): John S. Bell, "On the Einstein-Podolsky-Rosen Paradox", *Physics* 1, 195–200.
Birkhoff and Rota (1962): Garrett Birkhoff and Gian-Carlo Rota, *Ordinary Differential Equations*, Boston and New York: Ginn and Company.
Bohm (1952): David Bohm, "A Suggested Interpretation of the Quantum Theory in Terms of Hidden Variables" parts I and II, *Physical Review* 85, 166–193.
Bohr (1928): Niels Bohr, "The Quantum Postulate and Recent Development of Quantum Theory", *Nature* 121, 580–90, as reprinted in: Wheeler and Zurek (1983), 87–126.
Born (1926): Max Born, *"Zur Quantenmechanik der Stossvorgänge"*, *Zeitschrift für Physik* 37, 863–867. English translation in: Wheeler and Zurek (1983), 52–55.
Born (1949): Max Born, *Natural Philosophy of Cause and Chance, being The Waynflete Lectures delivered in the College of St. Mary Magdalen*, Oxford in Hilary Term 1948, Oxford: Clarendon Press.
Cassirer (1937): Ernst Cassirer, *Determinismus und Indeterminismus in der modernen Physik: Historische und systematische Studien zum Kausalproblem*. Göteborgs Högskolas Årsskrift, Bd. 42, No.3. Reprinted in: Ernst Cassirer (1957), *Zur modernen Physik*. Darmstadt: Wissenschaftliche Buchgesellschaft, 127–376.
Cassirer (1956): Ernst Cassirer, *Determinism and Indeterminism in Modern Physics: Historical and Systematic Studies of the Problem of Causality*, O. T. Benfey (trans.), New Haven: Yale University Press.
Cassirer (2009): Ernst Cassirer, *Nachgelassene Manuscripte und Texte, Bd. 18; Ausgewählter Wissenschaftlicher Briefwechsel*, John Michael Krois (ed.), Hamburg, Felix Meiner Verlag.
Cassirer (1981): Toni Cassirer, *Mein Leben mit Ernst Cassirer*, Hildesheim: Gerstenberg Verlag.
Dirac (1930). Paul Adrien Maurice Dirac, *The Principles of Quantum Mechanics*, Oxford: Clarendon Press.
Dirac (1958). Paul Adrien Maurice Dirac, *The Principles of Quantum Mechanics*, 4th edition, Oxford: Clarendon Press.

Du Bois-Reymond (1872): Emil du Bois-Reymond, Über die Grenzen des Naturerkennens: Die sieben Welträthsel; zwei Vorträge, Leipzig: Veit & Co., 1882.
Einstein, Podolsky, and Rosen (1935): Albert Einstein, Boris Podolsky and Nathan Rosen, "Can Quantum-Mechanical Description of Physical Reality Be Considered Complete?", *Physical Review* 47 (May 15), 777–780.
Frank (1932): Philipp Frank, *Das Kausalgesetz und seine Grenze*, Wien: Verlag Julius Springer.
Frank (1938): Philipp Frank, "*Bemerkungen zu E. Cassirer: Determinismus und Indeterminismus in der moderne Physik*", Theoria 4.Translated as "Determinism and Indeterminism in Modern Physics" in: Philipp Frank, *Modern Science and its Philosophy*, Cambridge, MA: Harvard University Press, 172–185.
French (2012): Steven French, "Unitary inequivalence as a problem for structural realism", *Studies in History and Philosophy of Modern Physics*, 43 (May), 121–136.
French (2014): Steven French, *The Structure of the World: Metaphysics and Representation*, New York: Oxford University Press.
French and Ladyman (2003): Steven French and James Ladyman, "Remodeling Structural Realism", *Synthese* 136, 31–56.
Gawronsky (1949): Dimitri Gawronsky, "Ernst Cassirer: His Life and Works", in: P.A.Schlipp (ed.), *The Philosophy of Ernst Cassirer* (Library of Living Philosophers, v.VI), Evanston, IL: Northwestern University Press, 3–37.
Haag (1996): Rudolf Haag, *Local Quantum Physics: Fields, Particles, Alegebras*, 2nd revised and enlarged ed., Berlin, New York, Heidelberg: Springer.
Hacking (1990): Ian Hacking, *The Taming of Chance*, New York: Cambridge University Press.
Heisenberg (1927): Werner Heisenberg, "*Über den anschaulichen Inhalt der quantentheoretischen Kinematik und Mechanik*", *Zeitschrift für Physik* 43 (1927), 172–198. English translation in: Wheeler and Zurek (1983), 62–84.
Helmholtz (1847): Hermann von Helmholtz, *Über der Erhaltung der Kraft; eine physikalische Abhandlung*, Berlin: Reimer.
Helmholtz (1878): Hermann von Helmholtz, "*Die Tatsachen in der Wahrnehmung*", as reprinted in: M. Schlick and P. Hertz (eds.), *Hermann v. Helmholtz: Schriften zur Erkenntnistheorie*, Berlin: J. Springer, 109–152.
Helmholtz (1896): Hermann von Helmholtz, *Handbuch der physiologischen Optik*, Zweite Auflage, Leipzig: Verlag von Leopold Voss.
Hollands and Wald (2010): Stefan Hollands and Robert Wald, "Axiomatic Quantum Field Theory in Curved Spacetime", *Communications in Mathematical Physics* 293, 85–125.
Howard (2011): Don Howard, "The Physics and Metaphysics of Identity and Individuality", *Metascience* 20, 225–251.
Jaffe (2008): Arthur Jaffe, "Quantum Theory and Relativity", in: R.S. Doran, C.C. Moore, and R.J. Zimmer (eds.), *Group Representations, Ergodic Theory, and Mathematical Physics: A Tribute to George W. Mackey*, Contemporary Mathematics 449, 209–245.
Ladyman and Ross (2007): James Ladyman and David Ross, *Every Thing Must Go; Metaphysics Naturalized*, New York: Oxford University Press.
Laplace (1814): Pierre-Simon, marquis de Laplace, *Essai philosophique sur les probabilities*, 6th ed. (1840), Paris: Bachelier, Imprimeur-Libraire de L'Ecole Polytechnique.
Laue (1933): Max von Laue, "*Materie und Raumerfüllung*", *Scientia* 54 (Dec.), 402–412.
Laue (1934): Max von Laue, "Über Heisenbergs Ungenauigkeitsbeziehungen und ihre erkenntnistheoretische Bedeutung", *Die Naturwissenschaften* 22 (June 29), 439–441.

Margenau (1954): Henry Margenau, "Advantages and Disadvantages of Various Interpretations of Quantum Mechanics", *Physics Today* 7 (No.10), 6–13.

Moore (1989): Walter Moore, *Schrödinger: Life and Thought*, New York: Cambridge University Press.

Nagel (1938): Ernst Nagel, "Review of Determinismus and Indeterminismus in der modernen Physik", Philosophy of Science 5 (April), 230–232.

Neiman (1994): Susan Neiman, *The Unity of Reason*, Oxford: Oxford University Press.

Neumann (1932): John von Neumann, *Der Mathematische Grundlagen der Quantenmechanik*, Berlin: J. Springer. Translation by R.T. Beyer, *Mathematical Foundations of Quantum Mechanics*. Princeton: Princeton University Press, 1955.

Rohrlich (1999): Fritz Rohrlich, "On the Ontology of QFT", in: Tian Yu Cao (ed.) *Conceptual Foundations of QFT,* New York: Cambridge University Press, 357–367.

Ruetsche (2011): Laura Ruetsche, *Interpreting Quantum Field Theories: The Art of the Possible*, New York: Oxford University Press.

Schrödinger (1929): Erwin Schrödinger, "Was ist ein Naturgesetz?" (Inaugural speech at the Universität Zürich, 9 December 1922), *Die Naturwissenschaften* 17, 9–11.

Schrödinger (1934): Erwin Schrödinger, "Über die Unanwendbarkeit der Geometrie im Kleinen," Die Naturwissenschaften 22, 518–520.

Segal (1959): Irving E. Segal, "The Mathematical Meaning of Operationalism in Quantum Mechanics", in: L.Henkin, P.Suppes and A. Tarski (eds), *The Axiomatic Method with Special Reference to Geometry and Physics*, Amsterdam: North Holland, 341–352.

Truesdell (1984): Clifford A. Truesdell III, *An Idiot's Fugitive Essays on Science,* New York, Berlin, Heidelberg: Springer-Verlag.

van Strien (2014): Marij van Strien, Continuity, Causality and Determinism in Mathematical Physics from the late 18th until the early 19th century, University of Gent Ph.D. dissertation.

Weizsäcker (1937): Carl Friedrich von Weizsäcker, "Besprechung von E. Cassirer, Determinismus und Indeterminismus in der modernen Physik", Physikalische Zeitschrift 38, 860–861.

Wheeler and Zurek (1983): J.A. Wheeler and W. Zurek (eds.), *Quantum Theory and Measurement*, Princeton: Princeton University Press,

Wightman (1976): Arthur Wightman, "Hilbert's Sixth Problem: Mathematical Treatment of the Axioms of Physics", *American Mathematical Society Symposium in Pure Mathematics* 28, 147–240.

Zee (2003): Anthony Zee, *Quantum Field Theory in a Nutshell,* Princeton: Princeton University Press.

Alan W. Richardson (Vancouver)
Holism and the Constitution of "Experience in its Entirety" Cassirer contra Quine on the Lessons of Duhem

For roughly a quarter century, as philosophers of science have expanded their philosophical curiosity and historical reach, neo-Kantian themes have been among the new (or renewed) trends in philosophy of science. The trend was given important impetus when Thomas Kuhn, in his presidential address to the Philosophy of Science Association, analogized his philosophical project not to any form of naturalism but to "Kantianism with movable categories".[1] At just that moment other philosophers of science—John Earman, George Reisch, and Michael Friedman prominent among them—were exploring structural similarities between Kuhn's philosophy of science and that of Rudolf Carnap and were doing so in part through an historical examination of the role of neo-Kantianism in Carnap's early philosophy.[2] Friedman has subsequently offered the most developed and most ambitious form of a renewed neo-Kantian philosophy of science.[3] It goes beyond Kuhn's by trying to use Kantian resources with a distinct Second Critique and critical theory flavor, to solve the problem of incommensurability and the rationality of revolutions. It is also deeply immersed in the philosophy of the self-described neo-Kantians of the early twentieth century, especially the Marburg neo-Kantians and, among them, especially the early work of Ernst Cassirer: his 1910 book, *Substanzbegriff und Funktionbegriff* and his 1921 exploration of the foundations of physics, *Von Einsteinschen Relativitätstheorie*.[4]

What is the shortest route into understanding the point of Friedman's "dynamics of reason"? Begin with the fundamentals of mature Carnapian philosophy: the distinction between the articulation of a logical framework and the empirical claims that can be articulated within that framework. For Carnap, analytic sentences constitute the logical structure of a given language; they constitute the evidential and meaning relations among the sentences of the language. Metalogical investigations, in turn, provide the meaning of philosophical terminology:

---

1 Kuhn (1990).
2 Earman (1993), Reisch (1991), Friedman (1993).
3 Friedman (1999, 2001, 2010).
4 Cassirer (1910, 1921), both translated in Cassirer (1953).

they allow you to speak intelligibly and precisely about meaning and justification, for example. Once a linguistic framework has been articulated (itself a project subject to the precise standards of metalogic), the philosopher can examine the range of empirical theories expressible on that framework. IF the language is an adopted language for empirical science, the philosopher can look at what empirical significance sentences actually formulated and adopted in the framework have, how they relate to observational sentences, and so forth. The heretofore unclear terms of traditional philosophy are converted into logical and metalogical terms that are precisely delineated; philosophy so constructed participates in the clarity and goals of science even as it helps to articulate how science achieves conceptual clarity and what goals science can properly adopt for itself.

If the analytic sentences constitute the logical framework and if there is, as Carnap insists, more than one such framework, then we have a set of evident issues. The more general sort of issue is how the logical frameworks relate to one another; this is very much the business of metalogic, the formal investigation of various logical systems. But if this is all meant to illuminate the progress of science, Carnap needs to consider the differences between a change of logical framework and mere changes in the acceptance and rejection of sentences expressible within that framework. Indeed, if the framework constitutes meaningfulness and the standard of evidence, then a change of framework seems to involve radical change of meaning and changes in what counts as evidence. On the one hand, that seems like a fair description—if a quite sketchy one—of what happens in scientific revolutions, making it seem like Carnap is on the right track. On the other hand, this does seem to be a pretty deep philosophical puzzle. Carnap's preferred answer invokes a theoretical/practical distinction: logical frameworks constitute theoretical reason, questions of evidence are only well-formed internal to a logical framework. But, there are practical reasons—reasons of efficiency, economy, etc.—that operate at the level of the adoption and replacement of a logical framework.

For technical, metalogical reasons, one might begin to think that, whatever promise on the epistemological side Carnap's views might hold, on the technical side he is in serious trouble. Metalogic has important self-referential capacities and well-known limitative results. Thus, for example, while the boundless range of possible linguistic frameworks might seem like a "logical fact", as a consequence of Carnap's strictures on what it means to articulate a language, the determination of what languages there are and what properties they have depends on the logical strength of the metalanguage the philosopher works within. This might begin to make you think that the sort of precision, clarity, and uncontroversiality that Carnap claimed for his philosophy just raise the questions of precision, clarity, and controversy to the metalanguage. Add to this certain difficulties—most famously scouted by W.V. Quine[5]—with Carnap's own attempts to draw an analytic/synthetic distinction for an empirical language, and you might begin to think that while the epistemology here is promising, the technical machinery of metalogic doesn't help.

Enter Thomas Kuhn.[6] Kuhn maintains a distinction between principles constitutive of meaningfulness and evidence and simple empirical claims. But his setting for this distinction is, in one of the many senses of that vexed term, importantly naturalistic. He speaks of scientific communities training young scientists in the practices and standards embedded in paradigmatic scientific achievements. In becoming a Newtonian or Einsteinian physicist you learn the crucial distinctions among aspects of the theories; you learn what counts as sensible criticism and is simple misunderstanding or the adoption of inappropriate standards of evidence. Kuhn doesn't tie this story to the articulation of difficult, technical logical distinctions. The epistemological vocabulary, so to speak, is given free rein—the clarification it needs is gotten through the structural analysis of paradigm articulation and change as well as through examples from the history of science.

The problem here is that you might well think that Kuhnian epistemology of science buys you too little. Famously, since paradigms constitute empirical meaningfulness for Kuhn, across paradigms there are no shared standards of meaningfulness; this is his famous incommensurability thesis. Across paradigms, scientists literally say things that cannot be understood in the other scientific language. But scientific revolutions involve change of paradigm. This leaves Kuhn with a seemingly irrationalist stance regarding scientific revolutions: holders of the new paradigm say things that cannot be understood for reasons that cannot be articulated from within the old paradigm. When called upon to discuss this further, Kuhn[7] sounded more like Carnap by invoking pragmatic considerations: there was a shared problem-solving understanding of science across paradigms and from within the new paradigm scientists could persuasively exhibit the problem-solving capacities of it and lead holders of the former paradigm to switch. Of course, this will only happen when the holders of the old paradigm begin to acknowledge that by its own standards the old paradigm is breaking down as a problem-solving device. The problem is this: if paradigms in a strict, not metaphorical, sense constitute the conditions of meaningfulness and evidence, then it is hard to see how scientists in one paradigm can even rec-

---

5 See Quine (1980).
6 Kuhn (2012).
7 Kuhn (1977).

ognize those in another as engaged in meaningful and successful problem-solving practices in the first place.

This is, then, the problem Friedman is trying to solve: how to give to the epistemological vocabulary itself enough structure and content to solve the Kuhnian incommensurability and irrationalism problems. The main ideas in his attempt are three. First, he builds back in some of the motivation and structure of Carnap's views. That is, he stresses how, within the mathematized natural sciences, mathematics itself plays the role of the conceptual technology or logical system. Contra the suggestions in Quine's diagnosis of the philosophical motives for and lessons from the demise of the analytic/synthetic distinction, the methodological role of mathematics is found not in its entrenchment but in its acknowledged immunity from empirical disconfirmation. The mathematics of tensor calculus and differential geometry were controversial in Einstein's time when he used them to formulate the general theory of relativity, but no serious scientist thought they might be empirically disconfirmed. Rather they thought they might have problems inherent in higher mathematics: inconsistency, vagueness, incoherence. But Friedman, in opposition to Carnap, does not attempt to explain that mathematics plays these roles (and not others) in the frameworks of empirical knowledge in virtue of their having a specific logical status, that is, their being analytic. The point is to exhibit and exploit the methodological and representational roles of mathematics not to explain them.

Second, Friedman notes that when scientists are in crisis they have a tendency to invoke the concerns and concepts of philosophy to sort their way through their crisis. This is Friedman's rather controversial place for philosophical meta-paradigms. This is not simply an apologia pro vita sua for philosophy,[8] it is an effort to indicate that there is more structure available to scientists in an epistemological crisis than Kuhn might have led us to believe. In particular, scientists have available to them the vocabulary of philosophy and the results of philosophy (or the general methodology of science) to help them sort through the sort of epistemological crisis they are having. After all, scientists do speak of confirmation and prediction and explanation and so on when they endeavour to explain the problems they are having and what solutions might look like.

Third, while this added structure limits the ways in which scientists can fail to communicate properly among themselves and, thus, makes instances of something looking like a genuine case of incommensurability less frequent, Friedman does allow that incommensurability is a problem not entirely solved by what has been said so far. Indeed, from an internal, forward-looking perspective, some-

---

8 As one commentator put it; see Richardson (2002).

times scientists are in a position much as Kuhn said they were in revolutionary moments: they have to join a community elaborating a framework that is by their own standards heretofore incomprehensible. Here, Friedman's thought goes directly back to Kant himself and thinks along the lines of communicative rationality in the manner of Jürgen Habermas. It works this way: scientists understand themselves to have a duty of communicative rationality to their historical predecessors and thus need to tell a story from the point of view of the later paradigm that explains what their predecessors were doing and what they were endeavoring to understand in their own vocabulary. Thus, the famous, "Einsteinian physics becomes Newtonian physics as the speed of light goes to infinity" sorts of limiting case arguments play a role in preserving a retrospectively rational and coherent story of scientific progress. Scientists may not always know what they do, but their rational commitments mean that they must understand (in their own terms) what they and their predecessors did.

The point of this summary is not to investigate the success of Friedman's project. The point is to present some of the motivating epistemological vocabulary in more detail and to excavate some of its sources. The plan for the rest of this paper is as follows. First, I will present some of the motivations for Friedman's views in a different direction—not by deriving them from Carnap and Kuhn but by looking at some of the historical resources Friedman uses to motivate his account and the language he takes from them. We'll be looking mainly at Kant, Hans Reichenbach, and Ernst Cassirer. Second, I will present an objection that despite Friedman's effort to peel us back from a problematic endorsement of analyticity to a less problematic endorsement of a relativized constitutive a priori, a substantially similar argument to Quine's epistemological argument against analyticity tells equally against the constitutive a priori. I will also present the historical claim found in the work of Don Howard that this argument was in fact stated in the historical moment of the development of the relativized constitutive a priori in Reichenbach and Cassirer by Albert Einstein and that this argument is substantially already to be found in the work of Pierre Duhem. Third, this will allow me to raise a puzzle: Carnap and Cassirer were familiar with and thought they were endorsing Duhem holism. Thus, their view was that holism was compatible with the articulation of the constitutive a priori. Cassirer, in fact, relied on Duhemian holism in articulating his view of the a priori element in physical knowledge. I will argue that attention to Cassirer's arguments can bring us farther down the road to articulating the epistemological vocabulary of neo-Kantianism and indicate how impoverished an epistemological view of science is that locates epistemological importance only in theory-testing. In other words, the essay, finally, attempts to provide more motivation to and resources for a neo-Kantian project with a robust account of constitution, whether Friedman would wish to go down this route or not.

In order for this essay to fit into the allotted space, while I will continue to note that the sort of constitutive a priori that Friedman endorses involves its relativization to theory or paradigm, I will not be speaking directly to the issues of rationality across paradigm change. I wish rather to give some more content to the neo-Kantian notion of constitution and, through some historical elaboration of themes in Cassirer, to indicate how the standard post-Quinean deployment of Duhemian holism begins from a highly impoverished language of the internal rationality of science. This vocabulary, which ties rationality considerations tightly to theory-testing, is too poor fully to engage with the ultimate points about the rational processes of science that the language of constitution is deployed to make.

1 Friedman on the Relativized A Priori

Friedman deploys historical resources throughout his account of the dynamics of reason. The two we will focus on are the methodological understanding of the synthetic a priori in Kant and the explicit development early in the twentieth century of a relativized synthetic a priori. It is the relativized a priori that both seems most illuminating of the structure of any given stage of the development of science and raises the specter of irrationalism and relativism. As I have said, here we shall set aside the latter issue and concentrate only on the idea of constitutive principles embedded within scientific theory.

As we all know, it was Kant who gave us the notion of the synthetic a priori and set the possibility of such judgments as the central concern of philosophy. According to the nominal definitions of synthetic and a priori, synthetic a priori judgments are judgments that are necessary and universal, knowable independently of experience, and yet tell us something about the way the world is. To say how such judgments are possible seems a hard task. Part of the difficulty of that task is mitigated by the more substantive and essentially Kantian version of the synthetic a priori: these principles don't just tell us this or that about the things there are in the world; they are constitutive of the objects of experience. Experience, considered as a form of knowledge of the world, would not be possible but for these principles. This, of course, connects us directly to the "Copernican revolution" in philosophy that Kant sought to effect—the a priori principles of the faculties of the mind, working in tandem, provide the structure by which it is possible to know objects in experience at all. How that works is the project of the Transcendental Aesthetic and the Transcendental Analytic in the *Critique of Pure Reason*.⁹

There are still several interpretative options open for figuring out what Kant is actually trying to do with his critical philosophy. Friedman follows a generally Marburg neo-Kantian line in arguing that the objects of experience that Kant is trying to show to be constituted by the forms of intuition and understanding are the objects of Newtonian physics. This is because Kant's whole articulation of the synthetic a priori begins with a trenchant understanding of something important about the structure of Newtonian physics. The three dimensional Euclidean structure of space, the one-dimensional continuous nature of time, and the three laws of motion in Newton constitute finally a framework within which true and objective motion can be distinguished from merely apparent and relative motion. Kant's critical theory of knowledge provides, for Friedman, an effort to philosophically explain how Newtonian physics has such structure and why such structure is necessary for empirical knowledge of (regular, law-governed) objects.

A simple example might suffice to make the point. Since ancient times it was well known that, for example, the apparent motion of the sun around the Earth from east to west once a day could be equally accounted for by a real motion of the sun or a real rotation of the Earth from west to east along its north-south axis. By the time of Newton it was possible to be put in very bad circumstances for holding (what the Church believed were the wrong) views on such matters. Newton understood that given the relativity of apparent motion, the only way to give physical significance to this question would be to have a theory of motion that distinguished between real states of motion and merely apparent states of motion. Together with the structure of space and time, this is what Newton's three laws of motion provide: the only real state of motion is a change of velocity, changes of velocity are caused by impressed forces, you can determine what the real changes of velocity are because forces balance in frameworks in inertial states of motion. Working from these principles—which together indicate that the center of mass frame for the solar system is the only frame in which forces always balance (assuming the solar system to be isolated)—and from matters of fact regarding the measurable masses of the sun and the planets, Newton could determine that the center of mass of the solar system is always quite close to the center of the sun. Thus, while both the sun and the earth undergo real rotations, from the perspective of the center of mass frame, the main real motion is the motion of the earth around the sun. Newton's laws of motion con-

---

9 Kant (1998).

stitute the framework within which the question is finally physically significant and answer the question in favor of the Copernican hypothesis.[10]

This methodological structure is carried forward in all Newtonian contexts. For example, because magnets cause deflections from rectilinear paths in some materials, magnets cause accelerations and thus there is a magnetic force. By mathematically precise measurements one can enunciate the form of the magnetic force law. The idea behind Friedman's Kant interpretation is that Kant was fully aware of this structure to the Newtonian system—as is amply attested in Kant's long discourse on Newtonian physics, his *Metaphysical Foundations of Natural Science*,[11] in which the principles of the pure understanding are linked to the methodological role of the Newtonian laws of motion. Kant was the philosopher of Newtonian science par excellence.

If the details of Kantian philosophy are so intimately tied to the fate of Newtonian science, then by the beginning of the twentieth century all could not have been well in the Kantian world. The rise of new types of logic, new forms of geometry, new types of physics all rendered it dubious that Kant was right about the a priori. For those impressed with Kant's own achievements, however, there were two evident ways forward that would not amount to a wholesale rejection of Kant's project. One way would be to grant that there are in fact necessary, universal, absolute synthetic a priori principles, but they were not the ones Kant suggested. Instead perhaps they were those that constituted the framework of the general theory of relativity. Or, perhaps, we haven't found them yet—our route toward enunciating the absolute a priori would only be through the progress of science and only the final science would lay out the ultimate a priori principles.

The other route would be to take the line explicitly endorsed by Hans Reichenbach in his 1920 book, *Relativitätstheorie und Erkenntnis A Priori*.[12] There Reichenbach distinguished between the synthetic a priori as the "necessary and universal" and the synthetic a priori as "constitutive of the objects of experience". On the basis of this distinction, Reichenbach argued that every scientific theory has principles that constitute the objects of that theory: Newtonian dynamics contained principles that constituted Newtonian forces and the objects that they act over; Einsteinian relativity has different constitutive principles, not a lack principles. In somewhat the same manner as Kant analyzed Newton's theory, the philosopher of science could discover those structural principles by

---

[10] Friedman has given this example in more detail in several places, most recently and most fulsomely in Friedman (2013).
[11] Kant (2004).
[12] Reichenbach (1920).

analyzing the knowledge created by other theories. Thus was born the relativized constitutive a priori. As their admiring mutual citation indicates, this idea was substantially laid out, though in less explicit language, in Cassirer's own Einstein book of 1921. Friedman offers a relativized constitutive a priori for the twenty-first century. But both projects—the universalist and the relativist—start from the notion of constitution; that is our chief stalking horse here.[13]

2 Was the Relativized A Priori Refuted Before the Fact?

The relativized a priori, as noted, raises troubling questions about the rationality of the change of a priori principles, problems Friedman attempts to solve, but may not fully succeed in solving. But a careful student of the history of analytic philosophy might think that the situation is more hopeless than that: she might think that no meaningful "constitutive" a priori/a posteriori distinction internal to scientific theories or languages can be drawn in the first place. This feeling might come from the arguments against the epistemological point of the analytic/synthetic distinction, already found in Quine. It is here that Quine deploys the "Duhem-Quine thesis" and suggests that no rational process could distinguish the analytic from the synthetic. The argument can be made just as easily for the a priori and a posteriori directly, one might suspect.

Quine deploys the "Duhem-Quine thesis" against the analytic/synthetic distinction toward the end of "Two Dogmas of Empiricism". His project at this point of the essay is to draw a connection between the two dogmas he has discovered; he does this by arguing that the analytic/synthetic distinction is motivated by (and ultimately, as he famously claimed, "at root identical" to) the dogma of sentence by sentence reduction to the language of experience. Here's how he makes the claim in the text:

> The dogma of reductionism survives in the supposition that each statement, taken in isolation from its fellows, can admit of confirmation or infirmation at all. My counter suggestion, issuing essentially from Carnap's doctrine of the physical world in the *Aufbau*, is that our statements about the external world face the tribunal of sense experience not individually but only as a corporate body.
>
> The dogma of reductionism, even in its attenuated form, is intimately connected with the other dogma: that there is a cleavage between the analytic and the synthetic. We have

---

[13] I consider the relations of the universalist and the relativized a priori in the neo-Kantians, especially Cassirer, in more detailed in Richardson (1998), chapter five.

found ourselves led, indeed, from the latter problem to the former through the verification theory of meaning. More directly, the one dogma clearly supports the other in this way: as long as it is taken to be significant in general to speak of the confirmation and infirmation of a statement, it seems significant to speak also of a limiting kind of statement which is vacuously confirmed, *ipso facto*, come what may; and such a statement is analytic.[14]

What is the argument here? As his invocation of the Duhem in a footnote to the text that was added in the 1961 version of the essay suggests, the argument can reconstructed this way: Traditional empiricism was based on the idea that each significant sentence carries its own consequences for experience and these consequences constitute that sentence's meaning.[15] This being the case, there might be some sentences—say the sentences of logic and mathematics or sentences that give meaning relations such as "All bachelors are unmarried" that no experience (or observation sentence) would refute. These are the analytic sentences.

But once we have seen from Duhem's work and from the way in which Carnap's effort in the *Aufbau* to translate all significant sentences into the language of sensation fails in principle, we will see that no epistemologically-significant analytic/synthetic distinction can be drawn. Why? Because no theoretical sentences carry individual consequences for experience; theoretical claims can only be tested against experience as a corporate body. Thus, on point of confirmation or infirmation by experience, all theoretical sentences are on equal footing: any sentence might, with sufficient ingenuity in making adjustments elsewhere in the system, be held as confirmed "come what may"; conversely, no sentence must be held true no matter how recalcitrant experience might be. Since the empirical testing of theory is the locus of rational deliberation regarding what is true or false, no rational process allows an epistemologically meaningful analytic/synthetic distinction to be drawn. Any such distinction then that is drawn is epistemologically meaningless and thus philosophically pointless.

If this argument works, then it would seem that an argument against the a priori/a posteriori distinction follows. (Indeed, you might think that the latter is the more direct argument here, since we don't have to go through the contortions of the theory of meaning.) If the sentences of scientific theory (or indeed, on Quine's view, everyday life) only have consequences in experience as a corporate body, then whenever theoretical expectations are refuted by the course of expe-

---

14 Quine (1980), 41.
15 The footnote in the text attaches to the sentence about the failure of the *Aufbau* and reads: "This doctrine was well argued by Pierre Duhem[, *La Theorie physique: son objet et sa structure* (Paris, 1906)] pp. 303–328. Or see [Armand] Lowinger[, *The Methodology of Pierre Duhem* (New York: Columbia University Press, 1941)], pp.132–140". Quine (1980), 41.

rience, logic never allows you to decide which theoretical sentences to discard and which to keep. Since any sentence might be discarded, then, in light of experience, there are no sentences that must be held true regardless of the course of experience. But that is as much as saying that there are no sentences that are knowable independently of experience. Duhemian holism about theory-testing is our greatest tool against drawing the a priori/a posteriori distinction. And, we might go on to say, since the analytic/synthetic distinction was brought in to explain the a priori/a posteriori distinction, no analytic/synthetic distinction will ever discharge its epistemological function.

Duhem made his argument for holism of theory-testing in 1906. The work on the relativized a priori that Friedman takes as his starting point is from the early 1920 s. It seems that a Duhemian argument would have been available to make against that work and, if it had been, a great deal of confusion might have been avoided. Now, as it happens, Don Howard[16] has been arguing for a long time that such an argument was made repeatedly by a fairly important figure in the early-twentieth-century arguments about physical methodology and the revolutions in physics: Albert Einstein. Here is a nicely distilled argument of this form that Howard has recovered in a review Einstein wrote in 1924:

> [The development of physics] does not, at first, preclude holding at least to the Kantian *problematic*, as, e.g. Cassirer has done [...]. Let me briefly indicate why I do not find this standpoint natural. A physical theory consists of the parts (elements) A, B, C, D, that together constitute a logical whole that correctly connects the pertinent experiments (sense experiences). Then it tends to be the case that the aggregate of fewer than all four elements, e.g. A, B, D *without* C, no longer says anything about these experiences, and just as well A, B, C, without D. One is then free to regard the aggregate of these three elements, e.g. A, B, C as a priori, and only D as conditioned. But what remains unsatisfactory in this is always the *arbitrariness in the choice* of those elements that one designates a priori, entirely apart from the fact that the theory could one day be replaced by another that replaces certain of the elements (or all four) by others.[17]

The main thrust of this argument is clear: the theory with A, B, C, D as parts only has experimental consequences as a corporate body, thus one would be free to take any proper subset of the parts as the a priori elements and consider the remaining parts as those that are structured by the a priori parts and are the locus of empirical import. But any such division in the theory is always arbitrary and does not identify or explain any genuine facts about the rational structure or progress of science.

---

16 Howard (1994, 2010).
17 Howard (2010), 346, quoting from Einstein (1924).

Indeed, if anything, this Einsteinian argument is even more directly geared to the Kantian conception of the a priori and thus the views that Friedman and his historical actors are attempting to articulate than is Quine's. Einstein, unlike Quine, is not talking about refutation in light of experience but the mere having of empirical content: only as a corporate body does physical theory have empirical content at all. In light of this fact, it is unclear why anyone would wish to locate empirical content in one rather than another portion of the theory, but it seems evident that, regardless of motivation, they will fail in the attempt.

3 The Historical Aporia

It is scarcely credible that Friedman has not noticed the Duhemian arguments that have been prominent in discussions of the analytic/synthetic distinction for over sixty years. But the situation is even stranger than that. Among those motivating Friedman's account, Carnap and Cassirer both explicitly understand themselves to endorse Duhemian holism and both view that issue as importantly distinct from questions of the a priori.

The case of Carnap, while not our principal concern here, is striking enough at least to display and comment upon briefly. In 1936 in *Logical Syntax of Language*, the first work in which his mature distinction between the analytic and synthetic sentences of a language was first drawn and used to account for the nature of logical and mathematical testing, Carnap writes:

> It is, in general, impossible to test even a single hypothetical sentence. In the case of a single sentence of this kind, there are in general no suitable L-consequences of the form of protocol sentences; hence for the deduction of sentences having the form of protocol-sentences the remaining hypotheses must also be used. Thus *the test applies, at bottom, not to a single hypothesis but to the whole system of physics as a system of hypotheses* (Duhem, Poincaré).[18]

Evidently, Carnap viewed holism of theory-testing as an entirely distinct issue from drawing the analytic/synthetic distinction. Moreover, the terms in which Carnap draws out the thesis of holism indicate why: in order to articulate the thesis of holism you need to have in hand the notions of synthetic sentence (hypothetical sentence), logical consequence (L-consequence), observation sentence (protocol sentence), etc. But those notions are among the notions in the meta-theoretical framework in which the analytic/synthetic distinction is drawn. In

---

18 Carnap (1936), 318.

Carnap's view the analytic/synthetic distinction and other metalogical notions in the logic of science allow us first to articulate precisely what the Duhemian thesis is.

The case that interests us, however, is the case of Cassirer. For, in his 1910 *Substance and Function*, Cassirer does not merely mention Duhem in passing, but cites Duhem's work repeatedly, positively, and often when crucial matters are at issue. It is evident that Cassirer believes that his own work builds on central themes in Duhem's work. Moreover, at a crucial moment in Cassirer's text he draws on the very passages in Duhem's 1906 book in which the canonical holist argument is made in order to draw a very different lesson from the one Quine and Einstein draw. It is worth looking in some detail at Cassirer's use of Duhem to see what the import of Duhem's work was taken to be in the German epistemological context that eventually made the move to the relativized constitutive a priori.

Before we get to Cassirer's direct invocation of the holism of theory-testing, we should note two things about the setting for that invocation in *Substance and Function*.[19] First, it is clear from the very structure of the work, that holism was no argument against the a priori for Cassirer. Cassirer's book begins with an account of the concepts and laws of logic—especially the new relational logic of the early twentieth century—and then moves on to a consideration of the concepts, objects, structures, and laws of mathematics. It is clear in these chapters that Cassirer simply presupposes that logic and mathematics are a priori. Indeed, he must presuppose this, for otherwise the epistemological problem he means to solve cannot even be articulated. That problem is, briefly, this: Mathematics allows you to see precisely how objective knowledge is possible. The mathematical relations that hold among mathematical objects are constitutive of those very objects: the number seven is constituted as the very number it is not by virtue of its essential sevenness but by virtue of the being the object it is within the system of objects determined by the relation of succession among the natural numbers. The question is: can we extend the way in which mathematical lawfulness constitutes the objects of knowledge to the realm of the empirical sciences, while allowing that an experiential, empirical element is involved in knowing both the laws and the objects (but not in mathematics proper)? Answer: yes, but it is complicated.

Second, holism is only one of the lessons Cassirer takes himself to have learned from Duhem and how he deploys the lessons of holism depends on

---

[19] For a larger introduction to the themes of Substance and Function, see Heis (2014). I have attempted to introduce the test to non-specialists in Richardson (forthcoming).

the prior lesson he finds in Duhem's work. In our times, Duhem's interest in the details of physical experimentation lead him to be cited as a precursor to the recent "move to practice" in philosophy of science. There is no doubt that Duhem, who was an experimental physicist, after all, is keenly interested in the practice of experiment. But if the "move to practice" means for current philosophers a lessening of our interest in theory, a move from "theory-centrism", then the main lesson of Duhem's interest in practice seems precisely the opposite. One of Duhem's main lessons about physical experimentation is that while pretty much anyone could experience what the experimentalist experiences when doing the experiment, only the experimentalist can render that experience relevant to physics and she can only do this because she can render the result in the language of physical theory. One of Duhem's favored phrases, and one that Cassirer repeats often, is "the result of an experiment in physics is an abstract and symbolic judgment".[20]

Duhem's claim is this. Most people if called upon could say on the basis of a relevant experience "The red line in the glass tube touches the line marked '20'". But that is not a fact relevant for the testing of physical theory. The fact that serves to test physical theory is "the temperature in the experimental system is 20 degrees Celsius". But to render the fact in this form is to speak the language of temperature, a theoretical concept, and to know that the glass tube is a mercury thermometer (whose behavior is itself understood only in and through our theories of thermodynamics), and to know why the temperature of the experimental set-up serves to test a theoretical claim in some portion of physics. A great deal of theoretical knowledge is brought to bear in rendering any fact of experience into a form relevant to physics. The fact is rendered in the symbolic form relevant to physics, the instruments used to establish the fact are modeled in theoretical physics, the experimental set-up is modeled in theoretical physics, and together they are brought to bear to test some claim in theoretical physics. This is why in Duhem's own account of holism we see two features: first, it is claimed that holism goes beyond the theory the physicist is trying to test to include the physics involved in understanding the experimental set-up and the behavior of the instruments. Second, it is claimed that holism is, therefore, an issue in physical experiment, not experiment in general. The behavior of instruments is always a matter for physics and in the work of experimental science generally, the physical theory governing the instruments is simply set aside.

---

[20] This is the heading of section two of chapter four of Duhem (1954), see 147.

We now have enough background to consider in some detail the specific passage in which Cassirer brings in the Duhemian argument for holism and to see what is at stake for him in so doing. Here is the passage:

> Even those thinkers who stress with all emphasis that *experience* in its entirety forms the highest and last check [Kontrolle] on all physical theory dismiss the naïve Baconian thought of the 'experimentum crucis'. 'Pure' experience in the sense of a mere inductive collection of scattered observations is never able to deliver the fundamental scaffolding of physics: because the power of mathematical form giving is denied to it. Only when the raw fact is represented and replaced by a mathematical symbol does the intellectual work of conceiving, which connects it systematically to the entirety of phenomena, begin.[21]

It is clear that Cassirer is reiterating the point about mathematical form being requisite for facts of experience to be facts for science. The point most relevant to the issue of holism is, however, absorbed in a phrase that might be easily overlooked and that is not clear on its face: "experience in its entirety" (*Erfahrung in ihrer Gesamtheit*). At stake for Cassirer is not "holism of theory-testing" but the entirety and unity of scientific experience. Bacon's mistake was not simply missing the structure of theory-testing but misconceiving the relation of theory to experiential fact in the first place.

Here is how Cassirer makes the point:

> We do not possess physical facts and physical concepts in pure isolation so that we could take a member from the first realm and could test whether a representation in the second corresponds to it: rather we possess the "facts" only in virtue of the entirety of concepts, as we, on the other hand, devise the concepts only with respect for the totality of possible experience.[22]

We might put the point as follows: For Cassirer scientific experience is a cognitive achievement. Experience in a form relevant to constructing and testing theory is formulated in the same language of mathematics that theory itself is. It is only in virtue of the harmony of the theoretical laws and the offerings of scientific experience that we can be said to possess facts in the first place. What is at issue for Cassirer is not a holistic structure to theory, but a holism of theory and experience and a demand of reason to bring recalcitrant facts of science under theoretical understanding.

---

21 Cassirer (1910), 195. Here and throughout I provide my own translation; cf. Cassirer (1953), 147.
22 Cassirer (1910), 194; Cassirer (1953), 147.

This is evident in the weight Cassirer places on exactly the considerations of this section of the book. Cassirer claims, in this section, to be solving "the core logical problem of physics", which he presents as a problem of circularity:

> The naïve view that the measures of physical things and processes inhere in them like sensible qualities and, like those qualities, only need to be read off, recedes ever more with the progress of physics. With this, however and at the same time, the relation between law and fact changes. For the explanation that we attain to laws insofar as we compare and measure individual facts now reveals itself as a logical circle. The law can only emerge from measurement because we have put it into the measurement in hypothetical form. However paradoxical this mutual relation might appear, it indicates exactly the core logical problem of physics.[23]

What is the solution to the core logical problem of physics? For Cassirer it is a matter of the modality of the laws, which begin as hypotheses and are only in the final analysis asserted as established. So, some laws must be in place as hypotheses in order for the offerings of experience to be formulated in the language of science and thus to test those theories. There is no guarantee, however, that the laws will be confirmed. For example, you have laws of thermodynamics and a model of an experimental set-up that indicate an experiment should result in a temperature reading of 420 degrees. But the result is 407 degrees. This is not just a recalcitrant experience leading to the overthrown of some portion of physics. It is a scientifically expressed "fact" without a lawful expression in the theories of physics. Physics progresses by heading back to theory perhaps to reformulate laws, perhaps to remodel the experiment (maybe this isn't a thermometer that works at these temperatures?), and so on. Neither the laws nor the fact are established until harmony is achieved between them. The goal of mathematized science is to subsume and explain all such facts—when this happens, we have "the entirety of experience" as a determinate object of knowledge.

From this perspective, it is easy to see that Quine's holism of theory-testing and even his eventual "web of belief" are not holistic enough. The offerings of sensation against which Quine claims science is tested stand as facts outside the scientific system: Quine attends neither to the issue of the scientific form of the facts nor to the ways in which changes to theory induced by acceptance of this fact eventually lead to theories that alter the understanding of the fact itself. Quine is a Baconian, whose epistemology presupposes a gulf between theory and fact, for whom experience "impinges" on the web of belief from the outside. For Cassirer science always works from within: the epistemological problem

---

[23] Cassirer (1910) 193–194; cf. Cassirer (1953), 146.

occurs when facts and laws, both couched in theoretical language, diverge; it is solved when the divergence is resolved.

Einstein's holism misses the role of mathematics in Cassirer's system. Mathematics is essentially a priori, not least because the whole epistemological problem of the identity or divergence of theory and fact is itself only precisely stated in the language of mathematics. (Only mathematics is a clear, law-governed way of talking about the identity or lack of identity between objects.) It also misses the way in which within any stage of scientific development the structural elements that form the a priori for that theory are not revealed by a unique factorization into the a priori and the a posteriori of any one argument or explanation, but through the recurring structural features that render any given problem situation uniquely determined. In classical physics, the a priori status of the conservation of momentum is not determined by factoring it out of a theory that only meets the tribunal of experience as a corporate body but by the fact that no momentum problem is set in the form of an equation and solved in mathematical terms except by the use of this principle. It plays a structural role in determining the objective features of physical objects.

4 How Does Cassirer Help?

What we have said about Cassirer helps, I believe, in giving further clarity and nuance to the notion of the "constitutive a priori". Cassirer's notion of constitutivity is quite strong: only in and through the mathematized language of scientific theory is experience itself a cognitive achievement relevant for science, capable of being used to test and further elaborate the system of the exact sciences. Moreover, there is a methodological drive not to understand the business of science to be completed until there is a harmony among the facts of experience and the theories of science such that no fact stands without theoretical comprehension. In the end, the manifold of experience behaves like a well-formed mathematical structure. Cassirer's use of Duhem indicates ways in which accounts of science that locate the rational processes of science in theory testing do not dig deep enough to fully engage the point of view from which the "constitutive a priori" is formulated.

Cassirer is interested in the conditions under which science achieves mathematized concepts and can serve to formulate facts of experience in a form capable of testing theory in the first place. The logic of factual determination for Cassirer goes well beyond the use of modus ponens and modus tollens in the schemata for theory-testing. For Cassirer it is concerned also with the construction of scientific concepts in the language of mathematics and the use of theory in the understanding of scientific instruments and in the rendering of experimental results in a form relevant to the test of theory. All these topics, for Cassirer, properly belong to the logic of the creation of objective knowledge in the exact sciences. Cassirer and Duhem, read on their own terms, can provide language for animating interest well beyond the canonical questions of analytic philosophy of science. Questions raised in trying to understand Cassirer's "entirety of experience" and its connection to theoretical understanding lead naturally to questions of inter-theoretic reduction and theoretical hierarchy. Whether the language of the "constitutive a priori" is ultimately language that animates our curiosity sufficiently and that ultimately also satisfies that curiosity, it is too early to tell.

Bibliography

Carnap (1936): Rudolf Carnap, *The Logical Syntax of Language*, Amethe Smeaton (trans.), Chicago: University of Chicago Press.
Cassirer (1910): Ernst Cassirer, *Substanzbegriff und Funktionsbegriff*, Berlin: Bruno Cassirer.
Cassirer (1921): Ernst Cassirer, *Zur Einsteinschen Relativitätstheorie*, Berlin: Bruno Cassirer.
Cassirer (1953): Ernst Cassirer, *Substance and Function*, William C. Swabey and Marie C. Swabey (trans.), New York: Dover.
Cassirer (1957): Ernst Cassirer, *The Philosophy of Symbolic Forms, Volume Three: The Phenomenology of Knowledge,* Ralph Manheim (trans.), New Haven: Yale University Press.
Duhem (1954): Pierre Duhem, *The Aim and Structure of Physical Theory*, Philip P. Wiener (trans.), Princeton, NJ: Princeton University Press.
Earman,(1993): John Earman, "Carnap, Kuhn, and the Philosophy of Scientific Methodology", in: Paul Horwich (ed.), *World Changes*, Cambridge, MA: MIT Press, 9–36.
Einstein (1924): Albert Einstein, "Review of A. Elsbach *Kant und Einstein*", *Deutsche Literaturzeitung* 45, 20–22.
Friedman (1993): Michael Friedman, "Remarks on the History of Science and the History of Philosophy", in: Paul Horwich (ed.), *World Changes*, Cambridge, MA: MIT Press, 37–54.
Friedman (1999): Michael Friedman, *Reconsidering Logical Positivism*, Cambridge: Cambridge University Press.
Friedman (2001): Michael Friedman, *The Dynamics of Reason*, Palo Alto, CA: CSLI Publications.
Friedman (2010): Michael Friedman, "Synthetic History Reconsidered", in: Mary Domski and Michael Dickson (eds.), *Discourse on a New Method*, Chicago and LaSalle, IL: The Open Court, 571–813.
Friedman (2013): Michael Friedman, *Kant's Construction of Nature*. Cambridge: Cambridge University Press.
Heis (2014): Jeremy Heis, "Ernst Cassirer's *Substanzbegriff und Funkstionsbegriff*", *HOPOS* 4, 41–270.

Howard (1994): Don Howard, "Einstein, Kant, and the Origins of Logical Empiricism", in: Wesley Salmon and Gereon Wolters (eds.), *Language, Logic, and the Structure of Scientific Theories*, Pittsburgh: University of Pittsburgh Press, 45–105.

Howard (2010): Don Howard, "'Let me briefly indicate why I do not find this standpoint natural': Einstein, General Relativity, and the Contingent A Priori", in: Mary Domski and Michael Dickson (eds.), *Discourse on a New Method*. Chicago and LaSalle, IL: The Open Court, 70.

Kant (1998): Immanuel Kant, *Critique of Pure Reason*, Paul Guyer and Allen Wood (trans.), Cambridge: Cambridge University Press.

Kant (2004): Immanuel Kant, *The Metaphysical Foundations of Natural Science*, Michael Friedman (trans.), Cambridge: Cambridge Press.

Kuhn (2012): Thomas S. Kuhn, *The Structure of Scientific Revolutions*. Chicago: University of Chicago Press.

Kuhn (1977): Thomas S. Kuhn, "Objectivity, Value Judgment, and Theory Choice", in: *The Essential Tension*. Chicago: University of Chicago Press, 102–118.

Kuhn (1990): Thomas S. Kuhn, "The Road Since Structure", in: Arthur Fine, Mickey Forbes, and Linda Wessels (Eds.), *PSA 1990*, vol. 2, East Lansing, MI: Philosophy of Science Association, 3–13.

Reichenbach (1920): Hans Reichenbach, *Relativitätstheorie und Erkenntnis A Priori*, Berlin: Springer.

Reisch (1991): George Reisch, "Did Kuhn Kill Logical Empiricism?", *Philosophy of Science* 58, 264–277.

Richardson (1998): Alan Richardson, *Carnap's Construction of the World*, Cambridge: Cambridge University Press.

Richardson (2002): Alan Richardson, "Narrating the History of Reason Itself", *Perspectives on Science* 10, 253–274.

Richardson (forthcoming): Alan Richardson, "Making Philosophy Functional: Ernst Cassirer's *Substance Concept and Function Concept*", in: Eric Schliesser (ed.), *Ten Neglected Classics of Philosophy*, Oxford: Oxford University Press.

Quine, W.V. (1980): "Two Dogmas of Empiricism", in: *From a Logical Point of View*, 2nd ed., Cambridge, MA: Harvard University Press, 20–46.

Jeremy Heis (Irvine)
Arithmetic and Number in the Philosophy of Symbolic Forms

The discussion of Cassirer's philosophy of mathematics in the literature has largely focused on the writings before the turn to the philosophy of symbolic forms.[1] In *Substance and Function* (SF)[2] Cassirer defends a version of structuralism, the view that mathematical objects are "positions in structures". In the paper "Kant und die moderne Mathematik" (KMM)[3], Cassirer defends a version of logicism, the view that mathematics is a branch of logic. There are good reasons why these claims would be of particular interest to Cassirer's readers. Structuralism has been perhaps the most widely defended and widely discussed philosophy of mathematics of the last thirty years or so, and Cassirer can with good justification be considered the first philosopher to defend mathematical structuralism. Moreover, Cassirer's version of logicism differs in interesting ways from Russell's and Frege's, and like structuralism, logicism continues to have its defenders to this day. In fact, Cassirer's logicism and structuralism both draw heavily on the work of the mathematician Richard Dedekind, whose work has received a bit of a recent revival among contemporary philosophers of mathematics.[4]

There has been comparatively little discussion in the literature of the philosophy of mathematics in the three volumes of the *Philosophy of Symbolic Forms*.[5] This is unfortunate, since Cassirer's philosophy of arithmetic[6] after the turn to *PSF* includes some fundamentally new ideas, and—as I'll argue—in some cases is opposed to the positions defended in *SF*. In *SF*, Cassirer employs a tran-

---

1 Gower (2000), Mormann (2008), Heis (2010), Heis (2011), Mormann and Katz (2013), Heis (2014), Yap (forthcoming). The revival in interest in Cassirer can perhaps be traced back to Benacerraf (1960), 162, where Benacerraf introduces the rough idea behind mathematical structuralism and acknowledges that the same idea is present in *SF*.
2 Cassirer (1923b).
3 Cassirer (1907).
4 Reck (2012).
5 Cassirer (1923a [*PSF1*], 1925 [*PSF2*], 1929 [*PSF3*]).
6 By "arithmetic" I'll always mean "scientific" arithmetic, the theory of the natural numbers that mathematicians refer to when they talk of "arithmetic." On the other hand, when I talk about "number," I'll sometimes mean "number" in scientific arithmetic, but I'll also sometimes mean number in non-scientific contexts. Arithmetic exists only in the symbolic form of science; number, as a category, appears in every symbolic form, including myth and language. (Thanks to Fabien Capeillères, whose comments helped me get clearer on this issue.)

scendental methodology that leaves no place for empirical psychology; *PSF* includes lengthy discussion of empirical work in the psychology of number. The logicism in *SF* rules out grounding arithmetic in any sort of intuition; in *PSF* Cassirer seems to endorse Poincaré's view that inferences in arithmetic are grounded in a pure intuition. The logicism of the pre-*PSF* writings eschews any kind of foundationalism; in *PSF*, Cassirer argues that pure arithmetic is "supported" by number in the symbolic forms of myth and language.

This chapter will have three parts. In the first part, I quickly review the chief features of Cassirer's philosophy of mathematics, drawing on the interpretation I have defended in a series of recent papers. In the second part ("Problems for Logicism in *PSF* 3"), I identify some positions defended in *PSF* 3 that are in tension with the pre-*PSF* philosophy of arithmetic, and I'll argue that this is no accident: the turn to *PSF* requires Cassirer to revise his earlier views, not just relocate them in a wider setting. In part III ("Number in the Symbolic Forms"), I canvass some of the results of Cassirer's discussion of number in myth and language, expression and intuition, explaining how number in these symbolic forms "supports" scientific arithmetic.

1 Overview of Main Features of Cassirer's Philosophy of Mathematics

In this section, I draw on the interpretation defended in Heis (2010, 2011, and 2014) to lay out three main features of Cassirer's philosophy of mathematics: *structuralism*, *developmentalism*, and *logicism*. My goal is to identify the places where Cassirer's thinking shifts as he moves to *PSF*. Because I have defended these interpretations elsewhere, I won't here give thorough justifications for my readings.

The basic idea of *structuralism* is that mathematical objects, such as numbers, are just positions in structures. More precisely, all of the essential properties of a particular natural number are irreducible relational properties between it and the other natural numbers. Cassirer finds this view expressed in Dedekind (1963):

> What is here [in Dedekind's work] expressed is just this: that there is a system of ideal objects whose content is exhausted in their mutual relations. The 'essence' of the numbers is completely expressed in their positions.[7]

---

7 Cassirer (1923b), 39.

That is, the number 2 is essentially the successor of 1 and the predecessor of 3. It is no part of the essence of 2 that it is, for example, the atomic number of helium, or indeed that it stands in any relations to physical or mental objects.

Dedekind calls the structure that contains the numbers "simply infinite system". A simply infinite system is an infinite collection whose structure can be graphically represented as a number line, as in the figure.

Fig. 1: A simply infinite system

In words, the simply infinite structure can be captured in the standard Dedekind/Peano axioms:
- The structure has a privileged position, called "0".
- Every position has a successor in the structure.
- 0 is not the successor of any position in the structure.
- Every position has no more than one successor in the structure.
- The principle of induction (discussed below in section 2).

Structuralism then asserts that arithmetic is the theory of the simply infinite structure, and that the numbers are just positions in that simply infinite structure.

For Cassirer, one of the appeals of structuralism is that it gives him a general strategy for arguing for the permissibility within pure mathematics of all the seemingly exotic new mathematical objects that were being studied in earnest in the late nineteenth and early twentieth century. Employing a "partner in guilt" strategy, Cassirer argues that since even the natural numbers themselves are just positions in structures, then negative, irrational, complex, hypercomplex, or transfinite numbers should equally be considered legitimate mathematical objects. Granted, the complex numbers constitute a different structure than the natural number structure, but both kinds of numbers are just ultimately positions in structures, and so these new exotic seeming numbers are "composed of no different logical stuff than these elementary objects".[8] Alternative philosophies of mathematics that ground mathematical objects in intuition or features of the empirical world might balk at the infinitary character of transfinite or real

---

[8] Cassirer (1957), 395.

numbers, or the apparent counter-intuitive character of complex numbers. Structuralism silences these worries.

Cassirer's defense of these new objects serves an important philosophical role. It had become the consensus view of mathematicians by 1900, and indeed a characteristic feature of their research, that the applicability of pure mathematical work to the empirical world was not a criterion of acceptability for a mathematical theory, so long as the work was internally consistent. Cantor called this attitude the "freedom of mathematics," and Cassirer endorsed it wholeheartedly: "no one will be permitted to try on philosophical grounds to set limits to the freedom of mathematics".[9] This non-revisionist attitude, I contend, follows from the characteristic Marburg Neo-Kantian "transcendental" method. Philosophy must begin with some fact, some given stock of cognitions, whose conditions it is the job of philosophy to investigate. In the case of theoretical philosophy, that fact is the fact of science, especially mathematical natural science. Because mathematical natural science is the starting point of philosophical investigation, philosophical results cannot contravene it—philosophy could never prove that that it is not a fact after all. "The modern development of mathematics thus created a new 'fact' that the critical philosophy, which does not seek to direct the sciences but to understand them, can no longer overlook".[10] Structuralism thus respects the "fact" of free mathematics.

For Cassirer, structuralism is only one part of a complete philosophical analysis of mathematics. Structuralism allows into the mathematical world any structure of mathematical objects that can be consistently characterized. But this is too weak; there are good mathematical reasons to think that mathematicians not only *can* investigate the properties of complex numbers, but that they *must* do so.[11] For example, the use of complex numbers provides a proof of the fundamental theorem of algebra, which is of course used to investigate even the most elementary mathematical objects, such as the natural numbers or curves in Euclidean space. For this and similar reasons, the introduction of complex numbers into mathematics was an inevitable historical development: it was dictated by what one might call the "logic" of mathematical conceptual change. This feature of Cassirer's philosophy, which one might call its *developmentalism*, insists that there is a "homogeneous logical structure of mathematics",[12] which can be uncovered by a transcendental philosophy taking all of the history of mathematics as a fact. Which questions are the important ones

---

9 Cassirer (1907), 48.
10 Ibid., 31.
11 Cassirer (1999), 51.
12 Cassirer (1957), 392.

to answer? Which objects are worth studying? What is the best way to prove a theorem? The answers to these questions, which determine the course of the history of mathematics, are not on Cassirer's view simply the expression of the caprice of this or that mathematician, but arise from applying a unitary mathematical method, which stays the same even as new mathematical theories are developed.

This developmentalism allows for a richer application of the transcendental method. After all, any attempt to follow the prescription "Take the best current mathematical natural science and identify the conditions of its possibility" will very quickly run into the difficulty that mathematicians often disagree, and leave the transcendental philosopher wondering which mathematics is supposed to be *the* fact which is given to philosophy. In cases of disagreement within the mathematical community, the transcendental philosopher can employ the fact of the history of mathematics to evaluate the conflicting claims of mathematicians. Which kind of mathematics is most consonant with the way mathematics has developed, and with the internal logic of that development? In the same way, facts about our best current mathematics can guide us in our transcendental analysis of the history of mathematics: what must the logic of mathematics' internal development be such that it could lead to the mathematics we have now? In this way, there is a back and forth in the transcendental analysis of the fact of current mathematics and of the fact of the development of mathematics. (This feature of Cassirer's philosophy—that there are multiple transcendental analyses that need to be accommodated with one another—will return again in a more significant form in section III of this paper.)

Logicism is the view that the primitive vocabulary of arithmetic consists of only logical vocabulary; that all arithmetical laws can be proved from logical laws; and that all of the rules of inference in arithmetic are logical rules of inference. It was vigorously and influentially developed in Frege (1884) and Russell (1903), and endorsed by Cassirer starting in KMM. There, Cassirer claims that Frege and Russell had shown that "logic and mathematics have been fused into a true, henceforth indissoluble unity".[13] Logicism, as Cassirer noted with enthusiasm, entails that mathematics is not empirical, and is not based on the intuitions of space and time. Cassirer's logicism, however, is distinctive in three ways. First, throughout his career Cassirer was hostile to the use of classes to found mathematics. He thought, for instance, that the natural numbers should be viewed fundamentally as ordinals (answers to the question Where in the sequence?) instead of as cardinals (answers to the question How many?). This con-

---

13 Cassirer (1907), 4.

ception of numbers, he believed, would remove whatever motivation there might be for viewing numbers as classes of equinumerous classes, as Frege and Russell did.[14] Second, Cassirer does not argue that the logicist analysis of number is an accurate analysis of the psychology of the everyday concept of number. Here he departs from Dedekind, at least on a plausible reading, who claimed that his logicist analysis of the natural number structure presents an accurate picture of the concept of number employed in everyday life, albeit unconsciously:

> From the time of birth, continually and in increasing measure we are led to relate things to things and thus to use that faculty of the mind on which the creation of numbers depends; by this practice continually occurring, though without definite purpose, in our earliest years and by the attending formation of judgments and chains of reasoning we acquire a store of real arithmetic truths to which our first teachers later refer as to something simple, self-evident, given in the inner consciousness.[15]

However, the transcendental method, as it was developed in the classic works of Cohen and Natorp and employed in *SF*, starts with the fact of science, not the fact of psychology. On this view, the results of an empirical study of the psychology of number have no place in the philosophy of arithmetic.

Third, Cassirer's logicism has no foundationalist ambitions. For many logicists, including Russell,[16] the appeal of logicism is that mathematics, whose certainty might otherwise be in doubt, gets to inherit the privileged epistemological status enjoyed by logic. Cassirer rejects this contention, because he does not believe that formal logic has a place of "honor and security"[17] not shared by mathematics or natural science. On his view, the most fundamental kind of logic is transcendental logic, the investigation of the preconditions of science. Since there is no epistemological route to "formal logic" except through an analysis of our best current science, taken as a fact, any attempt to ground the certainty of the latter in terms of the former is a fool's errand. Cassirer's logicism is thus a "transcendental" logicism: mathematics is a branch of transcendental logic—the science of the a priori principles that make (mathematical natural scientific) knowledge possible.

---

14 Cassirer (1923b), 53.
15 Dedekind (1963), 33–34.
16 Russell (1903), § 3.
17 Cassirer (1993), 132.

2 Problems for Logicism in *PSF*3

Cassirer returns explicitly to the philosophy of mathematics in Part III of *PSF*3. Though there is obviously a good deal of overlap in content between *SF* and this part of *PSF*3, Cassirer nevertheless departs in three significant ways from the kind of logicism developed in KMM and *SF*. First, Cassirer suggests that arithmetic is grounded in a sui generis intuition. Second, he argues for a place within the philosophy of symbolic forms for empirical results about the psychology of number. Third, he argues that number in the symbolic form of science is supported by number in the other symbolic forms, introducing a kind of grounding relation not envisioned in his earlier non-foundationalist logicism. After explaining each of these three points, I argue at the end of the section that the turn to the philosophy of symbolic forms required Cassirer to rethink some of his conclusions, even about scientific arithmetic.

Between the publication of *SF* in 1910 and *PSF*3 in 1929, mathematics faced the so-called foundational crisis. Partially in response to the paradoxes in set theory, formalists (led by Hilbert), intuitionists (led by Brouwer and Weyl), and logicists (led by Russell) presented rival foundational programs. Surprisingly, Cassirer shows little sympathy in *PSF*3 for logicism, and quite a bit of enthusiasm for various versions of intuitionism, especially those defended by Weyl and earlier by Poincaré.[18] Concerning the latter, Cassirer writes:

> Any attempt to deepen the foundations of the pure theory of numbers by conceiving this theory as a mere subdivision of a universal theory of sets and logically deducing the natural numbers from the concept of classes and sets is now consciously abandoned. Such deduction is replaced by complete [mathematical] induction. ... In this inference, ... it is recognized that the fundamental relation which connects one member of the numerical series with its immediate successor continues through the whole of the series and determines it in all its parts. In this sense a genuine a priori synthesis—as Poincaré, in particular, repeatedly stressed—actually underlies the principle of complete induction.[19]

Mathematical induction is the characteristic form of reasoning in arithmetic. Expressed schematically, an argument by induction looks like this:

> If φ is a predicate such that (i) $\varphi(0)$ is true, and (ii) for every natural number n, if $\varphi(n)$ is true, then $\varphi(n + 1)$ is true, then $\varphi(n)$ is true for every natural number n.

---

[18] In fact, I'll argue at the end of section 3 of this paper that Cassirer's sympathy with the intuitionism of Poincaré (and others like him, such as Brouwer and Weyl) is more limited than it may at first appear.
[19] Cassirer (1957), 376–377.

For example, if I wanted to prove that

(*) $1 + 2 + \ldots + n = n(n + 1)/2$,

I would begin by showing that this property is true of 0:

(i) $0 = 0(0 + 1)/2$

Then I would show that if the property holds of n, then it holds of $n + 1$:

(ii) $1 + 2 + \ldots + (n + 1) = (n + 1)((n + 1) + 1)/2$.

Together these results show that the property (*) holds of every number, since it holds of the number 0, and then keeps on holding true as the natural number sequence progresses one-by-one from zero.

An essential component of Frege's and Russell's logicism was the proof of the principle of induction from logical laws alone, which Frege first discovered in Frege (1879). This proof was important, since without it, the principle of induction remained a form of inference that is unique to arithmetic. Logical truths, however, are supposed to be general truths, applicable everywhere, and provable using only completely general forms of inference.[20] Insofar as logical truths are supposed to be general truths that apply to all subject matters, to claim that mathematical induction is a primitive form of reasoning, not further reducible, is to deny logicism. Poincaré was very clear about this, and argued that mathematical induction is therefore grounded in a kind of pure intuition, not in logic. In fact, Poincaré (in a passage that Cassirer was citing and summarizing in the passage from *PSF* 3 quoted in the last paragraph) argues:

> [Mathematical induction], inaccessible to analytical proof and to experiment, is the exact type of the *a priori* synthetic intuition ... [I]t is the affirmation of the power of the mind which knows it can conceive of the indefinite repetition of the same act, when the act is once possible. The mind has a direct intuition of this power.[21]

Once I know (*) holds of 0, I can use (ii) to show that (*) holds of 1, and I can then use (ii) again to show that (*) holds of 2. And so on. I thus become aware that I can always use (ii) to demonstrate that (*) holds of yet a further number, and I can thereby conclude that (*) holds of every number. This aware-

---

20 Frege (1884), § 3.
21 Poincaré (2001), § VI.

ness of my ability to keep on producing new demonstrations of (*) for yet further numbers Poincaré calls a "pure intuition" of this power of my mind.

Cassirer's endorsement of Poincaré's view is in open conflict with the logicism he earlier defended. Indeed, he seems to be reintroducing pure intuition after arguing strenuously against it in KMM and *SF*. Furthermore, to claim that mathematical induction is based in a pure intuition *of the power of the mind* seems to reintroduce psychological considerations into philosophy—the very sort of considerations that the transcendental method was meant to exclude. What explains this departure? In the rest of this section, I will argue that Cassirer's turn to the philosophy of symbolic forms explains it.

According to the philosophy of symbolic forms, there are multiple, irreducible symbolic forms. Science is now just one symbolic form, beside myth, art, and language. This fundamental idea already introduces complications for logicism. According to logicism, mathematical truths are logical truths, where a logical truth is a *general* truth, containing primitive terms that are used in thinking about *everything*, provable from premises that are used in thinking about *everything*. Would logicism require that arithmetical truths be provable from what is common to every symbolic form, or only to some symbolic forms (say, the symbolic form of science)? The former hardly seems plausible, and (as I'll show in the next section) Cassirer denies that scientific arithmetic, with its structuralist concept of number, could be derived from what is common to every symbolic form. On the other hand, if arithmetical truths are provable from what is general within the particular symbolic form of science, then we are faced with the question What would the relation be between arithmetic in the symbolic form of science and arithmetic in the other symbolic forms? What would logicism require?

In fact, Cassirer's willingness to introduce psychological content when approvingly referring to Poincaré's pure intuition of the power of the mind springs from a more general claim that there is a place for psychological facts within the philosophy of symbolic forms. He argues for this more general claim in Ch.1 ("Subjective and Objective Analysis") of part I of *PSF*3. Vol.3 of *PSF* concerns knowledge, the form of consciousness that is manifested in the symbolic form of science. Keeping with a traditional way of understanding knowledge,[22] Cassirer sees knowledge as the last step in a process that begins with perception, passes to intuition, and culminates in knowledge. Of course, as a transcendental philosopher, Cassirer doesn't want his epistemological analysis of perception and intuition to consist in merely descriptive empirical psychology. The transcenden-

---

[22] For instance, Kant argues that our (fully conceptual) knowledge depends on intuition, which depends on sensation.

tal question is not *quid facti*—How do we come to have the knowledge we have? —but the *quid juris*—What is the ground or justification for the knowledge we have?

Now, the form of knowledge can be revealed through the application of the transcendental method: knowledge is made manifest for us in the fact of science. Though perception and intuition are not made manifest in science in the same way, one might think that the structure of science gives us an indirect route into investigating the character of perception and intuition: What must perception and intuition be such that they can lead to knowledge, whose character is then revealed to us in the form of science? Cassirer believes that this strategy, which he finds in Natorp, is a step in the right direction, but is nevertheless inconsistent with the convictions underlying the philosophy of symbolic forms. Since the symbolic forms of language, art, and myth are all distinct modes of objectification, and not just pale copies or mistaken versions of science, it would be equally mistaken to treat perception and intuition as no more than steps on the way to knowledge.

To avoid this mistake, Cassirer argues that the forms of perception and intuition should be analyzed in light of the symbolic forms of myth and language, respectively. Since language and myth depend on intuition and perception, we can read back into perception and intuition the forms they need to have in order to make myth and language possible. We can thus avoid psychologism while respecting the fact that science is not the only symbolic form. This way of approaching perception and intuition give empirical psychology a role in epistemology. Both developmental psychology and psychological pathology (and even animal psychology) can help the epistemologist identify within perception and intuition distinct aspects that could be preconditions of myth, language, and ultimately, knowledge. Cassirer's strategy is to triangulate the forms of intuition and perception by approaching them through, on the one side, experimental results of empirical psychology, and, on the other side, the forms of myth and language catalogued in *PSF*1 and *PSF*2. Cassirer does this by aligning perception with the phenomenon of expression (the expressive function), which is manifested especially in myth, and by aligning intuition with representation (the representative function), which is made possible by language.

The introduction of empirical psychology into transcendental philosophy is not the only way in which the turn to the philosophy of symbolic forms leads to a revision of an earlier view. In the last section, I claimed that Cassirer's logicism in KMM and *SF* is distinctive in having no foundationalist pretensions, and indeed I claimed that the transcendental method rules out grounding arithmetic in something prior to it. But once Cassirer aligns the progression perception/intuition/knowledge with the progression myth/language/science, it is inevitable that science be seen as in some sense grounded in myth and language. In the preface to *PSF* 3, Cassirer writes:

> The third volume of *The Philosophy of Symbolic Forms* represents a return to the investigations with which I began my work in systematic philosophy two decades ago. ... But the question of the fundamental form of knowledge is now raised in a *broader and more universal sense*. In my book *Substanzbegriff und Funktionsbegriff* (1910) ... the form of knowledge as there defined *coincided essentially with the form of exact science*. Both in content and in method, the Philosophy of Symbolic Forms has gone beyond this initial formulation of the problem. It has *broadened* the concept of theory by showing that there are formative factors of a truly theoretical kind that govern the shaping not only of the scientific world view but of also of the natural world view implicit in perception and intuition. And finally, the Philosophy of Symbolic Forms was driven even beyond the natural world view of experience and observation, when the mythical world disclosed relationships which, though not reducible to the laws of empirical thinking, are by no means without their laws, and reveal a structural form of specific and independent character. In the first and second volumes of this work I have attempted to set forth these relationships. In the present volume we shall strive to bring out the newly acquired concept of "theory" in its full scope and entire range of formative potentialities. We shall see how *those other strata of spiritual life* that our analysis of language and myth has laid bare *support [unterbreiten und untergebaut]* the stratum of conceptual, *discursive knowledge*; and *with constant reference to this substructure [Unterbau]* we shall attempt to determine the particularity, organization, and architectonics of the superstructure [Oberbau]—that is, of science.[23]

Science is now "supported" by myth and language, and so—returning to the case that concerns us in this paper—arithmetic is the superstructure that is supported by the substructures, which are number in myth and number in language.

Clearly, the nature of this "supporting" relation needs to be made clear. The relation cannot be a logical relation, understood on the model of premises and conclusions in a formal inference, since these sorts of logical relations make sense only within the symbolic form of science. And this supporting relation cannot just be a causal relation, either, since this would reduce the *quid juris* to the *quid facti*, contrary to the transcendental character of Cassirer's inquiry. But this is a large question, which I cannot address any further here. In any case, once Cassirer takes seriously that scientific arithmetic is "supported" by number in perception and intuition (which can be triangulated through empirical psychology and the analysis of the symbolic forms of myth and language), the real possibility opens up that the earlier analysis of arithmetic in *SF* and KMM (which were based on a transcendental analysis of scientific arithmetic

---

23 Cassirer (1957), xiii.

alone) would need to be revised. After all, there are now whole new classes of data that Cassirer's philosophy needs to fit.

My point can be made in a different way. There are two contrasting models of the relation between the philosophy of the exact science in *SF* and in *PSF*: relocation and revision. On the relocation model, all of the positive claims made about exact science in *SF* can be carried over unaltered into the world of *PSF*, though with a new realization that the form of science is not the only form of objectification possible, and that the categories of exact science, such as number, appear in a different form in each of the other symbolic forms. On the revision model, the positive claims made about exact science in *SF* cannot all just be carried over unaltered into the world of *PSF*. Some of Cassirer's rhetoric suggests the relocation model. For instance, in the long quoted passage from *PSF* 3,[24] Cassirer talks about the move from *SF* and *PSF* as a move towards "broadening" the transcendental question, which might suggest that the old answers to the narrow question could remain unrevised. However, the latter part of that same quotation argues that the symbolic forms are not all independent of one another, but that the forms of myth and language "support" the form of science. I've been arguing on this basis for the revision model: *PSF*'s account of science must respect the fact that language and myth (whose character can be triangulated by looking at two other classes of data) support it; but an application of the transcendental method to exact science alone (as in *SF*) might not respect that fact.[25]

3 Number in the Symbolic Forms

In the previous section, I identified three ways in which the philosophy of arithmetic in *PSF* departs from *SF*. In *PSF*, Cassirer argues for a place within transcendental philosophy for empirical work on the psychology of number. In *PSF* Cassirer seems to endorse Poincaré's view that inferences in arithmetic are grounded in pure intuition. In *PSF*, Cassirer argues that pure arithmetic is "supported" by number in the symbolic forms of myth and language, introducing a kind of foundational project not present in *SF*. These latter two claims are particularly mysterious. What could Cassirer mean by calling mathematical induction a "genuine a priori synthesis"? In what way does number in perception and intuition support arithmetic in the symbolic form of science? In this final section,

---

24 Ibid.
25 In Heis (2010 and 2011), I was operating under the relocation model—an interpretive strategy that I now think was mistaken.

I'll address these questions by canvassing some of the claims Cassirer makes about number in the other symbolic forms. In particular, I'll argue that an understanding of how number in perception and intuition support the concept of number in science can explain what Cassirer thinks can play the role of the "intuition" of the "ability of the mind," which Poincaré says grounds mathematical induction.

To start, Cassirer is very clear that the structuralist concept of number as positions in a simply infinite structure does not appear in the other symbolic forms.

In myth, numbers are not mere positions, they are individuals with distinct sacred properties.[26] E.g., the number 7 is sacred, representing fullness, divinity, or blessedness. Moreover, in some languages, numerals are derived from words for body parts. In Sotho, "five" means "complete the hand" and "six" means "jump". In British New Guinea, the sequence in counting runs from the fingers of the left hand to the wrist, the elbow, the shoulder, left side of the neck, the left breast, the chest, the right breast, the right side of the neck, etc.[27] In each of these cases, the numbers are related in some essential way not just to each other, but also to parts of the human body. In other languages, there are distinct numerals for distinct kinds of things. E.g., in some Native American languages, there are different numerals for animate and inanimate things, and in the Klamath language different numerals are used depending on whether the objects to be counted are spread out on the ground, piled in layers, divided into heaps, or arranged in rows. This shows that numerals are being used to name an "intuitive quality": "As long as number is seen as a quality of things, there must fundamentally be as many diverse numbers and groups of numbers as there are diverse classes of things".[28] Numbers are therefore not positions in structures, but name certain intrinsic properties of intuited objects, just as color or shape words do. Cassirer concludes, then, that number in language is not independent of space and time, and is not non-empirical.

The longest discussion of empirical results concerning the psychology of number appears in the chapter devoted to psychopathology, where *inter alia* he discusses the arithmetical abilities of aphasics.[29] (Aphasics are especially interesting cases for Cassirer because his connection between intuition and language would be confirmed if an aphasic's linguistic impairment brought with it an impairment of representative functions.) Cassirer recounts some interesting experiments:

---

26 Cassirer (1955b), 140 ff.
27 Cassirer (1955a), 230.
28 Cassirer (1955a), 233.
29 Cassirer (1957), 248–261.

a) A patient says the numerals correctly in order and points to objects as he says the numerals. But he counts the same object multiple times, and at the end does not know how to answer the question How many?
b) A patient cannot answer the question Is 25>13? without counting up from 0 and seeing which number comes last.
c) A patient can answer 7+3 and 7−3 (or 10−3), but cannot know that 7+3−3=7 without counting out 7+3 then counting back 3 from 10.

Cassirer interprets case a) as showing that aphasics lack the ability to discretize, unify, and order, which he believes are three kinds of mental acts necessary for counting. For example, to count five objects, a subject needs to be able to do the following things:
1) Represent $a \neq b \neq c \neq d \neq e$. [act of discretion]
2) Recite the numerals in order.
3) Relate the objects 1–1 with the recited numerals. I.e., let a be 1, let b be 2, etc. [act of ordering]
4) Conclude: the number of objects is 5. [act of unity formation]

Cassirer's point is that language is essential to all four of these acts, and this explains why an aphasic may say the numerals correctly as he points at the counted objects, but nevertheless count the same object multiple times, and at the end not know how to answer the question How many?:

> For any adequate representation of the meaning of pure numerical concepts the support of language is indispensable. Only when specified in the word can the apartness of elements that is posited and demanded in the concept of number be fixated... And to this lack of distinction is linked an analogous deficiency in the seemingly contrary but actually correlative act of unity formation.[30]

Cassirer interprets cases b) and c) as showing that aphasics lack the ability to "recoordinize." For the competent language-user, each number can be thought of as a new 0. That is, to compute 7 + 5, I can begin at 7, treating it as 0, and count up 5 units from 7 in order to arrive at my answer. When I am asked to compute 7−3+3, I don't need to carry out 7+3 and then 10−3—as the patient in case c) did—because I can view 7 as my starting point from which I count up 3 and then count back 3. But I can't see that adding and subtracting 3 would just get me back to "where I started" unless I can conceive of 7 as a possible place to start, as a new 0. Similarly, the aphasic in case b) cannot just start counting

---

30 Ibid., 249–250.

at 13 to see whether 25 comes after it, because he cannot begin counting except at 0.

These facts about number in myth and language and about the empirical results of studies of aphasics illustrate how number in the other symbolic forms "support" scientific arithmetic, understood in Dedekind's way, as the non-empirical and non-intuitive science of positions in a structure. Consider, for instance, those languages that derive the numerals from the names of body parts that are pointed to when counting. Already here, linguistic thought is beginning to pull out "order in progression" as an essential aspect of number. After all, using the word for shoulder to mean 8 makes sense only when there is a canonical way to order the parts of the body: elbow after wrist, shoulder after elbow, etc.[31] Further, Cassirer argues that seeing what aphasics lack shows that number in intuition and language is an incipient form of number as Dedekind conceives of it. In fact, in the process of interpreting these aphasic cases, Cassirer writes:

> In his book *Was sind und was sollen die Zahlen?* Dedekind, a modern mathematician, reduces the whole system of natural numbers to a single basic logical function: he considers this system to be grounded in the 'ability of the mind to relate things to things, to make a thing correspond to a thing, or to image a thing in a thing.'[32]

Cases b) and c) show that the non-pathological representation of number in language allows for the ability to recoordinize. This ability, in turn, demonstrates that the numbers lack intrinsic characters. I can treat 7 as a new 0, 8 as a new 1, etc., because there are no intrinsic properties had by 8 that is not had by 1: each number is in itself identical to any other, and all that matters is the order in the progression. Case a) shows that the use of number in intuition already requires acts of discretion, ordering, and unifying, the very acts that Dedekind says are sufficient to characterize the number concept and thus ground arithmetic.

The structuralist concept of number is thus a further abstraction from the concept of number already present in language and intuition. In the same way, the ability to reason by induction is a more abstract form of reasoning implicit in language and intuition, where humans are already thinking of numbers as fundamentally what can be reached by repeated steps through an "order in progression." In these ways, number in the other symbolic forms "supports" number in exact science. According a standard foundationalist form of logicism, mathematical truths, whose *certainty* might otherwise be in doubt, gets to inherit

---

31 Cassirer (1955a), 238.
32 Cassirer (1957), 257.

the privileged epistemological status enjoyed by *logical truths,* from which the mathematical truths can be *proved*. The view in *PSF* obviously differs from this view in many ways. There is no suggestion at all that numerical thinking in myth and language is more certain than that in scientific arithmetic, or that the relation of support between the symbolic forms has anything to do with transference of certainty. What is given as a support for mathematics is not a stock of logical truths, but the forms of numerical thinking in myth and language, expression and perception. And to say that number in the other symbolic forms supports arithmetic in the symbolic form of science clearly does not mean that the latter is provable from the former. Instead, the concept of number as a position in a simply infinite system makes explicit what was implicit in number in language and myth. Put another way, in the progression from myth to language, the numbers are beginning to be freed of any intrinsic properties, and are shedding their relations to space, time, and experience. The concept of number as a position in a simply infinite system is the culmination of that progression, completing what was already started in the move from myth to language, expression to intuition.

The progression from number in the other symbolic forms to number in the symbolic form of science is, I believe, what Cassirer was getting at when he echoes Poincaré's claim that mathematical induction is grounded in a "genuine a priori synthesis". Initial appearances notwithstanding, this is not a return to an orthodox Kantianism in which arithmetic is grounded in pure intuition—where pure intuition is a kind of a priori representation that is distinct from conceptual representations and that is grounded in the constitution of the mind. The transcendental reflection on number in the various symbolic forms is Cassirer's replacement for an "intuition" of the "ability of the mind" that Poincaré says grounds mathematical induction. The truth of mathematical induction (as well as all the other Dedekind/Peano axioms of arithmetic) simply follows from the fact that numbers are no more than positions in a simply infinite system. And since the concept of number as a position in a simply infinite system is supported by number in myth and language, the principle of induction make explicit what was already implicit in number in the other symbolic forms, and is the end point in a progression that began with the move from number in myth to number in language. There is therefore no need within the symbolic form of science to try to prove the principle of induction on the basis of some prior theory of classes (as in logicists like Frege and Russell). In the same way, for Cassirer there is no need to appeal to some sui generis kind of non-conceptual "pure intuition," as in intuitionists like Brouwer or even Poincaré.[33] The move to *PSF* then explains the move toward letting mathematical induction be a primitive principle knowable by "a priori synthesis".[34]

Bibliography

Benacerraf (1960): Paul Benacerraf, *Logicism, Some Considerations*, Princeton Ph.D. Dissertation, University Microfilms.
Cassirer (1907): Ernst Cassirer, "Kant und die moderne Mathematik", *Kant-Studien* 12, 1–40.
Cassirer (1910): Ernst Cassirer, *Substanzbegriff und Funktionsbegriff. Untersuchungen über die Grundfragen der Erkenntniskritik*, Berlin: Bruno Cassirer.
Cassirer (1923a): Ernst Cassirer, *Philosophie der symbolischen Formen. Erster Teil: Die Sprache*. Berlin: Bruno Cassirer.
Cassirer (1923b): Ernst Cassirer, *Substance and Function,* William Curtis Swabey and Marie Collins Swabey (trans.), Chicago: Open Court.
Cassirer (1925): Ernst Cassirer, *Philosophie der symbolischen Formen. Zweiter Teil: Das mythische Denken*, Berlin: Bruno Cassirer.
Cassirer (1993): "Zur Theorie des Begriffs," as reprinted in: Bast, R. (ed.), *Erkenntnis, Begriff, Kultur*, Hamburg: Felix Meiner Verlag, 155–164.
Cassirer (1929): *Philosophie der Symbolischen Formen. Dritter Teil: Phänomenologie der Erkenntnis*, Berlin: Bruno Cassirer.
Cassirer (1955a): Ernst Cassirer, *The Philosophy of Symbolic Forms, Volume One: Language*, Ralph Manheim (trans.), New Haven: Yale University Press.
Cassirer (1955b): Ernst Cassirer, *The Philosophy of Symbolic Forms, Volume Two: Mythical Thought*, Ralph Manheim (trans.), New Haven: Yale University Press.
Cassirer (1957): Ernst Cassirer, *The Philosophy of Symbolic Forms, Volume Three: The Phenomenology of Knowledge,* Ralph Manheim (trans.), New Haven: Yale University Press.
Cassirer (1999): Ernst Cassirer, "Ziele und Wege der Wirklichkeitserkenntnis", in: Klaus Christian Köhnke and John Michael Krois (eds.), *Nachgelassene Manuskripte und Texte*, vol. 2, Hamburg: Felix Meiner Verlag.
Dedekind (1963): Richard Dedekind, "The Nature and Meaning of Numbers", in: *Essays on the Theory of Numbers*, Wooster Woodruff Beman (trans.), New York: Dover, 29–115.

---

33 This shows, I believe, that Cassirer's enthusiasm for intuitionism is quite limited: it does not extend to positing a faculty of pure intuition that can ground arithmetic. He is sympathetic with intuitionists' negative claims—Don't ground arithmetic in the theory of classes!—and with Poincaré's claim that the principle of induction can be treated as a primitive within scientific arithmetic.

34 I would like to thank the participants of the conference "The Philosophy of Ernst Cassirer: A Novel Assessment," and especially its organizer, Sebastian Luft. I owe a special debt to Pierre Keller, who has raised to me on numerous occasions the real possibility that Cassirer's views in *SF* would need to be revised in *PSF*, and not just relocated. Of course, all remaining faults are my own.

Frege (1884): Gottlob Frege, *Die Grundlagen der Arithmetik. Eine logisch-matheamtische Untersuchung über den Begriff der Zahl*, Breslau: Koebner.
Frege (1879): Gottlob Frege, *Begriffsschrift, eine der arithmetischen nachgebildeten Formelsprache des reinen Denkens*, Halle: Nebert.
Frege (1955): Gottlob Frege, *The Foundations of Arithmetic,* J. L. Austin (trans.), Oxford: Blackwell.
Gower (2000): Barry Gower, "Cassirer, Schlick and 'Structural' Realism: The Philosophy of the Exact Sciences in the Background to Early Logical Empiricism", *British Journal for the History of Philosophy* 8 (No. 1), 71–106.
Heis (2010): Jeremy Heis, "'Critical philosophy begins at the very point where logistic leaves off': Cassirer's response to Frege and Russell", *Perspectives on Science* 18, 383–408.
Heis (2011): Jeremy Heis, "Ernst Cassirer's Neo-Kantian Philosophy of Geometry", *The British Journal of the History of Philosophy* 19, 759–94.
Heis (2014): Jeremy Heis, "Ernst Cassirer's *Substanzbegriff und Funktionsbegriff*", *HOPOS: The Journal of the International Society for the History of Philosophy of Science* 4, 241–70.
Mormann and Katz (2013): Thomas Mormann and Mikhail G. Katz, "Infinitesimals as an issue of neo-Kantian philosophy of science", *HOPOS: The Journal of the International Society for the History of Phiilosophy of Science* 3, 236–280.
Mormann (2008): Thomas Mormann, "Idealization in Cassirer's Philosophy of Mathematics", *Philosophia Mathematica* 16 (No. 2), 151–181.
Poincaré (1902/2001): Henri Poincaré, "On the Nature of Mathematical Reasoning", W.J. Greenstreet (trans.), as reprinted in: *The Value of Science: Essential Writings of Henri Poincaré*, New York: The Modern Library, 9–19.
Reck (2012): Erich Reck, "Dedekind's Contributions to the Foundations of Mathematics", in: *The Stanford Encyclopedia of Philosophy*, E. Zalta (ed.): http://plato.stanford.edu/archives/win2012/entries/dedekind-foundations/.
Russell (1903): Bertrand Russell, *The Principles of Mathematics*, New York: Norton.
Yap (forthcoming): Audrey Yap, "Dedekind and Cassirer on Mathematical Concept Formation", *Philosophia Mathematica*.

Scott Edgar (Halifax)
Intersubjectivity and Physical Laws in Post-Kantian Theory of Knowledge Natorp and Cassirer

1 Intersubjectivity and Physical Laws in Post-Kantian Theory of Knowledge

Consider the claims that representations of physical laws are intersubjective, and that they ultimately provide the foundation for all other intersubjective knowledge. Those claims, as well as the deeper philosophical commitments that justify them, constitute rare points of agreement between the Marburg School neo-Kantians Paul Natorp and Ernst Cassirer and their positivist rival, Ernst Mach. This is surprising, since Natorp and Cassirer are both often at pains to distinguish their theories of natural scientific knowledge from positivist views like Mach's, and often from Mach's views in particular. Thus the very fact of this agreement between the Marburg School neo-Kantians and their positivist stalking horse points to a deep current of ideas that runs beneath the whole of the post-Kantian intellectual context they shared.

In fact, the view that representations of physical laws are intersubjective was ubiquitous in German-language philosophy in the late nineteenth and early twentieth centuries. Neo-Kantians and non-neo-Kantians alike, as well as philosophers and scientists on both sides of the debate between psychologism and anti-psychologism, maintain versions of this view. For example, Hermann von Helmholtz, the physicist and physiologist who set the program for the movement of physiological neo-Kantianism, maintains that representations of physical laws are "objective", and so intersubjective as well.[1] Alternatively, Hermann Lotze, whose anti-psychologistic metaphysics stood as an early and influential alternative to both neo-Kantianism and psychologism, defends the view that representations of physical laws are "universal" in the sense that they are intersubjective.[2]

In fact, Lotze's discussion can give the impression that the ubiquitous post-Kantian link between physical laws and intersubjectivity has a very simple ex-

---

1 Helmholtz (1977).
2 Lotze (1884), 2–3.

planation: physical laws are universal, and so they are precisely what can be represented universally. But of course, this is just a pun. Physical laws are (or aim to be) "universal" in the sense that they are exceptionless in space and time, whereas we want a philosophical explanation for why representations of them would be "universal" in the sense of being intersubjective. These two uses of the word 'universal' go back to Kant. But regardless of pedigree, equivocating between two different meanings of a word does not constitute a satisfying philosophical explanation. What we want to know is: why are representations of laws that are exceptionless in space and time intersubjective?

I aim to explain why, for Natorp and Cassirer, representations of physical laws are intersubjective. The guiding idea of the explanation I will offer is so simple as to be banal: physical laws are (or aim to be) valid across all regions and scales of space and time. But then, they are precisely what different subjects, with different positions in space and time, can all share identical representations of. Unfortunately, matters are not so simple. That simple idea turns out to be very difficult to articulate in a way that is consistent with Natorp's and Cassirer's (and even Mach's) accounts of the subject of knowledge—that is, the knower. Thus my task in what follows is to develop an account of that guiding idea that is consistent with their views.

To that end, I begin in §2 by placing this view in the context of their respective accounts of the objectivity of natural scientific knowledge. §3 considers Natorp's and Cassirer's accounts of subjectivity—that is, their accounts of the epistemic idiosyncrasy that some representations have, and that prevents those representations from being shared or available to all subjects universally. In §4, I argue that Mach provides surprising resources for further developing the idea of that epistemic idiosyncrasy. In the context of a discussion of Mach, I introduce the idea of what I call a *point of view*. I argue that it explains why certain experiences fail to be intersubjective, and also why representations of physical laws *are* intersubjective.

§5 faces the difficulty of interpreting these ideas in a way that is consistent with Natorp's, Cassirer's, and even Mach's views: I consider a simple explanation for why certain representations have points of view; I argue that neither Mach, Natorp, nor Cassirer can accept that explanation; and I consider their accounts of the relation between representations with points of view and the subjects who have those experiences. Finally, §6 makes it clear just how differently these ideas are developed in Natorp's and Cassirer's hands, as opposed to Mach's. Finally, I conclude in §7 by briefly considering the significance of the underlying agreement between Mach, Natorp, and Cassirer.

Finally, before anything else, I must stress how limited the ambitions of the present essay are. A completely convincing account of Natorp's and Cassirer's accounts of physical laws and intersubjectivity would have to do two things. First, it would have to trace the development of those accounts through all of their relevant writings. Second, it would have to attend to the differences between Natorp's and Cassirer's views, as well as their views' similarities. I make no attempt to do either of these things in the present essay. In what follows, I will draw from only enough texts to start sketching a picture of Natorp's views from the 1880 s to the 1910 s and Cassirer's views in 1910: namely, Natorp's 1887 essay, "On the Objective and Subjective Grounds of Knowledge", his 1888 book, *Introduction to Psychology according to the Critical Method*, his 1912 expansion of that book, *General Psychology according to the Critical Method*, and Cassirer's 1910 *Substance and Function*. Further, I will attend principally to points of overlap between Natorp's and Cassirer's views, often eliding details where their views differ. For those two reasons, the interpretation I defend below is necessarily provisional.

2 Three Elements of Natorp's and Cassirer's Conceptions of Objectivity

Enough throat-clearing. The question of why, for Natorp and Cassirer, representations of physical laws are intersubjective is ultimately a question about their views of the objectivity of natural scientific knowledge. We need to begin by seeing how that question emerges from their remarks about objectivity. There are multiple elements to both Natorp's and Cassirer's views of objectivity. Three of those elements are especially relevant for present purposes.

First, Natorp and (even more clearly) Cassirer maintain that our knowledge is objective when we represent objects determinately—that is, when we represent objects with definite conditions for their identities. On this view, having objective knowledge of an object requires that we have criteria for determining that an object we represent is the object it is, and not some other object.

Although Natorp and Cassirer have somewhat different views on this point, both maintain roughly that the identity conditions of objects are established in the context of a framework or structure that different individual objects are located in. The identity conditions of objects are given by different locations in this framework. Since those locations are well-defined and unique, they can constitute well-defined and unique identity conditions for objects.

The second element of both Natorp's and Cassirer's accounts of objectivity concerns the framework or structure within which objects have well-defined identity conditions. For both Natorp and Cassirer, those frameworks are constituted by—and so the objectivity of our knowledge is established by—relations in our experience that are constant or invariant over changes in the content of that experience. In other words, the framework is constituted by, and so our knowledge's objectivity is established by, *laws* in our experience. As Natorp puts it in 1887, "The objectification of appearance is carried out in the reduction to law; there is no other way".[3]

Cassirer has a somewhat more nuanced articulation of the idea that laws are objective, but he ultimately shares that view with Natorp. In a way that Natorp does not, Cassirer emphasizes that what is objective in our experience are *constant relations* between experiences. Throughout *Substance and Function*, Cassirer emphasizes the idea that objectivity consists in, as he variously puts it, constancy, invariance, permanence, or fixity in our experience. He emphasizes this idea again and again. For example,

> Whenever a *system of conditions* is given that can be realized in different contents, there we can hold to the form of the system itself as an invariant, undisturbed by the difference in contents, and develop its laws deductively. In this way, we produce a new "objective" form.[4]

But for Cassirer, the most significant expression of the idea that objectivity consists in constant relations within experience is his doctrine of "the universal invariants of experience". The universal invariants are those relations within our experience that do not just remain constant throughout all testing of a particular theory at a particular stage in science's evolution through history. They remain constant throughout the entirety of that evolution from theory to theory. The universal invariants are thus the relations that turn out to be constant across all changes in scientific theories throughout the entire history of science. But what is more, for Cassirer, these universal invariants are what ultimately constitute the object of knowledge. That is, it is ultimately in virtue of them that we can know *objectively*.[5]

Consequently, for Cassirer what is objective in our experience are the constant and permanent relations within it. But those constant and permanent rela-

---

[3] Natorp (1981), 255. And again in 1888: "As to the final objective grounds of the truth of knowledge, the issue called for is nothing other than the reduction of phenomena to laws of the highest order; the objectifying process would drive to the highest laws, which originally determine all objectivity of knowledge". Natorp (1888), 105. And in 1912: "Knowledge of objects is based on knowledge of laws ..." Natorp (1912), 154. That passage comes from a section of Natorp's *General Psychology* that he titles, none too subtly, "Objectification = knowledge of laws".
[4] Cassirer (1923), 40.
[5] Ibid., 268–270.

tions are, paradigmatically, physical laws. Thus for Cassirer, as for Natorp, our representations of physical laws are objective.

The connection between the first and second elements of Natorp's and Cassirer's theories of objectivity should be clear. Recall, the first element was that objects have their unique identity conditions defined by locations within some framework or structure. The second element is that the objectivity of our knowledge consists in constant, permanent relations within experience—paradigmatically, physical laws. For both Natorp and Cassirer, those physical laws, the constant, permanent relations within experience established by mathematical natural science, constitute the framework within which objects' identity conditions are defined.

The third element of Natorp's and Cassirer's theories of objectivity is intersubjectivity. Neither Natorp nor Cassirer emphasizes this idea as clearly as they emphasize the idea that laws or constant relations within experience are objective. Nevertheless, it is clear that both think objective knowledge must be independent of whatever representations happen to occur in the mind of an individual subject. They thus maintain that objective knowledge cannot be particular to an individual subject, and in that sense idiosyncratic. Natorp is especially clear about this in his 1887 essay:

> Objective validity signifies a validity that is independent of the subjectivity of knowledge—this is well established. What is to be objectively valid is to be valid apart from the givenness of its representation in this or that consciousness.[6]

First, Natorp tells us that objective knowledge must be "independent of the subjectivity of knowledge". He glosses that by saying that objective knowledge must be "valid apart from the givenness of its representation in this or that consciousness". That is, the "independence" of knowledge consists in the fact that it is independent of the minds of individual knowers. As he says later in the same essay, objective knowledge is knowledge that is "unanimously valid for all subjects in all circumstances".[7] In other words, objective knowledge is intersubjective.

For his part, Cassirer is clear enough in *Substance and Function* that he has the same view. Like Natorp, Cassirer thinks objective knowledge is independent of the individual knower. He says, for example,

---

6 Natorp (1981), 252.
7 Ibid., 256.

> No judgement of natural science is limited to establishing what sensuous impressions are found in the consciousness of an individual observer at a definite, strictly limited point of time.[8]

So for Cassirer, objective knowledge is independent of whatever representations happen to occur in the minds of individual knowers. In just that sense for Cassirer, objective knowledge is intersubjective.

However, with this third element of Natorp's and Cassirer's theories of objectivity, we arrive at our principal question. It is clear how the first element of their theories of objectivity relates to the second: laws and constant relations within experience constitute the structures within which objects' identity conditions are defined. But what connection is there between the second element and the third? On their view, representations of physical laws are objective, and objective representations are intersubjective. So for both Natorp and Cassirer, representations of laws must be intersubjective. But what philosophical explanation is there for this claim? What underlying commitments justify it for them?

3 Subjectivity and Epistemic Idiosyncrasy

If we want to answer these questions about Natorp's and Cassirer's accounts of intersubjectivity, recent work in historical epistemology suggests a fruitful interpretive strategy for us to pursue. Lorraine Daston and Peter Galison (2007), and most recently Ian Hacking (forthcoming), have argued that when historical figures appeal to a distinction between subjective and objective representations, the meaning of the term "objective" is fixed only in relation to the meaning of the term "subjective". Reciprocally, the meaning of the term "subjective" is often fixed in relation to the term "objective". Thus the concepts *objectivity* and *subjectivity* must be understood in relation to one another, as a pair.[9]

In fact, Natorp himself suggests that his view of objectivity can be understood only in relation to his view of subjectivity. In his 1887 essay, after he has begun the task of articulating his view of objectivity, including how it consists in intersubjectivity, he explicitly raises the question of why our representations of laws are objective and so too intersubjective. Then, to begin answering the question, he writes: "the answer to this will be found in the most direct way if we first succeed in understanding the meaning of that subjectivity which must

---

8 Cassirer (1923), 242.
9 Daston and Galison (2007), chapter 1.

be overcome in the representation of the object.[10] What follows is an important, if opaque, sketch of how Natorp conceives of subjectivity, details of which he would start to elaborate only in his book on psychology the following year. For now, what is important to notice is just that Natorp himself acknowledges that in order to understand his views of objectivity and intersubjectivity, we must first understand his view of subjectivity.

It is worth considering why the meaning of the concept objectivity can be determined fully only in relation to a corresponding concept of subjectivity. "Objectivity" is a term of epistemic success. It connotes an epistemic achievement. In contrast, "subjectivity" is a term of (at least partial) epistemic failure. Philosophers use the term to express a threat to epistemic success or an obstacle that epistemic achievement must overcome. But there is no way to understand what the epistemic achievement really amounts to without also understanding the epistemic threat or obstacle that it overcomes. To the extent that philosophers have different anxieties about different threats or obstacles to epistemic success, they will have different conceptions of exactly what kind of achievement that epistemic success amounts to. Thus, for example, Daston and Galison argue that as philosophers' and scientists' conceptions of subjectivity evolved over the course of the first half of the nineteenth century—as they came to have different anxieties about threats to knowledge—that evolution was accompanied by a parallel evolution in philosophers' and scientists' conceptions of objectivity.

Further, this point about how the concept of objectivity gets its meaning only in relation to the concept of subjectivity applies even more forcefully to the concept of intersubjectivity. For intersubjectivity is an epistemic achievement that overcomes the epistemic threat posed by subjectivity. Consequently, if we want to understand the details of how Natorp and Cassirer conceive of intersubjectivity and why they think representations of physical laws are intersubjective, we must also understand their conceptions of subjectivity.

As a first pass at those conceptions of subjectivity, Natorp and Cassirer make it clear that, for them, subjective representations are *idiosyncratic*. The mark of subjectivity is thus that subjective representations vary from one individual to another. On this view, representations are subjective if there is no shared standard with which we can judge that one individual's representation is correct and another individual's different representation is incorrect. The idiosyncrasy of such representations constitutes a threat to epistemic success: it means the representations fail to be shared by all individuals, and so fail to be intersubjec-

---

10 Natorp (1981), 256.

tive. In this respect at least, Natorp's and Cassirer's conceptions of subjectivity are entirely characteristic of post-Kantian theories of knowledge.

Thus Natorp, in his 1887 essay, explicitly contrasts objective (and so intersubjective) representations with representations that are valid only "for this or that consciousness"[11]—that is, representations that are idiosyncratic, that vary from individual to individual, and so are subjective. Further, he is explicit that what overcomes that subjectivity is a shared standard that is independent of any individual knower's representations, and that can be used to assess and compare different knowers' different representations.[12] In *Substance and Function*, Cassirer puts these points in almost identical terms. He says that "subjectively valid" representations are those "concerning momentary and *individual* experience" and that are "accidentally found together in *individual* consciousness".[13] He explicitly contrasts these subjective representations with representations that are "based in the object itself and independent of the condition of this or that sensing individual".[14]

Thus for Natorp and Cassirer, subjective representations are idiosyncratic; they vary from one individual to another. Still, this point on its own does not give us a full enough account of their conception of subjectivity to shed much light on their conceptions of intersubjectivity. In particular, it is not enough to explain why, on their view, our representations of physical laws are intersubjective. That explanation will come only with a much more detailed account of how Natorp and Cassirer think about the idiosyncrasy that subjective representations exhibit. It will be provided by an account of idiosyncrasy, as they conceive it, that makes clear exactly how that idiosyncrasy is overcome by our representations of physical laws.

4 Mach and the Idea of a Point of View

Ernst Mach—precisely the figure both Natorp and Cassirer come back to again and again as a stalking horse—provides an illustration of exactly the conception of idiosyncrasy that we need.

On its face, this is an implausible interpretive claim. First, Mach is precisely the kind of positivist that Natorp takes as his stalking horse in his 1887 essay. Second, one of the central philosophical aims of his 1888 and 1912 books on psy-

---

[11] Ibid., 252.
[12] Ibid., 252–253.
[13] Cassirer (1923), 245; emphasis added.
[14] Ibid., 246.

chology is to defend the view that psychology has a method that is fundamentally unlike the methods of natural science, a view that Natorp clearly intends to contrast with Mach's view that psychology has essentially the *same* method as natural science. Third, Mach is a radical empiricist, and has precisely the kind of empiricist, abstractionist account of concept-formation that Natorp criticizes explicitly as early as 1887 and that Cassirer takes to be his principal stalking horse in *Substance and Function*. Fourth, Mach has a very different conception of physical law than Natorp or Cassirer: on his view, laws are nothing but relatively stable relations between experiences that we attend to because it is useful for us to do so. But while Cassirer acknowledges that a physical law's fruitfulness for further scientific inquiry can be a reason to accept it,[15] neither he nor Natorp accepts the view that a law's usefulness for practical human ends constitutes a reason for science to accept it. Finally, Mach's theory of knowledge is an example of exactly the kind of psychologism that Natorp and Cassirer reject decisively throughout their writings, and at least in the case of Natorp's early arguments against psychologism, it is likely that Mach is above all the figure he has in mind as the target of his arguments.

But be that as it may, Mach illustrates a conception of idiosyncrasy that provides exactly what we are looking for—an explanation of why representations of physical laws overcome the idiosyncrasy of subjective representations. When I say that Mach *illustrates* that conception of idiosyncrasy, I mean it literally. He illustrates it with an image that appears in the introductory chapter of his 1884 *Contributions to the Analysis of Sensations*.

For Mach, this image is an illustration of what (relatively) subjective experience looks like. That is, he understands this to be an illustration of something close to immediate sensory experience. It is his sketch of what he sees from his left eye, as he sits in his office. He is looking out and seeing, in the extreme foreground, the side of his own nose; then, in the mid-ground, the length of his own body as he lies on some kind of lounge; and finally, in the background, he is looking out over his own feet to the windows on the opposite wall.

However, Mach's image also illustrates an important conception of the idiosyncrasy of subjective representations. Mach's picture illustrates what I will call a point of view. The image's point of view consists in the perspectival structure exhibited by the representations pictured. That is, it consists in the limited, partial spatio-temporal structure those representations exhibit. In general, we can say that a set of representations has a point of view just in case the regions and scales of space and time they represent are partial and limited. That is,

---

[15] Cassirer (1923), 317–318.

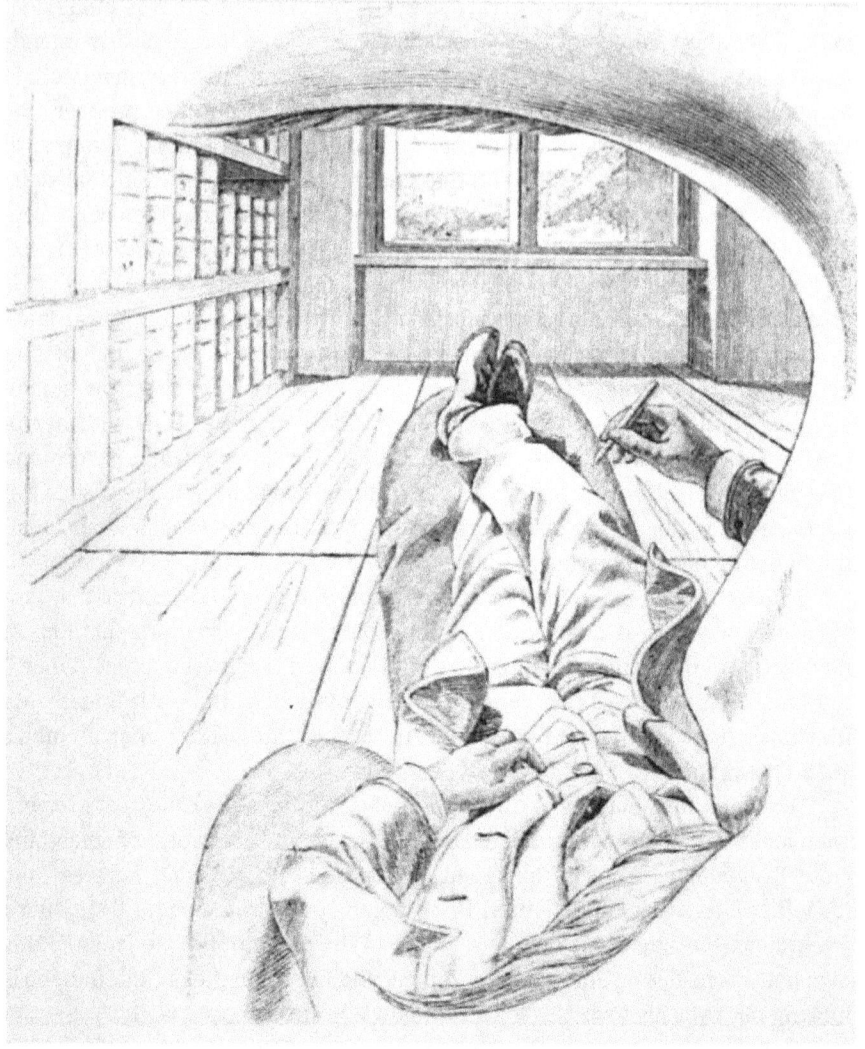

Fig. 1: Mach's Illustration of the Idiosyncracy of Subjective Representations

they do not represent space and time in their complete, all-encompassing totalities. Thus, for example, in Mach's illustration, we get representations of the region of space in one part of his office, and since it is a static image, only a single instant of time.

Representations that have a point of view in this sense will be idiosyncratic in just the way we are interested in. Since points of view are constituted by spatio-temporal structures that are limited and partial, it is always possible to have multiple points of view. But if there are multiple possible points of view, those points of view will be different—that is, they will represent different regions and scales of space and time. Consequently, different points of view will have different representations of whatever objects they represent. For example, representations of Mach's office from a point of view that is just outside the window in the background of his image would be different than the representations pictured in his image, structured as they are by their own point of view. But then, since different points of view will have different representations of the objects they represent, those representations will fail to be identical. The representations will not be shared by different points of view; they will be particular to their points of view, and thus will fail to be intersubjective. In just that sense, representations that have points of view will be idiosyncratic.

However, if points of view have the idiosyncrasy exhibited by subjective representations, then we can start to see exactly how representations of physical laws overcome that idiosyncrasy. We can start to see exactly why representations of physical laws might be intersubjective.

Physical laws are (or aim to be) universal, that is, exceptionless in space and time. That is, the more universal a law is, the more regions and scales of space and time it is valid for. If a law were absolutely universal, it would be valid for all regions and scales of space and time. But the more regions and scales of space and time a law is valid for, the more *points of view* it will be valid for. Since if the same law holds for different regions and scales of space and time, different points of view that represent these different regions and scales will nevertheless represent the same law. Thus despite their differences, different points of view will nevertheless represent the *same* law. In just that sense, representations of physical laws are what overcome the epistemic idiosyncrasy exhibited by points of view. In just that sense, representations of physical laws are intersubjective.

5 The Relation between a Point of View and the Subject of Knowledge

The key idea in the account I have just given is the idea of a point of view—that is, the idea of experiences that represent only limited, partial regions and scales of space and time. Those representations, in virtue of their limited perspectives, will be idiosyncratic, and so they will fail to be intersubjective. At the same time, representations of physical laws—laws that are (or aim to be) valid for all regions and scales of space and time—will not have that idiosyncrasy, and so will be intersubjective.

However, if the key idea is simply the idea of experiences that represent only limited, partial regions and scales of space and time, isn't there a much simpler way of thinking about them? And so isn't there a much simpler way of explaining why representations of physical laws are intersubjective?

Why not say this? There are a plurality of cognitive subjects—that is, knowers—at various points in space and time. These subjects' cognitive capacities are limited in at least this sense: their immediate or nearly immediate apprehension of the world around them is limited; that is, they do not immediately apprehend the totality of space and time as soon as they open their eyes, but rather have relatively immediate access only to what is in their vicinity. In this case, these subjects' representations will be of limited regions in space and time—that is, they will have points of view and the epistemic idiosyncrasy that comes with them. However, despite the fact that these subjects are situated at different places in space and time, they can all share identical representations of physical laws, since physical laws are (or aim to be) valid for all regions and scales of space and time.

The simplicity of this picture is attractive. Unfortunately, it is not a picture that we can attribute to Natorp or Cassirer, or even Mach. The picture makes at least two assumptions that all three figures reject.

First, the simple picture assumes that space and time exist, with determinate points in them that different subjects could be located at, and further, that space and time exist prior to or independently of the experience of the subjects located in them. Space and time must exist independently of the subjects' experience of them, because this picture invokes them to explain the limited, perspectival character of the subjects' experience. If space and time depended for their existence on the subjects' experience, they could not then provide a (non-circular) explanation of the perspectival character of that experience.

Second, the simple picture assumes that different subjects exist, and that their existence is independent of their experience. Once again, the subjects' existence must be independent of their experience, since the picture is invoked to explain the character of that experience.

Mach, Natorp, and Cassirer reject both of these assumptions. In *Analysis of Sensations*, Mach defends the view that (in a process that is partly unconscious and partly conscious) we construct our experience of space and time from simpler, more immediate sensory representations of extents and durations. But what is more, on the radically anti-metaphysical stance that he articulates, there is no space or time independently of or beyond the experiences we construct. Thus for

Mach, there is no space or time that is independent of experience, and that we could appeal to in order to explain experience's character.

At the same time, for Mach the subject is nothing but a provisional, if useful, collection of simple, sensation-like constituents of experience, constituents he calls "elements". The collection includes elements such as "colors, sounds, temperatures, pressures, spaces, times, and so forth," as well as "moods of mind, feelings, and volitions"[16]—the same kinds of elements that Mach thinks also make up objects. Some of these elements are collected together and put under the label "ego" or "I", because doing so makes it easier and more efficient for us to track important patterns and changes within experience. For example, Mach, suggests, grouping certain elements together under the label "I" makes it easier for us to reduce the number of painful elements in our experience and increase the number of pleasant elements.[17] Finally, if the subject is nothing but a useful collection of elements that are themselves constituents of experience, then the subject does not exist independently of experience. Thus Mach cannot accept appeals to the subject to explain anything about experience's character.

Although Natorp and Cassirer have very different views than Mach, they nevertheless also reject that picture. For both Natorp as early as his 1888 *Introduction to Psychology* and Cassirer in *Substance and Function*, space and time are the space and time represented in natural scientific experience.[18] Both reject as pre-critical metaphysics the idea that there could be any space or time independently of our natural scientific experience.

Both likewise reject the view that the subject exists independently of experience. On the view that Natorp defends in his 1888 and 1912 books on psychology, the subject is "reconstructed" within experience. In contrast, on his view, objective knowledge is "constructed" within experience. It is constructed, when the natural scientist begins with the limited and only partial lawlike relations within experience, and then establishes further lawlike relations of ever-increasing universality. Although, on Natorp's view, science will never succeed in establishing laws of absolute universality and so will never establish any absolutely objective knowledge, it nevertheless aims at that ideal.

Natorp is less clear than we might like about how philosophy and psychology "reconstruct" the subject of knowledge, but his view is clear enough for our purposes. Like the method of constructing objective knowledge, the method of

---

16 Mach (1890), 2.
17 Ibid., 19.
18 See, for example, the treatments of space in Natorp (1888), §§10–11, and Cassirer (1923), chapter 3.

reconstructing the subject of knowledge begins with experience containing limited and only partial lawlike relations. But then, the reconstructive method seeks to analyze apart these lawlike relations, revealing the less determinate experiences that had been made objective by the lawlike relations. Consequently, the reconstructive method seeks representations of lawlike relations of ever-*decreasing* universality. As the method isolates experiences of decreasing universality, those representations will be more and more subjective. Although, Natorp insists, this method will never succeed in revealing representations that are *absolutely* subjective, philosophy and psychology nevertheless aim at absolute subjectivity as an ideal for the reconstructive method.

For our purposes, what is important about this view is that for Natorp the subject is reconstructed within experience, rather than being independent of it. Thus Natorp must reject appeals to the subject to explain anything about experience's character.

Cassirer does not have an account of the subject of knowledge that is as well-developed as Natorp's. However, in *Substance and Function*, he is clear enough that he rejects any view on which the subject exists independently of experience. His explicit aim is to articulate an account of the subject that overcomes a hypostasized opposition between the subject and object of knowledge. That is, he wants to move decisively beyond the view that the subject and the object always stand in static opposition to one another, with an unbridgeable gap between them. He argues that the philosophical concepts of the subject of knowledge and the object of knowledge get their significance only in relation to the "universal functions of rational and empirical knowledge"[19]—that is, universal relations between experiences. Thus, he maintains, the subject and object always stand in a dynamic "correlation" to one another: as science establishes functional relations within experience of ever-increasing universality, there will be a parallel evolution of the concepts of the subject and the object that are defined in the context of that system of universal functions.

Admittedly, the details of Cassirer's account are far from clear. But what is clear from his account is that he cannot accept any view of the subject of knowledge on which the subject exists independently of experience and could explain anything about the character of that experience. For on his account, the concept of the subject gets its significance only in relation to a system of universal functions within experience.

So, like Mach, neither Natorp nor Cassirer can accept the view that the subject exists independently of experience, and whose existence in space and time

---

[19] Cassirer (1923), 309.

explains the character of its experience. Thus all three figures reject the two assumptions made by the simple explanation (considered at the beginning of this section) for why certain experiences represent only limited regions and scales of space and time, and thus why representations of physical laws are intersubjective.

However, if Mach, Natorp, and Cassirer all reject the view that subjects' locations in space and time explain why certain experiences represent only limited regions and scales of space and time, then what view can they have of the relation between those experiences and the subject that has them?

Mach and Natorp have views that have one philosophically interesting point in common, even if their views are ultimately very different. In effect, they take the natural view we have just considered and reverse the direction of its philosophical explanation. That is, they do not take the subject as basic and then appeal to it in order to explain why its experience exhibits a point of view. Instead, they take as basic—as a brute or given fact—that some experience represents only limited regions or scales of space and time. Then they appeal to that fact about experience in order to give their different accounts of the subject of knowledge.

As we have just seen, for Mach the subject is nothing but a collection of sensation-like elements we label "I". But some of the elements contained in the collection we label "I" will have spatio-temporal character. Mach says "spaces" and "times" are included among those elements, but also elements with color will also have shape and extension, and elements with tone or with tactile qualities will also have duration. Further, Mach's image illustrates the point that, on his view, the elements in the collection we label "I" will be arranged in a spatio-temporal structure that exhibits a point of view. However, crucially for Mach, the elements in the collection labeled "I" do not exhibit the spatio-temporal structure they do *because* they are representations of a subject that exists in space and time independently of experience. Rather, the fact that the elements are arranged in that particular spatio-temporal structure provides a partial explanation for why it is useful for us to group all of these different elements together under the label "I". That is, *because* the elements are contiguous in space and time, they capture only limited regions and scales of space and time, and are structured in such a way that it appears as if they flow outward from a single point, we find it useful to group them together in a single collection, and then name that collection "I".

For Natorp, as we have seen, psychology's reconstructive method produces a conception of the subject by revealing representations within experience of ever-decreasing universality. But then, the representations revealed by this method will be representations of increasingly limited and partial regions or scales of space and time. In other words, the reconstructive method seeks experiences that exhibit points of view. But then, on Natorp's view, it is precisely in virtue of the fact that these representations lack universality—and so represent only limited regions and scales of space and time—that they constitute the subject of knowledge. Thus for Natorp, the subject of knowledge is reconstructed precisely from experiences that exhibit points of view. So like Mach, Natorp does not appeal to the subject to explain why its experience has a point of view; rather he appeals to experience that has a point of view, in order to explain our conception of the subject.

6 Points of View in Natorp's and Cassirer's Theories of Knowledge

I have argued that Mach's views, and especially his image in the *Analysis of Sensations*, point us to a conception of points of view that we need in order to explain the link that Natorp and Cassirer maintain between physical laws and intersubjectivity. At the same time, no one could deny that Mach has a very different theory of knowledge than Natorp and Cassirer. We thus need to be very careful to identify exactly what views the Marburg School figures share with Mach and what views they do not.

The core of what their views share is this. First, certain sets of experiences represent only limited, partial regions and scales of space and time—that is, what I have called points of view. Second, those representations of limited regions and scales of space and time will differ from representations of different regions and scales of space and time. Thus, third, representations of physical laws—that is, relations between experiences that are stable across space and time and so are valid for different regions and scales of space and time—are precisely the representations that can be shared by different points of view.

However, if those claims are shared by Mach, Natorp, and Cassirer, Mach places them in a very different philosophical context than Natorp and Cassirer do. We have already briefly noted several important differences between Mach's theory of knowledge and Natorp's and Cassirer's, but there is one more difference we must be clear about.

For Mach, the representations that exhibit the limited spatio-temporal structures that constitute points of view are very close to immediate sensory experience. As we have seen, those representations are the sensation-like elements that, on his empiricism, are the ultimate constituents of experience. His illustration reflects that proximity to immediate sensory experience. The first thing one notices about his image is not the highly abstract point that it exhibits a limited, partial spatio-temporal structure. Rather, the first thing one notices is that the image is an illustration of a person's immediate (or nearly immediate) visual experience. Thus for Mach, what I have called a point of view is a paradigmatic feature of nearly immediate sensory experience.

However, the representations that exhibit points of view, as I have defined them, need not be immediate or nearly immediate sensory experiences. Indeed, for Natorp and Cassirer, they are not.

Natorp and, even more clearly, Cassirer are concerned above all with the objectivity and the intersubjectivity of the theories of mathematical natural science. The principal question of their theories of knowledge is not how an individual knower overcomes the idiosyncrasy and privacy of its immediate sensory experience, in order to have objective, intersubjective knowledge. Rather, as Cassirer makes especially clear in chapters 4–7 of *Substance and Function*, the principal question of his theory of knowledge is how a natural scientific theory can evolve to overcome its relative idiosyncrasy and subjectivity, in order to become relatively more objective and relatively more intersubjective.

In the context of this epistemological concern, which is more characteristic of the Marburg School, the representations that exhibit points of view are not in the first instance immediate sensory experiences. Rather, they are scientific theories at given stages in history. That is, at any point in history before the end of science, the theories of mathematical natural science will be partial, and will be valid for only limited regions and scales of space and time. But to say those theories are valid for only limited regions and scales of space and time is to say that they only represent limited regions and scales of space and time. It is to say they have points of view.

Consider two trite examples: Galileo's time-square law for bodies in freefall and Kepler's laws of planetary motion. At the end of the sixteenth century, Galileo established as an empirical regularity that the distance an object travels in freefall is directly proportional to the square of the time during which it falls. This was an empirical regularity that, to the extent that it was warranted by Galileo's evidence, was valid only within a certain region of space—namely, near the surface of the earth.

Just after the turn of the century, in 1609 and 1619, Kepler defended his three laws of planetary motion: first, that the orbit of a planet is an ellipse with the sun at one of its foci; second, that a line joining a planet to the sun sweeps out equal areas in equal intervals of time; and third, that the square of a planet's orbital period is directly proportional to the cube of the orbit's semi-major axis (that is, one half of the ellipse's long axis). To the extent that these empirical regularities were warranted by Kepler's evidence, they were valid only for describing planetary motion, and thus at a larger scale than that of terrestrial physics.

Each of these theories exhibits a point of view and the idiosyncrasy that comes with it. Since Galileo's time-square law is valid only near the surface of the earth, it represents only that region of space. Further, from the point of view of that region of space, Kepler's laws cannot be represented. Likewise, since Kepler's laws of planetary motion are valid only at the scale of astronomical bodies, they represent only that scale. But from the point of view of that scale of space, Galileo's time-square law cannot be represented.

It is not as easy to recognize the epistemic idiosyncrasy that results from different points of view when the representations that exhibit the points of view are natural scientific theories, rather than the (nearly) immediate sensory experience illustrated in Mach's image. But still, these theories do exhibit an epistemic idiosyncrasy in virtue of having points of view. The points of view exhibited by the theories cannot share representations. That is, representations within the spatio-temporal structure of one point of view cannot be identical to representations within the spatio-temporal structure of the other point of view. In exactly that sense, representations exhibiting either point of view fail to be intersubjective.

However, compare these two theories to a theory with laws that are relatively more universal: namely, the three laws of Newton's mechanics and his law of universal gravitation. Newton understood these laws to be absolutely universal. That is, he understood them to describe the motion of bodies in all regions and scales of space and time. Of course, we now understand these laws to be less than absolutely universal: they are not valid for objects traveling at speeds approaching the speed of light or for objects so small as to be on the scale of Planck's constant. Thus on our contemporary understanding, Newton's theory is valid only for limited regions and scales of space and time. Still, we can nevertheless recognize that the laws of Newton's theory are much more universal than Galileo's time-square law or Kepler's laws of planetary motion—that is, they are valid for more regions and scales of space and time. Thus the point of view exhibited by Newton's theory is much less limited than the ones exhibited by Galileo's and Kepler's theories.

For our purposes, the essential epistemological point is this. The laws of Newton's mechanics and his law of universal gravitation are universal enough that they are valid for the points of view exhibited by both Galileo's time-square law and Kepler's laws of planetary motion. That is, Newton's laws apply validly to both the region of space and time that Galileo's time-square law applies to and the region of space and time that Kepler's laws apply to. Thus from the point of view exhibited by Galileo's law, it is possible to represent Newton's laws. Similarly, from the point of view exhibited by Kepler's laws, it is possible to represent

Newton's laws. Further, the representations of Newton's laws from both points of view will be identical. Consequently, despite the fact that Galileo's law and Kepler's laws exhibit different points of view, those different points of view can nevertheless share representations of Newton's laws. In just that sense, the relative universality of Newton's laws makes them relatively intersubjective.

Thus, as Cassirer suggests repeatedly in chapters 4–7 of *Substance and Function*, the objectivity that science aims at requires that science represent experience in an ever-expanding extent of space and time. To take just one example of Cassirer's expressions of this idea, he says:

> We finally call objective those elements of experience that persist through all change in the here and now, and on which rests the unchangeable character of experience; while we ascribe to the sphere of subjectivity all that belongs to the change itself, and that only expresses a determination of the particular, unique here and now.[20]

What is subjective for Cassirer—what is particular, and so idiosyncratic—is what is tied to a limited, partial region or scale of space and time. Cassirer calls this perspective the "here and now". What is objective—what overcomes the idiosyncrasy and so is intersubjective—are relations in experience that are constant over regions in space and time beyond the "here and now". Paradigmatically, those relations are laws. So as natural science establishes laws that are constant across ever-increasing extents of space and time, its theories become less and less idiosyncratic. They become more and more intersubjective.

At the same time, on Natorp's and Cassirer's view, natural science will never arrive at a theory that is absolutely intersubjective. For example, we do not understand Newton's mechanics and law of universal gravitation to be absolutely universal. Because, on our understanding, Newton's laws do not apply validly to all scales of space and time, we recognize that they exhibit their own point of view, and representations of them are thus always at least partly subjective. We recognize the possibility that Newton's laws could be, and in fact have been, superseded by theories that are relatively more universal and thus relatively more intersubjective. Likewise, from the perspective of Natorp's and Cassirer's views, we must recognize the possibility for any natural scientific theory that it can be superseded by a theory that is relatively more universal and so too relatively more intersubjective.

It should be clear that the ideas of a point of view and the epistemic idiosyncrasy it brings must function very differently in the context of Natorp's and Cassirer's theories of knowledge than they do in Mach's views. For Natorp and Cas-

---

[20] Cassirer (1923), 273.

sirer, a point of view cannot in the first instance be the region and scale of space and time represented in immediate sensory experience. Rather, it must be the region and scale captured by representations of a natural scientific theory at a given stage in the history of science. That history then turns out to be one characterized by unending progress towards an ideal of theories that are absolutely universal—that is, theories that are valid for absolutely all regions and scales of space and time—and so too progress towards an ideal of theories that are absolutely intersubjective.

7 Conclusion

The crux of the interpretation of Natorp and Cassirer I have defended is the account of the epistemic idiosyncrasy—of how certain representations fail to be intersubjective—expressed by the idea of a point of view. On that account, some experiences represent only limited, partial regions and scales of space and time. But then, representations from the perspectives of those different regions and scales will be different. They will fail to be identical, and so will fail to be intersubjective. At the same time, if physical laws are valid for all regions and scales of space and time, then representations of them will be identical, regardless of what regions and scales of space and time they are represented from. In just that sense, representations of physical laws will be intersubjective.

However, I cannot conclude without emphasizing a final qualification of this account: it cannot be considered anything like a complete interpretation of Natorp's and Cassirer's views of subjectivity. My account is not even a complete interpretation of their views of the epistemic idiosyncrasy that is overcome by objective natural scientific knowledge. A complete interpretation would have to include an account of the connection they see between subjectivity or epistemic idiosyncrasy and the sensory representations studied by psychology and the physiology of the sense organs.

Nevertheless, the account I have offered constitutes one piece of a complete interpretation of Natorp's and Cassirer's views of subjectivity and of how that subjectivity is overcome in theories of mathematical natural science. Moreover, the piece I have offered is especially interesting, since it is a piece that, considered at a sufficient level of abstraction, Natorp and Cassirer share with one of the thinkers they most want to distance themselves from—Ernst Mach.

That two Marburg School neo-Kantians and a positivist share views about why some representations fail to be intersubjective but why representations of physical laws can be shared suggests that these views are not anomalies in post-Kantian philosophy. On the contrary, it suggests that these views were part of a deeper intellectual current, one that included not just Mach, Natorp, and Cassirer, but also Helmholtz and the other physiological neo-Kantians as well as post-Kantian metaphysicians like Lotze. For these figures, epistemic idiosyncrasy, failures of intersubjectivity, and ultimately subjectivity are connected in some way to locality, to situatedness in space and time. That idea can be articulated in different ways, and as Mach, Natorp, and Cassirer all show, it can be maintained even by figures who deny that space and time exist independently of the subject's experience of them. But however the view is articulated, it suggests that forms of knowledge that overcome failures of intersubjectivity will be forms of knowledge that extend beyond a particular, local, spatio-temporal situation—beyond, as Cassirer puts it, "the here and now". Hence the ubiquity in post-Kantian philosophy of the view that representations of physical laws, which aim to be exceptionless in all of space and time, are intersubjective. It is above all this view that, in the same year that Natorp's "On the Objective and Subjective Grounding of Knowledge" appeared, Friedrich Nietzsche parodied as the view that objectivity consists in "an eye turned in no direction at all"—*seeing* without any perspective of any kind, and so certainly no spatio-temporal perspective.[21]

Thus while the account of Natorp's and Cassirer's views I have offered does not constitute a complete interpretation of their views of subjectivity, it is nevertheless a piece of that view that was deeply embedded in their larger post-Kantian context.

Bibliography

Cassirer (1923): Ernst Cassirer, *Substance and Function*, Williams Curtis Swabey and Marie Collins Swabey (trans), Chicago: Open Court.

Daston and Galison (2007): Lorraine Daston and Peter Galison, *Objectivity*, New York: Zone Books.

Edgar (2008): Scott Edgar, "Paul Natorp and the Emergence of Anti-Psychologism in the Nineteenth Century", *Studies in History and Philosophy of Science* 39, 54–65.

Hacking (forthcoming): Ian Hacking, "Let's Not Talk About Objectivity", in: Flavia Padovani, Alan Richardson, and Jonathan Y. Tsou (eds.), *Objectivity in Science: Approaches to Historical Epistemology*, Boston Studies in Philosophy and History of Science, Dordrecht: Springer.

Heis (2014): Jeremy Heis, "Ernst Cassirer's *Substanzbegriff und Funktionsbegriff*", *HOPOS* 4 (No. 2), 241–270.

---

21 Nietzsche (1997), 87.

Helmholtz (1977): Hermann von Helmholz, "The Facts in Perception", Malcolm F. Lowe (trans.), in: *Epistemological Writings*, Robert S. Cohen and Yehuda Elkana (eds.), Dordrecht: Reidel, 115–163.

Kant (1997): Immanuel Kant, *Critique of Pure Reason*, Paul Guyer and Allen Wood (trans. and ed.), Cambridge: Cambridge University Press.

Kant (2002): Immanuel Kant, *Prolegomena to Any Future Metaphysics that Will be able to Come Forward as Science*, Gary Hatfield (trans.), in: *Theoretical Philosophy after 1781*, Cambridge: Cambridge University Press.

Lotze (1884): Hermann Lotze, *Logic: in Three Books, of Thought, of Investigations, and of Knowledge*, Bernard Bosanquet (trans.), London: Oxford University Press.

Luft (2011): Sebastian Luft, *Subjectivity and Lifeworld in Transcendental Phenomenology*, Evanston, IL: Northwestern University Press.

Mach (1897): Ernst Mach, *Contributions to the Analysis of Sensations*, C.M. Williams (trans.), La Salle: Open Court.

Natorp (1888): Paul Natorp, *Einleitung in die Psychologie nach kritische Methode*, Freiburg: J.C.B. Mohr.

Natorp (1912): Paul Natorp, *Allgemeine Psychologuie nach kritische Methode*, Freiburg: J.C.B. Mohr.

Natorp (1981): Paul Natorp, "On the Objective and Subjective Grounding of Knowledge" David Kolb (trans.), *Journal of the British Society for Phenomenology* 12 (No. 3), 245–266.

Nietzsche (2007): Friedrich Nietzsche, *On the Genealogy of Morality*, Carol Deithe (trans.), Keith Ansell-Pearson (ed.), Cambridge: Cambridge University Press.

Norbert Andersch (London)
Symbolic Form and Mental Illness: Ernst Cassirer's Contribution to a New Concept of Psychopathology

In his invitation to this conference, Sebastian Luft, its organizer, has rightly pointed out: "Ernst Cassirer's oeuvre is vast; it spans the history of philosophy, theoretical philosophy, the philosophy of mathematics, cultural studies and intellectual history, aesthetics, the study of language and myth and more." I am here today to speak about one of Cassirer's crucial fields of interest—which (for a number of reasons) has been ignored until recently: his focus on the make-up of consciousness and human psychopathology. Cassirer wrote in 1929:

> For what it [the philosophy of symbolic forms] is seeking is not so much common factors in being as common factors in meaning. Hence we must strive to bring the teachings of pathology, which cannot be ignored, into the more universal context of the philosophy of culture.[1]

This statement summarizes Cassirer's approach in shifting the focus on psychopathological theory from the brain and its localizations to the living interaction between the self and his/her social environment. This shift 'from substance to function' is not only of historical interest for philosophers but of very practical importance for patients and doctors in the actual public discourse how to liberate psychiatry from its damaging mantra of a primitive and merely descriptive symptomatology in its classification systems DSM and ICD.

Psychopathology is the study of significant causes and processes in the development of mental illness. While routinely its core aspects remain discussed among professionals in specific academic or clinical settings, the yield of these discussions is far from being irrelevant to the average individual or to the public in general. The 'International Classification of Diseases', version 10 (ICD10) and the 'Diagnostic and Statistical Manual of Mental Disorders', version IV (DSM IV) are the standard "classification-systems" used to identify mental disorder. They are introduced to ever more countries, regions and ethnicities by the WHO, the 'World Psychiatric Association' and numerous governments, administrations and insurance companies. At present they are used to classify and treat more than 100 million patients in more than 70 countries worldwide every

---

[1] Cassirer (1955), 275.

year. Critics claim that their content disregards the specific symbolic make-up of human culture; that it is not based on an underlying natural, relational or genetic order, and that it merely measures superficial descriptions of behavioral phenomena against a "norm" of individuals in the (post)industrialized milieu of the western cultures.[2]

In general science, no one doubts that human nature, our language, mathematics and our progressing tools of work-specification are based on and experienced as symbolic constructs. In its discourse, the quote of philosopher Ernst Cassirer that man is not the 'animal rationale' but the 'animal symbolicum'[3] has found its true confirmation.

Thus, in clinical psychiatry, one would expect symbolic formation to play a major role in the assessment and diagnosis of mental illness—especially since, in mental crisis, our symbolic matrix breaks down, the pattern-based construct of reality gets lost and our symbolic language is severely affected. But the symbolic message has not hit home and the breakdown of symbolic capacity in psychiatric patients continues to be ignored. Symbolic formation continues to be denied the role of providing building blocks to a universal model of consciousness and, subsequently, of psychopathology. Thus valuable opportunities for a new and different approach to treating mental crises remain unused.

After the turn of the millennium, with the crisis of psychopathology dragging on and desperate for new and original ideas, sign- and symbol related approaches have made their way back to the forefront of discussion. This approach is strengthened by the fact that not only Cassirer's, but also Whitehead's, Saussure's, Piaget's and Peirce's findings[4]—all of them founded on a mathematical-geometrical understanding of human interrelatedness and consciousness—have attracted researchers on an international scale. While present descriptive models produce 'object-like' diagnoses, as if they were able to retain their meaning independently of the patient's changing context, psychopathology is in fact desperate for new concepts that reflect the complex interactions and ever changing contexts that dominate human interrelations and their breakdown. Mathematically based and 'group-theory' based concepts have much to contribute to these—more relational and process related—templates of diagnostics, drawing from a multi-layered, parallel and integrated conception of consciousness and they may well in the near future produce a convincing synergic effect within an on-going debate.

---

[2] Berrios (1999), Gorostiza and Manes (2011).
[3] Cassirer (2006), 31.
[4] Smith (2001).

1 Philosophy and Psychiatry: Conflicting Approaches

Two highly acclaimed personalities, both psychiatrists and philosophers, Karl Jaspers and Ludwig Binswanger, had a major impact on the psychopathological discourse in the first half of the 20th century. Yet Jaspers' relentless and growing attraction to existentialism and Binswanger's turn towards a post-Fascist Heidegger in the 1940s marginalized their own early promising phenomenological approaches to psychopathology. Also, a strong post-war psychoanalysis in the USA disconnected itself in the mid-1950s from the psychiatric mainstream and was unable to look beyond the wealthy clientele and the transfixed papa-mama-child scenario. Explicitly, previous Gestalt- and symbol-research was left behind in the psychiatric discussion and could not catch up following the total disruption of their scientific networks during Fascism, enforced exile and the early death of their main protagonists. These are just a few of the reasons for the decline of the breadth of the psychopathological discourse and for the fact that a biological approach forced its way back to clinical 'superiority', promoting simple and standardized forms of diagnosis and treatment, be it ECT or psychopharmacology.

What remains in place in day-to-day practice are the early 20th century views of German psychiatrist and psychopathologist Emil Kraepelin[5]. Kraeplin was convinced that psychiatric diagnoses could be based on what he called 'natural entities of disease' (*natürliche Krankheitseinheiten*) and he proposed that 'dementia praecox' (later called 'schizophrenia') and 'manic-depressive illness' are distinctive complexes. His conclusions have been frequently challenged over the last 70 years and critical meta-research has never confirmed his findings.[6] The main conclusion of this critical meta-research is that such 'entities' may well exist in researcher's minds and in their descriptive models, but that they have no correlate in the reality of biological, social and clinical life. Nonetheless, Kraepelinean-based descriptive catalogues of symptoms remain the baseline tool of worldwide psycho-diagnostics and treatment. Further 'updated versions' will be published in 2014 and 2016 as DSM V and ICD 11. Despite claims by prominent mainstream psychiatrists that such systems "have outlived their usefulness"[7] there will be another increase of illness-'entities' from 350 to

---

5 Cf. Kraepelin and Lange (1927).
6 Cutting (2011).
7 Goodyer (2011).

about 400. To a lay person, this on-going diversification of descriptive diagnoses of individualized 'disorders' may look like a sign of scientific progress; instead it is only proof to the fact that the descriptive 'entity' approach is unable to grasp the underlying architectural and relational cultural framework which constitutes human consciousness and its symbolic fundaments.

There are two major failings preventing psychiatry from becoming a fully integrated member of the faculty of medical and scientific disciplines: one failing is based on the specific direction of psychiatric (and especially psychopathological) theories which went from an early (relational) magical, mythic, religious understanding of madness to a more brain-based substantial one, thereby defying the contemporary scientific mainstream, which has evolved from a focus on substances towards a focus on function and relational order (be it in mathematics, biology, physics, psychology, chemistry, etc.). The second failing is not having grasped the importance of man as the 'symbolic animal,' which situates psychiatry exactly on the borderline between biological and cultural patterns.

Both paradigm shifts have been neither understood nor digested by psychiatry. Both failings add up to a picture where contemporary psychiatry—in the public eye and in its clinical content—has become increasingly identified with the simplistic descriptive catalogue systems known as DSM or (parts of) ICD. Theoretical psychopathology has lost the breadth and depth of ideas and approaches that were found in the scientific community one hundred years ago. Both the aforementioned problems—a change from substance to function, and the importance of symbolic formation—were central aspects in the work of Ernst Cassirer during the 1920s. It is well worth reviewing some of his ideas about psychopathology, which got lost in the build-up to and aftermath of World War II, and re-evaluating their possible benefits for the future of psychiatry.

There have been numerous (pre- and post-Cassirer) attempts to acknowledge the importance of symbolic thinking in relation to consciousness, and to include findings on symbol theory in the canon of psychiatry and psychopathology. Their outcomes were often inconclusive, and, in the case of certain aspects of symptomatology, could not be generalized. Research results often contradicted each other. Ernst Cassirer's work, however, had from the outset a much wider frame in considering symbolic capacity as the centerpiece of human development, with symbols as the very tools of different levels of cultural development, which free mankind from the merely biological constraints of the animal empire. His three-volume work *Philosophie der symbolischen Formen*[8] provides the concept of a universally functional matrix of consciousness, based on a relational

---
[8] Cassirer (1923b), (1925), (1929).

model of 'invariants of human experience'. According to Cassirer, dysfunctions in its symbolic make-up—or the loss of established symbolic suspension systems—have a serious impact on human 'world-making', on psychiatric symptomatology and on the very concept of theoretical psychopathology. As a result of a new symbolic methodology, mental settings and clinical symptoms, which were seemingly contradictory beforehand, now emerge as compatible within a newly created, more abstract geometry of interrelations.

Discussions of the universal importance of signs and symbols in neurology gained momentum in the early 1920s, following Henry Head's research on symbolic thinking and expression.[9] His results showed that the symptoms of patients with cerebral lesions did not demonstrate a basic defect in the functions of speaking, reading or writing; instead he detected serious problems with symbolic meaning and categorical representation. The debate was further enhanced by Cassirer's first two volumes of his 'Philosophie der symbolischen Formen', and even more so by his special treatise on 'Die Pathologie des Symbolbewusstseins' in Chapter VI of the third volume from 1929. In this section, Cassirer refers to Head and his work:

> I myself became acquainted with Head's investigations only after the phenomenological analyses of perception in the first two volumes of this book [Philosophie der symbolischen Formen, Bd I&II] were largely completed. This made me attach all the greater importance to the indirect confirmation of my conclusions by Head's observations and the general theoretical view which he developed solely on the basis of clinical experience.[10]

Cassirer's much earlier publication *Substanzbegriff und Funktionsbegriff* (1910) had already initiated serious debates about 'paradigm changes' in the science of knowledge, but the impact of his *Philosophie der symbolischen Formen* is seen by today's historians as the 'semiotic turn' in the history of philosophy.[11]

Cassirer's ideas were widely discussed in German-speaking countries and beyond (the Soviet Union, France, US, Italy) throughout the 1920s and 1930s. They influenced well-known researchers in philosophy[12], neurology[13], psychiatry[14], psychology[15] and anthropology[16]. But it was Cassirer himself who modeled

---

9 Head (1921), (1926).
10 Cassirer, (1957), 209.
11 Krois, (2004).
12 Cf. Theodor Litt (1926), Susanne Langer (1948).
13 Cf. Kurt Goldstein (1934).
14 Cf. Ludwig Binswanger (1924).
15 Cf. Kurt Lewin (1947), Karl Buehler (1934), Foulkes (1964).
16 Cf. Elias (1937).

his developing philosophical work on the actual findings of this wider research and discourse-network. His closest cooperation on issues of consciousness and mental formation emerged in his day-to-day collaboration, discussion and clinical experience with neurologist Kurt Goldstein in the mid-1920s. From 1924–26 he maintained a lively scientific correspondence with psychiatrist Ludwig Binswanger[17] and tried to introduce symbolic thinking into the field of psychopathology, as did Goldstein in his main work 'The Organism' (1934) and Lewin (1949) in his psychological studies and field-research after immigrating to the US.

The rise of German Fascism and the subsequent war forced Cassirer—and the majority of scientists involved in the debate—into exile, destroying their research network and, more crucially, separating them from their philosophical and theoretical background. Cassirer's and Lewin's early death in 1945 and 1947, respectively, led to a marginalization of symbol- and 'Gestalt'-approaches and deprived them of the important role they had gained in the period between the two world wars. None of these theories ever made it back to the mainstream of German psychiatry and psychopathology, where too often post-war leaders in psychiatry and philosophy (e.g. Heidegger) were the same figures who had willingly cooperated with the Nazi regime.

2 Early Symbol Theory in Psychopathology: Finkelnburg, Silberer, Freud and Jung

Psychiatry, in its attempts to secure a permanent place among medical faculties, was understandably keen to distance itself from all forms of previous symbolic connections. Medieval healers and street gossip alike had thrived on real or invented symbolic connections in order to bind madness to magical, mythic and religious speculation. This is why during the first century of 'modern psychiatry' symbolic interpretation was synonymous with an unscientific approach to mental disturbance. Previous symbolic connotations had to be overcome—once and for all—by the biological allocation of (and rational thinking about) brain mechanisms. But fairly soon the importance of symbols was stressed again, albeit in the name of the newly adopted scientific paradigm. It was Finkelnburg who took to symbol-research[18], trying to work out the multitude of symptoms in aphasia. He concluded from his observations that the use of symbols amounted to a kind of artificial creation—of conventional signs—exclusively practiced by human be-

---

17 Cf. Andersch (2010).
18 Cf. Finkelnburg (1870).

ings, and that their proper usage, including a detached and abstract view on reality, got lost in the psychopathological process. Spamer[19], Kussmaul[20] and Pick[21] also presented clinical cases distinguishing the mere clinical loss of symbolic capacity from its representational importance as a tool fostering meaning and generalization.

Throughout the following decades a puzzling variety of clinical observations on symbolic formation were published, all of them looking at clinical symptomatology and psychopathology, ranging from a unilateral, regressive meaning of symbols to the very opposite view: that symbols are the indispensable cornerstones to the mature and social development of personality. Freud, Jones and Ferenczi focused on the regressive, pathognomic side, while Jung, Neumann, and Bachhofen highlighted the unifying, maturing and creative impact of symbols. Rank and Sachs portrayed the role of symbols as primitive tools of mental adaptation, while Mead and Pavlov put more emphasis on their importance as balancing forces and a means of saving mental energy. Silberer and Luria regarded symbols as natural forces of form- and pattern-building; Leuner and Lewin did the same, albeit more so from a Gestalt perspective. Psychoanalytic researchers such as Stekel, Szondi, Klein and Sechhaye conceived symbols to be facilitators in accessing suppressed mental complexes, while psychiatrists such as Hanfmann, Arieti, Kasanian and Bash considered symbols in their natural role of fostering human intelligence. While most researchers concentrated on very specific aspects in symptomatology, only Henry Head and, in particular, Ernst Cassirer took a more general approach prior to World War II to considering the role of symbols as the center point of the unfolding of man's cultural capacity—applicable to different categorical levels of meaning and 'world-making'. Subsequently they looked at certain forms of neurological and mental illness as a breakdown of symbolic formation.

Freud's psychoanalytic method was among the first attempts to take the psychopathological focus away from the brain and to replace it with the relational setting connecting subject and milieu, thus unconsciously shifting the approach 'from substance to function,' which only later was fully explored by Cassirer's philosophy. Before taking a more detailed look at Cassirer's philosophy it is interesting to consider the very different roles which both Freud and Jung—the best known contemporary protagonists in their field—attributed to the meaning of symbols.

---

19 Spamer (1876).
20 Kussmaul (1874).
21 Pick (1908).

Sigmund Freud, in his early publications, regarded symbol appearance as a typical sign either of the unconscious, the 'primary process' and basic dream experience, or psychopathological decline and regression.[22] Only dream symbols could (on rare occasions) rise to a position of transpersonal structural elements. Freud's connection of symbol building to pathological events and, even more so, exclusively sexual symptomatology was backed up by Ferenczi[23] and extended by Ernest Jones[24] who connected symbolic presentation to 'primitive thinking', thereby declaring Freud's verdict on symbols as the center-piece and dogma of psychoanalysis. Anna Freud[25] marginalized the meaning of symbols even more, calling them 'by-products of dream interpretation' and portraying them as the most basic access to 'Id'-impulses. This prompted an exclusion of the symbolic discourse from the center stage of psychoanalytical discussion.

Conceptualizing his own position, Freud had actually used (and obviously reinterpreted) the outcome of research carried out by his psychoanalytical colleague, Herbert Silberer. Silberer had explored symbolization efforts in much broader terms: as the general human and mental capacity to generate autoregulative forms in response to (uncontrollable) impulses.[26] Going even further, he came to the conclusion that those formed elements—which he had experienced during severe tiredness and loss of attention—do not appear at random, but have a structural similarity to the underlying pattern of the process, albeit not to its unique and concrete presentation. Silberer felt that "the process of symbol building, emerging during onto- and phylogenetic development, progresses to be an ever more differentiated and evolving process of knowledge ... (and) the only adequate expression of the achieved mental level."[27]

Sadly, his verdict on the dreaming process was ignored by Freud, as were Silberer's final far-reaching conclusions on the symbolic make-up of consciousness. Freud's interpretation of symbolism prevailed for the first half of the twentieth century, and it took major efforts and unfortunate disputes to redress his unilateral position, which finally rehabilitated Silberer and his early findings on the productive, protective and creative potency of symbols.

C.G. Jung—having split from Freudian psychoanalysis—elaborated his theories during the 1910s and 1920s without any closer affiliations to the lively contemporary discourse on symbols. In contradistinction to Freud's view, for Jung

---

22 Freud, (1894), (1900).
23 Ferenczi (1913).
24 Jones (1916).
25 A. Freud (1936).
26 Silberer (1912a), (1912b).
27 Eckes-Lapp (1988), 183.

the content of symbols has a major impact on the individuation process and the development of a mature inner self. Thus the symbolic process is an indispensable requirement and constant companion of the make-up of consciousness. Symbols are transformers of energy in assimilating mental complexes to the conscious part of our personality. Jung's emphasis is on the capabilities of symbols, on their pattern-based Gestalt, on their inner structure, on their ego-building format and on their unique power of anticipation. Highlighting the collective dimensions of symbols and their importance to generate preformed 'archetypical' pattern of mental energy, he brings in a completely new aspect to the psychological/psychiatric debate.

With respect to therapy, his view is that reinstating symbols between inner self and social environment can have an indispensable healing power. Jung and Cassirer never had any personal or other connections. While Cassirer fled into exile, Jung became the doyen of the Germanic branch of the Psychoanalytische Vereinigung under Nazi-rule. This makes a joint approach to the philosophy of symbols difficult to achieve, yet there are a surprising number of structural parallels to be found in both their theories.[28] Jung builds his concept on general laws of symmetry and mathematical geometry—as does Cassirer. Both show evidence of a similar complexity in building mental Gestalt, and both assume a multi-layered matrix of '*Sinnstiftung*' in the make-up of consciousness—which both consider to be not merely brain activity but a living process of interconnection.

3 Cassirer's Legacy: From Biology to Symbolic Formation

Cassirer's idea is that the endless variety of human culture and expression can be traced back and reduced to a small number of what he calls—referring to Plato—'*Bewegungsformen*'.[29] These underlying patterns are comparable to the very few elements that create the never-ending multitude of mathematical and chemical worlds, languages and music. Thus the multitude of human activities culminates in a limited variety of 'symbolic forms' such as magic, myth, religion, law, science, the arts and a few others; in other words, living complexes of balanced tension, like 'Gestalten', emerging from complementary contributions of subject and milieu, yet detached from their full direct involvement.

---

[28] Brumlik (1993), 143; Pietikainen (1998).
[29] Cassirer (1910), 435.

Most important to Cassirer in the architectural make-up of a symbolic form is the structural bond between its universal meaning and the external sign by which it is represented, leading to his 1922 definition: "Under a 'symbolic form' should be understood each energy of spirit [Geist] through which a spiritual [geistig] content or meaning is connected with a concrete sensory sign and is internally adapted to this sign."[30] Symbolic forms are stages of 'world making', which can be used as tools from a box, again and again in various settings. In Cassirer's thought, mankind's unique symbolic quality lifts it out of the animal empire and transforms it in such a profound way that man should no longer be called the 'animal rationale' (as Aristotle did) but 'animal symbolicum'[31]. It is also man's symbolic capacity which gets lost or altered in some forms of neurological dysfunction (e.g. aphasia or speech disorder) and in mental illness.

Cassirer based his assumptions on the findings of the biologist J. von Uexküll, a close colleague and friend at Hamburg University. He had stated that man shares his biological 'circle of functioning' with all animals, using a 'receptor' and 'effector' system, which keeps us adapted only to a certain part of our environment[32]. Cassirer widened this concept, proposing a "third link which may be described as the symbolic system, an intermediary world, a 'Zwischenreich', which stands between spirit and reality."[33]

In animal physiology, sense-perception is divided into more or less variable components and differentiates basic type-specific patterns from those which are random or related to a sole situation. But the human symbolic approach allows for an entirely new quality. Its pattern building—later to be used as the defining part of symbolic formation—is not a given, but has to be detected, extracted and used in an anticipatory way by human action (and working process) in several steps: by applying meaning to parts of his environment, by intensifying and connecting this meaningfulness, by separating it from the background into which it is built, and finally by using it as an abstract symbol or mental tool, independent of its first concrete usage.

Cassirer insisted on a sharp divide between signs and symbols. For him they represent two totally different realms: signs are part of the physical world of 'being' while symbols are central to human meaning and importance.

During his entire life Cassirer was never confronted with medical or psychiatric classification systems and could not have foreseen the problems they would

---

30 Cassirer (1922), 5; translated in Bayer (2001), 15.
31 Cassirer (2006), 31.
32 von Uexküll (1909).
33 Schilpp (1949), 874.

cause today.[34] Yet disputes about classification systems have not been as recent as most medical professionals might think. In the late eighteenth and early nineteenth centuries, descriptive catalogues of plants were seen as a major progress in a systematic approach to biology. Their publication was a public and financial success and led to a wave of botanical—and later on medical—classification catalogues.

French doctors, among them "Mentalists' dealing with 'mad and insane patients', picked up on the success of Linnaeus by applying botanical observations to mental classification systems. They were encouraged by Linnaeus himself, who—in a letter to the French doctor Boissier de Sauvage—expressed his view that "symptoms are in relation to illness what leaves and stems are to the plant."[35]

By coincidence it was the fierce critique of Linnaeus's cataloguing efforts by Goethe that motivated Cassirer to analyze more closely Goethe's generic approach versus Linnaeus's descriptive method. Goethe—obviously admiring Linnaeus's achievements as a biologist—was critical of his static descriptions and picture-related presentations of these living entities. He argued that visual presentation alone neglects their developmental stages and ignores the plants' general metamorphosis throughout their lifetime. Finally he criticized Linnaeus's relentless cataloguing efforts as a misrepresentation of nature.[36]

Cassirer undertook a sophisticated meta-analysis of Goethe's critique of Linnaeus, pointing out that Goethe focuses more on context and meaning than simply on the biological function. Goethe's observations capture the changing 'frames of reference', the plants' interrelations with environment and the mutual influences in this process—compared with the exactness and rigidity of the observational 'object' in Linnaeus's case. Goethe highlights the plants' genetic pathways more than their visual appearance, and tries to work out a general pattern in their development in contrast to seemingly concrete superficial similarities—which sometimes turn out not to be connected entities at all—thus misleading the observer's eye. Cassirer concludes that Goethe focuses on metamorphosis and Gestalt, as compared with the descriptive and associative visually substance-orientated approach of Linnaeus—an early methodological attempt to change the scientific focus from substance to function, highlighting its hidden yet underlying and progressing natural and relational order.

---

34 Berrios (1999).
35 Foucault (2005).
36 Krois (2004), 284.

Cassirer differs from Kant in his belief that the building stones of consciousness are not static categories but dynamic and evolving patterns: subjective correlatives of symbolic representation. Cassirer views the 'symbolic function' as the common element to all areas of knowledge, which, however, takes a specific form in each of these areas. In his early studies Cassirer[37] closely examines the progress of mathematical thinking and how its concrete and substance-bound terms are systematically replaced by functional relations and later on—using symbols only—by completely abstract terms of understanding[38]. He discovers that each of these mathematical views represents only one (out of a variety of possible forms) of 'world-making', yet each of them has a surprisingly stable inner logic and sense. Their inner laws of existence, representing a certain level of concrete experience, still remain valid under a new paradigm—fulfilling a role within a changed relational framework. Consequently, Euclidian geometry, which for centuries was seen as the natural final stage of its discipline (as its reality is proven by day-to-day experience) found itself replaced by a whole group of virtual, previously unimaginable, spheres: the Riemann geometries[39]. Most surprisingly these 'new geometries' emerge as complementary, yet independent, worlds, opening up our imagination to new and very different perspectives compared to the well-known (Euclidean) architecture of reality. All of them exist as parallel 'universes.' No one can be replaced by another, nor absorb or fully integrate their structures: even the 'old' Euclidean geometry remains valid within the 'new' matrix of structures as one continuously approximated limiting case. Yet Riemann geometries, despite their highly abstract architecture, are more than an entertaining virtual playground for mathematical specialists; they are of very practical use in solving complicated problems in the real world. Geometrical thinking, freed up from its previously limiting spheres, now has a capacity flexible enough to solve the riddles of Maxwell's theory of electro-magnetism and Einstein's theory of relativity.

Cassirer applied these notions of substance transmuting to function to cultural development. 'Symbolic formation' means to deconstruct this algorithm and to use its underlying pattern to understand how humans create a living wholeness (*Ganzheit*) out of the subject's changing level of experience and complexity, mutually connecting categorical elements with sensory ones: a marriage of complementary elements of subject and environment. Far from being naive, Cassirer knew all too well the incompatibilities between mathematical models

---

37 Cassirer (1902).
38 Ihmig (1997).
39 Riemann (1868).

based on exactness in ideal settings and the chaos of human existence and personal unreliability. He knew the unsolvable contradictions between frustration and fragmentation of everyday life, and our longing for an existence which makes some sense: there is an irreducible difference between axioms of geometry and the empirical statements derived from observation and measurement. The two cannot be directly compared since they belong to entirely different orders of object.[40] Yet we should not allow ourselves to be misled by this disparity; what we are going to set forth concerns logic only, and not ontology.[41] Nevertheless, we must not conclude that no mediation at all can obtain between these two levels. In spite of their specific differences they belong to the same genus, in so far as they share the function of objective knowledge. It is this common function whence their character derives; without the 'reference of ideas to an object' there is no perception.[42]

To allocate these contradictory elements to a single fixed and rigid relational order is not helpful, but requires a system able to change settings, thus managing a multitude of living tensions between different levels of subjectivity and their appropriate social frames within a moving matrix[43] which turns beliefs and ideologies into a virtual safety net. The wider framework of these 'symbolizations' constitutes a limited number of 'levels of world-making' and only in experiencing and integrating the full circle of their variety—and bringing them into a balanced equilibrium with our non-symbolic autoregulations in sleep and other regressions to our animal origins—will there be a minimization of mental vulnerability.

With regard to patients with an aphasic disorder, Cassirer explains a symptomatology which can also be observed in schizophrenic patients:

> Many patients who are not able to draw a sketch of their room can orient themselves relatively well on such a sketch if the basic schema is already laid down. If for example the doctor prepares a sketch in which the situation of the table where the patient usually sits is indicated by a point, the patient often has no trouble indicating the position of the stove, the window or the door on this sketch. Thus the truly difficult operation consists in knowing how to proceed in the spontaneous choice of a plan as well as the center of the coordinates. For precisely this choice unmistakably involves a constructive act. One of Head's patients expressly stated that he could not effect this operation because he could not correctly establish 'the starting point, but once it was given him everything was much easier.' We perceive the true nature of the difficulty when we consider how long it took science or

---

40 Cassirer (1944), 3.
41 Cassirer (1944), 5.
42 Cassirer (1944), 30–31.
43 Andersch (2007).

theoretical knowledge to perform this same operation with clarity and determinacy. Theoretical physics also began with 'thing space' and only gradually progressed to 'systematic space'—it, too, had to conquer the concept of a system and center of coordinates by persistent intellectual effort. Obviously it is one thing to apprehend the togetherness and apartness of perceptible objects, and another to conceive of an ideal aggregate of surfaces, lines, and points embodying a schematic representation of pure positional relations. Thus patients who can execute certain movements quite correctly are often baffled when they are expected to describe these same movements—that is, to differentiate them in universal, linguistically fixated concepts.[44]

While Cassirer, during his clinical studies, mainly saw neurological patients with speech disorders, Krois has highlighted that Cassirer's fundamental concept of symbolism is not a linguistic one, but includes ethnographic and anthropological aspects as well: "The linguistic model of semiotics regards the bond between the signifier and the signified as purely arbitrary and conventional, but Cassirer traced meaning back to a "natural symbolism" of image-like configurations in bodily feeling and perception."[45] This is why healthy persons with different levels of symbolic world-making will create a matrix of stable frames of a sequential and hierarchical order without even being aware of it. This further allows abstract ideas and theories to be grasped in anticipation and as mathematical concepts; moreover, it implements the unique universe of human existence as a system of transcultural valid symbols.

All 'symbolizations' remain unique in their complexity, quality and character; all provide some form of stability, like landmarks in the chaos of life. While, from a philosophical point of view, they are neither 'true' nor 'objective', among the average member of society they are perceived as reliable, well-functioning and pragmatic human intentions, corresponding well with their mutual field of resonance. Each of these paradigms in daily life is seen as incompatible with previous ones. Only from a very late integrative level of understanding do individuals get to use them as a box of tools, where the right one has to be chosen dependent on the actual requirements.

Cassirer differentiates between three types of reality and their corresponding symbolic forms. The expressive world is organized by myth, sign and signification. The representational world is organized by language. The conceptual world is organized by science. Each of these symbolic forms expresses a structure of consciousness achieved by the internal logic of the symbolic forms and

---

44 Cassirer (1957), 245–6.
45 Krois (1999), 531.

constitutes a major sphere of cultural activity. To know is to elicit order through the use of symbolic forms.[46]

4 Cassirer's Impact on Psychopathology (pre-WWII)

Cassirer's theories took much of their strength from discussions and clinical cooperation with leading contemporary psychiatrists, neurologists and psychologists such as Kurt Goldstein and Adhemar Gelb as well as Kurt Lewin and Ludwig Binswanger. The clinical cooperation between Goldstein and Cassirer in the early 1920s at Goldstein's 'Institute for Brain Injured Patients' (*Institut zur Erforschung der Folgeerscheinungen von Hirnverletzungen*) in Frankfurt was very fruitful for their mutual theoretical development towards a 'new psychopathology'. Goldstein adapted Cassirer's view that there is no hierarchy within different levels of world-making; the way brain-damaged patients try to express themselves verbally is neither disordered nor chaotic, as a superficial assessment might reveal. Instead it is a focused, vital and interactive effort in establishing a new Gestalt, a new equilibrium of correspondence with their environment. Having lost the more abstract tools of world-making, patients now refer back to the more concrete and sensory ones. In doing so, the patient changes from using symbols as patterns, which can be used in different situations, to a more basic form of expression, i.e. forging direct connections with the concrete field of their immediate experience. In this way they lose the capacity for symbolic adaptation to future contexts and situations in exchange for the remaining concrete management of presence[47]. Cassirer—reciprocally—studied Goldstein's clients, trying to understand what he later termed "the psychopathology of symbolic forms."[48] In 1929 Cassirer writes:

> I should scarcely have had the courage to go into it [the findings of the modern pathology of speech] more deeply if ... I had not also received the personal encouragement of the two authors [Gelb and Goldstein]. Here I must particularly thank Goldstein for demonstrating to me a large number of the pathological cases to which his publications refer and so enabling me to gain a true understanding of them.[49]

---

46 White (1946), 463.
47 Goldstein (1934).
48 Cassirer (2009), 71.
49 Cassirer (1957), 210.

Their close cooperation led to a special chapter in the third volume of Cassirer's main work, *Philosophie der symbolischen Formen*, entitled 'Zur Pathologie des Symbolbewusstseins' ('Towards the Pathology of Symbolic Consciousness')[50], and Goldstein integrated Cassirer's approach on 'symbolic formation' into his concept of psychopathology in his most important book *Der Aufbau des Organismus* (1934). It contained the very first systems and network theory based on principles, whereby the brain is regarded as working on different categorical levels, finding its concrete or abstract equilibrium depending on varying grades of complexity. The brain draws its potential from its ability to enact parallel levels of suspension (*Grundspannung und Erregungsbereitschaft*). All neuronal functions are guided by their subservience to the whole organism, even during a breakdown of the main cerebral activities. Learned functions are not strictly organized in local patterns, because their activities can be substituted by neighboring or different parts of the organism or changed to a different functional exchange level as such. The brain, seen from a systems approach, never switches to a mode of inactivity but endlessly moves between 'equilibriums of change' (*Verharren in Veränderung*).

Goldstein's model of adapted 'functioning' enables the therapist to look at the pathological process as a well-understood attempt at mental re-organization—compared with the traditional model of 'local damage'—and opens up the possibility of reconstructing a new level of symbol-based healing. This led to Goldstein's position (as summed up by Oliver Sacks), that:

> the unique value of pathology lies in 'illuminating the nature of health', and that pathological symptoms are a 'lawful variation of the normal life process', even if this involves a shrinkage or revision of self and world until an equilibrium of a radical new sort can be achieved. Symptoms are not isolated expressions of local damage but attempted solutions of healing. The task of the physician therefore is to help to achieve this new equilibrium and 'not force the patient to try and do the old things in the old way.[51]

Between 1924 and 1926 Cassirer maintained a lively scientific correspondence with the psychiatrist Ludwig Binswanger,[52] who wrote to Cassirer, after reading his first volume of *Philosophie der symbolischen Formen:* "Having worked out the term 'symbolic form' is of crucial importance for a psychiatrist—as soon as he acknowledges his main objective: to progress to a phenomenology of pattern

---

50 Cassirer (1929), 238–328.
51 Sacks (1995), 14.
52 Andersch (2010).

of thoughts which are continuously presented and performed by our main group of patients: the schizophrenics."[53]

Binswanger tried to introduce symbolic thinking and Gestalt ideas into the field of psychopathology. In his famous Zurich presentation of 1924, his audience expected him to continue to promote Freud's psychoanalysis; instead Binswanger emphasized the research outcomes of Cassirer, Goldstein and Gelb. There was an extensive exchange of letters between both of them, and joint ideas came so close that Cassirer wrote in 1926: "I have the very distinct impression, that finally the separating border between medics and philosophers has been broken down and both specialties can progress in joint cooperation."[54] Nevertheless, planned projects never came to fruition, as Binswanger made another theoretical turn towards Heidegger, having read his treatise *Sein und Zeit* in Husserl's *'Jahrbuch für Philosophie und phänomenologische Forschung'*. Heidegger's ideas had such an impact on Binswanger that he later apologized for his 1924 'errors'[55] and modelled his 'Daseinsanalyse' on an esoteric concept of Heideggerian linguistic self-references. He devoted his well-known publication *'Drei Formen missglückten Daseins'*[56] in particular to the new Heideggerian approach. But if we examine the cases which he presented, the patients' strangeness, their lack of resonance, their rigidity, their loss of perspective and their 'as-if' thinking all demonstrate a loss of making sense and a breakdown of symbolic formation which, in our view, can be much better explained by Cassirer's symbolic system than by Heidegger's 'Dasein' approach.

Cassirer referred to the example of transformation-groups in mathematics to clarify the way in which levels of world-making—based on underlying invariant structures—can be connected to one other and transformed into one another.[57] Thus certain qualities emerge as finally compatible although they had seemed mutually contradictory in the first place. In clinical terms this obviates the need for much of the sensual concreteness of symptomatologies:

> However, this phenomenon [i.e. Gestalt-structure] is related to a much more general problem, a problem of abstract mathematics; indeed, what else is this 'identity' of the perceptual form but what, in a much higher degree of precision, we found to subsist in the domain of geometrical concepts? What we find in both cases are invariances with respect to variations undergone by the primitive elements out of which a form is constructed; the peculiar kind of 'identity' that is attributed to apparently altogether heterogeneous figures in virtue

---

53 Cassirer (2009), 60.
54 Cassirer (2009), 93.
55 Binswanger (1994), 321.
56 Binswanger (1994).
57 Cassirer (1944).

of their being transformable into one another by means of certain operations defining a group, is thus seen to exist also in the domain of perception; this identity permits us not only to single out elements but also to grasp 'structures' in perception. To the mathematical concept of 'transformability' there corresponds, in the domain of perception, the concept of 'transposability'.[58]

5 Cassirer and the 'Gestalt-Movement'

Cassirer never considered himself a Gestalt theorist. Nevertheless, his philosophical writings, and especially his psychopathological research and publications, were strongly influenced by Gestalt ideas and influenced many researchers coming from a pure Gestalt background. In *Substanzbegriff und Funktionsbegriff* he explained:

> What is a given and what is known to us about the realm of consciousness are never isolated fragments, assembling to generate an observable impact. Instead it always is a well-constructed, sophisticated manifold, organized by interrelations of all kinds which, only due to our power of abstraction, can be separated in its different parts. The question cannot be put as how we can start with the isolated parts to achieve wholeness, but how, starting from wholeness, we get to its parts. Elements as such cannot exist without some form of inner relatedness; thus trying to extract their possible ways of relatedness from the sole elements is bound to failure.[59]

Cassirer agreed with the view of British neurologist Hughlings Jackson that the loss of speech (in aphasia) cannot be seen as a mere inability of word building, but rather a disorder in the construction of predicative sentences, "in general those determining the being, the kind or relatedness of objects."[60] In Cassirer's opinion, it is not the presence of Gestalt as a directly given phenomenon of nature which allows a full understanding of its formation. On the contrary, it is the escape from those concrete visual spheres into a virtual realm of relationships and structures which allows what the Greek word 'symbolein' actually means: the creation of wholeness, a symbolic form, deriving from complementary elements—like man and milieu. With regards to the underlying patterns of the contributing elements which facilitate this process, it is the abstract phenomenon of *prägnanz*, a term coined by Cassirer to explain the very transformation that makes Gestalt possible: "By 'symbolic pregnance' we mean the way (*die Art*)

---

58 Cassirer (1944), 25.
59 Cassirer (1923a), ch.8, II.
60 Head (1915), 132.

in which a perception as a sensory experience contains a meaning which it immediately and concretely represents."[61] The concrete superficial characteristics of both protagonists, even though their fascinating uniqueness first catches the observers' eye, are not the crucial issue. Individual elements as such cannot exist without some form of cooperation, and therefore trying to derive the actual relationship from the elements on their own is bound to fail. Moreover, "Whatever kind or form of the subject, this is why the point of view of a copying observance has to be replaced by an 'architectonical interconnectedness'."[62]

During the 1920s, certain practitioners in neurology and psychiatry saw the benefits of a Gestalt discourse. Binswanger[63], Goldstein[64] and Foulkes[65] were the most well-known professionals for fostering a Gestalt approach as part of their clinical practice. Gestalt ideas had a major impact on Kurt Lewin as well, in particular on his concepts of field-theory and action-research; they also had some influence on Moreno's psychodrama, on Leuner's 'symbol drama' and on Foulkes' theories on group-dynamics. But, despite its strong start, Gestalt theory failed to develop a convincing contribution to a theory of consciousness.[66] There is no doubt that its promising discourse was brutally halted by Fascism and World War II. Most of its theoreticians and researchers—Max Wertheimer, Karl Duncker, Wolfgang Koehler, Kurt Goldstein, Kurt Lewin, Sigmund Fuchs, Karl Buehler, Ernst Cassirer and many others—were driven into exile, and had their scientific work interrupted and destroyed, or were even murdered, as was Kurt Grelling in 1942.

The urgent necessity to understand the crucial connection between Gestalt- and Symbol-theory was never taken up. Cassirer's appeal to strengthen this approach and develop its theoretical perspective beyond the sensual realm of everyday (geometrical) experience—towards more virtual, abstract ideas of interconnectivity—was neglected by Goldstein as soon as their joint pre-war cooperation in Germany came to an end. Wolfgang Köhler's 'Isomorphie-Thesis' in its vague formulation of possible connections between mental and social existence, only added to an already existing confusion.[67] It gave rise to a series of misinterpretations, with the majority of researchers in the field even today siding with an interpretation of such parallel activity, a notion recently refueled by the

---

61 Cassirer (1957), 202.
62 Cassirer (1985), 20.
63 Binswanger (1924).
64 Goldstein (1934).
65 Foulkes (1948).
66 Ash (1998), 409–11.
67 Köhler (1929).

current vogue in research into mirror-neurons. A more comprehensive discussion of Köhler's—sometimes contradictory—remarks reveal that similarities in structure on both sides of the purported dualism only refer to the character of their relational make-up, while Gestalt-building requires further complementary components to achieve the final creative symbolic form of the ensuing figure. It was only Aaron Gurwitsch[68], who, referring to the works of Merleau-Ponty and Cassirer, followed this route, researching and exploring the missing link between Gelb's and Goldstein's concept of the 'concrete and abstract attitude' and Husserl's phenomenology.

In German psychiatry it was Klaus Conrad who resumed his wartime research on Gestalt in a number of well-received publications on the loss of Gestalt in psychosis.[69] He described several steps of '*Gestaltverlust*' and tried to apply them to a scheme built on Lewin's theory of mental suspension systems. Conrad's clinical considerations were much more flexible and complex in comparison with Kraeplinean theories, yet they remained very much tied to the concept of psychosis as a mere brain illness. His early death in 1962 brought an end to the Gestalt discourse in German mainstream psychiatry.

6 Cassirer's Impact on Psychopathology (post-WWII)

Nonetheless, behind the stage of public discourse Cassirer's ideas on the make-up of mental formation and psychopathology had a lasting influence on numerous scientists, a fact which has only emerged in recent decades through studies in the history of science. Luria, Leontief, Vygotsky, Bakhtin and Saporoshez in Russia modeled parts of their theories on Cassirer's ideas (or Goldstein's and Lewin's reception of Cassirer's philosophy), as did Bourdieu, van Ey, Canguilhem, Merleau-Ponty, Lacan and Foucault in France; Kasanian, Royce[70], Werner, Kaplan, Goodman, Hacker, Rappaport, Stack-Sullivan, Segal and von Bertalanffy in North America; Bash and Ciompi in Switzerland; Mayer-Gross, Elias and Bion in England; and Leuner, Conrad, Mentzos and Lorenzer in Germany.

Despite generous research funds in his American exile, Kurt Goldstein, Cassirer's closest clinical and philosophical friend and co-researcher, never managed to overcome the loss of his continental network and philosophical back-

---

68 Gurwitsch (1949).
69 Conrad (1958).
70 Royce (1965).

ground. His concept of abstract versus concrete attitude fell on deaf ears in the USA. His figure-background interpretation, which resembles Kurt Lewin's scheme, in that 'background' is conceived to be an abstract matrix of interrelations that are not represented on a pure phenomenological level, also remained misunderstood. Goldstein's early research on brain-injured patients (from World War I) was successfully repeated in a psychiatric setting with psychotic patients, but the results were obtained by Vigotsky and Luria in the Soviet Union[71] and thus remained sidelined in the USA by the impact of the 'cold war' in the late 1940s and 1950s. Goldstein's own appeasement policy of eradicating most of Cassirer's philosophical quotations from his own publications did not improve his standing. Moreover, it robbed Goldstein's readers of the very theoretical framework on which it was erected.

Integrating Cassirer's view and Gestalt theory, Russian psychologist AN Leontjew described 'Gestalt-building' by symbolic formation as a 'mechanism of building mechanisms' as early as the 1950s. Quoting research results from his colleague A.W. Saporoshez from 1958,[72] he pointed out that animal behavior never relies on a proper use of tools, and that typical copying activities in small children (echokinesis, echomimia, echolalia) come to an end early in the second year. It is then regularly replaced by 'copying' provided patterns, which are determined by *'Nachahmungshandlungen'*, a special form of copying activity. Their process of emergence is not fostered by a rewarding stimulus but by the unification of the child's own activity with its imagined purpose. This clearly contradicts the recent mirror neuron approach, suggesting instead that the early exhausting practice of storing sequences of outside experience gets replaced by a coding exercise via ever more complex categorization.

Most interesting is the fact that Jean Piaget,[73] from about 1930 on, established an understanding of diverse and added layers of how consciousness develops in children[74], which, based mainly on the semiotic philosophy of Saussure and the mathematical models of the Bourbaki-group, points to the incorporation of mental tools by which parallel ontologies and representational models of 'reality' come about. There is such a striking similarity between Cassirer-based concepts of psychopathology and those of Piaget that, despite the historical non-existence of dialogue between the two of them, researchers are now speaking of a joint "genetical semiology".[75] Promising attempts can also be detected in disen-

---

71 Vygotsky (1934).
72 Leontjew (1977), 295.
73 Piaget (1974).
74 Zlatev and Andrén (2009).
75 Fetz (1981).

tangling seemingly contradictory positions between the symbol concept of Cassirer and those of Freud[76], as well as showing up some surprising similarities between the theories of Cassirer and Jung.[77]

Group analysis, fostered and founded by S.H. Foulkes in England, owes much of its matrix-concept to Cassirer's ideas. Foulkes spent his German years as an assistant of Goldstein in Frankfurt in the mid-1920s when Goldstein and Cassirer cooperated on a daily basis on clinical cases.[78] The progressive clinical success of Luc Ciompi[79] was only possible because of his capacity to integrate Saussure's and Cassirer's structural and semiotic/symbolic thinking into mainstream psychiatry.

Hanscarl Leuner,[80] internationally renowned German psychiatrist and LSD researcher, was one of the few prominent figures after World War II who kept alive the approach of Goldstein, Lewin and Cassirer. Referring to Lewin's 'parallel dynamic systems of suspension' as a preemptive state of consciousness and Goldstein's idea of mental equilibriums, this allowed him to focus on varying levels of mental functioning, not just on a chaotic disorder of dysfunction and pathology. As a result, he was able to attribute the chaos following mental breakdown in psychosis (or emerging from LSD consumption in his research trials) to a mixture of damaged symbolic levels, prefabricated mental patterns and attempts at symbol-reformation, all of which can be seen as potential building stones of a new reality. Results of this comprehensive hallucinogenic research were, to Leuner, proof and confirmation of his theoretical approach. He cultivated a discourse on Lewin's idea of a new 'conditional-genetic psychopathology', one which was strongly opposed to the narrow Freudian interpretation of symbols as mere signs of pathology and the unconscious.[81] Leuner also categorized Jaspers' phenomenological and existentialistic approach as "rigid and fixated on substance," and further rejected Jaspers' widely adopted paradigms on mental illness as an "erroneous identification of appearance and phenomenon."[82] Attacking both godfathers of psychopathological discourse at the same time did not make Leuner many friends, and his theoretical papers, albeit strongly evidence-based in hallucinogenic research, proved too complicated to enter mainstream discussion. His meticulously formulated "transphenomenal dynamic

---

[76] Lorenzer (1970a); Lorenzer (1970b); Mentzos (1997); Mentzos (2009).
[77] Pietikainen (1998).
[78] Nitzgen (2010).
[79] Ciompi (1982).
[80] Leuner (1962).
[81] Leuner (1962), 109–12.
[82] Leuner (1962), 57–60.

mental steering system (tdyst)"[83] remains a hidden gold-mine of structuralist research. Leuner was fully aware of a partial parallelism of Gestalt- and symbol-processes and he remains the most successful innovator in implementing a '*katathymes Bilderleben*' or 'symbol theory' into clinical psychiatric practice. Over the years this approach emerged as a successful method of treatment, using imaginative 'symbols' to re-establish damaged bridges of interaction when dealing with severe forms of mental illness.

The closest structural link to the ideas of Cassirer and Goldstein was the French concept of '*pensée operatoire*', presented in 1978 by Pierre Marty and Michel de M'Uzan, which focused on plausible origins of psychosomatic illness. The term referred to the model of '*aggressivite fruste*', an unintegrated form of mental energy leading to somatic symptoms, a notion which had been formulated by Ziwar,[84] an Egyptian psychoanalyst. These authors described a '*relation blanche*', meaning a breakdown of the living interacting emotional contact, which became one-dimensional, without the skills of symbolization. Such patients, if seen from Cassirer's perspective, lack the capacity to abstract, remain unable to extract underlying patterns from a situation and use these 'categorizations' further to protect themselves, or to communicate or to jointly create an intersubjective reality with others. In both conceptions, individual psychopathology derives from the difficulty in blending concrete sensual interaction with dysfunctional patterns of abstract knowledge, and so such patients remain unfit to maintain social contact or open spheres of resonance (*Resonanzräume*) to practice creative life. This lasting frustration of a repetitive breakdown of the symbolic link, i.e. the failure to cope with the demands of milieu and future, finally leads to withdrawal, isolation and the resurrection of non-symbolic, autoregulatory realms of the past, with a regression into ontogenetically earlier patterns of biological and organic responses.

An important conference on 'Psychology and the Symbol' took place in Los Angeles in 1963 with presentations by Hacker, Bertalanffy, Rappaport and Royce.[85] Its whole focus was close to Cassirer's psychopathological approach and stressed the fact that symbols are freely created, and free from the imposed rules of physics and biology. Contributors to the conference further proposed that symbolization has a compelling rather than a compulsory quality, and that it is linked to emancipation, liberation and autonomy, but also to the continuing abuse of power, and that our symbolic repertoire is immensely variable

---

[83] Leuner (1962), 185–186.
[84] Ziwar (1948).
[85] Royce (1965).

but not inexhaustible, and limited by the possibilities of human Gestalt-perception and creation, qualities which break down in mental crisis.[86] For these reasons, the use of the 'symbolic concept' can help to understand and categorize a chaotic and contradictory set of previously disconnected symptoms. Strangely enough, the authors themselves—impressed by the overall 'success' of psychopharmacology—felt that their promising ideas were not yet powerful enough to be introduced into clinical psychiatry.

The evidence of hallucinogenic research during the 1970s (which a few years later came to a complete halt following a total ban on LSD and similar substances in the USA and Europe) provided a late clinical confirmation of Cassirer's theoretical approach.[87] Research results demonstrate the systematic deconstruction of layers of symbolization and consciousness as a result of artificial psychosis, and the subsequent reaction of the brain in trying to accommodate sudden vulnerability by using preformed neurological engrams.

Much attention has recently been given Fonagy's mentalization project,[88] whose findings on mental representation are presented as if totally disconnected from the historical roots of symbolic research. The project draws heavily on speculation about mirror neurons[89] and relies on the analysis of, particularly, childhood experiences, ignoring the emerging and changing complexity of symbolization as an ever-present process at all age levels. Symbolizing—as Allen and Fonagy[90] insist—can only start from a third-person perspective. In reality, symbolization is already present in magic and mythic (ambivalent) stages of the subject, albeit not carried by the subject himself or herself but by the complexity of the corresponding group.

7 A 'Matrix of Mental Formation'

Cassirer's view, expressed in today's terms, is that mental stability is not 'a function of the brain' but a functioning social construct, as is a good marriage, a decent education or respectable science. All are very much real and no 'myth', but not as a substance or an observable object in our brains, but as a relational order, wherein our brain plays a crucial role. Our different levels of consciousness are not just transmitter changes or simple representations of the outside

---

[86] Royce (1965).
[87] Baastians (1977); Grof and Halifax-Grof (1975); Leuner (1981); Pahnke and Richards (1966).
[88] Allen and Fonagy (2006).
[89] Gallese and Goldman (1998).
[90] Allen and Fonagy (2006).

world, but are the product of a creative tension between stabilized categorical patterns of the subject, growing in its complexity, and its social field or its later deconstructed elements. What is even more crucial is that the short-lived entities that the subject and environment are dealing with are not empirical sense data but symbols through and through. In a mental crisis this symbolic matrix breaks down, the pattern-based construct of reality gets lost, and symbolic language is severely affected.

Until now, Cassirer's approach to psychopathology has been marginalized and misunderstood, often confused with the concepts of contemporary philosophers, symbolists and Gestalt therapists. As a result, it has been left behind in the mainstream debates of psychiatry. It is crucial to understand that Cassirer's approach to symbolic formation is not based on the elementary application of a sphere of subjective fictional signs or terms to the perception of given objects in the surrounding environment. Instead, his concept requires the application of rules and structures that can be transferred from each of both spheres into the other. This means that the structure of each correlative element is not perceived as a given but is only created in the process of '*Gestaltung*' itself, thereby emerging as a complementary complexity of underlying patterns of both sides.[91] Cassirer's concept—and this is the major difference from Gestalt theory and a prerequisite to understanding his concept of 'Symbolic Formation'—can be extended to theoretical or virtual spheres which are no longer bound to an empirical construct of perception. Translated into clinical terms, this approach leads to a much wider understanding of a multi-layered architecture of mental health, which the German psychiatrist Blankenburg later termed: "*natürliche Selbstverständlichkeit*".[92] It allows for a fixed point of reference in defining 'mental illness', and it might help us understand yet unexplained symptom changes during the course of treatment.

Cassirer never developed a full system of 'symbolic formation', yet he had explicitly envisaged this possibility in the first volume of his 'Philosophy of Symbolic Forms':

> If there was a way to gain a systematic perspective over the different directions of that kind [i.e. the entirety of symbolic forms]—and: if there was the possibility of deconstructing it's typical and invariant pattern, as well as it's specific internal order and hidden differences, the ideal form of 'general characteristics' for the entirety of mental productivity might emerge—just as Leibniz had called for with regards to human knowledge in general.[93]

---

91 Ihmig (1997).
92 Blankenburg (1973).
93 Cassirer (1923), 18. Translation by Norbert Andersch.

Russian researchers have repeatedly stressed the point that human communication is always facilitated on different levels of semiosis,[94] and Portnov finally concludes: "the only way forward is not only to hint at the different levels of complexity among the semiotic layers, but to compare the structure of mental activity and consciousness to the different types and layers of the semiotic process."[95]

Here is the basic idea of the proposed 'Matrix' model: it combines a three-layered make-up of (1) basic patterns/codes of complexity, (2) meta-stabilities between individuals and milieu, and (3) a multitude of levels of 'symbolic formation'. Coding goes back to our instinct-driven behavior where patterns from the surrounding milieu ('*Wirkwelt*') are met by genetically complementary codes of rising complexity, established through past experience ('*Merkwelt*')—mainly expressed in immediate physical action.[96] Fixed meta-stabilities (as a second component) are likely to emerge only much later,[97] turning results of present live experience into patterns of interaction—thus modifying the settings and playing-fields of primates, including humans. Exclusive and unique (and attached to humans only) is the quality of the third step: symbolic pattern interference based on shared and anticipated intentionality among proactive humans, whose previously fixed meta-stabilities turn into flexible suspension systems that become symbolically connected to extra-cerebral signs—thus preserving memory for automatized repetitive usage, separated from the concrete content of the original context.[98]

Language is the main tool among others like gestures, mimicry, looks, dance, music, collective use of tools, etc. to expand figure building to lasting levels of world-making, like magic, myth, religion, law, politics, arts and others, which occur on a universal scale. Within these frames of mutual interaction, one can find more powerful paradigms and functioning hierarchies, yet they can well co-exist in a parallel fashion, creating a whole variety of different roles of cultural behavior; building various safety-nets for our daily undertakings, experiments, expectations, and protecting us in disappointments and failings. This model is a sophisticated map of accessible spheres; providing subjective intentions of varying complexities within their matching spaces of resonance. It is a guide to distinguish symbol-formation: preformed versus active,

---

[94] Seboek (1975).
[95] Portnov (1993), 275. Translation by Norbert Andersch.
[96] Cf. Uexküll (1909).
[97] Kriz (2001); Kelso (2008).
[98] Andersch (2007).

impulsive versus considered, spontaneous versus pre-planned; thus escaping from unilateral animal compulsion—still much alive in all humans.

Symbolic formation uses its capacity to identify underlying patterns in different contexts in order to not have to respond to every drive with an exhausting urge towards fulfillment. It protects us from being pressured towards immediate physical action, replacing it with ever more complex proactive planning—changing our environment into a habitat, which makes the gain of our needs more likely to be met—so that humans can stand back and delay immediate action for considerable periods, using saved energy to pursue new and different aims, emerging beyond our instinctive compulsion.

The draft model (Matrix) above is based on the assumption that the multitude and the uniqueness of the human personality emerges from a system of invariant pattern of a universal quality—in analogy (not comparison) to our anatomical architecture and its universal homogeneity. Those patterns of complexity merge into meta-stabilities via interference, only to change into 'symbolic forms' in human encounters, providing a vast variety of living suspension figures as the backbone of creative action between subjects and their resonating milieu. The 'Matrix of Mental Formation' is the cultural unfolding of re-presentation and consciousness—mainly replacing immediate, direct action with complex layers of mediated interference and resonance.

This is how the 'Matrix of Mental Formation' diagram should be 'read': the main aspect is the on-going cultural exchange between human intentionality (here on the left) and its natural and cultural milieu (on the right), and: the various cultural forms on the different levels of symbolic formation (middle). Without this 'dance of interaction', without this rapid repetitive proof of reality, human reaction would be reduced to either the inexperienced genetically transmitted patterns of behavior or to cultural conserves enforced by the group.

You can see in the graph that symbolic formation—the third element in the middle—does not exist from the beginning. Instead, it only emerges out of the original condition of universality (09), transitional symbiosis (1/8) and in- and ex-corporation between partners (2–7). It takes further steps of added complexity to set up related geometries to finally develop a mental membrane (0) between those contradictory—and figure-building complementary—entities, which in adult life we describe as subject and object (306, 405, 504, 603).

On the side of the subject, the contribution on the first level of 'symbol formation' (1/8) can only be a unilateral quality: either fascination, i.e. being totally taken in by the attraction of the surrounding magic complexity (8), or: repetition, intentionally acting out the same forward move again and again (1). On the next level (2–7), intentionality is the essence of change; ambivalent, thus adding to

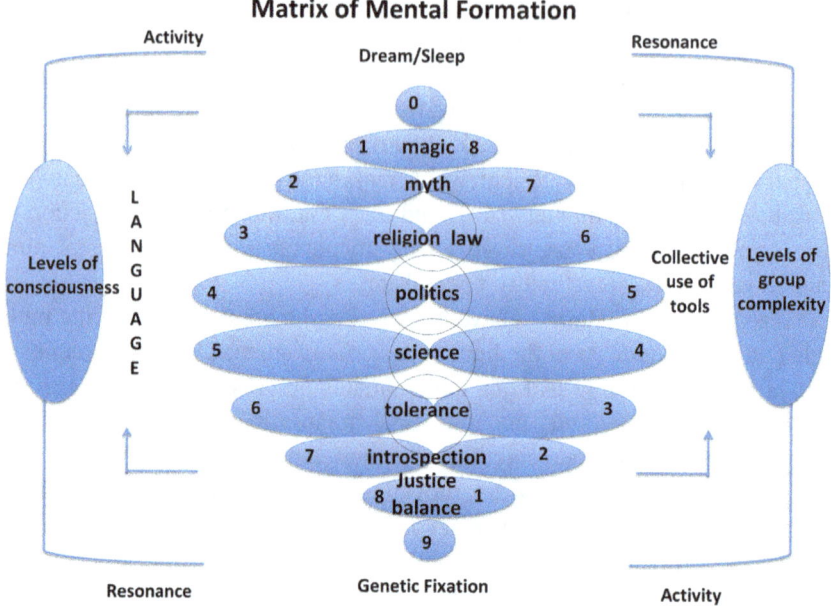

Fig. 1: The Matrix of Mental Formation

the intensification of contradictory feelings with a quality of roughly typifying or pursuing identification with the transitional object of choice.

On the third level, intentionality is represented in separation, identification (3) and (al)location in space and time (6); on the fourth level it unfolds by joint, authority-led cooperation (5) and body awareness (4). On the fifth level finally, there is structural thinking. This means 'abstract thinking'—i.e. moving virtual objects in relation to each other—a constellation which finds itself faced by a world of objects—the first time ever that individual complexity surmounts corresponding group knowledge. This is the mental paradigm of human existence in most (post)industrialized countries of the Western world. Progressing through the different subjective levels, there is a mounting complexity, an on-going emancipation, a setting-free of previous bindings finally leading to adult individualism (504), a newly-won freedom of choice and self-determination—but also the first level susceptible to break up again in a beginning mental crisis.

The process of becoming an individual is a long one. It requires a process of subject growth towards ever more complex, abstract behavior that then facilitates the carving out of complementary sensual elements out of the corresponding milieu. Only this on-going abstraction/deconstruction interference allows for the continuous creation of new levels of world making. It also proves that a mature and personal intentionality is a very late and very abstract level of existence —and one that comes at a price: the loss of contact to our early natural understanding of 'being in the world'; cut off from our magical, mythical and religious forms of self-evidence.

Cassirer's opinion is that gaining back those sensory and concrete aspects of our lives—lost during our transformation into a state of mature consciousness—cannot be achieved by regressing to those lost realms of previous experience. To the contrary: access to previous levels can only be gained by radically moving further on, from our present structural level of symbolization and consciousness (504), towards a newly built virtual sphere of integration (603). A deductive procedure that entails abandoning final thoughts of organic property or mere localization; now being replaced by ideas of mere function and changeable relatedness, drawn from underlying pattern in subject and object alike. Only the emergence of codes on both sides of the divide allows us to proceed to yet another virtual layer of symbolization—comparable to the building up of mathematical theories from substantial to differential to integral to infinitesimal, etc. It needs brave steps of further progress, which facilitates entrance into previous experiences—now from the other side of the divide—to reactivate and integrate the lost components from the early stages of our existence. Integration on this level (603) is the prerequisite for the final steps of mature symbol-creation (7–2) and self-control (8/1).

All levels of world-making—independent from their cultural content—are symbolically linked patterns of complementary complexity, or, expressed in mathematical, group-theoretical terms: the Matrix can be considered as a group with the connecting element of complementary complexity. They all represent a universal attempt of human groups to hand over and transform their common experience into relational complexities of individual group members. Each of these levels of the Matrix has a different quality in comparison with the previous one. All are worlds of their own making, and none of them can be absorbed or replaced by one of the others. Each one has its own cultural production and specific form of creation, which emerges as magic, myth, language, religion, politics, science, integration, creativity and self-control. They all are universal forms of existence beyond racial or regional differences. Nonetheless, it is a tragic fact that, due to their inner consistency and 'logic', all of these 'paradigms' lead to a bitter struggle to be accepted as the only way of existence and truth, including the efforts to eradicate the others. It takes quite a number of unwilling changes through different steps of this mental formation to give in to the experience that different ways of world building are not necessarily exclusive;

that their parallel variety increases flexibility and creativity, and that this newly gained capacity of frame-changing augments our mental stability instead of undermining it.

The 'Matrix' is a living object. It does not define the routes of human activity and consciousness, yet it provides a moving structure from which a probability can be drawn of how it might function. Nonetheless, it would be wrong to entirely replace terms of substance with terms of function. The new quality lies in developing a metamorphosis of '*Gestaltung*', in discovering a whole group of different fields of symbolic formation: a new creation at the interchange of patterns, both of them consisting of varying layers of substance and function. The Matrix shows no preference for the phenomenal (as in contrast to the virtual), no preference for the sensual (as in contrast to the abstract), and no preference for evidence-based relationship (as being superior to repetition or intensifying). There is an indispensable radical equality in all ways of world making, in that all of their aspects—concrete and abstract—come to the surface, albeit in an always-different constellation.

The brain as our neurological representation is only half of the symbolic Matrix—yet always happy to codify pattern of magic, myth and religion—totally unwilling to lend its cells, its binding-capacity and its membranes in an equal way to the more complex, new and different levels of cultural existence. Freeing up mental capacity out of its previous bindings, its neurological circles and preformed patterns is an exhausting process occurring between individuals and group. And it is only the attraction of intensity and the totality of merging patterns that guarantees progress in such cultural creations. Most helpful are music, language and the collective use of tools as they overwrite our old and fast instinct-reactions with the much slower indirect but reality-proven and powerful external symbolic forms.

The Matrix of Mental Formation is a permanent building-site, and it is only the lower floors of this building that seem ready or show a strong enough ability to be sustainable. Beyond that, the matrix shows on-going signs of deconstruction, which have to be repaired and renovated by the daily re-enacting of cultural experience. It demands the on-going use of language and collective work to keep the Matrix—and our consciousness, as its inner representation—alive. Longer periods of inactivity or isolation help to destroy this net of culture. It is also sometimes our laziness which allows it to be replaced by empty tradition and preformed patterns, and such a loss of spontaneity and creativity can, over a long period, and in isolation descend into early forms of mental illness or group-paranoia.

8 A New and Different Way of Thought

Ernst Cassirer centers his whole philosophical approach around the emergence of 'symbolic form' as the missing link between the individual biological being and civilization. In his opinion there is no human reality (*Wirklichkeit*) without or beyond 'symbolic formation'. The emerging human cultural world represents an irrevocable break with its organic animal tradition. This is reflected in the change of interaction between human intentionality and 'civilization', from instinct and preformed mental patterns to different levels of 'world-making' facilitated by symbolic forms. The latter appear on the human stage as magic, myth, language, religion, body experience, politics, science, the arts and others, taking the form of a universal metamorphosis of cultural creations, woven into a matrix of mental formation called consciousness.

It is 'symbolic formation' which provides the background, the safety-net and the sense of self to our fragile existence and our unsecured daily undertakings. During the first half of the twentieth century Cassirer's considerations seemed—and even now seem—a step too far for most psychiatrists who recoil from having their medical approach, or their patient's behavior, deconstructed into what looks like lifeless sequences of abstract patterns. Yet Cassirer was convinced that the growing knowledge about 'invariants of human experience' and the merger of categorical and sensual aspects in symbolic formation would bring up a more sophisticated picture of the uniqueness and variability of meaningfulness, which might help explain what even today are unexplainable and contradictory elements of psychiatric symptomatology.

Approached from such a 'symbolic' angle, "mental health" can be defined as the human ability to stabilize early patterns of personal experience and to successfully create, change and integrate, symbolic forms of social interaction, while at the same time establishing an equilibrium between the demands and intentions of self-regulation and environment, with further addition of its newly found results to human tradition.

Mental illness subsequently would no longer be misidentified as a mere dysfunction of the brain, but regarded as the inability to stabilize and/or integrate patterns of behavior into a social framework, leading to a breakdown of different and multiple layers of symbolic formation, while at the same time the balance between cultural interaction and the emergence of inner preformed patterns is continuously or constantly changed towards the latter. For psychiatry and psychopathology this route is still open; there should be organized efforts in collecting and coordinating findings on semiotic and symbolic research, in contributing to a 'science of meaning' or salience beyond the mere biological function of our animal brains and in integrating this important human source of knowledge into the regular discourse of our discipline.

Bibliography

Allen and Fonagy (2006): Jon G. Allen and Peter Fonagy (eds.), *Handbook of Mentalization-Based Treatment*, Chichester, UK: John Wiley and Sons.

Andersch (2007): Norbert Andersch, "Symbolische Form und Gestalt", *Gestalt-Theory* 29(4): 279–293.

Andersch (2010): Norbert Andersch, "Zur Pathologie des Symbolbewusstseins. Ernst Cassirers uneingelöster Beitrag zu einer radikalen Reform der Psychopathologie", in: B. Holdorff and E. Kumbier (eds.) *Schriftenreihe der DGGN*, Vol. 16. Würzburg: Königshausen und Neumann, 109–124.

Andersch (2012): Norbert Andersch, "Hanscarl Leuners Monographie: 'Die experimentelle Psychose' und sein Konzept einer 'konditional-genetischen Psychopathologie'", in: B. Holdorff and E. Kumbier (eds.) *Schriftenreihe der DGGN*, Vol. 18. Würzburg: Königshausen und Neumann, 197–212.

Andersch (2014): Norbert Andersch, *Symbolische Form und psychische Erkrankung. Argumente für eine neue Psychopathologie*. Würzburg: Königshausen und Neumann.

Andersch and Cutting (2014): Norbert Andersch and John Cutting, "Ernst Cassirer's Philosophy of Symbolic Forms and its impact on the theory of psychopathology". *History of Psychiatry* 25(2), 203–223.

Ash (1998): Mitchell G. Ash, *Gestalt Psychology in German Culture, 1890–1967. Holism and the Quest for Objectivity*. Cambridge: Cambridge University Press.

Baastians (1977): Jan Baastians, "The implications of the specificity concept for the treatment of psychosomatic patients". *Psychotherapy and Psychosomatics* 28(1–4), 285–293.

Bayer (2001): Thora Ilin Bayer, *Cassirer's Metaphysics of Symbolic Forms: A Philosophical Commentary*, New Haven: Yale University Press.

Berrios (1999): German E. Berrios, "Classifications in psychiatry: a conceptual history". *Australian & New Zealand Journal of Psychiatry* 33, 145–160.

Binswanger (1924): Ludwig Binswanger, "Welche Aufgaben ergeben sich für die Psychiatrie aus den Fortschritten der neueren Psychologie?" *Zeitschrift für die gesamte Neurologie und Psychiatrie* 91(3/5, Special Issue).

Binswanger (1994): Ludwig Binswanger, *Ausgewählte Werke*, Bd. 1, Heidelberg: Roland Asanger.

Blankenburg (1973): Wolfgang Blankenburg, *Der Verlust der natürlichen Selbstverständlichkeit*. Berlin: Springer.

Brumlik (1993): Michael Brumlik, *C.G. Jung zur Einführung*. Hamburg: Junius.

Bühler (1982): Karl Bühler, *Sprachtheorie. Die Darstellungsfunktion der Sprache*, Stuttgart and New York: Fischer.

Bühler (1960): Karl Bühler, *Das Gestaltprinzip im Leben der Menschen und der Tiere*. Bern: Hans Huber.

Cassirer (1902): Ernst Cassirer, "Descartes' Kritik der mathematischen und naturwissenschaftlichen Erkenntnis" in: Cassirer, *Leibniz' System in seinen wissenschaftlichen Grundlagen*, Marburg: Elwert'scheVerlagsbuchhandlung, 1–122.

Cassirer (1910): Ernst Cassirer, *Substanzbegriff und Funktionsbegriff: Untersuchungen über die Grundfragen der Erkenntniskritik*, Berlin: Bruno Cassirer.
Cassirer (1922): Ernst Cassirer, "Der Begriff der symbolischen Form im Aufbau der Geistewissenschaften", in: *Vorträge der Bibliothek Warburg, 1921–1922*, Leipzig: B.G. Teubner, 11–39.
Cassirer (1923a): Ernst Cassirer, *Substance and Function, and Einstein's Theory of Relativity*, WC Swabey and MC Swabey (trans.), Chicago: Open Court.
Cassirer (1923b): Ernst Cassirer, *Philosophie der symbolischen Formen. Vol. I: Die Sprache*, Berlin: Bruno Cassirer.
Cassirer (1925): Ernst Cassirer, *Philosophie der symbolischen Formen. Vol. II: Das mythische Denken*, Berlin: Bruno Cassirer.
Cassirer (1929): Ernst Cassirer, *Philosophie der symbolischen Formen. Vol. III: Phänomenologie der Erkenntnis*, Berlin: Bruno Cassirer.
Cassirer (1930): Ernst Cassirer, "'Geist und Leben' in der Philosophie der Gegenwart'", *Die Neue Rundschau* 41: 244–264, W. Brentall and P. Schilpp (trans.). In: Schilpp (1949), 855–880.
Cassirer (1944): Ernst Cassirer, "The concept of group and the theory of perception", A. Gurwitsch (trans.), *Philosopy and Phenomenological Research* 5(1): 1–35.
Cassirer (1953): Ernst Cassirer, *The Philosophy of Symbolic Forms. Vol I: Language*, R. Manheim (trans.), New Haven: Yale University Press.
Cassirer (1955): Ernst Cassirer, *The Philosophy of Symbolic Forms. Vol II: Mythical Thought*, R. Manheim (trans.), New Haven: Yale University Press.
Cassirer (1957): Ernst Cassirer, *The Philosophy of Symbolic Forms.Vol III: The Phenomenology of Knowledge*, R. Manheim (trans.), New Haven: Yale University Press.
Cassirer (1985): Ernst Cassirer, *Symbol, Technik, Sprache. Aufsätze aus den Jahren 1927–1933*, Hamburg: Meiner.
Cassirer (2006): Ernst Cassirer, *An Essay on Man*, in: B. Recki (ed.) Gesammelten Werke, Bd 23. Hamburg: Meiner.
Cassirer (2009): Ernst Cassirer, *Ausgewählter wissenschaftlicher Briefwechsel*, in: J.M. Krois, O. Schwemmer and C. Köhnke (eds.) Nachgelassene Manuskripte und Texte, Bd 18. Hamburg: Meiner.
Ciompi (1982): Luc Ciompi, *Affektlogik*, Stuttgart: Klett-Cotta.
Conrad (1958): Klaus Conrad, *Die beginnende Schizophrenie. Versuch einer Gestaltanalyse des Wahns*, Stuttgart: Thieme.
Cutting (2011): John Cutting, *A Critique of Psychopathology*, Berlin: Parodos.
Eckes-Lapp (1988): Rosemarie Eckes-Lapp, "Symbolbildung und Symbolik in psychoanalytischer Sicht", in: G. Benedetti and U. Rauchfleisch (eds.) *Welt der Symbole. Interdisziplinäre Aspekte des Symbolverständnisses*, Göttingen: Vandenhoek & Ruprecht, 172–199.
Elias (1937): Norbert Elias, *Über den Prozess der Zivilisation. Soziogenetische und psychogenetische Untersuchungen*, Frankfurt: Suhrkamp.
Ferenczi (1913): Sandor Ferenczi, "Zur Ontogenese der Symbole", *Internationale Zeitschrift für (ärztliche) Psychoanalyse* (1), 436–438.
Fetz (1981): Reto Luzius Fetz, "Genetische Semiologie? Symboltheorie im Ausgang von Ernst Cassirer und Jean Piaget", *Freiburger Zeitschrift für Philosophie und Theologie* 28, 434–470.

Finkelnburg (1870): Ferdinand Carl Finkelnburg, "Niederrheinische Gesellschaft in Bonn", Medicinische Sektion, Sitzung am 21. März 1870. *Berliner Klinische Wochenschrift* (37/8), 449–450, 460–462.
Foucault (2006): Michel Foucault, *History of Madness*, Abingdon: Routledge.
Foulkes (1983): Siegmund Heinrich Foulkes, *Introduction to Group Analytic Psychotherapy*, London: Karnac Books.
Freud A. (1936): Anna Freud, *Das Ich und die Abwehrmechanismen*, München: Kindler.
Freud (1894): Sigmund Freud, "Die Abwehr-Neuropsychosen", in: *Gesammelte Werke, Bd I*, Frankfurt: Fischer, 59–74.
Freud (1900): Sigmund Freud, "Die Traumdeutung", in: *Gesammelte Werke, Bd II & Bd III*, Frankfurt: Fischer.
Gallese and Goldman (1998): Vittorio Gallese and Alvin Goldman, "Mirror neurons and the simulation theory of mind-reading", *Trends in Cognitive Sciences* 2(12), 493–501.
Goldstein (1934): Kurt Goldstein, *Der Aufbau des Organismus*, Den Haag: Martin Nijhoff.
Goldstein (1943): Kurt Goldstein, "The significance of psychological research in schizophrenia", *Journal of Nervous and Mental Disorders* 97(3), 261–279.
Goldstein (1944), Kurt Goldstein, "Methodological approach to the study of schizophrenic thought disorder", in: J.S. Kasanin (ed.), *Language and Thought in Schizophrenia*, New York: Norton, 17–40.
Grof and Halifax-Grof (1975): Stanislav Grof and Joan Halifax-Grof, "Realms of the Human Unconscious", New York: The Viking Press.
Gurwitsch (1949): Aron Gurwitsch, "Gelb-Goldstein's concept of "concrete" and "categorial" attitude and the phenomenology of ideation", *Philosophy and Phenomenological Research* 10(2), 172–196.
Head (1915): Henry Head, "Hughlings Jackson on aphasia and kindred affections of speech", *Brain* 38, 1–190.
Head (1921): Henry Head, "Disorders of symbolic thinking and expression", *British Journal of Psychology* 11(2), 179–193.
Head (1926): Henry Head, *Aphasia and Kindred Disorders of Speech, Vol. I and II*, Cambridge: Cambridge University Press.
Heidegger (1927): Martin Heidegger, "Sein und Zeit", in: E. Husserl et al. (eds.) *Jahrbuch für Philosophie und phänomenologische Forschung*, V–XII. Halle/Saale: Niemeyer, 1–438.
Ihmig (1997): Karl-Norbert Ihmig, *Ernst Cassirers Invariantentheorie der Erfahrung und seine Rezeption des 'ErlangerProgramms'*, Hamburg: Meiner.
Jones (1916): Ernest Jones, "The theory of symbolism", *British Journal of Psychology* 9, 181–229.
Karpman (1943): Ben Karpman, "Environment and Heredity in the light of modern biology: a critical review", *Journal of Nervous and Mental Disease* 98(2), 154–163.
Köhler (1929): Wolfgang Köhler, *Gestalt Psychology*, New York: Liveright.
Kreitler (1965): Shulamith Kreitler, *Symbolschöpfung und Symbolerfassung*, München and Basel: Ernst Reinhardt.
Krois (1999): John Michael Krois, "Cassirer's 'Prototype and Model' of symbolism: its sources and significance", *Science in Context* 12(4), 531–547.
Krois (2004): John Michael Krois, "Ernst Cassirer's Philosophy of Biology", *Sign Systems Studies* 32(1/2), 277–295.

Kubie (1953): Lawrence S. Kubie, "The central representation of the symbolic process in psychosamatic disorders", *Psychosomatic Medicine* 15(1), 1–6.
Kussmaul (1874): Adolf Kussmaul, "Die Störungen der Sprache. Versuch einer Pathologie der Sprache", in: W.A. Erb (ed.) *Anhang zum Handbuch der Krankheiten des Nervensystems*, Bd. XII: Leipzig: Verlag F.C.W. Vogel.
Langer (1948): Susanne Langer, *Philosophy in a New Key*, New York: New American Library.
Leontjew (1977): Aleksej Nikolaevic Leontjew, *Probleme der Entwicklung des Psychischen*, Kronberg/Ts.: Athenaeum.
Leuner (1962): Hanscarl Leuner, *Die experimentelle Psychose*, Berlin, Göttingen, Heidelberg: Springer.
Leuner (1981): Hanscarl Leuner, *Halluzinogene: Psychische Grenzzustände in Forschung und Psychotherapie*, Bern, Stuttgart, Wien: Hans Huber.
Lewin (1926): Kurt Lewin, *Vorsatz, Wille und Bedürfnis*, Berlin: Julius Springer.
Lewin (1949): Kurt Lewin, "Cassirer's philosophy of science and the social sciences", in: E. Schilp (ed.) *The Philosophy of Ernst Cassirer*, Evanston, IL: Northwestern University Press, 271–288.
Lewin (1951): Kurt Lewin, *Field Theory in Social Science*, D Cartwright (ed.). New York: Harper.
Litt (1926): Theodor Litt, *Individuum und Gemeinschaft. Grundlegung der Kulturphilosophie*, Leipzig and Berlin: B. Teubner.
Lofts (2000): Stephen G. Lofts, *Ernst Cassirer. A "Repetition" of Modernity*, Albany: State University of New York Press.
Lorenzer (1970a): Alfred Lorenzer, *Sprachzerstörung und Rekonstruktion*, Frankfurt: Suhrkamp.
Lorenzer (1970b): Alfred Lorenzer, *Kritik des psychoanalytischen Symbolbegriffs*, Frankfurt: Suhrkamp.
Marty and de M'Uzan (1978): Pierre Marty and Michel de M'Uzan "Das operative Denken (pensée opératoire)", Psyche 32, 974–984.
Mentzos (1997): Stavros Mentzos, *Psychose und Konflikt*, Göttingen: Vandenhoeck und Ruprecht.
Mentzos (2009): Stavros Mentzos, *Lehrbuch der Psychodynamik*, Göttingen: Vandenhoeck & Ruprecht.
Nitzgen (2010): Dieter Nitzgen, "Hidden legacies. S.H. Foulkes—Kurt Goldstein—Ernst Cassirer", *Group Analysis* 43(3), 354–371.
Pahnke and Richards (1966): Walter N. Pahnke and William A. Richards, "Implications of LSD and experimental mysticism", *Journal of Religion and Health* 5(3), 175–208.
Piaget (1974): Jean Piaget, *Abriss der genetischen Epistemologie*, Olten und Freiburg: Walter Verlag.
Pick (1908): Arnold Pick, "Asymbolie, apraxie, aphasie", in: *Compte rendu des travaux du Ier congrès international de psychiatrie, de neurologie, de psychologie et de l'assistance des aliénés tenu à Amsterdam du 2 à 7 septembre 1907*, Amsterdam: Bussy, 341–350.
Pietikainen (1998): Petteri Pietikainen, "Archetypes as symbolic forms", *Journal of Analytical Psychology* 43(3), 325–343.
Riemann (1868): Bernhard Riemann, "Über die Hypothesen, welche der Geometrie zu Grunde liegen, aus dem Nachlass des Verfassers, mitgeteilt durch R. Dedekind", in: *Abhandlungen der Königlichen Gesellschaft der Wissenschaften zu Göttingen*, Bd. XIII 1866/1867, Göttingen: Dieterichsche Buchhandlung, 133–150.

Royce (1965): Joseph R. Royce (ed.), *Psychology and the Symbol. An Interdisciplinary Symposium*, New York: Random House.

Sacks (1995): Oliver Sacks, "Foreword", in: K. Goldstein, *The Organism. A Holistic Approach to Biology Derived from Pathological Data in Man*, New York: Zone Books, 7–14.

Saporoshez (1958): A.W. Saporoshez, *Die Bildung willkürlicher Bewegungen*, Habilitationsarbeit (Russ.).

Schilpp (1949): Paul Arthur Schilpp (ed.), *The Philosophy of Ernst Cassirer*, Evanston, IL: Library of Living Philosophers.

Silberer (1912a): Herbert Silberer, *Symbolik des Erwachens und Schwellensymbolik überhaupt. In: Jahrbuch fürpsychoanalytische und psychopathologische Forschungen*, Bd. III, Wien: Franz Deuticke, 621–660.

Silberer (1912b): Herbert Silberer, "Über die Symbolbildung. In: Jahrbuch für psychoanalytische und psychopathologische Forschungen", Bd. III, Wien: Franz Deuticke, 661–723.

Smith (2001): Howard A. Smith, *Psychosemiotics*, New York: Peter Lang.

Spamer (1876): Karl Spamer, "Über Aphasie und Asymbolie nebst dem Versuch einer Theoriebildung", *Archiv fur Psychiatrie und Nervenkrankheiten* 6, 496–542.

Vygotsky (1934): Lev Vygotsky, "Thought in Schizophrenia", *Archives of Neurology and Psychiatry* 31, 1063–1077.

von Uexküll (1909): Jakob von Uexküll, *Umwelt und Innenwelt der Tiere*, Berlin: J. Springer.

White (1946): Leslie A. White, "Miscellaneous: an essay on man. Ernst Cassirer", *American Anthropologist* 48(3), 461–463.

Ziwar (1948): Mostapha Ziwar, "Psychanalyse des principaux syndromes psychomatiques", *Revue Française de Psychanalyse* 12(4), 505–540.

Zlatev and Andrén (2009): Jordan Zlatev and Mats Andrén, "Stages and transitions in children's semiotic development", in: Jordan Zlatev, Mats Andrén, Marlene Johansson Falck and Carita Lundmark (eds) *Studies in Language and Cognition*, Newcastle: Cambridge Scholars, 380–401.

Part II: **Epistemology and the History of Philosophy**

Samantha Matherne (Santa Cruz)
Marburg Neo-Kantianism as Philosophy of Culture

1 Introduction

Although Ernst Cassirer is correctly regarded as one of the foremost figures in the Neo-Kantian movement that dominated Germany from 1870–1920, specifying exactly what his Neo-Kantianism amounts to can be a challenge. Not only must we clarify what his commitments are as a member of the so-called Marburg School of Neo-Kantianism, but also given the shift between his early philosophy of mathematics and natural science to his later philosophy of culture, we must consider to what extent he remained a Marburg Neo-Kantian throughout his career.

With regard to the first task, it is typical to approach the Marburg School, which was founded by Hermann Cohen and Paul Natorp, by way of a contrast with the other dominant school of Neo-Kantianism, the Southwest or Baden School, founded by Wilhelm Windelband and carried forward by Heinrich Rickert and Emil Lask. The going assumption is that these two schools were 'rivals' in the sense that the Marburg School focused exclusively on developing a Kantian approach to mathematical natural sciences (*Naturwissenschaften*), while the Southwest School privileged issues relating to normativity and value, hence their primary focus on the humanities (*Geisteswissenschaften*). If one accepts this 'scientist' interpretation of the Marburg School, one is tempted to read Cassirer's early work on mathematics and natural science as orthodox Marburg Neo-Kantianism and to then regard his later work on the philosophy of culture as a break from his predecessors, veering closer towards interests championed by the Southwest School.

In this paper, however, I argue that this way of interpreting Marburg Neo-Kantianism as well as Cassirer's relationship to it threatens to obscure one of the deep commitments shared by Cohen, Natorp, and Cassirer alike, viz., defending a systematic *philosophy of culture*, which accommodates both the mathematical natural sciences and the humanities. In order to bring to light the Marburg commitment to the philosophy of culture, I begin by calling into question the 'scientist' reading of the Marburg School that pits it against the Southwest School. I claim that although there are some important points of disagreement between the two schools, e.g., with regard to the notion of 'intuition,' there is a great deal that they agree on. In the first place, I show that they both endorse the basic tenets of Neo-Kantianism *in general* (Section 2). Moreover, I demonstrate that the Marburg and Southwest

Schools were united in rejecting 'genetic' interpretations of Kant in favor of an 'anti-psychologistic' interpretation, which placed emphasis on the logical conditions of knowledge in the mathematical natural sciences and humanities alike (Section 3). Once we begin to appreciate the continuity between the Marburg and Southwest Schools on these issues, we will be in a position to turn more directly to the Marburg approach to the philosophy of culture. To this end, we will consider not only how the Marburg Neo-Kantians use their distinctive 'transcendental method' to investigate the various regions *within* culture (Section 4), but also their attempts to account for the *systematic unity* of culture as a whole surprisingly by means of a distinctive form of 'psychology', which studies the consciousness of culture (Section 5). I conclude by claiming that this revised understanding of the Marburg School has implications for how we should understand Cassirer's relation to it: rather than read his *Philosophy of Symbolic Forms* as a break from his Marburg predecessors, we should treat it as a *critical revision* of Cohen's and Natorp's attempts to carry out the basic Marburg cultural project, which he continued to adhere to (Section 6).

2 Basic Neo-Kantian Commitments

Let's begin by situating the Marburg School within the Neo-Kantian movement more generally. In many ways, the Neo-Kantian movement arose in response to a worry about the continued value of philosophy in light of the rapid advancement of science in the mid-19th century: why would we continue to look to philosophy when science appeared to be capable and more reliable in providing answers to questions about the nature of the mind and world? The state of philosophy in the early 19th century did nothing to allay this worry, as the absolute idealism of Hegel and Fichte seemed to many to be little more than abstruse reasoning that had lost touch with the real world. This led many thinkers to endorse the 'positivist' idea that we should dispense with philosophy as a means of gaining knowledge and look exclusively to science to answer questions about the mind and world.

The Neo-Kantian movement emerged as a reaction against this positivist line of thought and as an attempt to justify the need for philosophy in the face of scientific progress. As the label for the movement suggests, the Neo-Kantians maintained that in order to vindicate philosophy, it was necessary to go 'back to Kant'.[1] But why Kant? For the Neo-Kantians, there are at least two reasons:

---

1 In *Kant und die Epigonen* (1865), Otto Liebmann critiques post-Kantian idealism and con-

first, Kant's philosophy gives us reason to doubt the underlying philosophical commitments of positivism, and, second, it offers a more satisfying analysis of how knowledge, whether in mathematics, natural science, or philosophy, is possible at all.

With regard to their criticisms of positivism, the Neo-Kantians argue that its proponents often make problematic assumptions with regards to metaphysics and epistemology. On the metaphysical side of things, the Neo-Kantians claim that many positivists are committed to a position we could call *'naïve realism'*, according to which subjects and objects form two ontologically independent realms.[2] On this view, neither the existence nor the properties of the entities in these realms depend upon each other. Epistemologically, the Neo-Kantians claim that positivists tend to endorse what we could call the *'copy theory'* of knowledge, which characterizes knowledge as a process in which our minds form a mental 'copy' of mind-independent objects.[3]

According to the Neo-Kantians, however, if we go 'back to Kant', then we will discover that endorsing either of these positions undermines one's ability to give a satisfying account of how we come to have knowledge, even in mathematics and natural science. To appreciate this, a few remarks about the basic Kantian framework for knowledge are in order. For Kant, knowledge is a matter of forming judgments that are *objectively valid*, i.e., they 'agree' with objects, and are *necessarily universally valid*, i.e., they are judgments that any judger at any time ought to make.[4] As such, from a Kantian perspective, any satisfying theory of knowledge must explain how we are able to form judgments that are valid in these ways.

Yet by Kant's lights, theories of knowledge that rest on naïve realism and the copy theory fall short on both of these counts. With respect to objective validity, Kant worries that if naïve realism is right, then it does not seem as if our judgment could 'agree' with objects: how could something non-mental agree with something mental?[5] As for necessary universal validity, Kant maintains that if

---

cludes each chapter with the phrase "*Also muss auf Kant zurückgegangen werden.*" While this is often cited as the origin of the phrase 'back to Kant', Willey (1978), 80 and Köhnke (1991), 128 note that this phrase does not originate with Liebmann, but had been used earlier by Kuno Fischer and Eduard Zeller.

2 Not all positivists adhere to this view: Ernst Mach, for example, endorses some version of phenomenalism.

3 See, e.g., Cassirer's Introduction to the first volume of *The Problem of Knowledge* in Cassirer (1957).

4 See, e.g., Kant (1902a), §18.

5 Kant (1902a), 282.

the copy-theory is correct, then our minds must conform to objects; in which case, the only access we have to objects is in the course of experience. But, echoing Humean worries about induction, Kant claims that if judgments arise only in the course of experience, they could never be necessary: "experience teaches me what there is and how it is, but never that is necessarily must be so and not otherwise."[6] Hence we would not be able to assert necessary universal validity of our judgments.

This line of thought represents a weapon for the Neo-Kantians to yield against positivism: insofar as positivism endorses some combination of naïve realism and the copy theory of knowledge, it will be in no better a position to explain how knowledge is possible than, say, Hegel or Fichte. What is needed instead, they argue, is a more philosophically viable account of knowledge, which can explain how objectively and necessarily universally valid judgments arise. To this end, they appeal to Kant and his so-called 'Copernican Revolution':

As Kant famously says in the Preface to the B edition of the first *Critique*,

> up to now it has been assumed that all our cognition [*Erkenntnis*] must conform to the objects; but all attempts to find out something about them *a priori* through concepts that would extend our cognition have, on this presupposition, come to nothing. Hence let us once try whether we do not get farther… by assuming that the objects must conform to our cognition.[7]

As we see in this passage, for Kant, as long as we suppose that our minds conform to objects (á la naïve realism and the copy theory), then we cannot make headway in our account of knowledge [*Erkenntnis*]. It is only if we reject that paradigm and instead conceive of objects as conforming to the conditions of knowledge that we will make any progress. Implicit in this line of thought are two Kantian commitments that become the foundation of the Neo-Kantian movement. The first is Kant's alternative to naïve realism, viz., '*critical*' or '*transcendental*' *idealism*, according to which the objects we have knowledge of are not 'things-in-themselves' or 'noumena', but rather 'appearances' or 'phenomena'

---

6 Kant (1902a), 294. See also Kant (1998), B3–4.
7 Kant (1998), Bxvi. It should be noted that the more recent Cambridge translations of Kant, e.g., the Guyer/Wood translation of the first *Critique*, render '*Erkenntnis*' as 'cognition' and while there are good reasons to think Kant himself distinguishes between 'cognition' [*Erkenntnis*] and 'knowledge' [*Wissen*], this is not a distinction the Neo-Kantians appear to make. Cassirer, e.g., in his English work *Essay on Man* (1944) never uses the term 'cognition', but only the term 'knowledge' in passages where he discusses ideas related to '*Erkenntnis*' from the *Philosophy of Symbolic Forms*. For this reason, I shall use the term 'knowledge' for '*Erkenntnis*', unless citing texts from Kant.

that conform to our minds. The second is his alternative to the copy theory, call it the *'critical theory of knowledge'*, which treats knowledge as the process through which objects conform to our minds.

More specifically, Kant characterizes knowledge as a process through which our minds *give form to* appearances[8]. He claims that there are primarily two mental capacities that are responsible for this: 'sensibility' [*Sinnlichkeit*], our passive sensible capacity for being affected by the world, and 'understanding' [*Verstand*], our spontaneous intellectual capacity for thought.[9] To each of these capacities he ascribes a priori forms, which appearances, if they are to be possible at all, must conform to: sensibility has the pure intuitions of space and time, while the understanding has the twelve 'pure' concepts or 'categories', like 'substance', 'cause', and 'reality'.

Kant maintains that once we appreciate that appearances are objects that conform to these a priori forms, then we will be in a position to account for how knowledge can arise. If the objects we are making judgments about are determined by the mind, then it is possible for those judgments to 'agree' with them; hence, objectively valid judgments become possible. Moreover, insofar as space, time, and the categories are constitutive of *our* minds, then any judgment in which I assert space, time, or the categories of appearances will be a judgment that I at any time and any other judger should make as well; in which case, Kant's view can also explain the possibility of necessarily universally valid judgments. Thus, on the Kantian account, the a priori forms of sensibility and understanding become the *conditions of the possibility of* knowledge.

However, for the Neo-Kantians, it is important that we recognize that Kant not only offered a general account of knowledge, but also that he endeavored to show that the knowledge we have in mathematics and 'pure' natural science rests on his critical presuppositions. Indeed, in the *Prolegomena* Kant orients the two parts of his investigation around the questions 'how is pure mathematics possible?' and 'how is pure natural science possible?' He claims that the answers to these questions hinge on critical idealism: it is only if our judgments in these fields are not about things in themselves, but rather about appearances that a priori conform to the mind that we will be able to issue knowledge claims like 'the shortest distance between two points is a straight line' and 'everything

---

8 Cf. Kant (1998), A20/B34, A93/B125.
9 Cf. Kant (1998), A50/B74-A52/B76. Though we cannot discuss this here, in the first *Critique*, Kant also highlights the contribution of a third capacity, the 'imagination' [*Einbildungskraft*], which mediates between sensibility and understanding. See, e.g., Cassirer (1907), Book 8, Section IV.

that happens is determined by a cause according to constant laws'.[10] For the Neo-Kantians this is especially pertinent since it indicates that in order to establish knowledge claims in the fields positivists are most concerned with, i.e., mathematics and natural science, one must resort to a Kantian explanation of the conditions of the possibility of knowledge.

Ultimately, then, we find that the rejection of positivism with regard to naïve realism and the copy-theory of knowledge and the endorsement of Kant's critical idealism and critical theory of knowledge constitute two of the basic commitments endorsed by (almost) every Neo-Kantian, Marburg and Southwest included.[11]

3 The Neo-Kantian Schools

In spite of agreement on these fundamental issues, different schools within Neo-Kantianism arose as a result of disagreement with respect to how to specify the a priori forms that serve as the conditions of the possibility of knowledge.[12] Among the first Neo-Kantians, there is a tendency to identify these conditions with the physiological and/or psychological organization of human beings.[13] This so-called 'genetic' variety of Neo-Kantianism is defended, for example, by Hermann von Helmholtz and Friedrich Albert Lange.[14] According to Helmholtz, who trained as a physicist, physician, and physiologist, Kant's a priori considerations should be read as anticipating the recent empirical discoveries, especially in the field of psychology, which had uncovered the physiological structures that make perception possible.[15] Meanwhile Lange in *The History of Materialism* (1866, 1st

---

10 Kant (1902a), 269, 295.
11 Alois Riehl is the notable exception as he was a Neo-Kantian who defended positivism.
12 For a discussion of the various schools within Neo-Kantianism, see Willey (1978), Köhnke (1991), Chignell (2008), and Pollock (2010).
13 This is not to say all the early Neo-Kantians endorsed the genetic approach; as Cassirer points out, Zeller and Liebmann focused on demonstrating the deficiencies in post-Kantian idealist and realist philosophy, in favor of a more 'epistemological' approach to the conditions of knowledge. Cf. Cassirer (1929), 215 – 6 and Cassirer (2005), 96.
14 See Cassirer (1943), 223. The precedent for 'psychological' readings of Kant had been set earlier in the 19th century by J.F. Herbart in his textbook *Psychologie als Wissenschaft neu gegründet auf Erfahrung, Metaphysik, und Mathematik* (1824 – 5) and J.F. Fries in *Neue oder anthropologische Kritik der Vernunft* (1828 – 31).
15 See Cassirer (1929), 215 and Cassirer (2005), 96. Citations to Cassirer's German texts that have been translated into English are to the English translations unless otherwise noted. Helmholtz was particularly interested in the philosophy of perception and there is disagreement as to what

ed.) argues at length against positivist assumptions about reality and offers as his alternative an idealist account that makes reality depend on the physio-psychological dispositions of the human being.

However, for the second generation of Neo-Kantians, which was dominated by the Marburg and Southwest Schools, the genetic approach to Kant is unacceptable. According to the younger generation, the genetic accounts endorse 'psychologism', the view that identifies psychological entities, e.g., actual mental acts or processes, as the source of logic and the conditions of knowledge, and members of both the Marburg and Southwest Schools argue that this is problematic on, at least, two counts.

First, they maintain that the genetic accounts leave out something that was of the utmost importance for Kant, viz., our *normative* experience of *values*.[16] Whether we consider values and norms relating to theoretical, practical, or other cultural domains, the Neo-Kantians claim that what is at issue is not how we *in fact* are, but rather how we *ought* to be, i.e., our sense of how we ought to think, how we ought to act, or how the world ought to be. However, they argue that all the genetic accounts have at their disposal is an analysis of the psycho-physiological dispositions that we in fact have, thus have no way of accounting for these important normative experiences.[17] As Cassirer makes this point against Lange:

> By extending this [genetic] interpretation to all parts of the Kantian system, Lange arrives at the conclusion... that even the "intelligible world," which was used by Kant as the foundation of ethics is a "world of poetry."... in this very implication, which threatened to transform the Kantian transcendental idealism into a *fictionalism*... the deficiencies of the empirco-physiological interpretation of Kantian Apriorism became clearly apparent.[18]

---

extent Helmholtz's theory of perception is truly Kantian (for discussion and references, see Hatfield (1991), 325–6.

16 See, e.g., Windelband (1907); Rickert (1913), (1921); Cohen (1904); and Natorp (1912a), 216–218.

17 As Kant makes this point about ethics in the *Groundwork*, "what is at issue here is not at all whether this or that does happen, but that reason by itself and independently of all appearances commands what ought to happen" Kant (1902a), 408.

18 Cassirer (1929), 215. Cassirer raises a similar objection against Riehl's positivism, claiming that, "through this confinement of philosophy to the pure science of knowledge, Riehl ends by allowing the theory of values to fall out entirely... This separation of knowledge from faith carried with it the danger that scientific value was attributed to natural knowledge exclusively, while the pure sciences of the mind (*Geisteswissenschaften*), the sciences of the historical reality of man's mental achievements, were deprived of their specific methodological foundation" Cassirer (1929), 216.

For these reasons, the Marburg and Southwest Neo-Kantians claim that if we are to remain in line with Kant's project as a whole, then we must give an account of the conditions of the possibility of the knowledge we have of values and norms.[19]

A second key objection members of both schools levy against the genetic theory is that it offers an unsatisfactory explanation of knowledge because it cannot account for the objective validity of our judgments.[20] They argue that by reducing the conditions of knowledge to the physio-psychological features of the human being, the genetic theory manages only to explain the *subjective* validity of our judgments, i.e., why we human subjects happen to make them, not why those judgments are *objectively* valid.[21] As Natorp frames this worry, with psychologism:

> [o]ne not only destroys logic, as the independent theory of the objective validity of knowledge, one also cancels out objective validity itself and changes it into purely subjective validity, if one attempts to support it on subjective grounds and to deduce it from subjective factors.[22]

Indeed, they take this to be a concern that Kant himself addresses in the B Deduction:

> If someone still wanted to propose...that the categories were... subjective predispositions for thinking, implanted in us along with our existence... in such a case the categories would lack the necessity that is essential to their concept. For, e.g., the concept of cause, which asserts the necessity of a consequent under a presupposed condition, would be false if it rested only on a subjective necessity, arbitrarily implanted in us... which is precisely what the skeptic wishes most.[23]

Thus it would seem even by Kant's own lights that the genetic approach side steps his core concern, viz., with explaining "how **subjective conditions of thinking** should have **objective validity**, i.e., yield conditions of the possibility of all cognition [*Erkenntnis*] of objects."[24]

For the Marburg and Southwest Neo-Kantians, then, in order to offer a proper account of knowledge, we must pursue an *anti-psychologistic* route, a route that investigates not the psychological conditions, but rather the *logical*, hence

---

19 We shall discuss how the Marburg School does this in more detail below.
20 For a discussion of Neo-Kantian approaches to psychologism, see Kusch (1995), 169–177; Anderson (2005); and Edgar (2008).
21 See Cassirer (1929), 215
22 Natorp (1981), 251.
23 Kant (1998) B167–8. Cf. Cassirer (1943), 224–5.
24 Kant (1998), A89–90/B122.

objective conditions of knowledge, i.e., the a priori concepts, principles, laws, structures, etc., that make objectively valid judgments possible.²⁵ In short, for these Neo-Kantians the only appropriate way to defend a 'theory of knowledge' [*Erkenntnistheorie*] is with what Kant calls a 'transcendental logic':

> a science, which would determine the origin, the domain, and the objective validity of such cognitions [*Erkenntnisse*]... it has to do merely with the laws of the understanding and reason, but solely insofar as they are related to objects *a priori*.²⁶

If we look at the relationship between the Marburg and Southwest School along these lines, then we find that they have a common goal, viz., offering an anti-psychologistic analysis of the a priori conditions of the possibility of knowledge, which extends to our knowledge of values and norms in the mathematical natural sciences and humanities alike. Yet the fact that the Marburg and Southwest Neo-Kantians share this as a common starting point tends to be overlooked because, as was mentioned at the outset, more often than not it is the differences between these schools that are highlighted. There are, in particular, two differences that I want to consider here.²⁷ The first concerns what type of knowledge each school focuses on. As the story usually goes, whereas the Marburg School is interested only in the knowledge we have in mathematics and natural science, the Southwest School privileges the humanities and is interested only in knowledge in normative fields.²⁸ The second difference that is often emphasized is connected to the role of 'intuition': while the Marburg Neo-Kantians endorse a version of 'logicism' according to which intuitions themselves are forms of thought, the Southwest School demands that intuitions be non-conceptual in character, serving as the 'given' on which thought is based. We shall return below to the genuine disagreement between these schools with regard to the notion of 'intu-

---

25 As Cassirer characterizes this anti-psychologistic approach: "in its very ideality, cognition-critique takes a strictly *objective* turn: it does not deal with representations and processes in the thinking individual, but with the validity relation [*Geltungszusasmmenhang*] between principles and "propositions" [*Sätzen*], which as such must be established independently of any consideration of the subjective-psychological event of thinking [*Denkgeschehens*]" Cassirer (2005), 97.
26 Kant (1998), A57/B81. See, e.g., Rickert's claim that the terms 'theory of knowledge' [*Erkenntnistheorie*], 'logic', and 'doctrine of truth' [*Wahrheitslehre*] are interchangeable (Rickert (1909), 170).
27 See Friedman (2000), 29–30 for a discussion of the difference between the two schools regarding the relationship between mathematics and logic.
28 See, e.g., Krois (1987), 72; Crowell (1998); Verene (2001), 10; Gordon (2010), 57–61; and Stati (2013). For a more detailed discussion of the relationship between the two schools, see Krijnen (2001), 77–93; Friedman (2000), 26–37; and Krijnen and Noras (2012).

ition'; here, however, our concern is with the first supposed difference. More specifically, given our primary interest is in Cassirer's relationship to the Marburg School, though there are reasons to worry about this way of depicting the Southwest School, we shall concentrate on issues surrounding their alleged scientism of the Marburg Neo-Kantians.[29]

To be sure, there are many reasons commentators have been led to this interpretation of the Marburg School. In the first place, the members themselves seem to endorse this position. According to Cohen, "Philosophy does not have to create things... but instead simply to understand and to re-examine how the objects and laws of mathematical experience are constructed."[30] As he makes this point elsewhere, "the chief question of logic and the foundational question of philosophy" is the question of the "concept of science".[31] Natorp, meanwhile, appears to suggest that 'thinking' and 'logic' are exclusively concerned with the objects of science:

> Thinking is in each case focused upon its particular object. An entirely new level of reflection is required to investigate, not the particular object, but the laws in accordance with which this and any *scientific object* in general first constitutes itself as an object. This new kind of reflection we call "logic".[32]

In light of these sorts of remarks, Cassirer himself tends to characterize Cohen and Natorp along scientist lines, claiming in the Introduction to the fourth volume of *The Problem of Knowledge* that:

> in the development of neo-Kantianism the theory of Cohen and Natorp is sharply opposed to that of Windelband and Rickert: a dissimilarity that flows of necessity from their general orientation, determined in the one case by mathematical physics, in the other by history.[33]

The critics of the Marburg School also took them to be engaging in a philosophical project that privileges mathematics and natural science. Heidegger, for one, claims that Cohen and Natorp interpret the first *Critique* as an "epistemology of

---

29 Rickert, for example, offers extensive analyses of natural science in *Kulturwissenschaft und Naturwissenschaft* (1926, $6^{th}/7^{th}$ ed.) and *Die Grenzen der naturwissenschaftlichen Begriffsbildung* (1929, 6th ed.).
30 Cohen (1885), 578. Translated by Patton in Cassirer (2005), 98.
31 Cohen (1902), 445. Translated by Kim (2008). Describing Cohen's project, Cassirer says, "For Cohen, Kant's system answers the truly fateful question of philosophy in general: the question of the relation between philosophy and science." Cassirer (1912), 95.
32 Natorp (1910), 10–11, my emphasis. Translated by Kim (2008).
33 Cassirer (1957b), 11.

mathematical natural sciences" and he argues that on this point, they are fundamentally mistaken because they overlook Kant's primary concern with metaphysics and ontology[34]:

> The intention of the *Critique of Pure Reason*, therefore, remains fundamentally misunderstood, if it is interpreted as a "theory of experience" or even as a theory of the positive sciences. The *Critique of Pure Reason* has nothing to do with a "theory of knowledge".[35]

So too does Rickert challenge the Marburg approach for placing too much emphasis in their interpretation of the first *Critique* on natural science instead of metaphysics:

> the main problem of [the first *Critique*] is not a theory of the experiential sciences [*Erfahrungswissenschaften*]. Rather, it revolves around the old, ever-recurring *problems* of metaphysics. The work on these problems becomes the foundation for an encompassing theory of worldview culminating in the treatment of issues in the philosophy of religion. The theory of mathematics and physics is merely *preparatory* for the treatment of these issues.[36]

More recently, the scientist interpretation of the Marburg School has manifested in two veins. In one vein, Marburg scientism has been emphasized by philosophers of science, like Michael Friedman, Alan Richardson, and Jeremy Heis, who are interested in establishing the historical roots of contemporary philosophy of science in Marburg Neo-Kantianism.[37] In another vein, commentators interested in Cassirer's relationship to the Marburg School have urged that while in his early work, like *Substance and Function* (1910) Cassirer endorsed the scientism of the Marburg School, with his declaration in the first volume of the *Philosophy of Symbolic Forms* that "the critique of reason becomes a critique of cul-

---

34 Heidegger (1997), 46.
35 Heidegger (1990), 11.
36 Rickert (1924), 153. Translated by Staiti (2013).
37 Heis, for example, claims that for the Marburg Neo-Kantians, "the proper object of philosophy is our best current mathematical sciences of nature. These sciences are the "fact" whose preconditions... it is the task of philosophy to study" Heis (2012), 8. In a similar vein, Richardson suggests that what is unique about Cohen and Cassirer's approach to epistemology is their scientific conception of experience: "The key to scientific Neo-Kantianism... is this: Unlike traditional empiricism, the neo-Kantians do not begin with a notion of experience as sensory impressions that serve as the subjective starting point of all knowledge... Rather, Cohen and Cassirer invite us to... understand the question of how objective knowledge of nature is possible in experience to be answered by a consideration of the preconditions of possibility of achieving a rigorously mathematized science of empirical nature" (Richardson (2003), 62). For discussion of the Neo-Kantian roots of contemporary philosophy of science, see Coffa (1991); Richardson (1998), (2003); Friedman (2000), (2005); and Stone (2005).

ture," he definitively with his predecessors.[38] In this vein, one could read his opening remarks to the first volume as a repudiation of Marburg scientism: his attention towards areas like language, myth, religion, and art, which fall beyond the purview of Cohen's and Natorp's concerns.

While there can be no doubt that the Marburg Neo-Kantians are deeply invested in defending a Kantian approach to mathematics and the natural sciences,[39] in what follows I argue that it is a mistake to think that this is the *only*, let alone the *primary* concern of the Marburg School. I show that Cohen, Natorp, and Cassirer alike are committed to the broader project of offering a systematic philosophy of culture. Although an analysis of science and mathematics constitutes an important component of this project, they, just as much as the Southwest Neo-Kantians, acknowledge that there are other regions of culture, like ethics, religion, and art that must be accounted for as well. Indeed, as we shall see, the Marburg School saw it as their task not only to elucidate each *particular* cultural sphere, but also to identify the unifying factor underlying our cultural experience *in general*. This systematic approach to culture is something they took Kant to have been heading towards in his three *Critique* and it is a task they think that those seriously committed to going 'back to Kant' must pursue even further.

---

38 Cassirer (1953), 80. Cassirer's claim about methodology at the outset of the first volume of the *Philosophy of Symbolic Forms* might suggest this as well: "[after *Substance and Function*] it gradually became clear to me that general epistemology [*Erkenntnistheorie*], with its traditional form and limitations, does not provide an adequate methodological basis for the cultural sciences. It seemed to me that before this inadequacy could be made good, the whole program of epistemology would have to be broadened" Cassirer (1953), 69. So too it has been suggested that he indicates his break from the Marburg School in his 1939 essay 'Was ist Subjektivismus?': "I myself have often been classified as a 'neo-Kantian' and I accept this title in the sense that my whole work on the field of theoretical philosophy presupposes the methodological basis that Kant presented in his *Critique of Pure Reason*. But many of the doctrines which are attributed to neo-Kantianism in the literature today are not only foreign to me, they are opposed and contradictory to my own opinion." Cassirer (1993), 201, translated and discussed by Rudolph (1998), 3. Other commentators who emphasize Cassirer's break with the Marburg School include Krois (1987), 36–7, 41, 44; Marx (1988); and Skidelsky (2011), 50–1, 65. For arguments that Cassirer did not break with the Marburg School, see Seidengart (1994), Orth (1996), Ferrari (2009), and Luft (2011), 277–280. We shall return to this issue in §6.
39 This is evident, e.g., in Cohen's *Kant's Theory of Experience* (*Kants Theorie der Erfahrung*) (1871/85) and the *Logic of Pure Knowledge (Logik der reinen Erkenntnis)* (1902), Natorp's *The Logical Foundations of the Exact Sciences* (*Die logischen Grundlagen der exakten Wissenschaften*) (1910), and Cassirer's first two volumes of *The Problem of Knowledge* (*Das Erkenntnisproblem*) (1906, 1907) and *Substance and Function* (1910).

4 The Transcendental Method

In order to bring out the Marburg commitment to the philosophy of culture, I want to begin with a discussion of what is arguably the 'core-thought' of this school, viz., the transcendental method. For the Marburg Neo-Kantians, going 'back to Kant' is not a matter of simply endorsing Kant's own doctrines. As Natorp makes this point, it was never the 'intention' [*Meinung*] of the Marburg School "to want or to expect to unconditionally adhere to Kant's tenets [*Lehrsätzen*]."[40] It is, instead, Kant's *way of philosophizing*, his *method* that the Marburg School endeavors to revive.[41]

Cohen calls Kant's distinctive philosophical method the 'transcendental method' and in his three-volume interpretation of Kant, he claims that Kant uses this single method in order to investigate theoretical, practical, and aesthetic philosophy in each *Critique* respectively.[42] Emphasizing the systematic role of the transcendental method in Cohen's Kant-interpretation, Cassirer says:

> Cohen gave for the first time a critical interpretation of the *entire Kantian system* which, with all its penetration into the specific detail of Kant's fundamental doctrines, sets, nevertheless, *one single systematic idea* into the center of the investigation. This is the idea of the "transcendental method".[43]

For the Marburg Neo-Kantians, however, the transcendental method is not merely of historical interest; it is the method they pursue in their own philosophical work.

So what exactly does the transcendental method involve? To answer this question, we shall follow Natorp in his 1912 article "Kant and the Marburg School" (*Kant und die Marburger Schule*) and his claim that the method involves two steps: first, orienting oneself around facts and second, uncovering the conditions of the possibility of those facts.

The *first step* concerns the starting point of philosophical investigation. Recall that in the early 19th century, philosophy was dominated by the abstract ver-

---

40 Natorp (1912a), 194. Translations of Natorp (1912a) are my own.
41 Natorp suggests that this is what Kant himself would have wanted: "Kant who understands philosophy as critique, as method, wanted to teach philosophizing [*Philosophieren*], but never "a" philosophy [*"eine" Philosophie*]" Natorp (1912a), 194.
42 *Kants Theorie der Erfahrung* (*Kant's Theory of Experience*) (1871/85), *Kants Begründung der Ethik* (*Kant's Foundations of Ethics*) (1877), and *Kant Begründung der Aesthetik* (*Kant's Foundations of Aesthetics*) (1889).
43 Cassirer, (1929), 215 (my emphasis).

sions of idealism defended by Hegel and Fichte and proponents of positivism rejected such 'high-flying' speculation as a route to truth. On this point, the Marburg Neo-Kantians agree with the positivists: one's account of what is true or what we can know needs to be grounded in facts in some sense. Yet this is a point they take Kant himself to have made already in the *Prolegomena*: "High towers and the metaphysically-great men who resemble them, around both of which there is usually much wind, are not for me. My place is the fertile bathos of experience."[44] For this reason, Kant restricts his account of knowledge in the first *Critique* and *Prolegomena* to what falls within the bounds of experience. As Cohen renders this point, Kant's theoretical philosophy takes the 'fact of experience' as its departure point.[45] It is, however, important to recognize that the Marburg Neo-Kantians take Kant to be using the term 'experience' in a technical sense to refer to our experience of the world in mathematical natural science.[46] In Cohen's words, "Nature is experience, which is mathematical natural science."[47] Thus, on the Marburg interpretation, the 'fact of experience' that Kant begins his theoretical philosophy with is the 'fact of mathematical natural science'.

Yet according to the Marburg Neo-Kantians, it is not just Kant's theoretical philosophy that is oriented around facts: they claim that the second and third *Critiques* are also guided by the respective 'facts' of ethics and art. In the second *Critique*, for example, Kant claims that our consciousness of the moral law is a 'fact of reason.'[48] As Cohen emphasizes, Kant says that this fact is "one that every natural human reason cognizes [*erkennt*]" and is given "so to speak [*gleichsam*], as a fact, that precedes all subtle reasoning about its possibility."[49] Meanwhile, in his analysis of Kant's aesthetic theory, Cohen argues (more controversially) that in the third *Critique*, Kant takes as his starting point the fact of "art as the cultural region [*Kulturgebiet*] in which aesthetic consciousness primarily operates."[50] He identifies the aesthetic consciousness at work in this realm as the

---

44 Kant (1902a), 373fn.
45 Cohen (1885), 255. Cohen translations are my own unless otherwise noted.
46 See Richardson (2003).
47 Cohen (1885), 501.
48 Kant (1902c), 31.
49 Kant (1902c), 91. See Cohen (1877), 224. By describing this as a 'so to speak fact' Kant does not mean to diminish its status, but rather to indicate that it is given to us in a way that is distinct from how facts are given in science, viz., through our distinctive consciousness of the moral law.
50 Cohen (1889), 144. See Guyer (2008) for a discussion of how Cohen's interpretation of Kant's aesthetics departs from Kant's own approach.

'feeling' [*Gefühl*] we have in the beautiful, i.e., the communicable feeling that is grounded in the free play of our cognitive faculties.⁵¹

Summarizing Kant's transcendental method, Cohen says:

> The transcendental method everywhere adheres to the stock of *cultural* facts [*Kulturthatsachen*], which are to be surveyed as to their conditions, to the 'fact of experience', the 'quasi fact', the 'analogue of a fact' of the moral law, and also to the works of the art of genius.⁵²

While Cohen takes Kant to pursue this method with respect to the theoretical, practical, and aesthetic facts at issue in each *Critique*, notice that he generalizes the point: the transcendental method begins with the 'stock of cultural facts'. Indeed, Cohen goes on to say that the "transcendental point of view [*Gesichtspunkt*]" does not just concern local issues related to, say, theoretical or moral philosophy, but rather 'systematic' issues related to culture in general.⁵³ Thus he claims in no uncertain terms that "culture forms the universe, the complex of problems [*Aufgaben-Complex*] for the transcendental method."⁵⁴

Natorp presents the transcendental method along similar lines in his article on the Marburg School, claiming that it must begin with "the existing, historically available facts of science, ethics, art, religion," indeed with the "entire creative work of culture."⁵⁵ To this end, he claims that although the Marburg Neo-Kantians are concerned with the facts pertaining to the mathematical natural sciences, they are equally concerned with the humanities [*Geisteswissenschaften*], e.g., with "social science [*Sozialwissenschaft*] (economics, jurisprudence, and education), history, the science of art [*Kunstwissenschaft*], and the science of religion [*Religionwissenschaft*]."⁵⁶ This is why Natorp insists that Marburg Neo-Kantianism must be understood as a 'philosophy of culture' [*Kulturphilosophie*].⁵⁷

What this line of thought reveals is that far from endorsing scientism, both Cohen and Natorp explicitly insist that Marburg methodology is oriented around the facts *of culture*. Indeed, as we see Natorp emphasize, they take as their starting point the *historical developing* facts of culture.⁵⁸ This has two important im-

---

51 See, e.g., Kant (1902d), §9; Cohen (1889), 222–3.
52 Cohen (1889), 190 (my emphasis).
53 Cohen (1889), 344.
54 Cohen (1889), 344.
55 Natorp (1912a), 196, 197.
56 Natorp (1912a), 216.
57 Natorp (1912a), 219.
58 To this end it has been suggested that the Marburg School shows its debt to Hegel (see, e.g., Verene 1969, 2011). While the emphasis on history is surely shared with Hegel, both Natorp and Cassirer insist on the differences between their views and Hegel's. According to Natorp, while

plications for how we understand the relationship of the Marburg School to Kant. In the first place, although they take their cue from Kant's investigation of the facts of experience, ethics, and art, they think that we need to *widen* the scope of philosophical investigation. Cohen and Natorp do this in their extensive analysis of religion and as Cassirer does in his analysis of language and myth.⁵⁹ As Cassirer describes this extension in the 1936 lecture, "Critical Idealism as a Philosophy of Culture":

> The problem of Kant is not bound to an inquiry into the special forms of logical, scientific, ethical, or aesthetical thought. Without varying its nature we may apply it to all the other forms of thinking, judging, knowing, understanding, and even of feeling by which the human mind attempts to conceive the universe as a whole. Such a synopsis of the universe, such a synthetic view, is aimed at in myth, in religion, in language, in art, and in science.⁶⁰

Furthermore, the Marburg Neo-Kantians claim that we need to be open to *revising* our understanding of these facts as they develop historically. On this point, they admit that Kant was too rigid, e.g., treating Euclidean geometry or Newtonian physics as *the* facts of experience; however, they take a proper philosophy of culture to be a philosophy that addresses how the human spirit unfolds over time.⁶¹ With respect to science, for example, Cassirer says:

> The "givenness" [*Gebenheit*] that the philosopher recognizes in the mathematical science of nature ultimately means the givenness of the *problem* [*Gebenheit des Problems*]. In its actual form the philosopher seeks and recognizes an ideal form, which he singles out, to confront it with the changing historical configuration as a standard for measurement.⁶²

This point, however, is one the Marburg Neo-Kantians take to apply to culture more generally: cultural facts should not be regarded as something 'given' [*gege-*

Hegel thinks that history progresses towards an 'absolute end' in which philosophy itself becomes 'absolute science', he insists that for the Marburg Neo-Kantians history and philosophy are involved in a never-ending process of development that could never be completed (Natorp 1912a, p. 211). Meanwhile Cassirer claims that critical idealism parts ways with Hegel's speculative idealism because Hegel sees history as the "self-actualization of the absolute idea... [which] is exempt from all conditions and all determinations of time," whereas Cassirer claims that critical idealism can understand culture only by remaining within it and its historical developments, Cassirer (1979b), 80.

59 See, e.g., Cohen's *Religion of Reason: Out of the Sources of Judaism* (1919), Natorp's *Religion innerhalb der Grenzen der Humanität* (1908), and the first two volumes of Cassirer's *Philosophy of Symbolic Forms*.
60 Cassirer (1979b), 70–1.
61 See, e.g., Natorp (1912a), 209–210 and Cassirer (1906), 14.
62 Cassirer (2005), 100.

ben] once and for all, but rather as something posed as a task or a problem [*aufgeben*] that can never be completed, but must rather be constantly undertaken anew.[63] For this reason, they saw no need for the transcendental method to adhere strictly to what Kant identifies as the relevant facts, but rather were open to revising Kant's views when they thought this was called for. In his *Ethics of Pure Will* (1904/1907), for example, Cohen claims that ethics should take as its starting point the facts related to the 'science of pure jurisprudence', i.e., the science that concerns how the will of human beings can be normatively constrained by laws. Meanwhile, Natorp claims that ethics should begin with the "practical forms of social order and of a life worthy of human beings."[64] In a theoretical vein, one of Cassirer's primary goals in *Substance and Function* (1910), *Einstein's Theory of Relativity* (1921), and *Determinism and Indeterminism in Modern Physics* (1936a) is to address the facts of mathematics and physics as they develop in the 19th and 20th centuries beyond Kant's more limited Euclidean and Newtonian paradigm.[65] Yet regardless of these extensions and revisions of Kant's views, the Marburg Neo-Kantians take their commitment to starting with the facts of culture to be in line with his transcendental method.

Once one has oriented oneself around these dynamic cultural facts, the Marburg Neo-Kantians claim that the *second step* of the transcendental method involves asking a 'transcendental question': what are the conditions that make the facts pertaining to each region possible in the first place?[66] For the Marburg Neo-Kantians, in order to answer this question, we must take our cue from the Copernican Revolution and specify the logical conditions that objects in each region conform to. According to Cohen, the transcendental method seeks to uncover the "general conditions of consciousness... in which the factual [*sachlichen*]

---

63 See Natorp 1912a, p. 199–200.
64 Natorp (1912a), 197.
65 With regard to the relationship between Cassirer and Cohen on the status of the historical development of science, Cassirer claims that although Cohen takes his cue from Newtonian physics in his *Logic of Pure Knowledge* (1902), in his Introduction to Lange's *History of Materialism*, he was "one of the first to point out the *philosophical significance* of *Faraday*, [and] he delved into the principles of *Heinrich Hertz's* mechanics... So, for Cohen, the orientation to science does not imply any commitment to its temporal, contingent form" Cassirer (2005), 100. Meanwhile, Cohen's assessment of *Substance and Function* is mixed: according to Moynahan, Cohen saw it as in line with the general spirit of his own theoretical philosophy, although he worried that Cassirer's emphasis on the idea of pure relation failed to do justice the role of the notion of the 'infinitesimal' at the core of Cohen's theoretical philosophy (Moynahan (2013), 122).
66 Cohen (1889), 144, see also Natorp (1912a), 197.

laws of culture find their source and totality [*Inbegriff*]."⁶⁷ This is how Natorp describes their target,

> The creative ground, however, of any such act of object-formation [*Objektgestaltung*] is law; in the end that original law [*Urgesetz*], which one still understandably enough designates as *logos, ratio,* reason [*Vernunft*].⁶⁸

Cassirer, meanwhile, tends to make this point in terms drawn from the first *Critique:* the 'transcendental' question concerns not so much the objects, as the "mode of knowledge [*Erkenntnis*]" on which those objects depend.⁶⁹

This being said, there is an important restriction that the Marburg School places on these logical conditions, which differentiates their view not only from the Southwest School, but also from that of Kant himself. This returns us to the issue of the Marburg Neo-Kantians' 'logicism' and their intellectualizing of Kant's theory of intuition. While Kant and the Southwest Neo-Kantians following him attempt to ground some facts in the a priori conditions of *sensibility,* as a capacity distinct from the understanding, the Marburg Neo-Kantians argue that this is a mistake. On their view, indeed on the view they think is more thoroughly Kantian, the mind is always active, never passive, hence there can be no independent, receptive capacity of sensibility; there is only our spontaneous capacity for thought. As Cassirer summarizes their position:

> Neither in its sensuous experience nor in its rational activity is the mind a *tabula rasa*... It is active in all its functions, in perception as well as conception, in feeling as well as in volition. There is no room left for a mere "receptivity" in addition to and outside the spontaneity of the human mind.⁷⁰

This is not to say that the Marburg Neo-Kantians deny that space and time ground the facts of culture in some sense; instead, they claim that these intuitions can actually be traced back to the activity of thought.⁷¹ Making this point, Natorp claims, "'intuition' no longer remains as a factor in cognition

---

67 Cohen (1889, 345.
68 Natorp (1912a), 197.
69 Kant (1998), A11/B25; see Cassirer (2005), 97 and Cassirer (1957a), 6.
70 Cassirer (1943), 226.
71 They argue that their position reflects Kant's own considered position, i.e., the one that he arrives at in the B Deduction in his analysis of the 'form of intuition'-'formal intuition' distinction in the B160–1 footnote, which his earlier views in the Transcendental Aesthetic should be revised in light of (see Natorp (1912a), 204 and Cassirer (1907), 571–586). For more recent discussion of this passage and the relevant secondary literature, see Allison (2004), 112–116, 223–5.

that opposes or stands against thought, instead it *is* thought."⁷² For the Marburg Neo-Kantians, then, the transcendental question about each region asks after the laws, principles, or modes of thought that make the facts within each cultural region possible.

To this end, they model their approach on the approach they take Kant to have pursued in each *Critique*. As they see it, in the first *Critique* Kant identifies the categories as the conditions of the possibility of the fact of experience⁷³; in the second *Critique*, it is the 'idea of freedom' that makes the fact of reason possible;⁷⁴ and in the third *Critique*, it is the 'subjective principle' of common sense that grounds our feeling in the beautiful.⁷⁵ Yet though the Marburg Neo-Kantians think that Kant employs the right strategy, they do not always concur with the specific conclusions that he draws. Cohen, for example, in the *Logic of Pure Knowledge* (1902) develops his theory of the principle of 'origin' [*Ursprung*] as the source of theoretical knowledge. Meanwhile in the *Logical Foundations of the Exacts Sciences* (1910), Natorp lays emphasis on the notion of '*fieri*' as the relevant theoretical grounds. Nevertheless, even if their own results differ from Kant's, the Marburg Neo-Kantians take their efforts to identify the logical conditions that make the facts of each cultural region possible to be in the spirit of the transcendental method as Kant established it.

5 Marburg Variations on the Unity of Reason

For the Marburg Neo-Kantians, however, a complete philosophy of culture cannot just address the logical conditions that govern *each* region; it must furthermore given an account of the underlying factors that make culture *as such* possible.⁷⁶ To this end, they wanted to elucidate something like Kant's 'unity of reason', i.e.:

---

72 Natorp (1912a), 204; see also Natorp (1910), Ch. 6, §2.
73 See, e.g., Kant (1902a), 319.
74 See, e.g., Kant (1902b), 461. While this passage is drawn from the *Groundwork*, Kant makes it clear in the Preface to the second *Critique* that even if in this later work he wants to maintain that consciousness of the moral law through the fact of reason precedes consciousness of freedom, nevertheless, freedom remains the '*ratio essendi*' of the moral law: "were there no freedom, the moral law would *not be encountered* at all in ourselves" Kant (1902c), 4fn.
75 See, e.g., Kant (1902b), §§20–22, 35–40.
76 Indeed, Cassirer suggests that in Cohen's work on the systematic unity of these various cultural forms that "the fundamental ideal of transcendental method comes to the fore yet again, with full acuity." Cassirer (2005), 105.

to be able to present [practical reason's] unity with speculative reason in *a common principle*; because in the end there can be *only one and the same reason*, which must differ merely in its application.[77]

Only for the Marburg Neo-Kantians, it is not just the unity of reason, but also the unity of culture that one must explain. And, as we shall find, rather surprisingly given their anti-psychologistic bent, there is a line of thought beginning with Cohen, then continuing through Natorp and into Cassirer according to which this task should be accomplished by means of a special sort of 'psychology', a psychology that deals not with particular acts of consciousness within an individual, but rather with consciousness as the source of the logical conditions of culture.[78]

To see this, let's begin with Cohen. As Cassirer emphasizes, Cohen's commitment to consciousness as the systematic ground of culture is evident in *Kant's Foundations of Aesthetics*.[79] He argues that our theoretical, practical, and aesthetic knowledge of the world "form a systematic unity [*Einheit*]" because they are all 'developments' or 'directions' of a more encompassing consciousness.[80] Indeed, Cohen suggests that, "consciousness, as the *principle* of all spheres of culture, is the source and condition for its value and end, and the foundation for its kind of development."[81]

However, this theme is not just one that Cohen pursues in his Kant interpretation; he had, in fact, hoped to develop this idea as the capstone to his own *System of Philosophy*, in a fourth planned, but never executed volume dedicated to

---

[77] Kant (1902b), 391, my emphasis. See also Kant (1998), Axx and Kand (1902c), 291. Although we could approach the unity of reason both from the perspective of its unity as a *terminus a quo* and a *terminus ad quem*, in what follows I will focus only on the former issue. This is not to say that the Marburg Neo-Kantians do not have a teleological view of where 'reason' or 'culture' is headed, e.g., in Cohen's philosophy of religion or Cassirer's third volume of the *Philosophy of Symbolic Forms*, but for the purposes of this paper, I shall have to set these issues aside.
[78] As I note below, there are reasons to think that in the late period of Cohen's and Natorp's philosophy, they veer away from this psychological project. Nevertheless, given that our interest is with their influence on Cassirer, what is important for our purposes is Cassirer's appropriation of this psychological project in his *Philosophy of Symbolic Forms*, which I discuss below.
[79] Cassirer (2005), 102 emphasizes this point. For a discussion of how Cohen's idea of 'origin' [*Ursprung*] plays a unifying role in his philosophy of culture, see Renz (2005).
[80] Cohen (1889), 95, 97.
[81] Cohen (1889), 96, my emphasis. Patton translation of Cassirer (2005), 102. Cohen makes this point in the context of criticizing pre-critical forms of idealism, e.g., Descartes's and Leibniz's, for having failed to appreciate the systematic unity of the various experiences we have of the world.

the topic of 'psychology'.[82] For Cohen, the *"problem of psychology"* in his sense is nothing other than the problem of the "unity of consciousness," more specifically, "the *unity of consciousness of unitary culture*".[83] Unlike in the earlier volumes of the *System*, in which he analyzed the cultural regions associated with theoretical knowledge, ethics, and aesthetics respectively, he intended this fourth volume as the "encyclopedia of the system of philosophy," which was to explain how consciousness made culture as such possible.[84] To this end, Cohen suggests that his proposed volume on psychology would be a study of 'man': "*the teaching of man in the unity of his cultural consciousness, as the development of this unity and the genetic connection of all its features and their embryos.*"[85]

While Cohen only sketched out the idea of a Marburg psychology, Natorp devoted much of his efforts towards clarifying what exactly such a psychology would involve, e. g., in his *Introduction to Psychology According to Critical Method* [*Einleitung in die Psychologie nach kritischer Methode*] from 1888 and in his *General Psychology According to Critical Method* [*Allgemeine Psychologie nach kritisher Methode*] from 1912.[86] On Natorp's view, we can approach knowledge from two different directions: either from the 'objective' or 'plus' direction by studying the various facts and 'objectivities' that pertain to each region or from the 'subjective' or 'minus' direction by studying the dynamic acts, the '*fieri*' of consciousness that those facts are grounded in.[87] Psychology, he argues, should concern itself with the latter, with what he refers to as the 'ultimate concentration' of each region into consciousness:

> the inner world of consciousness can no longer be logically ordered over, next to, or under [the worlds of theoretical knowledge, ethics, art, and religion]; to all of them, to *objectivizations of any kind and level* [**Objektsetzung jeder Art und Stufe**], it represents as it were the *counterpart*, the *turning inward*, the *ultimate concentration* of them all *into experiencing consciousness* [gleichsam die **Gegenseite**, eben die **Innenwendung**, nämlich die **letzte Konzentration** ihrer aller **auf das erlebende Bewußtsein**].[88]

---

82 For a discussion of Cohen's psychology, see Poma (1997), 147–153 and Zeidler (2001). As Poma notes, although Cohen never wrote this volume, he had been developing material for it in his lectures at Marburg 1905–06, 1908–9, and 1916 (Poma (1997), 148).
83 Cohen (1912), 426, 429. Translations of this text are my own
84 Cohen (1912), 432.
85 Cohen (1914), 11. Translation by Poma (1997), 153. Zeidler argues that Cohen abandons psychology because he comes to regard the philosophy of religion as the proper systematic capstone to his philosophy (Zeidler (2001), 141).
86 See also Natorp's "On the Objective and Subjective Grounding of Knowledge" (1887)
87 Natorp (1912b, 71). Translations of this text are my own. See also Natorp (1888), §14 and (1912b), 200
88 Natorp (1912b), 20.

According to Natorp, however, insofar as consciousness is the dynamic ground of objects, we cannot study it in the way that we study other objects. For this reason, he claims that we need to develop a distinctive method to study consciousness, which he labels the 'reconstructive' method.[89] This method begins with objects and then 'unravels' them in order to disclose the "psychological origin" and "subjective sources in consciousness," which condition them.[90] In so doing, Natorp suggests we reconstruct the immediate, concrete sources in consciousness that ground culture. Ultimately, he suggests that what we will uncover is the unitary source of culture, i.e., the "lawful ground, the unity of *logos*, of *ratio* in all such creative activity [*Tat*] of culture."[91]

By Natorp's lights, if we study consciousness in this way, i.e., by taking our cue first from objects and then reconstructing the subjective upon which those objects rest, then instead of lapsing into psychologism or 'subjectivism', psychology will retain its 'objective character':

> the law of objective formation [*objektiven Gestaltung*] can never be sought out other than in the objective formation itself... in the creation of the cultural life of humanity, at the same time it retains its rigorous *objective character*; thus it differs sharply from every "*psychologism*".[92]

Thus, by establishing the unitary source of culture through the reconstructive method, Natorp thinks we can arrive at an objective analysis of the subject that complements the rigorous analysis of the facts of culture.

If we now turn our attention to Cassirer, we find that he explicitly places his own *Philosophy of Symbolic Forms* within this tradition of Marburg psychology, albeit with some important corrections. Emphasizing, in particular, his relationship to Natorp's psychology, at the outset of the third volume, Cassirer analyzes

---

89 See, e.g., Natorp (1888), §13 and (1912b), Ch. 8
90 Natorp (1888), 101. See Cassirer (1957a), 53–4: "This psychology, as Natorp sees it, seems engaged in a mere labor of Penelope, unraveling the intricate fabric woven by the various forms of "objectivization" [*Objektivation*]."
91 Natorp (1912b), 197.
92 Natorp 1912a, 198; see also 208. Towards the end of his career, Natorp appears to have become dissatisfied with this approach insofar as it seemed to make the relationship between the subject and object still too external and did not yet fully get at the 'whole' of human life (Natorp (1921), 157). Thus he began to develop a 'general logic' instead, which was meant to overcome these difficulties, see, e.g., his 1921 essay in Schmidt's *Die Deutsche Philosophie der Gegenwart in Selbstdarstellungen:* Natorp (1921), 157–176, *Vorlesungen über Praktische Philosophie* (*Lectures on Practical Philosophy*) (1925), and *Philosophische Systematik* (*Philosophical Systematic*) (1958). See Cassirer (1925), 280, 291–6 for a discussion of these later developments.

the continuities and discontinuities between his approach and Natorp's.⁹³ On the one hand, he agrees with Natorp that what is needed in addition to studying facts that pertain to each region of culture is a reconstruction of the subjective sources in which those facts are grounded:

> We start... from the problems of the objective spirit, from the formations in which it consists and exists; however, we shall attempt by means of reconstructive analysis to find our way back to their elementary presuppositions, the conditions of their possibility.⁹⁴

As he puts it a few sentences earlier, "Our inquiry... aspires to find its way back to the primary subjective sources, the original attitudes and formative modes of consciousness."⁹⁵ Cassirer ultimately identifies these subjective sources as the three functions of consciousness, i.e., the expressive function [*Ausdrucksfunktion*], representative function [*Darstellungsfunktion*], and significative function [*Bedeutungsfunktion*], which he organizes the third volume of the *Philosophy of Symbolic Forms* around.

On the other hand, Cassirer argues that Natorp fails to do justice to these subjective grounds for two reasons. To begin, Cassirer argues that Natorp's survey of the relevant facts is incomplete: he claims that Natorp follows the 'trichotomy' of Kant's system adding only religion to it, while Cassirer himself claims that we need to acknowledge other regions of culture, like myth and language.⁹⁶ Furthermore, Cassirer argues that Natorp's account is problematic because he tends to *assimilate* everything to the model of mathematics and natural science by identifying *laws* as the subjective ground of every region.⁹⁷ From Cassirer's perspective, while this may be appropriate in the case of theoretical knowledge, the other regions of culture "move in different paths and express different trends of spiritual formation."⁹⁸ This is, in part, why Cassirer appeals not to the notion of 'law', but to the more general notion of a 'symbolic form' to capture what is common across the different spheres of culture. This is also why he thinks we need to distinguish between the sort of significative consciousness that dominates mathematical natural science and the expressive and representative forms of consciousness that dominate the other symbolic forms.⁹⁹ Indeed,

---

93 Cassirer (1957a), 51–57. For a discussion of Cassirer's relationship to Natorp, see Luft (2004).
94 Cassirer (1957a), 57.
95 Cassirer (1957a), 57.
96 Cassirer (1957a), 57.
97 Cassirer (1957a), 56.
98 Cassirer (1957a), 56.
99 Cassirer (1925), 296 suggests that the notion of the 'symbol' is perhaps the best way to describe what Natorp sees as the unifying factor of experience.

Cassirer argues that it is only if we acknowledge the distinctiveness of each mode of objectification that we will be able to fulfill our task in psychology: "These trends [of spiritual formation] must be kept sharply separate, each in its own peculiar determinacy, if the task of reconstruction is to succeed."[100]

At the same time, Cassirer does not give up on the Marburg idea that a philosophy of culture should also aim at exposing the unity that underlies culture more generally:

> all the various and complex systems of symbols that are contained in language, art, science, and mythical and religious thought... possess, in spite of their differences, an intrinsic unity... That unity which I am in the habit of calling the unity of symbolic thought and symbolic representations... is a condition of all the constructive processes of the mind, a force that pervades all our mental operations and energies.[101]

Indeed, for Cassirer, this is what is distinctive about us as human beings. This is why in the *Essay on Man*, he argues that we should not be defined as an '*animal rationale*', but as an '*animal symbolicum*'.[102] Although this emphasis on the symbol is surely distinctive in Cassirer, nevertheless his commitment to offering a 'psychology', which is properly understood as the study of humanity as the source of culture is a commitment he inherits from Cohen and Natorp.

6 Conclusion: Cassirer's Continued Commitment to Marburg Neo-Kantianism

We are now in a position to return to the question of Cassirer's status as a Neo-Kantian. In the first place, it is evident throughout his career, from the *Problem of Knowledge* to the *Essay on Man* that Cassirer adheres to basic tenets of Neo-Kantianism discussed in §2, i.e., he rejects naïve realism and the copy theory of knowledge in favor of critical idealism and a critical theory of knowledge. Moreover, it is clear that Cassirer along with the other members of the Southwest and Marburg Schools thinks we ought to pursue an anti-psychologistic route in order to specify the logical conditions on which our knowledge rests.

Yet matters become more complicated when we consider to what extent Cassirer remains a Marburg Neo-Kantian throughout his career. As was mentioned above, it has been suggested that we should read Cassirer's *Philosophy of Sym-*

---

100 Cassirer (1957a), 57.
101 Cassirer (1979b), 71.
102 Cassirer (1944), 26.

bolic Forms as a break away from the Marburg version of Neo-Kantianism defended by Cohen and Natorp, as well as Cassirer himself in his early works, like *Substance and Function*. In light of the preceding considerations, however, this interpretation of his relationship to the Marburg School becomes less convincing. In the first place, we have seen that the *interest* in a philosophy of culture in no way sets Cassirer apart, but rather places him squarely within the Marburg tradition. Furthermore, in order to study culture, Cassirer relies on the transcendental method; hence he also remains *methodologically* in line with Cohen and Natorp.[103] Finally, as we saw, with respect to his efforts to identify the 'unity' that underlies culture more generally, Cassirer also follows in Cohen's and Natorp's footsteps by endeavoring to offer a *psychology of culture*, which clarifies the roots of the symbolic forms in consciousness.

Still what about the alleged 'scientism' of Cohen and Natorp that Cassirer himself appears to attribute to them? We must be careful on his issue. On the one hand, it is clear that Cassirer, alongside Cohen and Natorp, does accord a certain privileged status to mathematics and natural science even in the *Philosophy of Symbolic Forms*. This is evident in the teleological organization of these three volumes, which situates myth, religion, and language as stages that lead towards the development of theoretical knowledge.[104] On the other hand, as we saw above in his discussion of Natorp, it is clear that Cassirer takes issue with the reduction or assimilation of every region of culture to mathematics and natural science. For him, it is important to recognize that there are distinctive acts of spiritual formation that underwrite each region and that we cannot treat these all as the exercise of reason and its laws. For Cassirer, the reductivist attitude not only leads Cohen and Natorp to a mischaracterization of fields like ethics, aesthetics, and religion, but also to the neglect of the more primitive forms of culture, which serve as the 'substructure' on which the 'superstructure' of mathematical natural science is based.[105] In this way, Cassirer's philosophy of culture certainly shifts away from the strict rationalism of his predecessors; however, this does not amount to a repudiation of the Marburg commitment to defending a philosophy of culture. Instead, it appears as a broadening of the

---

[103] See Ferrari (2009) and Luft (2011), 277–9.
[104] As Cassirer makes this point, "the Philosophy of Symbolic Forms now seeks to apprehend [the world view of exact knowledge] in its necessary intellectual mediations. Starting from the relative end which thought has here achieved [i.e., mathematics and natural science], it inquires back into the middle and the beginning, with a view to understanding the end itself for what it is and what it means" (Cassirer (1957a), xiv).
[105] Cassirer (1957a), xiii. See Friedman (2000), 100–101.

scope of the investigation and a revision of what in his view is the overly rationalist approach of Cohen and Natorp.

Yet from Cassirer's own perspective this would seem to be enough to keep him within the Marburg camp, for on his view, we should define Neo-Kantianism "functionally rather than substantially", i.e., as a "matter of a direction taken in question-posing" rather than as the defense of a particular "dogmatic doctrinal system."[106] Making a similar point in his Inaugural Lecture at the University of Göteborg in 1935, "The Concept of Philosophy as a Philosophical Problem," he claims that even though he extends the transcendental method to new areas, he retains a commitment to its way of posing questions:

> however much the type of problems may have changed, and its circumference may have been widened... I still believe that we need not give up the basic critical problem as Kant saw it and as he first established it... We must now direct the critical question to a completely new material, but we can and should maintain the form of this question.[107]

So even if Cassirer thinks the scope of philosophical investigation needs to be broadened to include new regions of culture, which Kant, Cohen, or Natorp neglect, or if he argues that we need a revised understanding of the symbolic, rather than wholly lawful grounds on which culture rests, insofar as Cassirer retains a commitment to asking about the conditions of the possibility of culture, his way of going 'back to Kant' retains the distinctive stamp of Marburg Neo-Kantianism.[108]

Bibliography

Allison (2004): Henry Allison, *Kant's Transcendental Idealism*, New Haven: Yale University Press.
Anderson (2005): R. Lanier Anderson, "Neo-Kantianism and the Roots of Anti-Psychologism", in *British Journal for the History of Philosophy* 13 (2), 287–323.
Cassirer, (1906): Ernst Cassirer, *Das Erkenntnisproblem in der Philosophie und Wissenschaft der neueren Zeit. Erster Band*, Berlin: Bruno Cassirer.
Cassirer, (1907): Ernst Cassirer, *Das Erkenntnisproblem in der Philosophie und Wissenschaft der neueren Zeit. Zweiter Band*, Berlin: Bruno Cassirer.

---

106 Heidegger (1990), 193.
107 Cassirer (1979a), 55.
108 I would like to thank Fabien Capèilleres, Massimo Ferrari, Jeremy Heis, Pierre Keller, Steve Lofts, Lydia Patton, Alan Richardson, the work-in-progress group at UBC, and the audience at the Marquette Cassirer conference for invaluable feedback on this paper.

Cassirer (1923): Ernst Cassirer, *Substance and Function, and Einstein's Theory of Relativity*, WC Swabey and MC Swabey (trans.), Chicago: Open Court.
Cassirer (1925): Ernst Cassirer, "Paul Natorp. 24. January 1854–17. August 1924", in: *Kant-Studien* 30, 273–298.
Cassirer (1929): Ernst Cassirer, "Neo-Kantianism", in *Encyclopaedia Britannica*, 14th ed., vol. XVI, 215–216.
Cassirer (1943): Ernst Cassirer, "Hermann Cohen, 1842–1918", in: *Social Research* 10.2, 219–232.
Cassirer (1944): Ernst Cassirer, *An Essay on Man*, New Haven: Yale University Press.
Cassirer (1953): Ernst Cassirer, *The Philosophy of Symbolic Forms. Vol I: Language*, R. Manheim (trans.), New Haven: Yale University Press.
Cassirer (1955): Ernst Cassirer, *Determinism and Indeterminism in Modern Physics*, Theodor Benfey (trans.), New Haven, Yale University Press.
Cassirer (1957a): Ernst Cassirer, *The Philosophy of Symbolic Forms. Volume Three: The Phenomenology of Knowledge*, Ralph Manheim (trans.), New Haven: Yale University Press.
Cassirer (1957b): Ernst Cassirer, *The Problem of Knowledge: Philosophy, Science, and History Since Hegel*. Trans. William Woglom. New Haven: Yale University Press.
Cassirer (1979a): Ernst Cassirer, "The Concept of Philosophy as a Philosophical Problem", in: *Symbol, Myth, and Culture: Essays and Lectures of Ernst Cassirer: 1935–1945*, Donald Philip Verene (ed.). New Haven: Yale University Press, 49–63.
Cassirer (1979b) "Critical Idealism as a Philosophy of Culture", in: *Symbol, Myth, and Culture: Essays and Lectures of Ernst Cassirer: 1935–1945*, Donald Philip Verene (ed.). New Haven: Yale University Press, 64–91.
Cassirer (1993): Ernst Cassirer, "Was ist Subjektivismus?", in: *Erkenntnis, Begriff, Kultur*, Hamburg: Meiner, 199–230.
Cassirer (2005): Ernst Cassirer, "Hermann Cohen and the Renewal of Kantian Philosophy", Lydia Patton (trans.), in: *Angelaki: Journal of the Theoretical Humanities* 10.1, 95–108.
Chignell (2008): Andrew Chignell, "Introduction: On Going Back to Kant", in *The Philosophical Forum* 39 (2), 109–124.
Coffa (1991): J. Alberto Coffa, *The Semantic Tradition from Kant to Carnap: To the Vienna Station*, Cambridge: Cambridge University Press.
Cohen (1871/1885): Hermann Cohen, *Kants Theorie der Erfahrung*. Berlin: Dümmler.
Cohen (1877): Hermann Cohen, *Kants Begründung der Ethik*. Berlin: Dümmler.
Cohen (1889): Hermann Cohen, *Kants Begründung der Ästhetik*. Berlin: Dümmler.
Cohen (1902): Hermann Cohen, *System der Philosophie, Erster Teil: Logik der reinen Erkenntnis*. Berlin: Bruno Cassirer.
Cohen (1904/1907): Hermann Cohen, *System der Philosophie, Zweiter Teil: Ethik der reinen Willens*. Berlin: Bruno Cassirer.
Cohen (1912): Hermann Cohen, *System der Philosophie. Dritter Teil: Ästhetik des reinen Gefühls, 2 Bde*. Berlin: Bruno Cassirer.
Cohen (1914, 3rd ed.): Hermann Cohen, *Einleitung mit kritischem Nachtrag zu F. A. Langes Geschichte des Materialismus*. Leipzig: Baedeker.
Cohen (1919): Hermann Cohen, *Die Religion der Vernunft aus den Quellen des Judentums*. Leipzig: Fock. Translated as (1972): *Religion of Reason: Out of the Sources of Judaism*. Trans. Simon Kaplan, New York: Frederick Unger.

Crowell (1998): Steven Crowell, "Neo-Kantianism", in: *A Companion to Continental Philosophy*, Simon Critchley and William R. Schroeder (eds.), Oxford: Blackwell, 185–197.
Edgar (2008): Scott Edgar, "Paul Natorp and the Emergence of Anti-Psychologism in the Nineteenth Century", in: *Studies in History and Philosophy of Science* 39, 54–65.
Ferrari (2009): Massimo Ferrari, "Is Cassirer a Neo-Kantian Methodologically Speaking?", in: *Neo-Kantianism in Contemporary Philosophy*, Rudolf A. Makkreel and Sebastian Luft (eds.), Bloomington: Indiana University Press, 293–314.
Friedman (2000): Michael Friedman, *A Parting of the Ways: Carnap, Cassirer and Heidegger*, Chicago: Open Court.
Friedman (2005): Michael Friedman, "Ernst Cassirer and Contemporary Philosophy of Science", in: *Angelaki* 10(1), 119–128.
Fries (1828–31): Jakob Friedrich Fries, *Neue oder anthropologische Kritik der Vernunft*, Heidelberg: Bey Mohr und Zimmer.
Gordon (2010): Peter Gordon, *Continental Divide: Heidegger, Cassirer, Davos*, Cambridge: Harvard University Press.
Guyer (2008): Paul Guyer, "What Happened to Kant in Neo-Kantian Aesthetics? Cohen, Cohn, and Dilthey", in *The Philosophical Forum* 39(2), 143–176.
Hatfield (1991): Gary Hatfield, *The Natural and the Normative: Theories of Spatial Perception from Kant to Helmholtz*, Cambridge: The MIT Press.
Heidegger (1990): Martin Heidegger, *Kant and the Problem of Metaphysics*, 5th ed, Richard Taft (trans.), Bloomington: Indiana University Press.
Heidegger (1997): Martin Heidegger, *Phenomenological Interpretation of Kant's Critique of Pure Reason*. Parvis Emad and Kenneth Maly (trans.), Bloomington: Indiana University Press.
Heis (2012): Jeremy Heis, "Ernst Cassirer, Kurt Lewin, and Hans Reichenbach", in *The Berlin Group and the Philosophy of Logical Empiricism*, Nikolay Milkov and Volker Peckhaus (eds.), Springer, 67–94.
Herbart (1924–5): Johann Friedrich Herbart, *Psychologie als Wissenschaft neu gegründet auf Erfahrung, Metaphysik, und Mathematik*, Königsberg: Unzer.
Kant, (1998): Immanuel Kant, *Critique of Pure Reason*, Paul Guyer, Allen Wood (trans.), Cambridge: Cambridge University Press.
Kant, (1902a): Immanuel Kant, *Prolegomena to Any Future Metaphysics*, in: *Kants gesammelte Schriften*, vol. 4, Deutschen (formerly, Königlichen Preussichen) Akademie der Wissenschaften (eds), Berlin: Walter de Gruyter.
Kant, (1902b): Immanuel Kant, *Groundwork to the Metaphysics of Morals*, in: *Kants gesammelte Schriften*, vol. 4, Deutschen (formerly, Königlichen Preussichen) Akademie der Wissenschaften (eds), Berlin: Walter de Gruyter.
Kant, (1902c): Immanuel Kant, *Critique of Practical Reason*, in: *Kants gesammelte Schriften*, vol. 5, Deutschen (formerly, Königlichen Preussichen) Akademie der Wissenschaften (eds), Berlin: Walter de Gruyter.
Kant, (1902d): Immanuel Kant, *Critique of the Power of Judgment*, in: *Kants gesammelte Schriften*, Deutschen (formerly, Königlichen Preussichen) Akademie der Wissenschaften (eds), Berlin: Walter de Gruyter.
Kant, (2004): Immanuel Kant, *Prolegomena to Any Future Metaphysics*. Gary Hatfield (trans.), Cambridge: Cambridge University Press.

Kant, (2012): Immanuel Kant, *Groundwork to the Metaphysics of Morals*. Mary Gregor, Jens Timmermann (trans.), Cambridge: Cambridge University Press.
Kant, (1997): Immanuel Kant, *Critique of Practical Reason*. Mary Gregor (trans.), Cambridge: Cambridge University Press.
Kant, (2002): Immanuel Kant, *Critique of the Power of Judgment*. Paul Guyer, Erich Matthews (trans.), Cambridge: Cambridge University Press.
Kant, (1902): Immanuel Kant, *Kants gesammelte Schriften*. Deutschen (formerly, Königlichen Preussichen) Akademie der Wissenschaften (eds), Berlin: Walter de Gruyter.
Kim (2008): Alan Kim, "Paul Natorp", in: *The Stanford Encyclopedia of Philosophy*, Edward N. Zalta (ed), URL = <http://plato.stanford.edu/archives/fall2008/entries/natorp/>.
Köhnke (1991): Klaus Christian Köhnke, *The Rise of Neo-Kantianism: German Academic Philosophy Between Idealism and Positivism*, R. J. Hollingdale (trans.), Cambridge: Cambridge University Press.
Krijnen (2001): Christian Krijnen, *Nachmetaphysischer Sinn. Eine problemgeschichtliche und systematische Studie zu den Prinzipien der Wertphilosophie Heinrich Rickerts*, Würzburg: Königshausen & Neumann.
Krijnen and Noras (2012): Christian Krijnen and Andrzej Noras (eds), *Marburg versus Südwestdeutschland: philosophische Differenzen zwischen den beiden Hauptschulen des Neukantianismus*, Würzburg: Königshausen & Neumann.
Krois (1987): John Michael Krois, *Cassirer, Symbolic Forms and History*, New Haven: Yale University Press.
Kusch (1995): Martin Kusch, *Psychologism: a Case Study in the Sociology of Philosophical Knowledge*, London: Routledge.
Lange (1866): Friedrich Albert Lange, *Geschichte des Materialismus und Kritik seiner Bedeutung in der Gegenwart*, Iserlohn: J. Baedeker. Translated as (1877–1881): *The History of Materialism and Criticism of Its Importance*. Trans. Ernest Chester Thomas, London: Trübner & Company.
Liebmann (1865): Otto Liebmann, *Kant und die Epigonen*, Stuttgart: Carl Schober.
Luft (2004): Sebastian Luft, "A Hermeneutic Phenomenology of Subjective and Objective. Spirit: Husserl, Natorp, Cassirer", *The New Yearbook for Phenomenology and Phenomenological Philosophy* 4, 209–248.
Luft (2011): Sebastian Luft, *Subjectivity and Lifeworld in Transcendental Phenomenology*, Evanston: Northwestern University Press.
Marx (1988): Wolfgang Marx, "Cassirers Philosophie—Ein Abschied von kantianisierender Letztbegründung", in: *Über Ernst Cassirers Philosophie der symbolischen Formen*, Helmut Holzhey and E. W. Orth (eds), Frankfurt: H.-J. Braun, 75–88.
Moynahan (2013): Gregory Moynahan, *Ernst Cassirer and the Critical Science of Germany, 1899–1919*, London: Anthem Press.
Natorp (1981): Paul Natorp, "On the Objective and Subjective Grounding of Knowledge", Louis Phillips, David Kolb (trans.), in: *Journal of the British Society for Phenomenology* 12, 245–266. Originally published, Natorp (1887): "Ueber objektive und subjektive Begründung der Erkenntniss (Erster Aufsatz)", *Philosophische Monatshefte* 23, 257–286.
Natorp (1888): Paul Natorp, *Einleitung in die Psychologie nach kritischer Methode*, Freiburg: Mohr.
Natorp (1908): Paul Natorp, *Religion innerhalb der Grenzen der Humanität*, Tübingen: Mohr.
Natorp (1912a): Paul Natorp, "Kant und die Marburger Schule", *Kant-Studien* 17, 193–221.

Natorp (1912b): Paul Natorp, *Allgemeine Psychologie nach kritischer Methode*, Tübingen: Mohr.
Natorp (1921): Paul Natorp, "Paul Natorp", in: *Die Philosophie der Gegenwart in Selbstdarstellungen*, vol. 1, Raymund Schmidt (ed.), Leipzig: Felix Meiner, 151–176.
Natorp (1925): Paul Natorp, *Vorlesungen über Praktische Philosophie*, Erlangen: Philosophischen Akademie.
Natorp (1958): Paul Natorp, *Philosophische Systematik*, Hans Natorp (ed.), Hamburg: Felix Meiner.
Orth (1996): Ernst Wolfgang Orth, *Von der Erkenntnistheorie zur Kulturphilosophie: Studien zu Ernst Cassirers Philosophie der symbolischen Formen*, Würzburg: Königshausen & Neumann.
Pollok (2010): Konstantin Pollok, "The 'Transcendental Method': On the Reception of the *Critique of Pure Reason* in Neo-Kantianism", in: *The Cambridge Companion to Kant's Critique of Pure Reason*, Paul Guyer (ed.), Cambridge: Cambridge University Press, 346–379.
Poma (1997): Andrea Poma, *The Critical Philosophy of Hermann Cohen*, John Denton (trans.), Albany: SUNY Press.
Renz (2005): Ursula Renz, "Critical Idealism and the Concept of Culture: Philosophy of Culture in Hermann Cohen and Ernst Cassirer", in: *Hermann Cohen's Critical Idealism*, Reinier Munk (ed), Dordrecht: Springer, 327–356.
Richardson (1998): Alan Richardson, *Carnap's Construction of the World*, Cambridge: Cambridge University Press.
Richardson (2003): Alan Richardson, "Conceiving, Experiencing, and Conceiving Experiencing: Neo-Kantianism and the History of the Concept of Experience", *Topoi* 22, 55–67.
Rickert (1909): Heinrich Rickert, "Zwei Wege der Erkenntnistheorie. Transcendentalpsychologie und Transcendentallogik", *Kant-Studien* 14, 169–228.
Rickert (1913): Heinrich Rickert, "Vom System der Werte", *Logos* 4, 295–327.
Rickert (1921): Heinrich Rickert, *System der Philosophie*, Tübingen: Mohr Siebeck.
Rickert (1924): Heinrich Rickert, *Kant als Philosoph der modernen Kultur. Ein geschichtsphilosophischer Versuch*, Tübingen: Mohr Siebeck.
Rickert (1926): Heinrich Rickert, *Kulturwissenschaft und Naturwissenschaft*, 6th and 7th expanded editions, Tübingen: Mohr Siebeck.
Rickert (1929): Heinrich Rickert, *Die Grenzen der naturwissenschaftlichen Begriffsbildung. Eine logische Einleitung in die historischen Wissenschaften*, 6th edition, Tübingen: Mohr Siebeck.
Rudolph (2008): Enno Rudolph, "Symbol and History: Ernst Cassirer's Critique of the History of Philosophy", in: *The Symbolic Construction of Reality: The Legacy of Ernst Cassirer*, Jeffrey Barash (ed.), Chicago: University of Chicago Press, 2–27.
Seidengart (1994): Jean Seidengart, "Die philosophische Bedeutung des Unendlichkeitsbegriffs in Ernst Cassirers Neukantianismus", in: *Neukantianismus, Perspektiven und Probleme*, E.W. Orth and Helmut Holzhey (eds.), Würzburg: Königshausen & Neumann, 442–456.
Skidelsky (2011): Edward Skidelsky, *Ernst Cassirer: The Last Philosopher of Culture*, Princeton: Princeton University Press.

Staiti (2013): Andrea Staiti, "Heinrich Rickert", in: *The Stanford Encyclopedia of Philosophy*, Edward N. Zalta (ed.), URL = <http://plato.stanford.edu/archives/win2013/entries/heinrich-rickert/>.

Stone (2005): Abraham Stone, "The Continental Origins of Verificationism", *Angelaki* 10(1), 129–143.

Verene (1969): Donald Phillip Verene, "Kant, Hegel, and Cassirer: The Origins of the Philosophy of Symbolic Forms", *Journal of the History of Ideas* 30(1), 33–46.

Verene (2001): Donald Phillip Verene, "Introduction: The Development of Cassirer's Philosophy", in Thora Ilin Bayer, *Cassirer's Metaphysics of Symbolic Forms*, New Haven: Yale University Press, 1–37.

Willey (1978): Thomas Willey, *Back to Kant: The Revival of Kantianism in German Social and Historical Thought, 1860–1914*, Detroit: Wayne State University Press.

Windelband (1907): Wilhelm Windelband, "'Kritische oder genetische Methode?'", in: *Präludien: Aufsätze und Reden zur Einleitung in die Philosophie*, 3rd ed., Tübingen: J.C.B. Mohr, 318–54.

Zeidler (2001): Kurt Zeidler, "Das Problem der Psychologie im System Cohens (mit Blick auf P. Natorp)", in: *Hermann Cohen und die Erkenntnistheorie*, Wolfgang Marx and E.W. Orth (eds.), Würzburg: Königshausen & Neumann, 135–146.

Steve G. Lofts (London/ON)
Cassirer and Heidegger: The Cultural-Event The *Auseinandersetzung* of Thinking and Being

1 Introduction: Reading Cassirer and Heidegger Outside of the Davos Paradigm

From the very beginning, our assessment of the relationship between Cassirer and Heidegger has been situated within the interpretative horizon of their 1929 meeting at Davos, Switzerland. Already at the time, the Davos *Auseinandersetzung* was seen as much more than an ivory-tower debate over Kant or a confrontation between two of Germany's most important thinkers. For Levinas, it was like "participating in the creation and the end of the world" that marked the "end of a certain humanism".[1]

The Davos debate, however, has been framed almost exclusively in terms of the problem of the proper interpretation of the productive imagination and the role of the schema. As the Davos conference focused on the question *Was ist der Mensch?*, the debate over Kant was subsequently understood as a fundamental clash between two antithetical conceptions of human existence, between spontaneity and thrownness, freedom and finitude. Between these two "normative *images* of humanity", as Peter Gordon puts it, no *media via* seemed possible.[2]

It is not surprising, nor entirely unjustified, that Davos has been understood as a paradigmatic event of its times and a watershed in European intellectual history. Cassirer is said to have defended the humanistic tradition reaching back through Humboldt and Kant to Pico, whereas Heidegger is said to have pointed the way to the new anti-humanistic tradition to come. Finally, this discussion is situated in the historical circumstances of the times, which took on particular significance given the fact that Cassirer was Jewish and Heidegger would become a member of the National Socialist Party.

Now, without questioning the value of the Davos paradigm, I would like to offer an *alternative* framing of the relationship between Cassirer's and Heideg-

---

[1] Levinas (2001), 35.
[2] Gordon (2010), 6.

ger's philosophical projects. As with any interpretative horizon, the Davos paradigm frames the issues in a certain way, assumes a certain starting point and, as such, excludes others.

Although Peter Gordon (2010) and John M. Krois (2004) have challenged our recollection of Davos, they nevertheless continue to affirm the basic framework of the Davos paradigm and see the relationship between Cassirer and Heidegger in terms of a fundamental struggle between the two antithetical positions of humanism and anti-humanism stemming from different interpretations of Kant. I would argue that this is a false starting point, that Cassirer and Heidegger are both searching to establish a new humanism: Cassirer through a radical transformation of classical humanism to the point of breaking with it; Heidegger through a Copernican revolution of the human—but both want to re-establish the "dignity of man", as Pico puts it, which is denied to human existence by the positivistic paradigms of naturalism and psychologism. I would emphasize that Levinas does not say it was the end of humanism *tout court*, but "the end of a *certain* humanism".

If I wish neither to set Cassirer and Heidegger off against each other, nor work within the Davos paradigm, what, then, do I want to argue and what is the framework in which my interpretation of their thought operates? In short, I want to argue: 1) that their projects share in the development of a new ontology as a response to a fundamental crisis in Western ontology; 2) that the philosophical projects of Cassirer and Heidegger are not antithetical, they are *different* and, through the opposition of their difference, they not only belong-together but require each other; 3) that to a certain degree Cassirer and Heidegger recognized this *rapprochement* of their respective philosophical projects; 4) that in their varied works, Cassirer and Heidegger were engaged in a mutual and reciprocal critical *Auseinandersetzung* and that this *Auseinandersetzung* helped define the content of their respective projects and ultimately influenced the trajectory of their thought in opposition to one another; finally, 5) that Cassirer's turn to culture and Heidegger's turn to ontology and the interconnection between these projects sets the stage for philosophy in the twentieth-century, which, after the turn to language and aesthetics, operates at the intersection of culture and ontology.[3]

---

[3] This article is but a *Darstellung* of a much larger project. Thus, the reader should view the following merely as a first draft and sketch of my interpretation of Cassirer's and Heidegger's projects—an interpretation which, admittedly, some may see more as a reconstruction. A full and complete presentation and defense of this interpretation will only be possible upon the completion of this project.

2 Toward a New Paradigm: Crisis and the Ontology of *Auseinandersetzung*

Cassirer and Heidegger must be situated in the context of the crisis in ontology that unfolds at the beginning of the twentieth century. The rapid progress in the positive sciences and the radical reorientation of socio-political life that took place in the course of the nineteenth century progressively challenged a number of fundamental ontological principles that can be traced back to Greek philosophy, in general, and to Aristotle, in particular: e.g., being, substance, nature, teleological order, essentialism, etc. In mathematics, a crisis broke out when it became apparent that mathematics was unable to ground its most basic principles. Given that since Descartes the sciences had been modelled on mathematics, the crises in mathematics escalated into a crisis in science. As Western culture had been founded on the concept of rationality, a crisis in the sciences undermined the principles that grounded the European world. In particular, as the modern philosophy of the subject had been built upon the principles of ancient ontology as they had been transmitted through medieval metaphysics, a collapse of these ontological principles threw into doubt the whole modern philosophical and political project. The crisis was not merely an ivory-tower affair: such popular works like Thomas Mann's *Death in Venice* (1912) and Oswald Spengler's *The Decline of the West* (1918) attested to the growing sense of malaise as the ontological ground gave way and with it, to speak with Levinas, one world came to an end and another had not yet fully come-forth; and with this, a secure sense of what it meant to *be* and what it meant to *be* human gave way to nihilism in all its forms.

Cassirer's and Heidegger's responses to the crisis develop out of a critical *Auseinandersetzung* with the metaphysical tradition. Both provide a critique of what I will call "the ontology of self-identity" as a "metaphysics of substance" (Cassirer) or an onto-theological "metaphysics of presence" (Heidegger). Implicit in both projects is the development of a new ontology that I will call the "ontology of the *Auseinandersetzung*", which operates at the heart of their respective ways of rethinking the human.

In the Western metaphysical tradition from Parmenides onward, being is equated with self-identity; something is if it is self-identical with itself, if, as Parmenides says, it "remains the same and in the same it abides by itself" (ταὐτόν τ' ἐν ταὐτῶι τε μένον καθ' ἑστιν εἶναι) (fr. 8.29). "For it is the same thing that can be thought and that can be" (τὸ γὰρ αὐτὸ νοεῖν ἐστίν τε καὶ εἶναι) (fr. B 3) (quoted by Plotinus, *Enneads* V, i.8). In Plato's *Timaeus*, being is defined as that which is always "self-identical with itself"; "being" in the *Phaedo*, 78c1-d7, for example, is said to "remain the same" (κατὰ ταὐτὰ ἕξει) and as such is never open to "alteration" (ἀλλοίωσιν). This conception of being, as ontological self-identity, continues to operate as the basic first principle of philosophy throughout the Western tradition, from Aristotle's definitions of *ousia* (οὐσία) and of god as the "self-sufficient prime mover" and Plotinus's conception of "the One" (ἕν) as pure self-identity ("for only being can be by itself" (μόνῳ γὰρ τούτῳ παρ'αὑτοῦ ἐστιν εἶναι) (lines 43–4)), through the autonomous self-identity of the Cartesian *cogito*, to the self-causing activity of the Spinozan *natura naturans*. Ultimately, something *is* because it is self-identical with itself; it possesses a permanent and consistent existence (*Bestand*) that is radically self-contained. The Greek οὐσία is translated into the Latin *substantia*, which in modern thought constitutes the being of the subject as a thinking substance. Descartes defines *substance* as something "that 'exists' in such a way as to depend on no other thing for its existence".[4] As such, what *is* is always autonomous and free of all external relations and constraints. It exists in-itself and, therefore, for-itself. It is the alpha and omega of its own existence, emanating out of itself into reality through its own auto-poetic activity, its own expression. The modern philosophy of the subject as well as the modern philosophy of nature is based entirely upon this ontology of substance, which is in turn based upon the ancient ontology of self-identity.

At first sight, Hegel seems to break from this tradition: for within the logic of being, something is what it is because it is *not* something else: it possesses an identity-in-difference: "Being" is because it is *not* nothing; identity is because it is *not* difference. Hegel introduces the "determinate negativity" of difference into the forming and configuring of being. In the final analysis, however, the determinate negativity is domesticated and proves to be only a logical moment in a more encompassing ontological identity. Every identity-in-difference is "sublated" (*aufgehoben*) into a higher ontological reality. This *Aufgehoben*, this "negation of the negation", continues until all difference has been sublated into the identity of Absolute spirit, until all reality has taken the form of an "identity of identity-and-difference". Absolute spirit is, in the final analysis, a "being-in-and-for-itself"—it is both Substance and Subject, a "living substance" as Hegel calls it. "Absolute spirit, while an identity that is eternally self-contained, is likewise an identity that is returning and has returned into itself".[5]

Cassirer and Heidegger seek to move beyond this tradition of ontology. The move from substance concepts to function concepts and from there to a tran-

---

4 Descartes (1985), 210.
5 Hegel (1991), § 554.

scendental critique of the hermeneutical horizons of culture that undertake the *Auseinandersetzung* of I and world begins from a critique of substantial metaphysics. Heidegger, for his part, sets out to think the ontological difference and the event of appropriation as the *Auseinandersetzung* of the human and being and this begins from a critique of the onto-theo-logical metaphysics of presence.

Elsewhere I have shown that *Auseinandersetzung* is a technical term for both Cassirer and Heidegger that refers not only to a critical engagement with another thinker or a tradition but designates the proper method of philosophy and more importantly constitutes the core principle structuring their respective philosophical projects.[6] For both, the logic of *Auseinandersetzung* marks a fundamental way to view relations and structures of reality. An *Auseinandersetzung* is a complex relational operation in which the oppositions (*Gegen-satz*) of difference coexist as the mutually defining opposing limits of each other; each is defined in its being, not through some self-identical essence that it contains in itself, but through the strife of opposition as the confrontation (*Auseinandersetzung*) with the limit of the other it is not. As such, each element carries within itself the trace of the other, which defines its position in the play of differences; or, in Hegelian terminology, it is the determinative negativity that sets apart and yet constitutes the relationship of belonging-together (*Zusammengehören*) in the opposition of thesis and anti-thesis, in the *Gegensätzlichkeit* that operates within the identity-in-difference but which can not be sublated into a higher ontological identity—which remains unsublatable [*unaufheblicher*] as Cassirer following Natorp puts it.[7] The Davos paradigm with its emphasis on Kant misses the importance of Cassirer's and Heidegger's critical *Auseinandersetzung* with Hegel to their respective philosophical projects.

For both, the truth is the whole—both critique the two-world theory of classical metaphysics based as it is on an ontology of self-identity as well as the subsequent false dichotomy between idealism and realism that stems from this ontology. Throughout Cassirer's philosophy we find a series of polar opposites which in the metaphysical tradition were thought as existing independently of each other but which in Cassirer's thought are always defined in terms of their identity-in-difference, in terms of their ontological correspondence as being differentiated and united through the symbolic structures of culture that sets each out of the other: form/matter, I/world, I/thou, subject/object, thought/being. We find the same tension between polar oppositions in both *Being and Time* (phenomenon/appearance, being/beings, authentic/inauthentic, signification/rele-

---

6 Lofts (2010).
7 Cassirer (1955a/2002a), 105/155.

vance, being-there (Da-sein) and not being-there (Death) etc.) and in particular in the later Heidegger where *Auseinandersetzung* is explicitly set forth as the core ontological principle of the event of being.

3 The *Auseinandersetzung* of the Critique of Culture and the Question of Being (*Seinsfrage*)

On numerous occasions, Cassirer and Heidegger gesture toward the interconnection of the critique of culture and the question of being (*Seinsfrage*) without, however, ever explicitly demonstrating the nature of this *rapprochement*. At Davos, they clearly state their differences but in such a way as to intimate the necessity of their own project to that of the other.

Heidegger succinctly states the problem from his perspective: "I believe that what I designate with the term Dasein cannot be translated by one of Cassirer's concepts".[8] In other words, a transcendental critique of culture, as an account of the *a priori* conditions of possibility of *a* world of significations, cannot account for the radical unique event of being and of *the* world. To explain, for example, the generic sense of language and its transcendental function in the formation and configuration of *a* world through the determination of the intelligibility of *this* world (*Weltverständtnis*), only accounts for what is common to every cultural world without being able to account for the uniqueness of any given world. From the perspective of a transcendental critique of culture, every historical culture is the same and it is necessarily unable to think the uniqueness of *that* world because it is unable to designate what is proper to *the* world qua world. As we shall see, what renders a world unique is *the* thinking of being as *the* event of being itself.

For Cassirer, Heidegger's existential phenomenology, beginning as it does from the radical finitude of Dasein, has no access to the realm of "trans-personal meaning" required for Dasein to exist in *a* shared world; Dasein's being-in-the-world is, after all, always a being-with (*Mitsein*). However, "there is no other way from one Dasein to another Dasein than through this world of form"[9]—nor, I would add, from Dasein to itself. In other words, "form" is the necessary vehicle of the disclosure of being—what Cassirer often calls life.

---

8 Hamburg (1964), 219.
9 Ibid., 220.

> Life [Cassirer maintains] cannot apprehend itself by remaining absolutely within itself. It must give itself form, for it is precisely by the 'otherness' of form that it gains its 'visibility' (*Sichtigkeit*), if not its reality (*Wirklichkeit*). To detach the world of life absolutely from form and oppose the two means nothing other than to separate its 'reality' from its 'visibility'.[10]

It is only through form that the ephemeral flow of life gains the "consistent existence" (*Bestand*) of an intelligible reality. Cassirer calls this process, by which the world of objective spirit sets out and unites, forms and configures life/being, the "great process of the '*Auseinandersetzung*' of the I and the world". Cassirer writes:

> We began with the view that the meaning and value of the individual symbolic forms could never be completely obtained if we were to see in each of them only a bridge between a finished "inner world" and a finished "outer world", between an "I" and a "non-I" as given and fixed starting points. They all had, rather, to be recognized as means for the creation of these polar opposites, as the mediums in which and only by virtue of which the "separation and setting out" ("*Auseinandersetzung*") of the I and the world takes place. [...] The apparent dualism, the rupture in "Dasein" (*der Riß im "Dasein"*), is in truth nothing other than the result of a necessary duality of "sight" ("*Sicht*"). This implies that life, without transgressing against itself, without as such being "outside itself," has broken away from itself, become transparent [*durchsichtig*] to itself, has become itself objective. Every symbolic form works in its own way and by its own means to bring about this turn from mere being-in-itself to being-for-itself and, at the same time, achieves with the objective configuration of culture that new way, that particular mode of consciousness that exhibits itself in the human.[11]

In other words, the event of being requires the transcendental structures of culture for there to be an event: as such, the event of a "living presence" is always a con-textual-event and would not be an event, in any strict sense of the word, if this were not the case. The symbolic forms do not "copy" an already existing and given reality. The symbolic act of *Auseinandersetzung* is thus *per*form*ative* in nature, in that it creates what it sets out, differentiates and unites; what *is* is only through the *per*form*ance* that we *are*, the history that we are. Thus, for Cassirer, one cannot separate the ontic historical world of culture from the existential-ontological worldliness of the world, the *Umwelt* of the Das Man from the Da-sein of Dasein in the way Heidegger does in *Being and Time* (BT).

To think the Cassirer's critique of culture and Heidegger's thinking of the event together is to conjoin the event of being with the transcendental structures of signification without reducing one to the other—it is to think them as the mu-

---

10 Cassirer (1957/2002c), 39/44 f.
11 Cassirer (1996/1995), 60 f./59.

tually defining opposing limits of each other; belonging-together (*Zusammengehören*) through and as the strife of their opposition as the confrontation with the limit of the other, each is *not*. As such, each carries *within* itself the *trace* of the other. They appear, of course, as antinomic because what *happens* (*Geschehen*), *the event* (*Ereignis*) *of being*, possesses some incalculable singularity that eludes the generality of signification—an event is non-repeatable, whereas the signification of what happens should be repeatable without loss of meaning. The cultural forms are world-forming but the world of signification they form is animated from within by the thinking of the event as the event of being itself. To think Cassirer and Heidegger together is to think beyond the false dichotomy between idealism and realism found in modern philosophy, between rationalism and empiricism, to think the per*form*ativity of the symbolic act that produces the cultural-event, the paradoxical antinomy of the per*form*ative cultural-event as the *Auseinandersetzung* of thinking and being.

4 Relevance (*Bewandtnis*[12]) and Significance (*Bedeutsamkeit*): The Worldliness of the World between 1925 and 1930

If one reads, in order, Heidegger's 1925 seminar *The History of the Concept of Time*, his 1927 version of *Being and Time,* and then his 1929–1930 seminar *The Fundamental Concepts of Metaphysics*, a number of interesting things become clear. First, one finds a constant evolution in Heidegger's understanding of the world and the worldliness of the world. In the 1925 seminar, we find a first draft of what will become division one of BT. One of the main differences is that here the analysis of world is centred around what in BT will be the *Umweltlichkeit* of the *Umwelt* and thus provides a phenomenological analysis of the concrete ontic life-world as the significant world of the factical life of Dasein that constitutes its average everydayness rather than an existentialistic analysis of

---

12 It is not possible to translate *Bewandtnis* into English. While "relevance" is not ideal it is better than "involvement" as it has been translated by John Macquarrie and Edward Robinson. The verb *bewenden* is derived from the Old High German *biwenten* which meant to turn toward, bring or come to the end (zum Ende wenden, zu Ende bringen oder kommen). It is the movement toward end that is the raison d'être, explanation or import of something. What is more, the *Bewandtnis* of something is largely implicit and as such often illusive and difficult to articulate: as it is often difficult to say, for example, where a conversation is going even if everyone senses that it is moving towards some outcome.

the worldliness of the world of BT—it is a transcendental-ontoloigical account of the world and not the existential-ontological account given in BT. By the time you get to the 1929–30 seminar, the world is already on its way to being understood in terms of the "clearing" and the human being has become world-forming. By 1935 with the writing of "The Origin of the Work of Art" and *Introduction to Metaphysics*, Heidegger has already entered into his famous turn which can be understood as a turn to language and art and as an "ontology of culture"—we will return to this in a moment. Reading backward, however, it becomes clear that the idea of the clearing and strife as the opening and truth of being is already operating, if only implicitly, in Heidegger's early understanding of *the* world. Second, in reading all three texts it becomes clear that Heidegger explicitly and repeatedly engages Cassirer on numerous points—developing his own ideas through this engagement.

In his 1925 seminar, Heidegger is more explicit than he is in BT in acknowledging the connection between average everydayness and mythical Dasein: although the

> task of conceiving Dasein in its everydayness does not mean describing Dasein at a primitive stage of its being [...] often the consideration of primitive forms of Dasein can more readily provide directions in seeing and verifying certain phenomena of Dasein, in-as-much-as here the danger of concealment through the self-interpretation through theory [...] is not yet so powerful.[13]

Of course, for Heidegger "The fundamental analysis of Dasein is just the right presupposition for an understanding of the primitive and not the reverse".[14] Heidegger sees mythical Dasein as an evolutionary stage that excludes the theoretical world, whereas average everydayness is a constant way Dasein is each and every day, thus collapsing the mythical and theoretical into one homogenous sphere—something that the later Heidegger will correct. Nevertheless, access to this everydayness is facilitated through an analysis of the mythical lifeworld. I would argue that for Cassirer the mythical world is a permanent structural mode of being of the human being—a life concretely lived in a world of significations—and thus is very much part of the everydayness of the human being. Mythical being as average everydayness is, however, only ever made manifest in being transcended, once it has become a foreign world and thus no longer *the world* in which one lives.

Now,

---

13 Heidegger (1992/1979a), 155/208.
14 Ibid.

> Worldliness, [Heidegger maintains,] is constituted in references, and these references themselves stand in referential correlations, referential totalities, which ultimately refer back to the presence of the work-world. It is not things, [Heidegger insists,] but references that have the primary function in the structure of *encounter* belonging to the world, not substances but functions, to express this state of affairs by a formula of the 'Marburg School'.[15]

Heidegger picks this up in the next lecture:

> In fact, the analysis we have given of the structure of the environing world could be explained in terms of this particular epistemology of the Marburg School, *but this would also spoil our understanding of the phenomenon*. To be sure, the contrast between the concepts of substance and function, to which the epistemology of the Marburg School attaches particular importance, *has without question permitted us to see something significant*.[16]

The move from substance to function is continued by Cassirer into a general theory of signification—each symbolic form produces its own mode of signification (*Bedeutung*). As such, each symbolic form is a hermeneutical horizon that gives meaning or sense (*Sinn*) to an historically concrete significance (*Bedeutsamkeit*) belonging to a historically concrete world. In the case of myth it is a world that is a lived significance, in the case of science it is the thought of a pure signification. Human existence (Dasein), for Cassirer, is a "life in 'significations' ['*Bedeutungen*']".[17] Now, for Heidegger the concept of function relation is still too linked to a mathematical concept of nature and the distinction between substance and function relations has not been adequately grounded. What seems clear is that Heidegger seeks to ground function relations (which Heidegger sees as belonging to the ontic world) in a theory of reference (which Heidegger sees as being the ontological structure of relations). He then defines, however, references as "signifying" (*bedeuten*). The worldliness of the world is thus the referential totality that Heidegger now calls significance (*Bedeutsamkeit*) that determines the being of ontic relations that form the world. Thus, for Heidegger too "Because Dasein, in its being, is signifying (*bedeutend*) itself, *it lives in significations (Bedeutungen) and can express itself in and as these significations*".[18]

Of course, the world for Cassirer is also a world of significance (*Bedeutsamkeit*); what then is the difference? And why would understanding the world in terms of the function relation "spoil our understanding of the phenomenon"? It would do so because, though *correct* with respect to the ontic immediacy of

---

15 Ibid., 200/271.
16 Ibid., 200/208, my italics.
17 Cassirer (2000/1961), 15/15.
18 Heidegger (2010a/1976b), 127/151, my italics.

the world of Dasein's average everydayness, it does not get to what is *essential*— but then what is the essential being of the world? A clue may to be found in a change Heidegger makes to his lecture notes to the plan for the "positive exposition" of the worldliness of the world: the third step was amended from "the determination of the basic structure of worldliness as the totality of significance (*Bedeutsamkeit*)" to "the determination of the basic structure of worldliness as the totality of relevance (*Bewandtnisganzheit*)". As the translator points out, the change from "totality of significance" (*Bedeutsamkeit*) to "totality of relevance" (*Bewandtnisganzheit*) "postdates the lecture course"—thus, it was made some time in 1926.[19]

In the original lecture, however, Heidegger already made an important confession concerning his use of the term "significance": "such delimitations [he says] point to a certain embarrassment in the choice of the right expression for the complex phenomenon that we want to call significance".[20]

The term *Bewandtnis* is almost certainly borrowed from Emil Lask, though Heidegger clearly attempted to imbue it with a new meaning—while Cassirer's analysis of the world is *correct*, it requires a grounding in what is essential, namely the being of the world which is grounded in the meaning of being (*Sinn von Sein*) which Heidegger will call primordial temporality. So, the ontic relations of the world are now grounded in the ontological structures of reference, which in turn are grounded in the existential structures of relevance, which is grounded in primordial temporality. The interconnection between significance and relevance forms the core of Heidegger's existential understanding of the world in BT. Cassirer's *Weltverständtnis* presupposes, Heidegger maintains, a pre-ontological *Seinsverständnis*.

What does Heidegger see in Lask's "transcendental empiricism"? Lask rejects the ideality of the idea and primacy of the subject in favour of the ideality of the object, of a "preformal something". Whereas, for example, Husserl understands intentionality beginning from the ideality of the idea and the activity of the transcendental subject, Lask grounds intentionality in a transcendental object. Lask separates knowledge from experience: the pre-theoretical, and thus pre-cognitive, structures are grasped in an immediate act of intuition; a "categorical intuition"[21] of the concrete primordial world beyond the world of signification and knowledge which, however, is already a categorized real object. The category of this real object is "nothing other than a particular objective relevance

---

19 Kisiel (1993), 388.
20 Heidegger (1992/1979a), 202/274.
21 Ibid., 69/93.

(*Bewandtnis*) that pertains to the material".²² The primordial truth against which judgements are measured first shows itself in "categorical intuition," which Lask calls "lived-experience" as distinguished from cognition or knowledge (*Erkenninis*). One lives in a pre-formal intelligibility without 'knowing' it as such. We are first 'lost' in meaning, given over in a "pure absorption" in lived-experience. The region of being is thus composed of entities: that is, of things that have being and of being that is the form of what is. "Form" thus receives its "signification" from the matter of being. "Objective *Bewandtnis*", for Lask, designates the concrete region of being of ontologically real differences. Significance, on the other hand, designates the interconnection between subjective validity and objective validity; but as such significance is limited to the cognitive sphere. In this short, and perhaps over simplified account of Lask, it is not difficult to recognize Heidegger's account of the pre-ontological *Seinsverständntnis*, we can see in *Bewandtnis*, which for Heidegger is grounded in temporality, the "pregnant existential structure" that grounds the historically contingent sphere of signification.

In the 1925 seminar, Heidegger inquires how it is that we understand *a* world that is not our own. That we understand our own historical world is one thing, but how is it that we are able to understand a foreign world? "It is, [Heidegger says,] because understanding is drawn from *the world* that there is the possibility of understanding *an* alien world or *a* world mediated by sources, monuments and ruins".²³ How are we to understand this "*the world*"? In BT it becomes clear that the referential totality of significance that is the structure of the ontic environmental world in which Dasein "lives" is historically contingent and thus not essential. What is essential is the totality of relevance that grounds it as the being of *the world*. Significance is the ontic reality of Dasein whereas relevance marks the existential being of Dasein. Thus, the "in order to" and "for the sake of which" of the totality of relevance resist any kind of mathematical functionalization in accordance with their phenomenal content. They are not something that is thought, something that is initially posited in thinking but rather are, as the being of *the world*, the existential structures of the significance of *the world*. They are the background contexts of the world and as such are therefore never themselves part of the world that is given. "The referential context of significance is anchored in the being of Dasein toward its own most being".²⁴

---

22 Lask (2003), 60.
23 Heidegger (1992/1979a), 243/334, my italics.
24 Heidegger (2010b/1979b), 120/123.

Now, understanding constitutes what Heidegger calls sight (*Sicht*)—but clearly there is a duality of sight; for, "In understanding *the world*, being-in is always also understood. The understanding of existence as such is always an understanding of *the world*".[25] What happens in anxiety, for example, is that Dasein can no longer sense the relevance of its being in and through the system of signification of *a world* in which it lives. *Although Dasein's lived world* is still there and the useful innerwordly things still possess a significance they now lack any relevance what so ever for Dasein. Anxiety takes away from Dasein the possibility of understanding itself in terms of *a world* of signification as the totality of references which in turn throws it back onto itself and upon the essential totality of relevance, namely upon its temporal being towards end as the ultimate meaning of its being.

Two final points on BT. First, it is not uncommon, nor entirely unjustified, that readers of BT often see a gulf between authenticity and inauthenticity. A close reading of Chapter four of Division two of BT, "Temporality and Everydayness", should dispel the reader from this reading of BT—it should at least indicate that this separation was not Heidegger's intent; even if in the final analysis it would appear that once the ontic realm had been separated from the ontological level in the way Heidegger does in Division one, it was no longer possible to bring them back together after the fact. It is through the hybrid concept of the "horizonal schema" that Heidegger attempts to bring the two levels together into a unitary phenomenon. "The unity of significance, that is, the ontological constitution of the world, must then also be founded in temporality. The existential and temporal condition of the possibility of the world lies in the fact that temporality, as an ecstatical unity, has something like a horizon".[26] Thus, "Authentic being a self is not based on an exceptional state of the *subject*, detached from the they, but is an existentiell modification of the they as an essential existential".[27] And yet, "The they-self is an existentiell modification of the authentic self".[28] The relationship between authenticity and inauthenticity is, to speak with Cassirer, the one in the other, the other in the one.

The second final point about BT, and I can only state this here and provide a few examples, is that at each critical step in his argument, Heidegger returns to a critical *Auseinandersetzung* with the philosophy of Cassirer. In section 11, "The Existential Analytic and the Interpretation of Primitive Dasein", Heidegger again reaffirms that average everydayness is "the *repetition* and the ontologically

---

25 Ibid., 142/146.
26 Ibid., 347/365.
27 Ibid., 126/130.
28 Ibid., 303/317.

more transparent purification of what is ontically discovered" in Cassirer's analysis of myth.²⁹ At the end of the critical section 18, "Relevance and Significance: the worldliness of the world", Heidegger returns to distinguish his concept of relevance from Cassirer's shift to function concepts maintaining that "functional concepts of this kind are ontologically possible only in relation to beings whose being has the character of pure substantiality. Functional concepts are always possible only as formalized substantial concepts".³⁰

Now, if we turn to Heidegger's 1929–30 winter seminar, which took place after Davos, Cassirer is again engaged in a central way. At the beginning of the seminar Heidegger speaks of the current philosophy of culture. He states:

> We have today a philosophy of culture concerned with expression, with symbol, with symbolic forms. [...] Here too almost everything is correct, right down to the essential. Yet we must ask anew: Is this view of the human an essential one? [...] yet the question remains as to whether setting the human out in this way concerns and grips human Da-sein, or indeed brings it to being, whether this setting-out that is oriented toward expression not only factically misses the essence of the human, but must necessarily miss it [...]. In other words, such philosophy attains merely the exhibition and setting-there [Dar-stellung] of the human, but never his Da-sein [being-there].³¹

It would be wrong to take this as a rejection of Cassirer. Heidegger often starts with something that is "correct" but not yet ontologically transparent. In these cases, the two levels must be thought together. Cassirer's transcendental exhibition and setting-there [*Dar-stellung*] of the human being must be grounded in an essential existential account of the *Da-sein* (being-there) of the human being—however inversely, the *Da-sein* (being-there) of the human requires its exhibition and setting-there (*Dar-stellung*) that comes about through the symbolic forms of culture. Towards the end of the seminar, at the heart of his analysis of logos in Aristotle that sets up the turn from the meaning of being to the truth of being, Heidegger now asks:

> Who forms the world? The human being, according to our thesis. But what is the human? [...] it is not the case that the human being first exists and then also one day decides amongst other things to form a world. Rather world-formation is something that occurs, and only on this ground can a human being exist in the first place. The human being as human is world-forming. [Or rather it is] the Da-sein in the human being [that] is world forming.³²

---

29 Ibid., 50/51.
30 Ibid., 87/88.
31 Heidegger (1995/1983), 75 f./111, my italics.
32 Ibid., 285/412.

Heidegger goes onto a very detailed and complex account of the symbol in Aristotle, which we cannot follow here. The symbol, however, now becomes "the condition of possibility of discourse (*Rede*)"[33] and it is the possession of the symbol that now sets the human as Dasein off from the animal who has world but is poor in world because it is not world-forming. This is why and how Dasein is world-forming. One is tempted to say here, that Dasein is, to speak with Cassirer, the being of the *animal symbolicum*. The world is now well on its way to being understood as the opening of being that is brought about in and through language and art, which, like Cassirer, undertakes an *Auseinandersetzung* of thinking and being.[34]

5 A Cassirerian Critique of Fundamental Ontology and Heidegger's Turn to Language and Art

Shortly after 1929, Heidegger entered that period often referred to as the "turn" (*Kehre*). While the overt references to Cassirer's work diminish, Heidegger's *Auseinandersetzung* with Cassirer's work continues and, as I argue in the next section, the two have more and more to say to each other: the turn marks a rapprochement of their projects. Before considering the nature of this turn, let me say a few words about Cassirer's critique of fundamental ontology which no

---

33 Ibid., 305/441.
34 Contrast this with what happens in BT where the world is understood in terms of the double horizon of the ontological referential totality of significance and existential totality of relevance into which Dasein is *thrown*. In section 34, "Dasein and Discourse: Language", Heidegger insists that discourse (*Rede*) is not language, but the existential-ontological foundation of language: language belongs to the historical and ontic surrounding cultural world in which Dasein "*lives*". In a marginal note, he states "thrownness is essential to language" (Heidegger (2010b/1979b), 151/160). The constitutive factors of language "are existential characteristics rooted in the constitution of the being of Dasein which first make something like language ontologically possible" (Ibid., 152/163). Heidegger insists that these constitutive factors of the ontological-existential structure of discourse must first be worked out in order to ground those approaches which attempt "to grasp the "essence of language" by orientating themselves to a single one of these factors and [which] have understood language [as] guided by the idea of "expression" ("*Ausdrucks*"), [...] "symbolic form" ("*symbolischen Form*"), communication as "statement" ("*Aussage*"), [as the] "manifestation" of lived-experience, [as] the "configuration" ("*Gestaltung*") of life" (Ibid., 152/163).

doubt would parallel his critique of Lask.[35] In keeping with the logic of *Auseinandersetzung*, Cassirer would no doubt have to maintain that a reversal of a two-world metaphysics is still a dualistic metaphysics: that one cannot separate the ontic from the ontological in the way Lask and Heidegger do; that the transcendental structures of signification and the existential relevance of being cannot be thought of as distinct but rather must be thought of as belonging-together in a relation of *Auseinandersetzung:* that Lask makes the same error that Husserl does when he separates form and matter and then inquires how the two can be conjoined, for "Whoever in this way converts the Kantian "dualism" of form and matter, which is a difference of signification and transcendental "validity", into a separation of things really existing next to and apart from each other, has thereby already missed the decisive point of view needed for the profound understanding of this difference".[36] Rather, there must be a strict unitary relationship between signification and relevance; between subjective and objective; between thinking and being—the key is to understand the nature of this unitary *relationship* without transforming it into a *relation* of self-identity, to understand how "the transcendence of the idea can be reconciled with the immanence of life"[37] is to think this unitary relationship in terms of the *Auseinandersetzung* of life and spirit. We must "resist the temptation of seeking to make differences of meaning and signification intelligible by tracing them back to ontologically real differences—of explaining them through realistic assumptions concerning the condition and the structure of the world of things".[38] All this is set out in the third volume of the *Philosophy of Symbolic Forms* and reading this Heidegger must have now recognized that the concept of relevance set out in BT as the pregnant objective existential-ontological structures of the world of signification, was too pragmatic and subjective.

Let us now consider Heidegger's turn. Effectively, Heidegger came to recognize that his approach in BT, beginning from the existential analytic of Dasein and attempting to move from it to the meaning of being remained embroiled in the metaphysical categories he was seeking to escape and as such was too

---

[35] Cf. Cassirer, *Erkenntnistheorie nebst den Grenzfragen der Logik, Aufsätze u. kleine Schriften* [1902–1921] (Bd. 9), 167. I would like to thank Massimo Ferrari and Anne Pollok for helping locate this reference. My paper was already completed before I was able to read this article and thus was not able to work it into the body of the text. It would appear, however, to correspond, point for point, with what has been worked out here based upon the principle of the *Philosophy of Symbolic Forms*.
[36] Cassirer (2013/1985a), 260/7 f.; cf. also Cassirer (1957/2002c), 196/228 ff.
[37] Cassirer (1998/1993), 866/42.
[38] Cassirer (1957/2002c), 122 f./142 f.

subjective. Heidegger realized that the primordial understanding of being, the *Seinsverständnis*, is itself *historical:* hence the turn marks a shift away from speaking about the meaning of being toward the truth of being that opens the world of meaning. As a result, the understanding of being, the form being gives itself, is determined by the unique historical epoch of the event of being. Being, to speak with Cassirer, now requires the otherness of historical cultural form, *Geist*, for its visibility and reality. Heidegger sets out four distinct epochs in the history of being: the ancient Greek world; the medieval world of the Middle Ages; the "modern" image world (*Weltbild*) of the subject; and finally, the late modern world of technological enflaming (*Ge-stell*) that transforms everything including the human being into a "standing reserve" (*Bestand*). There arises here a peculiar commensurability or correspondence (*sich entsprechen*) between the *Seinsverständnis-Weltverständnis* that structures the opening of each of these worlds. Whereas in BT Heidegger focused on the existential meaning of primordial temporality as what renders different worlds effectively the same, the focus now shifts to what renders a world unique; namely, its mode of thinking being in which the event (*Ereignis*) of being happens (*Geschehen*).

As a result, Heidegger's thought moves away from its initial focus on the *authentic totality of Dasein* to the *total authenticity of the community* as the *site* of thinking. This, in turn, brings a shift from the anticipatory resoluteness of authentic Dasein to the authentic destiny of a people determined by their myth as a mutual appropriation of being and man. Heidegger moves away from the disparaging account of *Das Man* and the referential totality of signification, which was said to level down the authentic existential disclosure of the being of Dasein. The human is now the shepherd of being. Language and art are now equiprimordially necessary in the foundation and consecration of the authentic gathering of the community as the opening of the historical world and the bringing forth of the event of being and the strife of the fourfold, the *Auseinandersetzung* of thinking and being: "In *Aus-einandersetzung*, a world comes to be" and "*aletheia* is not just the manifestness of beings, [...] it is rather, in itself, an *Auseinandersetzung*"[39] The relevance of useful things at hand gives way to a consideration of things that gather together and set out the fourfold and opening of the world in which they belong: Greeks and Greek things belong to a Greek world opened by way of a Greek understanding of being. And what of being? Heidegger realizes that in the end, *Seinsverständnis* is a *Weltverständnis* and not some primordial hidden ground—an objective *Bewandtnis* that determines signification. The term *Bewandtnis* disappears after 1930. Heidegger now begins

---

39 Heidegger (2002/1975), 66/91.

to speak of the nameless mystery of ~~being~~, *Seyn*, or the sacred that is concealed as the unthought (*Ungedacht*) in its disclosure in any one epochal understanding of being. It is a communal thinking of this nameless and figureless mystery that renders each epoch of the event of being unique and defines the unique meaning of a world and the community belonging to that world. Heidegger's turn in many respects can be interpreted as a response to Cassirer's critique of fundamental ontology. It warrants mention here that according to Cassirer, Heidegger "confessed [...] that for a long time he had been struggling with a review of [the] third volume, but for the moment did not know how to come to grips with the thing".[40]

6 Language and Art: the Mythical-Religious Dwelling in the Truth of Being of the Cultural-Event

In the later Heidegger, the ontological and ontic are rethought as belonging-together and this takes Heidegger back to an ontological interpretation of myth as the model of poetic dwelling in the truth of being. The thinking of being now takes place in and through language and great art, which founds and consecrates the authentic gathering of a community as the opening of the historical world and the bringing forth of being.

Let us return for a moment to Cassirer's theory of language, art and myth—which I have shown elsewhere is the model for Heidegger's later understanding of the fourfold of the world.[41] Both language and art hold a privileged place in Cassirer's theory of culture. In short, they are "the basic ways of objectification [...] the 'discursive' thinking in language and the 'intuitive' activity of artistic seeing and creating interact so as together to weave the cloak (*Kleid*) of reality".[42] For Kant, the term "discursive thinking" designates a mode of cognition by means of concepts—what he often called *tout court* "thought" (*das Denken*). Here, a "concept" is "opposed to intuition, for it is a universal representation, or a representation of what is common in several objects, hence a representation *insofar as it can be contained in various ones*".[43] Historical linguistic concepts now replace the pure and empirical concepts of Kant. It is now language and

---

40 Cited in Cassirer (2003), 184.
41 Cf. Lofts (2013).
42 Cassirer (1996/1995), 83/86..
43 Kant (2004), 589; see also 309.

not reason that introduces the internal relations that structure our cognition of the world. "The function of 'naming' becomes the starting point and vehicle for the function of objective determination—or, to put it a better way, for the function of the determination of objects. In naming a content, it first becomes ripe for observation and the pure intuition of objects. With the name, it acquires a constancy, a persistence, a permanence that is denied the fleeting contents of lived-experience that are given no names".[44] For Cassirer, "the entire character of language, understood in its proper sense, lies only in the act of its actual bringing forth (*Hervorbringen*)".[45] Through the linguistic formation of our perceptual understanding, things (*Sachen*) gain intelligibility and are thus brought forth. Strictly speaking, through this "bringing forth", they come into being as that which is given in perception and speech; thus, where there is no word, no thing can be given. Language does not "signify a being, rather it *is* a being".[46] However, picking up on Schelling's play between *Ding* and *Bedingend:* Cassirer insists that the being of language conditions the thing, as the being of the thing it things the thing. Language introduces the belonging-together (*Zusammengehören*) of content in thought or perception and simultaneously brings it forward out of a *background* of the undefined. This belonging-together goes beyond any "mere being-connected" (*bloßes Zusammensein*). Linguistic formation does not end with this setting in relief of content against a background; it also organizes this content internally in relation to other contents, which in the end determines its most basic sense.

However, as Kant reminds us, "thoughts (*Gedanken*) without content are empty, intuitions without concepts are blind." Without intuitive content, the linguistic relational structures that differentiate, delimit, form and configure our understanding of the world, as well as our critical thinking about the world that is given in our understanding, are empty formal rules of synthesis possessing no actuality. The names of language thus require, according to Cassirer, the "intuitive" activity of artistic seeing and creating. What, then, is the specific function of art?

> The visibility (*Sichtbarkeit*) of nature is the actual, even the only goal of artistic activity [...]. This "visibility", we must recognize, is neither a predicate attributed to things as such, as absolute things, nor does it consist in the simple passive possession of certain sense-data, certain optical sensations or perception. [...] "Things" attain a "look" (*Gesicht*) because spirit lends it to them through a particular kind of direction of activity. This activity is none

---

44 Cassirer (1995/1996), 73/72.
45 Cassirer (2013b/1993), 120/260.
46 Cassirer (1996/1995), 82/78.

other than that of artistic presentation. It does not imitate what has been seen; rather, its basic significance and true achievement consist in transforming the merely sensed or dully felt into something seen.[47]

To see, for Cassirer, is always, as Goethe said, "to see with the eyes of spirit" (*Sehen mit Geistes Augen*).[48]

> Once we have entered into [the artist's] perspective, we are forced to look on the world with his eyes. It would seem as if we have never before seen the world in this peculiar *light* [...]. By virtue of the world of art [this light] has become durable and permanent. Once reality has been disclosed to us in this particular way, we continue to see it in this shape".[49]

Cassirer is not interested in "aesthetics" in the traditional, modern sense—he is not interested in the artwork *qua aesthetical* object of experience for a subject, but as a formative-power (*energia*) from which the artwork as object originates, as the horizon that gives artworks their meaning as the origin of the work of art.

There is a pure synthesis of language and art, concept and sensibility, such that "The word is brought forth by the image and the image by the word, so much so that both live in one another; they are interwoven and exist in one another".[50] Together, they form and configure the textual fabric that gives life and being their reality and visibility. The mythical life-world is an absorption in the significations of language and art, a living of signification as the *feeling* of the life we are. Language and art name and figure the "nameless presence" of the *mana:* life is called forth and given the visibility and reality of *a* life. It is through the "mythical-poetic and the sensuous-plastic figures of the gods", then, that a people receives their god; accordingly, "the gods of Greece owe their origins to Homer and Hesiod".[51] The reality of mythical life is not found in the "narrative" dimension, but in concrete ritual activity. The cult is "the eternal process of the subject making itself identical with the essence of its being".[52] In the dance, the dancer does not represent the god, but becomes and, in fact, *is* the god. Thus, as such, "it is not by its history that the mythology of a nation is determined but, conversely, its history is determined by its mythology—or rather, the mythology of a people does not *determine* but *is* its fate, its destiny".[53]

---

47 Cassirer (1996/1995), 82f./80f.
48 Cited in ibid., 81/78.
49 Cassirer (1972), 146.
50 Cassirer (2014a/1985b), 358/147.
51 Cassirer (1955a/2002a), 82/11.
52 Cassirer (1955b/2002b), 219/258.
53 Ibid., 5/6.

However, beyond the fusional logic of the identity thinking of the magical-mythical, there is the religious-mythical as a relation of transcendence to a nameless and figureless mystery so absolute that has always already withdrawn into the alterity of its own difference: I am evoking Levinas here. The god or totem stands before mythical consciousness as the immediate sacred presence of the nameless *mana:* "In their mere existence and their immediate texture they contain a *revelation* and at the same time retain a kind of *mystery*; it is this interplay, this revelation that both discloses and conceals, that gives the mythical-religious content its basic trait, its character of the "sacred" (*Heiligkeit*)".[54] It is in the authentic existential structure of the opening of being as a lived-historical-world that the "earthly and celestial, human and divine" are brought forth and rendered visible by the formation and configuration of language and art. For Cassirer, the religious-mythical sphere has a fourfold structure that forms "the original actuality of all being—earthly and celestial, human and divine." (*In ihr, als ursprünglicher Wirklichkeit, bleibt alles Sein, irdisches wie himmlisches, menschliches und göttliches, beschlossen und gebunden)*".[55] "The word forms the power, out of which the gods themselves, the heavens (*Himmel*) and the earth (*Erde*) are brought forward (*hervorbringt*)".[56]

Now, compare this to Heidegger. For Heidegger, there exists a connection between "thinking" (*Denken*) and "poetizing" (*Dichten*). Poetizing involves the equiprimordiality of language and art. Receiving is always responding, a giving thanks, but it is also a poetic *evocation* of being itself. Cassirer and Heidegger: both employ a play on *sich entsprechen* and *se répondre*, to suggest that all correspondence between the I and the world, is a cor-responding (.[57] The French *se répondre* means something like "to correspond by responding to each other". In the English "cor-respondence", we should hear an agreement or conformity, a unity (or even identity) in difference, as well as a communication, for example, through an exchange of letters in which there is a mutual addressing and answering. The reciprocity between *entsprechen* and *sprechen*, "cor-responding" and "speaking", constitutes the basic structure of the relation of givenness in the encounter (*Auseinandersetzung*) between I and thou, I and world, the human and being.

For Heidegger, the human being poetically dwells in the fourfold of the earth and sky, divinities and mortals and in this way thinks the *Ereignis*, giving name and figure (*Gestalt*) to the epochal character of its manifestation, and thus poeti-

---

54 Ibid., 74/89.
55 Cassirer (1957/2002c), 164/185.
56 Cassirer (1955b/2002b), 190/247.
57 Cf. Cassirer (2014a/1985b), 357/146: cf. Heidegger (1958/1972), 77–79/23–24.

cally responds to being only because being gives itself poetically to man's own poetic evocation. The *Ereignis* is the belonging-together of the human and being, and thinking (*Denken*) is the setting out of the difference between being and beings that brings together and differentiates the poetic dwelling in the fourfold. Again, "In *Aus-einandersetzung*, a world comes to be" and "*aletheia* is not just the manifestness of beings, [...] it is rather, in itself, an *Auseinandersetzung*".[58]

All "great art", for Heidegger, is, in its very essence, a "poetizing" (*Dichten*), a *poiêsis*, that brings forth (*Hervorbringen*) beings into being. However, as "poetizing is the essence of language", language, too, is a bringing forth of beings into being. While at times we may speak of the "work of art", this is only shorthand for speaking about the poetic. Thus the work of art, as poetic, is the "setting-into-work of truth", and this takes place through the naming and figuring that brings what *is* into the truth of being—that is, the unconcealment of entities in their being and the illumination of the self-concealing of *Seyn*.

> It takes the "original" eye of the artist [Julian Young writes] to "thematize", to render "visible", being. [...] The role of the artwork is not to create but rather to "make visible" a world that already exists. [...] If the artwork does not *create* its world, what does? Heidegger's answer to this question is clear: not the artwork but rather "language" creates world. The artwork makes its advent"'within the clearing of what is, what has already happened unnoticed in language".[59]

Thus, language creates the "reality" of a world, art gives it its "visibility". Language and art are the poetic projecting forward that brings forth and sets into work the truth of being. Together they break open the world, giving to things their look (*Gesicht*) and to a people their outlook. "The projective saying is poetry, the myth (*Sage*) of the world and earth, and thus of the space of proximity and distance of the gods. The primordial language (*Ursprache*) is such a myth as the primordial poetry of a people, in which their world arises and their earth begins to close itself off as theirs".[60] "Out of the fourfold, the simple onefold of the four is ventured. This appropriating mirror-play of the simple onefold of earth and sky, divinities and mortals, we call the world".[61]

What is essential here, however, is that the thinking of being becomes the dwelling in the truth of being—it is a thinking of that which is concealed in the unconcealment of entities. Following the logic of the *Auseinandersetzung*,

---

58 Heidegger (2002/1975), 66/91.
59 Young (2001), 33 f.
60 Heidegger (1993/1977), 145/18.
61 Heidegger (1971/2000), 179/181.

what is essential to the being of the human being is to think (*Denken*) what is unthought (*Ungedacht*), but is most thought worthy, the self-concealing of *Seyn*. The 'un' in German is more powerful than in English: the *Ungedacht* is not just unthought but unthinkable and what provokes the authentic thinking that consecrates a community through the language and image of great poets and thinkers. As Heidegger puts it: "if the human is to find its way once again into the nearness of being the human must first learn to exist in the nameless".[62]

7 Conclusion: The Dignity of Man

When Pico inquires into the dignity of man, he seeks to determine what sets the human being off from the rest of reality, what renders the human being unique— in other words, he is asking *Was ist der Mensch?* For Cassirer the dignity of the human being is to be found in the symbolic: the human being is the symbolic animal. Wherever one finds the human being, one finds a linguistic-aesthetic being that gives an account of itself in a narrative story of its being; a narrative story that is lived out in the very flesh of its being in a pragmatic way. But one also finds a being that can become mindful of its being, that can take a distance from itself and retell the story of its being, thus reconfiguring itself, a being not just ontically free but ontologically free. The human being does not create the symbolic, rather, the symbolic is the being of the human being: the human being as human is always already in the symbolic. The symbolic forms are the transcendental horizons in and through which the human world comes to be, the horizons in which the human understands itself as the being that it is. The symbolic undertakes an *Auseinandersetzung* of I and world, a setting out that differentiates and unites the polar oppositions of reality. We might say that the symbolic as a whole is the house of being in which the human being makes itself at home by consecrating its own world and that in so doing participates in the event of being. But 'who' am I? Human no doubt, but what renders this human unique, this world unique? Does this too not belong to the dignity of man? This understanding is itself a unique act of being—I am this understanding and not another. And this understanding of my self cannot be divorced from an understanding that there is something rather than nothing: for, the understanding of my mortality that radically individuates me as a unique event is concurrent with an understanding of the event of being. For Heidegger, the dignity of

---

[62] Heidegger (1977/1976a), 223/343. For a more complete account of the sacred in Cassirer and Heidegger, see Lofts 2013.

the human being is found in the consecration and keeping watch over the unconcealed world, *that it is for sure*, however more essentially the human being is that being that is "held out into the nothing" and that keeps watch over what remains concealed—and in this way participates in the event of being. To think Cassirer and Heidegger together is to think the per*form*ativity of the symbolic act that produces the cultural-event, the paradoxical antinomy of the per*form*ative event as the *Auseinandersetzung* of thinking and being. This *Auseinandersetzung of the per*form*ative event* as the event of *Auseinandersetzung* does not fit into the traditional metaphysical classifications and dualisms but goes beyond them. The *performative event* never belongs to the sphere of immanence or to the sphere of transcendence; rather, its value consists precisely in the fact that it overcomes this opposition that arises from a metaphysical theory of two worlds. It is not the one *or* the other but represents the 'one *in* the other,' and the 'other *in* the one'. Cassirer is the thinker of the transcendental cultural forms of world configuration and formation; where as Heidegger is the thinker of the event: together they think the dignity of the human at the crossroads of the cultural-event.

Bibliography

Cassirer (1955a/2002a): Ernst Cassirer, *The Philosophy of Symbolic Forms, Volume One: Language*, Ralph Manheim (trans.), New Haven: Yale University Press; Ernst Cassirer, *Philosophie der symbolischen Formen*, Erster Teil, *Die Sprache,* in: *Gesammelte Werke* (henceforth ECW), Birgit Recki (ed.), vol. 11, Hamburg: Felix Meiner Verlag.

Cassirer (1955b/2002b): Ernst Cassirer, *The Philosophy of Symbolic Forms, Volume Two: Mythical Thought*, Ralph Manheim (trans.), New Haven: Yale University Press; Ernst Cassirer, *Philosophie der symbolischen Formen*. Zweiter Teil, *Das mythische Denken*, in: ECW, vol. 12, op. cit.

Cassirer (1957/2002c): Ernst Cassirer, *The Philosophy of Symbolic Forms, Volume Three: The Phenomenology of Knowledge,* Ralph Manheim (trans.), New Haven: Yale University Press; Ernst Cassirer, *Philosophie der symbolischen Formen*, Dritter Teil, *Phänomenologie der Erkenntnis*, in: ECW, vol. 13, op. cit.

Cassirer (1972): Ernst Cassirer, *An Essay on Man: An Introduction to A Philosophy of Human Culture*, New Haven and London: Yale University Press.

Cassirer (1996/1995): Ernst Cassirer, *Philosophy of Symbolic Forms, Volume Four: The Metaphysics of Symbolic Forms*, John Michael Krois and Donald Philip Verene (eds.), New Haven: Yale University Press; Ernst Cassirer, *Zur Metaphysik der symbolischen Formen*, in: *Nachgelassene Manuskripte und Texte,* vol. 1, John Michael Krois (ed.), Hamburg: Felix Meiner Verlag.

Cassirer (1998/1993): Ernst Cassirer, "'Life' and 'Spirit' in Contemporary Philosophy", Robert W. Bretall and Paul A. Schilpp (trans.), in: *The Philosophy of Ernst Cassirer* (Library of Living Philosophers, 6), Paul A. Schilpp (ed.), LaSalle, IL: Open Court Publishing

Company, 855–880; Ernst Cassirer, "'Geist' und 'Leben' in der Philosophie der Gegenwart", in: *Geist und Leben: Schriften zu den Lebensordnungen von Natur und Kunst, Geschichte und Sprache*, Ernst Wolfgang Orth (ed.), Leipzig: Reclam-Verlag, 32–60.

Cassirer (2000/1961): Ernst Cassirer, *The Logic of the Cultural Sciences: Five Studies*, Stephen G. Lofts (trans.), New Haven and London: Yale University Press; Ernst Cassirer, *Zur Logik der Kulturwissenschaften: fünf Studien*, Darmstadt: Wissenschaftlichen Buchgesellschaft.

Cassirer (2013/1985a): Ernst Cassirer, "The Problem of the Symbol and Its Place in the System of Philosophy", in: *The Warburg Years (1919–1933): Essays on Language, Art, Myth, and Technology*, S. G. Lofts with A. Calcagno (trans.), New Haven and London: Yale University Press, 254–271; Ernst Cassirer, "Das Symbolproblem und seine Stellung im System der Philosophie", in: *Symbol, Technik, Sprache: Aufsätze aus den Jahren 1927–1933*, Ernst Wolfgang Orth and John Michael Krois (eds.), Hamburg: Felix Meiner Verlag, 1–38.

Cassirer (2014a/1985b): Ernst Cassirer, "The Construction of the World of Objects", in: *The Warburg Years (1919–1933): Essays on Language, Art, Myth, and Technology*, S. G. Lofts with A. Calcagno (trans.), New Haven and London: Yale University Press, 334–362; Ernst Cassirer, "Die Sprache und der Aufbau der Gegenstandswelt", in: *Symbol, Technik, Sprache: Aufsätze aus den Jahren 1927–1933*, E. W. Orth and J. M. Krois (eds.), Hamburg: Felix Meiner, 121–151.

Cassirer (2014b/1993): Ernst Cassirer, "The Kantian Elements in Wilhelm von Humboldt's Philosophy of Language". In: *The Warburg Years (1919–1933): Essays on Language, Art, Myth, and Technology*, S. G. Lofts with A. Calcagno (trans.), New Haven and London: Yale University Press, 101–129; Ernst Cassirer, "Die Kantischen Elemente in Wilhelm von Humboldts Sprachphilosophie", in: *Geist und Leben: Schriften zu den Lebensordnungen von Natur und Kunst, Geschichte und Sprache*, Ernst Wolfgang Orth (ed.), Leipzig: Reclam, 236–273.

Cassirer (2003): Toni Cassirer, *Mein leben mit ernst Cassirer*, Hamburg: Felix Meiner Verlag.

Descartes (1985): René Descartes, *The Philosophical Writings of Descartes*, Cambridge: Cambridge University Press.

Gordon (2010): Peter E. Gordon, *Continental Divide: Heidegger, Cassirer, Davos*, Cambridge, MA: Harvard University Press.

Hamburg (1964): Carl H. Hamburg, "A Cassirer-Heidegger Seminar", *Philosophy and Phenomenological Research*, 25, 208–222.

Hegel (1991): G.W.F. Hegel, *Enzyklopädie Der Philosophischen Wissenschaften Im Grundrisse*, Hamburg: Felix Meiner Verlag.

Heidegger (1958/1972): Martin Heidegger, *What is Philosophy*, William Kluback and Jean T. Wilde (trans.), Boston: Twayne Publishers; Martin Heidegger, "Was ist das—die Philosophie?", in: GA, vol. 11, op. cit., 3–27.

Heidegger (1971/2000): Martin Heidegger, "The Thing" in *Poetry, Language, Thought*, Albert H. Hofstadter (trans.), New York: Harper & Row, 168–170; Martin Heidegger, "Das Ding", in: GA, vol. 7, op. cit., 165–189.

Heidegger (1977/1976a): Martin Heidegger, "Letter on Humanism", in: *Basic Writings: From Being and Time (1927) to The Task of Thinking (1964)*, David Farrell Krell (ed.), New York: Harper & Row, 213–266; Martin Heidegger, "Brief über den 'Humanismus'", in: GA, vol. 9, op. cit., 313–364.

Heidegger (1991): Martin Heidegger, *Kant und das Problem der Metaphysik*. in: *Gesamtausgabe* (henceforth GA), vol. 3, Friedrich-Wilhelm von Herrmann (ed.), Frankfurt am Main: Klostermann, 274–296.

Heidegger (1992/1979a): *History of the Concept of Time: Prolegomena*, Theodore Kisiel (trans.), Bloomington: Indiana University Press; Martin Heidegger, *Prolegomena zur Geschichte des Zeitbegriffes*, in: GA, vol. 20, op. cit.

Heidegger (1993/1977): Martin Heidegger, "The Origin of the Work of Art", in: *Basic Writings*, op. cit., 311–341; Martin Heidegger, "Der Ursprung des Kunstwerkes", in: GA, vol. 5, op. cit., 1–74.

Heidegger (1995/1983): Martin Heidegger, *The Fundamental Concepts of Metaphysics: World, Finitude, Solitude*, William McNeill and Nicholas Walker (trans.), Bloomington: Indiana University Press; Martin Heidegger, *Die Grundbegriffe der Metaphysik: Welt—Endlichkeit—Einsamkeit*, in: GA, vol. 29/30, op. cit.

Heidegger (2002/1975): *The Essence of Truth: On Plato's Cave Allegory and Theaetetus*, T. Sadler (trans.), London: Continuum; Martin Heidegger, *Vom Wesen der Wahrheit: Zu Platons Höhlengleichnis und Theätet*. In: *Gesamtausgabe*. Vol. 34. Friedrich-Wilhelm von Herrmann (Ed.). Frankfurt am Main: Klostermann.

Heidegger (2010a/1976b): *Logic: The Question of Truth*, Bloomington: Indiana University Press; Martin Heidegger, *Logik die Frage nach der Wahrheit*. In: GA, vol. 21, op. cit.

Heidegger (2010b/1979b): Martin Heidegger, *Being and Time: A Revised Edition of the Stambaugh Translation*, Albany: State University of New York Press; Martin Heidegger, *Sein und Zeit*, Tübingen: M. Niemeyer.

Kant (2004): Immanuel Kant, *Lectures on Logic*, J. Michael Young (ed.), Cambridge: Cambridge University Press.

Kisiel (1993): Theodore J. Kisiel, *The Genesis of Heidegger's* Being and Time, Berkeley: University of California Press.

Krois (2004): John Michael Krois, "Why Did Cassirer and Heidegger Not Debate in Davos?", in: *Symbolic Forms and Cultural Studies: Ernst Cassirer's Theory of Culture*, Cyris Hamlin and John Michael Krois (eds.), New Haven and London: Yale University Press, 244–262

Lask (2003): Emil Lask, *Die Logik der Philosophie und die Kategorienlehre—Die Lehre vom Urteil*, Jena: Scheglmann.

Levinas (2001): Emmanuel Levinas, "Is It Righteous To Be? Interviews with Emmanuel Levinas", Jill Robbins (ed.), Stanford, CA: Stanford University Press.

Lofts (2010): Stephen G. Lofts, "The Symbolic *Auseinandersetzung* of the Urphänomene of the Expression of Life", *Cassirer Studies* 3, 41–65.

Lofts (2013): Stephen G. Lofts, "Cassirer and Heidegger: Art, Language and the Thinking of the Textual-Event", *Cassirer Studies* 4, 81–121.

Young (2001): Julian Young, *Heidegger's Philosophy of Art*, Cambridge: Cambridge University Press.

Pierre Keller (Riverside)
Cassirer's Retrieval of Kant's Copernican Revolution in Semiotics

Ernst Cassirer's *Philosophy of Symbolic Forms* (hereafter: PSF) is a systematic attempt to retrieve Kant's Copernican revolution in metaphysics in its full significance and to bring that revolution up to date.[1] In retrieving Kant's Copernican revolution, Cassirer also fleshes out the fundamental significance of signs, of a general semiotics, for metaphysics. He draws on Kant's general account of signs to bring out the significance of semiotics for Kant's "revolution in thought". Kant's semiotics, his semiotica universalis, situates signs of all kinds, including the different characters that we form for ourselves as we engage with the world in his idea of philosophy and of the world as grasped from a cosmopolitan point of view.[2] The significance of signs is in this way ultimately tied up with the normative difference in the world that signs make to what we do or can do. Signs are not taken to be of isolated significance, their significance is tied to the process through which we reason things through for ourselves from the spatio-temporal and historical-cultural standpoint that we have in relation to the world as a whole. It is in the manner in which signs are caught up in the process through which we systematically come to terms with our own standpoint in the world that the Copernican significance of those signs is to be sought.

1 A Universal Characteristic

From the outset of PSF, Cassirer expresses his general sympathy with Leibniz's effort to comprehend the world in terms of the exact thought of logic and mathematics and to comprehend everything in terms of a "universal characteristic", a general system of signs.[3] A precise notation is key to the precise formulation of thoughts: "all truly strict and exact thought is sustained by the *symbolics* and *semiotics* on which it is based".[4] Cassirer never seems to waver from the view that only the modern logic and mathematics of relations is capable of expressing

---

[1] I develop this reading of the Copernican revolution and of the Critique(s) as a whole in a forthcoming book on *Kant's Experimental Pluralism*.
[2] Kant (1907-), 7:285.
[3] Cassirer (1957), 296.
[4] Cassirer (1955a), 86.

universally valid thoughts and truth.⁵ But Cassirer follows Kant's pragmatic anthropology and its conception of a "universal characteristic" or "universal semiotics"⁶ in extending the significance of the sign and symbol to all the forms of culture in terms of which human beings define themselves and their world. This includes especially those forms of culture not capable of the same universality that Cassirer ascribes to modern logic and mathematics. Symbols in general are now conceived as belonging to whole systems of signs that form symbolic systems, which, at the highest level of generality, Cassirer refers to as "symbolic forms"; these symbolic forms display both an internal systematicity in the signs that belong to them and also a systematic manner in which they are different from but also related to other symbolic systems, each of which has a systematic unity to it and all of which are part of a comprehensive differential whole of symbolic significance. Cassirer hopes thus to fulfill the "ideal of a 'universal characteristic', formulated by Leibniz for cognition ... for the whole of cultural activity".⁷

Cassirer had the ambition (in PSF) of describing everything in terms of the modern logical-mathematical notion of function and the functional relations between algebraic symbols. In defining such functions, we start from a set of structural formulae and a set of rules determining the structural permutations that are allowed. We are then able to generate new structural formulae by applying these rules to the former structural formulae. The outcome of each permutation is a possible object and, as such, subject to further permutation according to the rules. The generation of objects from principles for the establishment of functional relations between items in a structure can be extended from mathematics to elementary particles, atoms, molecules and chemical and biological substances and chemical and biological properties. In general, Cassirer's ambition is to dissolve substances into relational patterns of signification. Rather than thinking of mathematical or chemical formulae as part of a mathematical or chemical sign language that ultimately refers to substances, chemical (and other) substances are themselves for Cassirer nothing but signs with a certain functional relation to the whole field of signification in chemistry (physics, mathematics, etc.); they are the way the rules for structural modification in the field of chemistry (physics, mathematics, etc.) manifest themselves at different times and places. Modern physics moves more and more away from the notion of a thing that still pervades classical mechanics where

---

5 The importance of logic and mathematics for the universality of thought is emphasized by Friedman (2000), 156.
6 Kant (1907-), 7:285.
7 Cassirer (1955a), 86.

[s]pace and time ... in their absoluteness ... are still understood as thing-like concrete structures. The concept of mass in Newtonian physics also has this concrete substantial character. A piece of matter can be fixed as a self-identical thing and recognized in various locations in space as being one and the same [...] But precisely this substantiality of space, time, and mass has been progressively abandoned by modern physics.[8]

The notion of substance is progressively replaced by a comprehensive understanding of the world in terms of the structural abstractions and invariances under permutations of coordinates that can be articulated on the basis of that mathematical conception of function (especially in general relativity and quantum mechanics).

Cassirer comes to recognize however that something important is lost in a purely mathematical description of the world, something that is key to myth, but even to language, and also to music, and the arts and literature, and indeed to most of culture. What is missing is the subjective point of view from which we as human beings always view things. To preserve the subjective point of view, Cassirer finds that he must think of language and other non-mathematical systems of signs as always of only more limited generality: "The true ideality of language exists only in its subjectivity. Hence it is, was and always will be futile to attempt to exchange the words in the various languages for universally valid signs such as mathematics possesses in its lines, numbers and algebraic symbols."[9] Instead of giving up on the constitution of objects through functions, Cassirer extends the model to the different ways of viewing things that comprehend human culture. Each domain of human culture is to be understood in terms of the procedure by which the systematic pattern of signs in that domain is constituted. Cassirer's ambition is to develop a "grammar of the symbolic function as such",[10] a set of principles from which a whole of the different systems of signs may be generated, each of which in turn has a principle according to which it generates the signs (and with that the subjects and objects) in that system. Cassirer's idea is that the structure that a notation or system of symbols gives to thought and the rules that are implicit in systematically connecting those signs and symbols to each other provide the very basis for thought of any kind. As such they constitute the significance of subjects and objects of any kind for us. They are also conditions for the possibility of experience. Such systems of signs or symbolic forms make experience possible by making it possible for us to relate and contrast our experiences. But those signs have a significance

---

8 Cassirer (1927), 422.
9 Cassirer (1955a), 158.
10 Ibid., 86.

that is also ultimately tied at least indirectly to experience through the sensible character of all signs. The use that we put to signs is prior to our ability to refer to those signs as such. It is only gradually in the development of language, thought and mathematical logic that the distinction between the use and mention of signs develops.

Cassirer argues that thinking of everything as sign and in terms of the systematic relations between signs requires one to give up on the traditional dualism in idealism between the sensible and intelligible world, for "precisely the pure *function* of the spirit itself must seek its concrete fulfillment in the sensory world".[11] Thinking of the very identities of the self and of objects, but also of what is in and about us in a much less specific sense, as constituted by systems of signs, no longer allows a clear distinction between the sensible sign-design and its significance, to grasp it as sign and design is already to take it to have significance. For Cassirer

> the sign is no mere accidental cloak of the idea, but its necessary and essential organ…an instrument, by means of which this content develops and fully defines itself. It is, as it were, the fundamental principle of cognition that the universal can be perceived only in the particular, while the particular can be thought only in reference to the universal.[12]

2 Signs in Pragmatic Anthropology and Cosmopolitan Philosophy

Kant's pragmatic anthropology develops an account of our systematic use of signs for self-orientation that begins with the demonstrative "I". The account

---

11 Ibid., 87.
12 Ibid., 86. Kant does not think that logical propositions can be articulated in thought independently of language: "…we must use words in thought for judgments that we do not render as sentences" (Kant (1907-), 8:194n). This is because he thinks along the Platonic lines defended by Plato in the *Sophist* (263e), that "thought is dialogue with oneself,"; thought is internalized communication with others in which one communicates with oneself across different times (Ibid., 7:167; 194). Thought is so tied up with speech and the perception of sound that Kant doubts whether a person who is unable to hear and then to hear himself speak can be taught anything but the rudiments of thought. In the *Vienna Logic Lectures*, Kant goes so far as to reject the distinction between judgments and propositions because he does not think that propositions are distinguishable from their linguistic articulation in judgment: "Judgments and propositions are actually distinct according to standard speech. But when the logicians say: a judgment is a proposition clothed in words, that does not mean anything and this definition is worthless. For how can they think judgments without words" (Ibid., 24:934).

is firmly rooted in the unity of sensible sign and conceptual significance to which Cassirer aspires and which is a mark of Kant's pragmatic anthropology. Kant develops the essentially interconnected and temporal significance not only of cognition but also of feeling and desire. Cognition relates primarily to the present, it sustains a present representation of an object through successive states. In feeling we are pushed by our sense of general displeasure and discomfort from the past into the present and a hoped for better future.[13] Desire attracts us to act in the present on the basis of how our representation of the future that we would bring about is affected by our past.[14] The temporal interconnectedness of cognition, feeling and desire is reflected in the temporal difference that they make to the significance of signs (manifested in the difference that signs make in what we do).

For Kant, the faculty of signification, the faculty responsible for our use of signs, is defined as "the capacity for the cognition of the present as a means for connecting the representation of the past to what is foreseen [of the future]".[15] Thus signs are essentially temporal. The significance of the different systems of signs is tied up with the difference that they make in our (temporal) agency in the world, where the world is to be understood as the totality of significant relations in which a human agent stands. The role that signs play in connecting our world together for us gives our experience and consciousness their inherently temporal structure. For wherever human beings relate in any way to experience or to actual or counterfactual possibilities, they relate to them through signs and thus relate the present to the actual or possible past and future. The faculty of foresight, the capacity to anticipate similar, but different possible cases is key to our competence in the use of signs. Such foresight is also of decisive importance for practice,

> it interests more than any other because it is the condition of all possible praxis and of the ends to which the human being relates the use of his powers [...]. Recalling the past (remembering) occurs only with the intention of making foresight possible by means of it: generally speaking, we look about us from the standpoint of the present in order to decide something or to be prepared for something.[16]

The world as it is experienced from the point of view of pragmatic anthropology is a world in which we are situated as human beings that also has a systematic significance concerning what we do or might do systematically grounded in our

---

13 Ibid., 7:231.
14 Ibid., 7:251.
15 Ibid., 7:191.
16 Ibid., 7:185–186.

very situation in the world. It is the world understood in what Kant calls the world-citizen or cosmopolitan sense.

Kant pulls the different systems of signs connected to cognition, feeling and desire together in a general semiotics. This semiotics includes associations, images, figural syntheses of all kinds, schemata, linguistic expressions and a whole plethora of other epistemic signs. It also includes symbols and other aesthetic signs, and affects and passions that are signs of a less than constant character. But it most explicitly includes the natural and acquired characters that we have on the basis of the whole range of the different roles and capacities that we have as agents endowed with cognition, feeling and especially the desire that makes us agents. Kant treats our temperaments, talents and our individual, sexual and gender, folk, national and racial and even species identities in their cultural and historical development as part of a general characteristics or general semiotics.[17] All significance is tied up for human beings with the temporal and by implication also the spatial and cultural-historical relations between signs as they are relevant to what we are or might do.[18]

Our ability to experience and to think depends on our capacity as language speaking agents to see the significance of how things bear on each other in context and how they are relevant to what we do or can do. Kant links articulate thought even more closely to a sensibly perceptible pattern of signs and to language as inner speech than he ought to do so. He worries that those born deaf may be robbed of the ability to "hear" themselves and others think, and so of the ability to speak and with that they may be deprived of anything more than the "analogue" of articulate thought.[19]

Kant puts imagination front and center as the ability to grasp signs. The fundamental importance of our imaginative ability in our capacity as agents to recognize the relevance of different signs for each other and to see those signs as of other items, makes imagination and the different temporal structures of imagination involved in our cognitions, feelings, and desires of central significance. However the imagination itself comes to have a new significance. It is not so much a faculty of mental representation as it is the ability to connect the past and the future to the present through signs and the temporal structure of imaging. As such it is that faculty of sensibility that represents what is absent. Signs connect the past and the future to the present. They also connect our inner world to the outer world. Although not always spatial, as in the use of signs for thought

---

[17] Ibid., 7:285.
[18] Ibid., 7:191.
[19] Ibid., 7:155.

and inner speech, their very systematic significance for us is tied to their direct or exemplification or at least indirect relation to spatial patterns in the outer world. Kant employs a conception of language as dialogue and of thought as dialogue with oneself using a system of signs with intersubjective significance. This allows him to develop the process through which we first institute the inner world of our consciousness and even the dark ocean of unconscious awareness through the way in which we engage with the world in terms of a comprehensive inarticulate competence in signs and patterns.[20]

What we do is never without a relation to the different systematic contexts of signs and character. The development in both the child and in culture of the use of the sign "I" that many languages use for first personal self-reference is its starting-point,[21] but it is also an account of how such I-use develops not only in the individual agent, but in culture and in world-history. It is concerned with how the egoism inherent as a necessary illusion in the use of "I" can be overcome in favor of a cosmopolitan pluralism and a general cosmopolitan order of significance established. The word "I" serves as a fulcral sign through which the other signs in terms of which human beings understand themselves and their world gain their distinctive significance. Our ability to use the word "I" is connected with the development of our ability to reason. It involves the capacity to regard our own point of view and our own self as one among many actual and possible individuals. At the same time, self-reference tends to privilege each of our own standpoints for each of us. In taking one's own point of view as the only one, or regarding "oneself as containing the whole world in one's self", one is engaged in a kind of solipsism grounded in our ability to use the first person singular pronoun that needs to be combated in cognition, in aesthetic appreciation and in agency.[22]

While the first person plural pronoun includes the group with which one identifies in one's sense of self, it too involves a privileging of that wider sense of self and a kind of social solipsism. This is the conviction that the way the group with which we identify is entitled to a special status. We combat such solipsism by correcting our own point of view through the manner in which things appear to "another alien reason"; if our convictions do not hold up to the standpoint of "another alien reason" then they have the status of something of which we have persuaded ourselves (persuasion) rather than justified conviction.[23] But "educating oneself according to an alien reason" does not count as

---

20 Ibid., 7:136.
21 Ibid., 7:127.
22 Ibid., 7:130.
23 Ibid., A 821/B 827.

reasoning things through for oneself.[24] The appropriate attitude toward the standpoint of others is to take alien reason into consideration without giving up on one's effort to think things through for oneself.[25] "Pluralism" is the position according to which one recognizes that one has a standpoint in the world that is not the only one; it is "to regard oneself and to behave as a mere citizen of the world" rather than as a world unto oneself: "The opposite of egoism can only be pluralism, that is the way of thinking in which one is not concerned with oneself as the whole world, but rather regards and conducts oneself as a mere citizen of the world".[26] The way that Kant understands pluralism, it involves his Copernican turn, it involves taking a stand on how things are in general with respect to the world, while also recognizing that one has a position and particular point of view within the world. Pluralism ties the significance of epistemic and metaphysical commitments to what is relevant to what one can do from one's own vantage point in a world. The world in this cosmopolitan sense is not a collection of objects but a whole of differential significance for one. The world is that whole of possible matters of interest to oneself and to other that is systematically relevant to what one can do and to what others with whom one engages can do.

Kant's aim in his pragmatic anthropology is to establish the basis for such "pluralism" in cognition, aesthetic appreciation and moral, social and political conduct and thus to establish the basis in history for a comprehensive cosmopolitan pluralism. Politics cannot be excluded even locally because "freedom of the pen" is crucial to our ability to reliably check our own judgments against those of others; to prohibit books on theoretical topics even "offends humanity".[27] Freedom of publication and the freedom to review alternative views is even required for any freedom of thought at all because it is only through such confrontation with other views that one can distance oneself from mere prejudice.[28] Pluralism

---

[24] Ibid., A 836/B 864.
[25] Pluralism is connected to the parallax view that is involved in thinking things through for oneself by using other persons' perspectives and standpoints to grasp the approach that is systematically appropriate for one from one's own standpoint and perspective within the whole of the world (in the cosmopolitan sense): "Formerly, I viewed human common sense only from the standpoint of my own; now I put myself into the position of an alien reason outside of myself, and observe my judgments, together with their most secret causes, from the point of view of others. It is true, the comparison of both observations results in pronounced parallaxes, but it is the only means of preventing optical delusion, and of putting conceptions in regard to the power of knowledge in human nature into their true places" (Ibid., 2:349).
[26] Ibid., 7:130.
[27] Ibid., 7:128; 219.
[28] Ibid., 8:144.

requires that we check our judgments against those of others without relying slavishly on their judgments. We must "restrain our understanding by the *understanding of others*, instead of isolating ourselves with our understanding and judging *publicly* with our private representations, so to speak".[29] Kant insists that even mathematics cannot do without the kind of check against the judgments of others provided by unconstrained public discussion and presentation of results among peers and experts who have been socialized to a certain paradigm: "for if there had been no antecedent perceived pervasive agreement in judgment of the mathematician [*Messkünstler*] with the judgments of others who have pursued the subject with talent and effort, then one would not be spared the concern that one might have fallen into error somewhere".[30] An important part of Kant's pluralism involves participation in a set of shared practices and checking your way of proceeding against that of others. To be trained to follow the rule-guided practice correctly and to coordinate what we do with others involves being freed from "something subjective (for instance, habit or inclination) ... easily taken for something objective. This is precisely what the illusion consists in ... by means of which we are mislead to deceive ourselves in the application of a rule". While Kant insists on our individual autonomy in judgment, in holding ourselves accountable to principles, to do so pervasively is not at all a good idea. If you make it a habit of favoring your "own world" over "the common world", you are on your way to madness.[31]

Kant's pragmatic anthropology is framed from a cosmopolitan point of view. It is "world-knowledge ... that contains knowledge of the human being as *world-citizen*".[32] Pragmatic anthropology is knowledge of the world, but the world in terms of its relevance to what we can do and make of ourselves as members of the world as a community of self-governing reasoning agents. We relate to ourselves and to others as something that we define for ourselves through what we do: "because the human being is his own final end ... pragmatic [knowledge is] the investigation of what he as free-acting being makes of himself, or can and should make of himself".[33] Kant systematically develops the process of self-determination through the manner in which we come to understand and do justice to our own distinctive situation in the world.

---

29 Ibid., 7:219.
30 Ibid., 7:129.
31 Ibid., 7:219.
32 Ibid., 7:120.
33 Ibid., 7:119.

Kant's cosmopolitan conception of philosophy unifies the answers to all of the fundamental questions with which human beings are confronted[34]: "The field of philosophy in its cosmopolitan meaning can be brought under the following questions: what can I know?, what ought I to do?, for what can I hope?, what is a human being?".[35] The first question is answered in metaphysics according to Kant, the second in morals, the third in religion and the fourth in anthropology. The cosmopolitan conception of philosophy is of the world as a whole of ends and purposes to which our reason may and must be directed and of our reason itself as an ends-directed activity.[36] In the cosmopolitan conception of philosophy, all ends are brought together as a unity under the ultimate end of human endeavors. The cosmopolitan conception of philosophy is as such a "teleology of human reason"[37]; it is an account of how our reason develops from the context of natural and social purposes in which we cannot help but take ourselves to be involved as social rational animals.

Kant's pragmatic anthropology is part of his cosmopolitan conception of philosophy. In a note to the beginning of the second half of his pragmatic anthropology,[38] Kant indicates that the first half of the book addresses the question as to what a human being is in a general way and the second half addresses the question in terms of the signs or characters in virtue of which human beings may systematically be distinguished: "Anthropology // 1st Part // Anthropological *Didactic* // What is the human being? // 2nd Part // Anthropological *Characteristic* // How is the peculiarity of each human being to be cognized? // The former is at it were the doctrine of the elements of anthropology, the latter is the doctrine of method." Thus there is every reason to think that Kant addresses the question: what is a human being in the work, albeit implicitly. The notion of the world involved in Kant's pragmatic anthropology and in the cosmopolitan conception of philosophy is as the systematic relevance of signs to human action. It is an account of how we as human beings systematically relate to ourselves, to our situation and to the other things and human beings in the world in terms of what is of interest to us as human beings. Pragmatic anthropology is as a whole a "general semiotics" or "general characteristics" that is especially concerned with the distinguishing marks through which we as human beings define our character and relate to ourselves as natural and as socially responsible agents.[39] But

---

[34] Ibid., 9:24.
[35] Ibid., 9:25.
[36] Ibid., A 839/B 867.
[37] Ibid.
[38] Ibid., 7:283.
[39] Ibid., 7:285.

Kant's Anthropology also ties in the whole sensible world of cognition to our agency. In developing a character, we take direct and indirect control of the conscious and unconscious factors at work in affecting our decision-making. It is through the interlocutory signs of language and their internalization by means of "inner speech" and thought that we articulate our inner experience to ourselves. But the process of enlightenment requires that we situate ourselves properly in respect to all of the significative contexts in which we relate to ourselves and to the world through signs. It is thus my suggestion that it is in the use of signs to articulate our sense of ourselves and of what bears on what we do and what is of greatest importance to us that Kant sees the answer to the question: what is a human being? This answer is important to Kant because it is the basis for his conception of the most fundamental revolution in thought that human beings can undertake, the process of enlightenment.

3 Cassirer and Man as *Animal Symbolicum*

Cassirer takes up Kant's idea of a semiotic anthropology in the later twenties in his own anthropology.[40] Cassirer's effort to present PSF to an English speaking audience may be regarded as an attempt to rethink a broadly Kantian anthropology and theory of signs for the twentieth century. *An Essay on Man* (EM) is the core of Cassirer's response to the fourth Kantian question. Cassirer's answer to the question "what is a human being?" is that the human being is the animal that forms symbols for itself, signs that are not just of local, but also of general systematic import. Cassirer identifies the human being (man) as animal symbolicum,[41] as the creature that uses signs not merely for signaling emotive responses as animals do. Symbols are signs that reveal a "symbolic universe," an "ideal

---

[40] Cassirer refers to the section on signs from Kant's anthropology in some detail in conjunction with a discussion of the pathology of symbolic consciousness (Cassirer (1957), 211). In an 1870 lecture, Finkelnburg (Duffy and Liles (1979), 156–168) uses Kant's discussion (7:191ff.) to argue for a distinctive faculty that enables us to use conventional signs. Finkelnburg argues that linguistic disorders are a form of disorder he refers to as 'asymbolia'—a breakdown of the ability to use signs for the purposes of communication including gestures and mimicry and pantomime. Cassirer sees such disorders as breakdowns in our ability to engage in the kind of reasoning that occurs in the abstract significative use of signs. Discussing Finkelnburg, Cassirer provides an account of the different kinds of signs in Kant to which Finkelnburg refers. Cassirer draws on this passage and others for distinctions between different kinds of signs, especially the difference between schemata, symbols, and logical signs important to PSF (especially Kant's discussion of signification at 5:351ff.).
[41] Cassirer (1972), 26.

world" of comprehensive counterfactual significance to us as human beings.[42] Symbols are as such systematically significant for thought and action. In this way, Cassirer brings out the importance of the systematic account of signs for the notion of world. Symbols are signs that can be grasped by human beings not merely in their relations but in their abstract relatedness independently of any concrete experience in which they are exemplified.[43] They open up a world for us, but also allow us to transcend the spatio-temporal world.

Cassirer draws on Kant's idea that ours is "an understanding that needs images".[44] He clarifies Kant's grounding of our thought in images[45] by substituting symbols, systematically significant signs, for images; images are themselves for Kant a subclass of signs, of sensible objects endowed with conceptual significance. For Kant, as Cassirer emphasizes,[46] the very distinction between the actual and the possible is a function of the finite discursive intellect of human beings: "we cannot think without images and we cannot intuit without concepts … this dualism in the fundamental conditions of knowledge … according to Kant, lies at the bottom of our distinction between possibility and actuality".[47] For Kant we need a notation or visual pattern to be able to retain a complex pattern of significance across the flux of our different states of consciousness. Thus even the ability to think in the abstract terms of logic requires a notation, even if those have no more than the significance that they allow us to keep track of the structural relations between our thoughts and thus do not amount to what Kant would call a "symbol"; this sense of a logical sign-design in which imagery need play no substantive role in the meaning is what Cassirer has in mind when he thinks of all knowledge as symbolic: "Human knowledge is by its very nature symbolic knowledge […]. And for symbolic thought it is indispensable to make a sharp distinction between actual and ideal things. A symbol has no actual existence as a part of the physical world; it has meaning".[48] The development of human thought becomes the establishment of an "ideal world" of symbolic meaning that is distinct from and also not confused with actual objects. This is a distinction that Cassirer, again following Kant's interpretation of the import of Plato's *Republic* and its theory of ideas in the first Critique,

---

42 Ibid., 25; 60.
43 Ibid., 59.
44 Ibid., 80 ff.
45 Kant (1907-), 5:408.
46 Cassirer (1972), 56.
47 Ibid.
48 Ibid., 57.

also applies to the practical and the political.⁴⁹ The realm of the ethical is the realm of what ought to be rather than what is and here for Kant we start from what is rather than from the idea of what ought to be at our peril; this is how we succumb to illusion. The whole realm of the ideal or normative to which we relate in terms of our purposes or ends is the possible as it serves as a model for the actual. The terms in which we make sense of the world to ourselves are not limited except in earlier mythic phases of culture or in the case of psycho-pathology to immediate biological interests or to other more specific "practical interests" that we have as agents.⁵⁰ We are able to understand the world in terms of the abstract possibilities and systems of relations opened up by different forms of symbolization. Such possible worlds are not only important to the counterfactual conditionals of science, but also to the less abstract context of specific natural languages and art and music, as well as to religious ideals. This process of abstract symbolization is for Cassirer the process through which we emancipate ourselves from the limited sensible world inside Plato's cave, a world in which everything shows up in the light of perceived interests.⁵¹ For Cassirer, "[h]uman culture taken as a whole may be described as the process of man's progressive self-liberation. Language, art, religion, science, are various phases of this process".⁵²

It is crucial for Cassirer that we not run together the possible with the actual. Therein lies the danger in "primitive thought". Such thought fails to "differentiate between the two spheres of being and meaning. They are constantly being confused: a symbol is looked upon as if it were endowed with magical or physical powers".⁵³ Kant's *Anthropology*, in developing the significative power of the imagination in the use of signs, diagnoses the same "amazing tendency of the imagination to play with human beings leading them to confuse signs with things and to ascribe to those signs an inner reality as if things would have to accord themselves to those signs".⁵⁴ Kant sees this at work in the magical significance ascribed to numbers such as four and seven that are connected with the four phases of the moon and the period in which those phases recur (twenty-eight days broken into four phases gives seven). In astrology you find an even more extensive conception of invisible powers of influence that numbers and the trajectories of the celestial bodies are supposed to have on us. Such magical

---

49 Ibid., 60.
50 Ibid., 41.
51 Ibid.
52 Ibid., 228.
53 Ibid., 57.
54 Kant (1907-), 7:194.

and mythical thinking is never completely overcome and its emotional power is underestimated at one's peril as Cassirer shows in *The Myth of the State*. Kant too is attentive to the danger not just to the pursuit of truth, but also to the religious and political and social order of confounding signs and symbols with their referents. It counts for him as superstition and the task of overcoming it belongs to the process of enlightenment.

Cassirer recognizes that Kant's Critiques and the role of signs in them can be read as a kind of re-creation of this process of self-liberation and transcendence of the cave that Kant identifies with the process of enlightenment. There are two conflicting motifs in Cassirer's account of our symbolic nature both of which reflect an unresolved tension in his reading of Kant. On the one hand, Cassirer is inclined to see human development as a process through which human beings become capable of ever more abstract, structural, comprehensive and objective conceptions of things. From this vantage point, human emancipation consists in living more and more within an "ideal world" of language, literature, art, music, science and philosophy. In this ideal world, the abstract structural understanding of things replaces the understanding of things in terms of concrete objects and images. Theoretical physics, mathematics and logic are privileged in this ideal world because they are most independent of the sensible world. Cassirer's push toward a view from nowhere, as viewed from a theoretical point of view, is mitigated somewhat by the influence of Kant's Copernican revolution, which precludes human beings from occupying such a standpoint if it could even intelligibly be regarded *as* a standpoint. Even when he extols the emancipation of theoretical physics from imagery, he notes that there is a cost to such "impoverishment" and that it cannot be carried through completely.

As Cassirer himself belatedly recognizes, the project of enlightenment is not for Kant a purely theoretical matter, the cosmopolitan conception of philosophy puts what ultimately matters to us as human beings front and center and in that sense is engaged in a full-scale ascent from Plato's cave and a full-scale "turning around of the whole soul," it is not merely a cognitive change, but a change in one's underlying character and with that in the things to which one gives preference on the basis of one's faculty of feeling or of pleasure and displeasure and one's faculty of desire. EM especially in conjunction with his work *The Myth of the State* (MS) may be seen as Cassirer's effort at a rather abstract level to begin to redress the self-criticism that he had hitherto failed adequately to address the issues that are central to Kant's cosmopolitan conception of philosophy, the effort to tie all cognition to its relevance to the essential and the ultimate ends of human reason.

I am much more convinced that the question which is put here, the question of the connection of all knowledge to the essential aim of human reason itself, arises more urgently and imperatively than ever before, not only for the philosopher, but for all those of us who partake in the life of knowledge and the life of spirit and culture ... I do not exclude myself and I do not absolve myself. While endeavoring on behalf of the scholastic conception of philosophy, immersed in its difficulties as if caught up in its subtle problems, we have all too frequently lost sight of the true connection of philosophy with the world.[55]

4 Cassirer and the Copernican Revolution

Cassirer agrees with Kant that philosophy needs to start with the best contemporary science in order to get a grip on the underlying logical functions of thought as they are best understood in the present.[56] Cassirer no longer regards this as Newtonian mechanics, as Kant did. Such historical change in what is regarded as fundamental suggests historical relativism. But Cassirer responds to the worry about historical relativism by noting the continuity in the very idea of a history of science as a "unitary process".[57] The content of science may change but there has to be enough continuity in what science is about for it to be meaningful to talk retrospectively and prospectively of the history of science. Cassirer concedes that the historical character of the "fact of science" and the possibility of change in the "fixed stem-concepts of the understanding" do not emerge clearly in Kant in the way that they do "in modern idealism" of the Marburg school.[58]

In PSF, Cassirer endeavors to provide for the basis of the "unitary process of science" in what he calls, following Avenarius, "the natural world concept".[59] The "natural world concept" of everyday life is a world of felt significance, perception and direct representation of objects ("intuition") that grounds different theoretical articulations of things in terms of our concepts. Cassirer takes the natural world concept however everywhere to presuppose "the unity in multiplicity" that finds its explicit articulation in logical function and concept and that Kant finds in the distinctively human way of understanding things in terms of purposes or representations of parts in terms of their relation to a whole.[60] This is why such concepts are in the end, it would seem, as they are in Kant, to be under-

---

55 Cassirer (1981a), 59.
56 Cassirer (1995), 16–17.
57 Ibid., 17.
58 Ibid., 18.
59 Cassirer (1957), 297.
60 Ibid., 298.

stood in terms of the differential function within the "organic unity" of purposes. This is the way in which we are able to relate our different concepts to each other as nodes in a whole system of systems of signs.

Cassirer starts from a conception of the world as a whole, a representation of "unity in multiplicity" that gains its significance for us through our ability to maneuver our way about through different interlocking systems of signs. It is through signs, which are in their very nature a sensible manifestation of something conceptual, as Cassirer following Kant takes them to be, that we relate to the world.[61] This relationship is not extrinsic, signs are the "very organ," the very "unity in diversity of function" according to which we grasp but also constitute reality. Cassirer develops the conception of organic function and also applies it to all of the symbolic forms in their interrelatedness as well as to the internal functional structure of the organic forms.

Cassirer's conception of an organic unity of differentially significative function follows Kant's (and Leibniz's) organic conception of the relations of the different functions of cognition and of the relations between different sciences as it is laid out in the Architectonic of Pure Reason and B-Preface to the Critique.[62] This conception of organic unity is well entrenched in Kant's conception of systematicity in the first as well as in the other Critiques. The conception of purposive unity is also intimately related to his Copernican revolution according to which our standpoint in the world and our conception of ourselves as subjects, as well as what is object-like about us, is a function of the different ways in which we systematically relate our own standpoint to that of everything else. It reflects his conception of the ends-directed process in which our reason develops and unfolds as we engage with nature and history. It thus reflects Kant's conception of reason and science as a social expression of collective agency that systematically unpacks itself in our experience, the process of which is available to us through an experiment that everyone can perform with their own reason: "the nature of pure speculative reason … contains a truly articulated structure of members in which everything is for the sake of each member, and each individual member is for the sake of all, so that even the least frailty, whether it be a mistake (an error) or a lack, must inevitably betray itself in its use".[63] Cassirer recognizes that Kant's Copernican revolution involves not only the dependence of the object of our inquiry in its relation to the impersonal "subject of thought", but also the idea that the different contexts of our interest are systematically re-

---

61 Cassirer (1955a), 86.
62 Kant (1907-), A 832–833/B 860–861; B xxxviiff.
63 Ibid., B xxxviif.

lated and constituted by the manner in which all of our cognitive competences function together, in a whole in which everything relates as organ to the whole. Kant's Copernican revolution is intended to bring about a revolution in philosophy that will make metaphysics a science. The lesson that Kant learns from the history of science is that any discipline that is to yield cognition in the emphatic sense must be not only systematic, but also subject to intersubjective confirmation and disconfirmation through well-entrenched social practices. Science is itself such a social and historically situated practice as is philosophy. Philosophy can only purport to become a science insofar as it displays the systematic features of science. In science we engage with the world in terms of a set of systematically standpoint invariant conditions. These invariant conditions express themselves as laws that support counterfactual conditionals that allow us to predict certain outcomes from our interventions in the world. Our grip on these counterfactual conditionals is a function of our grip on possibilities and as Cassirer especially emphasizes in *Kant's Life and Thought* (KLT), this is a function for us as human beings of our grip on purposes or ends (*Zwecke*).

Cassirer recognizes the importance of Kant's conception of purposiveness, of "the contingency of the lawful" to Kant's whole conception of experience, modality and law.[64] As human beings we are forced to view things from the selective vantage point of our interests and purposes, even each science views things from a selective standpoint: "sciences (*Wissenschaften*) ... are all thought up from the vantage point of a certain general interest".[65] "Unity of purpose" (*Einheit des Zweckes*) is responsible for the kind of systematic unity under law to be found in any and all science and that defines for Kant the very conception of what is "scientific".[66] We can only understand laws as human beings in terms of regularities that we take to be significant for us. We cannot derive all laws from a single principle that we could grasp from a completely objective view from nowhere outside of our own standpoint. This is why Kant defines the kind of lawfulness that contingent matters have as their purpose-relevance: "the lawfulness of the contingent is called purposiveness".[67] Contingency is how laws manifest themselves to us as beings that occupy a changing standpoint from within the system of events governed by laws in virtue of those very laws who thus cannot take in the world from the view from nowhere. Our grip on uniformities is always a selective and interest-related one, it is always in terms of our purposes, any system-

---

64 Cassirer (1981b), 348 ff.
65 Kant (1907-), A 834/B 862.
66 Ibid., A 832/B 860.
67 Ibid., 5:404.

atic order that we recognize is thus a conformity to our purposes or purposiveness.

Kant thinks that the conditions for the possibility of experience and of transcendental philosophy unpack themselves in our very process of thinking through our own situation in necessary relation to other viewpoints. This leads him to the idea that "systems" of thought including the different philosophies and sciences all have a principle according to which they are produced "as the original germ in reason that merely develops itself and therefore are not only each in turn organized according to an idea, but are purposefully unified in a system of human cognition as members of a whole and allow an architectonic of all human knowledge".[68] In the *Prolegomena to Any Future Metaphysics*, Kant uses this idea of a germ that underlies the "self-development of reason" to characterize the synthetic method of the Critique as a whole. Unlike the analytic method of the Prolegomena, the Critique's synthetic method does not rely on the assumption of the fact of science or on the existence of practices that are committed to the existence of a priori knowledge: "This work is difficult and demands a reader resolved to think himself gradually into a system in which nothing yet is presupposed as given except reason itself, and thus who seeks to develop knowledge from its original germs without seeking the support of any fact".[69] This idea becomes in Cassirer (and in the later Kant) the genesis of the whole system of symbolic forms from "the spontaneous law of generation"[70] in terms of which human beings relate systematically to their world. The spontaneous law of generation also reflects the ascent to architectonic principles of systematic unification under the guise of the good that Cassirer recommends as Kant's appropriation of Plato.

> Kant saw the basic character of Platonic idealism in the fact that Plato did not stop with the "copy view of the physical world order: but elevates himself instead to a view of its "architectonic connection". In this sense the standpoint of the mere "copy view" must be exchanged for that of "architectonic connection" in every sphere of objectivity, no matter what kind or type it is. Such a sphere cannot, by the simple imitation and rendering of some given being, evidence the truth and objectivity which characteristically belongs to it, but accomplishes this rather in the meaningful order of the construction that it carries out by virtue of an original formative principle. It is well known how this basic thought has proven itself in the "Copernican revolution" that Kant executed in his attempt to lay the foundations of cognition.[71]

---

68 Ibid., A 835/B 863.
69 Ibid., 4:274.
70 Cassirer (1953), 81.
71 Cassirer (1981a), 425.

Culture becomes a social and interlocking, although not always superficially coherent, functional whole of paradigms in terms of which we implicitly systematically take things to be salient to our interests.[72] Culture forms an "organic whole" of symbolic function in which each of the different symbolic forms expresses itself differentially and functionally in the work of human culture, but in which the whole is also a unity of opposites[73]; this is in part because symbolic forms are only functionally related to each other and not related to each other in terms of an underlying identity.

Cassirer rejects the very notion of appealing to "an absolute reality which forms, so to speak, their [the symbolic forms'] solid and substantial substratum [...]. The realists always assume ... the so-called given which is thought to have some definite form, some inherent structure of its own".[74] The notion of a "mere raw material of sensation considered as something fundamentally alien to meaning ... is a mere fiction".[75] It is to be replaced by a "symbolic pregnancy" in which sensation is a mere difference (or following Cohen, "differential") in a whole of significant experience and not a "matter" to be "combined" with a "form" in order to generate experience.[76] Cassirer links the notion of 'symbolic pregnancy' to a rejection of faculty psychology (faculty psychology is for him nothing more than the 18th century form in which Kant's transcendental conception is formulated). The transcendental conception is "negated" by faculty psychology if such psychology is taken at face value.[77] The understanding is not something that stands in a causal relation to sense, but a normative-functional one in which the notion of sensory inputs loses all significance. The faculties of the mind have a functional relationship to one another that becomes unintelligible if their distinctness is understood as complete independence. Each is what it is only through the functional contribution it makes to the whole of cognition and to human agency.

Cassirer rejects the realist view for language, myth, religion and the other symbolic forms: "the analysis of reality in terms of things and processes, permanent and transitory aspects, objects and actions, do not precede language as a substratum of given fact, but language initiates such articulations, and develops them in its own sphere".[78] The symbolic forms are not themselves fixed either,

---

72 Cassirer (1946), 222–228.
73 Ibid., 68; 228.
74 Cassirer (1953), 8; 12.
75 Cassirer (1957), 195.
76 Ibid., 203.
77 Ibid., 194–195.
78 Cassirer (1953), 12.

but processes of signification through which a vocabulary of signs must first emerge that is responsible for "the spiritual construction of our world of "things".[79] Thus even language begins in a "state of indifference, a peculiar balance of feeling" between verb and noun forms and events and things.[80] Distinct subjects and objects emerge only gradually out of the process of culture. We first develop a general differentially sensory-affective sense of ourselves in relation to an indefinite natural and social world. But we do not do this by confronting a barrage of sense-data with a set of concepts that are supposed somehow to impose an order on them. General concepts only gradually emerge out of an experience that is both sensible and conceptual from the outset. Understanding the point correctly that the sensible and intellectual operate in signs as a unity allows one to understand Cassirer's notion of "symbolic pregnancy" as the (?) indissoluble unity of perception and perceptual significance. The fundamental conceptions of each science are "*symbols* created by the intellect itself" rather than "passive images" of things[81]; this extends down to the very manner in which observation and perception function in science. Symbolic unity of the sensible and conceptual is key to understanding the sense in which Cassirer is engaged in "overcoming the naïve copy theory of knowledge".[82] The naïve conception of correspondence and realism that goes with such a conception is also fundamentally revised. Cassirer rejects that "naive realism which regards ... reality as something directly and unequivocally given...".[83] Against this "myth of the given," he recommends Kant's Copernican revolution as an account of the "spontaneous law of generation" that provides "the measure and criterion for ... truth and intrinsic meaning".[84] Cassirer notes that the appeal to the relatedness of the object of cognition to cognition remains problematic and misleading until one sinks cognition into social and cultural activity (especially of science[85]). If one looks at the notion of cognition (*Erkenntnis*) in isolation from culture, then the full-force of Kant's Copernican revolution does not become obvious. Then it still seems as if objects have a kind of independent existence. But once one sees cognition as part of the process of culture the very being of objects comes to be seen as part of that cultural process that transforms what is perceived into a shared expression of what we do together in culture: "here being

---

[79] Ibid., 15.
[80] Ibid., 12.
[81] Cassirer (1955a), 75.
[82] Ibid.
[83] Cassirer (1953), 6.
[84] Ibid., 8.
[85] Cassirer (1955a), 80.

can only be apprehended in action".⁸⁶ This is an important insight of Cassirer's, which must be taken together with the social character of culture.

The ultimate import of this position is to do away with the "myth of the given" in a much more radical way than that later pursued by Wilfried Sellars under the influence of Cassirer's critique. In his review of *Language and Myth*,⁸⁷ Sellars notes that

> [i]n Cassirer's argument, however, this [Kant's Copernican] Revolution is given a "nominalistic" twist. The forms which bind together the thinking which is the generation of world-for-mind, are no longer the fixed pure schematized categories of Kant, but are instead conceived of as *essentially* bound up with the symbolism that would ordinarily be said to express them, and, consequently, as sharing in the *historicity* of human utterance.⁸⁸

Sellars notes the passage in which Cassirer rejects the realist's conception of what is given as what Sellars will later call "a myth"; he also notices that natural languages have analogous functions for Cassirer that give rise to similarities rather than strict identities of meaning. Cassirer limits strict identities of meaning to logical and mathematical symbolic systems; here what Sellars refers to as Cassirer's "nominalism" gives way to a Platonism. Sellars' own linguistic nominalism never transcends the nominalism of Cassirer's functional account of natural language. Not without justification, Sellars assumes that Kant's conception is that of "fixed pure schematized categories". For Cassirer, as Sellars interprets him (as on my reading, for Kant), language and thought are not to be understood as something that can be divorced from sensible signs, but are instead embedded in the whole historical-cultural and also natural functional interactive whole that gives those signs the significance that they have. Sellars is critical of the grounding of the symbolic function in culture. As a proponent of scientific realism, he argues for a psychological-causal grounding of language competence and a picturing relationship of language to the world (a version of the copy theory Cassirer eschews). Ultimately his demand for a psychological explanation of language leads to a tension between the semantic functionalism and linguistic nominalism that he shares with Cassirer and his psychological functionalism. Sellars's psychological functionalism constantly threatens to undermine the normativity of thought not only by limiting thought to the linguistic nominalism of language, but also by attempting to underwrite the understanding of natural language by the kind of psychological explanation of language that he finds lacking

---

86 Ibid., 80.
87 Sellars (1949).
88 Ibid.

in Cassirer. According to Cassirer's much more radical rejection of the "myth of the given", perception and all experience are understood to be an expression of our shared collective agency in culture, but also as agents who are part of the functional context of nature, and not as contents to which we can have causal or picturing relations.

Kant himself views cognition as the basis for objects in its role especially as the cognition of science and of a science of metaphysics. Kant thinks of science however not simply as a set of propositions but as a social practice, as a collaborative enterprise subject to check by others. Science is something, like the wider process of culture as a whole, that we do together. Even perceptual objects are not composites of sensations and our interpretations, but the process through which we make inchoate information our own and make it accessible to ourselves and others in thought and language. We do not have to give up on the idea that we are not only embedded in human culture, but also part of our natural environment. For there is an aspect of perception and all of our activities that is grounded in our natural functioning as living organism. But this engagement with the natural world is not a passive reception of data either, but an active proprioceptive kinaesthetic engagement with the world on the basis of the way in which our biological functions are embedded in our interactions with our environment.

The intimate connection between the systematic significance of signs and their sensible manifestation is not static for Cassirer; their significance unfolds through the development of a pattern in broadly sensible experience that includes our natural functional relation to our environment, but also the whole of human culture and all of human history. The fundamental distinctions in ontology between processes and things and the permanent and the transitory are constituted by, rather than presupposed by, language and thought and all of the symbolic forms and the distinctions with which language and thought work is tied up with the history of the languages and symbolic systems in terms of which they are articulated. This explains Cassirer's systematic commitment to understanding the historical development of the problem of knowledge. Here Cassirer follows an important line of thought in Kant's Copernican revolution, namely that the unpacking of the a priori significance of our judgments is not complete until we have been able to situate the practices in which they are grounded in a "History of Pure Reason", as the final section of the Critique is entitled.

5 Kant's Copernican Revolution

Cassirer rightly presents PSF as a reconstruction of Kant's Copernican revolution. His thought as a whole is firmly grounded in what he calls Kant's Copernican turn or revolution. However, Cassirer's conception of Kant's "revolution in thought" is very different from that now prevailing. For Cassirer rejects either of the alternatives that now prevail in the interpretation of transcendental idealism. On the dominant realist reading, objects, or at least things in themselves, are taken to exist completely independently of us and we are supposed to impose an order on them. On the representationalist or methodological reading, there are a set of methodologically solipsistic constraints on what is represented by us and these serve as limiting conditions on objects of experience. In contrast to such readings of Kant that take transcendentally or empirically real objects to have an existence that is independent of us, Cassirer takes the Copernican turn to be the very process in which subjects and objects come to be elicited from the indeterminate matrix of experience in the first place.

Kant does not fully explicitly call his "revolution in thought" modeled on the sciences a Copernican one anywhere. Thus in the most technical sense, the widespread view is correct that Kant does not identify his revolution as a Copernican one.[89] However, in following the modern scientific revolution, Kant proposes to follow "the first thoughts" of Copernicus.[90] He intends to shift to a knowledge-centered understanding of objects in which the perspective-relative appearances of objects are due to our changing standpoint within the system of relations of cognition and the perspective-independent features of objects are those features that are invariant with respect to changes in our standpoint as knowers.[91] Recapitulating two-centuries of celestial mechanics, Kant notes that Copernicus allowed the discovery of Newton's laws "by a true approach to the observed movements, but one going against the senses, seeking them not in the heavenly objects, but in the observer".[92]

The changing spatio-temporal standpoint of the observer is responsible for the way objects appear to us, while what is constant and constitutive of objects are the laws that systematically coordinate appearances from different spatio-temporal standpoints. These laws coordinating appearances are revealed by and to the cognition of knowers embedded in "the secure process of science";

---

89 Cf. Cohen (1985), 275 ff.
90 Kant (1907-), B xvi.
91 Ibid.
92 Ibid., B xxii.

such a process is secure only if it has an essentially social dimension to it. From the outset of the second edition of the Critique, Kant emphasizes that the secure process of science involves an essentially social dimension, and by implication so does his conception of metaphysics insofar as it is put on "the secure path of science". Science is only on a secure path when "different collaborators are able to agree in how to pursue a shared end" and in this way are able to cooperate with each other and build on their shared contributions; in this way they can confirm and disconfirm the results of their theories and experiments.[93] Thus the systematicity of science not only involves a comprehensive set of invariant laws, but also the social competence of investigators in coordinating with each other in the recognition of what counts as salient in their investigation of the laws and the phenomena that obey those laws (as they are salient to a particular science). Indeed the laws that we formulate as human beings are in the end governed by a sense of how those laws are to be coordinated with our collaborative ends as inquirers.

Kant engages in an experiment with our reason to determine whether we can come up with a coherent account of our reasoning about the world and our place in it.[94] This experiment with our reason initially seems to occur only *in foro interno*. But consonant with Kant's conception of the experimental method in science, the experiment actually depends on testing the results that one obtains from the first person point of view against the results of the reasoning of other persons, of an "alien reason". Agreement with the point of view of others is an indication of success, but no guarantee; one must also think things through for oneself. The object itself is something more than intersubjective agreement. The object is that in respect to which there is necessary agreement between those reasoning correctly about a certain subject-matter. It is this that one seeks to elicit as one thinks things through for oneself, but in a manner that attempts to do justice to the standpoints of others. The object is that which we conceive necessarily to present itself in the same way to any arbitrary self-consciousness and to be the way things are brought together under concepts in a possible universal self-consciousness.[95] This possible universal self-consciousness is always available to us only from the first person singular and plural points of view of mine or our representations, as the enabling condition of those representations and their differential conceptual significance.[96] But it provides the basis for a claim to standpoint independent truth that is crucial to Kant's conception.

---

[93] Ibid., B vii.
[94] Ibid., B xxff.
[95] Ibid., B 132ff. I develop this idea in detail in Keller (1998).
[96] Kant, op cit., B 134n.

The dependence of first and second points of view on a possible universal point of view is the basis on which Kant makes his claims to a priori knowledge in the Critique. Kant's confidence in his position is based on the systematic coherence of his take with that of all others who might reason things through to the end from their own distinctive vantage points. His claims to the "unalterability" of the principles of the Critique are based on

> the evidence drawn from the experiment showing that the result effected is the same whether we proceed from the smallest elements to the whole or return from the whole to every part (for this whole too is given in itself through the final intention of pure reason in the practical); while the attempt to alter even the smallest part directly introduces contradictions not merely into the system, but into universal human reason.[97]

Kant's experiment of pure reason in which we reason things through both from our own and from other persons' perspectives and from the unity of all of these possible perspectives extends to our social and practical commitments and leads Kant to connect our place in the universe with our place in the moral world-order.[98] These two orders are brought together in the comprehensive conception of world order in the cosmopolitan conception of philosophy. The whole of reason given in the accommodation of our theoretical knowledge to our practical commitments expresses the "true conception of philosophy" as "wisdom through the path of science".[99] This is philosophy from the cosmopolitan point of view. It is the integration of knowledge into the whole of our reason as governed by the ultimate and necessary ends that we have as reasoning agents.

Kant's Copernican move in metaphysics leaves to one side any theoretical claims about ultimate reality (about the world as it is in itself) and what Kant calls "the unconditioned" (that which is not affected by its relations to other things[100]). Instead, he looks systematically at the world from our own vantage point within the world. Efforts theoretically to retrieve the world as it is in itself from our own vantage point within the system of relations that is the world inevitably lead to contradictions between our essentially relational access to the world in which we are embedded and the effort to grasp the world as it is independently of any relations to us. The notion of a world as it is independent of and unmediated by this relational access is empty for us; it is available only to a kind of all-encompassing divine intellect that we cannot have. Kant exposes the nec-

---

97 Ibid., B xxxviii.
98 Ibid., 5:91–92; 162–163.
99 Ibid., B 878/B 850; 5:163.
100 Ibid., B xx-xxi.

essary illusion of taking our theoretical knowledge of objects presented to us in the systematicity of spatio-temporal experience also to be of something unconditioned by spatio-temporal causal relations (things in themselves that are independent of experience). The necessary illusion consisting in thinking that one can experience things independently of the conditions that go into one's being able to relate those things to one's own standpoint within experience (and as someone having experience). Kant then shows that our theoretical cognition is sunk into the social practices, including especially the individual sciences, in terms of which our judgments have the significance that they do. In such practices, we have a fundamental role as agents. Our practical cognition of ourselves is thus of something unconditioned by anything outside of the very social practices in which we are involved.[101] Once one has freed oneself of the idea of an object antecedent to knowledge and science to which knowledge must conform, then the possibility that science and our practices in general might be undermined by the causal connections between such objects becomes unintelligible.

In the first half of the Critique, the Transcendental Doctrine of Elements, our knowledge is shown to be substantively limited to what we can grasp systematically from our own spatio-temporal standpoint. In the "practical logic" of the Transcendental Doctrine of Method[102] Kant then offers a complex account of how theoretical cognition and propositional judgment concerning spatio-temporal objects and even logical relations are embedded in the pragmatic conditions provided by the social and historical practices of everyday life and of specific sciences that give our judgment their meaning. Kant views interaction in everyday and even in science as distinctively competitive. The competition between different points of view of different agents pursuing different ends and different disciplines with different conceptions of how to understand things is mitigated by the necessary and ultimate ends of inquiry. The normative commitments of shared inquiry as they manifest themselves to inquirers in a particular historical context are ultimately sunk into the unconditioned normative requirements on agency demanded by practical reason. Combining the perspective of the historical context of inquiry with the comprehensive normative constraints on agency, including truth telling, mutual aid and cooperation, and self-perfection, provides the basis for the realization of reason in history and a History of Pure Reason, the title of the last chapter of the Critique. This provides the final level of systematic unification in Kant's Copernican, or rather Keplerian, revolution.

---

101 Ibid., xxi.
102 Ibid., A 708/B 736.

It is no accident that the Critique ends with a section on the History of Pure Reason. Kant never explicitly encourages one to relativize his own standpoint or that of the best science of his day. Still Kant's own conception of unchangeable functions of thought and categories is an expression of his view that his philosophy is true and a coherent whole in which nothing can change without altering the character of the whole. For Kant, "there is only one truth" and thus every new philosophy is committed to regarding itself as "the one true philosophy" because it takes itself to be true and Kant's is no different: "So anyone who announces a system of philosophy as his own work says in effect that before this philosophy there was none at all".[103] This does not mean that Kant is oblivious to the historical and systematic importance of previous philosophy, but its significance is seen in the light of the critical philosophy. The same thing would apply to the sciences in general and chemistry in particular, even as those sciences have undergone a series of revolutions: "there is only one chemistry (Lavoisier's)".[104] We do not have to give up a standpoint-independent claim to truth either in the sciences or in philosophy or in morals even if we realize that that claim is itself standpoint dependent. The claims of phlogiston and oxydation chemistry or of rationalist and Kantian metaphysics will in a certain sense be incommensurable, and even oxydation chemistry (and Kant's metaphysics) come to be replaced by something more comprehensively explanatory. Just as Kant once thought that the phlogiston chemistry of Stahl was true and later that of Lavoisier, it is incumbent on us to rethink Kant's critical philosophy from our own historical standpoint as Cassirer has done. To do otherwise, would be to approach Kant's philosophy from the vantage point of an "alien reason" rather than thinking things through for ourselves as the cosmopolitan conception of philosophy requires.

Kant is quite clear in the second Preface to the Critique and in the Architectonic of Pure Reason that science and metaphysics have a historical development. The basic concepts of the understanding also have had a historical development and indeed a necessary historical development that goes back at least to Aristotle, as Kant's use of the term "categories" from Aristotle suggests.

> [P]hilosophizing is a gradual development of human reason through mere concepts and this cannot have proceeded or begun in an empirical way. There must have been a need of reason (a theoretical or practical one) that forced reason, first of all by common reason to go from judgments of things, for instance from heavenly bodies and their motions, back to their grounds and to their first grounds. But then one came up with purposes: but finally

---

103 Ibid., 6:207.
104 Ibid.

since one noticed that one could seek the rational grounds of all things, one began to enumerate one's concepts of reason (or of the understanding), prior to which one began to analyze thought in general without an object. The former occurred through Aristotle, the latter even earlier by the logicians.[105]

Kepler first formulates the crucial inertial laws of elliptical motion for the planets and thus gives the Copernican revolution its modern form. Kant extends Kepler's development of the Copernican model explicitly to history. The limited snap-shot observations that we make based on our own historical situation give us no more clues to the path of history than do our observations of the planets to the ultimate trajectory of the planets. But nevertheless we can predict the course of this trajectory "from the general ground of the systematic constitution of the edifice that is the world and from the little that we have observed".[106] Kant emulates Kepler's contribution in planetary science for history. Kepler "submitted the eccentric paths of the planets in an unexpected way to determinate laws" and "Newton explained these laws in terms of a universal natural cause".[107] Kant later returns to the same application of planetary science and the Copernican revolution to history:

> Perhaps it lies in our wrongly taken choice of the standpoint from which we view the way human things happen that it seems counter to sense [*widersinnig*[108]]. The planets viewed from the earth are sometimes retrograde, sometimes stand still, sometimes go forward. According to the standpoint of the sun, which only reason can take up, they proceed constantly in their rule-guided way in accordance with the Copernican hypothesis. But it pleases some, who are otherwise not unwise, to staunchly persist in the way of explaining appearances and to the standpoint to which they have once committed themselves: even if they get tied up in Tychonian cycles and epicycles to the point of absurdity.[109]

Kant now extends the Copernican hypothesis to a history in which we as human beings and agents in history make the decisive contribution. Kant is able to predict how history will go and thus make "history possible a priori" because he is himself involved "in bringing the outcome about" that he predicts.[110] Kant thus develops a new sense of the elliptical path that is crucial to relating the intelligible and the causal order of things: "the fate of the human race is … the outcome and handiwork of humanity's own free self-determination [...]. The course

---

105 Ibid., 240–241.
106 Ibid., 8:27.
107 Ibid., 8:18.
108 Cf. ibid., A x.
109 Ibid., 7:83.
110 Ibid., 7:79–80.

and path the intelligible determination takes, in the empirical causal process of events" is indicated by a "historical sign" the sympathy bordering on enthusiasm of spectators to the French revolution" who display their sympathy publicly.[111] Kant sees history as bound together for us in a unity of rememorative (past), demonstrative (present) and prognostic (future) use of signs in which the French revolution has a pivotal signification as a "historical sign". "A phenomenon such as the French Revolution was [rememorative sign], will never be forgotten [prognostic], because it has revealed a capacity for the better in human nature [demonstrative sign], the like of which no politician would have rationalized from the course of things until now, and which alone unites nature and freedom in accordance with the inner principles of right in mankind".[112] The engagement of observers for the cause of the French revolution is an engagement for the cause of self-governance and freedom from war that goes completely against their self-interest, a historical sign that we are capable of acting against our self-interest and for the cause of a cosmopolitan order and thus that history can be a forum for human progress and the expression of reasons for action that are unconditioned by causal antecedents in our self-interest. As such, Kant's conception of the trajectory of human history also becomes an account of the ultimate systematic unity of agents working together to give a comprehensive meaning to the whole of nature and culture from their own standpoints within nature and history. Philosophy and science are also equally caught up in this social and historical manner in which we as reasoning agents engage with ourselves and with the world because both philosophy and science presuppose a trajectory of inquiry that the participants in inquiry make possible through their very commitment to telling the truth in public.

Kant's Copernican revolution is the process through which we as human agents systematically socially relate ourselves to and come to terms with the demands of our particular stance in the world as agents. It is thus fundamentally as much about self-transformation as it is about abstract theoretical understanding. Cassirer does an impressive job of retrieving this conception from Kant, although it may be argued that he never integrates his interest in human rights and in the objectivity of science and the importance of the arts in a manner that quite achieves the dizzying level of systematic unity in Kant's thought. He never quite sees that for Kant academic or school philosophy gains its very significance from its differential contribution to the cosmopolitan conception of philosophy.

---

111 Cassirer (1981b), 406; Kant, op. cit., 7:85.
112 Cassirer, op. cit., 407; Kant, op. cit., 7:88.

Bibliography

Cassirer (1927): Ernst Cassirer, "The Problem of the Symbol and Its Place in the System of Philosophy", J. M. Krois (trans.), *Man and World* 11 (1978), 411–428.
Cassirer (1946): Ernst Cassirer, *The Myth of the State*, New Haven: Yale University Press.
Cassirer (1953): Ernst Cassirer, *Language and Myth*, Susanne K. Langer (trans.), New York: Dover Publication.
Cassirer (1955a): Ernst Cassirer, *The Philosophy of Symbolic Forms, Volume One: Language*, Ralph Manheim (trans.), New Haven: Yale University Press.
Cassirer (1955b): Ernst Cassirer, *The Philosophy of Symbolic Forms, Volume Two: Mythical Thought*, Ralph Manheim (trans.), New Haven: Yale University Press.
Cassirer (1957): Ernst Cassirer, *The Philosophy of Symbolic Forms, Volume Three: The Phenomenology of Knowledge*, Ralph Manheim (trans.), New Haven: Yale University Press
Cassirer (1972): Ernst Cassirer, *An Essay on Man: An Introduction to A Philosophy of Human Culture*, New Haven and London: Yale University Press.
Cassirer (1981a): Ernst Cassirer, *Symbol, Myth, and Culture: Essays and Lectures of Ernst Cassirer, 1935–1945*, Donald Philip Verene (ed.), New Haven: Yale University Press.
Cassirer (1981b): Ernst Cassirer, *Kant's Life and Thought*, James Haden (trans.), New Haven: Yale University Press.
Cassirer (1995): Ernst Cassirer, *Das Erkenntnisproblem in der Philosophie und Wissenschaft der neueren Zeit*, 2 vols., reprint: Darmstadt: Wissenschaftliche Buchgesellschaft.
Cassirer (2013/1985a): Ernst Cassirer, "The Problem of the Symbol and Its Place in the System of Philosophy", in: *The Warburg Years (1919–1933): Essays on Language, Art, Myth, and Technology*, S. G. Lofts with A. Calcagno (trans.), New Haven and London: Yale University Press, 254–271.
Cohen (1985), Bernhard I. Cohen, *Revolution in Science*, Cambridge, MA: Harvard University Press.
Duffy and Liles (1979): R.J. Duffy and B.Z. Liles, "A translation of Finkelnburg's 1870 lecture on aphasia as 'asymbolia' with commentary", *Journal of Speech and Hearing Disorders* 44, 156–168.
Friedman (2000): Michael Friedman, *A Parting of the Ways: Carnap, Cassirer, and Heidegger*, Chicago: Open Court.
Kant (1907-): Immanuel Kant, *Gesammelte Schriften*. Preussische Akademie der Wissenschaften (ed.), Berlin, New York: De Gruyter. References are in Akademie pagination, with the exception of the *Critique of Pure Reason*, which is referred to by means of the page numbers of the first and second editions, A/B.
Keller (1998): Pierre Keller, *Kant and the Demands of Self-Consciousness*. Cambridge: Cambridge University Press.
Sellars (1949): Wilfred Sellars, "Review of *Language and Myth*", *Philosophy and Phenomenological Research* 9 (1948–49), 326–329.

Simon Truwant (Leuven)
The Concept of 'Function' in Cassirer's Historical, Systematic, and Ethical Writings

The central concepts of Cassirer's thought are usually considered to be 'symbolic pregnance', 'symbol', 'symbolic form', and 'animal symbolicum'. In this paper, however, I will present the concept of 'function' as its most fundamental and pervading idea, thus honoring Cassirer's claim that "the fundamental principle of critical thinking is the principle of the 'primacy' of the function over the object".[1] In this way, I aim to clarify the coherence of Cassirer's monumental oeuvre: if we focus on his concept of function, I hold, we can see that his systematic investigations into human culture organically follow from his historical ones, and that his ethical reflections draw out the normative consequences of his systematic writings.

I will first discuss why and how Cassirer, in his first non-historical monograph *Substance and Function* (1910), develops the idea of functional unity (section 1). Then, I will show how this idea returns as a methodological guideline in the historical, systematic, and ethical phases of Cassirer's oeuvre. In his early, historical, writings (1906–1919), Cassirer tries to explain the continuity and progress in the history of thought while simultaneously acknowledging the rational legitimacy of each historical epoch (section 2). In his mature, systematic, writings (1923–1942), he likewise searches for a way to understand the unity of human culture without giving up the synchronic diversity of cultural domains (section 3). In his late, ethical, writings (1935–1946), Cassirer finally discusses the ethical and existential importance of recognizing both the structuring unity and irreducible plurality of our cultural world (section 4). Each time, I will argue, Cassirer relies on his early idea of a function to relate 'the one and the many'.

1 From Substance to Function

Inspired by contemporary developments in the fields of logic and mathematics, Cassirer argues in *Substance and Function* that traditional, substance-based, logic must be replaced by a critical, functional, one. He most explicitly criticizes Aristotle for initiating 'substance-thinking' and Berkeley for bringing it into psy-

---
[1] Cassirer (1955a), 79.

chology, but he actually considers this type of thinking to characterize Western thought as a whole, "in spite of all the manifold transformations it has undergone".[2] Because of this, I can leave aside here whether Cassirer's assessment of these two thinkers does justice to them or their mutual differences—unfortunately, little research seems to have been done on this topic so far[3]—and instead I will simply present his general critique and solution.

Cassirer holds that traditional logic orders concepts according to their degree of abstraction and therefore regards substance as the highest concept: this idea is said to unite the widest range of objects because it is independent of all specifying relations, be it with its own properties or with other entities:

> The category of relation especially is forced into a dependent and subordinate position by this fundamental metaphysical doctrine of Aristotle. Relation is not independent of the concept or real being; it can only add supplementary and external modifications to the latter, such as do not affect its real 'nature'.[4]

Cassirer sees two problems with this theory of concept formation. First, it implies that when the extension of our concepts increases, their intension decreases, and thus that a concept that is very limited in content represents the whole of reality. In Cassirer's words, the problem with substance-based logic is that if "all construction of concepts consists in selecting from a plurality of objects before us only the similar properties, while we neglect the rest, [...] a *part* has taken the place of the original sensuous *whole*" and "claims to characterize and explain" it.[5] Moreover, he later adds, this logical theory only allows for inductive inferences, but not for deduction.[6] Once all particularities—relations, properties, and modifications—are lost in the process of abstraction, there seems to be no way back to the variety of concrete objects. Hence, Cassirer concludes that rather than providing a grasp on reality, traditional logic estranges us from the empirical world:

> We reach the strange result that all the logical labor that we apply to a given sensuous intuition serves only to separate us more and more from it. Instead of reaching a deeper com-

---

2 Cassirer (1953), 8
3 One can find two early assessments of *Substance and Function* in Heymans (1928) and Hönigswald (1912)
4 Cassirer (1953), 8.
5 Ibid., 6.
6 Ibid., 19.

prehension of its import and structure, we reach only a superficial schema from which all peculiar traits of the particular case have vanished.[7]

Second, according to Cassirer, the process of abstraction is 'one-sided' or biased because it relies on only one of many possible principles of selection, namely the idea of similarity. Once more, the process of concept formation as it is understood by 'substance-thinking' leads to an impoverished view of the world. "In truth", Cassirer counters, "a series of contents in its conceptual ordering may be arranged according to the most diverging points of view", including "equality or inequality, number and magnitude, spatial and temporal relations, or causal dependence".[8] This variety of possible viewpoints implies that we should not merely represent a univocally given order of being, but must actively select the most appropriate rational criterion for relating the content of our perceptions. In sum, Cassirer criticizes the rigidity of both the procedure and the outcome of the traditional way of concept formation.

His solution to these problems consists in a reversal of the order between substance and relation in favor of the latter. We can distinguish three steps in this argumentation. First, he argues that a logic that takes substance as the highest concept only makes sense when it is supported, as it initially was for Aristotle, by a similarly substance-based *metaphysics*.[9] Such metaphysics considers substances as the highest ontological entities, the fundamental layer of all being. As a transcendental philosopher, Cassirer evidently does not endorse this view. It no longer makes sense for him to talk about substance as the substratum of the 'things in themselves', and to regard our logical concepts as representations thereof. Instead, we should understand substance as itself a logical concept that originates in the faculty of the understanding and allows us to structure the rhapsody of our intuitions prior to experience. In other words, the concept of substance represents a function of our knowledge rather than a metaphysical entity.

Second, Cassirer stresses that in order to avoid Berkeleyan psychology and draw out the full consequences of Kant's 'Copernican revolution', the shift from traditional metaphysics to transcendental philosophy must be complemented with the introduction of a new *logic*.[10] In contrast to Aristotelian logic, Kant's

---

7 Ibid.
8 Ibid., 16.
9 Ibid., 8.
10 Ibid., 11. See Gordon (2005), 134: "Now, physics abandons the notion of 'substance' and replaces it with a notion of 'function' anchored in nothing but the symbolizing capacities of human consciousness. This move, Cassirer noted, was essentially a restatement of the Kantian

transcendental logic regards the concept of substance as only one of the twelve categories by means of which we order the manifold of perceptions and make truth claims. This concept has neither ontological nor logical priority over the other categories, but is one of many possible 'points of view' for relating and comparing phenomena. Hence, rather than indicating that which is independent of all relations, the concept of substance expresses a particular type of objective relationship between perceptions.[11] Cassirer concludes from this the logical priority of relations over concepts: "It is the identity of this generating relation, maintained through changes in the particular contents, which constitutes the specific form of the concept".[12] He later adds that "the relation of necessity ... is in each case decisive", while "the concept is merely the expression and husk of it".[13]

Finally, Cassirer understands these logical relations as 'functions' in the *mathematical* meaning of the term. He holds that they relate to phenomenal objects in the same way that a universal mathematical 'law of arrangement' (y) relates to a series of variables ($x_1, x_2, ...$), namely as a pure relation that indicates a specific 'direction of objective reference' but has no fixed meaning of its own. Understood as such, the concept of function is much better suited for representing the empirical world than an abstract concept such as 'substance'. Because the mathematical function is nothing but "a universal *rule* for the connection of the particulars themselves",[14] it "does not disregard the peculiarities and particularities which it holds under it, but seeks to show the *necessity* of the occurrence and connection of just these particulars".[15] We can, in this case, also 'return' from the function to its variables: "When a mathematician makes his formula more general, this means not only that he is able *to retain* all the

---

idea of the Copernican revolution"; and Luft (2005), 29: "As it turns out retrospectively, the critical historical study of *Substance and Function* is merely an exemplification of the change in framing philosophical problems in the wake of idealistic (transcendental) philosophy. The shift from a substantialist account, which conceives of objects as 'substances', i.e. *independent* of their conceptualization, to a functionalist account, which frames phenomena in a meaningful 'series' of function, is *equal* to the shift from considering objects as they exist independently, to considering them *in so far as they are experienced*".

11 See also Cassirer (2001a), 485: "In this way, the relation moves to the center of the system of categories: it does not signify one of the classes of categories, as Kant thought, but is simply 'the' category, of which all particular ways of connecting of which our knowledge is capable—especially the forms of space of time—are nothing but individual subspecies".
12 Cassirer (1953), 15.
13 Ibid., 16.
14 Ibid., 20.
15 Ibid., 19, 23.

more special cases, but also *to deduce* them from the universal formula".[16] Cassirer's concept of function thus eradicates the two problems that he has with the traditional theory of concept formation: its attention to logical relations that validate the particulars overcomes the problem of the poor meaning of the concept of substance, and the consequent relativity of the rational point of view overcomes the one-sidedness of the selection procedure on the basis of similarity alone.

2 Cassirer's Historical Writings (1906–1919): A Functional Account of the History of Thought

In "The Concept of Philosophy as a Philosophical Problem" (1935), Cassirer holds that despite the many forms that philosophy has taken through the ages—ranging from pure idealism to hardcore realism—its task has always been the same, namely to understand the unities of being and knowing:

> Philosophy claims to be the real, the true unified science; the whole of its striving and its conceptual longing appears to be aimed at absolute unity, at the unity of being as well as the unity of knowledge. But this unity in no way corresponds to an immediate unity of itself, its intellectual structure.[17]

Cassirer here reiterates the main thesis of some of his earliest writings, the first three volumes of *The Problem of Knowledge* (1906, 1907, 1919), namely that the fundamental problem of both philosophy and science has always been that of the relation between 'the one and the many'.[18] He alternately understands this as the problem of subjectivity and objectivity or form and matter. Throughout the ages we have, however, understood this issue differently. According to Cassirer, then, paradigm shifts between two epochs in the history of thought do

---

16 Ibid., 19.
17 Cassirer (1979a), 51..
18 At least in recent times, these 'historical writings' have gained much less attention than Cassirer's 'systematic writings', the three volumes of *The Philosophy of Symbolic Forms* in particular. For an extensive account of Cassirer's view of history and philosophy's relation to it, see, nevertheless, Bast (2000) and Plümacher (2004), 250–263. The first three volumes of *The Problem of Knowledge* have not yet been translated to English, which means that all following quotes from these works present my own translations from the original German. The fourth volume, *Philosophy, Science, and History since Hegel* (1950), on the other hand, was first written in English and translated to German in 1957.

not result from a novel answer to the same problem, but rather from an original reinterpretation of this problem itself:

> This is one of the first and most characteristic philosophical accomplishments of each epoch, that it reformulates the *problem* of the correlation between being and thinking [...] In this delineation of the *task* consists, even more than in their particular solutions, the originality of each productive era.[19]

First, Cassirer holds that the basic concepts of our worldview—matter, form, object, and subject—have repeatedly been redefined, and did not always mean the same thing: "The concepts of 'subject' and 'object' are no given and evident possession of thought; each truly creative epoch must first acquire them and actively coin their meaning".[20] Kant, for example, according to Cassirer no longer understood matter and form as "original determinations of being" but as "structures of signification".[21] Second, our redefining of these concepts also alters their mutual relation:

> Not only the *content* changes, so that, what previously belonged to the objective sphere is transferred to the subjective one, but the meaning and *function* of both basic elements simultaneously also shifts. The great scientific epochs do not inherit the ready-made schema of opposition to realize it with various, interchanging, contents, but first conceptually construct both opposing terms.

After Kant's 'revolution in the way of thinking' (*Revolution der Denkart*; *CPR* B xi) —to stick with this example—the unity of our knowledge constitutes rather than copies the unity of being. The relation of dependence between knowing and being has thus turned upside down, but is also rendered much more intimate. With Kant, Cassirer claims, it becomes clear that "all disagreement about the problem of being in the end always originates from a different or conflicting understanding of the problem of truth, its actual source".[22] Third, It is possible that concepts that are problematic in one era become central to the next: "We thus notice that a concept, which appears in one epoch as a source of contradictions, becomes a tool and necessary condition of all knowledge in the next".[23]

---

19 Cassirer (1999), 7. See also Cassirer (1979b), 68–69.
20 Cassirer (1999), 7.
21 Cassirer (1957), 9–10.
22 Cassirer (2000a), viii..
23 Cassirer (1999), 4. With regard to the Enlightenment, for example, Cassirer holds that "all those philosophical concepts and problems, which the eighteenth century simply took over from the past, move into new positions and undergo a characteristic change of meaning. They are transformed from fixed and finished forms into active forces, from bare results into im-

On these grounds, the problem of the relation between the one and the many takes on radically different forms in the subsequent philosophical and scientific epochs, as each of them is established by "a new intellectual orientation".[24] It consequently seems impossible to perceive any real progress in the history of thought: "In the actual crucial epochs of knowledge, the many basic intuitions do not relate to each other according to a steady, quantitative, development, but in the most sharp dialectic contradictions".[25] Cassirer wonders, however, if it might not be possible

> to discern in this continuous [historical] transformation, if not a consistent, permanent, *content*, then at least a unified *goal*, towards which the ideal development strives? Is there in this process, if there are *no persistent elements* of knowledge, *nevertheless a universal law* that prescribes meaning and direction to this evolution?[26]

In 1906, Cassirer has not yet developed the conceptual distinction between a substantial and functional unity. Nevertheless, the idea behind it is clearly already present in the introduction to the first volume of *The Problem of Knowledge*. The flaw of any metaphysical understanding of the history of thought, he there answers his own question, is that it assumes a substantial substratum that remains the same throughout the different epochs and allows for a cumulative progress in our understanding of the world. A critical approach, on the other hand, searches for a merely ideal continuity, "which is all we need in order to talk about a unity of its process" and which is "the real a priori of history".[27] Only the latter approach can account for true, not merely gradual, differences between the historical epochs.[28]

---

peratives." This, he concludes, "is the really productive significance of the thought of the Enlightenment" (Cassirer (2009b), xiii– hereafter indicated as 'PE').
24 Ibid., 33. Cassirer specifically elaborates on the intellectual orientation of the Enlightenment in *The Philosophy of the Enlightenment* (1932), an on that of the Renaissance in Cassirer's *Individual and Cosmos in Renaissance Philosophy* (1927) and *The Platonic Renaissance in England* (1932).
25 Cassirer (1999), 4.
26 Ibid., 5; italics added.
27 Ibid., 13.
28 Cassirer's functional account of the history of thought informed Hans Blumenberg's view on the transition from the pre-modern to the modern age in *The Legitimacy of the Modern Age*. According to Blumenberg, we cannot understand the secularized worldview of the latter as a translation of the Christian worldview of the former, as Karl Löwith holds in *Meaning in History*, but their incommensurability does not preclude a common task either. This task, Blumenberg argues in Cassirer's spirit, originates in the perennial metaphysical questions that the human being has asked throughout the different ages. The constant, ideal, factor in the history of human thought

What Cassirer suggests here is, further, clearly a transcendental move: rather than to focus on what the different epochs pose as facts, the philosopher should take an interest in their subjective conditions of possibility. The goal of critical philosophy, he later proclaims, is to achieve the 'self-understanding of reason'.[29] Progress in our philosophical knowledge should not be measured quantitatively but methodologically: what the philosopher must strive for is, according to Cassirer, not a continuous growth of our knowledge, but a better delineation of what we can possibly know.[30]

For Cassirer, then, Kant's transcendental method marks a crucial contribution to the history of philosophy that informed all post-Kantian thinkers. In the third volume of *The Problem of Knowledge*, he discusses the thought of Jacobi, Reinhold, Aenesidem, Beck, Maimon, Fichte, Schelling, Hegel, Herbert, Schopenhauer, and Fries, and holds that, despite *prima facie* severe differences, they are all deeply indebted to this method. On the one hand, Cassirer even admits that the many disagreements between the different Neo-Kantian schools have become so profound by the beginning of the twentieth century that Kant's legacy seems to have dissolved in a number of dispersed and even contradictory ideas.[31] At the same time, however, he regards the dispersion of Kant's thought not as a sign of its decline, but as an indication of its success; it confirms his belief that the heart of transcendental philosophy lies not in a specific doctrine to which it adheres but in its multi-applicable method: "The result of the critique of reason cannot, as a finished product, be brought down to a number of dogma's. It is what it is only by means of the manner in which it was accomplished, and by means of the method upon which it is grounded".[32] Cassirer thus

---

lies, then, in the questions we pose and not in the progress among the answers that the different epochs have formulated in response to them. Consequently, these answers stand in a functional, rather than a substantial relation to each other (Blumenberg (1996), 35–8, 74–5, 79).

29 Cassirer (2000a), 1.

30 See Cassirer (2004a), 342 and Cassirer (1979a), 54. In *Einstein's Theory of Relativity* (1921), Cassirer defends a similar view of the history and task of science: "No single astronomical system, the Copernican as little as the Ptolemaic, can be taken as the expression of the 'true' cosmic order, but only the whole of these systems as they unfold continuously according to a definite connection. [The scientific] concepts are valid, not in that they copy a fixed, given being, but in so far as they contain a plan for possible constructions of unity, which must be progressively verified in practice, in application to the empirical material. But the instrument, that leads to the unity and thus to the truth of thought, must be in itself fixed and secure. If it did not possess a certain stability, no sure and permanent use of it would be possible; it would break at the first attempt and be resolved into nothing. We need, not the objectivity of absolute things, but rather the objective determinateness of the *method of experience*" (Cassirer (1953),,322).

31 Cassirer (2000a), 1.

32 Ibid., 2.

views the evident diversity among post-Kantian thinkers as a surface phenomenon of a single underlying method. In fact, he holds, this diversity should be applauded: "Despite their mutual conflicts, the many attempts to revive Kant's thought stand in a relation of ideal continuity with regard to each other. Together, they accomplish a task that none of them separately could entirely grasp".[33] The transcendental method, which consists in a 'direction of question-posing', allows for a manifold of applications, each of which confirms its validity and increases its value.

This functional definition of Kantianism serves Cassirer well in a number of ways. First, it allows him to regard (Neo-)Kantian philosophy an ongoing rather than a dead movement. Very different thinkers can, according to Cassirer, legitimately consider themselves to respect the spirit of Kant's writings, as long as they adhere to the transcendental method. As he puts it in the Davos debate, "the term 'neo-Kantianism' must be determined functionally rather than substantially. It is not a matter of the kind of philosophy as dogmatic doctrinal system; rather, it is a matter of a direction taken in question-posing".[34]

Second, Cassirer's formal characterization of transcendental philosophy can accommodate the fact that there have been, and still are, both realist *and* idealist continuations of Kant's thought; that there are inspiring epistemological *and* ontological readings of his work; and that, for example, both continental phenomenology *and* certain tendencies in analytic political philosophy are born from his insights. It also explains why the paradigm shifts in natural science, psychology, and neurobiology, may pose new challenges to the Neo-Kantian thinker, but do not designate the end of transcendental philosophy.[35] Kant's methodology transcends the domains and doctrines to which Kant or his successors have applied it, so that its value remains unimpaired by scientific revolutions.

---

33 Ibid.
34 Cassirer (1990), 274. See also Cassirer (2004c), 308: "The individual thinkers who belong to this movement differ from each other in their interpretation of the Kantian doctrine as well as in the results which they reach from the Kantian premises. But, notwithstanding differences of detail, there is a certain methodological principle common to all of them". In a funeral oration for Cohen, Cassirer further holds that his former teacher also always considered the 'Marburger Schule' as "held together not by connected results, but by a shared ideal direction of inquiring and questioning" (Cassirer (2004b), 290).
35 Cassirer (1999), 12. In the first volume of *The Problem of Knowledge* (*EP I* 12) and in 'Goethe und die mathematische Physik' (*ECW:9* 302), Cassirer opposes the at that time increasingly popular interpretation of Kant's philosophy that reduces it to a mere defense of Newtonian science. Moreover, in *Einstein's Theory of Relativity*, he defends the validity of the theory of relativity from a transcendental perspective.

Third, Cassirer's focus on the methodological novelty of Kant's philosophy allows him to extend its field of application to all human interests and their corresponding cultural domains:

> The problem of Kant is not bound to an inquiry into the special forms of logical, scientific, ethical, or aesthetical thought. Without varying its nature we may apply it to all other forms of thinking, judging, knowing, understanding, and even of feeling by which the human mind attempts to conceive the universe as a whole.[36]

Cassirer's philosophy of symbolic forms sets out to transcendentally ground the truth claims of such diverse meaning systems as language, myth, science, etc., while making use of the same, transcendental, method.

In sum, Cassirer aims to transcend the ongoing disputes about Kant's philosophy by emphasizing its task and method. In light of its task, Cassirer holds, this philosophy subscribes to the perennial quest for an accurate understanding of the relation between matter and form that constitutes the ideal continuity or functional unity of the entire history of thought. In light of its method, he later adds, it introduces a novel, transcendental, approach to this problem that in turn constitutes a functional unity between a variety of seemingly incommensurable Neo-Kantian positions. For the sake of contemporary philosophy, Cassirer finally suggests that we adapt this approach to a systematic investigation of the different domains of culture.[37] This is indeed the task that Cassirer takes up in his mature thought.

3 Cassirer's Systematic Writings (1923–1942): A Functional Definition of Culture

In the opening lines of *The Phenomenology of Knowledge* (1929), Cassirer announces a "return to the investigations with which I began my work in systematic philosophy two decades ago", but also immediately adds that "both in content and in method, the Philosophy of Symbolic Forms has gone beyond this initial formulation of the problem".[38] Indeed, Cassirer's mature philosophy draws out the consequences of the functional logic he established in *Substance and Function* within the framework of a philosophy of culture. The logical theory

---

36 Cassirer (1979), 70–71.
37 Cassirer (1999), 11.
38 Cassirer (1957), xiii.

that was initially meant to found scientific knowledge ("mathematical-physical objectivity") now serves the understanding of our scientific as well as our natural and mythical worldviews, and eventually our cultural world as a whole.

First, the symbols around which Cassirer's mature philosophy centers—space, time, number, causality, and self—correspond for the most part to the functional concepts that he lists in *Substance and Function*: "We can conceive members of series ordered according to equality or inequality, number and magnitude, spatial and temporal relations, or causal dependence".[39] Second, Cassirer repeats that it should be "the pure relation which governs the building of consciousness and which stands out in it as a genuine a priori, an essentially first factor".[40] Like the concept of function, the symbol expresses nothing but a rational relation between our sensations:

> Consciousness cannot devote itself in every moment with equal intensity to all the various sense impressions that fill it; it cannot represent them all with equal sharpness, concretion, and individuality. Thus it creates schemata, total images into which enter a number of particular contents, and in which they flow together without distinction. But these schemata can be no more than abbreviations, compendious condensations of the impressions. Where we wish to see sharply and exactly, these abbreviations must be thrust aside; the symbolic values must be replaced by 'real' values—that is, by actual sensations.[41]

Third, the meaning of both the functional relations and the symbols are consequently dependent on a certain intellectual perspective. In *Substance and Function*, Cassirer already stated that

> the similarity of certain elements can only be spoken of significantly when a certain 'point of view' has been established from which the elements can be designated as like or unlike [and which is] something distinctive and new as regards the compared contents themselves.[42]

In his mature philosophy, the idea of a 'point of view' and the varieties thereof becomes even more important. Cassirer now distinguishes the symbolic spheres of myth, language, art, religion, natural science, history, law, economics, technology, and politics, arguing that each of them sheds a particular light on the symbols that structure our perception of the world. While our sensations are al-

---

39 Cassirer (1953), 16.
40 Cassirer (1957), 203.
41 Ibid., 192–193.
42 Cassirer (1953), 25.

ways loaded with conceptual meaning, a specific "direction of vision"[43] in turn always determines this meaning prior to experience:

> If we designate the various kinds of relation—such as relation of space, time, causality, etc.—as R_1, R_2, R_3, we must assign to each one a special 'index of modality,' u_1, u_2, u_3, denoting the context of function and meaning in which it is to be taken. For each of these contexts, language as well as scientific cognition, art as well as myth, possesses its own constitutive principle that sets its stamp, as it were, on all the particular forms within it.[44]

Within a specific symbolic form, our understanding of the world is "guided by one and the same fundamental spiritual function",[45] but each form has its own function and thus ascribes a different meaning or 'modality' to the same symbols. There consequently is no one-on-one relationship between the functional relations among our perceptions and the point of view from which they are understood: all the symbols that Cassirer mentions—space, time, number, causality, self—occur within each symbolic form—myth, language, science, art, religion, etc. We can perceive a line, which is itself already a spatial construct (symbol), in very different and yet equally meaningful ways, depending on the cultural context (symbolic form): as a geometrical figure, a geographical border, an aesthetic ornament, a mythical dividing line between the profane and divine, or a religious symbol.[46] Likewise, causal relationships are constitutive of both the scientific and mythological worldview, even though these views promote a respective genetic and teleological conception of causality,[47] and even though they express universal laws in the former and magical inferences in the latter case.[48] "Here again", Cassirer holds, "it is not the concept of causality as such but the specific form of causal explanation which underlies the difference and contrast between the two spiritual worlds". These examples show that the decisive interpretative mark of the symbols stems from the cultural point of view in light of which we employ them at a given time:

---

43 Cassirer (1957), 138.
44 Cassirer (1955a), 97.
45 Cassirer (1957), 41.
46 Ibid., 202–204. In *Symbolic Forms and History*, John Michael Krois offers a similar overview of the different conceptions of time that we use in our daily lives: lived time ("as we normally conceived it", with changing rhythms), mythic thought time (in which "the ages of life—youth, maturity, and old age—are occupied like spaces"), scientific clock time (which "progresses constantly without any reference to human feelings"), calendar time ("which, unlike clock time, has a distinct beginning"), and the action time of technology ("in which things that would otherwise be inaccessible to us are made present"; Krois (1987), 204–205.
47 Cassirer (1955b), 20.
48 Ibid., 48.

> All cultural objectivity must be defined not thing-wise but functionally: this objectivity lies neither in a metaphysical nor an empirical-psychological 'reality' which stands behind it, but in what [each symbolic form] itself is and achieves, in the manner and form of *objectification* which it accomplishes.⁴⁹

The Phenomenology of Knowledge offers further insight in the relation between these points of view and the modalities of the symbols, when distinguishing between expressive, representational, and signifying functions that correspond to the forms of mythical thought, language, and science,⁵⁰ and *The Logic of the Cultural Sciences* contributes to this by introducing the 'characterizing functions' that are constitutive of the human or cultural sciences.⁵¹

On the basis of these different types of functions—which I cannot elaborate on here—the different symbolic forms shed "a light of their own" on the symbols and ascribe a particular "grammar" to the human world.⁵² As a result, the worlds of myth, art, science, etc., have little in common with each other. In fact, if each type of function "presupposes and applies entirely different standards and criteria",⁵³ their claims can only be measured on the basis of their own standards, but not assessed from another viewpoint: "None of these forms can simply be reduced to, or derived from, the others; each of them designates a particular approach, in which and through which they constitute their own aspect of 'reality'".⁵⁴ Moreover, Cassirer holds that each symbolic form lays an absolute claim to the world:

> In the course of its development every basic cultural form tends to represent itself not as a part but as the whole, laying claim to an absolute and not merely relative validity, not contenting itself with its special sphere, but seeking to imprint its own characteristic stamp on the whole realm of being and the whole life of the spirit. From this striving toward the absolute inherent in each special sphere arise the conflicts of culture and the antinomies within the concept of culture.⁵⁵

---

49 Ibid., 14; translation modified.
50 Cassirer (1957) 448–453; Cassirer (2004a), 260–261.
51 Cassirer (2000), 70–73.
52 Cassirer (1979b), 71–76.
53 Cassirer (1955a), 91.
54 Ibid., 78, 177; Cassirer (1945), 170.
55 Cassirer (1955a), 81, 82; Cassirer (1996), 224. In Cassirer (1979a), 61, Cassirer even adds that "without the claim to an independent, objective, and autonomous truth, not only philosophy, but also each particular field of knowledge, natural science as well as the humanities, would lose their stability and their sense".

The same questions that Cassirer raised earlier in a logical (*Substance and Function*) and a historical context (*The Problem of Knowledge*), now recur in the cultural context that interests him the most: how can we, given the irreducible manifold of our cultural domains, conceive of the unity of culture as a whole? How can we, *a fortiori*, reconcile the existence of this manifold with the absolute claims of the symbolic forms? We could assume that Cassirer's answer will once again follow the same, functional, logic. From the point of view of an encompassing philosophy of culture, the viewpoints of the symbolic forms after all appear as variables themselves, for which we must find a higher functional unity and interpretative point of view.

point of view point of view'				?					
function'				?					
point of view	myth	language	art	religion		science		politics	
function	space		time		number	causality			self
variables	x	x	x	x	x	x	x	x	x	x

Fig. 1: Rendering of the Order of Symbolic Forms, First Suggestion

The obvious candidate for the role of 'über-function' in Cassirer's thought is his idea of culture. For Cassirer, our cultural world has no substantial identity, no fixed content of its own, but only exists in the interplay between the heterogeneous symbolic forms that, each in their own way, attempt to explain the unity of our world:

> Upon closer scrutiny the fundamental postulate of unity [of being] is not discredited by this irreducible diversity of the methods and objects of knowledge [...] Instead, a new task arises: to gather the various branches of science with their diverse methodologies—with all their recognized specificity and independence—into one system, whose separate parts precisely through their necessary diversity will complement and further one another. This postulate of *a purely functional unity* replaces the postulate of a unity of substance and origin, which lay at the core of the ancient concept of being. [...] Instead of dogmatic metaphysics, which seeks absolute unity in a substance to which all the particulars of existence are reducible, such a philosophical critique seeks after a rule governing the concrete diversity of

the functions of cognition, a rule which, without negating and destroying them, will gather them into *a unity of deed*, the unity of a self-contained human endeavor.[56]

This unity of deed—or unity of 'work', as Cassirer calls it in *The Metaphysics of Symbolic Forms* (ca. 1940)—is that of human culture as a whole. The ideal continuity between the different symbolic forms lies, then, like the continuity between the different philosophical epochs, in the shared task of all cultural domains to grasp the relation between the universal and particular in a meaningful way: "The various forms of human culture are not held together by an identity in their nature but by a conformity in their fundamental task".[57]

However, Cassirer's talk of 'human deed', 'endeavor', or 'task' suggests a second candidate for the role of functional unity between the different symbolic forms, namely human consciousness:

> With all their inner diversity, the various products of culture—language, scientific knowledge, myth, art, religion—[are] multiple efforts, all directed toward the one goal of transforming the passive world of *impressions*, in which the spirit seems at first imprisoned, into a world that is pure *expression* of the human spirit.[58]

Although Cassirer's writings often refer to human consciousness as the seat of all symbolic formation, he almost never thematizes it. Even *An Essay on Man* (1945) mainly engages in an overview of the different symbolic forms and rather briefly addresses the issue of human subjectivity explicitly. The reason for this is that, for Cassirer, just as we cannot perceive an 'object in itself', we cannot perceive a 'subject in itself' either: "However deeply we may penetrate into the formations of the sensuous-spiritual consciousness, we never find this consciousness absolutely objectless, as something absolutely simple, prior to all sensations and distinctions".[59] Instead, Cassirer holds, we must approach "the question of the structure of the perceptive, intuitive, and cognitive modes of consciousness [...] by means of reconstructive analysis" starting from the problems of cultural

---

56 Cassirer (1955a), 77; my emphasis. See also Cassirer (1945), 228: "Philosophy cannot give up its search for a fundamental unity in the ideal world. But it does not confound this unity with simplicity. It does not overlook the tensions and frictions, the strong contrasts and deep conflicts between the various powers of man. These cannot be reduced to a common denominator. They tend in different directions and obey different principles. But this multiplicity and disparateness does not denote discord or disharmony. All these functions complete and complement each other. Each one opens a new horizon and shows us a new aspect of humanity".
57 Cassirer (1945), 223.
58 Cassirer (1955a), 80–81.
59 Cassirer (1957), 97.

life "to find our way back to their elementary presuppositions, the conditions of their possibility".[60] In other words, all that we can know about human consciousness we must gather from a transcendental investigation of our cultural accomplishments: "The content of the spirit is disclosed only in its manifestations; the ideal form is known only by and in the aggregate of the sensible signs which it uses for its expression".

Accordingly, for Cassirer, human subjectivity can only be understood as the unity of the rational capacities that constitute different worldviews: "We take subjectivity as a totality of functions, out of which the phenomenon of a world and its determinate order of meaning is actually built up for us".[61] This unity, he specifies in *An Essay on Man*, is not grounded in an identical substance, but must be understood as a functional continuity:

> The philosophy of symbolic forms starts from the position that, if there is any definition of the nature or 'essence' of man, this definition can only be understood as a functional, not a substantial one. We cannot define man by an inherent principle that constitutes his metaphysical essence—nor can we define him by an inborn faculty or instinct that may be ascertained by empirical observation. Man's outstanding characteristic, his distinguishing mark, is not his metaphysical or physical nature—but his work. It is this work, it is the system of human activities, which defines and determines the circle of 'humanity'.[62]

On this ground, Cassirer also substitutes the traditional definition of the human being as *animal rationale* for the original title of *animal symbolicum* (*EM* 26). He holds that "reason is a very inadequate term with which to comprehend the forms of man's cultural life in all their richness and variety": it does no justice to the diversity of our experience, and it may suggest a substantial substratum as the essence of human being. Cassirer's idea of the symbol, in contrast, refers to the variable and essentially interactive and co-constitutive relationship of the human being with its surroundings.

Whether one locates the functional unity of the symbolic forms in our cultural world ('objectivity') or in the *animal symbolicum* ('subjectivity'), depends on one's (current) philosophical interest and perspective. This viewpoint, Cassirer holds in *The Metaphysics of the Symbolic Forms* (ca. 1928), is generically different from that of the symbolic forms: "Philosophical knowledge [...] does not cre-

---

60 Ibid., 57.
61 Cassirer (1996), 50.
62 Cassirer (1945), 67–68, 222; see also Cassirer (2007), 313: "The term 'Geist' is correct; but we must not use it as a name of a substance—a thing [...] We should use it in a functional sense as a comprehensive name for all those functions which constitute and build up the world of human culture".

ate a principally new symbol form, it does not found in this sense a new creative modality—but it grasps the earlier modalities as that which they are: as characteristic symbolic forms".[63] More specifically, the nature and task of philosophy is, according to Cassirer, to enhance "the self-knowledge of reason" through "both criticism and fulfillment of the symbolic forms".[64]

Philosophy can criticize the symbolic forms by countering their absolutizing tendencies: "it grasps these forms as the active intellectual construction of reality, not as directed toward some external 'Absolute'". On this basis, it can point out the one-sidedness of our cultural domains: "We must strive to comprehend every symbol in its place and recognize how it is limited and conditioned by every other symbol".[65] In the first volume of *The Philosophy of Symbolic Forms*, Cassirer calls this a 'highly significant insight' of critical philosophy:

> With this critical insight, science renounces its aspiration and its claim to an 'immediate' grasp and communication of reality. It realizes that the only objectification of which it is capable is, and must remain, mediation. And in this insight, another highly significant idealistic consequence is implicit. [...] We are forced to conclude that a variety of media will correspond to various structures of the object, to various meanings for 'objective' relations.[66]

Further, once we acknowledge the relative character of the cultural domains, we can attempt to establish their mutual harmony. In this way, philosophy can also 'fulfill' the symbolic forms by placing them in the larger context of a cultural world that is much richer than the one they could account for on their own. From the internal, limited, perspective of science or religion, the cultural domains necessarily compete with each other for the title of most accurate explanation of the world. From the detached perspective of Cassirer's transcendental philosophy of culture, on the other hand, they offer equally valid human *worldviews* that together constitute our culture as a whole:

> In the boundless multiplicity and variety of mythical images, of religious dogmas, of linguistic forms, of works of art, philosophic thought reveals the unity of a general function by which all these creations are held together. Myth, religion, art, language, even science,

---

[63] Cassirer (1996), 226; Cassirer (2009a), xiii.
[64] Cassirer (1996), 226. One should recall at this point that Cassirer in the first volume of *The Problem of Knowledge* also already called the 'self-understanding of reason' the goal of critical philosophy (Cassirer (1999), 1).
[65] Cassirer (1996), 227. See also Cassirer (1953), 447: "Each particular form [must] be 'relativized' with regard to the others, but [...] this 'relativization' is throughout reciprocal and [...] no single form but only the systematic totality can serve as the expression of 'truth' and 'reality'".
[66] Cassirer (1955a), 76.

are now looked upon as so many variations on a common theme—and it is the task of philosophy to make this theme audible and understandable.[67]

For Cassirer, then, philosophy is the ultimate or 'highest' human viewpoint, in so far as it seeks for a unity between the symbolic forms that does not compromise their mutual differences.

point of view'	philosophy								
function'	culture / symbolic consciousness								
point of view	myth	language		art	religion		science		politics
function	space		time		number		causality		self
variables	x	x	x	x	x	x	x	x	x

Fig. 2: Philosophy as Highest Viewpoint

4 Cassirer's Ethical Writings (1935–1946): The Normative Task of Philosophy

In his late writings, Cassirer increasingly emphasizes the import of maintaining harmony between the symbolic forms: to neglect either the diversity or unity of our cultural life, he argues, can have severe ethical or existential consequences.

On the one hand, an exaggerated dominance of one of the symbolic forms over the others would not only lead to a one-sided, but possibly also to an inhumane worldview. In *Form und Technik* (1930), Cassirer warns that a culture that reduces all meaning to what is considered meaningful from a technological viewpoint would inevitably violate certain human rights.[68] A similar but subtler problem arises when the difference between certain symbolic forms becomes blurred. Cassirer's famous example of the merging of two cultural domains is

---

67 Cassirer (1945), 71. Luft also characterizes the philosopher as a "disinterested and uninvested observer", in contrast to, for example, the religious or scientific attitude (Luft (2004), 36). About the 'Sonderstatus' of philosophical reflection, I further recommend Kreis (2009), 459–475; and Ulrich (2012), 297–319.
68 See Cassirer, (2004e), 139–183.

that of the Nazi ideology that he discusses in *The Myth of the State* (1946).⁶⁹ This ideology, he explains, efficiently but illegitimately merged mythological and political discourses, the tragic results of which are well known. In today's Western society, we can discern the same phenomenon in the emergence of technocracies, which tend to erase the distinction between economics and politics. Such 'antinomies of culture',⁷⁰ Cassirer emphasizes more and more toward the end of his life, are not just a philosophical, but also an ethical issue: "Without intellectual and moral courage, philosophy could not fulfill its task in man's cultural and social life".⁷¹

On the other hand, exclusive attention to the differences between the symbolic forms would lead to an equally undesirable situation. In fact, Cassirer identifies the neglect of their ideal connection with each other through the *animal symbolicum* as the cause of the general crisis of culture that haunted Europe at the beginning of the twentieth century. In *An Essay on Man*, he holds that previous ages have always been marked by "a general orientation, a frame of reference, to which all individual differences might be referred".⁷² The symbolic forms of myth, religion, and science have consecutively dominated our culture, taking up the role of the highest viewpoint on the human world.⁷³ In the twentieth century, however, such dominant perspective has disappeared:

> An established authority to which one might appeal no longer existed. Theologians, scientists, politicians, sociologists, biologists, psychologists, ethnologists, economists all approached the problem from their own viewpoints. To combine or unify all these particular aspects and perspectives was impossible.⁷⁴

---

69 Cassirer (2009b).
70 Cassirer (1955a), 81.
71 Cassirer (2009b), 296. The fact that Cassirer never acknowledges a symbolic form of ethics suggests, moreover, that this ethical character is not a late addition, but actually an intrinsic feature of his conception of philosophy. In Kreis (2010), Kreis explains that there is no place for ethics as a distinct symbolic form in Cassirer's philosophy of culture since the role that it would have is already taken up by, on the one hand, the symbolic form of law (cf. Cassirer (1939),) and, on the other hand, philosophy, in so far as it secures the ethical development and self image of each form and the subject as whole (Kreis, (201), 361–4). Freudenthal (2008), 190 and Recki (1997), 67, 72–8, confirm the ethical character of Cassirer's philosophy as a whole, thus countering Krois' in my view less successful argumentation for ethics as a separate symbolic form (Krois (1987), 142–171).
72 Cassirer (1945), 21.
73 See Orth, (2004), 71: "*Kultur wird bestimmt je nach dem Akzent, den eine grade führende Einzelwissenschaft oder eine speziell orientierte philosophische Richtung [setzt]*".
74 Cassirer (1945), 21.

Paradoxically, Cassirer explains, as the various cultural domains developed and gained more and more independence, we lost sight of their original, shared, task. As a consequence, the human being became lost amidst what seems to be a mere manifold of conflicting viewpoints, facing a "crisis in man's knowledge of himself":

> No former age was ever in such a favorable position with regard to the sources of knowledge of human nature. Psychology, ethnology, anthropology, and history have amassed an astoundingly rich and constantly increasing body of facts. Our technical instruments for observation and experimentation have been immensely improved, and our analyses have become sharper and more penetrating. We appear, nevertheless, not yet to have found a method for mastery and organization of this material. When compared with our own abundance the past may seem very poor. But our wealth of facts is not necessarily a wealth of thoughts. Unless we succeed in finding a clue of Ariadne to lead us out of this labyrinth, we can have no real insight into the general character of human culture; we shall remain lost in a mass of disconnected and disintegrated data that seem to lack all conceptual unity.[75]

We already know from his systematic writings that, according to Cassirer, this conceptual or ideal unity is rooted in the human being conceived as 'animal symbolicum'. Furthermore, we know that it requires critical philosophy to grasp this unity: only the detached perspective of philosophy allows us to recognize not just the substantially incommensurable claims of the symbolic forms but also their shared function and, on that basis, their potential harmonious coexistence. In his late works, Cassirer ascribes an existential weight to this insight: "In our time, it is not only a general methodological demand, but a general cultural fate that couples philosophy with the special disciplines of knowledge, and which binds them closely to each other".[76] As Cassirer sees it, in order for us to once again be able to orient ourselves amidst the variety of symbolic forms, we need the encompassing perspective of a critical philosophy that offers us a coherent account of both ourselves and our cultural world as a whole.

In conclusion, Cassirer's philosophy of culture has an ethical task in so far as it is capable of deconstructing ideologies like Nazism. It has existential import, further, because it can establish the human being's central place in its diversified world, lending us a sense of orientation and our world a sense of unity. Cassirer's 'clue of Ariadne' for holding these matters together is usually taken to be his symbol concept. I hold however, that it is more accurately identified as his idea of a functional unity. This idea structures and connects each phase of Cas-

---

75 Ibid., 22.
76 Cassirer (1979a), 61.

sirer's thought, and ultimately gives way to his ethically charged conception of philosophy.

point of view'		ethics							
function'		culture / symbolic consciousness							
point of view	myth	language		art	religion	science		politics	
function	space		time		number	causality			self
variables	x	x	x	x	x	x	x	x	x	x

Fig. 3: Rendering of the Order of Symbolic Forms, Second Suggestion

Bibliography

Bast (2000): Rainer A. Bast, Problem, Geschichte, Form. Das Verhältnis von Philosophie und Geschichte bei Ernst Cassirer im historischen Kontex,. Berlin: Dunker & Humblot.

Blumenberg (1996): Hans Blumenberg, *Die Legitimität der Neuzeit*, Frankfurt am Main: Suhrkamp.

Cassirer (1939): Ernst Cassirer, *Axel Hägerström: Eine Studie zur Schwedischen Philosophie der Gegenwart*, in: Göteborgs Högskolas Arsskrift 45, 1–119.

Cassirer (1945): Ernst Cassirer, *An Essay on Man*, New Haven: Yale UP.Cassirer (1953): Ernst Cassirer, Substance and Function, William C. Swabey and Marie C. Swabey (trans.), New York: Dover.

Cassirer (1955a): Ernst Cassirer, *The Philosophy of Symbolic Forms*, Volume One: Language, Ralph Manheim (trans.), New Haven: Yale University Press.

Cassirer (1955b): Ernst Cassirer, *The Philosophy of Symbolic Forms*, Volume Two: Mythical Thought, Ralph Manheim (trans.), New Haven: Yale University Press.

Cassirer (1957): Ernst Cassirer, *The Philosophy of Symbolic Forms*, Volume Three: The Phenomenology of Knowledge, Ralph Manheim (trans.), New Haven: Yale University Press.

Cassirer (1979a 1935): Ernst Cassirer, *The Concept of Philosophy as a Philosophical Problem*, in: *Symbol, Myth, and Culture: Essays and Lectures of Ernst Cassirer 1935–1945*, Donald Phillip Verene (ed.), New Haven: Yale UP.

Cassirer (1979b 1936): Ernst Cassirer, *Critical Idealism as Philosophy of Culture*, in: Symbol, Myth, and Culture, op. cit..

Cassirer (1990 1929): Ernst Cassirer, *Davos Disputation between Ernst Cassirer and Martin Heidegger*, in: *Martin Heidegger, Kant and the Problem of Metaphysics.*, Richard Taft (trans.), Indianapolis: Indiana UP.

Cassirer (1996): Ernst Cassirer, *Philosophy of Symbolic Forms*, Volume Four: The Metaphysics of Symbolic Forms, J.M. Krois/D. P. Verene (eds.), New Haven: Yale University Press.

Cassirer (1999 1906): Ernst Cassirer, *Das Erkenntnisproblem in der Philosophie und Wissenschaft der neueren Zeit*; Erster Band, in: *Gesammelte Werke* (henceforth: ECW), vol. 2, Hamburg: Meiner Verlag.
Cassirer (2000a 1919): Ernst Cassirer, *Das Erkenntnisproblem in der Philosophie und Wissenschaft der neueren Zeit*; Dritter Band: *Die nachkantischen Systeme*, in: *ECW*, vol. 4, op. cit.
Cassirer (2000b 1942): Ernst Cassirer, *The Logic of the Cultural Sciences.*, Stephen G. Lofts (ed.), New Haven: Yale UP.
Cassirer (2001a 1914): Ernst Cassirer, *Charles Renouvier, Essais de critique générale*, in: ECW, vol. 9, op. cit.,.
Cassirer (2001b 1921/1924): Ernst Cassirer, *Goethe und die mathematische Physik. Eine erkenntnistheoretische Betrachtung*, in: ECW, vol. 9, op. cit.
Cassirer (2004a 1927): Ernst Cassirer, *Das Symbolproblem und seine Stellung im System der Philosophie*, in: ECW, vol. 17, op. cit.
Cassirer (2004b 1928): Ernst Cassirer, *Beiträge zu: Hermann Cohen; Schriften zur Philosophie und Zeitgeschichte*, in: ECW, vol. 17, op. cit.
Cassirer (2004c 1929): Ernst Cassirer, *Beiträge für die Encyclopedia Britannica*, in: ECW, vol. 17, op. cit.
Cassirer (2004d 1929): Ernst Cassirer, *Formen und Formwandlungen des philosophischen Wahrheitsbegriffs*, in: ECW, vol. 17, op. cit.
Cassirer (2004e 1930): Ernst Cassirer, *Form und Technik*, in: ECW, vol. 17, op. cit.
Cassirer (2007 1945): Ernst Cassirer, *Structuralism in Modern Linguistics*, in: ECW, vol. 24), op. cit.
Cassirer (2009a 1932): Ernst Cassirer, *The Philosophy of the Enlightenment*, Fritz C.A. Koelln and James P. Pettegrove (trans.), Princeton/Oxford: Princeton UP.
Cassirer (2009b): Ernst Cassirer, *The Myth of the State*, New Haven: Yale UP.
Freudenthal (2008): Gideon Freudenthal, *The Hero of Enlightenment*, in: Jeffrey Andrew Barash (ed.), *The Symbolic Construction of Reality: The Legacy of Ernst Cassirer*, Chicago: The University Press of Chicago, 189–213.
Gordon (2005): Peter Eli Gordon, *Myth and Modernity: Cassirer's Critique of Heidegger*, in: New German Critique 94, Secularization and Disenchantment, 127–168.
Heymans (1928): Gerard Heymans, *Zur Cassirerschen Reform der Begriffslehre*, in: Kant-Studien 33 (No. 1–2), 109–128.
Hönigswald (1912): Richard Höningswald, *Substanzbegriff und Funktionsbegriff: Kritische Betrachtungen zu Ernst Cassirers gleichnahmigen Werk*, in: Deutsche Literaturzeitung 33, 2821–2843.
Kreis (2010): Guido Kreis, *Cassirer und die Formen des Geistes*, Berlin: Suhrkamp.
Krois (1987): John Michael Krois, Cassirer: *Symbolic Forms and History*, New Haven: Yale UP.
Luft (2004): Sebastian Luft, *Cassirer's Philosophy of Symbolic Forms: Between Reason and Relativism; a Critical Appraisal*, in: Idealistic Studies 34 (No. 1), 25–47.
Orth (2004): Ernst Wolfgang Orth, *Von der Erkenntnistheorie zur Kulturphilosophie, Studien zu Ernst Cassirers Philosophie der symbolischen Formen*, Würzburg: Verlag Königshausen und Neumann.
Plümacher (2004): Martina Plümacher, *Wahrnehmung, Repräsentation und Wissen: Edmund Husserls und Ernst Cassirers Analysen zur Struktur des Bewusstseins*, Berlin: Parerga Verlag, 2004.

Recki (1997): Birgit Recki, *Kultur ohne Moral? Warum Ernst Cassirer trotz der Einsicht in den Primat der praktsichen Vernunft keine Ethik schreiben konnte*, in: *Kultur und Philosophie: Ernst Cassirers Werk und Wirkung*. Dorothea Frede und Reinold Schmücker (eds.), Darmstadt: Wissenschaftliche Buchgesellschaft, 58–78.

Ulrich (2012): Sebastian Ulrich, *Der Status der 'philosophischen Erkenntnis' in Ernst Cassirers 'Metaphysik des Symbolischen'*, in: Birgit Recki (ed.) Philosophie der Kultur—Kultur des Philosophierens: Ernst Cassirer im 20. und 21. Jahrhundert. Hamburg: Meiner Verlag, 297–319.

Guido Kreis (Bonn)
The Varieties of Perception
Non-Conceptual Content in Kant, Cassirer, and McDowell

There is a distinctive Kantian approach to perception that involves a commitment to a specific kind of conceptualism. Philosophers in the Kantian tradition typically argue that the application of concepts of some sort is a necessary condition for having a perception, in the sense that these concepts are necessarily required already in the very act of perceiving. It is not clear, however, whether this claim inevitably entails the further, and more radical, claim that the representational content of a perception is itself conceptual—or, more precisely, propositional. In what follows, I argue that although a Kantian approach to perception is committed to conceptualism in some sense, it is not committed, and indeed must not commit itself, to the claim that all perceptual content is propositional. In order to defend this line of argument, I shall have a closer look at four different stages of classical and contemporary Kantian philosophy of perception. I begin by discussing some main aspects of Kant's initial account of intuition in the *Critique of Pure Reason* (1). I will then introduce John McDowell's claim that all perceptions have propositional content, which he actually shares with the early philosophy of Ernst Cassirer (2). But this account of perception is far too narrow, and has to be emended by means of two revisions. The first is due to McDowell's own acknowledgment, expressed in his more recent writings, that the content of perception is in at least one important sense non-conceptual and hence non-propositional (3). The second revision is due to Cassirer's highly original account in his *Philosophy of Symbolic Forms* of the plurality of different kinds of perception. It provides, as I will argue, the most compelling solution to the puzzles of conceptuality and non-conceptuality of perception in the Kantian tradition (4).

1 Avoiding the Myth of the Given: Kant

In the introduction to his *Critique of Pure Reason*, Kant uses a well-known metaphor to illustrate one of the guiding principles of his transcendental epistemology. He says that "there are two stems of human cognition, which may perhaps arise from a common but to us unknown root, namely sensibility and understanding, through the first of which objects are given to us, but through the second of which they are thought".[1] Kant uses the metaphor of the two stems to illustrate a philosophical thought. Human cognition contains occurrences (representations or *Vorstellungen*) of two generically different kinds: those which have been *made by* the human mind, on the one hand, and those which have been *given to* the mind, on the other. One of the points Kant wants to make here is that the representational content of occurrences of the one kind cannot possibly be reduced to the representational content of the occurrences of the other, contrary to how proponents of both the empiricist and the rationalist tradition would have it. For classical empiricists like Locke or Hume the content of conceptual representations can be traced back, at least in principle, without loss to the representational content of our sensual impressions, from which the content of our concepts and ideas is derived by modes of intellectual reflection and abstraction. By contrast, rationalists like Leibniz or Wolff used to treat sensual representations as a subspecies of conceptual representations, claiming that the content of a perception is nothing else but the content of an unclear and indistinct concept.

Contrary to any reductionism of these sorts, Kant insists on the mutual irreducibility of the contents of sensual and conceptual representations. His main point here is a 'logical' one, in the sense that he wants to point out two different *necessary conditions* of empirical knowledge. For our empirical judgments to be instances of empirical knowledge, it is a necessary condition that they contain conceptual representations which have been *made by* the thinker, on the one hand, and it is just as much a necessary condition that they contain intuitive representations that have been *given to* the thinker, on the other. The latter of these conditions is the crucial one for Kant's theory of perception. What is particularly interesting here is that he reinvents the empiricist notion of the given within the methodological context of a 'logical' (or 'transcendental') analysis of necessary conditions of experience. Our contemporary debates over perception have somehow lost this strong connection between the idea of givenness and the idea of necessary conditions of experience. I shall come back to this at the end of my paper.

Nevertheless, Kant's metaphor of the two stems is somewhat risky. It might invite us to view the sensible and the conceptual in the manner of two isolated layers of the human mind. The first layer would contain given sensations, and the second would consist of conceptual activities operating *on* these sensations. Empiricists for example typically claim that there is a basic layer of the human mind containing immediate sense data, and an additional 'upper' layer where

---

[1] Kant (1998), A 15/B 29.

the more mediated conceptual work is done. This dual layer view is frequently combined with a foundationalist account in which the supposed ground layer is claimed to function as an ultimate justificatory basis for our empirical beliefs and judgments. The difficulties with this picture have been revealed in the logical positivists' debate about protocol sentences. In the layer conception, sense data are claimed to have non-conceptual content. But at the same time they are said to have the rational force to count as reasons for empirical beliefs, which in turn requires that they have an essentially predicative and hence conceptual structure. This pair of mutually inconsistent claims about sense data— that they are both conceptual and non-conceptual—is a form of what Wilfrid Sellars famously called 'the myth of the given'.[2]

But Kant's metaphor of the two stems neither expresses a dualistic layer conception of the human mind, nor can it be blamed for falling back into a mythical account of the given. Admittedly, the metaphor *does* suggest that the faculties of sensibility and understanding, and their respective representations, can (and even ought to) be investigated separately in philosophical inquiry. But at the same time, it is one of Kant's main concerns to emphasize the merely *methodological* character of this operation. At the beginning of his analysis of sensibility, Kant points out that in "the transcendental aesthetic we will therefore first isolate sensibility by separating off everything that the understanding thinks through its concepts, so that nothing but empirical intuition remains".[3] And he gives a complementary characterization of his method at the beginning of his analysis of the understanding: "In a transcendental logic we isolate the understanding (as we did above with sensibility in the transcendental aesthetic)".[4] The *methodological* isolation of sensibility and understanding, being the result of transcendental reflection,[5] does *not* entail any acknowledgement of real isolation of intuition and concepts. Quite the contrary, intuition and concepts always already work together in experience. This is what Kant claims in one of the most frequently quoted passages from the *Critique*:

---

[2] Compare Sellars (1997), 68–69: "One of the forms taken by the Myth of the Given is the idea that there is, indeed *must be*, a structure of particular matter of fact such that (a) each fact can not only be noninferentially known to be the case, but presupposes no other knowledge either of particular matter of fact, or of general truths; and (b) such that the noninferential knowledge of facts belonging to this structure constitutes the ultimate court of appeals for all factual claims— particular and general—about the world".
[3] Kant (1998), A 22/B 36.
[4] Ibid., A 62/B 87.
[5] Cf. ibid., A 260–8/B 316–24.

> Without sensibility no object would be given to us, and without understanding none would be thought. Thoughts without content are empty, intuitions without concepts are blind. It is just as necessary to make one's concepts sensible (i.e., to add an object to them in intuition) as it is to make one's intuitions understandable (i.e., to bring them under concepts).[6]

This idea of an interwoveness of intuitions and concepts in experience makes it clear that Kant does not advocate a dualistic conception of the mind in which intuitions and concepts would belong to two radically isolated layers. But the very idea of interwoveness in turn seems to raise a new, and even more intricate, worry. If the deliverances of the senses are always already embedded in the exercise of conceptual capacities, it is not at all clear how Kant could do justice to his initial anti-rationalist motive that the representational content of intuitions cannot possibly be reduced to the representational content of concepts, since it now seems natural to suppose that the former is in one way or other 'shaped' or even determined by the latter. Moreover, and more radically, the very idea of givenness itself, initially introduced as a necessary transcendental condition of empirical judgments, seems to be in danger of being entirely empty. So Kant's idea of an interwoveness of intuitions and concepts in experience naturally leads us to the following two questions:

(*a*) Is the application of concepts (the exercise of conceptual capacities) a necessary condition for having a perception or an intuition?

(*b*) Do perceptions or intuitions have conceptual content?

The 'interwoveness'-passage quoted above (A 51/B 75) seems to suggest positive answers to both questions. If intuitions really do need concepts in order not to be blind, then it might seem inevitable that the exercise of conceptual capacities is a necessary condition for having an intuition, and also that the latter *therefore* has conceptual content.

But on closer inspection, neither of these conclusions is necessitated by what Kant is saying *here*, since the claim that intuitions without concepts are blind apparently *does* leave open the possibility of there being intuitions without concepts—*blind* intuitions, to be sure. An obvious candidate for intuitions of this kind would be what Kant calls "obscure representations" in his *Anthropology*, characterizing them as "representations that we have without being conscious of them".[7] Obscure intuitions—representations which we *unconsciously* entertain—do not presuppose the application of either pure or empirical concepts. And although they would necessarily have to be blind intuitions, one might

---

[6] Ibid., A 51/B 75 (translation modified).
[7] Kant (2006), 23–26. For a detailed discussion of blind intuitions, see Grüne (2009).

very well try to grant them a constitutive role in the whole of Kant's theory of experience. One might point out that for Kant, after all, the very function of an intuition *is* "to present us with particulars".[8] Similarly, it has been argued that intuitions play the elementary semantic role of fixing the references of our empirical judgment's singular terms.[9] The idea is here that singular judgments form the basic propositional elements of experience. But in order for them to count as *empirical* judgments, the argument goes, they necessarily presuppose an essentially non-propositional (and pre-predicative) *acquaintance* with spatio-temporal particulars *by help of which* the reference of our empirical judgment's singular terms is *fixed*. Blind representations might then be exactly those elements of the human mind in which this basic semantic function is actually fulfilled. Or else one might try to conceive of a blind intuition as a "veridical intuitional cognition without concepts" in the sense of an informational state of the human mind, allowing us to acknowledge mental states of this kind even in non-rational animals.[10] It is far from clear, though, how one could successfully avoid a fallback into the myth of the given on any of these lines. This is particularly pressing with those interpretations that try to ascribe to blind intuitions in themselves an immediate justificatory force for empirical and practical beliefs. Robert Hanna for instance has somewhat darkly referred to blind intuitions as delivering "the body's own reasons"[11]—an interpretation of Kant that, in his own words, "explicitly deflects and trumps The Myth of the Given".[12]

There are not very many passages in the *Critique of Pure Reason* that might support a reading of that sort, but there are some. There are altogether three passages, to be found in one single paragraph, in which Kant seems to be explicitly subscribing to the claim that intuitions do not necessarily require the categories: "objects can indeed appear to us without necessarily having to be related to functions of the understanding" (A 89/B 122); "appearances can certainly be given in intuition without functions of the understanding" (A 90/B 122); "intuition by no means requires the functions of thinking" (A 91/B 123). Any *non-conceptual* (in the sense of *non-categorical*) interpretation of Kantian intuitions will have to rely on these passages. But it is far from clear that they can really yield the desired textual support. It is essential to take into account the specific dia-

---

8 Allais (2009), 384, cf. 405–409.
9 Rohs (2001).
10 Cf. Hanna (2005), 99, with reference to Evans (1982), chapters 2–7 (cf. Hanna (2005), 85–86). Evans' doctrine of informational states is the target of Lecture III in McDowell (1996).
11 Hanna (2011), 327.
12 Hanna (2014), supplement.

lectical situation of Kant's argument here. The passages in question appear in the first section of the transcendental deduction of the categories, which, according to Kant, is "the explanation of the way in which concepts can relate to objects *a priori*" (A 85/B 117). The deduction is thus designed to show that intuitions, being the sort of representations in which objects show up for us, are dependent on the application of categories. Now it seems natural to suppose that in the first section, when Kant tries to establish the very idea of this kind of deduction, the categories cannot be taken as necessary conditions of intuitions without begging the question: Kant cannot take for granted as a starting point for the transcendental deduction a claim that appears to be its conclusion. Hence, he is dialectically obliged to assume the opposite claim that intuition by no means requires the functions of thinking, which, after all, seems to be exactly how common sense would have it here in any event. But then again, the result of the transcendental deduction shows that this common sense belief is simply wrong. What the deduction demonstrates is that it is *not* the case that intuition by no means requires the functions of thinking.

Quite the contrary: according to Kant, the exercise of the categories is both a necessary and sufficient condition of (the unity of) intuitions. This is explicitly stated in another famous passage from the *Critique*:

> The same function that gives unity to the different representations *in a judgment* also gives unity to the mere synthesis of representations *in an intuition*, which, expressed generally, is the pure concept of understanding.[13]

What Kant here says is that the categories are responsible not only for the unity of judgments, but also for the unity of intuitions. But on that account it is impossible for us to have an intuition without at the same time applying categories. In light of this claim from the 'metaphysical' deduction (which receives its appropriate justification only in the transcendental deduction), we can now see more clearly that the thought that blind intuitions might play a constitutive role in human experience is indeed an empty thought for Kant. It is impossible that blind intuitions (obscure representations that we have without being conscious of them) could ever exhibit that very unity of consciousness which is necessarily required for any representation *in order to count as an element of the human mind at all*: "something would be represented in me that could not be thought at all, which is as much as to say that the representation"—in this case—"would be nothing for me".[14] Blind intuitions as such cannot in principle

---

13 Kant (1998), A 79/B 104–105.
14 Ibid., B 132.

belong to the human mind at all. Hence, whatever and wherever they may be, they could never in principle perform any positive cognitive function in the human mind.[15]

Kant's answer to the first of the above mentioned questions is hence positive: the application of the categories is a necessary condition for having an intuition. With regard to the second question, though, this answer can be interpreted in quite different ways. A natural reading of the 'same function'-passage at A 79/B 104–105 would be that the unity of an intuition is effected by the categorical unity of concepts *in a judgment*. This in turn would strongly support the claim that the representational content of an intuition is conceptual, and hence suggest a positive answer to the second question. This is essentially the account of perception and intuition that Ernst Cassirer in his early writings, particularly in *Substance and Function*, and John McDowell in his lectures on *Mind and World* have tried to draw from the *Critique of Pure Reason*. But this is, as we shall see in more detail in the following sections, not the only possible, and not even the most conclusive, reading of the passage in question.

But on any reading, the *given* Kant is talking about is always already embedded in the conceptual context of empirical judgments (and, as we might add, their linguistic expressions). It is true for Kant that intuitions stand in *causal relations* to the environment of the observer, but it is their being embedded in conceptual and linguistic structures that *also* gives them the *rational force* to count as reasons for empirical beliefs. The myth of the given does not even arise on that account. Kant does not want to get rid of the given in general; he wants to get rid of the inconsistent, 'mythical' version of it. And this is why his account of intuitions has become so interesting for both Cassirer and McDowell. It remains to be seen, though, whether this broadly 'Kantian' line of reasoning about perception and intuition can still give sufficient weight to the initial sense of the idea of giv-

---

[15] At this point one might try to draw on Kant's distinction between *intuitions* and *perceptions*: whereas the application of categories is a necessary condition for having the former, this might not be the case for having the latter (the idea would then be that in contrast to intuitions, perceptions occur on a *proto*-propositional level of experience). But this is not so. In a careful analysis of the relevant passages from the A-deduction Christian Wenzel (2006), 417–426, has shown that for Kant even perceptions (and, following the argument of the deduction, representations of just *any* kind) presuppose the application of categories, or else they could not count as elements of the human mind at all. Cf. in particular Kant (1998), A 115: "On them [viz., the categories] is grounded, therefore, all formal unity in the synthesis of the imagination, and by means of the latter also all of its empirical use (in recognition, reproduction, association, and apprehension) down to the appearances, since the latter belong to our consciousness at all and hence to ourselves only by means of these elements of cognition".

enness: the one that was at work when givenness had been introduced as a necessary transcendental condition of empirical judgments.

2 Perceptions Have Conceptual Content: Cassirer (I) and McDowell (I)

Cassirer's early account of perception is contained in his systematic writings on the philosophy of science. In *Substance and Function*, Cassirer understands the Kantian notion of *experience* exclusively in the sense of *scientific experience*, following one of the main strands of Cohen's interpretation of the *Critique of Pure Reason*. Accordingly, Cassirer's paradigm case of perception is observation in scientific experiments. He refers to the account of experiments in physics that can be found in Pierre Duhem's *Aim and Structure of Physical Theory*. According to Duhem, observation in scientific experiments always requires a certain interpretation against the holistic background of a whole theory:

> An experiment in physics is the precise observation of a group of phenomena, accompanied by the interpretation of these phenomena; this interpretation replaces the concrete data really gathered by observation with abstract and symbolic representations that correspond to them by virtue of physical theories accepted by the observer.[16]

This idea of a holistic integration of the particular observational content into the whole of a physical theory is crucial for Cassirer's own account. Holism has been decisive for Kantian thinkers early in the twentieth century long before it became popular through the works of Quine. In *Substance and Function* Cassirer writes:

> ...each particular phase of experience has a 'representative' character, in so far as it refers to another and finally leads by progress according to rule to the totality of experience. [...] The enlargement [...] places the individual in the system. [...] Hence if we understand 'representation' as the expression of an ideal rule, which connects the present, given particular with the whole, and combines the two in an intellectual synthesis, then we have in 'representation' no mere subsequent determination, but a constitutive condition of all experience. Without this apparent representation, there would also be no presentation, no immediately present content; for this latter only exists for knowledge in so far as it is brought into a system of relations, that give it spatial and temporal as well as conceptual determinateness.[17]

---

[16] Duhem (1991), 147 (translation modified). On Cassirer's reception of Duhem, see Ferrari (1995).
[17] Cassirer (1923), 284.

What Cassirer points out here is that an observation in scientific experiments can have a determinate content *only* if the relevant concepts of a theory (and the inferential relations between them) are *represented* in the particular observational content in question. Observations are, to borrow a well-known term coined by Norwood R. Hanson, *theory-laden*.[18] What is decisive for Cassirer, though, is that the relevant concepts that give any particular observational content its specific determinateness are not an addition, not an interpretative *surplus* to what is given, but instead have to be seen as constitutive elements of what is initially itself given—of what the very observation in question consists in. Sensible and conceptual elements are interwoven and united at the very first layer. And this is to say that we do not have any layers at all in (scientific) observation. Cassirer has extended this account of perception to cases of non-scientific perceptions in the third volume of his later *Philosophy of Symbolic Forms*. Cassirer here accounts for perceptions and observations of linguistic human subjects in general. Consider the following passage:

> [T]here is no seeing and nothing visible which does not stand in some mode of spiritual vision, of ideation. A seeing and a thing-seen outside of this 'sight,' a 'bare' sensation preceding all formation, is an empty abstraction. The 'given' must always be taken in a definite aspect and so apprehended, for it is this aspect that first lends it meaning. This meaning is to be understood neither as conceptual in a secondary sense nor as an associative addition: rather, it is the simple meaning of the original intuition itself.[19]

The argument from *Substance and Function* can be clarified by help of this passage. Any instance of perception is a perceiving *of* something *in* a specific conceptual aspect. Having a sheet of paper in my hands, I might for instance perceive this object in front of me with respect to its whiteness, that is, perceive that this object in front of me is white. This in turn requires me to be a competent participant of the language game of attributing the predicate *white* to perceivable objects in my environment. Perceiving this object in front of me *as* white requires my mastery of judgments of the form "This is white" or, more generally, "This is F", or even "This x is F". Cassirer labels this kind of perception 'perception of things' (*Dingwahrnehmung*). We might summarize his account by help of three constitutive claims:
(1) There is no perception of things without concepts. (There is no 'bare' perception of things.)

---

18 Cf. Hanson (1958), 19: "There is a sense, then, in which seeing is a 'theory-laden' undertaking. Observation of x is shaped by prior knowledge of x".
19 Cassirer (1957), 135 (translation modified).

(2) In a perception of things, I perceive something in light of a specific aspect: that something x is of a certain kind F.
(3) The perceiver of things is required to be a competent user of the relevant predicates.

This is certainly one way to spell out Kant's original claim that the categories are responsible not only for the unity of judgments, but also for the unity of intuitions.[20] It is, actually, a prominent way in the Kantian and Neo-Kantian tradition.[21]

Cassirer's account of perception of things is quite close to John McDowell's theory of perception in his 1994 lectures on *Mind and World*. This is, of course, no mere coincidence. As commentators like Michael Friedman have emphasized,[22] McDowell has been strongly influenced by Wilfrid Sellars's interpretation of Kant, and McDowell himself frequently refers to the relevant passages of the first *Critique*. McDowell has become famous in the contemporary debate for his claim that the *content* of a perception is, for example, *that this object in front of me is white*, and hence propositional. McDowell arrives at this claim from a different starting point, though. He begins with Sellars's critique of the myth of the given, and then proceeds by confronting two quite extreme positions of contemporary epistemology. On one end of the spectrum, McDowell finds radical empiricists, who want to justify empirical beliefs by help of the merely causal input of the senses. On the other end, there are radical coherentists like Donald Davidson, who want to justify empirical beliefs exclusively by help of their inferential relations to all other beliefs of one's web of beliefs, where coherence and consistence are supposed to count as *sufficient* conditions for empirical truth. In McDowell's view, both parties go wrong and make complementary mistakes: Radical empiricists are guilty of falling back into the myth of the given, whereas radical coherentists lose the grip to the actual world, since they portray the web of empirical beliefs (in McDowell's now well-known formula) as "a frictionless spinning in a void".[23]

---

[20] In his recent outline of the argument of *Substance and Function*, Jeremy Heis (2014), end of section I, also stresses this point and refers to Cassirer's interpretation of Kant's theoretical philosophy in the second volume of *Das Erkenntnisproblem* (1907).
[21] In his *Philosophy of Symbolic Forms*, Cassirer also claims that this has to be extended pluralistically to the varieties of different kinds of perception. I shall come back to this in section 4.
[22] See Friedman (2002).
[23] McDowell (1996), 11.

McDowell's solution to this dilemma is twofold. To get rid of the inconsistent claims of the empiricist myth of the given, McDowell recommends that we accept the following three claims:
(4) All perceptions have their positions in the space of reasons.
(5) All perceptions are conceptual.
(6) All perceptions have propositional content.

According to McDowell, there can be no instance of human perceiving, knowing and acting outside the space of reasons. For human beings like us, there simply is no radically non-rational or a-rational sphere. So even perceptions must be conceptual, and they must have propositional content, since this is the only way to credit them with the rational force of counting as reasons for empirical beliefs. The upshot is that McDowell recommends positive answers to both of the aforementioned Kantian questions: not only is the exercise of conceptual capacities a necessary condition for having a perception or intuition at all, but the representational content of perception and intuition is in itself propositionally structured and hence conceptual. Subscription to *both* of these claims (positive answers to *both* of the Kantian questions) defines what one might call *strong conceptualism* with regard to perception and intuition.[24]

In addition to his anti-empiricist move, McDowell wants to avoid the coherentists' threat of a "frictionless spinning in a void" by means of a so-called "direct realism". According to McDowell, that this object in front of me is white, amounts to the fact that this object in front of me appears to be white for human perceivers in suitable circumstances.[25] As McDowell sees it, my perception of this object's being white is not a mediate and indirect representation, but an immediate and direct presentation and manifestation of the object itself to me:

---

[24] Note that Cassirer's account of perception in *Substance and Function* is also committed to strong conceptualism in this sense, since he there subscribes to claims (1) and (2), which are obvious equivalents for McDowell's claims (5) and (6). (The picture is somewhat different with respect to Cassirer's later *Philosophy of Symbolic Forms*, though, since perception of things is now just *one* form of perception *among others*. I shall have to say more about this in sect. 4.)—My use of the term *conceptualism* differs from Hanna's use of the same term (see, e.g., Hanna (2014), supplement) in that Hanna does not distinguish the two quite different aspects of Kantian conceptualism that are captured in questions (*a*) and (*b*), respectively (cf. section 1 of this paper).
[25] McDowell is here drawing on the Lockean doctrine of secondary qualities (see, e.g., McDowell (1985), 133–141). Allais (2007), 468–76, has pointed out that Kant's original account of perception can also be reconstructed in terms of Lockean secondary qualities, thus amounting to the claim that "perception is directly presentational". Allais (2007), 468.

(7) In all perceptions, a state of affairs that obtains with respect to a certain object makes itself directly manifest to the perceiver.

McDowell's proposal in *Mind and World* has provoked an extensive debate about whether the content of perception is conceptual or non-conceptual. One result of this debate is the conviction—explicitly shared by McDowell himself in his more recent writings—that at least some revision of the strong conceptualist account of perception in *Mind and World* is necessary. The point is not that on closer inspection we should feel forced to dismiss the Kantian picture altogether. The point is rather that even within the Kantian framework this account of perception is too narrow. McDowell cannot do justice to the—potentially unlimited—*richness* of each particular perception. If the content of a perception would itself be propositional, then just one particular propositional content—for example, *that this object in front of me is white*—would cover *everything* that can be experienced in *this* particular perception. Accordingly, in order to complete our picture of strong conceptualism, we should add this somewhat hidden implication of (4) to (7) to our list:

(8) The propositional content of a perception includes everything that can be experienced in this particular perception.

But then, to perceive *different* aspects of the same object—for example, that this object in front of me is rectangular—one would need to have *different* perceptions. But this is certainly not the way we normally perceive things, since *one and the same* perception can apparently be experienced *in (infinitely) many different* aspects. And this account of perception is certainly not capable of capturing one of the most important strands in Kant's doctrine of intuitions. For Kant, it is quite essential that each particular intuition in itself contains an infinite "manifold of representations"[26] and not just one single aspect of a given spatio-temporal particular. So the strong conceptualism both of Cassirer's *Substance and Function* and of McDowell's *Mind and World* can neither do justice to the phenomenology of perception, nor to Kant's initial ideas. This is why we need two revisions of strong conceptualism. The first is due to McDowell himself and leads us to an acknowledgment of the essentially non-conceptual nature of perceptual content without leaving Kant's broader conceptual framework of the categories. The second revision can be found in Cassirer's mature account

---

[26] Cf. Kant (1998), B 129: "The manifold of representations can be given in an intuition that is merely sensible, i.e., nothing but receptivity [...]".

of the variety of different forms of perception in his *Philosophy of Symbolic Forms*. To these two revisions I shall now turn.

3 Perceptions Have Non-Conceptual Content: McDowell (II)

The starting point for McDowell's own revision[27] of the strong conceptualism of perception in *Mind and World* is once again the familiar passage from the 'metaphysical deduction' of Kant's *Critique of Pure Reason*:

> The same function that gives unity to the different representations in a judgment also gives unity to the mere synthesis of different representations in an intuition, which, expressed generally, is called the pure concept of understanding.[28]

McDowell now recommends a reading of this passage that differs significantly from his earlier interpretation. As before, he takes Kant to be claiming that the categories are responsible not only for the unity of judgments, but also for the unity of intuitions. But the idea is now that the categories can be responsible for the unity of an intuition *without* bringing about this unity *in judgments*. The categorical unity of intuitions and the categorical unity of judgments, both of which are the result of the application of the categories, can actually be brought about in two quite distinct operations. Following McDowell, this idea forces us to distinguish two different senses of the term "conceptual". In the first sense, "conceptual" means "categorical", and in this way we refer to an *a priori* form of thinking. In the second sense, "conceptual" means "predicative", and in this way we are referring to the propositional structure of particular judgments. Now McDowell recommends that we read the crucial passage from Kant in the following way: *all* that Kant is claiming here is that all intuitions are conceptual in the *first* sense, in the sense of being *categorical*; they have and display a categorical unity. To put it in a different way: There is an *a priori* form of thinking that captures the content of an intuition in a unifying way.

What is most important, though, is that this categorical form does *not* itself enter into the *content* of the intuition. The intuitional content as such does not have a predicative structure, and we do not entertain this intuitional content in an explicitly articulated manner. The content of an intuition is *non*-conceptual

---

27 Cf. McDowell (2007a), 345–9 (sect. IV), and McDowell (2008).
28 Kant (1998) A 79/B 104–105.

in the *second* sense of "conceptual", in the sense of being essentially non-propositional. And this is because in every intuition there are always many aspects that the observer has not yet been aware of, and even some that the observer *never* becomes aware of. McDowell thus writes:

> So I am acknowledging that at least some of the content of a typical world-disclosing experience is not conceptual in that sense [viz., in the sense that it never becomes the content of a conceptual capacity].[29]
>
> I used to assume that to conceive experiences as actualizations of conceptual capacities, we would need to credit experiences with *propositional* content, the sort of content judgments have. And I used to assume that the content of an experience would need to include *everything* the experience enables its subject to know noninferentially. But both these assumptions now strike me as wrong.[30]

Here McDowell explicitly withdraws the most provocative claim in *Mind and World*. He no longer claims that perceptions and intuitions have propositional content. They are not conceptual in the second sense. Instead, they are conceptual in the first sense: they are categorical. McDowell thus gives a positive answer to the first of the aforementioned Kantian questions (the application of categories is a necessary condition for having a perception or intuition), and a negative answer to the second (the propositional content of a perception or intuition is non-conceptual). The point is that one actually can give a positive answer to the first question without thereby being committed to a positive answer to the second. Strong conceptualism of perception and intuition is after all *not* an inevitable consequence of the idea of an interwoveness of concepts and intuitions in experience.

This leads to the following picture. Basically, the content of an intuition consists of a manifold of aspects (Kant's "manifold of representations") that can be carved out by means of particular singular judgments in which predicates (empirical concepts) are applied to the intuitional content in order to determine its aspects. So my intuition of this object in front of me contains the aspect that might be carved out as "white", the aspect that might be carved out as "rectangular", and many other aspects. We might say, and McDowell actually does say, that the content of an intuition is *potentially conceptual* in the second sense: it may be determined, step by step, by different empirical concepts in different predications, and hence has "a potential for discursive activity".[31] This whole picture implies two things: everything we know of the content of an intuition

---

29 McDowell (2007a), 347.
30 McDowell (2008), 258.
31 McDowell (2008), 265.

is something we know through the predicative use of concepts; but there is always more contained in an intuition than has yet been determined.

There are two other central claims from *Mind and World*, however, that have survived McDowell's own revision. The first is that every intuition still entitles us to the belief that certain states of affairs obtain, for example that this object in front of me is white and rectangular. Intuitions still have the rational force to count as reasons, and hence they still have their positions within the space of reasons. The second claim that has survived revision is McDowell's version of direct realism. So to sum up, we get the following picture of McDowell's revised conceptualism of perception and intuition:

(9) All intuitions have their positions in the space of reasons.
(10) All intuitions are conceptual in the first sense (= categorical).
(11) All intuitions have non-propositional content (are non-conceptual in the second sense).
(12) In all intuitions, states of affairs that obtain with respect to a certain object make themselves directly manifest to the perceiver.
(13) The content of an intuition can never be fully determined.

In this revised version, McDowell's account of perception clearly has very strong affinities to the accounts of perception in the Kantian tradition. Claims (9) to (13) capture quite nicely Kant's theory of intuitions. They are also quite close to Cassirer's account of perception of things within the plurality of symbolic forms. Nevertheless, a second revision is in place here.

To see why, it may be useful to call attention to some main motives for the recent debate between McDowell and Hubert Dreyfus. Dreyfus has attacked *Mind and World* from the background of Merleau-Ponty's *Phenomenology of Perception* and Heidegger's analysis of Dasein in *Being and Time*.[32] What Dreyfus attacked in particular is McDowell's claim that all perceptions are rational as well as conceptual. Dreyfus criticizes this, from Merleau-Ponty's point of view, as a paradigm case of *hyper-intellectualization* of perception.[33] All instances of our everyday-life understanding, perceiving, and acting, in Dreyfus's view, simply do not involve anything rational or conceptual; they have to be seen as entirely unreflective and non-conceptual instead. Rationality, reflection, and concepts come into the play only at a later point, when we leave our natural openness to the world. And what philosophy has to do, according to Merleau-Ponty, is to make

---
[32] Dreyfus (2005). I will not go into the details of the debate; see Dreyfus (2007a and 2007b), and McDowell (2007a and 2007b). Schear (2013) is a collection of essays on the various aspects of the debate, including recent papers by Dreyfus and McDowell.
[33] See Merleau-Ponty (1962), § 10.

transparent this very phenomenology of perception. Against this, McDowell argued—unsurprisingly at this point—that Dreyfus is guilty of falling back into the dualistic layer conception of the human mind. So instead of assuming that there is a 'myth of the mental' at work in McDowell (as Dreyfus puts it), we would do better to assume that there is a 'myth of the disembodied intellect' at work in Dreyfus (as McDowell puts it).[34] The intellect, in Dreyfus's picture, is something that only comes into the play when we leave our natural openness to and natural understanding of the world.

This is exactly the point where we should return to Cassirer's *Philosophy of Symbolic Forms*. From Cassirer's point of view, both McDowell and Dreyfus are right in certain respects, and wrong in others. McDowell is right in claiming that nothing is sensible without at the same time being spiritual (*geistig*), as Cassirer would have it. Dreyfus is right in observing that there are cases of perception that do not presuppose the use of concepts. Dreyfus, on the other hand, is wrong in claiming that perception is mindless or spiritless at all. And finally, McDowell is wrong when he says that there is no perception other than perception of things—that is, perception in the context of concepts and linguistic expressions. This account of perception is still too narrow in that it cannot do full justice to the phenomenological richness of the varieties of perception. There is indeed, Cassirer points out, a *variety* of different kinds of perception of which perception of things is just one single kind.

4 The Varieties of Perception: Cassirer (II)

If one is looking for a philosophical approach to perception that might be able to reconcile Kantian intuitions with phenomenological insights without being susceptible to the reservations about either of them, Cassirer's *Philosophy of Symbolic Forms* is certainly one of the most promising candidates. As can be seen from the very title of its third volume, *The Phenomenology of Knowledge* (alluding to Hegel as well as to Husserl), it was one of Cassirer's main objectives to integrate that which remains compelling in Husserlian phenomenology into the broader framework of both a Kantian theory of experience and a Hegelian dialectic of the symbolic forms of world disclosure.[35] I shall not go into the details of the ar-

---

[34] McDowell (2007), 349.
[35] For a reconstruction of Cassirer's transition "from subjectivity to lifeworld as a world of culture" (with Natorp and Husserl as leading figures) see Luft (2011), in particular chs. 9–10. Cassirer's discussion of Heidegger's version of phenomenology didn't enter the third volume of the *Philosophy of Symbolic Forms* (the manuscript was completed in 1927 just before Heidegger's

gument and the architecture of Cassirer's *Philosophy of Symbolic Forms* here.[36] Instead, I will concentrate on the varieties of perception within the philosophy of symbolic forms, and on perceptions of expression in particular, since here Cassirer most clearly answers the systematic problems raised by the McDowell/Dreyfus debate. One of Cassirer's earliest statements on the idea of the varieties of perception can be found in the second volume of the *Philosophy of Symbolic Forms*:

> On sharper analysis even the apparently 'given' proves to have passed through certain acts of linguistic, mythical, or logical-theoretical 'apperception'. Only what is *made* in these acts 'is'; even in its seemingly simple and immediate nature, what is thus made proves to be conditioned and determined by some primary meaning-giving function. And it is this primary, not the secondary, formation which contains the true secret of all symbolic form, which must forever arouse new philosophical amazement.[37]

There are three important principles at work in this passage. The first might be called the *plurality principle:* there is not just one single kind of perception of the human mind or spirit, but a plurality of different kinds of perception instead. To put it in Cassirer's terms: each symbolic form has its own specific kind of perception, and if we change from myth to language or from language to science, "perception" does not always mean the same thing, since we have to take into account different modes of "linguistic, mythical, or logical-theoretical 'apperception'", as he puts it.[38] The structure and the content of perception change from one symbolic form to another. Just as no single symbolic form could ever be reduced to any of the others, so no particular kind of perception could ever be reduced to any other.[39] The task of a philosophy of symbolic forms with respect to perception is therefore twofold: it has to analyze the specific features of each particular kind of perception, and it has to reconstruct the interrelations of these kinds within the system of symbolic forms. This is precisely what Cassirer is aiming at in the third volume. Secondly, Cassirer implicitly presupposes the *'expressivist' principle* of the boundedness of the spiritual to the sensual: everything that is mental or spiritual is essentially bound to its being expressed in sensual formations (*Gestalten*). This principle is adopted from the 'expressivist'

Being and Time was published), and was deferred to the 1929 Davos debate (on this, see Friedman (2000) and Stephen Lofts' paper in this volume).
36 I have tried to do this in Kreis (2010).
37 Cassirer (1955), 94.
38 Aesthetic perception would of course be another obvious (and quite important) kind.
39 This is the point in Cassirer's calling the specific symbolic structures of each of the kinds of perception 'Urphaenomene'.

tradition of Humboldt, Herder, and Hegel, where particular emphasis was given to the boundedness of thought to language. And thirdly, and conversely, Cassirer employs the *principle of symbolic pregnance:* there is nothing sensual, 'material' or 'natural' that would not at the same be saturated ('laden') with the spiritual.

This last principle immediately leads us to the core of Cassirer's integration of the phenomenology of perception into the Kantian framework of a theory of experience. Cassirer frequently refers to modern Gestalt psychology in his *Phenomenology of Knowledge,* and the upshot is that although there really are several different kinds of perception, there cannot be one single case of a 'bare' perception entirely lacking the spiritual: "I want to emphasize most emphatically that a 'mere' perception, as it were, a bare perception entirely lacking any function of signification, is in no way a phenomenon given to us directly, in our 'natural stance' to the world".[40] Cassirer tries to take into account the innovations of phenomenology and Gestalt psychology *without* falling back into a dualism of isolated layers of the human mind:

> ... we again and again had to reject [...] the conception that the process of 'symbolic formation' is a mere reconstruction of a given world of sensation or of a ready-made world of perception—as if merely to the latter, taken as a basic and original layer, a kind of intellectual 'superstructure' had to be added. We saw that instead each particular intellectual *viewpoint* itself already determined *that which* perception as such *consists in*—that neither can be separated and isolated from each other.[41]

The principle that there is nothing sensual that would not at the same time be saturated with the spiritual prevents Cassirer from falling back into anything like a 'myth of the disembodied intellect' (which was McDowell's point against Dreyfus' reception of Merleau-Ponty[42]). Rather, the central idea is that of a thoroughgoing embodiment of the intellectual (or, more broadly conceived, the spiritual), and an equally thoroughgoing, complementary saturation of the sensual with the intellectual (or spiritual). Compare in particular Cassirer's definition of symbolic pregnance:

> By 'symbolic pregnance' we mean the way in which a perception as a 'sensory' experience contains at the same time a certain non-intuitive 'meaning' which it immediately and con-

---

[40] Cassirer (1938), 123 (my translation).
[41] Cassirer (1996), 50–51 (translation altered).
[42] John Krois (1987), 58, rightly emphasizes that Merleau-Ponty, though frequently referring to Cassirer's *Phenomenology of Knowledge* in his *Phenomenology of Perception,* entirely misses the point in terming symbolic pregnance a "new *cogito*" in a Cartesian fashion. Merleau-Ponty (1962), 296.

cretely presents. Here we are not dealing with merely 'perceptive' data, on which some sort of 'apperceptive' acts are later grafted, through which they are interpreted, judged, transformed. Rather, it is the perception itself which by virtue of its own immanent organization, takes on a kind of spiritual 'articulation'—which, being ordered in itself, also belongs to a determinate order of meaning.[43]

Once again, Cassirer recommends that we regard the isolation of the sensual and the spiritual in perception as a purely methodological isolation, and not as a real one. In the real life of a human perceiver, sensual and spiritual aspects are always interwoven from the very beginning. The point is that any perception whatsoever displays as its content *at least that* 'meaning' or 'sense' which is constituted by the *immanent* organization and articulation of the sensual aspects of this very perception *itself.*

What is particularly important here is that kind of perception which Cassirer calls the *perception of expression* or *expressive perception* (*Ausdruckswahrnehmung*) in contrast to the perception of things.[44] In a perception of expression, one typically experiences one's own environment as displaying to oneself an expressive, *vital* quality: what is in front of me expresses itself, for example, as threatening, cheerful, or lovely. Consider the following descriptions of expressive perceptions:

> *Concrete* perception [...] is never directed exclusively toward the 'what' of the object but encompasses its mode of appearance in its entirety—the character of the luring or threatening, the familiar or uncanny, the soothing or frightening, which lies in this appearance purely as such and independently of its objective interpretation.[45]
>
> For the reality we apprehend is in its original form not a reality of a determinate *world of things*, being against and face to face with us; rather it is the assuredness of a vivid efficacy that we experience.[46]
>
> That which here presents itself as 'reality' is not a totality of things endowed with definite 'characteristics' and 'marks' by which they can be recognized and distinguished from one another; rather it is a manifold and plentitude of original 'physiognomic' characters.[47]

The essential point here is that expressive perceptions are an immediate disclosure of the world in one of its vital characters on specific occasions. One would entirely miss the point if one would read these passages as a description of

---

[43] Cassirer (1957), 202 (translation altered). On the significance of symbolic pregnance, see Krois (1987), 52–57.
[44] Cf., among others, Krois (1987), 57–62; Friedman (2000), 103–104; Lofts (2000), 91–96.
[45] Cassirer (1957), 67 (translation altered).
[46] Ibid., 73 (translation altered).
[47] Ibid., 68 (translation altered).

'mere' subjective appearances in contrast to objective perceptions of things. Cassirer repeatedly emphasizes the fact that perceptions of expression in themselves, phenomenologically, cannot be characterized by help of the subjective/objective contrast that is typical for other kinds of perception in more elaborated (conceptual) contexts. An expressive perception is, as it were, a vivid experience of vitality that is immediately saturated with reality. Since it is *not* mediated by generic terms and predicates, as Cassirer is eager to emphasize, it is somewhat misleading to give a verbal description of its content at all. We misleadingly describe the expressive experience of something threatening with the help of the concept of being threatening, whereas the content of the experience is not the result of the application of that concept. The interesting point now is that two quite different features are united in this account: expressive perceptions are perceptions in which we *directly* experience something *given* to us, *without* at the same time being 'bare' or spiritless occurrences, since the principle of symbolic pregnance definitely applies to them (in fact, expressive perception is the paradigm case of symbolic pregnance). Perceptions of expression in their pure form occur in myth, but according to Cassirer, they occur as well in, for example, language, art and politics. Without an analysis of perceptions of expression our overall theory of perception would be incomplete.

A perception of expression is a non-conceptual perception in a more radical sense than a perception of things. Whereas the latter is at least potentially conceptual in the sense that its infinitely rich manifold of aspects has the potential for being carved out with the help of empirical concepts in predicative judgments, the non-conceptual content of a perception of expression would lose its specific character by being interpreted through the predicative use of concepts. Whereas in the case of a perception of things any rendering of perceptual content in the general forms of "This is F", "that this is F", "the F-ness of this" and the like would be a case of making this content explicit in one of its infinitely many aspects, any rendering in one of these forms in the case of a perception of expression would be a complete *transformation* and hence a *loss* of its specific perceptual content. This contrast enables us to give a more accurate technical account of perceptions of expression. In the case of a perception of things, its non-conceptual content can always be adequately made explicit with the help of concepts, and hence it can be described as having a *general* meaning in the following sense: (*a*) each of its aspects can occur as the spiritual aspect of infinitely many perceptions on infinitely many different occasions (the concept 'white' for example is at play in all perceivings of white objects); (*b*) each of its aspects is a universal meaning type that can be instantiated in infinitely many meaning tokens to infinitely many different objects (the concept 'white' for example can be attributed to all white objects); and (*c*) each of its aspects is publically accessible and shared by all competent speakers of a natural language (the concept 'white' for example is accessible to all competent participants in the language game of attributing expressions like "white", "*weiß*", "*blanc*", "*blanco*" and the like to perceivable objects in the environment). By contrast, in the case of a perception of things its non-conceptual content would be significantly transformed by the application of concepts, and therefore it can be described as having a *singular* 'meaning' in the following sense: (a^*) it occurs in just one particular perception on one particular occasion, and cannot occur on different occasions in exactly the same way; (b^*) it is the 'meaning' of just one particular perception, and cannot be the 'meaning' of any other perception; and (c^*) it is entirely bound to the particular individual person who is entertaining it, not being capable of being experienced in exactly the same way by any other person. Singularity in this sense is the defining feature of perceptions of expression.

It should be clear by now that this conception is by no means simply a sophisticated repetition of sense data empiricism, nor a fallback into the myth of the given. The reason for this is quite simple: *despite* its specific singularity, *any* perception of expression is always in itself laden with 'meaning' and thus already situated in the realm of the spiritual. This leads us to another detail in Cassirer's revision of McDowell's revised conceptualism as captured in claims (9) to (13). Against McDowell's employment of the Sellarsian conception of a space of reasons, we can draw the broader notion of a space of the spiritual from Cassirer's *Philosophy of Symbolic Forms*.[48] All we have to secure here is that perceptions of all kinds have their place within this broader space of the spiritual. This is in perfect accordance with a positive answer to the first of the Kantian questions: as a sub-system of spirit as a whole, even the cases of expressive symbolization, and of expressive perception in particular, are subject to the categories (as Cassirer tried to show in rich detail in the second volume of his *Philosophy of Symbolic Forms*). But there is simply no need to restrict ourselves to that one and only kind of perception that can successfully be placed within the all too narrow space of reasons. So from Cassirer's *Phenomenology of Knowledge* we can draw the following *additional* claims to (9)–(13) as a second revision of strong conceptualism:

(14) All perceptions of expression have their positions in the space of the spiritual.
(15) All perceptions of expression are categorical.
(16) All perceptions of expression have non-propositional content.

---

[48] I am indebted to Jeremy Heis and Sebastian Luft for pointing this out to me.

(17) In all perceptions of expression, reality in one of its vital aspects makes itself directly manifest to the perceiver.
(18) The content of a perception of expression can never be fully captured with the help of concepts.

I'd like to mention one final issue here. So far, the need for an account of perceptions of expression has been motivated on phenomenological grounds: it is a phenomenological fact that some cases of perception are expressive rather than conceptual. There is another argument, though, to show the *indispensability* of an account of expressive perceptions in a philosophy of symbolic forms. One might call it a 'transcendental argument', and here is a brief (and informal) sketch of it. Remember that Kant employed the metaphor of the two stems of human cognition. As I read it, one of the thoughts Kant wants to illustrate with it is the following: For our empirical judgments to be instances of empirical knowledge, it is a necessary condition that they contain representations that are *given to* the thinker. This claim should hence be taken as the starting point for the argument. Suppose now, by *reductio*, that perception of things is the only kind of perception within the human mind. But then, as we have seen, the best account of this kind tells us that everything we explicitly know of the content of a perception of things is that which he have explicitly carved out and determined with the help of predicates. We cannot possibly know, on that account, the content of a perception *as* something that has been given, but only as something that has been actively determined in a conceptual activity. One might try the following trick: The one thing that could speak in favor of givenness is the fact that we experience a *progress* of our empirical beliefs—a progress that might be interpreted as a progress from one perception to another. This is what Kant says in the *Critique of Pure Reason:* "Nothing is really given to us except perception and the empirical progress from this perception to other possible perceptions".[49] But clearly, what now accounts for the givenness of our perceptions is the dynamic of our web of beliefs and therefore a feature of an essentially conceptual structure.[50] This line of thought might even lead us to the extreme consequence that perceptions of this kind are identical with thinking itself, which is exactly what Natorp claimed in his 1912 portrayal of the Marburg School: "What is called 'intuition' no longer remains as a factor in experience alien to thinking and as a counterpart face to face with thinking; instead, intu-

---

[49] Kant (1998), A 493/B 521.
[50] For a recent version of this idea, see Brandom (2009), 94–105.

ition *is* thinking".⁵¹ And this is definitely unacceptable. But even if we don't want to subscribe to this extreme view, the crucial point here is the following: if there is only one kind of perception within the human mind, i.e., perceptions of things, we can't guarantee that it contains any given elements at all. We can't then guarantee that a necessary transcendental condition of empirical knowledge is fulfilled. But it is the main task of the transcendental method to demonstrate how empirical knowledge is possible. Hence, there must be at least one other kind of perception: perceptions in which we directly experience something given to us. And these are perceptions of expression. This is a 'transcendental argument' in favour of perceptions of expression.

Bibliography

Allais (2007): Lucy Allais, "Kant's Idealism and the Secondary Quality Analogy", *Journal of the History of Philosophy* 45 (No. 3), 459–484.

Allais (2009): Lucy Allais, "Non-Conceptual Content and the Representation of Space", *Journal of the History of Philosophy* 47 (No. 3), 383–413.

Brandom (2009): Robert B. Brandom, "History, Reason, and Reality", in: *Reason in Philosophy: Animating Ideas*, Cambridge, MA: Harvard University Press.

Cassirer (1923): Ernst Cassirer, *Substance and Function*, W.C. Swabey and M.C. Swabey (trans.), Chicago: Open Court.

Cassirer (1938): Ernst Cassirer, "Zur Logik des Symbolbegriffs", in: Ernst Cassirer, *Gesammelte Werke*, Birgit Recki (ed.), Vol. XXII, Hamburg: Meiner, 2006, 112–139.

Cassirer (1955): Ernst Cassirer, *The Philosophy of Symbolic Forms, Volume Two: Mythical Thought*, Ralph Manheim (trans.), New Haven: Yale University Press.

Cassirer (1957): Ernst Cassirer, *The Philosophy of Symbolic Forms, Volume Three: The Phenomenology of Knowledge*, Ralph Manheim (trans.), New Haven: Yale University Press.

Cassirer (1996): Ernst Cassirer, *Philosophy of Symbolic Forms, Volume Four: The Metaphysics of Symbolic Forms*, J.M. Krois/D. P. Verene (eds.), New Haven: Yale University Press.

Dreyfus (2005): Hubert Dreyfus, "Overcoming the Myth of the Mental: How Philosophers Can Profit from the Phenomenology of Everyday Expertise", *Proceedings and Addresses of the American Philosophical Association* 79, 47–65.

Dreyfus (2007a): Hubert Dreyfus, "The Return of the Myth of the Mental", *Inquiry* 50, 352–365.

Dreyfus (2007b): Hubert Dreyfus, "Response to McDowell", *Inquiry* 50, 371–77.

Duhem (1991): Pierre Duhem, *The Aim and Structure of Physical Theory*, Philip P. Wiener (trans.), Princeton: Princeton University Press.

Evans (1982): Gareth Evans, *The Varieties of Reference*, John McDowell (ed.), Oxford: Oxford University (Clarendon) Press.

---

51 Natorp (1912), 204 (my translation).

Ferrari (1995): Massimo Ferrari, "Ernst Cassirer and Pierre Duhem", in: Enno Rudolph, Bernd-Olaf Küppers (eds.), *Kulturkritik nach Ernst Cassirer*, Hamburg: Meiner, 177–196.

Friedman (2000): Michael Friedman, *A Parting of the Ways: Carnap, Cassirer, and Heidegger*, Chicago: Open Court.

Friedman (2002): Michael Friedman, "Exorcising the Philosophical Tradition", in: Nicholas H. Smith (ed.), *Reading McDowell: On Mind and World*, London/New York: Routledge, 2002, 25–57.

Grüne (2009): Stefanie Grüne, *Blinde Anschauung: Die Rolle von Begriffen in Kants Theorie sinnlicher Synthesis*, Frankfurt am Main: Klostermann.

Hanna (2005): Robert Hanna, "Kant and Nonconceptual Content", *European Journal of Philosophy* 13, 247–290. Reprinted in: Robert Hanna, *Kant, Science, and Human Nature*, Oxford: Oxford University Press, 2006, ch. 2.

Hanna (2011): Robert Hanna, "Beyond the Myth of the Myth: A Kantian Theory of Non-Conceptual Content", *International Journal of Philosophical Studies* 19: 323–398.

Hanna (2014): Robert Hanna, "Kant's Theory of Judgment", *The Stanford Encyclopedia of Philosophy* (Summer 2014 Edition), Edward N. Zalta (ed.): <http://plato.stanford.edu/archives/sum2014/entries/kant-judgment/>, supplement: "The Togetherness Principle, Kant's Conceptualism, and Kant's Non-conceptualism".

Heis (2014): Jeremy Heis, "Ernst Cassirer's *Substanzbegriff und Funktionsbegriff*", *HOPOS: The Journal of the International Society for the History of Philosophy of Science* 4 (No. 2), 241–270.

Kant (1998): Immanuel Kant, *Critique of Pure Reason*, Paul Guyer and Alan W. Wood (trans. and ed.), Cambridge: Cambridge University Press.

Kant (2006): Immanuel Kant, *Anthropology form a Pragmatic Point of View*, Robert B. Louden (trans.), Cambridge: Cambridge University Press.

Kreis (2010): Guido Kreis, *Cassirer und die Formen des Geistes*, Berlin: Suhrkamp.

Krois (1987) John Michael Krois, *Cassirer: Symbolic Forms and History*, New Haven: Yale University Press.

Lofts (2001): Stephen G. Lofts, *Ernst Cassirer: A "Repetition" of Modernity*, Albany: State University of New York Press.

Lofts (2015): Stephen G. Lofts, "Cassirer and Heidegger: The Cultural-Event", in this volume.

Luft (2011): Sebastian Luft, *Subjectivity and Lifeworld in Transcendental Phenomenology*, Evanston, IL: Northwestern University Press.

McDowell (1985): John McDowell, "Values and Secondary Qualities", as reprinted in: John McDowell, *Mind, Value, and Reality*, Cambridge, MA: Harvard University Press, 131–50.

McDowell (1996): John McDowell, *Mind and World*, with a new introduction by the author, Cambridge, MA: Harvard University Press.

McDowell (2007a): John McDowell, "What Myth?", *Inquiry* 50, 338–51.

McDowell (2007b): John McDowell, "Reply to Dreyfus", *Inquiry* 50, 366–70.

McDowell (2008) John McDowell, "Avoiding the Myth of the Given", in: John McDowell, *Having the World in View*, Cambridge/Mass.: Harvard University Press, 256–72.

Merleau-Ponty (1962): Maurice Merleau-Ponty, *The Phenomenology of Perception*, Colin Smith (trans.), London: Routledge.

Natorp (1912): Paul Natorp, "Kant und die Marburger Schule" *Kant-Studien* 17, 193–221.

Rohs (2001): Peter Rohs, "Bezieht sich nach Kant die Anschauung unmittelbar auf Gegenstände?", in V. Gerhardt and R. P. Horstmann (eds.), *Akten des IX. Internationalen Kant-Kongresses*, vol. II, Berlin: De Gruyter, 214–228.

Schear (2013): Joseph K. Schear (ed.), *Mind, Reason, and Being-In-The-World: The McDowell-Dreyfus-Debate*, London: Routledge.

Sellars (1997): Wilfred Sellars, *Empiricism and the Philosophy of Mind*, reprinted with an introduction by Richard Rorty and a Study Guide by Robert Brandom, Cambridge, MA: Harvard University Press.

Wenzel (2005): Christian Helmut Wenzel, "Spielen die Kategorien nach Kant schon bei der Wahrnehmung eine Rolle?", *Kant-Studien* 96, 407–426.

Part III: **The Philosophy of Culture Today**

Anne Pollok (Columbia/S.C.)
The First and Second Person Perspective in History: Or, Why History is 'Culture Fiction'

Who would hold that history is a dialogue? It sounds somewhat striking to concentrate on the second-person perspective in Cassirer's account of history, since it is obviously true that the past may somewhat "speak *to* us", but that it cannot "speak *with* us" in a truly dialogical sense. What is here and now contrasts with what is stored away in the past, as two different levels of fluidity. Symbols, as the expressions of past consciousness, are no longer in flux as the present ones are, but need to be actively reconstructed, or revivified by the historian. With Cassirer's dynamic view[1] on symbolic forms, however, this reconstruction can be understood as a movement from both sides, from the past and from the present.

The literature on Cassirer's philosophy of symbolic forms and its relation to history does not discuss how our relationships with others, as participants in a dialogue, shape this particular practice of using and understanding symbols.[2] The main reason for this lack of discussion is presumably due to Cassirer's own vagueness on the issue. In the end, it is entirely unclear whether or not 'history' is in fact a symbolic form (as Cassirer would seem to suggest in *An Essay on Man*)[3], or a basic means of discovering said forms. Cassirer is also notoriously unclear whether he means history as the temporal unfolding of events or our retrospective account of it (*Geschichtswissenschaft*). This paper focuses on the 'intersubjective mechanics' of the historical understanding[4] that provides a per-

---

[1] I should add that I mainly focus on Cassirer's late work, based on the *Philosophy of Symbolic Forms*, but with the main weight placed on his writings and unpublished papers from the 1930's and 40's. I do not claim that the earlier works lack an historical perspective—which, in light of his masterful treatments of the history of science, or the "problem of knowledge" more generally, but also his wonderful captures of, say, the life and work of Immanuel Kant, or of Leibniz' philosophy, would amount to nearly complete nonsense. My restriction here is due only to pragmatic reasons: a paper on Cassirer's take on history as a whole might end up being a book, not a paper.
[2] I refer here mainly to Krois (1987), but also to the lack of discussion of history at all in the Cassirer volume of *Synthese*, vol. 179 (2011).
[3] Also in his 1942 lecture "The Philosophy of History", Cassirer (1979), 121–41. See for example ibid., 126–27. Göller (1991), 237, leaves the issue open as well, even though he explores both options.
[4] Here, *understanding* translates *Verstehen*, not as a faculty, but as a process. The overall structure of this process is reflected in Cassirer's discussion of the distinction between scientific and cultural concepts; see Cassirer (1961/2000), 433/74.

spective on history as *Geschichtswissenschaft*. Not as a merely 'objective' account, but as a living interaction between the past and the present.⁵ This understanding, I will conclude, marks history as a fruitful and peculiarly artful symbolic *method* that elucidates the intersubjective character of symbolic forms more generally.

Cassirer links the understanding and account of the historical development of the symbolic forms, also somewhat surprisingly, to art as a creative mode of understanding. Thus, I likened 'history' in this sense with the term "culture fiction". I will discuss the functions and constraints of this peculiar form of *Geschichtswissenschaft* in the last section of this paper. Before we get there, however, we need to clarify the particular position of history in general within Cassirer's overall "philosophical anthropology". So, in short, this paper will first characterize Cassirer's notion of history as directed towards our use and the development of symbolic systems. Only after that will we be in a position to define the historians' attempts to capture past significative activities in their accounts of what our 'history'—the story of us getting here—is.

To justify this view, I will first give an overview of historical reconstruction in general that is mostly informed by Cassirer's *Philosophy of Symbolic Forms* (1923–29) and later works, in particular *An Essay on Man*, where he treats history most explicitly.⁶

Then, I will discuss the notions of individuality and universality in historical understanding. History deals with individual agents and their actions. These actions are, however, not erratic expressions of an individual spirit that nobody can ever access (thus making all historical understanding impossible); rather, they contain a universal element that renders them comprehensible. This universal aspect—and this is the key to my interpretation of Cassirer—is nothing else than an intersubjective dimension of the symbolic. Beginning from an assessment of the role of "work" as a basic phenomenon, I will then try to capture the intricate interplay of the "I" as the source of such works, and the "You" as

---

5 I follow here Göller's nomenclatura in Göller (1991), see 225. See also Cassirer himself in his lectures (Cassirer (1979), 138): he calls it the difference between the *res gestae* ("the facts, the events, the deeds of the past"), and our "recollection" of said events (*Geschichtsschreibung*, or *–wissenschaft*).

6 Here, I should direct the reader's attention to Bast's monumental study (2000) on Cassirer's view on history that covers all of Cassirer's works. It does not contain a treatment of the second person perspective, however, a thought that became dominant in particular with the *Logic of the Cultural Sciences*. This is an interesting change from Cassirer's concentration on the History of Ideas in his earlier works.

the addressee, to penetrate into the tightly woven net of past and present expressions of consciousness as a dialogue among *animalia symbolica*.

1 Cassirer's Argument for Historical 'Reconstruction'

The historical perspective as such is deeply ingrained in Cassirer's philosophy, which Skidelsky characterizes as the "historization of Kant's transcendental subject".[7] This historicized transcendental subject must, on the one hand, be understood as the 'symbolic animal' that situates herself in a time-continuum, thereby creating her identity within a temporal perspective. On the other hand, this being must be understood as oriented toward other subjects, by using symbols as a means to address these others, or by interpreting the symbols used by others —even if this usage is situated in a distant past. The second person perspective[8] accounts for both parties in a historically guided self-understanding. On the one hand, the agent orients herself towards other agents existing both in the past and in the present. But same as she also addresses agents in the future with her works, so can past agents be understood as being oriented towards her. We address ourselves to others, and this practice of reaching out leads us back to ourselves again.[9]

E.W. Orth defends the thesis that Cassirer actually uses the philosophy of symbolic forms to cope with the historicity and culturicity (*Kulturhaftigkeit*)[10]

---

7 Skidelsky (2008), 125.
8 To be sure, we do not refer to normative second-personal reasons as described by Darwall (2006). Those pertain to reasons of and for 'free and rational agents' (ibid., 9). For our knowledge of history (which represents a claim of a different sort, and also another kind of normativity) it does not quite matter whether the person on the other end (the person or event that we seek to understand) was free or rational. It is useful to suppose that (only given the circumstances), but not necessary. It is a somewhat epistemic second person perspective, even though still also the perspective on an agent: history seeks to know/understand what people *did*. We may even want to know what reasons people had. But we will not hold them accountable in the same way as we hold our contemporaries accountable for, to repeat an example by Darwall, stepping on our feet.
9 See Cassirer (2002c/1957), 207–213/182–188. See also Steve Lofts discussion of *Auseinandersetzung* in this volume.
10 I follow Steve Lofts' recommendation for a translation of *Kulturhaftigkeit*. It should mean, roughly, that science or philosophy are embedded within human culture, or are affected by their origin in human activity, which, for Cassirer, is always the cultural activity of symbolization.

of both philosophy and the sciences.[11] Thus, to view something historically is a method by which to detect how the use of symbolic forms has created these specific sorts of cultural activities. History, viewed this way, appears as a means to understand the inner order of these forms (note that this is a *dynamic* order that unfolds and changes over time) and their interaction with each another.[12]

In *An Essay on Man*, Cassirer discusses history as a symbolic form.[13] In a parallel vein as science, history is a 'system' with a particular structure.[14] Accordingly, "historical thought" is a specific mode of consciousness that implies a particular "process of judgment".[15] Here, Cassirer does not reflect on the issue that every symbolic understanding contains a temporal perspective. In his philosophy it is extremely hard (or, let us concede: perhaps impossible) to disentangle the historical perspective from any of the other symbolic forms that he treats rather extensively in the three published volumes, or from art.[16] The historical perspective is one key technique in our discovery and justification of each form; this holds true even for science as the most abstract such form. The historical "modes of knowledge"[17]—in contrast to purely scientific ones—are not, however, concerned with a (causal) explanation of objects or events, but with what Cassirer calls the "characteristic".[18] Before we can decide whether history is a symbolic form, or a higher-order method of rediscovery, let us concentrate on its particular "process of judgment" that marks historical understanding as a particular reflection on our mode of being in the world.

---

11 Orth (1993), 17.
12 This does not mean, however, that history is the only and most important method. As Cassirer makes it clear in *An Essay on Man* (Cassirer (1972), 77), the "general structural principles underlying these works" cannot be detected merely historically. But if we can reconstruct a historical perspective in the formal, not material, sense, we might gain an insight into the "unity of [human] action" (ibid., 78) that created these particular works.
13 Cassirer lists history explicitly in the second part of the expositional chapter "The Definition of Man", see ibid., 76. It is interesting, however, that history drops from the list in all subsequent enumerations (ibid., 76–77). History remains a *"vinculum functionale"*, but somehow morphs into a "historical method".
14 Ibid., 186.
15 Ibid., 188.
16 Lauschke (2007) and Bundgaard (2011), for example, reconstruct art very convincingly as the fourth symbolic form.
17 Cassirer (1972), 188.
18 However, Cassirer explicitly rejects the distinction by Rickert and Windelband, who characterize science as nomothetic, and history as idiographic (see also Cassirer (1961/2000), 416/58). For Cassirer, both of these symbolic systems exhibit lawfulness and particularity. What marks their difference, rather, is the mode of symbolical retraction: thinking scientifically requires other functions than the process of historical reconstruction and revivification.

To explain physical events scientifically we trace them back to the space, time and the causal relations that brought them it into being. Our understanding of historical events does not operate along the same logic. We need to identify the event as taking place in its place and in its time; but we cannot then infer from any antecedent cause to its effect. We do not just want the "skeleton" of events (which we could get that way), but "we wish to reconstitute [all the works of man, and all his deeds] into this original state, we wish to understand and feel the life from which they are derived"[19]—to ultimately understand "human life" more generally. To achieve this, we seek to understand the agents, not merely the actions. In his Yale lecture notes Cassirer refers to this complex issue as the "historical 'character'" that brings together the particular and the universal in a special way: "In history, there always appears a new factor which is not analyzable into simpler elements".[20] On this 'elementary' stage, we discover the historical agent, or the individual, that brought the elements of said historical events into that particular configuration. To 'understand' an historical event, the historian needs to 'understand' the agents—and for this she needs not only explanation and description, but also "symbolic interpretation"[21], a new, "highly difficult and complex 'hermeneutics'".[22] Understanding history, then, involves our consideration of the various symbolic expressions of particular consciousness(es) in past times. It means an understanding of the *dynamics* of history, or what Cassirer calls the *"analysis of becoming"*.[23]

In *An Essay on Man* Cassirer states, as an ideal case of historical understanding, that such a symbolic expression must be sustained without interruption.[24] Otherwise, ultimate verification whether we are still expressing the same thing will become impossible. But even if we cannot fulfill this criterion of constant revival (and for most historical events or agents, we really cannot), there is hope. Instead of Simmel's "Tragedy of Culture",[25] Cassirer does not think the 'objectification' of ourselves in our works will alienate them from us. A human expression cannot become unreadable *per se*. It "always retains a trace of human

---

19 Cassirer (1972), 198.
20 Cassirer (1979), 128. One source of this view could be Goethe. In his essay "Goethe und die geschichtliche Welt", Cassirer discusses Goethe's insistence of historical knowledge as knowledge of personalities, not of 'facts'. These personalities point to the essence of history and life, as a "living continuity" (*lebendige Kontinuität*) (Cassirer (2004b), 367).
21 Cassirer (1972), 196; see also Cassirer (1979), 129–130.
22 Cassirer (1961/2000), 456/97.
23 Ibid.
24 Cassirer (1972), 199.
25 See Cassirer (1961/2000), part V.

life, awaiting retrieval in the act of sympathetic interpretation".[26] The relationship between historical 'facts' and contemporary understanding is indeed mutual: Our historian can capture systems of meaning of previous cultures, because she shares the ability to use 'functions within human symbolic systems' with the historical agent. This does not mean that this understanding is without problems, but it does say that it is fundamentally possible.

For Cassirer, expressing ourselves in symbolic forms is a necessary component of our own life. "[L]ife cannot *apprehend* itself [*Selbsterfassung*] by *remaining* absolutely within itself. It must give itself form; for it is precisely by this 'otherness' [*Andersheit*] of form that it gains its 'visibility' [*Sichtigkeit*], if not its reality [*Wirklichkeit*]".[27] That is, in order to grasp ourselves we need to express or disclose ourselves by means of symbols. This means to turn something internal into an external form as a means of self-understanding. This externalization is not, however, just important for me as the agent (or creator of symbolic forms) as an expression of myself. A description of the scenario, of the activity of expression, is incomplete if we only look at it from this one side. The creation of an object also serves to address others. Or, more radically stated, this creation marks the creation of the subject herself. Since it is through her work that she is recognized by others, and therewith constituted and acknowledged by them as an agent, and a participant in the intersubjective exchange of symbols that creates our world.[28] Or, as Cassirer puts it in the *Logic of the Cultural Sciences:* "the "I" and the "You" are not two fundamentally distinct "*conditions*" but the poles of a "mutual *communication*" that—together—constitute the cultural world".[29]

Let us now look a bit deeper into the issue of how we understand past symbolic systems, and therewith, engage with past symbol users.

Historical understanding is not a reproduction but, as Cassirer somewhat obscurely says, "the reverse, of the actual historical process".[30] Since we need to understand and feel its "real life",[31] we need to understand how this particular action was an expression of spirit in a particular situation. For this, the historian needs to preserve her objects, but she also needs to decipher them again.

How exactly does this 'reversion' of the actual process look like? Cassirer characterizes our capacity for symbolization thusly:

---

26 Skidelsky (2008), 184.
27 Cassirer (2002c/1957c), 39/46.
28 See Cassirer (1995/1996), 125/130–131, also Cassirer (1961/2000), 433/75.
29 Cassirer (1961/2000), 406–411/49–53.
30 Cassirer (1972), 198.
31 Ibid.

> All works of culture originate in an act of solidification and stabilization. Man could not communicate his thoughts and feelings, and he could not, accordingly, live in a social world, if he had not the special gift of objectifying his thoughts, of giving them a solid and permanent shape.[32]

The historical event itself is thus just one attempt to stabilize fluctuating thoughts and to give them a permanent shape. The agent in history solidifies. The historian, however, does the "reverse": she makes the solid liquid again. This, of course, is not easy. Whereas we create symbols and meaning in our own everyday life, the historian only has the embodiment of such symbols from a past life. She must bring those back to life—she has to "reconstruct the real life that is at the bottom of all these single forms".[33] Or, as Cassirer formulates it in *An Essay on Man:* The first step in historical understanding is an "ideal reconstruction"[34]; that is, our remembrance of these symbols as they were meant initially. This reconstruction is not, however, just a 'reproduction'. Cassirer refers to it as "a new intellectual synthesis—a constructive act".[35] In other words, the historian needs to detect the dynamic, inner side of these solidifications, their "life". "The task of history does not consist merely in making us *acquainted* with the existence and life of the past, but in teaching us how to *interpret [deuten]* it".[36] Since this interpretation is no mere intellectual exercise, we must be able to "integrate [this knowledge] into our interior and [must be] able to transform" it.[37] Since human symbolism is always in flux—and therefore also always needs reconstruction—the historian needs to "revivify" the symbols to render them intelligible again.[38] "The historian must learn to read and interpret his documents and monuments not only as dead remnants of the past but as living messages from it, messages addressing us in a language of their own".[39] Thus, history is more than a mere narrative, but a rediscovery of a form of life. It is a "living form"[40] that does not just stand for itself, but is through our under-

---

32 Ibid., 299.
33 Cassirer (1979), 139.
34 Cassirer (1972), 189.
35 Ibid., 199.
36 Cassirer (1961/2000), 434/76.
37 Ibid.
38 Cassirer (1979), 138.
39 Cassirer (1972), 191.
40 Ibid. Of course, the reference to Friedrich Schiller, whom Cassirer discusses in the previous chapter on "art" (see ibid., 180), is palpable here.

standing also integrated into our own life. For the historian, time thus "possesses and retains a peculiar presence".⁴¹

Another distinction might help to clarify the difference between history as the treatment and setting of past events (*Geschichtsschreibung*, but also *Geschichtswissenschaft*) and the process itself (*Geschichte*). With Cassirer, we can translate this distinction in Wilhelm von Humboldt's conception of *ergon* and *energeia* that the latter introduced to distinguish between the stable and the dynamic aspects in in language. The objects of *Geschichtswissenschaft* that the historian immerses herself in (the *ergon*) just hint at the *energeia* that created them: starting from the products of becoming, history guides us back to the principles of such becoming.⁴² To really understand them means to uncover the energy behind them, and therefore to make them speak again. This also explains why Cassirer calls symbolic forms *energeia*, not *ergon:* were they just the fixed forms of, say, writing, they would be not more than the lifeless embodiment of our thinking. Symbolic forms point beyond this. They are more than a mere fixture of thought: they are the unfolding of thought that is attached to, but not exhausted in, a physical form. Understanding the production of an *ergon* means to reflect on the creative process (the *energeia*) of setting one's thoughts into a work. Living in history means this process of setting (as *Setzung* in contrast to fixture). Understanding said process needs the historian to translate any set form back into the process that led to it.

2 Symbolic Interpretation and the Second-Person Perspective

What is the specific character of such "symbolic interpretation"⁴³? Cassirer explains the difference between historical and scientific interpretations (of 'facts')

---

41 Cassirer (1961/2000), 435/76.
42 In a wider frame, this is exactly the task of the philosophy of symbolic forms. They should uncover the "very principle of becoming" of all human works. The version of history that I reconstructed here is a richer version of Cassirer's own, more restricted, account of history that he offers in *An Essay on Man*. Or, to put it more clearly: my reconstruction of history portrays it as a function within the philosophy of symbolic forms, not a prerequisite of Cassirer's own discovery of the function of symbolism.
43 In the *Logic of the Cultural Sciences* Cassirer calls this a "double interpretation" that uncovers the "characteristic manner" in which the object is constituted (Cassirer (1961/2000), 415/57.

with an example that he also⁴⁴ uses to illustrate the 'interpretation' (or mere recognition) of symbols. When I see signs, I *physically* see nothing different than I saw the second before I realized I am looking at signs. For example, I don't see anything physically different than haphazard lines on a stone, even in the moment when I understand that these lines may mean something. So, I still see nothing else, and at the same time I 'see' more—I look 'behind' the material manifestation of signs into their symbolic dimension: "They begin to 'speak' to me".⁴⁵

For Cassirer, the symbol is a "representation of consciousness as a whole which is necessarily contained or at least *projected* in every single moment and fragment of consciousness".⁴⁶ We understand this "projection" when we look at the above-mentioned stone and understand that it has something to tell us. We would not be able to understand the function of such signs at all, were it not for this intuitive capacity of ours, "an original spiritual process which belongs to the very essence of consciousness".⁴⁷ This is our personal capacity to participate in the production and interpretation of symbolic forms.

In history, we look at works⁴⁸ and not stones. Our understanding of such works, however, is piece-meal: we do have remnants, that is, 'things' or 'objects' that we seek to interpret as 'works' and that still speak to us in a sense. A coin was not made with a specific message in mind, and still it is imbued with meaning; it signifies something, may it be just an ordinary method of payment. Such objects can be read symbolically within a wider framework of other, more openly intentional symbols that contain a message. For example, the coin points toward not only a method of payment but also to the entire mechanism of the markets that functioned through this method. Hence, every coin helps, so to say, to paint an encompassing picture of the past. And every coin thus points way beyond itself.

---

44 See Verene's footnote, Cassirer (1979), 135. Consider also Cassirer's example for the different moments of perception in his essay from 1927, "Das Symbolproblem und seine Stellung im System der Philosophie", in Cassirer (2004a), 257–58: here he describes the different ways in which we can perceive a line—aesthetically, mathematically, and so on. Nothing of the brute physical facts (which, *nota bene*, Cassirer does not qualify as the 'other' of our thought, but as a moment in thought itself) changes. What rather changes is our appraisal of them.
45 Cassirer (1979), 136.
46 Cassirer (2002a/1955a), 39/105. This is the first stratum, or what he calls "natural symbolism", that serves as the basis for "artificial symbols" in language, ritual, and art.
47 Ibid., 39/106.
48 "*Das Zeugnis durch das Gezeugte, Erzeugte*—das ist das Thema des historischen Verstehens". Cassirer (1995/1996),162/164, with further references.

On the next plane, historical remnants speak to me from a particular perspective—"all historical facts are characteristic facts".[49] The historian has to collect material, only to then start the real job: she "has to complete [those fragments] and to synthesize them; to bring them into a coherent order, to show us their unity and consistency".[50] Most of the time, she has to figure out how the remnants studied actually can have a meaning. What looks like a mere object served a specific purpose once—only if the historian understands this relation can the object "tell" us something of its creator. The coin gains in personality, so to say, when the *Lebenswelt* in which it held meaning begins to come forward.

Reconstruction from a few leftovers, however, is a very hard task. In order to actually 'know' whether I, the historian, guessed correctly, I need to have much more than a few symbolic tokens. Ideally, I need to be able to reconstruct at least one or two complete symbolic systems of the culture I am interested in. Realistically, such deciphering of past symbolic systems is a movement back and forth between discovering the foreignness of a particular symbol and relating it back to more familiar symbolic systems. This synthesis of interpretations that the historian uses is, on a smaller scale perhaps, the same as the symbolic synthesis that defines our 'social being'. Man "creates verbal symbols, religious symbols, mythical and artistic images—and it is only by the totality, by the system of these symbols and images, that he can maintain his social life—that he is able to communicate with other human beings and make himself understood by them".[51] Accordingly, a complete, ideal understanding must cover all these areas. However, this happens very rarely; but this does not mean it ceases to be the ideal historical method. This holistic communication and construction of a social life can happen over time and thereby allow a historian to understand a former social life. For this communication to be successful, however, she must at least aim at grasping more than one symbolic structure of a past culture.

The above mentioned requirement—to know the 'totality' of symbolic forms in order to understand a certain time and a certain culture—leads us to another, more straightforwardly intersubjective issue. Understanding such works must also involve the 'social' dimension of each such creation that was already hinted at in Cassirer's talk of the "social dimension" of human life in general. In his notes for the prospective fourth volume of the *Philosophy of Symbolic Forms*, Cassirer holds that "every work is as such not that of an individual, but proceeds from *cooperative, correlative action* [*Wechselwirkung*]. It bears witness to 'social

---

[49] Cassirer (1972), 212.
[50] Cassirer (1979), 137.
[51] Cassirer (1979), 137.

action'. 'History' and 'culture' can be *understood* only as social phenomena".[52] No symbol can be formed in a mere private language, but needs an addressee. In the *Logic of the Cultural Sciences*, Cassirer explicitly calls culture an "intersubjective world" in which participants form various systems of interaction.[53] Mutual recognition is one strong component of this world. We need to understand such social dimensions in history as well, since we would not be able to grasp the meaning of past phenomena and events if we overlooked how deeply intersubjective communication in symbolic systems is woven into our cultural being.

The understanding of the temporal dimension of our symbolic systems via the 'works' of past agents thus demands a deeper understanding of the structure of symbolic interpretation. And this structure is fundamentally dialogical: I understand a work only if I *presuppose* that it is indeed a work, not an object. That means: I understand and interpret it as being purposively created to address a 'reader'. On the other hand, I create a work not just for my own pleasure, or, with Cassirer, to get a grasp on the world, but also with an addressee in mind. Thus, the gap between past and present is indeed bridged from both sides.[54] Historical and *mutual* understanding is the texture of human life.

Giving shape to our experiences is thus in need of stabilization from two sides. On the one hand, the agent reaches out for the more fixed form of symbols. On the other hand, such symbols only really mean something, or, have a life, if they are shared in a wider praxis of symbolization—this includes the "reading", or interpretation of symbols by others. Our expression (and consolidation) of life in symbols needs acknowledgement from the others, or such symbols mean nothing, even for me alone. This, as I understand Cassirer, is also true for the set forms of past life that the historian studies.

Accordingly, Skidelsky calls Cassirer's philosophy the "self-consciousness of culture".[55] Such philosophy examines the implicit tendencies in myth, art, science and other symbolic forms. It investigates into the ways in which each field constitutes itself in its peculiar attempt to give shape to reality. This "shape giving" is, of course, not to be understood as an inherent characteristic of any field in itself, but it is the particular kind of "work" that human beings do. The notion of "work"—may it be in the loose meaning of 'human creations', or in the more specific meaning as a basic phenomenon of life—already includes a social di-

---

52 Cassirer (1995/1996), 156/159.
53 Cassirer (1961/2000), 433, 74–75.
54 It should be noted that R.G. Collingwood presents a strikingly similar idea in his account on a philosophy of history. See the posthumously published compilation, Collingwood (1946), 294, 304.
55 Skidelsky (2008), 102.

mension. It refers to its creator as well as to its perceiver. The historian as one such perceiver never just passively observes, but actively shares in the existence of a work as a *meaningful* entity.[56]

Now we still need to show that this social dimension functions not only within a contemporary time frame (synchronically, as it were), but also diachronically—where an earlier symbolic objectification is in need of its later interpretation. Beginning from his notes for the *Metaphysics of Symbolic Forms* and its discussion of the basic phenomena and their relation to the interaction of "life" and "spirit" up to the writings and notes of his last decade, we will see that Cassirer offers an intersubjective interpretation of our historical mode of being.

3 How Basic Phenomena Establish Meaning

For Cassirer, the realm of "life" and "spirit" is not one of unity, but of dynamic rupture. Both are not simply there, but always active—which puts the thus created objects into a dynamic tension. As Cassirer presents it in the intended fourth volume of the *Philosophy of Symbolic Forms*, this dynamic rupture is triadic, formed by the three basic phenomena, the "I", the "you", and the "works". At first glance, it seems obvious that Cassirer's discussion of the second moment, the "you", should facilitate his main argument for the fundamental intersubjective direction in understanding and creating symbolic systems. However, it does not quite work out so easily.

It is striking that in the first exposition of the second basic phenomenon,[57] Cassirer employs the term "*du*" only once: as the 'other' that we first experience as an outer reality (as a 'counter-action' that resists our will).[58] It may perhaps be inferred as the addressee of the categorical imperative, and as the source of recognition (which can only come about through the "ought",[59]—but all this remains too much within the boundaries of the acting subject (the "I") to justify any focus on a self-standing second person perspective.

---

56 With reference to Dilthey, see Cassirer (1995/1996), 160–162.
57 Ibid., 134–135/139–140.
58 Later, in his discussion of the basic phenomena in relation to metaphysics, Cassirer relates the second phenomenon to Fichte's *Wissenschaftslehre* and clarifies the inter-subjective dimension (see ibid., 154–155/156–157 also 137). In relation to the theory of knowledge, the "You" steps back to make room for a philosophy of the "will" (see ibid., 179–186/177–182). Still, this "You" is understood more as the outward direction of the "I", hardly as an equally grounded second person.
59 See ibid., 186/182.

The reference to the other as a person and, most importantly, to an addressee is much clearer in the third moment, that of the "work". When the "I" objectifies herself in her work, she simultaneously gains self-understanding through expression—but she also loses control over the product of this expression. The work joins a sphere other than the "I"; it becomes its own basic phenomenon. Cassirer stresses the enduring "being" of these works. They are not aimed at and exhausted by a particular effect, but they "outlive" the moment.[60] These works are not directed at one aim in neither present nor future, but meant to be realized time and again. Such works *defy* time. This does not mean, however, that they are non-directional. They are addressed to 'recipients' in a wider sense: ideally speaking, anyone should be able to read or re-create them. Hence, the author alone can never hold complete control over the work. It "extends over the centuries. It only becomes clear in the total course of its consequences and interpretations [*in seiner totalen Wirkung und Auslegung*]"[61] by others. To create such works is a mode of reaching out to the other, since such works are to be understood, apprehended, and realized by others. In his Yale Seminar on Symbolism and Philosophy of Language from 1941/42, as well as in the *Logic of the Cultural Sciences*, Cassirer refers to this phenomenon from a different perspective: "Man is constantly looking back to his past and looking forward to his future. His consciousness of the present moment always involves an act of recollection and an act of anticipation".[62] Here, he regards our capacity to understand ourselves and our works within a timeline in which the conscious subject is not the starting point itself, but reaches beyond herself into both the past and the future. This is the perspective of any 'reader' of such works as previously mentioned: works of past people are understood both in their historical time frame, as well as in regards to us (as their future). Anticipation serves as an important moment in morality, or, we may state more generally, in 'normativity': "Man has to choose his way towards the future; he has to intervene in the course of things

---

60 See ibid., 187/183. Mind the striking similarity to Cassirer's notion of *"das Bleibende im Leben des Geistes"*, which he explicates in the opening paragraph of his 1916, "Der Begriff der Symbolischen Form im Aufbau der Geisteswissenschaften" (Cassirer (2003), 76). Our spiritual being is a dynamic entity, its essence is "becoming", which, in turn, can only be apprehended when it is elevated into something enduring—the dynamic, in other words, is not visible if we don't have something enduring that we use as a contrast or foil. But to do that, we need to capture what is enduring in the dynamic, that is, we need to hold it fast. In the cultural sciences we can only do this through the works that represent our spiritual being. We just need to be sure, however, that we concentrate not just on the work's physical presence, but on its function—otherwise we kill off the dynamic and will never understand anything of it (see ibid., 78).
61 Cassirer (1995/1996), 125/131.
62 Cassirer (2005), 290, see also 289, and Cassirer (1961/200), 382–383/26.

and events".⁶³ Such reaching out into the future creates a practical demand, or, with Cassirer, an "ideal".⁶⁴ Man therewith is "actively" interested in the future.⁶⁵ "Human life cannot persist without incessantly changing its forms. It does not persevere in its present state; it has always to go beyond this state" to create a "symbolic eternity".⁶⁶ To create a future, we need to reach into the past as well. We thus build on previous peoples' attempt to create this 'symbolic eternity', i.e. their culture.

This temporality is constituted by our awareness of works and other persons. In the mythical state, "[w]e do not need to infer 'other minds'; we experience the other directly, 'immediately', with more certainty and more immediately than the being of things".⁶⁷ In mythical consciousness, everything is fundamentally animated. Thus, all 'works' are primarily perceived as external and personal forces, not as the product of spirit. Things are different in the historian's non-mythical attempts to uncover past agents via their works. When the historian interprets such works, she aims at the force behind these 'objects', in short: the person. In the *Logic of the Cultural Sciences*, Cassirer is even clearer on this double-faced relation of agents and works:

> There is no perception that does not intend a determined 'object' and that is not directed toward it. But this necessary objective reference presents itself to us in a twofold direction, which we can briefly and schematically characterize as a direction toward the 'it' and a direction toward the 'you'.⁶⁸

Therefore, again, empirically speaking we may discover the historical agent through her works, but we can only discover her because we had to assume her to be there.

There is one more thing to consider from the side of the producer of said forms. Of course, different pieces of historical evidence serve a different purpose.

---

63 Cassirer (2005), 297.
64 Ibid., 298.
65 Therefore, again, our interest in history is also practical, as a means of self-knowledge and self-direction: "What he seeks in history is not a mere speculation on past events; it is a guide to decisions and actions that are directed to the future". (ibid., 290) This also points against Bayer's argumentation that the second basic phenomenon is situated in the present (see Bayer (2001), 133).
66 Cassirer (2005), 290–291.
67 Cassirer (1995/1996), 120/124. This also helps to explain why myth is the primordial symbolic form—everything is personalized; everything is animated, just because an "object" is so much farther removed from our understanding.
68 Cassirer (1961/2000), 396/39.

A novel serves a different role in remembrance than a statue, a war-diary, or a haphazard collection of newspaper articles. Different kinds of works are hence various embodiments of an intention to be understood, and this does something to the degree of trust that the historian should have in her sources. I certainly do not want "the world" to read my diary, but I might wish for it to read my books. Hence, I may present things differently in my published work than in other writings. This difference can even amount to blatant deceit: The statue reminding us of some great war tends to gloss over the loss and pain that this war also entailed. When Napoleon addressed himself to posterity, he was certainly not always honest.

Deceit as the intention to be understood in a certain (positive) way in order to cover up more base desires is a type of historical fake-work that can perhaps never be completely ruled out But it can be kept at bay through the use of a careful historical method that reconstructs whole situations from various viewpoints. The historian does not simply believe her object, but puts it into the wider framework of its environment. No statement is taken for granted, but must always be tested. Additionally: even a seemingly faithful, personal entry in a diary can be a lie to oneself and can consequently lead the trusting reader astray. On the other side of the spectrum, every deceitful or euphemistic representation addressed to posterity (as with various types of monuments, or Napoleon's utterances) can claim a historical present itself that has a certain effect. They create another perspective of the event described. The interplay of such artificial perspectives and the cautiously critical perspective of the historian herself is a good example of Cassirer's idea of "revivifying", after all.

Our receptivity to works by other agents is due to our own trajectory into the future. In order to be able to actively shape the future we want, we need to be able to understand who and where we are. And we can more efficiently do so when we see how we arrived there. Present possibilities, but also the historical interpretative frameworks of past events influence our understanding. As Steve Lofts put it quite wonderfully, "meaning is possible only in living dialogue, in a dynamic process of exchange, of reading which is a rewriting, rewriting in the sense that one rethinks the idea in order to understand it, but also in the sense that one appropriates the idea to oneself".[69]

---

[69] Lofts (2000), 13.

4 The Culture of History: An Ongoing Renaissance

Cassirer diagnoses a desire of all cultures to defy death by creating the "symbolic eternity" already mentioned. Symbolic forms allow us to grasp our world and give it shape. This does not mean, however, to 'arrest' our worldview in one fixed symbolic expression. For our expression to count as a genuine "work" at all, it does not suffice to be done once. The reality of a symbolic expression is that it is repeated over and over again.[70] Not as a passive remaking, but as an active re-creation that is not necessarily bound to the one person that initially created it. This weaves a net of respective re-creations throughout time: The content of "truly great works of culture ... exists for us only by virtue of the fact that it is continually taken possession of [*angeeignet*] anew and as a result always created anew".[71]

This constant re-creation is a combination of the old and the new, and it offers a peculiar connection of the personal and the universal: We enter the hermeneutic circle from our very own direction, with our very own 'baggage'.[72] But instead of viewing this as a problem, Cassirer embraces this particular perspective. Without personal experience, so his argument goes, we would not understand another person's experience at all. Historical truth is always a "personal truth",[73] even though that seems a *contradictio in adiecto*. A character on the one side, the present, reaches out to another character on the other side, the past. In the same vein, the works of the past also reach out towards the future, in their sheer will to be understood.

In the concluding chapter of the *Logic of the Cultural Sciences*, "The 'Tragedy of Culture'",[74] Cassirer once more stresses that understanding cannot be achieved by the subject relating to its object by somehow putting herself into it—

---

[70] "In order to endure, the works of man must be constantly renewed and restored". Cassirer (1979), 199. See also the notes for his Seminar on Symbolism and Philosophy of Language, Cassirer (2005), 292–294: in his discussion of Diotima's teaching of immortality in Plato's *Symposium* Cassirer calls this "symbolic immortality".
[71] Cassirer (1961/200), 469–470/111.
[72] The questions we ask of the past are "put and dictated by the present—by our present intellectual interests and our present moral and social needs". Cassirer (1972), 192.
[73] Ibid., 201.
[74] In his critical discussion of Simmel's claims, and more general against "sensualist" theories "which believes to have understood an ideal concept by making it a copy of an objective existence", see Cassirer (1961/2000), 467/108.

we must place ourselves "in an active relation to the other",[75] which is a process of *communication*, not of classification. I do not know that there is a "you" because I project myself there. I can only know it when I accept the dialogue, not impose a monologue with two roles. My interpretation of a work serves as the "bridge that leads from one I-pole to the other".[76] Naturally, when you start the walk, you already assume such an end-point; otherwise you would not step onto the bridge. And, to stay within the analogy: Same as a bridge, the work itself must remain flexible. It will never be completely comprehended or exhausted, but it "becomes the mediator between I and you, not by transporting a finished content from the one to the other but in that the activity of the one is kindled by that of the other".[77]

And here we get ever closer to the term "culture fiction" as embraced at the beginning of this paper. Historical comprehension via works is closely related to understanding art as a symbolic form, in that it requires the 'reader' to be not only a passive recipient, but to creatively reconstruct the works. In language, "[t]he recipient does not take the gift as he would a stamped coin. For he can take it up only by *using* is, and in this use he imprints upon it a new shape".[78] Likewise, historical evidence is never just 'taken in', but can only be understood as a piece of a larger puzzle. Through interpretation, such 'use' has its effect on the piece of evidence itself, in that it re-shapes, or re-creates the essence of such a work through its renewed understanding. As such, historical understanding of symbolic objects serves as a tool for world-understanding and self-recognition.

All such understanding is hence a creative process, a process of *Aneignung* [of making something one's own], which re-creates the object through the attempts to understand it. "The creative process must always satisfy two different conditions: on the one side, it must tie itself to something permanent and existing, and, on the other, it must always be open to a new employment and a new approach that changes this existence".[79] To be sure, in the particular context of this statement, Cassirer is referring to the artist. However, this also applies to understanding history: as the author of a work ties the existing and the new together in order to form something according to her will, and to effect something; similarly, the reader needs to take these objects in and to make them her own. The historian does not rewrite her material. If I investigate the events that

---

75 Ibid., 267/108.
76 Ibid., 469/110.
77 Ibid., 469/111.
78 Ibid., 473/114–115.
79 Ibid., 474/116.

stand behind and may have influenced Descartes' creation (and its withholding) of *Le Monde* (1664), I do not just write them up anew to my liking. It is necessary, however, to give every piece of evidence a *frame* of reference, a framework within which it speaks to us in the present in a way that we can understand, and that we can justifiably and coherently relate to what we know about Descartes (as a researcher, a philosopher, etc.). Like the artist, who is bound to vocabulary, material and personal capability and therefore cannot just freely invent things,[80] the historian is bound to both her own time (such as her language and thus her ultimate frame of reference) and to the demand for the coherence of the historical evidence. The evidence speaks to her, both in the language of its time and her own time. "Science fiction" plays with projecting and expanding the natural laws as we know them into an unknown realm of the future. "Culture Fiction" needs to accept a body of evidence, and it needs to frame this body within a possible, and rich, lively environment, or frame of reference. Science Fiction seems to work best where it is most closely modeled after the world as we know it. This might be true as well for Culture Fiction: it is most convincing if it does not present us with the past as something closed off and gone, but as having its own capacity to live.

The goal of historical understanding could be reformulated thusly: to immerse oneself into the other and therewith find oneself anew "in a new and deeper sense".[81] The understanding of past works in this demanding way offers a *"source of power"*[82] for one's self-understanding. In the end, Cassirer does not quite make an argument for history as the faithful archive of human deeds. Instead, he supports the idea of what I call an 'informed renaissance'. We invent ourselves anew through a deeper understanding of what we were.[83]

---

[80] See ibid., 467/116.
[81] Ibid., 470/112.
[82] Ibid., 471/112.
[83] My heartfelt gratitude goes to Sebastian Luft, organizer of this conference, for his kind invitation and impeccable hospitality at Marquette in June 2014. I am also indebted to comments and criticism by all participants, especially Olga Knizhnik, Pierre Keller, Guido Kreis, Samantha Matherne—and in particular Simon Truwant and Steve Lofts, who read and ingeniously commented on a later version of this paper. All remaining mistakes, however, are entirely mine.

Bibliography

Bast (2000): Rainer A. Bast, *Problem, Geschichte, Form. Das Verhältnis von Philosophie und Geschichte bei Ernst Cassirer im historischen Kontext*, Berlin: Duncker & Humblot.

Bayer (2001): Thora I. Bayer, *Cassirer's Metaphysics of Symbolic Forms: A Philosophical Commentary*, New Haven and London: Yale University Press.

Bundgaard (2011): Peer F. Bundgaard, *The Grammar of Aesthetic Intuition: On Ernst Cassirer's Concept of Symbolic Forms in the Visual Arts*, Synthese 179, 43–57.

Cassirer (1961/2000): Ernst Cassirer, *Zur Logik der Kulturwissenschaften: fünf Studien*, Darmstadt: Wissenschaftlichen Buchgesellschaft; Ernst Cassirer, *The Logic of the Cultural Sciences: Five Studies*, S. G. Lofts (trans.), New Haven and London: Yale University Press;

Cassirer (1972): Ernst Cassirer, An Essay on Man: *An Introduction to A Philosophy of Human Culture*, New Haven and London: Yale University Press.

Cassirer (1979): Ernst Cassirer, Symbol, Myth, and Culture: *Essays and Lectures of Ernst Cassirer 1935–1945*, Donald Phillip Verene (ed.), New Haven and London: Yale University Press.

Cassirer (1995/1996): Ernst Cassirer, *Zur Metaphysik der symbolischen Formen*, in: *Nachgelassene Manuskripte und Texte* (hereafter: ECN), vol. 1, J.M. Krois (ed.), Hamburg: Felix Meiner Verlag; Ernst Cassirer, Philosophy of Symbolic Forms, Volume Four: The Metaphysics of Symbolic Forms, J.M. Krois and D. P. Verene (eds.), New Haven: Yale University Press.

Cassirer (2002a/1955a): Ernst Cassirer, *Philosophie der symbolischen Formen, Erster Teil, Die Sprache*, in: *Gesammelte Werke* (henceforth ECW), B. Recki (ed.), vol. 11, Hamburg: Felix Meiner Verlag; Ernst Cassirer, The Philosophy of Symbolic Forms, Volume One: Language, Ralph Manheim (trans.), New Haven: Yale University Press.

Cassirer (2002b/1955b)): Ernst Cassirer, *Philosophie der symbolischen Formen. Zweiter Teil, Das mythische Denken*, in: ECW, vol. 12, op. cit.; Ernst Cassirer, The Philosophy of Symbolic Forms, Volume Two: Mythical Thought, Ralph Manheim (trans.), New Haven: Yale University Press.

Cassirer (2002c/1957c): Ernst Cassirer, *Philosophie der symbolischen Formen, Dritter Teil, Phänomenologie der Erkenntnis*, in: ECW, vol. 13, op. cit.; Ernst Cassirer, *The Philosophy of Symbolic Forms, Volume Three: The Phenomenology of Knowledge*, Ralph Manheim (trans.), New Haven: Yale University Press.

Cassirer (2003): Ernst Cassirer, *Aufsätze und kleine Schriften* (1922–1926), in: ECW, vol. 16, op. cit.

Cassirer (2004a): Ernst Cassirer, *Aufsätze und kleine Schriften* (1927–1931), in: ECW, vol. 17, op. cit.

Cassirer (2004b): Ernst Cassirer, *Aufsätze und kleine Schriften* (1932–1935), in: ECW, vol. 18, op. cit.

Cassirer (2005): Ernst Cassirer, *Vorlesungen und Studien zur philosophischen Anthropologie*, in: ECN, vol. 6, op. cit.

Collingwood (1946): R.G. Collingwood, *The Idea of History*, Oxford: Oxford University Press.

Darwall (2006): Stephen Darwall, *The Second-Person Standpoint*, Cambridge and London: Harvard University Press.

Göller (1991): Thomas Göller, *Ernst Cassirer über Geschichte und Geschichtswissenschaft*, Zeitschrift für philosophische Forschung 45, 224–248.
Krois (1987): John Michael Krois, *Cassirer: Symbolic Forms and History*, New Haven and London: Yale University Press.
Lauschke (2007): Marion Lauschke, *Ästhetik im Zeichen des Menschen*, Hamburg: Meiner.
Lofts (2000): Steve G. Lofts, *Ernst Cassirer: A 'Repetition' of Modernity*, Albany: State University of New York Press.
Orth (1993): Ernst W. Orth, *Cassirers Philosophie der Lebensordnungen*, in: Ernst Cassirer: Geist und Leben, E.W. Orth (ed.), Leipzig: Reclam, 9–30.
Skidelsky (2008): Edward Skidelsky, *Ernst Cassirer: The Last Philosopher of Culture*, Princeton and Oxford: Princeton University Press.

J Tyler Friedman (Milwaukee)
Cassirer's Critique of Culture and the Several Tasks of the Critic

In his 1935 inaugural lecture at the University of Gothenburg, where Ernst Cassirer had just assumed an academic post, the exiled philosopher reflects on the *conceptus cosmicus* of philosophy; that is, the connection of philosophy to the world as opposed to the scholastic conception in which philosophy primarily engages in a dialogue with itself. As usual, Cassirer mines the history of thought for resources that might shed light on the present and in this instance he cites Kant's "Architectonic of Pure Reason" in order to inquire whether we have retained Kant's own ideal of philosophy as "related to the world."[1] Siding with Albert Schweitzer, Cassirer gestures towards the "crumbling of our spiritual and ethical ideals of culture"[2] embodied by the National Socialist regime that had forced him from Germany. It was, in part at any rate, the derelictions of theoretical philosophy, too enamored of its subtle, scholastic problems that allowed the masses to be swayed by illegitimate claims to truth and justice.

Cassirer's speech ends with a clarion call for philosophy—that is to say, philosophers—to take up the mantel of Enlightenment humanism in response to the *crisis* of contemporary culture. Etymologically speaking, as the term appears in the work of Galen and Hippocrates for instance, "crisis" denotes the turning point in a disease. With time, however, the semantic range of the term has broadened to encompass any situation in which immediate, drastic, and decisive action is required.

In the world of Galen and Hippocrates, a crisis called for a doctor. But what sort of a practitioner does the crisis that Cassirer faced in 1935 require? Given the context of his lecture, it is clear that Cassirer has 'the philosopher' in mind. But the philosopher is not the only individual whose station is to assess the various products of culture. "I am much more convinced," claims Cassirer, "that the question ... of the connection of all knowledge to the essential aim of human reason itself, arises today more urgently and imperatively than ever before, not only for the philosopher, but for all of us who partake in the life of knowledge and the life of spiritual culture."[3] The critic is also responsible for overseeing the health and welfare of culture, and while the philosopher plays an essential role in var-

---

1 Cassirer (1979a), 59.
2 Cassirer (1979a), 60.
3 Cassirer (1979a), 59.

ious manifestations of critique/criticism, within Cassirer's thought there are tasks of the critic in which the philosopher qua philosopher does not participate.

It is the aim of the present essay to adumbrate the several tasks of the critic that fall out of Cassirer's critique of culture. In the process, we shall also assess the relationship between Cassirer's conception of critique and that of his predecessors who stand at the head of the tradition of which Cassirer is a member. We shall see that Cassirer's position is situated between the hardline insistence on objectivity in critique that marks the views of Kant and Hegel and the diametrically opposed view that critique or criticism cannot and should not strive to be anything other than an expression of one's own subjectivity.

A brief foray into the etymology of "critique" will help us understand the core meanings that inform not only the meaning of "critique," but also the family of terms to which it is related.[4] This point of departure will also combat the tendency to read pejorative connotations into these terms, since, in English, they usually imply faultfinding or negative valuation more generally—as is suggested by the common qualification '*constructive* criticism.'

The proximal source of the term "critique" is the French language, but it is in ancient Greek that we reap the benefits of etymology. "Critique" derives from κριτική, a shortened form of κριτική τέχνη, "the critical art."[5] Relatedly, κριτικός, translatable as "capable of judging"[6] or "able to discern,"[7] becomes *criticus* in Latin and, eventually, "critic" in English. The ancient Greek term at the root of both "critique" and "critic" is the verb κρίνειν "to separate, divide, judge."[8] Interestingly and importantly, the term "criterion"—that according to which the critic critiques—has a similar provenance; namely, the ancient Greek term κριτήριον, meaning a "means of judging" or a "test."[9]

One consequence of this peek into the etymological background of "critique" is that we are unable to derive from it an unassailable definition of the task of the critic. Simply, the meaning is too broad and thus delimiting the task of the critic would require fixing an understanding of equally vague terms. The critic, so the etymologist tells us, is an individual who is capable of judging. But what exactly is the critic capable of judging? What is the domain of the critic? How do we judge who is and who is not capable of judging?

---

[4] Also illuminating is the history of the concept of critique. Cf. Schneiders (1985) and Röttgers (1975).
[5] Klein (1971), 374.
[6] Klein (1971), 374.
[7] Skeat (2005), 145.
[8] Klein (1971), 374.
[9] Hoad (1996), 229.

What constitutes a suitable criterion for critique? The questions proliferate and, ironically, are in need of a capable judge to settle them.

1 Kant's Critique

For certain philosophers, these questions can be distilled to a single question: how is the judgment of the critic to establish universal validity? If the objectivity of critique were suitably demonstrated then the critic could go about her task with clear conscience. This question is powerfully answered in the methodology set out by Immanuel Kant's *Critique of Pure Reason*, and this particular approach to the question of critical objectivity has shaped subsequent conceptions. One of the hallmarks of the critical tradition beginning with Kant is that it avoids trying its object in a "foreign court of judgment,"[10] and, thereby, it establishes the objectivity of its activity. "One can regard the critique of pure reason as the true court of justice for all controversies of pure reason," writes Kant, "for the critique is not involved in these disputes ... but is rather set the task of determining and judging what is lawful in reason in general."[11] While Kant's immanent critique, as it emerges in the *Critique of Pure Reason*, is applied to speculative reason (i. e. reason as it determines its objects *a priori*), its core insight was taken up in less abstract, theoretical, philosophical registers.[12] The German Romantics, for example, as Walter Benjamin writes in his dissertation on *The Concept of Criticism in German Romanticism*, the "cardinal principle of critical activity since the Romantic movement ... is, judging works of art by immanent criteria."[13] For instance, this principle can be found in the first two of Goethe's three questions of art criticism: "1) what was the artist trying to do? 2) How well did he or she do it? 3) Was it worth doing?"[14] The immanent impulse is also found in the libretto of Wagner's *Der Meistersinger*: "Wollt ihr nach Regeln messen, Was nicht nach eurer Regeln Lauf, Der eig'nen Spur vergessen, Sucht davon erst die Regeln auf! ... Eu'r Urtheil, dünkt mich, wäre reifer, Hörtet ihr besser zu."[15]

---

10 Hegel (2002), 210.
11 Kant (1998), 649.
12 And, of course, in the *Critique of Practical Reason and Critique of the Power of Judgment*, Kant applies immanent critique to reason in its practical mode and as it makes teleological and aesthetic judgments, respectively.
13 Benjamin (2004), 155.
14 Archer (2003), 115.
15 Wagner (1904), 51.

Kant's celebrated Copernican Revolution can in fact not be thought apart from the establishment of critique as immanent. When we suppose that objects of experience conform to our manner of knowing them, then once we have determined the conditions for the possibility of experience, we have identified non-arbitrary criteria according to which we may evaluate the prima facie validity of knowledge claims. To take a common but significant example, if all possible experience is by definition spatio-temporal experience then we may dismiss out of hand claims to knowledge of a being [viz. God] that exists outside of space and time.

It is for this reason that Kant understands the critique of pure reason to be primarily of a negative significance. As "the mere estimation of pure reason, of its sources and boundaries,"[16] the critique of pure reason can account for the conditions of possibility for synthetic *a priori* judgments in pure mathematics and pure natural science. The critique can also thereby explain the possibility of metaphysics as a science and the desiderata of putting metaphysics on such a secure path. However the results won in the investigation prove to be of little value when its comes to the amplification of our metaphysical knowledge. Instead, since the critique deals not with the traditional objects of metaphysics (e.g. God, freedom, and immortality) but with the possibility of human beings' mode of cognition as it functions *a priori*, the utility of the critique of pure reason is primarily "the purification of our reason, and for keeping it free of errors"[17].

This purification, especially when used to illustrate the overreaching of philosophical theories, is where Kant's critique (as *krinein* "to separate, decide") becomes criticism (as *kritikos* "able to make judgments"). This subtle shift in the meaning and significance of critique emerges especially clearly in Kant's remarks on the discipline of pure reason. In "The discipline of reason with regard to its polemical use,"[18] for instance, Kant issues directives for proper critical practice with respect to "the defense of [pure reason's] propositions against dogmatic denials of them."[19] When the subject matter is merely speculative, so long as both parties 'speak reason,' polemical disputes concerning the use of pure reason pose no threat to the common good. In fact, such conflicts serve to cultivate reason: "Thus instead of charging in with a sword, you should instead watch this conflict peaceably from the safe seat of critique, a conflict which must be exhausting for the combatants but entertaining or you, with an outcome

---

[16] Kant (1998), 149.
[17] Kant (1998), 149.
[18] Kant (1998), 643.
[19] Kant (1998), 644.

that will certainly be bloodless and advantageous for your insight."[20] Note that the transformation of critique from *krinein* to *kritikos* is also a transformation of philosophy from the "scholastic concept" (*Schulbegriff*) to the cosmopolitan concept (*Weltbegriff*)[21], in which philosophy acts on the world instead of merely circumscribing the limits and possibilities of philosophy's realm of permissible action in the world. And it was philosophy's failure to move from scholastic concerns to cosmopolitan activity that Cassirer identified as playing a crucial part in the crisis of contemporary culture.

2 Critique in Early Hegel

Critique also appears as an explicit theme in Hegel's early thought. In fact, the 1801 essay "On the Essence of Philosophical Critique Generally, and its Relationship to the Present State of Philosophy in Particular"[22] picks up nicely where we left off with Kant's "The discipline of reason with regard to its polemical use;" seeing as Hegel's essay reads like a how-to manual informing the would-be critic of her task.

In Hegel's hands, the topic of critique commences with the question of a standard [*Maßstab*, literally: measuring rod]. As a form of evaluation, critique requires —"presupposes,"[23] [*vorausgesetzt*] writes Hegel—a measure with which to evaluate the matter at hand. One might say that an 'in terms of which' belongs to the intentional structure of critique. The standard is also the philosophical focal point of critique, for it contains the tacit philosophical commitments, presuppositions, and sharp edge with which the critic bushwhacks her way through the thicket of things to be judged.

Hegel warns against two forms of debilitating dependence that undermine the suitability of a standard and, along with it, the validity of the critique that utilizes this standard. First, the critical standard must be independent of the critic. If critique is to come forth with the clean conscience of objectivity and disinterestedness—as Hegel claims its essence demands—then it must wash its hands of everything subjective. When this condition is not met, "what appears is only two subjectivities in opposition; things that have nothing in common with one

---

20 Kant (1998), 647.
21 Kant (1998), 694.
22 This essay—the introduction to *The Critical Journal of Philosophy*—was co-written by Schelling; a fact that I ignore here. For speculation of Schelling's contribution to the piece cf. Hegel (2002), 207 f.
23 Hegel (2002), 209.

another come on stage with equal right for that very reason; and ... criticism transposes itself into a subjective situation and its verdict appears as a one-sided decision by violence."[24] Thus the critique will lack the force and compellingness appropriate to its nature. "That's just *your* opinion," protests the object of critique.

If the individuality of the critic vitiates critique, so does deriving the standard from the individuality of the object being critiqued. Said differently, Hegel forbids the derivation of a critical standard from "the singular appearance [*einzelnen Erscheinung*],"[25] i.e., the particular thing in question. While this may appear as an abandonment of immanent critique, it is in fact only a commitment to a certain 'type' of immanent critique, or rather, a commitment to a rigorous understanding of objectivity that also leads us into the metaphysical background animating Hegel's conception of critique.

The only critical standard capable of vindicating criticism's aspirations for universal validity is the standard derived "from the eternal and unchangeable model of what really is [*von dem ewigen und unwandelbaren Urbild der Sache selbst*]."[26] In his critique essay, Hegel's preferred term for this eternal and unchangeable model is the Idea [*Idee*]. Thus, philosophical criticism requires the Idea of philosophy while art criticism requires the Idea of art, and so on. It is the Idea watching over the critique, so to speak, that accounts for different 'types' of criticism. The objectivity of critique is grounded on the objectivity of its standard, which ensures that the critic is not judging on the basis of personal taste or some such subjective standard.

How is the critic to gain access to, say, the Idea of philosophy? "The fact that philosophy is but one, and can only be one, rests of the fact that reason is but one,"[27] writes Hegel. And it is "because the truth of reason is but one, like beauty, that criticism as objective judgment is possible in principle"[28]. The Idea of philosophy does not exist in the realm of Platonic Ideas; rather, following Kant's Copernican Turn, the Idea of philosophy is understood as immanent to reason itself; namely, as reason in an adequate mode of self-cognition. In another formulation and in terms that point to the idiom of the *Phenomenology of Spirit*, Hegel also defines philosophy as "a cognition of the Absolute"[29]. Philosophy is nothing but reason turning towards itself in a critical mode. And, as Karin

---

24 Hegel (2002), 276.
25 Hegel (2002), 208.
26 Hegel (2002), 208.
27 Hegel (2002), 209.
28 Hegel (2002), 210.
29 Hegel (2002), 209.

de Boer points out, Hegel holds "that reason actually appears in the guise of historical philosophical systems that do not allow it to achieve adequate self-knowledge."[30] Thus the critical standard is the exact same criterion that determines—*by definition*—the success of any historical philosophical system. Because the standard of critique (the Idea of philosophy, the Idea of art, etc.) is immanent to the object (a philosophical system, a work of art, etc.), critique is capable of objective, intersubjective validity.

3 The Transcendental Dimension of the Critique of Culture

Cassirer himself makes it clear that he understands his work as continuing the grand tradition of idealism that arises out of Kant.[31] "It is not the things themselves," explains Cassirer, "but the possible determinations of things, their determination by the different modes of cognition, that proves to be the true problem of a new idealism."[32] In other words, it is Kant's prioritization of "the problem of accessibility"[33] over the problem of objectivity that distinguishes his transcendental idealism from the dogmatic idealism of Berkeley and the skeptical idealism of Descartes, and paves the way for the critical idealism of the Marburg School and Cassirer. In fact, it is the immanent status of Kant's critique that made possible Cassirer's critique of culture. "Instead of measuring the content, meaning, and truth of intellectual forms by something extraneous which is supposed to be reproduced in them," writes Cassirer in a characterization of Kant's Copernican revolution, "we must find in these forms themselves the measure and criterion for their truth and intrinsic meaning."[34]

---

30 De Boer (2012), 86.
31 In *Critical Idealism as a Philosophy of Culture*, for example, Cassirer carefully distinguishes between the idealism of Berkeley and Kant before associating his own project with the latter.
32 Cassirer (1979b), 70.
33 Cassirer (1979b), 69.
34 Cassirer (1946), 8. Kant also gestures at what we shall see to be the ethical dimension of critique. In "the discipline of pure reason with regard to its polemical use," he prefigures Cassirer's insistence on holding apart the claims made from within different symbolic frameworks. "Thus let your opponent speak only reason, and fight him solely with the weapons of reason. For the rest, do not worry about the good cause (of practical reason), for that never comes into play in a merely speculative dispute." Kant (1998), 646.

While Cassirer adopts Kant's analytical task of studying modes of cognition, his more expansive definition of reason[35] implies that the work of transcendental critique is far from finished. In Cassirer's framework, the critique carried out in Kant's first Critique would pertain to one of the numerous modes of cognition, namely that of the symbolic form of science. A similar parsing of the structures constitutive of, for example, mythical thinking is also necessary. Fortunately, doing so does not require that we start at square one since we find "the same universal forms of intuition and thought which constitute the unity of consciousness as such and which accordingly constitute the unity of both the mythical consciousness and the consciousness of pure knowledge."[36] Thus the task of a transcendental critique of mythical reason involves laying bare the distinctive "tonality"[37] [*Tönung*] taken on by the forms of intuition (i.e. space and time) and the categories according to which this irreducible type of experience takes shape. For instance, Cassirer situates mythical space in "a kind of middle position between the space of sense perception and the space of pure cognition, that is geometry."[38] Like the space of perception, mythical space is founded on individual feeling; 'here' and 'there' are never the mere abstract coordinates of geometric space, but are rather tied up with the embodiment of human beings as well as "mythical feeling values."[39] Nevertheless, mythical space, like the metric space of Euclidean geometry, also strives towards universality. While the content of this universality is different, Cassirer identifies a functional similarity insofar as mythical space operates as a schema by virtue of which incommensurate elements can be brought into relation. For instance, in totemic conceptions of the world, everything is endowed with membership of a totemic group, which is "the expression of relationships which are felt and understood to be quite real."[40] These originally felt relationships are then given spatial expression, which are frequently organized according to cardinal directions and other organizational schemes. This analysis of space in mythical thinking is, of course, but one ele-

---

35 Oswald Schwemmer attributes Cassirer's broadened understanding of reason to the influence of Goethe who "stresses the variety of sensible and especially of creative forms of action and life." Schwemmer (2004), 5. The influence of Kant, as it relates to Cassirer's understanding of reason, comes in the form of the *unity* of reason's activities: "[The various symbolic forms] possess, in spite of their differences, an intrinsic unity." Cassirer (1979b), 71.
36 Cassirer (1955), 60.
37 Cassirer (1955), 61.
38 Cassirer (1955), 83.
39 Cassirer (1955), 85.
40 Cassirer (1955), 86.

ment of one symbolic form. The completion of the critique of culture requires that all of the symbolic forms be submitted to this transcendental critique.⁴¹

How does the transcendental dimension of the critique of culture stand with respect to immanent critique? As we have seen, the polysemic character of 'critique' requires that we untangle its manifold senses. In its transcendental practice, critique (as *krinein* "to separate, decide") is perhaps best understood as preparatory for, instead of an instantiation of, immanent critique; since, as the notion emerges in the thought of Kant and Hegel, immanent critique primarily concerns critique practiced as *kritikos* "able to make judgments." Thus with the transcendental dimension of the critique of culture we have not yet reached the threshold beyond which immanent critique most clearly emerges. Recall that Kant's critique of pure reason seeks not only the elements of reason but also the laws of its pure use. The critical task for which the immanence of critique's standard is pertinent arises when we assess whether particular philosophical theories have exercised pure reason in a lawful manner. So while this transcendental critique is a condition for the possibility of immanent critique/criticism, (seeing as they provide the resources that are necessary to distinguish between permissible and impermissible claims), it largely sidesteps the question of immanence.

4 The Ethical Dimension of the Critique of Culture

The transcendental critique of culture is tasked with presenting the *sui generis* character of the symbolic forms. It is, in other words, a descriptive enterprise. But its descriptive results are not without normative import. There is a concrete, practical consequence of the transcendental critique of culture, in which the ethical significance of Cassirer's critique as well as its immanent character come to the fore.

In order to approach the ethical aspect of the critique of culture, let us take a step back in order to consider who carries out the transcendental critique. This researcher strives "to comprehend every symbol in its place and recognize how it is limited and conditioned by every other symbol."⁴² Doing so entails that this individual not prioritize any one symbolic form over the others, and this requires that the researcher not be entirely immersed in any one form. This is Cassirer's presentation of the unique position occupied by the philosopher. That philoso-

---

41 Concerning the question of how many symbolic forms there are, cf. Luft (2004), 35.
42 Cassirer (1996), 227.

phy does not constitute a symbolic form unto itself is implied by Cassirer's definition of philosophy, which, he characterizes as the "self-knowledge of reason"[43]. Importantly, the achievement of this self-knowledge secures for the philosopher a panoptic grasp of the equal nobility and field of validity of each paradigm and prepares her to supervise their interrelations.

While there is no experience that is not symbolically clad, the philosophical vantage point involves always keeping one foot outside the symbolic forms, so to speak; or, rather, it involves never immersing oneself in a single form to the extent that the other forms are made to relinquish their inherent rights in order to conform to one form that has been placed on the pedestal of Truth. Describing the task of philosophy, Cassirer writes that it

> has to grasp the *whole system* of symbolic forms … and it must refer each individual in this totality to its fixed place. If we assume this problem solved, then the rights would be assured, and the limits fixed, of each of the particular forms of the concept and of knowledge as well as of the general forms of the theoretical, ethical, aesthetic and religious understanding of the world.[44]

Thus by grasping the whole system of symbolic forms in the transcendental critique of culture, the philosopher has achieved a standpoint that allows her to assure the rights of each symbolic form. This task of defending the plurality of ways that human beings experience the world is what is referred to as the ethical dimension of Cassirer's critique of culture.[45] One noteworthy consequence is that, in this way, the traditional dualism of rational/irrational breaks down. No longer does scientific thinking have exclusive rights over the domain of rationality while myth and religion are denigrated or dismissed out of hand. Because the transcendental critique of culture illustrates the rational structure of mythical and religious consciousness, the ethical critique of culture must deem scientific consciousness itself 'irrational' when it arrogates to itself exclusive ownership of rationality.

In what respect is this ethical task 'critical?' In our brief etymological excursion we saw that critique involves separation and categorization and, on that basis, judgment and decision. The transcendental dimension of the critique of culture categorizes concrete cultural products and thereby studies the various manners of symbolically parsing the world. On this basis, we once again find the subtle shift in the meaning and task of critique; namely, where the *krinein*

---

[43] Cassirer (1996), 226. Also cf. Hegel (2002), 209: "For reason…when it becomes object for itself in its self-cognition (and hence philosophy)…"
[44] Cassirer (1923), 447.
[45] Cf. Luft, 2004, 37.

("to separate, decide") of the transcendental critique becomes the *kritikos* ("able to make judgments") of its ethical counterpart. Once the transcendental critique has categorized the symbolic forms, it is the critical task of the ethical critique to oversee their separation. This task is necessitated by an inherent tendency of the symbolic forms to "turn against their own 'system of signs'—so religion turns against myth, cognitive inquiry against language, the scientific concept of causality against the sensory-anthropomorphic-mythic conception of causality, and so forth."[46] In short, while the transcendental critique traces the demarcating lines between the symbolic forms, the ethical critique is required to enforce this separation and to ensure that the claims made in a particular symbolic modality do not transgress the 'limits fixed' by the transcendental critique. For example, in *The Myth of the State*, Cassirer diagnoses the ascendance of myth to a political stage that ought to be reserved for a different mode of rationality.[47] And it is this overreaching that was at the heart of the cultural crisis that Cassirer addresses in his University of Gothenburg inaugural lecture, "The Concept of Philosophy as a Philosophical Problem," with which we began this essay.

With this so-called ethical dimension of the transcendental critique, we see that Cassirer's critique is indeed an immanent critique. In the Preface to his *Phenomenology of Spirit*, Hegel writes, "If the refutation [of a philosophical principle] is thorough, it is derived and developed from the principle itself, not accomplished by counter-assertions and random thoughts from outside."[48] Utilizing the criterion of one symbolic form to critique another is unlawful and bound to fail for the reasons that compelled Kant and Hegel to ground their critiques immanently. We saw that Hegel understands that a critique whose criterion is not drawn from the object it is critiquing will not only fail to convince the opposition of its objectivity, as he explains in his *Logic*, "Genuine refutation must penetrate the power of the opponent and meet him on the ground of his strength; the case is not won by attacking him somewhere else and defeating him where he is not."[49] In other words, not only might critique that is not grounded immanently fail to convince its interlocutor, it may miss the mark altogether. And this is the error of conflating symbolic forms. Myth is not science manqué, which is what science presupposes when it critiques the mythological understanding of the world according to its own criterion for truth.[50]

---

46 Cassirer (1996), 226.
47 Cf. Fabien Capeillères' essay in the present volume.
48 Hegel (1977), 13.
49 Hegel (1969), 581.
50 The failure to appropriately ground critique occurs not only in the interactions of the different symbolic domains of a given culture, but also in the encounter of two different cultures. In

5 Subjective Critique

What conception of critique stands opposed to the sort of immanent critique favored by philosophers in the wake of Kant? Must it be unreflective and naïve? A consideration of H.L. Mencken's views on the subject show that it needn't be, though this particular conception will prove to be philosophically inadequate (albeit willfully) and, in Cassirer's framework, will fall *within* a symbolic form instead of being poised to evaluate the claims of particular symbolic forms. Mencken is a fitting figure to consider a different conception of critique for three reasons. First, Mencken was himself a practicing critic who actively commented on various domains of culture throughout the first half of the twentieth century, as such he will serve as a useful reference point when we consider the task of the Cassirerian critic of culture as she functions in the everyday world of culture. Second, Mencken is explicit in his understanding of what the task of the critic is and he provides grounds for this conception that are well worth philosophical examination. Third, Mencken's presentation of the task of the critic, in contradistinction to Kant and Hegel, allows the individuality (or, subjectivity) of the critic to participate in the critical process. We shall see that the task of the Cassirerian critic of culture that takes place within a given symbolic framework is also more amenable to the introduction of subjectivity than were Kant and Hegel.

Mencken's view of criticism, as it is formulated in *Footnote on Criticism*, is a passionate embrace of subjectivity in criticism that is regarded as fatal—a contradiction in terms, even—in the view of Hegel. This position, however, does not derive from a failure to understand or consider the concerns that animate the philosophical tradition's demand for objectivity and scientific rigor. Rather, we shall see, Mencken regards this demand as based on misguided epistemological convictions. "Let us forget all the heavy effort to make a science of [criticism]," writes Mencken in a pithy formulation of his stance, "it is a fine art, or nothing."[51]

In Mencken's view, the critic is neither policeman nor pedagogue but rather "a general merchant in general ideas ... an artist working in the materials of life

---

comparing the Western and African cultural standards of good musical tone, LeRoi Jones writes, "A blues singer and, say, a Wagnerian tenor cannot be compared to one another in any way. They issue from cultures that have almost nothing in common, and the musics they make are equally alien. The Western concept of 'beauty' cannot be reconciled to African or Afro-American music...For a Westerner to say that the Wagnerian tenor's voice is 'better' than the African singer's or the blues singer's is analogous to a non-Westerner disparaging Beethoven's Ninth Symphony because it wasn't improvised." Jones (1963), 30.

51 Mencken (1982b), 183.

itself."⁵² The only difference between the critic and the artist as traditionally understood is that, instead of choosing paint or marble as her medium, the critic is animated by "feelings inspired, not directly by life itself, but by books, pictures, music, sculpture, architecture, religion, philosophy—in brief, by some other man's feelings about life."⁵³ For the Menckenian critic, however, this secondhand starting point is merely the *terminus ad quem* of criticism. If the critic is a genuine critic (which for Mencken means a genuine artist) and "if his feelings are in any sense profound and original, and his capacity for self-expression is above the average of educated men—then he moves inevitably from the work of art [or religion, or philosophy] to life itself."⁵⁴ And it is this transition that marks the difference between criticism and mere reviewing. The latter is "devoted to diluting and retailing the ideas of his superiors," to being a "mere cataloguer and valuer of other men's ideas."⁵⁵

It is therefore not the case that Mencken's conception of critique fails the test of objectivity so much as it resolutely, not to mention truculently, *refuses* objectivity. According to this paradigm, demanding the effacement of subjectivity from criticism (as the practice's ideal or essence) would be as unreasonable and absurd as demanding of Picasso that his cubist portraits recall their subject with photographic accuracy.

Mencken's revaluation of criticism's values is grounded by epistemological convictions, which, one suspects, derive from his engagement with Nietzsche. In short, jaded or enlightened by a historical perspective, Mencken is skeptical of the notion of absolute truth: "What the world turns to, when it has been cured of one error, is usually simply another error, and maybe one worse than the first. This is the whole history of the intellect in brief."⁵⁶ And if truths remain always provisional then it would be presumptuous and ill informed to rest assured that one's own position will stand the test of time.

Thus, according to Mencken, the genuine critical impulse is not to educate, to moralize, or to diagnose. The motive of the critic "is no more and no less than the simple desire to function freely and beautifully, to give outward and objective form to ideas that bubble inwardly and have a fascinating lure in them, to get rid of them dramatically and make an articulate noise in the world."⁵⁷ And this lib-

---

52 Mencken (1982b), 179.
53 Mencken (1982b), 178.
54 Mencken (1982b), 179.
55 Mencken (1982b), 180.
56 Mencken (1982b), 182.
57 Mencken (1982b), 177.

erating disregard for absolute truth and genuine dialogue with one's interlocutor obviate the need to ground critique immanently.

6 A Further Task of the Critic

This antipode to the traditional philosophical conception of critique leads us to two matters that will orient the remainder of this essay. First, we will assess Cassirer's place on the continuum of objectivity-subjectivity, as it pertains to critique. As we have seen, Kant and Hegel are proponents of a hardline position demanding objectivity (in Hegel: the total effacement of subjectivity[58]) in critique. Mencken, on the other hand, regards objectivity as an unreasonable demand and therefore embraces subjectivity as the proper critical standpoint. We will find Cassirer somewhere in between these two extreme positions.

Our second remaining question concerns the exhaustiveness of our analysis. We have seen that the transcendental and ethical dimensions of the critique of culture fall within the purview of the philosopher, who, by definition, is not oriented by any one symbolic framework. However, these two dimensions do not exhaust the tasks implied by a critique of culture, and a consideration of where Cassirer is situated on the continuum of objectivity-subjectivity will help us to answer the question: what is the task of the critic of culture that takes place from *within* a given symbolic form?

The development of culture, claims Cassirer, is a dialectical process. To this extent, Cassirer sounds very much like Hegel. However, whereas for Hegel, the dialectical movement of consciousness ultimately terminates in Absolute Knowing, for Cassirer, culture never comes to a final rest: "Any equilibrium that may occasionally appear to have been attained … is never more than an unstable balance, which can at any moment change into a new movement."[59] We have already seen how Hegel's metaphysical convictions inform his stance on the task of the critic: criticism is to assess whether and to what degree the Idea (of philosophy, of art, etc.) comes to adequate expression in the object being criticized. The Idea is the condition of the possibility for and guarantor of objec-

---

[58] It is perhaps not entirely fair to associate Kant with this extreme position, seeing as he acknowledges the difficulty—the impossibility, even—of achieving the completely objective stance of the idea: "It would be very boastful to call oneself a philosopher in this sense and to pretend to have equaled the archetype, which lies only in the idea." Kant (1998), 695. While it may remain unattainable, the ideal of objectivity can serve as a limit idea after which the philosopher-critic must strive.

[59] Cassirer (2000), 123.

tivity. And if, for example, "The real subject of art is not ... the Absolute of Hegel [or the Idea of art],"[60] then the art critic has lost the criterion by virtue of which Hegel was able to explain and uphold the essential objectivity of critique.

However, Cassirer's rejection of the Absolute does not lead him to take refuge in the Charybdis that stands diametrically opposed to the insistence on the complete effacement of subjectivity from critique. In other words, the critic is not merely an artist beholden to nothing more than her whims. If we reject the Menckenian conception of critique, it is not to dismiss the stance whole cloth, but only as an account of critique as such. Considered on the continuum of objectivity-subjectivity, with Mencken the pendulum swings too far in the other direction—albeit, we shall see, a direction to which Cassirer is not hostile, since, because there is no absolute criterion that must orient the critic's judgments, there will prove to be more leeway in viable critical positions. Ultimately, however, Mencken's conception comes at too high a cost: the total elimination of normative force from critique. And the persuasiveness that critique retains is owed to its charm. Indeed, in an especially provocative moment, Mencken goes so far as to assert that to make a thing "charming ... is always a million times more important than making it true."[61] If we remain committed to some normative notion of truth, then the critic is, in Mencken's picture, more of a sophist than a philosopher. Cassirer's philosophical method of dialogue with the history of philosophy as well as his emphasis of culture as an intersubjective space suggest that Mencken's solipsistic conception of critique, which is devoid of responsibility to its interlocutor, would be unsuitable for Cassirer.

In fact, with Mencken, we find a conception of critique that is no longer within the purview of the philosopher. As we saw, Mencken maintains that the critic is an *artist*. And in Cassirer's framework, this implies that the critic would operate within the symbolic form of art, which disburdens the Menckenian critic of the transcendental and ethical dimensions of critique that we saw to be elements of Kant's conception. In itself this is no objection to Mencken's conception of critique, but if we are after the task of the critic that is implied by Cassirer's critique of culture, to reach a destination that is unconnected to the route travelled suggests that something has gone awry.

The demands on the Cassirerian critic of culture cannot be as stringent as those made by Kant/Hegel nor as lax as those made by Mencken. By turning to our final question—what is the task of the critic that emerges from within a

---

60 Cassirer (1954), 201.
61 Mencken (1982b), 182.

symbolic form?—we will win a more contoured and complete understanding of the nature of critique as it emerges from Cassirer's thought.

Although Cassirer doesn't focus on the terms 'critique' or 'criticism' in his discussion of the "Tragedy of Culture," this study from *The Logic of the Cultural Sciences* provides fertile ground for thinking about the task of the critic. In the study Cassirer is in conversation with Georg Simmel, who he believes to have formulated the so-called tragic character of culture "with complete decisiveness."[62] The putative tragedy concerns a conflict woven into the fabric of culture as such, whereby the liberatory power that culture is thought to possess is seen as collapsing into self-alienation.[63]

Cassirer rejects the tragic conception of culture on two accounts. First, it stems from the view that the works of culture constitute "the simple *opposite* to that which the I requires by its very nature" instead of understanding these works as "a *prerequisite* for [the I] to find and understand itself in its own essence."[64] Thus the tragic conception of culture finds self-alienation where Cassirer finds the condition for the possibility of self-discovery. A work of culture is not "something merely objective, an existing and given thing"[65] to be consumed and digested. This misunderstanding, in conjunction with the never-ending proliferation of these works, culminates in the I's realization that it is ineluctably unable to enjoy all of culture's gifts and consequently instead of drawing "from culture the consciousness of its own power" it finds only "the certainty of its own intellectual powerlessness."[66]

The situation is different, however, if we reject the conviction that the self's externalization in the works of culture constitutes an unbridgeable gap between and instead come to understand that the belief in knowledge of self and others that "could dispense with all symbolism and all mediation through the word and image, rests on a self-deception."[67] Instead, as mentioned, Cassirer maintains that these works are "a *prerequisite* for [the I] to find and understand itself in its own essence."[68]

The second reason that Cassirer rejects the tragic conception of culture is that the process never comes to an end: "just as little as there is an ultimate vic-

---

62 Cassirer (2000), 105.
63 In his discussion of the tragedy of culture, Skidelsky points out that it takes on different contour at different stages of Simmel's career. Cf. Skidelsky (2011), 181–183.
64 Cassirer (2000), 108.
65 Cassirer (2000), 105.
66 Cassirer (2000), 105.
67 Cassirer (2000), 53.
68 Cassirer (2000), 108.

tory so there is no ultimate defeat."⁶⁹ And because culture never comes to rest in an Absolute, a better characterization of the never-ending oscillation between the cultural forces of renewal and conservation would be to speak of the "drama of culture,"⁷⁰ in which one of these forces may temporarily gain the upper hand, but in so doing serves to heighten the "inner friction"⁷¹ that will give way to something new. This process can be clearly seen in the phenomenon of renaissances, epochs in which the fund of cultures past are made manifest as "the conglomeration of huge potential energies" instead of as "inert masses,"⁷² as the tragic conception of culture would have it. Insofar as they return to what has come to pass, a renaissance is not without a conservative impulse. But in a true renaissance this return to and conservation of the past results in an epoch bringing forth something new. The dramatic dialectic of culture thus requires both the forces of renewal and conservation. Without the former there is no forward movement. Without the latter culture becomes unmoored from its past and lacks the foundation and oedipal friction that forward movement requires. Renaissances are also illustrative of the aforementioned way that both individuals and epochs undergo a process of self-discovery and constitution through their engagement with the works of culture. The fact that the healthy forward march of culture requires the perpetual conflict of the forces of renewal and conservation will have implications for the task of the critic.

Let us end by returning to our starting point, Cassirer's lecture "The Concept of Philosophy as a Philosophical Problem." As he comes to the end of his remarks, Cassirer issues a *cri de coeur* for more practically-minded intelligentsia. Contra Hegel, Cassirer rejects the famous aperçu "What is rational is real; what is real is rational." Instead, he claims, "reason is never a mere present; it is not so much an *actual*, as it is a constant and ever *actualizing*, not a *given* but a *task* ... we must seek [reason] in the continual self-renewing work of spirit."⁷³ Of course, this work of spirit is not to be entrusted with its own unfolding and self-realization. Instead we ourselves are responsible for the actualization of rationality and this entails not only our contributions to the plurality of culture, but also our defense of it—a defense that belongs to the tasks of the critic. The most authentic expression of the critical spirit as it acts from within a given symbolic form consists in a participation in the "real and most significant

---

69 Cassirer (2000), 124.
70 Cassirer (2000), 124.
71 Cassirer (2000), 113.
72 Cassirer (2000), 113.
73 Cassirer (1979a), 62.

function"[74] of a work (be it a lyric poem, a law, or a philosophical theory): to function as a cultural digestif and catalytic; to assist in the reception works such that they become the source of new cultural creations; to reveal works of the present and of the past as conversations with different ways of understanding the world.[75] Understood in this light, the task of the critic can be reduced neither to nay- nor yeasaying, although a recognition that the engine driving culture is a tension between the forces of conservation and renewal entails that the critic need not (and perhaps even *cannot*) be denied the right to criticize in the name of her subjective inclinations. Still, mere finger wagging, which does nothing to point a way forward—even if this way forward be conservative in nature—is unworthy of the name 'criticism' or 'critique.'

The critic is to assist in the reception of a work so as to foment further activity, thereby preventing culture from becoming stagnant and one-sided. This task, which takes place at the pre-philosophical level of operating from within a symbolic form, has important consequences for the 'higher level' tasks of a critique of culture. It is precisely when culture slumbers in its conservative mode that ideologies and institutions are able to take on the appearance of the Absolute towards which culture had been striving. Enthroned thusly, these ideologies and institutions are able to apply their standard of truth in the sort of unwarranted manner that we have seen it to be the ethical task of the critique of culture to oppose.

Bibliography

Archer (2003): Steven Archer, Cynthia Gendrich, Woodrow Hood, *Theatre: Its Art & Craft*, San Diego: Collegiate Press.
Benjamin (2004): Walter Benjamin, *The Concept of Criticism in German Romanticism*, in: *Walter Benjamin: Selected Writings, Volume 1: 1913–1926*, Marcus Bullock and Michael W. Jennings (eds.), Cambridge: Harvard University Press, 116–200.

---

74 Cassirer (2000), 110.
75 Interestingly, the critic as catalyzer is the task that Mencken prescribes in his earlier criticism essay "Criticism of Criticism of Criticism." "It is [the critic's] business to provoke the reaction between the work of art and the spectator. The spectator, untutored, stands unmoved; he sees the work of art, but it fails to make any intelligible impression on him…But now comes the critic with his catalysis. He makes the work of art live for the spectator; he makes the spectator live for the work of art." Mencken (1982a), 176. In his later criticism essay, "Footnote on Criticism," Mencken dismisses his earlier position: "[The critic] is not even trying to discharge the catalytic office that I myself, in a romantic moment, once sought to force upon him." Mencken (1982b),181.

Cassirer (1923): Ernst Cassirer, *Substance and Function, and Einstein's Theory of Relativity*, WC Swabey and MC Swabey (trans.), Chicago: Open Court.
Cassirer (1946): Ernst Cassirer, *Language and Myth*. Susanne K. Langer (trans.), New York: Dover Publications Inc.
Cassirer (1953): Ernst Cassirer, *The Philosophy of Symbolic Forms. Vol I: Language*, R. Manheim (trans.), New Haven: Yale University Press.
Cassirer (1954): Ernst Cassirer, *Essay on Man*, Garden City: Doubleday Anchor Book.
Cassirer (1955): Ernst Cassirer, *The Philosophy of Symbolic Forms. Vol II: Mythical Thought*, R. Manheim (trans.), New Haven: Yale University Press.
Cassirer (1979a): Ernst Cassirer, *The Concept of Philosophy as a Philosophical Problem*, in: *Symbol, Myth, and Culture: Essays and Lectures of Ernst Cassirer: 1935–1945*, Donald Philip Verene (ed.). New Haven: Yale University Press, 49–63.
Cassirer (1979b) Ernst Cassirer, *Critical Idealism as a Philosophy of Culture*, in: *Symbol, Myth, and Culture: Essays and Lectures of Ernst Cassirer: 1935–1945*, Donald Philip Verene (ed.). New Haven: Yale University Press, 64–91.
Cassirer (1996): Ernst Cassirer, *The Philosophy of Symbolic Forms. Vol IV: The Metaphysics of Symbolic Forms*, John Michael Krois (trans.), John Michael Krois and Donal Phillip Verene (eds.), New Haven: Yale University Press.
Cassirer (2000): Ernst Cassirer, *The Logic of the Cultural Sciences*, S.G. Lofts (trans.), New Haven: Yale University Press.
De Boer (2012): Karin De Boer, *Hegel's Conception of Immanent Critique: Its Sources, Extent, and Limit*, in: *Conceptions of Critique in Modern and Contemporary Philosophy*, Ruth Sonderegger & Karin de Boer (eds.), London: Palgrave Macmillan, 83–100.
Hegel (1969): Georg Wilhelm Friedrich Hegel, *Hegel's Science of Logic*, A.V. Miller (trans.), Amherst: Humanity Books.
Hegel (1977): Georg Wilhelm Friedrich Hegel, *The Phenomenology of Spirit*, A.V. Miller (trans.), Oxford: Oxford University Press.
Hegel (2002): Georg Wilhelm Friedrich Hegel, *Introduction: On the Essence of Philosophical Critique Generally, and its Relationship to the Present State of Philosophy in Particular*, in: *Miscellaneous Writings of G.W.F. Hegel*, Jon Stewart (ed.), Evanston: Northwestern University Press, 207–225.
Hoad (1996): T.F. Hoad (ed.), *The Concise Oxford Dictionary of English Etymology*, Oxford: Oxford University Press.
Jones (1963): LeRoi Jones, *Blues People: Negro Music in White America*, New York: Harper Perennial.
Kant, (1998): Immanuel Kant, *Critique of Pure Reason,* Paul Guyer, Allen Wood (trans), Cambridge: Cambridge University Press.
Klein (1971): Ernest Klein, *Comprehensive Etymological Dictionary of the English Language: dealing with the origin of words and their sense development thus illustrating the history of civilization and culture*, New York: Elsevier Publishing Company.
Luft (2004): Sebastian Luft, *Cassirer's Philosophy of Symbolic Forms: Between Reason and Relativism; A Critical Appraisal, Idealistic Studies* 34, 25–47.
Mencken (1982a): H.L. Mencken, *Criticism of Criticism of Criticism*, in: *The American Scene: A Reader*, Huntington Cairns (ed.), New York: Vintage Books, 169–176.
Mencken (1982a): H.L. Mencken, *Criticism of Criticism of Criticism*, in: *The American Scene: A Reader*, Huntington Cairns (ed.), New York: Vintage Books, 169–176.

Mencken (1982b): H.L. Mencken, *Footnote on Criticism*, in: *The American Scene: A Reader*, Huntington Cairns (ed.), New York: Vintage Books, 177–189.
Röttgers (1975): Kurt Röttgers, *Kritik und Praxis: Zur Geschichte des Kritikbegriffs von Kant bis Marx*, Berlin: de Gruyter.
Schneiders (1985): Werner Schneiders, *Vernünftiger Zweifel und wahre Eklektik: Zur Entstehung des modernen Kritikbegriffes*, Studia Leibnitiana 17, 143–161.
Skeat (2005): Walter W. Skeat, *An Etymological Dictionary of the English Language*, Mineola: Dover Publications Inc.
Skidelsky (2011): Edward Skidelsky, *Ernst Cassirer: The Last Philosopher of Culture*, Princeton: Princeton University Press.
Schwemmer (2004): Oswald Schwemmer, *The Variety of Symbolic Worlds and the Unity of Mind*, in: *Symbolic Worlds and Cultural Studies: Ernst Cassirer's Theory of Culture*, Cyrus Hamlin and John Michael Krois (eds.), New Haven: Yale University Press, 3–18.
Wagner (1904): Richard Wagner, *Die Meistersinger von Nürnberg*, W.P. Bigelow (ed.), New York: American Book Company.

Sebastian Luft (Milwaukee)
The A Priori of Culture: Philosophy of Culture Between Rationalism and Relativism. The Example of Lévi-Strauss' *Structural Anthropology*

1 From Kant's Transcendental Idealism to Cassirer's Symbolic Idealism: The Project of a Philosophy of Culture

When Cassirer declares, in the Introduction to the first volume of *The Philosophy of Symbolic Forms,* that the critique of reason should come forth as a critique of *culture,* this is more than a rhetorical pronouncement. His ambitions are grand: what Kant had achieved for reason and *a fortiori* for natural science, Cassirer wanted to achieve for culture writ large. This all-encompassing scope, however, was not something he dreamt up in the armchair. Indeed, he was led to a large-scale philosophy of culture, as focused around the concept of the symbolic, through his research into linguistics, mythology, theory of science and, not least, his vast and encompassing historiography of philosophy and of modern science. He can be called *the* scholar of modernity *par excellence*, if we mean by 'modernity' the totality of cultural and intellectual tendencies ongoing since the Renaissance and still informing our very worldview.

Insofar as culture is the name for the totality of the deeds and achievements of the human being—a being that is more than just an *animal rationale*—a broadening of the critique of reason to that of culture suggested itself in the wake of Kant. To subject culture as a whole to a philosophical critique that is obviously indebted to Kant was motivated by Cassirer's belief that the type of critique Kant enacted with respect to reason would be equally possible with respect to other forms and expressions of the human species. Such a *philosophy* of culture, in other words, would only be possible if *other* regions of human beings' activity and creativity would equally be shown to be governed by general principles, such that all of these regions would have their own logics in the comparable (though not mutually reducible) or parallel manner in which reason cognizes nature.

Kant himself, of course, projected the critique, firstly of *pure* reason, to also investigate other *applications* of reason, such as practical reason and teleological reason. But as Kant would have readily agreed, the human being is not comprised wholly of reason but also of linguistic capacities, religious beliefs, artistic expression, emotions, volitions, and so on. All of these make up the human being, such that a focus on reason would seem far too narrow. Though Kant would have agreed with this view of the human being, he factually relegated these other parts of the human being to the "impure", pragmatic investigation in the *Anthropology*. The pragmatic view of the human being opens up the view to a consideration of the human being as defined by his or her race, gender, nationality, climate, thus individual traits that yield very interesting results, not the generalities of what make up the human being *as such*. Such an account does not achieve the standard Kant had himself set up for philosophy, namely to be an a priori discipline. The *Anthropology* may be considered part of Kant's *philosophy*, but not of his *transcendental philosophy*.

This bifurcation causes a split in his account of the human being, irritating interpreters to this day, especially since the three replies to which the three Critiques give answers are supposed to be equal to the question, *"Was ist der Mensch?"* To Cassirer, among other critics, the split Kant declared between pure and impure investigations, such that the account of the human being as a person with emotions, having been exposed to particular climates, and so on, would be the topic of an anthropology with pragmatic intent, is not satisfactory, since it would declare everything human, which is not part of "pure reason", to be a merely empirical matter and hence fall out of the purview of philosophy as a *critical* enterprise. Hence, something is fundamentally problematic, not so much with Kant's architectonics, but with the ambiguous place of the human being in it. Or put differently, it is not clear what status an anthropology in his system is to have—if it is ostensibly not part of the *critical* system.[1]

It was for these reasons—the loss of the transcendental dimension in the investigation of the "impure" elements in the human being and the unclear status of anthropology—that already Cassirer's predecessors in the Marburg School claimed, against Kant, that critical philosophy had to be enacted in *all* spheres

---

[1] I realize this view of Kant's *Anthropology* and the place of it within the Kantian overall system has come under closer scrutiny among Kant scholars recently, but since this presentation here is done for the sake of setting up the critical system of Cassirer's *Philosophy of Symbolic Forms*, my claim here does not amount to a substantial contribution to the scholarship on Kant. For a good overview over and a case for Kant's *Anthropology* belonging to his critical system, cf. Louden (2002).

of culture, starting out with a "factum of science" in each region. In this light, the factum of science and the factum of freedom were just particular instances of a critical treatment of all forms of human expression, the sum total of which is "culture". To put it differently, the members of the Marburg School hold and defend the view that culture is more than just a haphazard arrangement of human creativity with no internal and discernible structure; to the contrary, the Marburg doctrine and the Marburg members maintain that culture is a *fundamentally systematic* expression of human nature, such that culture can rightfully be divided into different regions with their own *sui generis* structure and material (not just formal) lawfulness. Because culture is of such an internal makeup, it can be subjected to a critique; more precisely, to a critical investigation of *sui generis* different regions. Thus, the philosophy of culture is to make good on the promise of an anthropology in a *transcendental register*—something that is putatively inconceivable to Kant.

Hence, that the critique of reason had to be unfolded so as to become a critique of culture as a critical investigation into the conditions of possibility of each region of human spirit's expression, was already a program issued by Cohen, the founder of the Marburg School. However, one motivating factor in Cassirer's development of his own philosophy of culture in terms of symbolic formation was the nagging suspicion that Cohen's take on culture was, despite all better intentions, still too oriented by a scientific or logicist bent that would stifle the wealth of cultural expression human beings are capable of. Thus, while still committed to Cohen's idea of critique, Cassirer's look at culture is a decidedly more modern one, both in method and scope. This is at least Cassirer's claim as he switched from the logicist to the functional paradigm.[2]

Indeed, Cassirer was more sensitive to the material wealth of culture than Kant's formalism and Cohen's formal logicism were capable of grasping. While Cassirer initially took over the general directions of culture more or less from the canon—cognition, art, religion—he added language and myth (and later some others). Here, his guiding idea was that each cultural form had *its* own, original, and irreducible internal manner of functioning, its "logic", that is incommensurable with other forms and hence merits its own investigation. These forms, accordingly, were not to be judged by the measuring rod of logic or science alone. Instead, each cultural expression has its own internal functional principle by which individual objects are connected with others, so as to constitute its functional nexus, its meaningful *Verweisungszusammenhang* (nexus of

---

[2] What I say here in broad strokes and far too abbreviated, is to be found in greater detail in Luft (2015).

reference), as phenomenologists might call it. What he wanted to systematize, hence, was the totality of the human spirit insofar as it manifests itself in cultural forms that are universally discernible despite different individual manifestations in *cultures* (with a lower-case 'c').

How does this work concretely? Grasping each functional nexus could be achieved by a focus on the concept of the symbolic. Each individual thing is more properly understood as a symbol and thereby as part and parcel of a particular symbolic order. Rather than positing the traditional opposition between the individual and the universal, Cassirer takes from Goethe the concept of the special/the unique (*das Besondere*) that stands exemplarily for the context as a whole, such that each thing has a symbolic *pregnancy*. A symbol is the bearer of a meaning context which it itself instantiates. The context, insofar as it is a "necessary formal point of view", is, however one among many. And an account of this totality is Cassirer's notion of "systematic philosophy". Of the latter, he writes already in the final pages of *Einstein's Theory of Relativity* of 1921,

> ... it is the task [of systematic philosophy], which extends far beyond the theory of knowledge, to free the idea of the world from this one-sidedness. It has to grasp the *whole system* of symbolic forms, the application of which produces for us the concept of an ordered reality, and by virtue of which subject and object, ego and world are separated and opposed to each other in definite form, and it must refer each individual in this totality to its fixed place.[3]

Hence, Kant's transcendental idealism becomes in Cassirer's work a symbolic idealism. That is, we are not in touch with the world as it is in itself but only in the way that it shows itself to us. However, the world reveals itself to us essentially in *different* meaningful manners, corresponding to the ways in which we construct the world as a cultural whole. These meaningful contexts are what he calls the symbolic forms, and it is the task of a philosophy of culture as an account of the symbolic universe to discern these different symbolic forms and to describe their different and distinct manners of functioning in a manner that does justice to each in its own "logic", hence non-reductively.

But being a symbolic idealism in the way described, this account is decidedly philosophical, i.e. in the form and fashion of *transcendental* philosophy, insofar as these symbolic forms are interpreted as forms of intuition, of viewing the world, by laying our spirit into things. These forms are, in other words, the conditions of the possibility of viewing and experiencing the world, however in different manners. The light which our gaze shines upon the world is broken up in

---

3 Cassirer (1953), 447.

refractions. This symbolic-idealistic account could be called, thus, a *pluralized* transcendental aesthetics, insofar as the ways of "seeing" the world in an extended sense are not restricted to the time and the space Kant discerns as the experience of physical nature. Following the Kantian script, but pluralizing it, each transcendental aesthetics had to be justified by its own transcendental logic. And, these forms are more than just manners of passively observing the world, but these ways of understanding the world are at the same time, as Goodman has called it, ways of world-*making*. The overall claim is a transcendental-philosophical one, in that these forms are the necessary manners in which we as human beings experience the world as a cultural universe of our own making. What Cassirer wanted to get at, thus, was, as the title of this essay indicates, an account of the *a priori of Culture*. This will suffice for an unfolding of the systematic background. I would now like to introduce a systematic problem, which I then shall proceed to answer in the spirit of Cassirer, but with the help of Lévi-Strauss and Merleau-Ponty.

2 The General Problem of a *Philosophy of Culture*

It is at this point—that a philosophy of culture can be a transcendental enterprise—that I would like to raise a systematic problem that follows from precisely this philosophical theory, namely that of the *status* of this account, which is to describe the system of Culture in a *universal* manner, vis-à-vis the *particular* cultures in which human beings encounter themselves. Cassirer saw the problem, but although he was, as is clear from his many writings, sensitive to cultural differences and open for empirical studies of cultures, and drew heavily from them, he nonetheless (from what I can tell) did not meet it head-on. But this does not mean that it should not be possible to address this problem in Cassirer's spirit, in fact I do believe it is; and I also believe one can answer it in this very spirit. To segue into the systematic problem, I shall begin from the opposite side of this philosophical account, namely an *empirical* account of culture as it is to be found in contemporary cultural studies or anthropology.

An *empirical* anthropological account of the human being and its cultural achievements would presumably agree that culture is a variegated, plural, but also in certain respects structured realm with its different manifestations; structures that can be described scientifically and with certain methods. However, by focusing on plural and essentially different forms of culture or different *cultures*, an account of each different cultural form and its own internal structure is just that—an *empirical* account of, say, the burial rites of a certain tribe in native Americans. The anthropologist's aim is to understand this particular culture, or a certain aspect of it, *from within*, i.e., not by imposing our prejudices and biases (Western, heterosexual, etc.) on it, but by trying to do justice to it on its own terms. But precisely here lies the problem for the empirical anthropologist: the description of the concepts, values and norms guiding a certain culture threatens, despite best intentions to get *inside* of it, to unjustly colonize (to use a contemporary term) that other form of culture, since one inadvertently remains on the outside. So even when one thinks one has *gotten inside of it,* one *may always* be mistaken. To cite a phenomenological trope, the alien nature of the other —be it another human being or another culture—resists being made familiar, and if I make it familiar to me, it is no longer the alien.

But if we are able to resist this overbearing attitude and find ways to confine ourselves to the specifics of this particular culture on its own terms, this means that the account given of culture cannot be but an account *relative to it.* But is such a fidelity to this particular culture different from my own even possible? Can I ever completely rid myself of my Western/male/heterosexual forms of seeing and thinking when trying to describe what I see with my Western-trained eyes and my Western-thinking mind? Do not the concepts and categories that I inadvertently use already carry my entire Western "baggage" along with it? This stripping-myself of my familiar habits is impossible; or if I pretend I can achieve it, it will be done in a manner that is again familiar to myself. It is impossible to entirely get outside of my "frame of reference", in which I have been acculturated.

But if one bites the bullet and admit that one cannot rid oneself of this way of seeing and understanding, then one has to admit, as well, that there is no way one *can* truly give a just account of that other culture. Thus, the first problem of a *universal* account is that it is at the expense of what this other culture is about in its *particularity,* or that such a universal account is one that is demanded only from my Western perspective, which results in the Westerner not seeing this particularity *in its particularity,* but only in what *she wants to see,* blinded by her quest for universalism.[4] The quest for universality turns out to be just another method of domination. The alternative is that one gives up the universal view-

---

[4] Interestingly, Lévi-Strauss gives what could be called an inverse example of a so-called savage, when exposed to our culture, seeing only what he wants to see—not because he wanted to find universalities but because "all these things [that fascinated him when visiting New York] brought his own culture into the picture, and what he did was to seek evidence of that culture in certain aspects of ours" (Lévi-Strauss (1960), 25). This observation will become crucial further down as I turn to the way in which Lévi-Strauss deals with "invariances" in culture.

point and then one is left with nothing but a local account that is not communicable to another cultural standpoint, without fundamentally distorting it.

Yet, is this a fair description of what the fair-minded and benign anthropologist does? Is the latter not trying to extract the *particularity* of this particular culture, from within that culture, by immersing herself into this other culture and attempting to give a just account of it? But again one must be clear about this person's agenda: This immersion in the foreign culture is not done for the sake of a description of this particularity in and of itself—although that might be a first and preliminary task. Indeed, in so doing, is the anthropologist not trying to bring to the fore the *universality* of culture, that which we all have in common, no matter whether we are Western, non-Western, black, white, yellow, and so on? An anthropologist who would not have this ambition even to a *minimal* extent would not deserve the title of a researcher, but only that of a storyteller. But once again, one can ask, *is there* such a universality, such an a priori, such that tradition A and tradition B could be interpreted as enacting the *same* cultural form, however in *different* manners? Is this not to overlook particularities that cannot be universalized? Is not, to vary the reproach mentioned earlier, this dream of a universal account dreamt up in the Western armchair?

The problem that I want to point to, which appears as one between universalism and particularism, may also be called the quandary between rationalism and relativism. The problem presents itself as follows: If I want to give a philosophical, i.e., *universal* account of what culture "in itself" is, by describing what human beings as cultural creatures have in common, I threaten to overlook forms of culture that do not fit neatly into this scheme. Moreover, the scheme that I draw up has, by necessity, blind spots and biases since it is drawn up from a certain standpoint, although the investigator believes, or hopes to believe, to be in a position *above* particularities. But as raising herself above particularities, there is always the threat that certain elements of my particular situation remain with me. I take this to be a critique that is launched at this rationalistic account from different sides, for instance from scholars working in philosophy of race, feminism, and others. One can even go one step further, following Gadamer, that a universally valid standpoint is not only unattainable, but also not desirable. If this last point is not to be taken as self-contradictory, since it is putatively spoken with the claim to universal validity, it must be construed differently; I will return to this suggestion in the conclusion, as I believe Merleau-Ponty gives us the resources to avoid the skeptical conclusion.

Thus, the ideal that such an account aims at, I call rationalistic insofar as it strives for an account of what culture *in itself* is, and insofar as it claims to arrive at universal, general traits of culture that we all partake of. The problem with such an account has been indicated: it might not be *possible* to arrive at an a priori of culture; and moreover, it might not even be *desirable* insofar as, even if it might succeed (by what standards would we ascertain this?), it would by necessity overlook those particularities that do not fit the scheme. Or worse, it would declare those that do not fit as uncultured, barbaric, subhuman, and we all know to which excesses these exclusions have led. In this vein, it has been suggested that the very ideal of universality is one that came into being in a particular culture—the West—and that, far from thereby leaving its very particularity behind, has included in its benign ideal also those of oppression (against women, non-whites, non-heterosexuals etc.). I take this critique—a variation of Adorno/Horkheimer's thesis of the dialectic of the Enlightenment—very seriously. I take its point to be that the benign universal is in truth, and can only be, a "bad universal", since its very constitution is based on exclusion. The result would be that to even seek out this universal is a wrong-headed attempt. It is *this* move that I disagree with; I shall argue that we are beholden to find the "good" universal, the correct a priori, though it will look different than the Enlightenment doctrine might have it, which I would call a naïve Enlightenment (and its rationalism equally naïve).

So for these reasons, a "rationalistic" account, as much as a philosopher might desire it, might not be so desirable for the sake of an account of culture, or it could only be given at the expense of eliminating those particularities that do not fit this universalistic account. It would be, by necessity, one-sided, squinting, and simply blind to the differences that our species is ostensibly capable of achieving. To demand a rationalistic, universalist account of the sort sketched would be to do injustice to all the flowers that bloom in the garden of culture.

But the alternative does not fare much better either. If we abandon the rationalist framework and instead focus on the peculiarities of cultural differences, the following problem ensues: If we give up the ambitions to attain a universal account of culture, we are left with accounts that are relative to the specific cultural form we encounter. We, presumably (assuming it is possible), immerse ourselves into a specific culture and try to account for it "from within" without the claim that what we are describing is of any universal nature. What one insists on, then, is the radical difference between different cultures and cultural forms such that no universalistic claim whatsoever is ever attempted. But then we end up in a purely relativistic account, whereby each cultural form we encounter is believed to have its own specific particular nature that cannot be understood in terms of another; this claim entails, in effect, that of a radical incommensurability amongst cultures. This was the paradigm of cultural anthropology for certain period of its work, in which it was influenced by the postmodern paradigm of difference. To take radical difference seriously was in effect a prohibition against attempting to compare different cultures with respect to what they have in common. But this sentiment is itself blind to the observation that it, too, is made from an absolute standpoint. But in this case, we end up with a self-contradictory relativism. For, the claim that all cultures have their own specific forms of functioning is obviously claimed to be true across the board, and hence the claim to relativism is itself not relativistic. But this may be a cheap shot. A more substantial point is the following.

Indeed, one can dismiss this relativism on more than just this logical ground. From a descriptive point of view, and even conceding that all one can do is view different cultures from without, the claim seems to be simply false. For, despite there being some clearly visible differences between cultures, the evidence that we have things in common simply outweighs that of the differences that separate us. For instance, there is, one could say, the general rule of behavior called politeness towards others, and although this simple rule of behavior is enacted differently when observed from without, it is quite obvious that it is meant to deliver on the same rule, from within: be polite to others. To give another example, let us take the difference between Westerners and other cultures is the consciousness of time. There are numerous stories about a Westerner visiting a foreign culture and being stumped by certain arrangements, where words like "soon" or "right away" have quite different meanings. But this difference in the evaluation of time durations obviously points to the fact that all cultures have *a sense of time*. Thus, the general claim that human cultures have a meaningful sense of time duration does not contradict the different understandings of these senses. They might be different as observed from without, but from within, even if there are material differences, nevertheless there exist structural commonalities (such as alternating periods of rest and work).

To bolster this claim with another purely empirical observation, there seems to be a sea change in anthropology, where precisely "what we have in common" is, in current scholarship, increasingly emphasized vis-à-vis the paradigmatic differences between us.[5] The weight here is placed on the emphasis that there are only *seemingly* differences between us, which exist, however, merely on the surface level, pointing to deeper commonalities. When we immerse ourselves in different cultural forms and try to understand them *from within,* it becomes revealed that "really" what we find are such deep commonalities and that the differences are owed to contingent factors, such as language, climate or geography. To utilize the parlance of an "account from without" and "from within",

---

[5] I here refer to a study by the renowned anthropologist Christoph Antweiler (2009). Antweiler motivates his project by the simple gesture towards the paradigm shift in his discipline for some years now, which is not due to certain theoretical developments in anthropology, but simply a result of the fading dominance of postmodernism.

some behaviors we engage in are similar from without and are comparable without further ado, such as the use of utensils for eating. But, if the paradigm of commonality is correct, an immersion into a certain activity *from within*, explicating why it is done from the person's first person perspective, can not only be understood from another first person standpoint, but can point to a *deeper* commonality than the one encountered from without. What one finds, if this thinking is correct, is a *deep commonality* on the level of inward *meaning*, despite different outward *expression*. But given that this novel paradigm is one that has emerged only recently, it is entirely possible that the pendulum will swing back again in the future. So much for the objectivity of science.

But if there is more plausibility on the side of the paradigm of cultural commonality, are there after all commonalities such that a universal account of culture is in reach after all? This brings us back to the rationalistic paradigm that was shown to be precarious earlier. How can we get further from here? Can we avoid the seesaw of rationalism and relativism? It is at this point that I want to turn to Lévi-Strauss' structural anthropology to move the issue forward. Clearly, he saw this problem—he calls it the problem of invariance—and tried to find a way to account for it despite cultural differences and in a way that overcomes the unfruitful opposition between a relativistic particularism and a rationalistic universalism. I believe the way in which he does so offers an interesting way out of the conundrum just presented. However, it was not until it was clearly articulated by the philosopher Merleau-Ponty that the full impact of the anthropologist Lévi-Strauss' achievement can be fully appreciated from a philosophical standpoint. But what Merleau-Ponty—who was, by the way, an attentive reader of Cassirer—articulates, is, I argue, precisely the spirit of Cassirer in which a satisfactory answer to this conundrum can be given.

So let me turn to Lévi-Strauss next, and I will conclude, in Part IV, with Merleau-Ponty's interpretation of the former's work.

3 Lévi-Strauss on "Invariance in Anthropology"

To begin with, there are no (obvious) traces of Cassirer in Lévi-Strauss' works, yet when he defines culture, in his great *Structural Anthropology*, as a "system of symbolic communication",[6] the affinities to the former are plain. It is Lévi-Strauss' general claim that we live in a world of symbols with meaning and in

---

[6] Lévi-Strauss approvingly cites Tylor's "famous definition of culture" that he restates above, cf. Lévi-Strauss (1963), 68.

which there is a discernible structure of this meaning that we are able to analyze. Lévi-Strauss, however, places special emphasis on the notion of communication via language as the main manner in which culture plays itself out in the interaction between human beings. (Such an understanding would surely be too narrow, for Cassirer, but this shall not detract us from pursuing Lévi-Strauss' line of thought, which I follow by way of his essay "The Problem of Invariance in Anthropology"[7]) The general structure of communication is that of *exchange* as the structural occurrence that guides communication. One of his main claims is, furthermore, that the different systems of communication are governed by a level of complexity that is more or less *equal* in all forms of communication, such that the so-called savage mind is no less "primitive" than the so-called "civilized" mind. Thus, there is no teleology in cultural development from lower to higher, if that is to mean from primitive, simple to ever more complex levels; rather, each cultural form has its *sui generis* level of complexity. (This certainly is a claim Cassirer would agree with.) This has led to the term "primitive" as a descriptor for savage peoples in effect disappearing. This thesis is the ground upon which a comparison between different "minds" of peoples becomes possible in the first place, and if such a comparison is indeed feasible, the question regarding the invariance of cultural expressions raises itself naturally, as he realizes. How then does Lévi-Strauss account for this invariance?

Lévi-Strauss begins by considering the idea of incest, which appears as a taboo in different manners in many different cultures; if we do find it in many cultures, we seem to be justified in calling it an invariant trait across cultures. To be sure, here, as in all empirical sciences, we encounter the problem of the number of samples being sufficiently representative to make general claims. But this is not so much Lévi-Strauss' concern; rather, he is interested in the structure of this taboo. It is the structural comparison, not taboo per se (which might be interpreted or understood very differently in different cultures) that he is after. His first observation is that its treatment points in each known case to its structurally common meaning: its prohibition. Next, he is after the structural commonality which may not be visible at first sight, but which does emerge in a deeper *structural* comparison. In this context, Lévi-Strauss compares a myth stemming from North American Iroquois and the familiar Oedipus legend, which bear a similar structure, such that Lévi-Strauss' comparison can conclude with the interesting observation that "the brother-sister incest of the Iroquois myth [constitutes] a permutation of the that between mother and son in the Oe-

---

7 Lévis-Strauss (1960).

dipus legend".[8] The question is, what does this affinity or similarity mean, which permits permutations to arise in the first place? He asks, accordingly, "Does the analogy spring from deeper reasons? In effecting the comparison, have we not touched on a significant fragment of a whole?"[9] Could such a comparison suggest, in other words, that there is something like a basic story in the deep structure of *the human mind* such that narrating it inevitably leads to similar and overlapping story lines (the lesson being, in this particular case, that "the very precautions taken to avoid incest serve only to render it inevitable"[10])? Is there something like a universal grammar or language that is the *condition of the possibility* of these overlapping stories, with their moral norms, to crop up in different cultures, where a cross-influence is both temporally and geographically impossible? Is do we find here such an a priori, which becomes discernible in this comparison and which is the condition of the possibility of these differences all pointing to a deeper commonality?

But comparisons are not all that simple; they have to be "wrested from the phenomena". That is to say, invariances are not always visible from without and each individual myth adheres to its own "weird logic", such that the comparison can only be made with some creativity. Thus for instance, Lévi-Strauss claims that another form of permutation of one identical "essential" myth might actually be its *inversion*. For example, the theme of summer and winter might appear in different myths, where they signify their opposite: "a summer or a winter equally endless, but one of which would be shameless to the point of corruption, the other pure to the point of sterility".[11] What this suggests is that there is a "relationship, not external and in fact but internal and *in reason*, and this is why civilizations as different as those of classical antiquity and primitive America may associate them independently from each other".[12] This would mean, finally, that if this is true and investigated to the fullest possible extent, that there is indeed an "invariance" among cultures across the board and the onus would be on the anthropologist to find these in what are only seeming and "external" differences. These invariances exist; they only need to be discovered through special research methods, such as linguistic comparative analyses.

The question thus is that of the "universality of human nature",[13] which raises itself for the anthropologist at exactly this juncture. Can we justifiably assume

---

8 Ibid., 20.
9 Ibid.
10 Ibid.
11 Ibid., 22.
12 Ibid., italics added.
13 Ibid., 23.

such a universality across the board? What kind of universality are we talking about? Lévi-Strauss *rejects* the biologistic interpretation of Durkheim, who claims that the commonality of all human beings lies in us all having the same "instincts".[14] Hence, we cannot assume a naïve objectivism that would be based on our common human nature due to our biological makeup. But what kind of commonality are we talking about, then? It is at this point that he himself brings his colleague at the *Collège de France*, Merleau-Ponty, into the discussion, in particular the latter's reflections concerning what anthropologists do. He, Lévi-Strauss, the anthropologist, approvingly cites Merleau-Ponty, the philosopher, when the latter observes, "each time the anthropologist returns to the living sources of his knowledge, ... he spontaneously philosophizes".[15] That is to say, in comparing cultures "furthest removed from himself"[16] and attempting to understand them, the researcher is compelled to "philosophize", and that is precisely to find *common ground* between them and hers. Merleau-Ponty, thus, avers that it is the natural tendency of the anthropologist to philosophize, that is, to find invariances that are not visible to the plain eye, so to speak, and Lévi-Strauss agrees that this is something she *should* do.

But Lévi-Strauss brings up an objection at this point. There is, as he points out, a "fear" among honest anthropologists in such universalizing, namely that what one picks out when one tries to universalize might be bound to a certain fad and fashion within my own culture; that one, thus, is blinded by these contemporary fashions and misses the true invariance—or discerns the wrong one. Yet, this problem vanishes when one realizes that all research, with its questions and problems, is guided by problems *du jour*, such that "there is no guarantee that in its present forms [a certain theory that we entertain] does not proceed from a similar illusion".[17] That is to say, the notion that research in trying to find invariances could ever start out in an ideal realm with no particular questions in mind that are relative to today, is illusory. In fact, as Lévi-Strauss demonstrates, in the example of surrealism, it has "transformed our sensibilities"[18] that have aided us in understanding of forms of "exotic life and thought lacking in our predecessors".[19] It is entirely legitimate, in other words, that we only begin to see certain things in *other* cultures when certain fashions in our own let us begin to develop sensitivities that allow us to see things that we simply did

---

14 Ibid.
15 Ibid., 24.
16 Ibid.
17 Ibid., 25.
18 Ibid., 26.
19 Ibid.

not have "on the radar" before. One striking instance of this casual attitude to fads and fashions is newer research into sexual mores in late antiquity, where a new kind of focus on the issue of slavery *in conjunction with sexuality* has for the first time highlighted the fact that the alleged sexual libertinism was essentially due to the exploitation of enslaved people for sensual pleasures.[20] In this light, the early Christian rejection of free-for-all *porneia* takes on a very different shape, namely it reveals itself as the insistence on equal human rights. This striking observation has certainly gotten us closer to "the truth" of middle- and high-class members of the ancient Roman Empire, and it was only able to come about through a combination of two topics that had hitherto been treated in a completely unrelated manner.

Thus, the fashionableness of certain fads within cultural anthropology, as in every science, should not lead to a rejection of the idea that what we are finding are commonalities. Let us quote Lévi-Strauss again:

> Let us then resist the charms of a naïve objectivism, while we understand that the very precariousness of our position as observers provides us with unsuspected guarantees of objectivity. Insofar as so-called primitive societies are very far removed from our own, we may encounter in them those 'acts of general functioning,' ... which may well be 'more universal' and have 'more reality'. In these societies ... one grasps men, groups, and behaviors. ... one sees them move as if mechanically, one sees masses and systems.[21]

This passage requires some unpacking. Where do the "unsuspected guarantees of objectivity" and "acts of general functioning" come from? Lévi-Strauss' point seems to be that the distance between them and us, even if these other societies are "very far removed from our own", actually helps us to see them as "masses and systems". That is to say, no matter what the difference—and *greater* difference might actually be of help here, presumably because the "exotic index" is larger—what we see in these other societies is that there *is* a systematicity and there *is* an ordered set up of behaviors that move "as if mechanically". This "mechanism" is not meant to reduce them to *automata*; rather, it means they have an internal mechanism, a detectable structure, even in its alien nature, *since my own society has one itself too*. I might not (yet) be on the inside, but I see *that there is such an inside systematics* that I can understand if I try hard enough, because my own society works according to its own mechanics that I *happen* to know intimately.

---

20 I refer here to the new work by Kyle Harper (2013). Cf. also the review of it in New York Review of Books, vol. LX/20, 2013.
21 Lévi-Strauss (1960), 26.

It is the task, then, of the anthropologist to immerse herself in that other society, to the extent that it is possible—since some of these societies might not longer exist—and to try to spell out the *logic* of these systems other than my own. Once this first step is accomplished, I can take the second one of comparison, as Lévi-Strauss has sketched in the above-mentioned examples, with the creative task of showing that the invariance is something that only emerges as the result of some "unpacking" of what appears to be a convoluted "logic" on both sides, pointing to a deeper invariance (the one being the inversion of the other, or an analogous one). The "philosophical" task, to use Merleau-Ponty's terminology, would be to spell out the Logic (with a capital 'L') of the ways in which the variances can arise from the deeper invariance, in other words, to turn around the "logic of discovery" of invariances from variances to a "logic of emergence" of variances from the invariance. It is thus an a priori-constructive task, not an a priori regressive one, but the first cannot occur before the second. This philosophical method, as should be clear, is nothing but a rephrasing of the transcendental method the Marburg School developed.

Do I thusly arrive at a universal account of culture and the human being? Yes, but not in a simple manner of a timeless a priori. Lévi-Strauss' answer is to suggest that this question cannot be asked without taking into consideration the historicity of humanity in its cultural development. The idea that we could give one universal account of the human species would be just as mechanistic as social philosophy's 18th century dream of transforming "men into machines".[22] That is to say, the theories we engender with respect to the human species and culture would be as historically changing as human civilizations change, but what they do point to is the "permanent possibility of man, over which social anthropology would have a mission to stand watch, especially in man's darkest hours",[23] an equally ceremonious as well as mysterious phrase on which Lévi-Strauss' account ends. What is the philosophical upshot of this discussion? Let us turn to the philosopher's interpretation of the anthropologist's thoughts on his work.

4 Merleau-Ponty and the "Lateral Universal"

Thus, the invariance that anthropology arrives at has, one can infer, an ideal or universal form ("man's permanent possibility" of being a cultural being in the

---

22 Ibid., 27.
23 Ibid., 28.

face of these "darkest hours"), but it is something the account of which will change based on the interests *du jour* that drive researchers. Yet, this does not spell a relativism, since on Lévi-Strauss' account, what we gain is a larger picture through shifting perspectives that give us different insights, which may contradict one another at first, but give way to a new commonality, a new agreement. In this sense, Lévi-Strauss would presumably be in agreement with what the contemporary philosopher of science, Martin Carrier, dubs the "epistemic stance", which is that stance which welcomes scientific plurality for the sake of reaching commonality. This "pluralism, which brings controversy to the forefront and which determines essential parts of scientific rationality, must be reined in and satisfied through a common striving for commonality. Pluralism then comes to an end and yields to a consensus".[24]

Since scientific interests change just as historic societies do, there will always be *new* universal traits we discover and new general theories about them. Thus, we can presume that there is such an a priori, such an invariance, but it is not the timeless invariance of mathematical axioms. This does not mean that something like logic, in turn, becomes time-bound and historical, which would lead to an egregious relapse into psychologism. Instead, it seems to suggest that we need to accept that there are different *kinds* of a priori, and the a priori of culture, in this light, is an historically developing one—without a *telos*, at least according to the suggestion of Lévi-Strauss—that the expansion of knowledge will yield richer accounts of the common traits of human beings and culture. The question is now, once again, *what kind* of an a priori is this?

Indeed, where Lévi-Strauss leaves the philosophical reader wanting is an exact account or definition of the type of universal that we are achieving. It is here that I turn, in conclusion, to Merleau-Ponty's interpretation of Lévi-Strauss structural anthropology. Merleau-Ponty adds another and final element to the kind of universals that we are seeking here in the spirit of Cassirer. Being a phenomenologist, one can perhaps guess how Merleau-Ponty will explain the possibility of understanding another society, or the other more generally. The obvious answer lies in the phenomenological theory of intersubjectivity, more precisely its explanation of mutual understanding: through *empathy*. To begin with, Merleau-Ponty emphasizes that the commonalities that Lévi-Strauss alleges to find between different societies are *structural*, not of the form of a timeless substance. Structure, he insists, is "no Platonic idea",[25] but something malleable and fluid. As he writes, commenting on Lévi-Strauss' example cited earlier,

---

[24] Carrier (2013), 12.
[25] Merleau-Ponty (1964), 117.

> ... the reason why contemporary American society has rediscovered a path in its mythology which has already been taken in another time or place [as shown, in ancient Greece] is not that a *transcendent archetype* has been embodied [in different times...], it is that this mythical structure offers a way of resolving some local, present tension, and is recreated in the dynamics of the present.[26]

Structure, thus, recurs differently, but societies *are structured*, such that a comparison between them must be made as to their structural functioning, thereby "resolving certain local tensions" in favor of a larger consensus (to use Carrier's term). It is on this basis that a comparison can be made, not to the extent that different societies embody ideal archetypes, but instead something else, a structural a priori, presumably. To see what kind of an a priori this is, one has to ask, how a such comparison can be made, which does not presume a view from nowhere. This is Merleau-Ponty's question.

Despite his laudatory presentation of Lévi-Strauss' work, Merleau-Ponty is nagged by the question, "up to what point can the comparison go? Will we end up finding, as sociology in the correct sense of the term would have it, universal invariants?", later adding, "like a chemical table of elements".[27] Ideally, one could imagine the "program of a universal code of structures",[28] and he is surprisingly positive about it; but he warns that such an envisioned "formal structure" or a "formal portrait of societies or even general articulations of every society do not constitute a metaphysics".[29] Instead, as Merleau-Ponty phrases his vision in a very compressed manner,

> ... the ideal models or diagrams traced out by a purely objective method are instruments of understanding. The elementary which social anthropology seeks is still elementary structures. ... The variables of anthropology ... must be met with sooner or later on the level at which phenomena have an immediately human significance.[30]

---

26 Ibid., italics added.
27 Ibid., 118.
28 Ibid.
29 Ibid., 119.
30 Ibid. In Merleau-Ponty's emphasis on *understanding* these structures as those of lived-experience, he seems to me to be making a point made by Dilthey at the end of the 19th century, who makes the distinction between explanatory (natural) and understanding (spiritual/human) sciences, insisting that the latter are, by their germane paradigm, sciences as well. This is not an historical reference but points to the timeliness of the discussion regarding the status of human vs. natural sciences between Dilthey, Windelband, and Husserl around 1900.

What we thus arrive at is

> a sort of *lateral universal* which we acquire through ethnological experience and its incessant testing of the self through the other person and the other person through the self. It is a question of constructing a general system of reference in which the point of view of the native, the point of view of the civilized man, and the mistaken views each has of the other can all find a place—that is, of constructing a more comprehensive experience which becomes in principle accessible to men of a different time and country.[31]

Let us elaborate on what Merleau-Ponty here suggests with the highly interesting notion of "lateral universal". Essentially, although it sounds highly original, I do not think he is creating a new category here. If I am not mistaken, all he is doing is reminding us of the type of universal we can *hope* to achieve in human affairs: it is not a universal of the type of a Platonic archetype—which we do in fact achieve in eidetic sciences—but a universal that can only reveal itself in the interaction between human beings who make their best efforts to understand one another. It is a universal that is achieved, in other words, through empathy between human beings. The term "empathy" is not meant as a magical trick out of the hat, but the insistence, emphasized by phenomenologists since Husserl, that any understanding of human beings can only be gained when I try to understand the other, that means, a re-creation of the *other's* point of view from within her *within me*. If I do this with respect to the other, and the other with respect to me, there is no high hope of ever getting it completely right; Merleau-Ponty indeed includes the "mistaken views each has of the other" in the attempt to understand one another. The universal is not timeless and fixed, but historical and changing, it is subject to fads and fashions, and can also be entirely wrong-headed and up for revision.

But the universal understanding that is *achievable* can only be one from one's *first person stance* across another *first person stance*, which does not reach a universal that would or could ever be acknowledged from a *third person perspective*. The best we can do is reach a mutually enriching account of our first person accesses to the world. This is the important *phenomenological* element that Merleau-Ponty adds to this understanding of what an a priori of human beings and human culture *could ever be*. And it supplements Cassirer's theory of symbolic formation as an a priori theory of cultural symbolism insofar as any understanding of the symbolic forms we have in common can only start out from my own radically individuated first person perspective, even though, or precisely because, this first person perspective is always already imbued by the gen-

---

[31] Ibid., 120.

eral shapes of spirit—and vice versa. Hence we constantly move in a hermeneutical circle.

If this universality is claimed to be "lateral", then no claim to "a universal human nature" or "culture as such" is made, if these are understood in substantial, Platonic terms. Human beings and their culture is something that occurs over the course of history, and generally discernible cultural forms and their invariant structures can only be understood in a functional or structural manner as they play themselves out *over the course* of this history. And this is precisely Cassirer's claim, which cuts through the Gordian knot of relativism and rationalism (or historicism and Platonism, as Lévi-Strauss might put it). The only normative claim involved here would be the *general possibility* of such a lateral universal; in other words, mutual understanding is always possible when the effort is made, and the universal reached is never one that may be imposed on others from above. This would be a fundamental misunderstanding of this (type of) universal. Even something like "universal human rights" would have to fall under the scrutiny of this understanding of universal: it is not a Platonic archetype that we attempt to grasp as clearly as possible, only to impose it on others—and us. Even "universal human rights" would have to be worked out in a lateral, that is to say, horizontal and not vertical manner and in an ongoing conversation between human beings caught up in their histories and their cultures. Only then can one hope to arrive at something like the a priori of Culture, which will never be complete, but always underway, ever to be refined and corrected. Finally, an understanding of such an a priori is also not achievable in the armchair but in immersing oneself in the muddy waters of culture. That is, the philosopher hoping to work on an a priori of culture needs the empirical anthropologist; and the latter, once she attempts to discover universal traits, in effect already philosophizes. The difference between them is always only relative, never completely opposed, just as the empirical and the a priori are relative differences on a sliding scale. This conclusion invokes one last time the spirit of Cassirer's empirical philosophizing or philosophical empiricism in the search for an a priori of culture.[32]

---

[32] Thanks to Clark Wolf (Marquette University) for his corrections of grammar and style of this essay. I thank the following people for helpful comments on an earlier version of this essay: Steven Lofts, Grant Silva, Jennifer Marra, J Tyler Friedman, and the participants of the conference in Milwaukee in June 2014.

Bibliography

Antweiler (2009): Christoph Antweiler, *Was ist den Menschen gemeinsam? Über Kultur und Kulturen*, Darmstadt: Wissenschaftliche Buchgesellschaft.
Carrier (2013): Martin Carrier, "Werte und Objektivität in der Wissenschaft", *Information Philosophie* 4 (December), 8–13.
Cassirer (1953): Ernst Cassirer, *Substance and Function and Einstein's Theory of Relativity*, William C. Swabey and Marie C. Swabey (trans.), New York: Dover.
Harper (2013): Kyle Harper, *From Shame to Sin: The Christian Transformation of Sexual Morality in Late Antiquity*, Cambridge and New York: Harvard University Press.
Lévi-Strauss (1960): Claude Lévi-Strauss, "The Problem of Invariance in Culture", J. H. Labadie (trans.), *Diogenes* 8 (No. 31), 19–28.
Lévi-Strauss (1963): Claude Lévis-Strauss, *Structural Anthropology*, Claire Jacobson and Brooke G. Schoepf (trans.), New York: Basic Books.
Louden (2000): Robert Louden, *Kant's Impure Ethics: From Rational Beings to Human Beings*, Oxford: Oxford University Press.
Luft (2015): Sebastian Luft, *The Space of Culture: Towards a Neo-Kantian Philosophy of Culture (Cohen, Natorp, and Cassirer)*, Oxford: Oxford University Press.
Merleau-Ponty (1964): Maurice Merleau-Ponty, "From Mauss to Lévi-Strauss", in: *Signs*, Richard C. McClearly (trans.), Evanston: Northwestern University Press, 114–125.

Curtis L. Carter (Milwaukee)
After Cassirer:
Art and Aesthetic Symbols in Langer and Goodman

Throughout the nineteenth century and beyond, both philosophical aesthetics and European and American art underwent significant changes. Just as traditional rationalist philosophical views of how to comprehend the world came unraveled, so a gradual shift in Western art occurred as it moved from the representational styles that had reigned supreme from Classical art and Renaissance art to the modern period. Image making in painting and sculpture, for example, had previously consisted mainly of representing landscapes, portraits, and historical, religious, and mythical subjects. Images in traditional arts also included imaginary subjects such as fairies, and unicorns.

A quotation from Goethe written in 1809, which comments on the landscape art of Caspar David Friedrich, succintly expresses the relation of art and nature in pre-twentieth century Western art.

> An artist who holds fast to nature with earnestness and truth, who unfolds his inner self in his works, and strives toward significance, ... this artist can never lack the support of the public, for he brings new things to light ... and since already in the simple, characteristic, true imitation of Nature an appreciable level of art is attained, there is no reason why the old and tried rules should not be strictly observed.[1]

Viewing Friedrich's drawings from this perspective, Goethe proceeds to illustrate the point in a description of one of Friedrich's drawings viewed in an 1808 Weimar exhibition:

> In the first of the four large drawings we see over high hills lit by the rays of the rising sun, and over the tops of dark trees towards the edge of the sea, which, ruffled by a light breeze, is making barely perceptible waves. In the distance rises the steep coastline of an island. On a nearby hill a cross has been erected under tall trees, which bend towards each other to form a natural arch or temple [...].[2]

While never entirely abandoned in the subsequent history of art, representational art began to give way in the late nineteenth century with the emergence of Im-

---
1 Goethe (1980), 229.
2 Ibid., 229.

pressionist painting. Impressionist painting explored perceptual sensations of natural light, atmosphere, and movement while moving away from representation. Textured surfaces consisting of short stiff brush strokes and mixed colors replace the smooth glazed figurative surfaces of traditional paintings.

The new forms of art such as Expressionism and Cubism at the beginnings of the twentieth century focused on the inner forms of feeling and ideas of the individual artist's experiences, or on abstract form. Aesthetic concepts based on rationalist principles positing a correspondence between artists' images and the external worlds of nature and civilization were no longer suited to account for this new art. Empiricism focused on sensations and aimed at describing or analyzing surface perceptual features of art, which proved insufficient for interpreting the broad scope of new art. As it turned out, positivist empiricism had little interest in the arts. Instead, the positivists turned their attention to science and to replacing traditional metaphysics with the development of formal logical or mathematical symbol systems.

Since modern art forms no longer employed representation as the dominant means for art making, it became necessary for aesthetics to search for alternative ways of understanding art. Developments in art were accompanied by efforts of philosophers such as Ernst Cassirer, Susanne Langer, and Nelson Goodman to introduce their respective aesthetic theories featuring symbols. These philosophers base their approaches to art, language, myth, and science on their respective theories of symbols. My presentation here will consist of a brief look at Cassirer's philosophy of symbols as it applies to the arts, and then an examination of how central ideas in Cassirer's thought subsequently took root in the respective aesthetic theories of Suzanne Langer and Nelson Goodman.

1 Cassirer and Art Symbols

Basing his philosophy of symbols in part on an understanding of ideas found in the writings of idealist philosophers Vico, Kant, and Hegel, Cassirer set forth his main ideas on the formation of symbols in his three volume *The Philosophy of Symbolic Forms,* first published respectively in 1923, 1925, and 1929. A fourth volume assembled from Cassirer's unpublished manuscripts by John Michael Krois and Donald Verene was published in 1996.[3] This fourth volume is believed by the editors to represent Cassirer's intention to produce a fourth volume. A shorter

---

[3] Cassirer (1996).

version of his system, *An Essay on Man*, published in 1944, includes a chapter devoted to art symbols.

Running throughout Cassirer's philosophy is the notion that human experience, and our attendant world or worlds, exists in the form of symbols. Hence, a primary activity of humans is the generation of different forms of symbolism. Among the symbolic forms that Cassirer addresses are language, science, myth, religion, history, and art. He is particularly adamant in the claim that science based on empirical data and logic is only one form of symbolism, and that the other symbolic forms are necessary to a full understanding of the human domain. In other words, empirical data and logic, however useful, are not the measure of all that contributes value and meaning to human life. Hence, the symbolic forms of language, myth and art, as well as religion, history, and technology, provide complementary approaches to our understanding of human life.

Cassirer, in effect, views the metaphysical traditions of rationalist philosophers, who seek to match up a set of rational principles and whatever else there is in their accounts of the world, as yielding unsatisfactory accounts of human life. Similarly, constructed logic, mathematical symbols and empiricism based on sensory data are relegated to a more limited role than their perpetrators have envisioned.

As noted, our main concern here is with Cassirer's treatment of art symbols and its subsequent influence. There is, however, a problem in choosing to focus on Cassirer's art symbols and the aesthetic. He never devotes a volume of his major work, *The Philosophy of Symbolic Forms*, to art as he does, for example, to myth. Art is thus arguably the least well attended to symbolic form in Cassirer's philosophy.

Our first task then, is to establish the significance of art in Cassirer's treatment of symbols. In addressing this question, it is important to note that art appears in virtually every iteration of the forms of symbols throughout Cassirer's publications. He is unwavering in his inclusion of art among the formative symbols necessary to articulate the human spirit. It appears that art clearly exemplifies the necessary features possessed by other acknowledged symbolic forms such as language, myth, and religion.[4] In an essay he published in 1930 shortly after the publication of Volume III of *The Philosophy of Symbolic Forms*, Cassirer affirms Goethe's commentary on the forces of attraction and repulsion concerning art's relation to the world. "There is no surer way of evading the world than

---

4 Symbolic forms including art share in common two features: they contribute to human understanding and are way of world making. See also Hendel (1955a), 48.

through art ... ." and "There is no surer way of binding oneself to it than through art".⁵

Catherine Gilbert's essay, "Cassirer's Placement of Art", situates Cassirer's discussion of art symbols in the context of philosophical aesthetics and examines art's place with respect to other symbolic forms. Gilbert also takes note of the absence of a major volume on art in Cassirer's writings, but argues nevertheless that, "The aesthetic symbol [i.e. art] is, then, for Cassirer, symbol at its height".⁶ Harry Slochower echoes this claim when he argues that, "art problems are not simply an integral part of Cassirer's philosophy but the most characteristic amplification of his method and system".⁷ Method here refers to the dialectical interplay in Cassirer's theory of symbols between particulars as in works of art and the functional unity of the whole of the symbolic forms that comprise consciousness.

Current studies on Cassirer's understanding of art symbols continue to affirm the importance of art in his philosophy of symbols. Fabien Capeillères essays on art in Cassirer's thought published in *Cassirer Studies* I, II, and IV are of particular interest for their treatment of the various problems that arise with respect to Cassirer's views on art and symbolic form. Among the topics being investigated in these volumes: Cassirer's relation to art historical and cultural investigations at the Warburg Institute for Cultural studies and the art historical work of Panofsky (Volume I), an examination of the materials concerning art in the manuscript "K for Kunst" assembled by Krois and Verene as Volume IV of *Philosophy of Symbolic Forms* (Volume II), and an examination of art critique in reference to philosophy, and its application in Cassirer's aesthetics to art as a field of symbols which participates in world-constructing, versus its application to art as a field of objects.⁸ Capeillères and other current studies concerning Cassirer's views on art symbols are more than sufficient evidence that this topic remains viable for continued investigation.

A letter from Cassirer to Paul Schilpp sent during the preparation of the volume of the *Library of Living Philosophers* featuring Cassirer might explain in part his failure to produce a volume of *The Philosophy of Symbolic Forms* dedicated to art. This letter of May 13, 1942 is cited in the introduction of Krois and Verene to their presentation of the previously unpublished Volume IV of *The Philosophy of Symbolic Forms*. Here, "Cassirer noted that in the first sketch ... of his *Philosophy of Symbolic Forms* he had considered a volume on art, but the malice (*Ungust*) of

---

5 Cassirer (1949), 870.
6 Gilbert, (1949), 609.
7 Slochower (1949), 633.
8 Capeillèrs (2008, 2009, 2011). See also Capeillèrs (2013).

the times had caused him to put it off again and again".⁹ He stated in the 1942 letter to Schilpp that he now intended to present his aesthetics.

Perhaps this task was begun in the chapter on art in his *Essay on Man* written during his tenure at Yale University and published in 1944, the year prior to Cassirer's death. In fact, his most extended discussion of art symbols appears as a chapter in this late work. Three unpublished lectures, "Language and Art I", and "Language and Art II", and "The Educational Value of Art" made available in *Symbol, Myth, and Culture,* a collection of Cassirer's essays and lectures edited by Verene and published in 1979, offer additional comments on art symbols and art.¹⁰

The overall message seems to be that a well-formed understanding of culture will embrace art and a wide range of symbolic forms. Throughout, his discussion of symbolic forms takes place in a rich context of the history of both philosophy and art. The former is informed by the philosophies of Vico, Kant, and Hegel. The latter is fueled by his engagement with the Warburg Institute and Panofsky's views on art history, as noted by Capeillères.

For Cassirer, art originates in imagination and gives us "the intuition of the form of things ... as a true and genuine discovery".¹¹ Art offers a perspective that differs from ordinary seeing as well as from the impoverished abstractions of science based on facts or purported natural laws. Both of these focus on "constant and common features" of things. "Aesthetic perception exhibits a much greater variety and belongs to a much more complex order than our ordinary sense perception".¹² According to Cassirer "The artistic eye is not a passive eye that receives and registers the impression of things. It is a constructive eye, and it is only by such constructive acts that we can discover the beauty of natural things. Hence, the greatness of an artist is characterized by an ability to "elicit from static materials a dynamic life of forms".¹³ This process depends on "formative acts of contemplation" which differ from the "acts of theoretical objectification, by scientific concepts and constructs".¹⁴ In effect, art "teaches us to visualize, not merely to conceptualize or utilize things [...]. Art gives us a richer more vivid

---

9 Cassirer (1996), xxiii. The letter to Schilpp is in the Library of Living Philosophers Collection at the University of southern Illinois Carbondale.
10 Cassirer (1979a and 1979b)145–195. See also Cassirer (1979c), 208–209, 211–212.
11 Cassirer (1956), 184.
12 Ibid., 185.
13 Ibid., 193.
14 Ibid., 204.

and colorful image of reality, and a more profound insight into its formal structure".¹⁵

2 Langer and Cassirer

Among the philosophers who have continued to explore ideas found in Cassirer's writings on art as a symbolic form is the American philosopher Susanne Langer. Langer is credited as being the most effective in carrying forward aspects of Cassirer's notion of symbolic forms. Langer's interest in Cassirer's ideas extends to both aesthetics and myth, as she translated Cassirer's book on myth as a form of symbolic life.¹⁶ Here, our discussion will focus on Langer's views of aesthetic symbols. My point will not be to show that Langer simply adopts Cassirer's ideas concerning art symbols. Rather, she takes his core notion of symbolic form and then develops her own contributions to the understanding of art symbols.

Evidence of Langer's connections to Cassirer is found in her various references to his *Philosophy of Symbolic Form* found throughout her writings. For example, Langer's *Philosophy in a New Key* (1941) includes five different citations referring to Cassirer. Additional citations of Cassirer appear in Langer's *Mind: An Essay on Human Feeling* (three volumes: 1967, 1972, and 1982), in Philosophical Sketches (1962) and also in her discussion of Cassirer's views on language and myth.

Perhaps Langer's most explicit commentaries on Cassirer's contributions to philosophy of symbols are found in the essay, "On a New Definition of 'Symbol'" published in her *Philosophical Sketches*, and in a passage found in *Mind: An Essay on Human Feeling* I, where she discusses the import of art.

> It was in reflecting on the nature of art that I came on a conception of the symbol relation quite distinct from the one I had formed in connection with all my earlier studies, which had centered on symbolic logic. This new view of symbolization…had been highly developed in Cassirer's *Philosophie der symbolischen Formen*. In many years of work on the fundamental problems of art I have found it indispensable.¹⁷

Langer again affirms her indebtedness to Cassirer's *The Philosophy of Symbolic Forms* in *Mind: An Essay on Human Feeling I*, where she acknowledges his "ad-

---

15 Ibid., 236.
16 Cassirer (1946).
17 Langer (1962a), 58.

mirable scholarship and awareness of its implications" for differentiating among the different symbolic forms necessary to accommodate different modes of thought. In her words,

> Since the publication of that pioneering work *[The Philosophy of Symbolic Forms]* a number of books and articles have appeared ... but none, so far as I know, has gone on to develop the differences among the forms beyond those, which Cassirer indicated.[18]

Judging from their respective comments on art and symbols, it would appear that Langer and Cassirer are in agreement on many points. They both recognize the importance of acknowledging a range of symbol systems including language, art, myth and symbolic logic, mathematics and the natural sciences. Both agree that the symbols in the respective cultural systems function according to different principles, and contribute in different ways to the creation of human life. Art symbols for Cassirer and Langer are considered generative of aspects of life that go beyond what is received through sense data representing the external world. Hence intuition, feeling, and sensuous form are terms that resonate in the views of both Langer's and Cassirer's views concerning aesthetic symbols.

Langer defines art as "the practice of creating perceptible forms expressive of human feeling", which includes painting, sculpture, architecture, music, dance, literature, drama and film.[19] She holds the view that, "The primary function of art is to objectify feeling so that we can contemplate and understand it".[20] Hence, art symbols give access to the inner life not otherwise accessible through symbols used in language, mathematics and the empirical sciences. Form, or 'significant form', as Langer refers to it in *Philosophy in a New Key*, where she considers form in reference to music, is the means by which art symbols articulate feeling.[21] "Expression" as used by Langer does not mean the ordinary venting of feelings. Instead, Langer's uses expression to refer to the presentation of an idea of feeling as conveyed by an artistic symbol. Art thus contributes to understanding, albeit not by way of concepts.

Langer would agree with Cassirer's notion that human understanding requires thinking beyond rationalist conceptions of prior developments in philosophy and scientific views of both the external world and human consciousness. In short, both thinkers ask us to abandon chauvinistic claims of science or symbol systems based on symbolic logic to exclusive rights as the measure of all

---

18 Langer (1967a), 80–81.
19 Langer (1962b), 85.
20 Ibid., 90.
21 Langer (1950).

human understanding. In doing so, Langer and Cassirer point to a holistic view of reality, which is created out of the available varieties of symbols. This shared holistic view does not assign normative or hierarchical relationships among the various forms of symbols. Rather, it finds value in recognizing the cognitive worth of all the forms of human symbols.

Given this brief exposition of key points in the aesthetics of Langer and Cassirer, it seems that they are in agreement on the central themes in their respective aesthetics. In short, by introducing art into their philosophies of symbolism alongside language, myth and other forms of symbolism, both Langer and Cassirer insure that human beings are not limited to a singular approach to constructing a world view of reality, but can choose a single specific point of view and pass from one aspect of things to another.[22]

3 Cassirer and Langer on Language and Art

In order to take a closer view of Langer's relation to Cassirer's views on symbolic forms it will be useful to consider their respective views on language and art. As we have seen, Cassirer's aesthetics emerges from the main currents of the history of philosophy running from Plato through Vico, Kant, Hegel. However, Cassirer's early work was in epistemology, philosophy of science and logic. (There is not time to develop these connections, but the references throughout Cassirer's texts as well as in the interpretations of scholars such as Donald Verene and others will support this claim.)[23] Langer also began her studies of symbols from her initial work in symbolic logic as noted previously.

However, their views of art emerge from out of different directions. Cassirer's discussion is richly grounded in the history of philosophy, whereas Langer bases much of her study of symbols in biology and psychology. In keeping with his grounding in the history of philosophy, Cassirer's essay on "Language and Art" offers a broad overview of philosophical issues concerning the different uses of language from Plato through Croce. He takes note of the significance of language as a primary form of symbolism and explores its different uses. Among these uses, for example, are ordinary language, poetry, and scientific language. Underlying his argument here is the claim, shared by Langer, that art contributes to cognitive understanding in ways that are not accessible to

---

[22] Cassirer (1956), 217; Langer (1967b), 205–206.
[23] Verene (1979), 2.

non-art symbols, including language.[24] Cassirer argues that the artist focuses on the pure expressive form of things achieved through creative intuition of the human systems. In other words, art is not comprised of logical propositions or empirical descriptions. This point of view is in contrast to that of the engineer or scientist whose interest lies in empirical facts or the physical qualities of things.[25]

At this point Langer begins her attempt to address more fully the question of the differences between language symbols and art symbols, which she noted that Cassirer had not completed. In her quest to answer the Positivists' neglect or dismissal of art, Langer argues for art's intellectual credibility by giving it a "logic" of its own. Art's logic functions parallel to logic as found in symbolic logic, mathematics, and the languages of the empirical sciences. A remark from chapter four of *Philosophy in a New Key* suggests that this distinction arises out of a desire to free cognitive activity from a limit, which follows from the post-Wittgensteinian and post-Carnapian analysis of language.[26]

Her solution introduces a distinction between discursive and presentational symbols. Discursive symbols operate in language systems with syntactical and semantic features. Syntax provides construction rules for well-formed units of a language, and semantic rules establish guidelines for creating a vocabulary of meaningful units capable of interpretation such as words that represent objects.

Langer includes art in the category of presentational or non-discursive symbols that do not require syntactic or semantic rules. For example, in the case of a painting:

> Visual form-lines, colors, proportion, etc. are just as capable of articulation, i.e. of complex combination as words. But the laws that govern this sort of articulation are altogether different from the laws of syntax that governs language. The most radical difference is that visual forms are not discursive.[27]

The core of Langer's explanation of the logic of art symbols, as she explains in *Mind: an Essay on Human Feeling I,* lies in the notion that the artist projects the *idea* of a feeling through the artwork. Projection, as Langer notes, has multiple dimensions as it applies to art symbols. In this case, she intends it to be under-

---

[24] Cassirer (1979a) 145–165. See also Cassirer (1979b), 185–186, for further comments on the relation of art and language.
[25] Cassirer (1979a), 159.
[26] Langer (1967b), 86, 87.
[27] Ibid., 93, 94.

stood to mean that the expressive object (art) projects or expresses in some perceptible form the artist's *idea* of feeling, "the symbolization of vital and emotional experience for which verbal discourse is peculiarly unsuited".[28] Citing Ivy Campbell-Fisher, Langer agrees that the created form in art expresses "the nature of feelings conceived, imaginatively realized, and rendered by a labor of formulation and abstractive vision".[29]

Langer offers in support of her distinction between language and painting these arguments, which we can only summarize here:
a. Presentational symbols (art) express the form of feelings generated by the productive action of the work in expression.
b. Discursive symbols present their constituent elements sequentially, while paintings present theirs simultaneously.
c. Elements in language have fixed meaning, whereas the elements in a painting do not.
d. The rules for combining elements in language are few enough to allow for syntax, and the conventions are more binding than painting.[30]

There is not time to examine Langer 's case for the division of language and art symbols according to discursive versus presentational symbols as I have done elsewhere.[31] One difficulty is that nowhere in her comparison of the vocabularies that distinguish language and painting does Langer establish what the units of comparison might be.

If, as Langer believed, no one since Cassirer had proceeded beyond what he established to account for the differences among the various forms of symbols, we may acknowledge Langer for undertaking this challenge. It is sufficient to our aims here to note that Langer's differentiation of language and art symbols extends beyond the discussion of the differences among forms of symbols offered by Cassirer. Her solution to the problem seems closer to logical solutions of analytic philosophers such as Carnap than to those likely to be found starting from the metaphysical sources found in the historical authors (Vico, Kant, Hegel) as understood by Cassirer.

---

[28] Langer (1967a), 80.
[29] Ibid., 90.
[30] A fuller development of Langer's argument appears in ibid., 90, 102.
[31] Carter (1974).

4 Goodman and Cassirer

After Cassirer and Langer, Nelson Goodman (1906–1998), is arguably the philosopher to pay most attention to art symbols. Goodman thought of his work as belonging to the main stream of philosophy, but on his own constructed path. In this respect, he proposed to substitute his constructed symbol systems for the structures of the world, mind, and concepts. According to Goodman, the symbol systems of the sciences, philosophy, perception, the arts, as well as everyday discourse, constitute ways of world making. *The Structure of Appearance*, Goodman's first major book, reaches back to Carnap's *Aufbau (The Logical Structure of The World)* and offers a general theory of the systematic logical experience and actual construction of specific symbol systems. In *The Structure of Appearances*, Goodman follows Carnap in recognizing a plurality of logics and languages whose rules are fixed by convention instead of by one universal logic.[32]

Goodman's main connections to Cassirer are acknowledged in the first chapter of his 1978 book, *Ways of Worldmaking* where he offers a warm tribute to Cassirer's philosophy of symbols. *Languages of Art* also contain a reference to Cassirer's *Philosophy of Symbolic Forms II* in conjunction with their respective discussions of metaphor. A third reference to Cassirer can be found in a supplementary reading list to Chapter 3 of *Problems and Projects*.[33] In *Ways of Worldmaking*, Goodman cites as common themes shared with Cassirer, "… The multiplicity of worlds, the speciousness of 'the given', the creative power of the understanding, the variety and formative function of symbols" as being integral to his own thinking. Goodman's aim is to explore further such questions as these: "In just what sense are there many worlds? What distinguishes genuine from spurious worlds? … What role do symbols play in the making? And how is world making related to knowledge?"[34] The task of exploring these themes in depth would be well beyond the scope of this essay, but I will bring to light

---

[32] Goodman, (1951), 114 ff.
[33] Goodman (1978a). This first chapter of *Ways of World-making* was read at the University of Hamburg on the 100th anniversary of the birth of Ernst Cassirer. See also, Goodman (1978b), 77; Goodman (1972), 147.
[34] Goodman (1978a), 1. In this passage Goodman appears to attribute the theory of multiple worlds to Cassirer. However there is some question as to whether Cassirer understands multiple worlds in the same sense as Goodman who clearly holds to a plurality of worlds or world versions. Cassirer seems to entertain a holistic view in which multiple worlds are in some sense reconciled. This is a point for further investigation. Goodman's multiple worlds are perhaps linked together in the sense that each correct multiple world may contribute to understanding. The test of a multiple world version is its cognitive effectiveness. See Scheffler (1985).

here a brief exposition of Goodman's treatment of art symbols in order to show in parallel how his views complement, or go beyond those of Cassirer and Langer.

In *Languages of Art* (1968) Goodman presents his theory of art symbols in the context of a more general theory of symbols. Through careful individuation of the different kinds of symbolism represented in painting, music, dance, literature and the other arts, he offers a fresh structure for addressing key problems in aesthetics. His theory of art and other forms of symbols is based on the view that the use of symbols beyond immediate practical needs is for the sake of understanding or "cognition in and for itself". Understanding draws upon the urge to know or delight in discovery, and leads to enlightenment. The uses of symbols for communication and other practical or pleasurable uses are secondary. The criteria for judging symbols, whether in the sciences or the arts, depend on how well a symbol serves its cognitive purposes: "how it analyzes, sorts, orders, and organizes", and how the symbols participate in the making and transformation of knowledge.[35]

In an effort to show how pictures, music and dance performances, literary texts and buildings shape our experience as partners of the sciences, Goodman analyzes the various art forms with respect to semantic and syntactic differences. Here, he offers an alternative to Langer's claim that the arts lack syntax and semantics, which she allows only for language as a discursive symbol system. (As noted previously, Langer assigns the arts to a category of presentational symbols with their own non-discursive symbolic features.) For example, according to Goodman, paintings are considered syntactically dense symbols due to the inability ability to differentiate characters in the compositional schemes (shapes, brush marks etc.) of the works. Whereas, music allows for a greater degree of syntactic disjointness, and finite differentiation in its compositional schemes (constructing combinations of sounds with some possibilities for establishing notational systems).[36]

Using his recasting of the characteristics of art symbols, Goodman identifies three distinct forms of reference applicable to art symbols: representation, expression, and exemplification. Representation, he argues, is a matter of habit and familiarity rather than being based on natural resemblance. Understanding what a picture represents is a matter of invoking a range of cognitive resources including discerning its pictorial properties in reference to pictorial conventions and may involve complex connections to historical, scientific or mythical refer-

---

[35] Goodman (1968).
[36] Goodman (1978b), 179–198.

ences.³⁷ Exemplification is symbolizing by means of sample; it refers to the relation between a sample and the features in its referents. For example, a musical work might exemplify its harmonic or rhythmic properties. Or a painting might exemplify its colors, shapes, or textures. Familiarity with the symbol system in question is necessary to identifying the properties being exemplified. Artistic symbols according to Goodman, can exemplify only those properties they actually possess. Expression, the third form of reference in Goodman's account of symbols, entails metaphorical exemplification. For example, a painting, which is not literally expressing sadness, may metaphorically express the feeling of sadness.

While introducing a radically new form for understanding art symbols with considerably more detailed features than were offered by Cassirer or Langer, Goodman also tackles other central problems in aesthetics. For example, he replaces the question, "what is art?" with the question, "when is art?" In addition, he supplants aesthetic properties as the means of identifying art. Instead he substitutes the various syntactic and semantic properties operative in the respective art forms. As well, Goodman dismisses the relevance of artists' intentions. Gone too are attempts to proffer spurious distinctions between scientific understanding and art. For Goodman, they represent two complementary means for making and understanding our worlds. Similarly, art and philosophy are complementary means of world making; a claim that Goodman set out to demonstrate in actually creating a notable dance-theater work, *Hockey Seen*. *Hockey Seen* incorporates dance, theater, music, drawings, costumes, theater design, and elements from a hockey game with ideas contributed by Goodman.³⁸ His aim in this work was to present an application of his philosophical theories expressed in *Languages of Art* in the making of an actual work.

5 Art and the Philosophy of Art Symbols

Perhaps it is useful to conclude this discussion with some questions. First is the question concerning what motivated these philosophers to push beyond ideas their predecessors had offered concerning art's place in human understanding? No doubt these efforts were substantially driven substantially by their interest in addressing, and hopefully solving, the puzzles raised by art as a form of human symbolic activity in relation to language and the sciences. We find cumulative references in all three of our candidates presented here to the philosophical

---

37 Goodman (1988).
38 Carter (2009).

groundings for addressing the problems in their respective predecessors running from Plato to their contemporaries. As we have seen, for Cassirer the main sources of understanding problems in aesthetics were Vico, Kant, and Hegel. For Langer, the sources were symbolic logic, Cassirer's philosophy of symbols, and the biological sciences. For Goodman, Cassirer's views on the role of symbols in worldmaking and his interest in symbolic logic, especially Carnap's ideas provided useful starting points for his investigations into the philosophy of symbols.[39]

I would like to propose that the concurrent changes in the arts developing during the lives of the three philosophers' explorations of art's role in cognition, and its relation to other forms of symbols, may have provided additional incentive for their interest in championing the importance of art symbols. Goodman, for example was an avid collector of art including modern art, as well as Seventeenth Century Dutch, and art from China, India and American tribal arts. Between 1928 and the early 1940's he ran an art gallery in Boston. In addition to *Hockey Seen*, Goodman's most ambitious venture into the arts, he initiated projects relating to music, dance, and Picasso's art, over the course of his life.

The art of the era during which our three aestheticians formulated their views concerning art symbols contrasts sharply with the representational art epitomized in Goethe's elegant tribute to the artist Caspar David Friedrich noted at the beginning of our discussion.

Following the invention of photography some fifty years earlier, the artists of the twentieth century continued to invent new forms of art. In the words of the eminent twentieth century art historian Meyer Shapiro,

> ... The ideal of an imageless art of painting was realized for the first time, and the result was shocking—an arbitrary play with forms and colors that had only a vague connection with visible nature. Some painters had discovered that by accenting the operative elements of art—the stroke, the line, the patch, the surface of the canvas—and by disengaging these from the familiar objects altogether, the painting assumed a more actively processed appearance, the aspect of a thing made rather than a scene represented, a highly ordered creation referring more to the artist than to the world of external things.[40]

One outcome of these developments was the notion that the aim of art need not be narrating a story or copying nature, but rather to "express a state of feeling,

---

39 Apart from the citations noted in footnote 33, the extent of Goodman's connection with Cassirer is not known. Catherine Elgin, Goodman's colleague and co-author, reported that she did not recall Goodman's having discussed Cassirer's work during their association.
40 Shapiro (1978), 142.

an idea...or to create a harmony of colors and forms".[41] This shift corresponds to the view shared by Cassirer and Langer that art is a means of expressing inner feelings or ideas as well as their common task of studying the forms of consciousness or unconsciousness that generate them. The shift also is consonant with Goodman's view that art participates in the cognitive contributions to understanding.

The art and the theories of the Russian-born Wassily Kandinsky (1866–1944) will serve to illustrate the changing climate for art during the period in question. In an invitation issued to artists in 1909 announcing the formation of a "New Association for Artists of Munich", Kandinsky states, "Our point of departure is the thought that the artist, in addition to the impressions he received from the external world, from nature, continuously collects experiences in an inner world".[42] Perhaps reflecting Hegel's view "of a necessary perpetual spiritual progression away from dependence on the external world", Kandinsky argues in his book, *Concerning the Spiritual in Art* for a principle of "inner necessity" that would liberate art to establish a new aesthetic of symbols emphasizing inner feelings and artistic form over representation of the external world. Kandinsky's view did not exclude impressions from the external world, but his ideas and artistic practice clearly places the focus on art's origins in the inner life of the artist.[43]

While one cannot cite direct contact between Cassirer and Kandinsky, it seems plausible to suggest that a prominent philosopher interested in art, and living in Germany during the first decades of the twentieth century, would be aware of innovative artistic developments taking place there. Kandinsky developed as an artist while living in Munich between 1896 and 1914, and at the Bauhaus (first in Weimar then in Dessau and finally in Berlin) between 1922 and 1933, the leading site of innovative development in the arts in Europe at the time.

In particular, artists' shift from images linked to external reality in the Twentieth century, including nature, to images originating in the inner life of individual artist's called for explanation not available in traditional rationalist aesthetics.[44] The seeming formless expressions of feelings and the plethora of newly invented forms now appearing in art invited new investigations in aesthetics of the sort undertaken by Cassirer and later by Langer and Goodman.

Correspondence, if not causal connections between the interests of our philosophers considered here, and the developing shift in the practices of art from representation to abstraction and expression, is a subject calling for further in-

---

41 Ibid.
42 Kandinsky (1909), 67.
43 Heller (2003), 68.
44 Shapiro (1978), 145–146.

vestigation. In any event, the shift in art practices exhibited in Kandinsky's art and other modern artists corresponds nicely with the shifting focus of aesthetics from representational theories to expressionist theories and leading to philosophies of art symbols such as those under consideration in our discussion here.

Such radical developments in art and aesthetics inevitably raised new questions. Were these new developments to be interpreted as a sign of a deteriorating culture, hence warranting hostility to the novelties of modern art and philosophy, and, deservedly, their being subjected to criticism? Or might these changes signal that new developments in art and philosophy, as in physical science and technology, are necessary components of an invigorative society?

One difference between art and philosophy is that art generates personal responses through which one identifies with, or rejects particular works of art on the basis of personal feelings. This is not necessarily the case in philosophy or in science and technology where the acceptance and the uses of products and ideas does not depend as much on personal feelings as in changes of outlook. Hence, there is an even greater need for aesthetic theories that will help to assimilate new artistic developments into the understanding of individuals, clarify art's societal roles, and sustain art's place in the on-going stream of philosophical and other cultural investigations.

This discussion brings us to the second set of questions: How have the reflections on symbolic forms in the writings of Cassirer, Langer, and Goodman contributed to these undertakings? Without implying that each had the exact same aims in their treatments of symbolic forms, I conclude that they are all working toward a similar end of clarifying the nature, types, and functions of particular symbolic forms. Cassirer effectively presents the argument that symbols are the means by which humans form their conceptual worlds, and he perceives the importance of recognizing differences between art and the other symbol systems that contribute to this task of worldmaking. He finds the origins of art symbols in imagination or intuition, but does not fully account for the variations in how or why the symbols operative in art and elsewhere differ, apart from noting differences in their functions. Langer and Goodman carry on this project introducing further distinctions among the types of symbols and the ways in which they function based on their logical features. Each of these philosophers has at least made a strong case for the continuing relevance of art as an important means of constructing and understanding our worlds. Together they have shown that art symbols contribute an enriching form of symbolism to human understanding, essential and complementary to language, the sciences, and other forms of symbols.

Bibliography

Capeillères (2008): Fabien Capeillères, "Art Esthetique et Geisstgechichte: Appropos des Relations entre Warburg, Cassirer et Panofsky", *Cassirer Studies* I (2008), 77–100.
Capeillères (2009): Fabien Capeillères, "'K' for 'Kunst'. Cassirer's Pages on Art for PRs IV with a note on Francis Bacon", *Cassirer Studies* II (2009): 11–50.
Capeillères (2011): Fabien Capeillères, "Art Critique as a Philosophical Science?", *Cassirer Studies* IV (2011), 65–81.
Capeillères (2013): Fabien Capeillères, "Artistic Thinking within Cassirer's System of Symbolic Forms: A Brief Reassessment", unpublished paper presented at *The Seminar on Aesthetics* symposium, "Cassirer and the Aesthetic—Expression, Representation, Significance", University of Oslo, February 28, 2013
Carter (1974): Curtis L. Carter, "Langer and Hofstadter on Painting and Language: A Critique", *Journal of Aesthetics and Art Criticism* 32 (1974), 331–342.
Carter (2009): Curtis L. Carter, "Nelson Goodman's *Hockey Seen:* A Philosopher's Approach to Performance", *Congress Book II, XVII International Congress of Aesthetics*, Jale Erzen (ed.), Sanart, 60–67.
Cassirer (1946): Ernst Cassirer, *Language and Myth,* Susanne Langer (trans.), New York: New York: Harper and Brothers.
Cassirer (1949): Ernst Cassirer, "'Life' and 'Spirit' in Contemporary Philosophy", R. W. Bretall and P. A. Schilpp (trans.), in: *The Philosophy of Ernst Cassirer* (Library of Living Philosophers, 6), P. A. Schilpp (ed.), LaSalle, IL: Open Court Publishing Company, 855–880.
Cassirer (1956): Ernst Cassirer, *An Essay on* Man, New York: Doubleday & Company.
Cassirer (1979a): Ernst Cassirer, "Language and Art I", in: Donald Phillip Verene (ed.), *Symbol, Myth, and Culture: Essays and Lectures of Ernst Cassirer 1935–1945*, New Haven and London: Yale University Press.
Cassirer (1979b): Ernst Cassirer, "Language and Art II", in: Donald Phillip Verene (ed.), *Symbol, Myth, and Culture,* op. cit.
Cassirer (1979c): Ernst Cassirer, "The Educational Value of Art", in: Donald Phillip Verene (ed.), *Symbol, Myth, and Culture,* op. cit.
Cassirer (1996): Ernst Cassirer, *Philosophy of Symbolic Forms, Volume Four: The Metaphysics of Symbolic Forms*, J.M. Krois/D. P. Verene (eds.), New Haven: Yale University Press.
Gilbert (1949): Catherine Gilbert, "Cassirer's Placement of Art", in: P.A. Schilpp (ed), *The Philosophy of Ernst Cassirer,* op. cit.
Goethe (1980): J.W. von Goethe, "Caspar David Friedrich", in: John Cage (ed.), *Goethe on Art,* Berkeley and Los Angeles: University of California Press.
Goodman (1951): Nelson Goodman, *The Structure of Appearance,* Cambridge, MA: Harvard University Press.
Goodman (1968): Nelson Goodman, "Art and Inquiry", *Proceedings of the American Philosophical Association, Eastern Division,* 5–19.
Goodman (1972): Nelson Goodman, *Problems and Projects,* Indianapolis: Bobbs Merrill Company.
Goodman (1978a): Nelson Goodman, "Words, Works, Worlds", in: *Ways of Worldmaking,* Indianapolis: Hackett Publishing Company, 1–22.
Goodman (1978b): Nelson Goodman, *Languages of Art,* Indianapolis: Bobbs Merrill Company.

Goodman (1988): Nelson Goodman, "Confronting Novelty", in: *Reconceptions in Philosophy & Other Arts & Sciences,* Indianapolis and Cambridge: Hackett Publishing Company.

Heller (2003): Reinhold Heller, "The Blue Rider", in: *Schoenberg, Kandinsky, and the Blue Rider,* Esther da Costa Meyer and Fred Wasserman (eds.), New York and London: Scala Publishers, 2003.

Hendel (1955a): Charles W. Hendel, "Introduction", in: Ernst Cassirer, *Philosophy of Symbolic Forms, Volume I,* New Haven: Yale University Press.

Kandinsky (1909): Wassily Kandinsky, 1909 Invitation, New Association of Artists Munich, as cited in: Reinhold Heller, "The Blue Rider", op. cit.

Langer (1950): Susanne Langer, "The Principles of Creation in Art", *The Hudson Review* 2 (No. 4), 515–534.

Langer (1962a): Susanne Langer, "On a New Definition of Symbol", in: Susanne Langer (ed.), *Philosophical Sketches,* Baltimore: Johns Hopkins Press.

Langer (1962b): Susanne Langer, "The Cultural Importance of Art", in: *Philosophical Sketches,* op. cit.

Langer (1967a): Susanne Langer, *Mind: An Essay on Human Feeling I,* Baltimore: The Johns Hopkins Press.

Langer (1967b) Susanne Langer, *Philosophy in a New Key,* Cambridge, MA: Harvard University Press; original publication 1942.

Scheffler (1985): Israel Scheffler, "The Wonderful Worlds of Goodman", in: *Inquiries: Philosophical Studies of Language, Science and Learning,* Indianapolis: Hackett Publishing Company.

Shapiro (1978): Meyer Shapiro, *Modern Art: 19th and 20th Centuries; Selected Essays,* New York: George Braziller.

Slochower (1949): Harry Slochower, "Ernest Cassirer's Functional Approach to Art and Literature", in: P.A. Schilpp (ed.), *The Philosophy of Ernst Cassirer,* op. cit.

Verene (1979): Donald Phillip Verene, "Introduction", in: *Symbol, Myth, and Culture: Essays and Lectures of Ernst Cassirer 1935–1945,* op. cit.

Jennifer Marra (Milwaukee)
Humor as a Symbolic Form: Cassirer and the Culture of Comedy

In an attempt to understand human beings' relationship to humor, theories have been offered from sociological, psychological, biological, and philosophical perspectives.[1] While philosophers have explored humor from within each field, none have succeeded in accounting for humor as a totality, that is, in a way that can explain or predict all instances and objects of humor; and in some cases it has been claimed that such a unified account is impossible.[2] As humor exists in all cultures and all times, the confusion surrounding this topic represents a substantial lack of philosophical understanding of human experience. It is from this perspective that I approach the work of Ernst Cassirer and his philosophy of symbolic forms. I believe that the problem is not, as some philosophers claim, that it is impossible to give a unified account of humor, but rather that humor is already unified as what Cassirer would call a "symbolic form". Symbolic forms are perspectives from within which the world is comprehended, they are the "organs of reality"[3], each with its own laws and logic, and they are the conditions for the possibility of experience of any sort. "For the mind," he says, "only that can be visible which has some definite form; but every form of existence has its source in some peculiar way of seeing, some intellectual formulation and intuition of meaning."[4] Reason, or science, is one of these forms, and Cassirer believes that Kant articulated the laws and logic of that form in *The Critique of Pure Reason*. But there are other forms as well, including myth, art, and language, among others, and "each of these is a particular way of seeing, and carries within itself its particular and proper source of

---
[1] I would like to thank Stephen Lofts, Fabien Capeillères, Norbert Andersch, and Philip T. L. Mack for their extremely helpful comments, as well as all participants at The Philosophy of Ernst Cassirer: A Novel Assessment (2014) and the Lighthearted Philosophers' Society (2014) conferences for their questions and recommendations. While I was not able to pursue all avenues and suggestions for this paper, I am indebted to these scholars for the helpful guidance in future research. Special thanks to Sebastian Luft, Stephen Lofts, and Alan Richardson for their encouragement in pursuing this project.
[2] See Ribeiro (2009), wherein he offers an account which he sarcastically claims is "pitched at roughly the same level of detail, and intended to have roughly the same level of inclusiveness" as those of Hobbes and Kant.
[3] Cassirer (1946), 8.
[4] Cassirer (1946), 8.

light."⁵ Cassirer's philosophy of culture is the study of these forms and their respective internal structures. Thus my aim is twofold: to show that humor is a symbolic form, and that understanding humor in this way avoids the problems of the classic theories of humor.

As Cassirer himself claims that his list of symbolic forms is not exhaustive, conceptual space exists for humor to be included. I aim to show that the root of the problem in the philosophy of humor is rooted in a misunderstanding of the foundational classification of humor, and that this problem is solved when humor is understood as a symbolic form. I will begin by detailing the nature of Cassirer's symbolic forms. I will follow this by differentiating humor from comedy, laughter, trait, and genre. Then I will summarize the four most popular theories in the philosophy of humor. I do this for two reasons: first, to show that philosophers of humor have fallen victim to category mistakes in their study of humor; and second, to show why each theory fails to give a unified account of humor. In the next part, I will turn to Cassirer's own words regarding humor in order to make the case for understanding humor as a symbolic form. In the final section, I will show how Cassirer's normative command to keep symbolic forms distinct is particularly striking when we consider humor as a form.

1 Cassirer's Philosophy of Symbolic Forms

What exactly is a symbolic form? Cassirer explains that Kant's critique only gives us *part* of the human story, and in order to tell the whole tale we need to critique other aspects of our existence, or, other symbolic forms, and learn the laws and logic of them. He names art, myth, language and religion among these forms, but leaves the list open to additions as the human spirit progresses and more forms reveal themselves. As "products of the human spirit"⁶, symbolic forms "shape the character and destiny of culture"⁷ and "reflect the realities of cultural experience."⁸ The relationship between the human being and the forms is expressed as necessarily bidirectional:

---

5 Cassirer (1946), 11.
6 Cassirer (1953a), 78.
7 Itzkoff (1977), 83.
8 Itzkoff (1977), 98.

> Man lives with *objects* only in so far as he lives with these *forms*; he reveals reality to himself, and himself to reality, in that he lets himself and the environment enter into this plastic medium, in which the two do not merely make contact, but fuse with each other.[9]

He continues, "it is solely by their [the forms'] agency that anything real becomes an object for intellectual comprehension, and as such is made visible to us."[10] Thus symbolic forms are the conditions for the possibility of experience, driven and molded by the human spirit, and they are as fluid as that spirit.

The symbolic forms, then, can be considered as the abstract categories that objects of experience express; that is, objects of experience can only be experienced insofar as they fall under the forms. Objects, as Cassirer claims, can represent any and all symbolic forms, and the form they take will depend upon the form within which we are operating. If I am operating within the form of myth, for example, I will understand a tree as a representation of divinity or the spirituality of nature. If I am operating from within the form of science, I will understand the tree as part of a complex ecosystem. The tree itself remains the same, it is my *confrontation* with the tree that changes depending upon the internal structures of the form from within which I confront that tree. In other words, my perspective dictates the form for which a given object will stand as a representation.

Importantly, Cassirer is also very clear about the forms' relationships to each other. Each form has its own domain, he says, and none should be confused for or conflated with another: "Though they all function organically together in the construction of spiritual reality, yet each of these organs has its individual assignment..."[11] Each form has its own domain, its own criteria, and its own logic, and the domain of one form ought never be confused with the domain of another. For example, when one uses rational categories, which fall under the form of science, in order to judge the validity of religion, which falls under the form of myth, he speaks past his interlocutor. Religion has different criteria for truth than reason does, and one should assess religion *from within religion's form* if one wants to understand it. To use scientific categories is to in effect "miss the point" of religion, to attempt to "explain it away" instead of gain an understanding of its logic and influence. The same is true of the inverse; religion's categories and criteria cannot be used to understand or explain science because it does not have the tools or perspective to do justice to that which does not belong to its form. In other words, to judge religion by the categories of reason, or vice versa, is a normative failing in that "utilizing mythological cat-

---

9 Cassirer (1946), 10.
10 Cassirer (1946), 8.
11 Cassirer (1946), 9.

egories in rational discourse contorts rationality itself,"[12] or vice versa. This normative command regarding the boundaries of symbolic forms will become key in the final section of this paper.

Given the nature of the forms, the method by which a philosopher of culture must proceed is by first identifying which forms are existent, and then articulating the internal structures of that form from within that form. In this paper, I will only focus on the former, making a case for the existence of the symbolic form of humor. The existence of the form is foundational to any work concerning what that form entails, or, as Cassirer explains of the philosophy of symbolic forms as such, "it is not a question of what we see in a certain perspective, but of the perspective itself."[13] Thus my goal here will be to show that conceptual space exists for humor as a symbolic form, and that doing so will solve the root of a foundational problem in the philosophy of humor.

2 The Philosophy of Humor

Let us turn now to the study of humor. When we speak of humor itself, we are not speaking exclusively of a character trait like wit, nor are we referring only to a literary or entertainment genre, though these things are included under the category of humor. Humor is also not identical to comedy or laughter. Laughter is not always provoked by humor; often people laugh when they feel anxious, uncomfortable, or scared. Laughter is not always an indication that one is experiencing humor.[14] Comedy is an event intended to provoke laughter, such as a stand-up comedy performance. Laughter is the goal of the event, but this goal need not be met in order for the event to be comedy.[15] Humor, as the broad category, is not always confined to comedy nor must it provoke laughter.[16] Laughter, comedy, wit, and genre can be *objects* of humor, but humor need not be tied to laughter, comedy, wit, or genre. Humor can encompass all of these things, though it is not dependent on any one of them. Humor as the broad category is that which I will argue is a symbolic form.

Historically, there are four main theories in the philosophy of humor: Superiority, Relief, Relaxation, and Incongruity. The Superiority theory, credited mainly to Plato and Hobbes, states that the reason I laugh when a man slips on a ba-

---

12 Luft (2004), 38.
13 Cassirer (1946), 11.
14 Provine (2012), 40.
15 Richards (2013), 28.
16 Morreall (1987), 4.

nana peel is because I feel superior to him.[17] Laughter is the result of malice in the soul, a vice, which signals one's sense of superiority over another. To laugh at another is to shift power away from him and to oneself; this is why jokes at the expense of religious icons or political leaders have historically been banned or punished.[18] According to this theory, when I laugh I am always laughing at, never with, an object or person. Evidence for this theory of humor can be found everywhere from the medieval jester to the pratfalls of Chevy Chase to the self-deprecating standup of Louis CK. In contemporary discourse, this theory has been unanimously dismissed as an all-encompassing theory of humor, even by those who feel that it does have some explanatory power in certain situations.[19] This theory approaches the question of humor politically and sociologically; in order for me to feel superior to the object of my laughter, I must consider myself and the object in terms of a power hierarchy. That is, this theory presupposes humor as contingent on social hierarchies and asks for causes within the mind of an individual in relation to another.

The Relief and Relaxation theories are similar in that both claim that laughter is necessary for some sort of release. The former claims that we need to laugh to release excess energy, energy that is normally released through aggression or sexual activity. Laughter allows me to "release the pressure valve" in a socially acceptable way.[20] Proponents claim that we need to laugh to release physical tension in the body, tension which builds up due to every day or extraordinary stresses.[21] We can see evidence for the Relief theory in every high school hallway, though this theory loses steam when trying to explain humor in many cases of wordplay.

Both the Relief and Relaxation theory can explain why we enjoy laughter and seek it out, but they don't seem capable of explaining why certain objects stimulate a humor response and others do not. Most importantly, neither ex-

---

17 Morreall (2009), 4.
18 Recent developments regarding North Korea's response to a film called *The Interview* is a perfect example of this. The film, a comedy, portrays the assassination of North Korean leader Kim Jong-un. As of 23 December 2014, North Korea has been found responsible for hacking the movie studio, Sony, in an attempt to prevent the films' release in the United States, as well as threatening terrorist action against theaters that screen the film. See Brooks Barnes and Michael Cieply's piece in the New York Times, accessed 23 Dec 2014: http://www.nytimes.com/2014/12/24/business/media/sonys-the-interview-will-come-to-some-theaters-after-all.html?hp&action=click&pgtype=Homepage&module=second-column-region&region=top-news&WT.nav=top-news&_r=0
19 See Gilbert (2004) as well as Morreall (1987) and (2009).
20 Morreall (2009), 16.
21 Morreall (2009), 25.

plains humor itself since it is not humor that is the goal but laughter, and laughter has no necessary connection to humor (think of nervous laughter, for example; the body relaxes, but there is no humorous stimuli). The Relief theory approaches the question of humor psychologically, while the Relaxation theory approaches humor biologically. They ask for causes within the mind or body, respectively, in order to explain physiological needs for laughter. Laughter may be accounted for in these theories, but humor is not.

The Incongruity theory, which finds its origin in Kant's *Critique of Judgment*,[22] is the most popular and widely accepted of the four theories among contemporary philosophers of humor. As its name implies, this theory claims that humor arises from the incongruous, such as when an expected pattern is suddenly disrupted. Jerry Seinfeld's observational humor relies on this model: take an ordinary or mundane object or event and expose it as ridiculous or absurd.[23] This theory prioritizes the status of the object; it asks how the stimuli must be organized or presented in order to be found funny. This approach is both linguistic as it applies to jokes and aesthetic as it applies to presentation. Theorists have taken pains to tweak and adjust this theory in order to make it universally applicable, though these attempts have failed, particularly when we consider that "a sudden disruption of pattern or expectation" is also how we describe the experience of trauma.[24] There have also been difficulties in massaging this theory to explain why it is that we continue to find jokes funny on repeated tellings; if humor depends on toying with my expectations, and I know what to expect from a joke I've already heard, incongruity cannot explain why I would still find the joke funny. Furthermore, the theory fails to explain how it is possible for the same object to inspire humor in one person but not in another. If humor is dependent on the organization of the object, then insofar as an object is properly organized it should be found universally humorous. But experience shows that even the funniest joke or image is never appreciated by everyone who encounters it.

Each theory fails to provide a universal account for humor. For three of the theories this is due to a category mistake; the Superiority, Relief, and Relaxation theories are not philosophies of humor, they are philosophies of laughter. Since laughter has no necessary connection to humor these theories do not, and cannot, explain humor itself. The Incongruity theory does not commit this category mistake and does search for an explanation of humor itself, however, as I have

---

[22] See Kant (2000), 333.
[23] Morreall (2009), 11.
[24] Brison (2000), 104.

shown, it is not capable of providing a universal account. It is my claim that the struggles in understanding humor will continue so long as humor is approached from within other fields such as science (the biological, psychological, and sociological approaches of the Relaxation, Relief, and Superiority theories, respectively), language (the linguistic approach of verbal Incongruity) or art (the aesthetic approach of visual/auditory Incongruity). The strides we make when we approach humor from within these fields will be strides within those fields, not within the study of humor; the Relaxation theory, for example, certainly tells us more about the human body than it does about humor itself. To consider humor as *only* scientific, *only* linguistic, or *only* artistic, is in effect to "miss something" about humor and our relationship to it. Thus it is my contention that our foundational understanding of humor is misguided, and in the following sections I will provide a solution to this problem.

3 Cassirer on Humor

Cassirer had a great respect for humor, as we see in his study of the subject in *The Platonic Renaissance in England* (henceforth PRE). Here Cassirer praises Shaftesbury's insistence that humor is a means of social critique, saying that for him:

> Humor represents that fundamental attitude and disposition of the soul in which it is best equipped for the comprehension of the beautiful and the true. [This is the attitude] in which the soul gains the proper standpoint for judgments concerning questions of faith and knowledge and concerning religion and philosophy.[25]

That is, the remarkable way in which Shaftesbury used comedy was to expose its effect on the soul. By placing oneself in the standpoint of the comic, one can expose implicit or hidden truths in the dogmatism of religion and philosophy. Shaftesbury understood comedy as a means to truth, a way of encouraging the relinquishment of unquestioned ideas. Cassirer continues:

> Humor need not justify itself before religion, but religion before humor... One must ask oneself the general question as to what part the various types and species of the comic have had in the formation of the modern work and what latent energies seek expression in these types.[26]

---

[25] Cassirer (1953b), 168.
[26] Cassirer (1953b), 169–170.

Here we see that Cassirer finds humor to be an influential cultural force, and that questions concerning its instantiations are worthwhile to say the least. The suggestion here seems to be that objects of humor can, in all their "various types and species", be a powerful litmus test for truth. But it is not only this, as the last half of the quotation indicates. It would be worthwhile, he says, to see how these types and species work themselves out in the human story, and to discover the nature of the spirit that has and will continue to work its way through this story.

On the basis of these quotations, one may claim that while it is clear that Cassirer finds *comedy* to be culturally important, it is not clear that he would consider *humor itself* to be a symbolic form. In fact, his discussion of comedy takes place in a section devoted to the study of art. So it seems that Cassirer himself subsumes comedy under the symbolic form of art; if humor has any chance of being its own form, it must not be capable of being subsumed under another. The question is: should we understand humor as Cassirer does, as a representation of the form of art?

Cassirer does seem to collapse comedy into art, and appropriately so, since comedic writing such as that of Shaftesbury and literature in general can indeed represent objects of art if approached in that manner. But when Cassirer speaks of "the comic", he is no longer speaking from within the form of art. While he does not explicitly acknowledge the distinction, Cassirer does treat comedy and "the comic" as different categories; "comedy" as particular objects capable of being understood within the form of art, and "the comic" as an abstract category. For example, the comedies of Shakespeare and Cervantes as introduced in *Essay on Man* are objects of art,[27] but for Cassirer they can also be objects of the symbolic forms of history[28] or language.[29] These comedies are then particular objects, individual representations of a symbolic form, not the form itself, and they can thus be interpreted as representations from within any number of symbolic forms.[30] This is in opposition to when Cassirer speaks of "the comic" and how its "various types and species" have formed the modern world and the "latent energies" which "seek expression in these types."[31] Here I take "the comic" to be what philosophers of humor today would simply call the broad category of "humor", that is, that thing which encompasses all energies, types, species,

---

27 Cassirer (1944), 158.
28 Cassirer (1944), 222.
29 Cassirer (1944), 168.
30 Cassirer (1946), 85.
31 Cassirer (1953b), 170.

and objects of humor, the umbrella under which all instantiations of humor fall. Take the following for example:

> Thus in the power of the comic lives the power of love which will and can understand even that form of the world which the intellectual must abandon and surmount... From the different kinds and varieties of the comic, from sarcasm and jest, from satire and irony, emerges the new approach, the *original form of humor*, with increasing clarity and self-consciousness. This humor must first be stripped of its multifarious cloaks and disguises, but it stands before us finally as an *original and independent entity*.[32]

This "stripped down" humor, the humor which can instantiate in many different varieties as an *original form* with clarity and self-consciousness, sounds very much like a symbolic form. Later in the text he uses the language of form again in regard to humor when speaking of Shakespearean comedies:

> The *form of humor* now to prevail is not unsuitable to the immediate presence of suffering, or even death. It is no longer confined to mere play of the mind... Humor henceforth takes its place in the heart of Shakespeare's world, forming everywhere the medium of reconciliation of all the opposites which this world comprehends. ... The element of nobility, indeed of humility, characterizes *true* humor, as distinguished from mere wit. For in the world of humor the apparent truth of things proves over and over again to be mere show. But humor can sense the real immanent truth behind show and acknowledge it as such. ... In the *realm of humor*, too, epochs meet and intermingle in strange ways. For humor looks before and after; it helps to usher in the vital shapes of the future without renouncing the past.[33]

But what do we do about the claim that Cassirer is speaking of objects typically considered as within the form of art? Does humor really just collapse into art? If we are to distinguish humor as its own symbolic form, we may want to differentiate it from others. Humor can easily be distinguished from the forms of science and history; science is in the business of searching for "truth in universal law hypotheses" and naturalism,[34] while history is in the business of depicting "historical forces, conflicting human purposes, and the significance of events";[35] while humor can instantiate in jokes and commentary *about* these forms, we certainly would not say that either of these describe the domain of humor proper. The same is true of language; if humor can exist outside of the spoken or written word, it cannot fall exclusively within the realm of language, although of course

---

32 Cassirer (1953b), 171–172, emphasis added.
33 Cassirer (1953b), 178–179, emphasis added.
34 Krois (1987), 132–3.
35 Krois (1987), 134.

language does come into play in humors' objects, as it does, Cassirer claims, in all objects. But the form of language cannot encompass the humor of Charlie Chaplin. If we considered only how Chaplin's silent films call to mind referents and nominatums, we would surely be missing the point. Humor is not myth, regardless of the fact that the genre of comedy in ancient Greece has close connections to mythical understandings of the world. Indeed, the close connection between humor and myth supports my claim that humor is its own symbolic form, as Cassirer claims that myth is prior to all other forms.

The most difficult distinction to make is between humor and art, and given that Cassirer was not himself taking up the task of carving out humor as its own form it is reasonable that he would collapse the two together. The best I can do here is show where art and humor diverge. Krois defines the symbolic form of art as such: "Art confronts us with a world of ideal imaginative forms, in which we can recognize the possibilities and realities of human feeling and experience as a lived personal reality."[36] Certainly objects of humor can produce these effects. But does humor proper consistently and perfectly correspond with this definition? I believe it does not.

Oftentimes objects of humor as such do not present us with ideal forms, but rather expose the sometimes embarrassing truths of the world in which we live. Take the following bit on the concept of reverse racism by standup comedian Aamer Rahman:

> I could be a reverse racist if I wanted to. All I'd need would be a time machine…and I'd convince the leaders of Africa, Asia, the Middle East, Central and South America to invade and colonize Europe, right, just occupy them, steal all their land and resources, set up some kind of like, I don't know, trans-Asian slave trade… I'd make sure I'd set up systems that privilege black and brown people at every conceivable social political and economic opportunity. … If after hundreds and hundreds of years of that I got on stage at a comedy show and said, 'hey, what's the deal with white people? Why can't they dance?" that would be reverse racism.[37]

What we have here is certainly not idealization.

Furthermore, humor also does not always deal with exposing human feeling. It can focus on introspection of the individual in her engagement of the world, but can also focus on the world divorced from the individual. We can find humor in things, objects, and ideas that have no obvious relationship to us *as individuals*, such as the humor we find in puns and other wordplay. We are not engaged in self-conscious introspection when we laugh at a pun, nor do

---

36 Krois (1987), 134.
37 Rahman (2010).

we contemplate our relationship to the universe. Wordplay does not make us "recognize the possibilities and realities of human feeling and experience as a lived personal reality", yet it is most certainly humor. These counterexamples show that humor, whatever its domain, cannot be confined to the domain of art as Krois articulates it. Humor and art, humor and language, humor and myth are not the same things, and cannot be reduced to one another. Thus just as each symbolic form is irreducible to another, we have seen in our previous examination of contemporary theories of humor and in our distinction between humor and art that humor itself cannot be reduced to or understood through any one symbolic form.

4 Humor as a Symbolic Form

Thus a positive definition of humor can be given in terms of humor as a symbolic form analogous to, for example, art. Art is a symbolic form, and representations of this form include painting, sculpture, poetry, music, etc. Humor is a symbolic form, and representations of this form include comedy as genre, wit, satire, irony, absurdity, etc. Humor and objects of humor are different things, just as art and objects of art are different things. Objects of humor, properly speaking, are objects that can represent the symbolic form of humor, while humor is itself a symbolic form. When operating from within the form of humor, I can consider any object as a representation of humor just as I could, from within the form of myth, consider any object as a representation of myth. To understand humor in this way is to avoid the pitfalls of previous theories.

I believe it would be quite impossible to explain or understand certain aspects of human experience without understanding humor as a symbolic form. In fact, there are some actions that human beings do that can only be explained if we understand the human spirit as something that seeks out and engages in humor, such as novelty objects. There would be no reason for a thumb drive shaped like a thumb or a set of plastic wind-up chattering teeth to exist where it not for the sake of humor alone.

One may object, however, that not everyone looks at chattering teeth and finds them humorous. Or, that not everything can be an object of humor in the way that anything can be an object of art or myth. And for something to be a symbolic form, it must be the case that you can take any object and interpret it as a representation of that symbolic form. What can we make of these objections? First of all, someone who is not looking from within the form of humor will probably not find the chattering teeth funny. And this is fine for our theory; any object is a representation of any form from within which it is being studied.

So the chattering teeth can be understood in any number of lights, but in order to understand it in its totality and in its relationship to the world we experience, to know why such a thing is created and the purpose of that creation, we must understand it in terms of humor.

Secondly, as regards the possibility of any object being recognized as a representation of the form of humor, we again have no problem. In fact, it explains why some people can find any and everything funny, even those things that can make others feel morally queasy. We can look at a tree and see it as a representation of science, myth, art, or language, etc. Can we also see it as a representation of humor? Certainly, trees can be immensely funny given the appropriate perspective. There's certainly nothing *preventing* the tree from representing the form of humor. It may not be as obvious to us that it can be done with a tree in the way it can be done with language or art, but that may be because many of us are out of practice, undereducated, or simply unaccustomed to placing ourselves within the form of humor to view the world. Just as it may take an education in myth to be capable of understanding any object as a representation of that symbolic form, it also may take an education in humor in order to understand any object as a representation of the form of humor. In other words, just because it may not be intuitively obvious that any given object can be considered from within the form of humor does not mean that the form of humor does not exist.

Here I have shown that conceptual space exists for humor to be considered a symbolic form. It is irreducible to any other form, it is a unique perspective with which to view and understand the world, it instantiates in objects that cannot be understood outside of the form itself, and it is capable of being represented by any object that is confronted from within it. Cassirer himself recognized the importance and influence of humor, and spoke of it as if it were a form, regardless of the fact that he never explicitly included it in his list of existent forms. Understanding humor as a symbolic form not only explains why each theory of humor can be both correct and incorrect (as objects can stand as representations of any form dependent upon the perspective), but also why no unified account has been successful (none of the forms from within which humor has been approached have the tools or capabilities of subsuming humor as such). Humor as a symbolic form solves this problem by showing that these aforementioned approaches have been misguided—humor is a form unto itself—and that humor must be recognized and appreciated in this way if progress in the study of humor is to made and human experience is to be better understood.

5 Normative Implications

Why take such pains to reveal humor as its own symbolic form, irreducible to art or any other? What is at stake in my analysis, and what are the implications of this conceptual distinction? I believe understanding humor in this way has a great deal of explanatory power. Recognizing humor as a symbolic form allows us to understand the right and wrong ways humor has been used in culture and society. This has to do directly with Cassirer's normative command to keep the boundaries of symbolic forms strict, that is, to never use the laws and logic of one form to gauge the truth or falsity of another.

As discussed earlier, Cassirer explains that "[i]t is no longer a matter of simply deriving one of these phenomena from the other, of 'explaining' it in terms of the other—for that would be to level them both, to *rob* them of their characteristic features."[38] But doing so is not just a faux pas in analysis—it can in fact be extremely dangerous, as Cassirer witnessed for himself as a Jew during the Nazi regime. He explains in *The Myth of the State* that the Nazis used the myths of race worship in order to justify historical and philosophical, and later scientific, claims of the Aryan man's factual superiority and need to embrace his inevitable destiny.[39] As Luft explains, Cassirer's claim here is that by subjecting myth to the laws and logic of science and philosophy "fascist rhetoric consisted precisely in mixing symbolic forms, deliberately overstepping boundaries"[40] with the goal of allowing myth to infiltrate and overturn rational discourse.

Cassirer's normative argument becomes very powerful when the form in question is humor. Humor, as we know, can instantiate in the form of mockery. Mockery creates in-groups and out-groups—those being laughed at and those doing the laughing. This is a key step in what human rights scholar Gregory H. Stanton has called "organized genocide",[41] that of classification. Socio-politically, humor has been and continues to be used today to undermine and dehumanize others. Marginalized groups are often victims of mocking humor, and in the particular example of Germany, the dehumanization of the Jews instantiated in casual jokes long before organized genocide. Jokes become part of the mythos of the culture, that is, when any group of people is the consistent butt of popular jokes, that group of people becomes, in the minds of the majority, jokes them-

---

38 Cassirer (1946), 9, emphasis added.
39 Cassirer (1955), 281.
40 Luft (2004), 38.
41 Stanton (1996).

selves. When a group becomes a joke, and that joke is classified as different from another, the joking group will begin to think of the mocked group as "lesser". It is a short distance from mocked to marginalized to silenced to dehumanized, and once a group has been placed outside of the realm of the human, it becomes morally permissible to treat them as mere objects, in whatever form that may take. This is why, even today, marginalized and leftist groups are incredibly sensitive to humor and its objects; to joke about another can be a first step to dehumanizing her.

Humor is one of the most subtle and efficient ways in which to plant beliefs and emotions into a person or society precisely because it is not something we associate with seriousness. Humor spreads quickly and the conclusions of humor can infect a large cultural community in a short amount of time. Punch lines and humorous images and associations become part of the vernacular of a people, and if the target of this humor is a particular group of people, then humor can work to undermine and dehumanize those people. Humor is often at work in genocide. Over the course of decades, the Jews were made into objects of laughter, then, in a matter of years, they were made into objects of fear. With humor laying the groundwork, the dehumanization of the Jews had penetrated the cultural ethos of the nation, had put in the minds of the Germans and others that Jews were a "different sort of thing" than them.

The force of Cassirer's warning against conflating symbolic forms can be seen clearly in circumstances where humor is hijacked by political, mythological, or scientific forms. Humor exists in all cultures, at all times. When mocking humor against a group becomes commonplace in the cultural ethos, propagandists can point to that humor as *evidence* for claims made from within other forms; for example, a joke which states a particular Jewish person is morally inferior (referring to someone as a "Shylock", for example) can be used as evidence for the *biological* inferiority of all Jews ("all Jews are Shylocks, it's in their blood"). As such, an unscientific object, the joke, is made subject to scientific criteria, biology, and the butt of that joke, the Jewish people, pay the price. By mixing the forms in this way, humor and science become distorted, the truths of humor are taken up as if they were the truths of science, and suddenly a cultural community believes that the dehumanization mythos can be, and in fact is, rationally supported through scientific criteria.

The Nazis, of course, are not the only group who has used this tactic; the American forces released their own humorous and later dangerous portrayals of Nazis (and more recently, Muslim and Middle Eastern peoples) in order to dehumanize them and create a cultural tolerance for war and death. This is a popular tactic not only reserved in times of war, as American and other societies continue to hijack humor and use it as a basis to support claims of biological inferiority of nonwhites, women, homosexuals, and other marginalized groups. The consequences of this insidious use of humor is culturally tolerated genocide, colonialism, racism, sexism, and homophobia, to name just a few.

Here we can see the normative force of Cassirer's plea for separation of the symbolic forms. None of the forms, he claims, should be considered an absolute stance through which all other forms must be subjected.[42] It is imperative that we understand the symbolic forms, humor included, as equally important and relevant to the understanding of human experience while at the same time fundamentally distinct. Krois explains that forms should never be forced or expected to "sacrifice their integrity by making one of them into the measure of the others."[43] The consequences of not heeding this warning can be, as we have seen, staggering. These cultures of comedy can be destructive to human life and moral progress, and it is an abuse of the form of humor when its objects are subjected to the laws and logic of another form.

6 Conclusion

My study of humor as a symbolic form is, of course, incomplete. I have taken the first step in showing humor to be a symbolic form and expressing the importance of understanding it as such within the totality of culture. The next step is to begin work on classifying the internal truths and structures of the form of humor from within humor itself, and to articulate the criteria, domain, and logic of it. I would like, in future projects, to study the "invisible" misuse of humor as that which helps create and sustain dominant cultural narratives of the inferiority of women and nonwhites. Such an abuse is similar in kind to the explicit, genocidal use explored in this paper, however it is so engrained and so much a part of the culture it is often overlooked, if explored at all. In doing so I ultimately hope to explore ways in which humor properly understood as a symbolic form may be able change this destructive discourse, or more humbly, weaken and expose it.

Bibliography

Brison (2002): Susan J. Brison, *Aftermath: Violence and the Remaking of a Self*, Princeton: Princeton University Press.

---

42 Luft (2004), 37.
43 Krois (1987), 107.

Cassirer (1944): Ernst Cassirer, *An Essay on Man*, New Haven: Yale University Press.
Cassirer (1946): Ernst Cassirer, *Language and Myth*. Susanne K. Langer (trans.), New York: Dover Publications Inc.
Cassirer (1953a): Ernst Cassirer, *The Philosophy of Symbolic Forms. Vol I: Language*, R. Manheim (trans.), New Haven: Yale University Press.
Cassirer (1953b): Ernst Cassirer, *The Platonic Renaissance in England*, James P. Pettigrove (trans.), London: Thomas Nelson and Sons Ltd.
Cassirer (1955): Ernst Cassirer, *Myth of the State*, Garden City, NY: Doubleday & Company, Inc.
Cassirer (1979a): Ernst Cassirer, "Critical Idealism as a Philosophy of Culture", in: *Symbol, Myth, and Culture: Essays and Lectures of Ernst Cassirer*, New Haven & London: Yale University Press.
Cassirer (1979b): Ernst Cassirer, "Language and Art I", in: *Symbol, Myth, and Culture: Essays and Lectures of Ernst Cassirer*, New Haven & London: Yale University Press.
Gilbert (2004): Joanne R. Gilbert, *Performing Marginality: Humor, Gender, and Cultural Critique*, Detroit: Wayne State University Press
Itzkoff (1977): Seymour W. Itzkoff, *Ernst Cassirer: Philosopher of Culture*, Boston: Twayne Publishers.
Kant (1998): Immanuel Kant, *Critique of Pure Reason*, Paul Guyer & Allen Wood (trans.), New York: Cambridge University Press.
Kant (2000): Immanuel Kant, *Critique of the Power of Judgment*. Paul Guyer & Eric Matthews (trans.), New York: Cambridge University Press.
Krois (1987): John Michael Krois, *Cassirer: Symbolic Forms and History*, New Haven and London: Yale University Press.
Lipman (1991): Steve Lipman, *Laughter in Hell: The Use of Humor during the Holocaust*, London: Jason Aronson Inc.
Luft (2004): Sebastian Luft, "Cassirer's Philosophy of Symbolic Forms: Between Reason and Relativism; A Critical Appraisal", *Idealistic Studies* 34, 25–47.
Morreall (1987): John Morreall, *The Philosophy of Laughter and Humor*, Albany: SUNY Press.
Morreall (2009): John Morreall, *Comic Relief: A Comprehensive Philosophy of Humor*, Oxford: Wiley-Blackwell.
Neher (2005): Allister Neher, "How Perspective Could be a Symbolic Form", *The Journal of Aesthetics and Art Criticism*. 63, 359–373.
Provine (2012): Robert R. Provine, *Curious Behavior: Yawning, Laughing, Hiccupping and Beyond*, Cambridge: Harvard University Press.
Rahman (2010): Aamer Rahman, "Reverse Racism". *Fear of a Brown Planet*. YouTube. Uploaded 28 Nov 2013. Last accessed 26 Dec 2014. https://www.youtube.com/watch?v=dw_mRaIHb-M.
Ribeiro (2008): Brian Ribeiro, "A Distance Theory of Humor" *Think* 6, 139–148.
Richards (2013): Richard C. Richards, *A Philosopher Looks at The Sense of Humor*, Healing Time Books.
Stanton (1996): Gregory H. Stanton, "The 8 Stages of Genocide", http://www.genocidewatch.org/images/8StagesBriefingpaper.pdf, 26 Dec 2014.

Fabien Capeillères (Paris/Princeton)
Cassirer on the "Objectity" of Evil
The Symbolic Constitution of
Der Mythus des 20 Jahrhunderts[1]

What is clear is that men's concern for their standing in the eyes of their comrades was not matched by any sense of human ties with their victims. The Jews stood outside their circle of human obligation and responsibility.[2]

For us, Europe after the war is less a problem of frontiers and soldiers, of top-heavy organizations or grand plans, but Europe after the war is a question of how the picture of man can be re-established in the breasts of our fellow citizens.[3]

Considering the philosophical analyses and deconstructions of Nazism almost contemporary to this historical phenomenon, the essays that immediately come to mind are those of Adorno and Horckheimer, Hannah Arendt or Günter Anders, perhaps Eric Voegelin. Only a few specialists of either myth or neo-Kantianism would think of Ernst Cassirer: he is still too often inadequately considered merely a philosopher of science or an historian of ideas.[4] Furthermore, his last and posthumous book, *The Myth of the State,* suffers from a relatively, and not completely undeserved, bad reputation.[5]

The purpose of this article is to correct these views and to show *de facto* that the philosophy of symbolic forms offers an effective tool to analyze Nazism. Cassirer's claim was that in order to understand Nazism (as well as what he called Bolshevism and Fascism) we have to consider it, first and foremost, as a political myth:

---

[1] The first draft for this article goes back to a conference given at the symposium: *Ernst Cassirer: Kulturkritik im 20 Jahrhunderts* in Weimar and published as Capeillères (1995). I would like to thank Sebastian Luft for giving me the opportunity to further elaborate this question and give shape to what will hopefully become part of a chapter of a long-planed book about the Olympian's philosophy. The talk "What is a Symbolic Form?" given at the conference "The Philosophy of Ernst Cassirer: A Novel Assessment" (Marquette University, 2014), is part of an article published in *Cassirer Studies* V (Bibliopolis ed., Napoli, 2015) I did not wish to republish here.
[2] Browning (1992), ch. 8.
[3] Moltke (1948), quoted in Frei (1993), 195.
[4] In April 1933, at the very beginning of his exile, Ernst Cassirer wanted to write "a philosophical refutation [*Widerlegung*] of the National Socialist movement in the hope to galvanize the German intellectuals" (Cassirer (1981), 197). His wife "strongly" dissuaded him for the safety of the relatives and friends still in Germany.
[5] This unfortunate book is the source of endless misinterpretations of Cassirer's doctrine, mainly because it is considered independently from PSF II, *Mythical Thought*. See infra note 10.

> Historians and politicians, philosophers and psychologists, sociologists and economists have made the greatest efforts to account for this phenomenon. They have studied the special conditions under which the modern 'myth of the state' has developed and has come to its full strength. I do not contest the results of these various analyses, nor do I underrate their value. But to my mind they do not suffice to answer the principal question. ... What is myth and what is its place in man's cultural life?[6]

The end of the paragraph from which this passage is taken makes clear what Cassirer had in mind. What is needed for an accurate understanding of Nazism is a *philosophical "theory* of myth in the proper sense",[7] which is precisely what he offered in the second volume of his *Philosophy of Symbolic Forms* (hereafter: PSF). As will become clear, the reasons are somewhat simple: *Das mythische Denken* brought to light the relationship between myth and what Cassirer called the phenomenon and function of expression by which two fundamental aspects of the political myth are explained. The first is its *affective* dimension, the fact that it is rooted in and strives to overcome the strongest feelings, (fear, angst, etc.) and eventually transfigures them into other strong affective moods such as collective enthusiasm or nationalistic fervor. Second, and correlatively, the book showed that expression is the function constituting the figures taken by subjectivity and inter-subjectivity. It is hence the function configuring originally the early formations of the whole inter-subjective field, from the smallest groups (family, phratry) up to the political structures and institutions.

Indeed, the philosophy of symbolic forms provides answers to these questions that Arendt explained were impossible not to ask spontaneously: "Why the Jews?" "What is the nature of the totalitarian regime?"[8] Furthermore, just as in the case of Arendt's consideration of Eichmann's case, where her interest led to other matters (the banality of evil and its treatment by justice), Cassirer's query was actually directed by another and more fundamental epistemological question, that of the role played by myth and religion in the symbolic edification of a world, *including* the constitution of individual and social identities as well as law. I will show how it also offers an explanation regarding the constitution of evil. This expression is here to be understood in two senses: we will examine how mythic consciousness configures an object it then calls "evil", and how this "objectity" (coined here in analogy to "banality") of evil is that of neither rational consciousness nor ethical, religious consciousness. At this level of inquiry, the question is not so much "*why* (the Jews)?" but "*how?*": how is the sym-

---

[6] Cassirer (2008), 167. Cassirer works are quoted in *Gesammelte Werke*, as well as in *Nachlassene Manuskripte und Texte*. Unless otherwise mentioned, all translations are mine.
[7] Ibid., 168.
[8] Arendt (2006), 286.

bolic objectification of the totalitarian state produced? How did the figure of the "Jew" become the figure of absolute evil in Nazi ideology? etc. The reason for this methodological limitation is that the analysis is essentially phenomenological, it examines modes of the transcendental constitutions of objects and values. At another level, Cassirer also attempted to answer the "why"—"Why the Jews?" Although his answer may be less convincing, it still deserves mention. All these questions are architectonically organized by an overarching question pertaining to philosophical anthropology: How was such a reconfiguration of humanity by the Nazi mythical consciousness possible?

In order to reconstruct Cassirer's analysis and to apply it to Nazi thought, I will follow Cassirer's own methodological path. Volume II of PSF, *Mythical Thought*, to which the first chapters of *The Myth of the State* explicitly refer the reader (as does Chapter 4 of his *A. Hägerstöm*, "Law and Myth"[9]), provides the conceptual tools for a symbolic and phenomenological analysis of Nazism by showing the mode of constitution of the first figures of inter-subjectivity and their relationship with mythical thinking. As is evident in the very structure of the first two volumes, Cassirer analyzed the symbolic forms by following a triple articulation: he untangled the "forms of thought", the "forms of intuition" and finally the "forms of life". If one follows this constitutive structure of a symbolic form, one should be able to scrutinize Nazism's "form of thought" in order to expose the form of its core operative categories, then study its "forms of intuition" in order to bring to light its conception of spatiality, temporality and the functions performed by the use of numeration. Finally, Nazism's "form of life" reveals its conception of subjectivity and its figures of inter-subjectivity. This is, of course, the essential moment, when it comes to understand the relation of myth to politics.

Second, to the extent that one of the distinguishing features of myth is to subjugate all other symbolic forms and use them to its end, philosophy requires an analysis of Nazi language (the rhetoric by which propaganda transformed German and gave a new shape to everyday language as well as some literature)[10], of the so-called "Nazi science", of Nazi art[11] and historiography.

---

9 Cassirer (2005), 81.
10 For obvious reasons of space I had to cut a part devoted to the Nazi form of intuition as shaped by its use of language. Cassirer was indeed very sensitive to this aspect of myth in general and Nazi Germany in particular. In *The Myth of the State*, while mentioning this change of the function of language, he referred to a book without giving the reference. It is Pächter (1944). The foreword, "The Spirit and Structure of Nazi Language", is in perfect harmony with Cassirer's ideas on this topic.

Third, *The Myth of the State* sketched an "exoteric", i.e., popular, historical and genetic study of the conceptions of the State that lie at the basis of the actual figures of totalitarianism. The complementarity of the two works is not only quite explicit, it is also the norm for an author who, throughout his work, always unified history and systematic philosophy. This book did not aim at an explanation of the *myth* (of the state). For this purpose, after an extremely short, introductory first part dedicated to what myth is *not*, it directs the reader back to *Mythical Thought* to learn what it actually *is*. Rather, it examined the models of the conception of state that mythical thought had at hand in its attempt to produce a totalitarian racist state: "We are able to write the history of the race-myth and to give the name of its authors—from Gobineau and Huston Steward Chamberlain up to Hitler and Rosenberg".[12] The status of this book is that of an updated chapter to the second volume of PSF, and to consider it independently is a sure way to never set foot into Cassirer's doctrine.[13]

Ultimately, such a study allows for a philosophical, as well as social (ethnological one might even say) understanding of the institutions we continue to call the "Third Reich" and the implementation of the Shoah. More fundamentally, this all too brief and schematic analysis of the myth of the twentieth century still shows how the philosophy of symbolic forms provides a powerful tool for understanding the socio-political field: it brings to light the modes of constitution and the necessary relationships of the figures of subjectivity and inter-subjectivity, of institutions, of all the cultural fields understood as symbolic forms—myth, religion, language, art, technology, economy, law, state and history, to quote Cassirer's most extensive inventory. Thus, it can be argued that, as suggested by a recent book,[14] once enfranchised from a caricatured reputation of rigid and obsolete neo-Kantianism, the philosophy of symbolic forms is able to offer a significant renewal of "critical theory".

---

11 One can now read an English translation of Eric Michaud's very remarkable book, Michaud (1996). It is not at all a Cassirerian exegesis of Nazi art, but as "a journey inside Nazi myth, following the metaphors and bringing to light a structure" (ibid., 11) it is a work that, I believe, very harmoniously resonates with Cassirer's.
12 Cassirer (2008), 198.
13 One of the latest examples of this curious kind of exercise can be found in Mali (2008), 135 ff., in which, for instance, the fundamental function of expression is not mentioned even once.
14 Cornell and Panfilio (2010).

1 Myth and its Narratives: *Der Mythus des 20 Jahrhunderts*

I will start this Cassirerian analysis of Nazism with the same methodological question Cassirer raised at the opening of PSF Volume II: according to the fundamental postulate of transcendental method proper to critical philosophy, the inquiry ought to start with a fact, with an existing object.[15] If we are to analyze the Nazi myth, where do we find it? The Nazi myth can be apprehended at the intersection of two narratives: on the one hand Alfred Rosenberg's book *Der Mythus des 20. Jahrhunderts*, on the other hand the institutional internal history of the "Third Reich". Of course, other stories could be substituted or added to the first: *Mein Kampf*, Hitler's and Goebbels' speeches, etc. But when it comes to concision, a tight bundle of reasons point towards the first book.

First of all, Rosenberg's personality and political functions designate him as the initial ideologue of the Nazi Party. His ties with the party date back to the beginning: he was its 123rd member.[16] He joined the National Socialist Society for German Culture (1928) and one year later founded the *Kampfbund für deutsche Kultur* (integrated in 1934 into the *Reichsverband für deutsche Bühne*). In 1933, Hitler nominated him as *Beauftragter des Führers für die Überwachung der gesamten geistigen und weltanschaulichen Schulung und Erziehung der Partei und gleichgeschalteten Verbände* (DBFU, 1934), thus offsetting the growing importance of Goebbels as propaganda minister. Schematically said, the latter propagates an ideology forged by the former. As the "acting officer for the Führer regarding the supervision of all the spiritual and world-vision education and upbringing of the Party and the assimilated associations," Rosenberg had ideological oversight over all political and cultural bodies and created institutions (such as the *Hohe Schule der NSDAP*) for the development of the "National Socialism's worldview": he was the "*Weltanschauungdirigent*".[17]

To reach such functions and exert them for a while implied full recognition and direct support from Hitler (a support Rosenberg held until 1943). Otto Strasser reports that the "Führer" told him: "Rosenberg's ideology is an inalienable part of National Socialism ... Rosenberg is a precursor, a prophet—his theories are the expression of the German soul. A good German cannot repudiate

---

[15] Cassirer (2002b), ix. About this question and the specificity of myth, see Holzhey (1988), 196–197.
[16] His card was number 623 but numbering started at 500. Hitler's was number 555 (he attempted to falsify his card in order to be number 7!).
[17] *Margaretenstraßenchronik*; quoted in Piper (2005), 640.

them".¹⁸ These words, reported by a somewhat unreliable source, are confirmed by one of Hitler's conferences in which he said: "Rosenberg is one of the most penetrating thinkers in all the issues of worldview".¹⁹ This reputation was quite widespread and his supporters made sure to spread it. In a very characteristic hagiographic essay, the preface to *Blut und Ehre*, Thilo von Trotha did not hesitate to write that Rosenberg was "the father of the National Socialist literature" and, citing *NS Funk*, that he unearthed "even in their smallest elements, the spiritual foundations of the National Socialist movement".²⁰

The Myth of the Twentieth Century is the most complete expression of this ideology.²¹ The oldest parts of the book date back to 1918 and it was almost completed in 1925. It summarizes the texts published by Rosenberg since 1919, particularly in the *Völkischer Beobachter* (of which he became director in 1921). ²² It was published in 1930 when its author became a member of the Reichstag and editor of the monthly booklet of National Socialism. *The Myth* not only synthesized Rosenberg's former writings, it also integrated and systematized other sources, especially *Mein Kampf*, in the same way that his 1922 commentary, *Das Parteiprogramm. Wesen, Grundsätze und Ziele der NSDAP* integrated, systematized and made explicit the program written by Hitler and Drexel.²³ Indeed, in the preface, Rosenberg claimed not to present the Party's official doctrine. But this posture was strategic: it spared Hitler's susceptibility,²⁴ and helped preserve

---

18 Quoted in Piper (2005), 642. For another echo regarding Hitler's ambivalence about *Der Mythus*, see Cecil (1972), 101 ff .
19 Quoted in Billig (1963), 28 (It refers to document 746, protocol for a conference from June 8 1943, in which Hitler criticized Rosenberg's total lack of political pragmatism regarding the strategy towards Soviet Union.).
20 Trotha (1939), 8–9. See also for instance Bäumler (1943), viii..
21 Readers should not regard the 'bible of National Socialism' (*Mein Kampf*) as the most advanced expression of Nazi ideology, either. That dubious honor should probably go to Alfred Rosenberg's 1930 *The Myth of the Twentieth Century*; cf Foxman (1999), xix.
22 The vast majority of Rosenberg's texts can be found in four volumes: *Blut und Ehre* (Aufsätze von 1919–1933), *Gestaltung der Idee* (Reden und Aufsätze von 1933–1935), *Kampf um die Macht*, (Aufsätze von 1921–1932), *Tradition und Gegenwart*, (Reden und Aufsätze von 1936–1940). The first writings are collected in *Schriften und Reden*, Bd. 1 (Schriften aus den Jahren 1917–1921), Hoheneichen-Verlag, München, 1943. A significant number of documents of all sorts are listed in Billig (1963).
23 Partially republished in Rosenberg (1939), 105 ff. It is a commentary on the program written by Drexler and Hitler (February 24, 1920; paragraph 11 is Feder's). Feder's program, *Das Programm der NSDAP und seine weltanschaulichen Grundgedanken*, first volume of the *National-Socialist Bibliotheque* (with Gottfried Feder himself as director) dated from 1927.
24 *Mein Kampf* is presented several times by its author as the only dogmatic ground for the NSDAP.

the Party's official doctrine vis-à-vis the Church. It is evident that the book unified and developed the themes outlined in articles and editorials that the author published in both official journals of the NSDAP, of which he also was the editor. The book is thus, in its genesis, contemporary with the birth and establishment of the Nazi party. With nearly a million and a half copies printed,[25] alongside *Mein Kampf*, *The Myth* is thus often referenced to clarify the party's ideology.[26]

It is true that Rosenberg has sometimes been considered at the margins of the efficient core of the political apparatus of the party. Vis-à-vis the Church he did not follow the line set by Hitler; a fact that—for example—delayed the release of *The Myth*. He irritated Goebbels as well as Goering and sometimes opposed trends such as those of Himmler. His ideological line vis-à-vis the East collided with the political and strategic realities of the Reich.[27] Furthermore, in private, Hitler[28] and Goebbels[29] mocked his intellectualism. Such elements drove few historians to minimize his role. For instance Reinhard Bollmus wrote that "the chief work of A. Rosenberg, *The Myth of the Twentieth Century*, was never recognized within the party as the founding representation of the National Socialist world view".[30] This book, then, would not be a good candidate to analyze, even partially, the symbolic constitution of Nazi thinking.

However, three remarks are in order: First, we must distinguish between the man and his work, the latter exceeding the former by far. Second, the fact that a handful of leaders, often totally cynical, distanced themselves from the man—who was totally convinced and somehow naïve—his book and its doctrine (which was also conveyed by many other sources) in no way diminishes the significance and impact of this ideology on the rest of the socio-political body. Third, even taking into account Hitler's desire to keep *Mein Kampf* as the movement's founding book, the perverse games he played to ensure sole reign, his effort to spare the Church that Rosenberg's book would offend and finally some pragmatic and strategic requirements such as those regarding the Eastern territories, *The Myth of the Twentieth Century* remains one of the most adequate ex-

---

25 By the end of 1942, 1,080,000 copies of *The Myth* had been printed. Like *Mein Kampf*, it was widely distributed in a small pocket edition printed on India paper.
26 In 1940, when Bormann considered the publication of a small guidebook for the principles of National Socialism, he turned to Rosenberg (mentioned by Billig (1963), 20).
27 However, Cecil (1972) shows in his ch. 9 that Rosenberg's politics for the East might have been much more efficient than the one actually implemented!
28 See Picker (1951), 275.
29 Krebs (1959), 166.
30 Bollmus (1970), 9.

pressions of Nazi *Weltanschauung*, to the point that it became a general expression, the title of the book serving as a metonymy to describe Nazi ideology.

Therefore one should agree with Piper's conclusion:

> The purpose of the National Socialists was not 'National Socialism as a political religion' but a worldview State [*ein Weltanschauungstaat*], an ideological totalitarianism in place of any religion. ... Thus, insofar as the Third Reich was a *Weltanschauungstaat*, Rosenberg had great importance. He represented the ideological dimension of this totalitarian State, and as such, he left his mark on it.[31]

In fact, even the *Führerstaat*, based on the myth of the providentiality and infallibility of the Führer and seeing in him the origin of all legitimacy and legality,[32] is possible only within a larger structure, within a "worldview" that makes it possible and in which it participates. Ideologically, the supremacy of the Führer originates in the National Socialist Idea he embodies,[33] he is the archetype of the Type (the Ideal represented) and the State is only a means to the realization of this Idea. The relationship between the ideological dogma (*The Myth*, *Mein Kampf*), the political leader, the party organization, propaganda and society are hence perfectly well defined and articulated in the Nazi ideological corpus.

We could sum up the position of Rosenberg vis-à-vis the Party and the role of *The Myth* with a metaphor: in a totalitarian state that ignores the *reality* of the distinction between the legislative and the executive, the ideology of the myth serves as legislative or it at least presents the origin of laws (e.g. with the Nuremberg Laws in 1935, Rosenberg's writings became embodied in the law and efficient as such). The distance Rosenberg sometimes had to suffer is that which separated the Ideal from its realization in the executive. In this sense and to this extent, his book not only configured what is called propaganda and ideology; to submit it to philosophical critique is also a strictly political criticism.

We can therefore conclude that, at least for a partial and brief study of Nazism as mythical thinking, Rosenberg's book and its connection to the social and institutional reality offers a reasonable starting point for Cassirer's transcendental method. Furthermore, Cassirer referred to the metonymical use of this title

---

[31] Piper (2005), 646. Hitler clearly described the National Socialist State as a part of the National Socialist world vision (see for instance Hitler (2002), 378).
[32] According to Cassirer (1981), 189–190, when Ernst heard about a decree claiming, "Law is what suits the Führer" he said: "If tomorrow all law scholars in Germany do not raise like one man to protest this text, Germany is lost". As we know the most (in)famous response was Carl Schmitt's justification of Hitler in Schmitt (1934).
[33] See for instance Rosenberg (1939), 161 ff.

when he labeled the third chapter of the *Myth of the State* "The Myth of the Twentieth Century" and, as we have seen, mentioned its author.

We now have to identify the conditions for the emergence of the myth of the twentieth century. Cassirer points to three: 1) an anthropological paradigm crisis —the crisis of self-knowledge; 2) an economic, social and political crisis; 3) the possibility for consciousness to let the basic strata of (phenomenological) constitution, "the function expression" characteristic of mythical thinking overwhelm all other functions. This is what we will now examine in the two following sections.

2 The Grounds for the Myth of the Twentieth Century: The "Crisis of Self-Knowledge"

Studies of Nazism emphasize that the movement grew amid crisis. However, the assessment of the nature of this crisis differs according to the field of study. For some it was historico-political (e. g. highlighting the humiliation of the Versailles Treaty, the difficulties of the Weimar Republic); it was economic for others (often Marxists); others emphasize social considerations such as the "disenchantment of the world" (Max Weber). Cassirer is no exception. It requires a crisis for the mythical consciousness to be able to subjugate the entire consciousness and its *cosmos intellectualis*, but what kind of crisis? Cassirer does not reject the reality of other crises, however the most fundamental one in his eyes is that of self-knowledge. This is the initial diagnosis for Cassirer's assessment of the intellectual and political situation of his time.

This assessment opens *An Essay on Man:* facing the plurality of answers to the question "What is Man?", our modern theory of the human being has lost its intellectual center. We acquired instead a "complete anarchy of thought".[34] Cassirer, using the work done in the *Erkenntnisproblem* for his anthropological query, outlines the genesis of the present lack of unity:

> Even in the former times, to be sure there was a great discrepancy of opinions and theories relating to this problem. But there remained at least a general orientation, a frame of reference, to which all individual differences might be referred. Metaphysics, theology, mathematics and biology successively assumed the guidance for thought on the problem of man and determined the line of investigation.

---

34 Cassirer (1972/2006), 21/26. The following quotations come from the same page. A similar diagnostic opens the 1944 article "Philosophy and Politics", in Cassirer (1979), 226 ff.

In other words, the unity of methodological paradigms, which the successive volumes of *Erkenntnisproblem* had followed, allowed for a unity of the conception of the human being: "the real crisis of this problem manifested itself when such a central power capable of directing all individual efforts ceased to exist". This conclusion is relatively common at the time within philosophy itself: it is in line with, for instance, those of Schweitzer, Jaspers, Husserl and Scheler (to whom Cassirer refers in the same text).[35]

What is the specific character of this crisis? "The personal factor became more and more prevalent, and the temperament of the individual writer tended to play a decisive role. *Trahit sua quemque voluptas:* each author seems in the last count to be led by its own conception and evaluation of human life". The absence of a dominant paradigm that would offer a unitary and universal conception of the human produces individualism and relativism of both truth and values immanent to each field of culture. The theoretical dimension of this observation hence concerns, for sure, this particular site of knowledge that we call philosophical anthropology, but it also concerns all other fields of knowledge which participate in the comprehensive anthropological question, as conceived by Kant when he claimed that all the problems of philosophy could be brought back to the question "What is Man?" The crisis therefore results from an intellectual lacuna, itself the consequence of a collapse, which is evident in the political sphere, but also in the philosophical sphere. Let's briefly examine these two specific occurrences of the crisis.

According to Cassirer, the political field undergoes this general process of disintegration. During the nineteenth century, political thought, exploring new ways, seemed to have reached "the sure path of a science". Certainly,

> the different economic, sociological, and philosophical schools by no means agreed in their general views. They followed different ways of investigations and they strove for widely divergent political ideals. Nevertheless there was one point on which all seemed unanimous. They had the same conception and meaning of the task of a political theory.[36]

The philosophical ideal of the nineteenth century that was "shared by all the pioneers of modern political, economic and social thought—seems suddenly to fall into pieces"; as we shall see, that is when both the content and the basic

---

35 A. Schweitzer's conception of this crisis, as apprehended by Cassirer, is well studied by Gaubert (1996),17–32.
36 Cassirer (1944b/2007a), 165/251. Cassirer read the published paper and said, "A good article, even if not a word is from me!" See Cassirer (1981), 296.

form of political thought underwent a radical transformation, going from rationalism to myth.[37]

Philosophy also played a role in this crisis, as it appears particularly in the criticisms Cassirer addressed to Spengler and Heidegger in "Philosophy and Politics" (1944) and later in *Myth of the State*.[38] Cassirer showed how the rejection of a unifying conception, universal and critical, of both truth and humanity also implied the rejection of the value that this concept of humanity had for practical action, namely the status of a regulative ideal.

In Spengler, Cassirer critiqued the concept of destiny, a concept that governs *Der Untergang des Abendlandes*. "His system is a system of historical fatalism. And his judgment is that our cultural life is doomed once and for all. We can not escape our fate and we can not avert the danger". [39] This concept of destiny is none other than the mythical category of history and, in Spengler, it leads not only to the denial of the practical ideal of action, but also to a flat pessimism.

The criticism of Heidegger's position is conducted in two stages: first, Cassirer claimed that the analytic of Dasein was interesting, but that it is illegitimate to be limited to that sphere. One example is provided by a note on the concept of space in the third volume of the *Philosophy of Symbolic Forms:* "Our own study and our own problem differ from those of Heidegger primarily in that, instead of dwelling on this level of 'being available' [*Zuhandenen*] and its mode of 'spatiality', without contesting them, we question beyond them".[40] During the Davos debate Cassirer generalized this objection, insisting on the fact that from Dasein to Dasein, the only authentic relationship is through the world of forms. Hence, one has to strive towards universality. We then reach what the philosophy of symbolic forms considers as moments of a common world. Cassirer's criticism also addressed a core Heideggerian element, the temporality of Dasein, which appeared to bear all the characteristics of a mythical structure of temporality. Again, I can not be clearer than Cassirer, who, summarizing Heidegger's thesis, wrote:

> The philosopher can not strive for an 'objective', universally valid truth. He can only give the truth of his individual existence, and this existence has always an individual character. It is bound up with the historical conditions in which the individual lives. ... [The *Geworfenheit*] is one of the fundamental and unalterable conditions of human life. ... Man has to accept the historical conditions of his existence; he has to submit to his fate.[41]

---

37 Cassirer (1944b/2007a_, 165/251. See also Cassirer (1972/2006), 3/7.
38 Ibid., 289 ff./ 283 ff.
39 Cassirer (1979), 227.
40 Cassirer (2002c/1957), 169/173–174.
41 Cassirer (1979), 229.

There are two essential criticisms: the inability to reach the inter-subjective sphere and a theory of history that invalidates the principle of action.

Cassirer's conclusion was very stern, since, even if he explicitly recognized that it was not philosophy, and thus neither the thought of Spengler nor that of Heidegger, that spawned Nazism, it nonetheless failed to condemn it: "as soon as philosophy no longer trusts its own power, as soon as it gives way to a merely passive attitude, it can no longer fulfill its most important educational task". The paragraph ends with the words: it "can no longer do its duty". Looking back at sources not available to Cassirer, we now know that philosophies certainly did not cause this ideology, but some did occasionally feed it. We will have to go back to this point, which is linked to the duty that Cassirer assigned to philosophy and which is immediately connected to his political task.

With this analysis, Cassirer was able to determine the danger posed to civilization by this global crisis of self-knowledge: the lack of a unified design and of a humanist critique of humanity left open the possibility that a mythical conception of humanity became the cement of a new unity, no less mythical. We shall now examine this dramatic substitution.

3 How Could a Mythical Anthropology be Substituted for a Rationalist Anthropology? The "Function of Expression" and Politics

3.1 The Enduring Presence of Myth and Expression

We have just considered the first condition as a result of which a mythical anthropology may follow a rationalistic anthropology: the latter must be in crisis (and, in particular two critical fields of this anthropology, politics and philosophy, are not able to provide remedies). According to Cassirer, it was a dearth, not an excess, of rationality that led to Nazism.

In addition to a second condition, which consists of a socio-economic crisis I will address in a moment, a third condition is the transcendental possibility of what may *look like* a regression by which, in the human mind, rational thought gives way to mythical thinking.[42] Cassirer found the answer in the phenomeno-

---

42 This idea of myth being completely wiped out by rationality over the progress of history (and then suddenly reappearing out of nowhere to overthrow rationality) is one of the most common and widespread misreadings of Cassirer's doctrine. It appeared right after the publication of *The Myth of the State* (for instance in E. Vögelin's otherwise positive and moving review: Vögelin

logical moments (in the Hegelian sense), in the successive levels of symbolization characterized as the functions of "expression" (characteristic of myth), "presentation", and "pure signification" (well illustrated by contemporary science). The empire of myth is not a regression: neither myth nor expression have ever disappeared. Rather, what happens is 1) an imbalance, a strong disharmony within the fundamental symbolic functions: presentation and pure signification actually give way to expression instead of canalizing and complementing it; 2) a displacement; for if myth and expression can be wonderful as elements of art, religion or language, they are a major threat when they invade politics and reign over all other cultural forms.

> Myth is not only a transient but a permanent element of human culture. It cannot be entirely superseded; it cannot be extirpated root and branch. Man is not only an '*animal rationale*' he is and remains a mythical animal. ... [I]n the field of religion, of art, of language, this fusion and interlacement of disparate elements seems to be no serious danger. They do not enfeeble or contradict each other; they assist and complete each other. In religion, in language, in poetry myth appears—to use the Hegelian term—as an '*aufgehobenes Moment*'. It is not completely destroyed; it is in a sense saved and preserved.[43]

It is to this progression and stratification of the symbolic process that Cassirer refers in a metaphoric way in *The Myth of the State* and in his article in *Fortune*:

> Modern civilization is very unstable and fragile. It is not built on sand but on a volcanic soil. For its first origin and basis was not rational, but mythical. Rational thought is only the upper layer on a much older geological stratum that reaches down to a great depth. We must always be prepared for violent concussions that may shake our cultural world and our social order in its very foundations.[44]

The function of expression is completely immanent to thinking; it forms its first moment and its first layer. It can be overcome but not suppressed. Since it is the fundament and the medium of myth, myth can always rise again and overthrow rationality.

It is then necessary to understand how, from being transcendentally *possible*, this resurgence became *historically effective*. Or, in other words, why, after a constant struggle in history, mythical consciousness seems to take over and impose totalitarianisms in Europe after the First World War. It is at this point that Cassirer brought into account what I have designated as a second condition,

---

(1947), 445–447) and is still alive and well in contemporary readings. As we will see, Cassirer's texts claim the opposite: not only is myth always present in culture, but it is necessary!
43 Cassirer (2008), 172.
44 Cassirer (1944b/2007a), 206/264. Also Cassirer (2008), Conclusion.

namely, historical, economic, political, social and psychological determinations. After noting that the myth resurfaces when the individual feels threatened and that the usual defenses do not seem to effect it, Cassirer adds:

> In the times of inflation and unemployment Germany's whole social and economic system was threatened with a complete collapse. The normal resources seemed to have been exhausted. It was the natural soil upon which the political myths could grow up and in which they found ample nourishment.[45]

It is important to realize that when Cassirer refers to these social, political and economic states of affairs, the main point for his philosophy of myth is not their objective reality, it is their *emotional impact*.

> The political and economic pressure was everywhere keenly felt. Everything that promised to relieve or to remove this pressure was greeted with enthusiasm. It did not matter if these promises were possible or probable. Mythical thought is emotional thought.[46]

Mythical consciousness resurfaces, when facing fear, desire and frustration, a rationality already in crisis becomes increasingly impotent. Cassirer intends to explain the possibility for historical conditions to produce a return of mythical consciousness, and thus to account for its emergence in German society after the First World War.

What are the channels of this resurgence? In the redeployment of mythical thought, the political field holds a privileged role we must now circumscribe.

3.2 Myth, "Expression", and Politics

The political field is indeed, to use Cassirer's volcanic metaphor, the crater from which lava and ash will spread over the whole of society. It is from this particular site, politics, that myth extends its grip on the whole culture:

> It is not by chance that all new myths maintain and defend a 'totalitarian' conception of the state. By this conception every appeal to any other tribunal is from the very beginning declared null and void. There is nothing in the world to restrict the power of the myth of the state. To mythicize man's political life means at the same time to mythicize all other human activities. There exists no longer a separate sphere that has value of its own. Philosophy,

---

45 Cassirer (1961/2007b), 278/273.
46 Cassirer (2008), 196.

art, religion, science are under the control of the new ideal. The hybrid of myth and politics becomes omnipotent and irresistible.[47]

For a neo-Kantian philosopher, this may seem a curious concession to Hegelianism. Indeed, for Hegel, the state, in its historical development, is the final phase of Objective Spirit, hence the all-encompassing figure, to the point that it has been commonly argued that even the figures of Absolute Spirit (art, religion and philosophy) could in their reality only unfold *within* the state (i.e., politics). In contrast, for Kant morality prevails and remains the ultimate, synoptic, *but not encompassing*, perspective: it fulfills the function of a regulative ideal for judgment. This is precisely Cassirer's point: to elevate the state to an ultimate figure governing all others, or, in Hegelian terms, to raise it to a figure against which the others are 'without-right', is characteristic of a mythical conception of the state. The *Machtstaat*, this modern Leviathan, embodies the contemporary mythical figure of the state. We should note that Cassirer rejoins here, at the political level, a theoretical reading of Hegel initiated by his master Hermann Cohen when the latter saw in the deployment of the Hegelian system the development of "the mythical power of the Idea".[48]

At least two points deserve to be highlighted and explained here. First, with such remarks, Cassirer acknowledges that a symbolic form is (illegitimately) likely to overwhelm and submit all the others. We must also, then, understand why this empire is exerted via politics and we must base our apprehension on transcendental grounds.

In the *Philosophy of Symbolic Forms* our author had already noted that each symbolic form has a tendency to set itself up as the one and only standard of effective reality and truth.[49] The basis of this impulse is a fetishization: failing to properly grasp the methodological functional process of knowledge, consciousness reifies the result. Instead of articulating the different methods specific to each field and defining their domain of validity, this result is erected as the only standard of truth. In a sense, this epistemological form of 'totalitarianism' produces only methodological disasters: it results, at worst, in the hegemony of a given paradigm of knowledge on all other fields. The problem we face here is different because the perspective is not only theoretical but also practical; the con-

---

47 Cassirer (1944b/2007a), 166/253.
48 This criticism of the Hegelian State, developed since 1916, is more subtle that it may appear. Cassirer distinguished Hegel's influence on political *theory* and his impact on political *life*. Then he tried to save Hegel from caricatures made in these two different fields. The clearer texts are his 1937 lectures in Oxford, when he was also addressing British Hegelianism.
49 For instance Cassirer (2002a/1955a), 21/20.

sequences are more dramatic. However, the intellectual process is the same: all thought submits to one of its instances.

What is the origin, in the modern myth, of the predominance of state? The importance of politics is to be found first of all at the very root of mythical thinking, in what Cassirer called "the phenomenon of expression". Briefly said—we will return to this point later—this locution refers to the fact that in the phenomenological genesis of consciousness, the first objectification is an *expressive living* figure, a *living* figure whose main characteristic is to express *affects*. In other words, the first "object" of consciousness is an emotional "subject" and the first form of "inter-subjectivity" consists in the confrontation of two personified affects, frightening and frightened, threatening and threatened, etc. The world of myth, precisely because it is constituted by the 'function of expression' is a world of affective subjects, a world of living things that virtually ignores all inert forms of the object. The essential points here are that 1) myth originally gives shape to the elements of its world thanks to this function of expression; 2) that these figures are the correlative figures of subjectivity and inter-subjectivity (no inert, objective thing); and 3) that this configuration is so to speak cut out of an affective fabric, and the unity of its world is maintained by and within an *affective feeling of unity of life*.

The significance of politics comes from the special relationship that social rules and laws have with mythical thinking. For now, let's just notice the trivial nature of this thesis when we focus on its factual dimension: the first form of social rules are rituals, the first form of law is mythical prohibition and it is clear that science, history, art and philosophy won their independence by fighting against mythical and religious forms of bans and jurisdictions.

The importance of the state in the modern myth (that is, in societies where other symbolic forms and other areas of culture have become independent) comes from the capacity of the absolute state to maintain the *substantial unity of the world of myth*. Beyond a small group's psychological inclination for domination, which such a state may serve, the substantial unity of the absolute state avoids the fragmentation and alienation of such crises as we have indicated, or the "tragedy of culture" denounced by Simmel. What is characteristic of the myth of the twentieth century, and what is brought to a climax by the Nazi myth, is the unity of the *structure* of the absolute state and the *emotional, affective* dimension of mythical consciousness (a character that is not necessarily immanent to *dictatorships:* the state is then not really an absolute state, since society remains deeply split and lacks the unity of feeling—the fervor, the enthusiasm).

The transition from absolute state to totalitarian state is made by hypertrophy of negation: in the former, the unification still maintains a semblance of diversity, of differences. Certainly, both in Hegelian or Cassirerian terms this state is an *abstract universal* in that it does not fully recognize particularities in order to bring them to the status of singularities; however, they can remain within the state. The totalitarian state instead is the paroxysm of abstract universality in that, first, internally, it requires full participation of the individual (who then gains recognition and full integration) and second, it totally negates all forms of otherness, a denial that is not an exclusion but rather a destruction. We will see further examples.

It is on the grounds of these relationships between mythical consciousness and politics that the philosopher undertakes the deconstruction of the myth of the state and the myth of the twentieth century.

Once all the conditions mentioned above are present, the crisis of self-knowledge as a global anthropological crisis may actually lead to a dramatic substitution: under the influence of affects (anxiety, fear, etc.), the place left vacant by a rationalist and critical anthropology will be invaded by a mythical anthropology in which politics dominates theoretical fields—transforming them to be used for its ends—and the practical and aesthetic fields. We can then observe the work of mythical consciousness: faced with angst, impaired by the crisis of self-knowledge and feeling trapped by the collapse of the socio-historical conditions of existence, the themes analyzed in *The Myth of the State*—the hero, race, absolute state—undergo a new synthesis, a mythical fusion giving rise to the myth of the twentieth century. The latter, as a magic solution to the global crisis, must propose a new paradigm of self-knowledge, a new image of a glorious humanity promised a bright future. This also results in an identity and recognition finally conquered, both of which were painful problems in Germany's case.

4 An Analysis of the Myth of the Twentieth Century

Rosenberg's *The Myth of the Twentieth Century* is a striking example of these configurations of the mythical concept of humanity produced by the Nazis. It presents an amazingly clear synthesis and the impact of the myth it expresses cannot be underestimated. What are the dynamics of this book and what is the structure and mode of constitution of the myth it expresses?

The book begins with a general diagnosis of the crisis:

> Today, all the external struggles for power are externalizations of an internal collective collapse. Already, *all* the 1914 state systems have fallen, despite some partial formal survival. Equally collapsed are social, religious and world-intuitive [*weltanschauliche*] knowledges

and values. No chief principle, no sovereign idea dominates unquestionably the life of the peoples [*Völker*].⁵⁰

Of course the essence of this crisis and its causes are very different from those identified by Cassirer. But socially and existentially, the discomfort and the uneasiness are similar. And the book is dedicated to "all those who are internally separated from their community, but who have not yet reached the end of their fight for new cosmic [*weltanschaulichen*] relationships". Lashing old ideals,⁵¹ it is presented precisely as a new unifying conception of the human: "The common man [*Die Kärrner*, literally: the carters] may, in the relatively near future, complete the building of the new worldview.⁵² ... This is the task of our century: forging, from a new myth of life, a new type of man".⁵³ The distinctiveness of these paragraphs is to work out the emotional unity of mythical consciousness. Unlike traditional populism, Rosenberg was not satisfied with manipulating the traditional doleances (to have a job, increase of income, access to social strata perceived as superior and their distinctive external signs, etc.) or forms of recognition (coalescence of identity in particular groups). He aimed at a deeper level, which also allowed him to address a wider audience. He aimed directly at the emotional feeling of separation from the living unity of society. In doing so he consciously and deliberately sought to fill the space vacated by a rationalist and functional conception of the human in order to substitute it with a mythical, substantial and emotional conception.

The *Philosophy of Symbolic Forms* stated that "The authentic overcoming of myth must be based on its knowledge and recognition: only through the analysis of its spiritual structure can be determined, on the one side, its authentic meaning, on the other side its limits".⁵⁴ But it was a theoretical statement. *The Myth of the State* and the articles written during the same period echo the practical meaning of this statement. What is at stake now is not only to understand mythical thinking and to assign to it its place within the system of knowledge, neither is it to reject scientific knowledge of everything that still belongs to expression as a form of symbolism; the goal now is to find a way to ruin myth's political grip on

---

50 Rosenberg (1942), 1.
51 "Humanity, universal church, the autonomous [*selbstherrliche*= not only autonomous but its own master] subject separated from the totality of blood are no more supreme values for us|". Ibid., 22.
52 Rosenberg plays with a saying: "*Wenn die Könige bauen, haben die Kärrner zu tun*" (When the kings build, the people are busy).
53 Ibid., 2.
54 Cassirer (2002b), xiv. See also Cassirer (2005), 81–82.

all cultural forms and the resulting configuration of humanity. Both projects, although tightly related, are quite different. If the latter presupposes the former, which also means that *The Myth of the State* is doctrinally grounded in and presupposes the *Philosophy of Symbolic Forms*, it also imposes a particular reading of the seminal work: it is necessary to highlight the supporting structures of the deconstruction of modern political myth. In order to do this, I will follow the path of Cassirer's methodological reflection.

How is the study of myth in the philosophy of symbolic forms constructed? Cassirer, seeking to produce a critique of the phenomenology of mythical consciousness, structured his reflection in three stages following the analytical order of the transcendental method: myth is first considered as *Denkform* (a form of thought), then as *Anschauungsform* (a form of intuition) and finally as *Lebensform* (a form of life). Applied to the myth of the twentieth century, this analysis provides a good insight into its constitution. Within the limits of this short essay, it is only possible to give brief examples; I will give priority to the mythical *Lebensform* because, first, it is the point where myth reaches its concrete deployment; second, it clearly shows the reconfiguration of the concept of humanity that led to the most disastrous consequences.

4.1 The Myth of the Twentieth Century's Form of Thought

One of the main theses of Cassirer's analysis of mythical thought is that it is not devoid of categories such as those found, for example, in classic physics (causality, etc.), but that the form of these concepts is different in each symbolic form. The National Socialist use of the basic categories of thinking is similar to the mythical use. Thus, by the principle of concrescence brought to light by Cassirer,[55] mythical thought dissolves that which in the Kantian table of categories was the middle term: regarding quality, reality knows no determined limitation because negation itself is denied; therefore the part is undifferentiated from the whole, the property stands for the thing itself, etc. Similarly, regarding relation, causality is not the formal and general law governing the succession of a previously analyzed diversity, but it is thought as a principle emanating from the nature of the substance it only prolongs. This emanation depends in the end on the first principle established by mythical thought as a form of life. Thus the Nazis attributed all the ills of the world to Jews not in the form of experimental causality, which links an individual phenomenon to another, but as contamination, as

---

55 Cassirer (2002b/1955b), 78–79/131.

an emanation due to a harmful substance; it is the *identity* of the *substance itself* that is expressed as contamination, not an *effect* of the substance that exerts a measurable action understandable by a formal mathematical law. The acts are not individual effects of an individual, determined cause, but by virtue of making the part equivalent to the whole, the acts involve the whole community, thus completely dissolving individual responsibility into collective responsibility:

> But what is absent or, at least, entirely undeveloped in primitive society ..., is the concept and ideal of *individual* moral responsibility. ... In the current German political system] if there is any 'moral' subject, the community, the nation, the race are held answerable for its actions. The acts are good or evil according as they are done by a super-race or an inferior race.[56]

The persecutor's responsibility is also non-existent, since it is the German people embodied by the Führer who act, which at the same time provides the agent with the feeling of total participation in the substantial unity of the whole, the German nation. As Göring so aptly said, "my conscience's name is Adolf Hitler".[57] It is also not necessary, in order to be persecuted, to be responsible for a particular crime, since here too the part—the individual—stands for the whole—the hated race.

4.2 The Myth of the Twentieth Century's Form of Intuition

The philosophy of symbolic forms examines myth as a form of intuition in order to apprehend the "*intuitive* unity that precedes and grounds all developments it undergoes in 'discursive' thinking".[58] It then identifies all key schemata that implement the fundamental opposition (sacred and profane), namely the mythical use of space, time and number.

In its constitution of space, time and number, the myth of the twentieth century follows the intellectuals procedures used by mythical consciousness. The fundamental opposition it reveals, however, is not so much the delimitation of the sacred and profane but rather the struggle between life and death.

In myth, space has an affective content and value: north is the source of light and life, south is synonymous with darkness and death. Within the unity of life, these principles apply to geography as well as to peoples and nations: northern

---

56 Cassirer (1944a/2007a), 121.
57 "*Ich habe kein Gewissen! Mein Gewissen heißt Adolf Hitler*". Rausching (1940), 77; ch. 7 titled: "*Ja! Wir sind Barbaren!*"
58 Cassirer (2002b), 85.

countries are the origin of the race of heroes, those having clear, light skin, hair and eyes, while the southern countries are the cradle of the hated races, people with darkest skin. "Aryan" invasions are similar to daylight rising on Earth, a principle of life regaining its territories over darkness, etc.

Regarding the question of the relation of myth's form of intuition to law and state, a few pages in *Mythical Thought* are particularly interesting. Cassirer noticed, following Nissen's analysis of the *Templum* and its relation to antique land survey, that this activity of spatial delimitation is the origin of borders setting and hence of property, both private as well as public.[59] It is clear all throughout the *Myth of the Twentieth Century* that, as just mentioned, the delineation of limits and borders follow the initial principles of the "life struggle", of "blood against blood", and the original setting of its own "*templum*": north/light/life against south/dark/death and the conquest of the Earth being similar to the course of the sun propagating light and life. But there is one more interesting element about property. Rosenberg's doctrine of property first seemed to remain within the classic rational doctrine of property, which roots its legitimacy and its limits in work.[60] However, the concepts of property and work are immediately redetermined by the criteria of life, blood and of a people's solidarity.[61] In these pages, which develop a chapter titled "The Nordic-German Law", the underling principle is summarized by Hitler: "Law is what serves the Führer" as the incarnation and safeguard of the ideal of the race/life.[62] The concepts of work and the worker are hence determined anew in an organicist conception where both fulfill their role for the accomplishment of the unity and health of the *Volk*.[63]

The Reich's eternity is suggested by a magical invocation of numbers that no longer perform their mathematical function: *Der thousandjahre Reich*, etc. What rational thought (the functions of "presentation" and "pure meaning") conceives as purely *quantitative* is here, for mythical thinking and the function of expression, *qualitative:* the *thousand years* of this Reich, which did not last twelve, are

---

59 An interesting analysis of Cassirer's text can be found in Favuzzi (2012), 107 ff.
60 Rosenberg (1942), 585: "Truly, in its authentic meaning property is nothing else then concreted work"; "*geonnene Arbeit*" can literally be translated "*coagulated* work".
61 Rosenberg (1942), 564, 589.
62 Rosenberg clearly saw that the opposition between law and politics boiled down to the opposition between morals and power (ibid., 571). When wondering which should be the prevailing term his answer was: "Law and politics are not absolute essentialities, but are only specific effects determined by distinguished men." And to quote a "principle of law from Nordic pre-historic times": "Law is what Aryan men decide to be right" (ibid., 571–572); "A German state has as its first duty to create laws which meet these basic requirements [race protection, race breeding and race hygiene]" (ibid., 577).
63 See ibid., 584.

to be understood not as a separate quantifier for a determined historical periodization, but as a unity expressing an eternal substance coming to its historical advent. It convenes "one of the oldest and most widespread of motives in all mythologies, the thought of the 'millennium'—of a period of a thousand years in which all hopes shall be fulfilled and all evils shall be removed".[64]

4.3 The Myth of the Twentieth Century's Form of Life

Regressing to the ultimate conditions of the possibility of mythical consciousness, Cassirer investigates myth as a form of life in order to find the first "*Ur-Teilung*", the originary division/judgment from which myth's forms of thought and forms of intuition derive, "this first division [that] contains the germs of all subsequent divisions which remain conditioned and governed by the former".[65] In particular, Cassirer looks for the principle ruling the procedure by which the correlative figures of subjectivity and inter-subjectivity are delineated upon the common background of the feeling of life. For the starting point of mythical feeling is in the feeling of the unity of life; this feeling is produced by the concretion of the first perceptual physiognomic elements, a dynamic whose emotional tone is, in particular, that of sympathy, understood in the anthropological sense. It forms the base of the feeling of the unity of life. According to this feeling, "The I feels and knows itself only as far as it grabs itself as a member of a community, as long as it sees itself as integrated with others in the unity of a clan, a tribe, a social group".[66] We can thus grasp how the I understands itself and others through the examination of the communities it delineates on the background of the affect of community of life (both in the sense of something that is unified and shared, and of a social group). Different communities are thus, in a way, both terms within a reciprocal determination between the I and the figures of otherness, and species of this global genre.

The essential point here is that none of the terms—neither a determined figure of the I nor that of otherness, be it another I or a group—exist before this synthesis. The activity of differentiation that leads me to conceive myself in separation from another I or from a group, which is a prelude to further progressive determinations by which I become a concrete I, is a process that is not carried out by presupposing the concept of the human. It is from within the first living

---

64 Cassirer (2008), 197, 271.
65 Cassirer (2002b), 86.
66 Ibid., 205.

community that this concept will gradually emerge. In other words, the community is, as human community, not a given, but the product of a process of objectification, insofar as the concept of humanity is itself fluctuating:

> the development of myth shows first with peculiar clarity that the awareness of even the most universal form of the human species, even the gender whereby man abstracts itself from the background of the totality of forms of life, aggregate itself with similar others in a particular natural 'species', is not initially given as the *starting point* of the mythical and religious world view, but should only be understood as a mediated product, as a *result* of this worldview. The limits of the species 'man' are for the mythical and religious consciousness in no way stable, but perfectly fluctuating boundaries.[67]

The myth of the twentieth century's primordial accomplishment is a new determination of the concept of the human. Understanding Nazism as a figure of the symbolic form of myth allows us to eventually *philosophically* understand how it became possible that, in the eyes of ordinary men, "The Jews stood outside their circle of human obligation and responsibility".[68]

If we want to follow the principles of a Cassirerian hermeneutics, we must seek to understand the principle for the original division by which the general feeling of life is instituted and from which all subsequent divisions and classifications will follow. We have seen how the explicit goal of *The Myth of the Twentieth Century* is to forge "from a new myth of life, a new type of man",[69] and we should now notice how, in a characteristic manner, the "myth of life" comes first, as the informing power for the new humanity. How then is this "myth of life" deployed?

The first chapter, "Race and Race' Soul" is immediately rooted in what, in Cassirer's view, constitutes the ground of mythical thought: the feeling of life. "A feeling of life, young and yet acknowledged as original [*uralt*], begins to strive into shape [*drängt nach Gestaltung*]". What figure does that feeling of life take? Its fundamental and encompassing dimensions must first be noted: "a *worldview* is born and begins a voluntary confrontation with the old forms [*Formen*], consecrated usages and established customs. Not historically anymore but

---

[67] Ibid., 209. This is an essential and recurring point: "Only through a progressive concentration, through a gradual stricture of this universal feeling of life that it takes as its starting point does myth attain gradually a specific feeling of human community". Ibid.. See also ibid., 16.
[68] Browning (1992), 73.
[69] Rosenberg (1942), 2.

fundamentally. Not on specific areas but over all. Not on the boughs but also on the roots".[70]

What is the specific content of this feeling? Its supreme principle is "life's" immediate expression, that is "blood", and it operates as the fundamental rule: "one can build and maintain values only where the law of blood determines the ideas and actions of men."[71] Life is thus conceived as identical to blood. The first outward expression of blood is race and its internal expression is the soul: "*But soul means race seen from the inside, and vice versa race is the outside of a soul*".[72] Two points are essential to the understanding of the Nazi myth's *Lebensform*. Firstly, and typically for mythical thinking, the terms "life", "blood", "race", and "soul" do not denote rational distinctions referring to the same objective reality, rather they are expressions of the same *affect*. This emotional, qualitative content immediately erases the distinction between part and whole. The soul, for example, is both collective and individual. Furthermore, with blood and race we are not at all dealing with a biological conception of life but with a classification that claims to be "spiritual" (hence the association with the "German spirit"); this aspect will also explain, further down in the diversification/classification, the completely non-scientific essence of the Nazi "typology", "physiology", and "medicine". In other words: the concept of nature found in the Nazi myth is not the heir of the natural sciences; rather it derives from (the highly inaccurate understanding of) a certain romanticism and it ultimately relates not to actual science but to a "mystical" conception of nature, life, blood and race.[73]

How, then, does the process of configuration by which the feeling of life will differentiate into specific shapes and figures operate?

Rosenberg starts with the first principle, the feeling of life that is given, which appears and manifests itself as blood.

> A new image [*Bild*], complex and colorful, of the history of earth and man unfolds gradually today, when we reverently recognize that the confrontation between blood and environment [*Umwelt*], between blood and blood, represents for us the last reachable phenomenon [*Erscheinung*].[74]

---

70 Ibid., 21.
71 Ibid., 22.
72 Ibid., 2.
73 See, for instance, ibid., 119–120, 141–142.
74 Ibid., 23.

It is in this emotional texture that all the other figures, all the other specifications, will, so to speak, be cut out. We must now consider how myth conceives of the differentiation process itself, then we will examine the production of the elements according to two directions: the subordination (species in a genus, etc.) and coordination (species standing next to each others within a genus).

Rosenberg never hesitated to appropriate humanity's greatest works, be they German—Bach, Kant, Hölderlin—or not—Homer, Da Vinci, etc. Here, it is Goethe who is invited to offer the main schema that explains the genesis and process of the differentiation of life. Life does not appear as such but only through diversified apparitions [Erscheinungen]. The original phenomenon [Urphänomene] is that of the fight that produces these apparitions and dispatches them according to polarities. The above quotation continues thus: "But this recognition immediately brings the knowledge that the struggles of blood and the forebode mystic of the phenomena of life [Lebensgeschehens] are not two separate things but one and the same, presented under different aspects".[75] Hence, as in *Mein Kampf*, rather then a logical and scientific process of class-building corresponding to ontological material and distinct entities, we are here dealing with a mystique of expression.

Once the basic process and its status have been assessed, we can examine the directions it takes. It is quite simple: along what would be, in logic, the axis of subordination (or: the splitting of genre in homogeneous species and of species in individuals), it is the purity and power of life that is used as a criterion. Along what would be the axis of coordination, opposites in the original split (because we deal with a "struggle"), the terms are not only logical or architectonic opposites, they are *antagonists*. Let's examine the first terms of these classifications.

The first great architectonic dichotomy is made according to a Manichean division into two opposing classes. Identity is gained negatively, conquered through the initial fight of life. The polarities are posited as expressions of the struggle of life, two bloods, two races, two souls, the antagonisms of life and death, health and disease, creativity and parasitism. The principle of the "good soul", of the "living soul" or the "revived" one is "honor", while the principle of the "evil" or "malignant" soul is "gold" (the principle of "contaminated" soul, producing for example Christianity, is "love"). Regarding the "type", that is the real unity of race and soul, the "Aryan" opposes the "Jew", etc. This Manichaeism is hardly tempered by a diversity of intermediate races between

---

75 Ibid,

"Aryan" and "Jewish" because the extremes are absolutized: "Jew" is a "*Gegenrasse*".[76] If its principle is the "parasitism" it is precisely because it "does not have an organic soul-figure [*organische Seelengestalt*] and therefore also no race-figure [*Rassengestalt*]". [77] "*Gegenrasse*" means an absolute anti-race, the originally negative and formless. It is tempting to say that if it is not the *Nichts* that *nichtet*, it certainly is the *gegen* that *gegent!*

Along the axis of subordination, the classificatory and axiological principle is at first very simple: there are initially only two terms, two sides, the good one and the bad one. However, because of the "parasite" principle, intermediaries are introduced. The proximity to the type set by the first dichotomy then becomes a criterion: the more blood is pure, the more the race is pure, the more life is present, healthy and vibrant, the more the individual embodies the type, the Aryan etc. Remoteness is thought according to the terms of weakening, degeneration, etc.

For Cassirer, the constitution of classes in mythical thought involves more than classificatory principles. The successive determination of classes within the phenomenon of life is accomplished by a correlation between the sphere of the divine or of the figurate ideal and the personal identification of the agent of this classification. Thus mythical consciousness acquires identity through a correlation with ancestors, family gods and phratry gods, tribe gods and finally with gods of the city and the nation. The core of this process of identification is the objectification of an *activity*. Cassirer relied for example, on the correlation between human activities such as breeding, farming and agriculture and the special gods associated with these activities. Quoting Usener, he showed that agrarian sacrifice among the Romans consisted of the evocation of twelve gods, each corresponding to one of the laborer's activities. Thus, the different areas of activity are set and organized by a theological system that is its figurative reproduction. Cassirer can then claim that "in the plurality of his divine figures, man not only intuits external manifestations of natural objects and forces, but he sees himself in them, in the concrete variety and particularization of its functions".[78] A pantheon is thus the mirror in which a society shows its identity through the figuration of activities. Three essential components of mythology: theogony, anthropogony and historiography collaborate in the constitution of

---

[76] Ibid., 462.
[77] Ibid., 461. The organicity is that of a 'Goethean' (!) morphology. It does not contradict the physiognomical claims to identifications, but simply means that there is an "external figuration" constituted of "degenerated" borrowed characters.
[78] Cassirer (2002b), 240.

this identity.[79] This direction of research provides several levels of exegesis: one allows for an understanding of the identity humans give themselves via objectifications in the figures of gods and heroes; another sheds light on the structuration of the social and political fabric in groups and institutions of a state apparatus. I can only sketch here the first level.

The pantheon of *The Myth of the Twentieth Century* is quite meaningful. As we have seen, first comes the deification of blood and race, which are immediately rooted in a mythical genealogy. Among the many pages that could be cited, here is an example. After mentioning the Atlanteans as the origin of authentic humanity, Rosenberg continues:

> we may still not have figured out where the original land [*Urheimat*] of the Nordic race was ... but no results will change the *unique* grand factual principle [*Tatsache*] that the 'sense of the history of the world' radiated from the north on all the Earth, carried by a blond, blue-eyed race, which, in several large waves, set the spiritual face of the world, even where it was to disappear. Here are these periods of travel: in fact, the raid of the Atlanteans over North Africa, that of the Aryans over India and Persia ... the itinerant German peoples ... the colonization of the world by the German Occident.[80]

A nation of warriors conquering the world. The reinterpretation of the pantheon and the meaning of the Greek heroes is an equally amazing example: Theseus fighting the Amazons is the embodiment of the chapter on "State and Gender", which assigns women the only function of reproduction and thereby their participation in the preservation of the purity of the race. Unify these two narratives and you have, for instance, Himmler's *Lebensborn eintragen Verein*.

Ever since this origin, war is declared against the *"Gegenrasse"*:

> The light Aryans, noticing and becoming aware of the elusive phenomenal images, dug a ditch between them as conquerors, and the dark brown faces of the Hindus. Following this separation between blood and blood, the Aryans formed for themselves a picture of the world so deep and vast that even today, it can not be surpassed by any philosophy, even after long conflicts with the always more invasive representations begotten by sub-races.[81]

The genealogy and history of the "German people" is written from the perspective of this fight. We encounter here and again, in their dynamic work of separation and their relation with the first principle of life, the categories we mentioned

---

[79] It is interesting to note that Rosenberg was fully aware of the importance of these components and explicitly worked them out as constitutive moments (for instance, cf. ibid., 678).
[80] Ibid., 27–28.
[81] Ibid., 28.

earlier: the opposition of the two forms of life, both spiritual principles—honor and gold—and their racial characters—North / Light, South / Dark, etc.

The opposite terms of this mythological classification have dramatically different statuses: what is at stake in this opposition is the new delineation between mankind and its other. Everything that comes from the negative side, from "evil blood", is cast out of the limits of humanity, which, with this opposition, finds its new circumscription. The concept of blood is anterior to a 'biological' determination of the human species, but since in its expressions it unfolds both along a spiritual axis—the soul—and a natural axis—race—"the racial history is both natural history and mystique of the soul".[82] We are hence really dealing with a new determination of humanity. I already mentioned how the 'positive' side of the polarity is constructed by the objectivization of gods, heroes, etc. Rosenberg was also very clear about the status of otherness, of this other which forms the opposite term, the shapeless "*Gegenrasse*":

> above all is singled out *one* result: parasitism. This concept is not to be understood here as an ethical value, but as the qualification of a life-legal (organic) fact, just as we speak of parasitic phenomena in the animal or vegetal life. When a barnacle insidiously invades the body of a Jonah Crab, grows more and more in it and sucks its last vital forces, the process is identical to that of the Jews infiltrating society through an open wound in the people, feeding on its racial and creative strength until its fall.[83]

In many ways Rosenberg's concept of "*Gegenrasse*" and of its "parasitism" is much worse than his naturalist examples. At least, the real parasite has very determined identity and figures, it shares with its host a common minimal genre, animality. Whereas the "counter-race" is "shapeless", "figureless", it has only "borrowed degenerated characters": it only *imitates* humanity, only has its ("degenerated") *appearance*, but in fact *does not belong* to it.

5 Why the Jews?

Up to this point, we can understand how the myth of the twentieth century expelled the Other, the "*Gegenrasse*" from the realm of its new circumscription of humanity; what remains unintelligible is why this Other was "the Jew", why the cardinal *ur-Teilung* commanding the differentiations within the myth's form of

---

[82] Ibid., 23.
[83] Ibid., 461.

life set the "Jew" as the opposite of the "Aryan".[84] The explanation we are looking for cannot, of course, be found at an explicit level within the myth itself.

First, Cassirer takes careful note of the unprecedented and radical nature of what he faces:

> To speak here of mere 'anti-Semitism' seems to me to be a very inadequate expression of the problem. Anti-Semitism is not a new phenomenon; it had existed at all times and under all forms. But the German form of persecution was something entirely new. ... It was a mortal combat—a life and death struggle which could only finds its end in the complete extermination of the Jews.[85]

Second, considering the reasons for this extermination, he took into account specific problems: personal antipathy and aversion, repeated bias deeply anchored in culture, hatred and fanaticism, how easy it was to attack a small minority, etc. The anthropological theory of the scapegoat was also taken into account. However, none of these reasons could explain the choice of the Jews as a symbolic substrate: Cassirer concluded: "All this may be true, but it is only a half-truth".[86]

Reaching the whole truth is only possible by assessing the mythical nature of Nazism. The strength of this regime rested neither on it economy, nor on any of its "material weapons": "*ideology* was the strongest and at the same time, the most vulnerable point in the[ir] whole political system".[87] In other words it is its mythical nature that made both the strength and the weakness of Nazism. What does this have to do with the Jews?

> In the history of mankind they [i.e. the Jews] had been the first to deny and to challenge those very conceptions upon which the new state was built. It was Judaism which first made the decisive step that led from a *mythical* to an *ethical* religion.[88]

Because of the historically proven ability of Judaism to transform myth, the Jews where considered the most lethal threat to the myth of the twentieth century.

Cassirer's explanation has often been either caricatured or relativized in various ways: psychological—a late reaction and reconsideration of his own Judaism by a philosopher overwhelmed by guilt; doctrinal—is not Judaism itself es-

---

84 This question does not neglect other mass assassinations. The massacre of communists, resistants, and SA obey different mythical principles. They were enemies, not an "anti-race". The only exception could be the Roma (Gypsies).
85 Cassirer (1944a/2007), 125–126/207–208.
86 Ibid., 125/207.
87 Ibid., 115/197.
88 Ibid.

sentially mythic?, etc. So it obviously needs some explanation before any assessment of its value can be made.

Whether we share it or not, Cassirer's conception of Judaism is deeply rooted in that of his master and friend Hermann Cohen. In other words, the Judaism he opposed to myth is neither that of our local day school, nor that of a spontaneous reading of basic texts. It is an understanding of Judaism as a religion that has succeeded in transforming itself through its own history and in transforming *muthos* into *ethos*. As such it is the very opposite of Nazism's ideological technology, which, by the extension of myth to politics, negated ethics. Of course, to illustrate his argument in a non-philosophical journal, Cassirer did not go into an explanation of Cohen or of Judaism as a "religion of reason", but he gave some clear examples:

Judaism as a religion of reason rather then of sentiment or imagination,

> has from its very beginnings attacked and rejected all these mythical elements which had hitherto pervaded and governed religious thought. The classical expression of this rejection is to be found in the words, 'Thou shall not make unto thee any graven image, [n]or any [manner of] likeness *of any thing* that is in heaven above, or that *is* in earth beneath, or that *is* in the water under the earth: Thou shalt not bow down unto them, nor serve them'. Here we have the complete break with mythical thought. For imagery is at the very core of mythical thought. To deprive myth of imagery is to ensure its decay.[89]

It would be too long to develop this line of thinking here, but Holzhey described it in a wonderfully compact and accurate sentence: "Cassirer conceived of religious consciousness as the critical reason of mythical consciousness".[90]

Judaism did not only deprive mythical thought of its constitutive elements, visual and textual imagery, it also and even more fundamentally renewed and redirected its fundamental energy, thereby accomplishing this '*Aufhebung*' we have mentioned. "Can religion survive myth? ... Ethical thought had to take precedence over mythical thought".[91] Myth, in its fundamental element—feeling, affect—is a paradox in that it consists in a self-alienation. Consciousness extraposes an entity it then hypostasizes and entirely submits to in all sorts of ways. Despite an originary, productive spontaneity, the feeling is dominated by passivity. Judaism as ethical religion re-instaurates spontaneity and activity at the core of the religious feeling. It is, in this regard too, a lethal concurrent to the myth of the twentieth century, which, by invading politics, deceptively seems to accom-

---

89 Ibid. 117/199.
90 Holzhey (1988), 193.
91 Cassirer (1944a/2007), 117/199.

plish a liberation of the passive mythical feelings into active ones, like fervor and enthusiasm.

Finally, Cassirer made sure to highlight the principal steps by which Judaism rose to the status of ethical religion and how these steps were in total contradiction and conflict with the myth of the twentieth century: The Prophets (Cassirer quotes Isaiah 1: 11, 13) redirected and transformed the meaning of rituals. Judaism, essentially with its conception of monotheism, shifted the realm of obligation from the collective to the individual, thereby producing a moral subject (instead of the community, the nation or the race). Prophetism put an end to nationalism with a concrete universalism. It promoted an ideal of perpetual peace. Cassirer summarized:

> If we compare this conception of man's ethical, social and religious life to the 'myth of the twentieth century' we feel at once the fundamental and striking difference. The prophets are inspired by the ardent wish for a perpetual peace; our modern myths tend to the perpetuation and intensification of war. The prophets dissolve the physical bond between God and man: the bond of blood relationship. The modern myths, on the other hand, acknowledge no other duty than that which arises from the community of blood. The German leaders promised to the German people the conquest of the whole world. What the prophets promised was not the glory of the Jewish nation but its decline and fall in the deepest misery. The political myths enthrone and deify a superrace: the prophets predict an age in which all the nations shall be united under the worship of God. There is no point of contact and no possible reconciliation between these two conceptions.[92]

So to the question "Why the Jews?" Cassirer offered a strictly philosophical answer that complemented the psychological and sociological ones: because the worse enemy of a political myth is an ethical religion. For Cassirer, the best example we have of such a religion is not Protestantism, as Hegel thought, but Judaism.

6 Conclusion

When we ask: "What did a philosopher do?"—Did Cassirer write a political philosophy? Did he produce an analysis of Nazism? What did he do against Nazism? —we ask, in the best case, a *historical* question and, in the worst, a *psychological* question. In this context, the only *philosophical* question is: "What can a philosophy conceive of?" My claim is that, although Ernst Cassirer never wrote a trea-

---

92 Ibid., 123/206.

tise on political philosophy,[93] and although he only suggested what his understanding of Nazism was, and utilized a strategy against Nazism that was too subtle, realistic and modest to be easily understood, his philosophy of symbolic forms, as a philosophy of culture, offers perhaps not the best, perhaps not the easiest, certainly not the most fashionable, but still a reasonably good tool to analyze modern and contemporary political phenomena. The "myth of the twentieth century" is only one example; I strongly believe capitalism is another one, but this is another story.

Bibliography

Arendt (2006): Hannah Arendt, *Eichmann in Jerusalem: A Report on the Banality of Evil*, New York.
Bäumler (1943): Alfred Bäumler, *Introduction to: Alfred Rosenberg, Schriften und Reden*, vol. 1, München: Hoheneichen-Verlag.
Billig (1963): Joseph Billig, *Alfred Rosenberg dans l'action idéologique, politique et administrative du Reich hitlérien, Les inventaires des archives du Centre de documentation juive contemporaine*, Paris: Editions du Centre.
Bollmus (1970): Reinhard Bollmus, *Das Amt Rosenberg und seine Gegner, Zum Machtkampf im nationalsozialitischen Herrschaftssystem*, Stuttgart: Deutsche Verlags-Anstalt.
Browning (1992): Christopher Browning, *Ordinary Men: Reserve Police Battalion 101 and the Final Solution in Poland*, New York: HarperCollins.
Capeillères (1995): Fabien Capeillères, *Cassirer and Political Philosophy*, in: *Cassirer-Forschungen: Kulturkritik nach Ernst Cassirer*, Enno Rudolph and Bernd-Olaf Küppers (eds.), Hamburg: Meiner, 129–142.
Cassirer (1944a/2007a): Ernst Cassirer, *Judaism and the Modern Political Myths*, Contemporary Jewish Record, vol. VII (No. 2), April 1944; in: *Gesammelte Werke* (henceforth ECW), Birgit Recki (ed.), vol. 24, Hamburg: Felix Meiner Verlag.
Cassirer (1944b/2007a): Ernst Cassirer, *The Myth of the State*, Fortune, vol. XXIX (No. 6), June 1944; in: ECW, vol. 24, op. cit.
Cassirer (1961/2007b): Ernst Cassirer, *The Myth of the State*, New Haven: Yale University Press; Ernst Cassirer, The Myth of the State, in: ECW, vol. 25, op cit.
Cassirer (1972/2006): Ernst Cassirer, *An Essay on Man*, New Haven: Yale University Press; Ernst Cassirer, An Essay on Man, in: ECW, vol. 23, op. cit.
Cassirer (1979): Ernst Cassirer, *Symbol, Myth and Culture: Essays and Lectures of Ernst Cassirer, 1935–1945*, Donald P. Verene (ed.), New Haven and London: Yale University Press.
Cassirer (2002a/1955a): Ernst Cassirer, *Philosophie der symbolischen Formen, Erster Teil, Die Sprache*, in: ECW, vol. 11, op. cit.; Ernst Cassirer, *The Philosophy of Symbolic Forms*, Volume One: Language, Ralph Manheim (trans.), New Haven: Yale University Press.

---

[93] One can find an analysis of Cassirer's conception of the state, including its relation with myth, in Müller (2003).

Cassirer (2002b/1955b): Ernst Cassirer, *Philosophie der symbolischen Formen, Zweiter Teil, Das mythische Denken*, in: ECW, vol. 12, op. cit.; Ernst Cassirer, *The Philosophy of Symbolic Forms, Volume Two: Mythical Thought*, Ralph Manheim (trans.), New Haven: Yale University Press.

Cassirer (2002c/1957): Ernst Cassirer, *Philosophie der symbolischen Formen, Dritter Teil, Phänomenologie der Erkenntnis*, in: ECW, vol. 13, op. cit.; Ernst Cassirer, *The Philosophy of Symbolic Forms, Volume Three: The Phenomenology of Knowledge*, Ralph Manheim (trans.), New Haven: Yale University Press.

Cassirer (2005): Ernst Cassirer, *Axel Hägerström: Eine Studie zur schwedischen Philosophie der Gegenwart; Thorilds Stellung in der Geistesgeschichte des achtzehnten Jahrhunderts*, in: ECW, vol. 21, op. cit.

Cassirer (2008): Ernst Cassirer, *Zu Philosophie und Politik*, in: *Nachgelassene Manuskripte und Texte*, vol. 9, John Michael Krois (ed.), Hamburg: Felix Meiner Verlag.

Cassirer (1981): Tony Cassirer, *Mein Leben mit Ernst Cassirer*, Hildesheim: Gerstenberg Verlag.

Cecil (1972): Robert Cecil, *The Myth of the Master Race: Alfred Rosenberg and Nazi Ideology*, London: Batsford Ltd.

Cornell and Penfilio (2010): Drucilla Cornell, and Kenneth Michael Panfilio, *Symbolic Forms: for a New Humanity; Cultural and Racial Configurations of Critical Theory*, New York: Fordham University Press.

Favuzzi (2012): Pellegrino Favuzzi, *Critica al mito e origine del diritto e della società in Ernst Cassirer*, in: *Simbolo e cultura: Ottant'anni dopo la Filosofia delle forme simboliche*, Fabrizio Lomonaco (ed.), Milan: Franco Angeli, 103–116.

Foxman (1999): Abraham Foxman, Introduction to: Adolf Hitler, *Mein Kampf*, New York: Mariner Books Edition.

Frei (1993): Norbert Frei, *National Socialist Rule in Germany: The Führer State, 1933–1945*, Oxford and Cambridge: Blackwell.

Gaubert (1996): Joël Gaubert, *La science politique d'Ernst Cassirer*, Paris: Kimé.

Hitler (2002): Adolf Hitler, *Mein Kampf*, Ralph Manheim (trans.), Boston and New York: Houghton Mifflin Co.

Holzhey (1988): Helmut Holzhey, *Cassirers Kritik des mythischen Bewusstseins*, in: *Über E. Cassirers Philosophie der symbolischen Formen*, Hans-Jürg Braun, Helmut Holzhey, and Ernst Wolfgang Orth (eds.), Berlin: Suhrkamp.

Krebs (1959): Albert Krebs, *Tendenzen und Gestalten der NSDP*, München: Deutsche Verlags-Anstalt

Mali (2008): Joseph Mali, *The Myth of the State Revisited: Ernst Cassirer and Modern Political Theory*, in: *The Symbolic Construction of Reality: The Legacy of Ernst Cassirer*, Jeffrey A. Barash (ed.), Chicago: University of Chicago Press.

Michaud (1996): Eric Michaud, *Un Art de l'Éternité, l'image et le temps du national-socialisme*, Paris: Gallimard; translated as: Eric Michaud, *The Cult of Art in Nazi Germany*, Janet Lloyd (trans.), Stanford: Stanford University Press, 2006.

Moltke (1948): Helmuth James Graf von Moltke, *A German in the Resistance: The Last Letters of Count Helmut James von Moltke*, 2nd ed., Oxford: Oxford University Press.

Müller (2003): Peter Müller, *Der Staatsgedanke Cassirers*, Würzburg: Königshausen & Neumann.

Pächter (1944): Heinz Pächter in association with Hellman, Pächter, and Pätel, *Nazi-Deutsch: A Glossary of German Usage*, with Appendices on Government, Military and Economic Institutions, New York: Frederick Ungar Publishing Co.

Picker (1951): Henry Picker, *Hitler Tischgespräche im Führrerhauptquartier*, 1941–1942, Berlin: Athenäum-Verlag.

Piper (2005): Ernst Piper, *Alfred Rosenberg: Hitlers Chefideologe*, München: Karl Blessing Verlag, 2005.

Rasuching (1940): Hermann Rausching, *Gespräche mit Hitler*, New York: Europa Verlag.

Rosenberg (1939): Alfred Rosenberg, *Blut und Ehre*, Aufsätze von 1919–1933, Thilo von. Trotha (ed.), München: Eher Verlag.

Rosenberg (1942): Alfred Rosenberg, *Der Mythus des 20. Jahrhunderts*, München: Hoheneichen-Verlag.

Schmitt (1934): Carl Schmitt, *Der Führer schützt das Recht. Zur Reichstagsrede Adolf Hitlers vom 13 Juli 1934*, Deutsche Juristen-Zeitung 39.

Trotha (1939): Thilo von Trotha, *Forward to: Alfred Rosenberg, Blut und Ehre (Aufsätze von 1919–1933)*, 22nd ed., München: Zentralverlag der NSDUP.

Vögelin (1947): Eric Voegelin, *Review of The Myth of the State*, The Journal of Politics, vol. 9 (No. 3), August 1947, 445–447.

Subject index

Aesthetics 1 f., 4 – 6, 8, 12 – 16, 20 f., 25
– Transcendental A. 385
An Essay on Man 1 – 5, 7 – 9, 11, 15 f., 19
Animal symbolicum 1 f., 10 f., 15 f., 19 f., 24
Anthropology 1 – 17, 20
Antiquity 12, 14
A posteriori 9 – 11, 17
A priori 1 – 13, 15 – 19, 22, 25, 28
Arithmetic 1 – 3, 5 – 12, 15 – 17
Art 1 – 22, 24, 26, 29, 31
Axiom 3, 7, 13 f., 16, 21

Biology 4, 8 – 11, 14, 23
– Philosophy of b. 40

Cartesian 236, 330
Category 1 – 4, 6, 8 f., 11 f., 18, 20
Causality 2, 4 – 6, 8, 11 – 13, 15 – 24
Chemistry 2, 4, 8 – 10, 27
Cogito 4, 18
Comedy 1 f., 4 f., 7 f., 10 f., 15
Communication 4, 6, 10 – 12, 15, 17, 21, 26
Concept 1 – 28, 30 f., 36
Consciousness 1 – 27, 29 – 31
Copernican Revolution 1 – 4, 6 f., 14 – 18, 20, 22 f., 28 f.
Cosmology 8
Crisis 1 – 5, 7, 9 – 12, 14, 17 – 20, 24 f., 28
Critic 1 – 3, 5 – 7, 10, 12 – 18
Critique 1 – 16, 18 f., 21 f., 24 – 27
Critique of Practical Reason 3
Critique of Pure Reason 1, 3 – 5, 7 – 9, 11 – 13, 20, 22
Critique of Judgment 424
Culture 1 – 26, 29 f., 32

Davos 1 f., 5 – 7, 9, 11, 14, 17
Determinism 8 – 10, 17, 22, 24, 30
Determinism and Indeterminism in Modern Physics 1, 17
Dialectic 7 f., 16 – 18
– Transcendental Dialectic 6, 11 f., 22

Einstein's Theory of Relativity 1, 4, 6, 8 f., 12, 17
Empathy 16, 18
Empiricism 2 – 4, 8 – 11, 13, 16, 19 – 22, 30 f.
Energy 1, 3, 5, 7 – 10, 13, 15, 19, 23, 26 f., 29 – 31
Epistemology 1, 3, 5 – 8, 10 – 12, 14, 16, 18, 20, 25 f., 36
Ethics 5, 7, 12 – 17, 19, 21, 25, 30
Ethnology 20
Experience 1 – 26, 29 – 31, 35
Expression 1 – 25, 27 – 30

Fact/factum 383
Form 1 – 31
Foundationalism 2
Freedom 1, 3 f., 8 f., 19, 22, 25 f., 28 f., 31 – 33
Function 1 – 24, 26 f., 29 – 31

Geometry 4 f., 8 f., 12 – 14, 16
Gestalt 3, 6 f., 9 – 11, 15, 17 – 21, 23 – 25

History 1 – 20, 22, 24 – 31
Holism 1, 5 – 8, 11 – 17, 27 – 29
Humanism 1 f., 5
Humanity 1, 3, 6, 8, 11 f., 15 – 19, 22 – 25, 27 f.
Humor 1 f., 4 – 15

Idea 1 – 24, 26, 29 f.
Idealism 1 f., 4 – 9, 11 – 16, 18, 20 – 24, 29 – 31
Idealization 2 – 4, 7, 10 – 16, 18
International Classification of Diseases (ICD) 1
Interpretation 1 – 25, 28 – 30, 33
Intersubjectivity 1, 3, 5 – 8, 16 f., 21
Intuition 1 – 23
Intuitionism 7, 17

Jew/Jewish 233, 431 f., 435 f., 453, 457 – 462
Judaism 16, 29 – 31

Judgment   1–11, 13–15, 18–20, 22, 26 f.
Justification (*quid iuris*)   1 f., 4, 6, 8, 10, 21

Knowledge   1–32

Language   1–26, 29–31
– Philosophy of l.   4, 353–356
Logic   1–19, 21 f., 25 f., 29
– symbolic l.   406–414
– transcendental l.   40, 128, 209, 292, 315, 385
Logicism   1–3, 5–10, 15, 18
Logic of the Cultural Sciences   2, 6, 8, 11, 13 f., 16

Mathematics   1–18, 21, 23, 25, 30
– Pure m.   125, 205, 364
Matrix of Mental Formation   24, 27 f., 30 f.
Metabasis eis allo genos   49
Metaphysics   1–5, 7–18, 22, 24 f., 27, 36
Method   2–28
– Transcendental m.   12–13, 126–134, 202, 213–226, 395, 439–442, 453
Middle Ages   7, 17
Myth   1–32
– M. of the Given   278–280, 313–333

Nature   1–22, 24, 28 f., 32, 34
Neo-Kantianism   1 f., 4–6, 8–12, 15 f., 18 f., 24–28
Norm   2, 4, 6–9, 12, 31
Normativity   1, 3, 13, 21
Number   1–16, 18, 20 f., 26, 29 f., 33

Objectivity   2–19, 21, 24, 26 f., 29, 31
Ontology   1–5, 9, 11–13, 15, 18, 22
– Fundamental o.   247–250

Perception   1–25
Phenomenology   2, 6, 9 f., 12 f., 15 f., 18–21
Phenomenology of Spirit   6, 11
Philosophy   1–32, 36
– Transcendental p.   2–4, 7–10, 12, 17 f.
– Cosmopolitan p.   262
Philosophy of Symbolic Forms   1–13, 15–23, 25, 32
Physics   1–25, 27–30, 36

Platonism   6, 9, 11, 13–16, 19, 21
– Neo-P.   24
Politics   3, 7–9, 11–17, 19–21, 26, 29–31
Positivism   3 f., 6 f., 13 f.
Primitive Thinking   8
Principles   1–13, 15–21, 23, 25–29, 31
Psychiatry   1–4, 6, 19 f., 22, 24 f., 31
Psychoanalysis   3, 8 f., 17
Psychologism   1 f., 7–10, 16, 22
Psychopathology   1–7, 13, 15–17, 20–23, 25, 31

Quantum Mechanics   1–6, 10, 12–17, 19–25, 27–31, 33 f., 36

Race   286, 382, 387, 431, 438, 451–465
Rationalism   1, 7 f., 10 f., 19, 25
Realism   3–6, 8, 11–13, 15, 20 f., 24 f., 29, 35
Reason   1–30
– Pure r.   71, 78, 283, 363 f., 367–369, 382
Relativism   1, 6 f., 9 f., 15 f., 19
Relativity   1–9, 12, 20, 22, 24, 32, 34
Renaissance   1 f., 5–9, 11, 16–18
Representation   1–22, 24 f., 27–35

Science   1–31, 34
Sciences   1–5, 7, 9–19, 23 f., 26 f., 30
Scientific Revolution   1–3, 5 f., 9 f., 13–15, 23
Semiotics   1 f., 6, 10, 14
Sexuality   14
Solipsism   7
Space   1–23, 25–35
Spirit   2–17, 19–21, 23 f.
Structuralism   1–4, 25, 27–31, 34, 36
Structure   1–22, 24–27, 30–35
Subjectivity   2–8, 12–17, 19–22
Substance   1–5, 7–12, 14, 16 f., 19 f., 22, 24, 30
Substance and Function   1–5, 7–14, 17, 19, 25, 30
Symbolic Pregnancy   4, 19 f.
Symbols   1–16, 20, 22–25

Technology 3–5, 11f., 16, 30
The Myth of the State 1, 3f., 9, 11–14, 17–19
Theory 1–25, 28f., 31–36
The Platonic Renaissance in England 7
Time 1–24, 26, 28–34

Unity 1f., 4–10, 12–22, 24f., 29
– U. of reason 219f., 368
Universal 1–12, 14–20, 23–29, 31
– Lateral u. 359–399
Universalism 6f., 10, 31

Work 1–30
World 1–31, 34

Index of names

Andersch, N.   163–198
Arendt, H.   436
Aristotle   172, 235–236, 246–247
Avenarius, R.   273

Benjamin, W.   363
Bell, J.   68
Binswander, L.   165, 168, 177–179, 181
Blumenberg, H.   295
Bohm, D.   66, 87
Bohr, N.   66–67, 69, 82–83
Borcherds, R.   98–99
Born, M.   65–67, 79, 86, 88, 93
Brouwer, L.E.J.   129, 139
Bruno, G.   15
Brunschvig, L.   21–22
Burtt, E.   21, 24

Cantor, G   126
Capeillères, F.   404–405, 435–468
Carnap, R.   45, 47, 84, 103–107, 112, 114–115, 410–411
Carrier, M.   18, 396
Carter, C.   401–417
Cei, A.   57–59
Cervantes, M.   426
Chaplin, C.   428
Cohen, H.   4, 12–14, 16, 19, 128, 201, 210, 212–221, 225–226, 277, 383, 464
Conrad, K.   182
Copernicus, N.   18, 281
Cusanus, N.   15

Daston, L.   146
Davidson, D.   322
de Broglie, L.   66, 77
de Boer, K.   268
de Saussure, F.   164, 184
Dedekind, R.   124–125, 128, 137
Descartes, R.   236, 358
Dirac, P.   65–68, 80–81, 89, 92
Dreyfus, H.   327–328, 330
du Bois-Reymond, E.   41, 44–45, 73–74

du Bois-Reymond, P.   34, 41–44
Duhem, P.   17–18, 107, 111–120, 320

Earman, J.   103
Edgar, S.   141–162
Einstein, A.   31–32, 52, 55, 66, 68, 86, 106–107, 113–115
Euler, L.   20
Exner, F.   83–84

Ferrari, M.   11–29
Fichte, J.G.   202, 204, 352
Finkelnburg, F.C.   168, 269
Frank, P.   52–53, 72, 84–85
Frege, G.   35, 123, 127–128, 130
French, S.   51, 55–59, 88
Freud, S.   169–171, 184
Friedman, J T.   361–380
Friedman, M.   54, 103, 105–111, 114, 211, 322
Friedrich, C.D.   401

Gadamer, H.-G.   2–3, 387
Galison, P.   146
Galileo   15, 17–19, 23, 25–26, 157–159
Gelb, A.   177, 179, 182
Gilbert, C.   404
Goebbels, J.   439, 441
Goldstein, K.   168, 177–179, 181–185
Goodman, N.   411–416
Gordon, P.   1, 233–234
Göring, H   454
Gurwitsch, A.   182

Haag, R.   97–98
Habermas, J.   5
Hacking, I.   73–74
Hamilton, W.R.   89–91, 9–94, 97
Hanson, N.   321
Head, H.   167, 169
Hegel, G.W.F.   4, 202, 204, 215–216, 236, 328, 361, 365–378, 449, 451, 465
Heidegger, M.   165, 168, 179, 210, 233–256, 327, 445–446

Index of names

Heis, J.   123–140, 211
Heisenberg, W.   65–67, 69, 82–83, 92
Hilbert, D.   45, 94, 129
Himmler, H.   441, 461
Hitler, A.   438–441
Hobbes, T.   422
Howard, D.   107, 113
Husserl, E.   2–4, 24, 179, 328, 444

Jackson, H.   180
Jaspers, K.   165, 444
Jordan, P.   65–67, 69
Jung, C.G.   169–171

Kandinksy, W.   415–416
Kant, I.   4, 14, 18–20, 50, 69, 75–76, 78, 86, 108–110, 174, 202–208, 214–219, 250–251, 259–287, 294, 296–298, 313–320, 324–326, 334, 361–378, 381–385, 419–420, 424, 453
Keller, P.   259–288
Kepler, J.   17–19, 157–159, 286
Köhler, W.   181–182
Koyré, A.   16, 21, 23–25
Kraeplin, E.   165, 182
Kreis, G.   313–337
Krois, J.M.   1, 176, 234, 300, 433
Kuhn, T.   16, 26, 69, 103–108

Ladyman, J.   51, 55–56
Lagrange, J-L.   90, 96
Lange, F.A.   206–207
Langer, S.   406–416
Langevin, P.   66
Laplace, P.-S.   44–46, 71–76, 85, 90
Lask, E.   243–244, 248
Leibniz, G.W.   11, 70–71, 259–260
Lembeck, K.-H.   14
Lenzen, V.   46
Leuner, H.   184–185
Levinas, E.   233, 253
Lévi-Strauss, C.   386, 390–399
Lewin, K.   168, 182–184
Liebmann, O.   203–204
Linnaeus, C.   173
Lofts, S.G.   233–258
Lorentz, H.A.   66

Lotze, H.   141–141, 161
Lovejoy, A.   21
Löwith, K.   295
Luft, S.   163

Mach, E.   23, 141–142, 148–160
Mahnke, D.   24
Mann, T.   235
Margenau, H.   53–54, 82, 87
Marra, J.   419–434
Matherne, S.   201–231
McDowell, J.   313–335
Mencken, H.L.   372–375, 378
Merleau-Ponty, M.   182, 327, 330, 390, 393, 395–399
Meyerson, E.   21–23
Minkowski, H.   96
Mormann, T.   31–63

Nagel, E.   84
Nagel, T.   49
Natorp, P.   12–14, 26, 38–39, 50, 128, 132, 141–149, 152–160, 201, 208, 210, 212–213, 215–219, 221–226, 237, 334
Newton, I.   19, 109, 158–159
Nietzsche, F.   161
Nowak, L.   42–43

Orth, E.W.   343

Parmenides   235
Pauli, W.   66
Peano, G.   35
Peirce, C.S.   164
Piaget, J.   164, 183
Planck, M.   55, 69
Plato   19, 171, 235, 262, 270–272, 276, 422
Plotinus   235–236
Poincaré, H.   98, 129–131, 138–139
Pollok, A.   341–360
Poisson, S.D.   65, 91–92

Quine, W.V.   77, 85, 105–107, 111–112, 114–115, 118, 320

Reichenbach, H.   84, 107, 110–
Reisch, G.   103

Richardson, A.   103–121, 211
Rickert, H.   201, 211
Rosenberg, A.   4384–442, 451–462
Ross, D.   56
Russell, B.   35, 123, 127–130
Ryckman, T.   65–102

Sacks, O.   178
Saxl, F.   83
Scheler, M.   444
Schelling, F.W.J.   251
Schiller, F.   11, 347
Schlick, M.   50
Schrödinger, E.   65–69, 77, 81, 83–84, 93–94
Schweitzer, A.   361, 444
Segal, I.   99
Sellars, W.   279–280, 315
Servois, J.   14
Shaftsesbury   425–426
Shakespeare, W.   426–427
Skidelsky, E.   343
Silberer, S.   170
Sluga, H.   1
Sokolowski, R.   2–3

Spengler, O.   235, 445
Spinoza, B.   236
Stanton, G.   431
Strong, E.   24–25

Truesdell, C.   72
Truwant, S.   289–311

van Fraassen, B.   35, 40, 55, 59–60
von Goethe, J.W.   4, 173, 252, 345, 384, 401, 403–404, 459
von Helmholtz, H.   74–75, 141, 161, 206
von Laue, M.   86
von Mises, R.   45
von Neumann, J.   67–68, 95–96
von Uexküll, J.   172
von Weizsäcker, C.F.   85–86

Warburg, A.   15
Weber, M.   443
Weyl, H.   47, 129
Whitehead, A.N.   164
Wightman, A.   97
Wigner, E.   48, 94
Windelband, W.   20

www.ingramcontent.com/pod-product-compliance
Lightning Source LLC
Chambersburg PA
CBHW070603230426
43670CB00010B/1385